TITLE

Hidden in Plain Sight: Politics and Design in State-Subsidized Residential Architecture

EDITORS

Rui Jorge Garcia Ramos
Virgílio Borges Pereira
Marta Rocha Moreira
Sergio Dias Silva

COPY-EDITING AND PROOFREADING

David Tucker

PUBLISHER

Park Books

GRAPHIC DESIGN AND PAGINATION

Cristina Amil
Sergio Dias Silva

COVER IMAGE

Affordable Houses Estate of Agualva-Cacém
(Archs. Alberto Pessoa and João Abel Manta, Landscape Arch. Gonçalo Ribeiro Telles, Sintra, 1965–1976)
© Tiago Casanova / University of Porto, Faculty of Architecture

© 2021 Faculdade de Arquitectura da Universidade do Porto and Park Books AG, Zurich

© for the texts: the authors
© for the images: the artists / see image credits

Park Books
Niederdorfstrasse 54
8001 Zurich
Switzerland
www.park-books.com

Park Books is being supported by the Federal Office of Culture with a general subsidy for the years 2021–2024. This book had the support of nation funds from FCT–Fundação para a Ciência e Tecnologia through the Centre for Studies in Architecture and Urbanism, Project Reference UIDB/00145/2020.

All rights reserved; no part of this publication may be reproduced, stored in a retrieval system or transmitted in any form or by any means, electronic, mechanical, photocopying, recording, or otherwise, without the prior written consent of the publisher.

The [MdH XXX] code refers to the record numbers in the Mapping Public Housing Database, available at http://mappingpublichousing.up.pt/en/database/

ISBN 978-3-03860-261-3

Hidden in Plain Sight
POLITICS AND DESIGN IN STATE-SUBSIDIZED RESIDENTIAL ARCHITECTURE

Editors
RUI JORGE GARCIA RAMOS
VIRGÍLIO BORGES PEREIRA
MARTA ROCHA MOREIRA
SÉRGIO DIAS SILVA

Photo Essay by
TIAGO CASANOVA

 PARK BOOKS

Table of Contents

7   Preface
JOSÉ MIGUEL RODRIGUES

9   How Many Names Make the History of Housing?
RUI JORGE GARCIA RAMOS

1. HOUSE, PHILANTROPY, AND SOCIAL ECONOMY (1910–1933)

19   The "Housing Issue" in Portugal: Between the End of the Monarchy and the Republic
PAULO M. ALMEIDA

33   Republican Affordable Housing: Art, Hygiene, and Modern Architecture in Portugal
ELISEU GONÇALVES

47   Science and Technique in the Service of More Modern and Salubrious Cities
ANA CARDOSO DE MATOS

59   Homes Fit For Heroes
MARK SWENARTON

2. HOUSE, FAMILY, AND STATE (1933–1946)

81   Frankfurt am Main: A Shared Life
CARMEN ESPEGEL

101   Corporatism and Affordable Housing in the Portuguese Urban Environment (1933–1974)
PAULA BORGES SANTOS AND JOSÉ MARIA BRANDÃO DE BRITO

127   Progressively Picturesque, Reluctantly Modern: Building a Timeline of the Casas Económicas (1933–1974)
SÉRGIO DIAS SILVA

141   Plain Façades and Exuberant Rooms: A Tour of Casas Económicas
ELIANA SOUSA SANTOS

153   Between the Survey of Rural Housing and the Survey of Popular Architecture: The Housing of Settlers by the Internal Colonization Board (1936–1960)
FILIPA DE CASTRO GUERREIRO

169   The Portuguese People as Peaceful and Intuitive Artists: Propaganda, Folk Art, and the Legitimation of Salazar's New State
VERA MARQUES ALVES

3. HOUSE, NEIGHBOURHOOD, AND DENSITY (1946–1968)

181   Post-War Portugal: Between Conservatism and Modernity
MARIA FERNANDA ROLLO

195   Boosting Perspectives from the Neighbourhood of Alvalade
JOÃO PEDRO COSTA

211   "From User to Dweller": Observation, Consultation, and Involvement Processes in Housing Solutions, 1950s and 1960s
TIAGO LOPES DIAS

227   A Singular Path in Portuguese Housing: Reviewing the Work of the Habitações Económicas—Federação das Caixas de Previdência
MARIA TAVARES

239   Housing Programmes and the Construction of the Portuguese City: the Realization of Modernity in the First Half of the Twentieth Century
TERESA CALIX

255   State, Social Housing, and the Changing City: Porto's 1956 "Improvement Plan"
VIRGÍLIO BORGES PEREIRA AND JOÃO QUEIRÓS

271   Not Houses but Cities—Not Designs, but Designers. 1950s Italy: the INA-Casa Neighbourhoods
ORSINA SIMONA PIERINI

4. HOUSE, URBAN SPRAWL, AND REVOLUTION (1968–1974)

293   Urban Planning and Development Agency Housing Estates in Spain: Bigador's Operational Urbanism (1939–1969)
LUIS MOYA

311   Olivais and Chelas: a Large-Scale Housing Programme in Lisbon
TERESA VALSASSINA HEITOR

335   The Impossible Transition: Marcelo Caetano's Final Shutdown (1968–74)
MANUEL LOFF

353   Before April: The Housing Issue
JOSÉ ANTÓNIO BANDEIRINHA

5. NEW HYPOTHESIS FOR OLD PROBLEMS

373   European Collective Housing in the Post-War Period: Thermal Retrofitting and Architectural Impact
FRANZ GRAF AND GIULIA MARINO

383   Typo-Morphological Laboratories During the 20th Century: a General Overview on the State-Subsidized Multifamily Housing Projects in Portugal (1910–1974)
GISELA LAMEIRA

401   Between Preservation and Transformation of State-Subsidized Multifamily Housing Buildings: Current Paradigms in the Scope of the "Improvement Plan" for the City of Porto
LUCIANA ROCHA

419   The New State, Architecture and Modernism
JOANA BRITES

437   Readings and Re-Readings of the Estado Novo
VICTOR PEREIRA

450   Agualva-Cacém
PHOTO ESSAY BY TIAGO CASANOVA (2018)

Preface

JOSÉ MIGUEL RODRIGUES
Architect, Professor and Director of CEAU-FAUP

This book reports on the research undertaken into public housing policies and their architectural and urbanistic expression at a given moment in history, presented in the form of a curatorial overview. It has always seemed to us that State-sponsored housing merited a study such as this one, which helps to re-establish the State's important role in guaranteeing the right to housing for all, without exception. The Centre for Studies in Architecture and Urbanism (CEAU) readily welcomed the research proposal and was most enthusiastic about being able to accompany the highly relevant work undertaken by the team of researchers participating in this study, in collaboration with other authors from a range of different geographies and chronologies. Hidden in Plain Sight is thus a beautiful operative title for the anthology of academic essays that this book has brought together and placed in dialogue with one another, and now, through its publication, in dialogue with all of us. As befits a work of academic research, the book reveals a discovery that, in a certain sense, was already there before our eyes that do not see (Le Corbusier dixit) and that only the researcher's trained eye is able to identify and make visible, which is the very hallmark of the research into architecture and urbanism that the CEAU undertakes and promotes. The series of studies that can now be read (and observed) here will therefore undoubtedly represent a milestone in the history of research into State-funded housing, both from the point of view of the diverse range of converging perspectives that it contains and, above all, for its defence of the importance of housing in past, present and future public policies. It is with this expectation in mind (in other words with the hope that this book may influence policymakers, who play such a decisive role in safeguarding citizens' basic rights, and, undoubtedly, also architects, whose mission is to think about and design a possible future that is accessible to all) that the research centre from the Faculty of Architecture of the University of Porto proudly associates itself with the initiative of this book and with its authors.

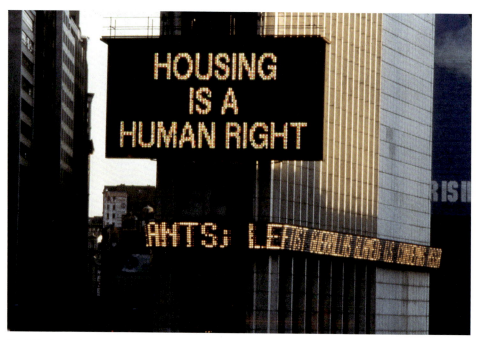

Fig. 1 Martha Rosler, "Housing Is a Human Right," 1989; Frame from Spectacular animation, Times Square, New York; Sponsored by the Public Art Fund under its program, "Message to the Public"
© Martha Rosler; Courtesy of the artist and Mitchell-Innes & Nash, New York

How Many Names Make the History of Housing?

RUI JORGE GARCIA RAMOS
University of Porto, Faculty of Architecture, Centre for Studies in Architecture and Urbanism

Hidden in Plain Sight: Politics and Design in State-Subsidized Residential Architecture

The Mapping Public Housing Research Project (MdH), that reached its final stage in the end of 2019, was the result of a years-long interest in what could be called *ordinary housing*. A group of colleagues and researchers in architecture wondered about a secondary production by Portuguese architects, one that anonymously fills in the streetscape, is absent from trade publications or from architectural history and criticism of the 20th century, and is even forgotten in resumes. The pertinence of that interest was confirmed by a series of piecemeal investigations in the first years of the 21st century, based on surveys and on contact with the authors of these forgotten designs. It focused on the subject of housing for the masses, housing for generic clients, and housing for profit, and on the study of the estates that shaped the city, expanding and inhabiting it and that, in some cases, became what we now call new centralities and peripheries. Risking a quest for an understanding of these houses, estates, and city blocks, one humbly accepts the gargantuan dimension, or perhaps sheer impossibility, of the task. A house, a housing block or an estate form fragments of the city that were erected by a multitude of uncharted names and tales: promoters, designers, builders, and inhabitants assembled a location, lot by lot, street by street, through persistent processes that may not be crystallized and seldom have a discernible end.[1]

BIOGRAPHY

Rui J. G. Ramos is an architect and Full Professor at the Faculty of Architecture, University of Porto (FAUP). He teaches the Project Studio in the Integrated Master's Degree and Theory 2 / Architecture for Today in the PhD Programme in Architecture.

He developed an architectural practice in his own office between 1983 and 2003. Now, he is a researcher at the Centre for Studies in Architecture and Urbanism, and he was the Principal Investigator of the interdisciplinary project "Mapping Public Housing: A Critical Review of the State Subsidized Residential Architecture in Portugal 1910–1974" (FCT 2016–2019). His main study areas are the spatial devices of the house; the relation between culture and forms of dwelling; mass housing programmes; and, currently, developing a renewed understanding for an "inclusive architecture" from aging to sustainability, of which he has published works, available at <http://bit.ly/ruijgramos>.

He has held several leading roles in the UP, including Vice Rector for Facilities and Operation (2014–2018), and he is now President of the FAUP Scientific Council.

[1] Rui Jorge Garcia Ramos, "Quantos nomes fazem uma rua na história da cidade?," in Joana Marques and Rui J. G. Ramos (coord.), *Reconstituição Biográfica dos Arquitectos Representados na Exposição de 1953: "Marques da Silva—Exposição Conjunta das Principais Obras do Mestre e de Alguns dos Seus Discípulos"* (Porto: FIMS, FAUP–CEAU, 2015, 10–14).

These researches are forcibly focused on long-term architectural phenomena, practices, and mentalities, resuming the teachings of the remote Annales school and resetting the investigation agenda to what may be called a social history of architecture; in tune with other sectors, they confront elitist singularizations with a sum of complementary narratives.[2]

These works definitely set a trailblazing tone in the disciplinary field of architecture by shedding light on parallel realities, such as the promotion of popular estates, rural colonising, the small houses so to the liking of Salazar in the first housing programme started in 1933—the Casas Económicas (CE, Affordable Houses)—, and the experiments in modern housing throughout the territory, from Trás-os-Montes to the Algarve; or even on the "b-side" housing production of offices such as those of Ventura Terra, Raul Lino, Marques da Silva, Couto dos Santos, Leonel Gaia, Arménio Losa, Cassiano Barbosa, etc. These and other familiar and unfamiliar names designed *ordinary housing* while worrying about the lack of commissions or while developing the *great works*, creating a parallel testing ground for the rationalization and minimization of the house, enhancing the instruments that would later serve as basis for the official state approach to social and affordable housing initiatives.[3] This book is set, therefore, in the continuity of those previous researches and of the research project *Mapping Public Housing: A critical review of the State-subsidized residential architecture in Portugal (1910-1974)*, funded by the Fundação para a Ciência e Tecnologia (FCT–Foundation for Science and Technology). It establishes the logical reunion of an ensemble of apparently scattered interests and researches, gathering sectorial investigations produced with the goal of bringing up architectural assets on the subject of programmed housing in Portugal, planned or directed by the state, with direct or indirect public financing, fixing it as an epistemological tool, duly referenced, documented and open to other and future investigations, and not limited to the field of architecture.

By making the research available in an online database (open to public access and available for completion and growth), steps are taken towards identifying a large built architectural heritage. There we find today a qualified urban fabric, somewhat under risk of deprivation, urging the evaluation of an identity strategy that focuses on sustainability and qualification of housing and of housing estates in urban areas. This heritage, for the first time identified as an ensemble, is not only a part of a cultural history of Portugal, in political, economic, and social terms but it is, first of all, a disregarded part of the history of Portuguese architecture.

---

[2] This aspect was also mentioned by Dana Arnold: the history of architecture set as a dialectic of different epistemologies, not in chronological and progressive fashion but in a convergence of simultaneous readings; an idea precociously raised by José-Augusto França in 1963. When prefacing the Art History of the 19th century, he mentioned that that work dared to present itself as a contribution of a cultural anthropology of the Portuguese 20th century, and through it to a full knowledge of the century. Finally, in the same text, he noted how "its enlightenment could only come from a pluridisciplinary work, only effectively conducted in a joint reading of the conclusions taken from surveys developed in other cultural domains and other historical series, something that was too soon to achieve in Portugal." Dana Arnold (ed.), *Reading architectural history* (Routledge, 2002). José-Augusto França, "Prefácio," in *A Arte em Portugal no Século XIX*, (Lisbon: Bertrand, 1966 [1st ed. 1963], 13 e 17). Ricard Bucaille and Jean-Marie Pesez, "Cultura Material," in Ruggiero Romano (dir.), *Enciclopédia Einaudi*, vol. 16 (Imprensa Nacional, Casa da Moeda, 1989, 11–47).

[3] We note, among others, the works of Ana Tostões, Eliseu Gonçalves, Filipa Guerreiro, Filipa Serpa, Gisela Lameira, João Pedro Costa, José A. Bandeirinha, Luciana Rocha, Maria Tavares, Marta Rocha, Ricardo Agarez, Rui J. G. Ramos, Sérgio Dias Silva, Teresa Calix, Teresa Heitor, Tiago L. Dias, Vanda Maldonado e Pedro Borges, Virgílio B. Pereira and João Queirós, etc.

A narrative is being built, claiming the right to narrate and hear the voices of *others* that, extensively and diffusely, built different types of housing across the country. Within their specific circumstances, those houses transformed and improved the quality of life—at least for some. This historiographic propensity challenges an "insistently ideological critic that refrained the development of a disciplinary autonomy"[4] by inhibiting a look over this vast heritage and substantially altering the understanding of its circumstances and period of creation, and of the role of architecture and its modernity throughout the Portuguese 20th century. It is no longer admissible to ignore the extensive phenomenon that is the production of housing for the masses in Portugal between 1910 and 1974.

The purpose is not to whitewash the role which architects and other actors set for themselves by accepting commissions for works of affirmation and glorification of an authoritarian regime, and so becoming political instruments.[5] Nor it is to ignore how housing and the access to a dignified home became weapons for the regime that, with its view set on abolishing class divisions through corporatist organisation, intended domination of the socially and economically weak, and the exploration of their failings by imposing rules for moral and civic conduits in tune with total obedience to a repressive political power. It is impossible to observe these architectural phenomena and ignore their context. Housing and politics are two sides of the same coin, included in the first actions of the Estado Novo along with others that limited access to education, established a thorough system of censorship and created a propagandistic façade for a deep structure of social control. Programmed housing was, from the start of the regime in 1933 with the Casas Económicas, part of a complex staging of *salvaging* the original Republican initiative,[6] placing it in the service of a corporatist network of institutions directly supervised by Salazar himself.[7] This bureaucratic structure led a policy of social control over a specific electing group, able to afford a resoluble rent and life insurance, mandatory elements that came with a single-family house with a flower garden and a kitchen garden, far from the vices and dangers of the tavern, as put by Salazar. With these small houses, Salazar wanted, in an early stage, to forswear the socialist phalanstery, breeding ground for promiscuity and revolution in the people (an entity he feared so much) but simultaneously to fight the image of misery and insalubrity spread through town and country. However, this and other expectations turned out to be unfounded. At the end of World War II, opposition movements felt safe enough to denounce the destitute living conditions of a large section of the population. The *indigents,* as the regime called them, with no resources to own a house and therefore not subject to

[4] Ana Tostões, "O desafio da arquitectura africana e o teste do tempo: modernidade em Angola e Moçambique", in *Arquitetura Moderna em África: Angola e Moçambique*, ed. Ana Tostões (Lisbon: FCT), 4.

[5] Jorge Ramos do Ó, *Os Anos de Ferro: o Dispositivo Cultural Durante a "Política do Espírito" 1933–1949* (Lisbon: Estampa, 1999 [1993])

[6] Rui J. G. Ramos, Eliseu Gonçalves, and Sérgio Dias Silva, "Política e arquitetura habitacional: um Mapa da intervenção do estado na habitação," in Joana Brites and Luís Miguel Correia (eds.), *Obras Públicas no Estado Novo* (Coimbra: Imprensa da Universidade de Coimbra, 2020).

[7] António Ferro, "Salazar princípio e fim," in *Entrevistas de António Ferro a Salazar* (Lisbon: Parceria A. M. Pereira, Livraria Editora, 2003 [1938]), 169.

political manipulation, brought up the reality of an underdeveloped country where rampant poverty, hunger and poor living conditions were present not only in cities but also in rural settings. In this context, a political struggle opened a scar within the institutional core of the regime, as a set of young technicians fought for a more cosmopolitan view of progress, one that could only be achieved through the electrification and infrastructuring of the country and by new types of houses that could tackle the housing issue with faster and more cost-effective solutions. It is interesting to note how this struggle inside the regime opened up new understandings of the housing problem and made it more receptive to solutions which until then were unthinkable. Modernity was the inevitable architectural response when a new generation of architects took control of the design of collective housing blocks and estates. They were at the helm of the new Casas de Renda Económica (CRE–Affordable Rents Houses) programme from 1945, using the accumulated capital of the Federação das Caixas de Previdência (FCP–Federation of Provident Funds) through their design office, the Habitações Económicas (HE–Affordable Housing). From this programme, a small revolution in the design of housing for the masses took place, taking the principles of modern architecture and revising them for the Portuguese reality, set on reformulating ways of life and, above all, on achieving houses *for the larger number.*

In spite of the almost 600 estates and eighty-two thousand houses built by dozens of housing programmes and related initiatives, the aggregate public participation in housing between 1910 and 1974 reveals a somewhat slim scale of intervention in view of the dimensions of the problem. The stable launch of housing initiatives with public intervention or support grew considerably after the epic period of the regime and after World War II, with noticeable influence in the transition from traditional forms of construction to a building industry and in the consequential job creation. An apparent reduction in investment in housing in the 1960s set the background to soaring discussions of housing politics of the post-1974 revolution: the Intermediary Development Plan for 1965–67 included, for the first time, a topic on housing; a colloquium on housing policies took place in the Laboratório Nacional de Engenharia Civil (LNEC–National Laboratory for Civil Engineering); and the Fundo de Fomento da Habitação (FFH–Fund for Housing Development) was created. The transition to democracy, however, uncovered the limitations of the Estado Novo intervention in housing, as, in 1974, 52 per cent of houses in Portugal did not have water supply, 53 per cent had no electricity, 60 per cent had no sewerage, 67 per cent had no bathroom and, in general, 600,000 houses were needed.[8]

[8] António Fonseca Ferreira, *Por Uma Nova Política de Habitação* (Porto, Afrontamento, 1987).

The distribution of programmes in time shows the hesitations of the regime as to what it needed to focus on, equalizing, dimension-wise, initiatives with variant goals. From the corporatist approach of the Casas Económicas, more deeply connected to the state's political vertex, and of the more independent Casas de Renda Económica, to the *charitable* approach of the Casas para Famílias Pobres (CFP–Houses for Poor Families), the political elites went back and forth looking for the best targets for housing policies.[9]

The inefficacy of the central state's structure was more perceptible when, at the end of the 1950s, a collaboration between the Ministério das Obras Públicas (MOP–Ministry for Public Works) and the two largest municipalities gave rise to intense interventions with fast results, as the Plano de Melhoramentos do Porto (Plan for the Improvement of Porto) and the Plano de Novas Construções da Cidade de Lisboa (Plan for New Constructions in the City of Lisbon) rapidly equalled the production of other decades-long programmes.

The Estado Novo's intervention in the discussion of and search for solutions for the housing problem was, as we have seen, hesitant, even scarce. Its architectural importance and the political charge and significance the dictatorship attributed to the topic cannot, however, be denied.[10] Set as a closure to the research project, this book takes on an attempt to prelude larger works. The object of study, the time lapse, and the specific circumstances warn us of the impossibility of definitive answers. If a conclusion may be drawn, after a long research journey—with a debt owed to the many collaborators of this project—it is the presence of a complex organization. Because there is no simple formula to encompass lengthy phenomena that crossed several political systems, from the monarchy to the complex Estado Novo machine, reductive answers are dangerous. Permanent variables were crossed, divided , and modified in hierarchic branches, more subtly or less so, in precise , and ambiguous fashion, in variably sized partnerships between private initiative, financial goals, philanthropy, local government, and central state. Any attempt to synthesize this reality or to approach one of its topics must always stress what preceded it and what it precedes, in a chronological and diachronic movement, knowingly gathering the social, geographical, economic, technic, and architectonic factors that build up politics.

That is, perhaps, the safest of the observed realities—that the social, geographical, economic, technical, and architectural are always used as instruments for political action. To observe the architectural production of housing is to accept the impurity of its practice as part of processes that generate impasses. There are no simple answers.[11]

[9] Ramos, "Política e arquitetura habitacional."
[10] Ibid.
[11] Ibid.

This book follows a time sequence in its chapters—1 House, Philanthropy, and Social Economy 1910–1933, 2 House, Family, and State 1933–1946, 3 House, Neighbourhood, and Density 1946–1968, 4 House, Urban Sprawl, and Revolution 1968–1974. Its interior allows for space to invoke diverse thematic, architectural, sociological, historical, national, and international alignments. Avoiding isolation of the core subject, an effort was made to open intersection hypotheses that unexpectedly place the reader in a larger reality, vital to an understanding not only of the Portuguese housing issue, but also to its integration in the period's housing discussions in a Western context, when other precocious experiments and alternative paths were tested within other political regimes. As the architectural question is seldom exclusively architectural, invitations were extended to bring other views from the fields of history, political science, sociology, and cultural studies, hoping that our colleagues from other disciplinary fields are also interested in architecture, or in the clarification of the architectural dimension of their questions. In the final chapter—5 New Hypothesis for Old Problems—but already when closing the previous chapter, a new time is set up. The housing question before the 1974 Revolution is analysed as the premise to the post-revolutionary initiatives that were sprouting, and the architects authoring modern housing for the FCP–HE became active figures in the revolutionary process of April 1974. This shows how illusive, even if momentarily useful, it is to shelve arguments in separate containers as, particularly in the Portuguese case, the continuity of the ways of doing is vivid and follows a millenary tradition. The book closes with a focus on the pertinence of the effect of these architectures in the built environment of recent decades and its heritage value. Recognition of its spatial qualities and coherent designs is urgent, as they modelled urban spaces of identity that, in some cases, have significantly increased in financial value but that are in need of non-destructive and non-intrusive conservation strategies for preservation of their identity and typo-morphological characteristics. The book gathers a set of essays that opens up possibilities and sets space for doubts, but mostly opens up new paths, in continuity, for research on housing.

BIBLIOGRAPHY

Arnold, Dana (ed.). Reading Architectural History, Routledge, 2002.

Bucaille, Ricard, and Jean-Marie Pesez. "Cultura Material," in Ruggiero Romano (dir.), Enciclopédia Einaudi, edited by Ruggiero Romano, vol. 16, 11–47. Lisbon: Imprensa Nacional, Casa da Moeda, 1989.

Ferreira, António Fonseca, Por Uma Nova Política de Habitação. Porto: Afrontamento, 1987.

Ferro, António. "Salazar princípio e fim." In Entrevistas de António Ferro a Salazar, 169. Lisbon: Parceria A. M. Pereira, Livraria Editora, 2003 [1st ed. 1938].

França, José-Augusto. "Prefácio." In A Arte em Portugal no Século XIX, 13–17. Lisbon: Bertrand, 1966 [1st ed. 1963].

Ó, Jorge Ramos do, Os Anos de Ferro: o Dispositivo Cultural Durante a "Política do Espírito" 1933–1949. Lisbon: Estampa, 1999 [1st ed. 1993].

Ramos, Rui Jorge Garcia, "Quantos nomes fazem uma rua na história da cidade?" In Reconstituição Biográfica dos Arquitectos Representados na Exposição de 1953: "Marques da Silva— Exposição Conjunta das Principais Obras do Mestre e de Alguns dos Seus Discípulos", edited by Joana Marques and Rui J. G. Ramos, 10–14. Porto: FIMS, FAUP-CEAU, 2015 [digital edition].

Ramos, Rui Jorge Garcia, Eliseu Gonçalves, and Sérgio Dias Silva. "Política e arquitetura habitacional: um Mapa da intervenção do estado na habitação." In Estado Novo e Obras Públicas, edited by Luís Miguel Correia and Joana Brites. Coimbra: Imprensa da Universidade de Coimbra, 2019 [no prelo].

Tostões, Ana. "O desafio da arquitectura africana e o teste do tempo: modernidade em Angola e Moçambique." In Arquitetura Moderna em África: Angola e Moçambique, edited by Ana Tostões. Lisbon: FCT, 2013, 4.

Innauguration of the Social Estate of Cascais in 1933, a municipal initiative that followed legislation from the First Republic but was appropriated by the dictatorship for propaganda, as were other housing initiatives.

Empresa Pública Jornal O Século, Albuns Gerais no. 25, doc.0257H
PT/TT/EPJS/SF/001-001/0025/0257H. Image from ANTT.

1. HOUSE, PHILANTROPY, AND SOCIAL ECONOMY (1910–1933)

Many years of legislative discussion placed housing in the centre of political action, but the first housing law in Portugal was published only in 1918, in the context of social unrest following a disastrous participation in World War I. Sparse and limited initiatives failed to create a momentum for the development of housing by or with the support of the State. Germany was at the forefront of public housing investment and Portuguese politicians and technicians were aware.

The "Housing Issue" in Portugal: Between the End of the Monarchy and the Republic

PAULO M. ALMEIDA
University of Porto, Faculty of Arts and Humanities,
Transdisciplinary Research Centre "Culture, Space and Memory"

ABSTRACT

In Portugal, the "housing issue" gained ground in the last decades of the 19th century. It became a public and political debate that had no visible achievements, despite the economic expansion and industrialization that had taken place in the last quarter of the century, in which medical hygienists, journalists and some public decision makers were beginning to gain prominence. The debate emphasized the need to support private initiative in the construction of hygienic housing for the working class as a way of combating poverty and insalubrity in cities. Initially neglected, the need for intervention from public initiatives, the state, and local authorities, gained a preponderance in this debate over time and ended up being present in all political proposals on the matter. It was not until the beginning of the 20th century, in the early years of the Republic, that the first public promotion initiatives appeared, while at the same time safeguarding a legal framework for private promotion, which showed no interest in investment in social housing aimed at the popular and working classes. The first examples of social housing in Portugal came from municipal initiatives, specifically in the city of Porto, with apparent genuine interest in addressing the housing issue and correcting unhealthy situations. Soon after, two Republican governments, from opposite political fields, launched the first state initiatives, which were very limited to the urban reality that they sought to combat. The housing developments launched during the Republic were attacked in the regime itself and were later used as a vehicle for political propaganda in favour of authoritarianism. In this chapter we will analyse, from a historical perspective, the beginnings of public concerns with the housing of the working classes and the first measures for dealing with the housing crisis felt in the main cities. We will present a picture of the environment of profound changes that the country went through at the turn of the 19th to the 20th century, recognizing the urban housing issue and how it was approached by the public authorities.

BIOGRAPHY

Paulo M. Almeida has directed his research to issues related to social housing and Estado Novo, after the completion of the Master's thesis in Contemporary History at the Faculty of Arts of the University of Porto, "Favor, reward and social control" (2010), about the Casas Económicas (Affordable Houses) iniatives by the Portuguese authoritarian regime launched in the city of Porto between 1935 and 1965. He is a researcher at CITCEM–Transdisciplinary Research Centre "Culture, Space and Memory" since 2010, integrated in the Trading Value group. He published the article "Economic neighborhoods of Porto: The house as a political weapon," in the collective work "Family, Space and Heritage" (2011). Currently, he prepares his Ph.D. in History at the Faculty of Letters of the University of Porto, under the theme "Social Housing in Estado Novo (1933–1974)—Policies, Models and Processes." Professionally he has worked as a journalist in the Portuguese written press since 1992.

PORTUGAL IN CHANGE: "PAUPERISM," SALUBRITY, AND HOUSING IN THE CITIES

The turn of the century in Portugal was characterized by major social, economic, and political transformations. The 19th century was a period of civil wars, migrations, and epidemics, which assisted in the consolidation of liberalism without erasing many of the characteristics of the *Ancien Régime*. The beginning of the 20th century, which was preceded by a strong economic upturn and then followed by a serious financial crisis, was marked by the establishment of the Republic, a period of great instability, which included participation in World War I, problems of supply of essential genres and intense agitation among workers.

In the period that we are interested in analysing, in a broader perspective, between 1860 and 1930, the Portuguese population increased progressively, with unequal rhythm, but always with high physiological indexes, i.e., a high mortality rate, associated with a high birth rate. The population varied between 3.8 million people in 1864 and 6.8 million in 1930. Between these dates, Portugal faced successive migratory waves, which removed tens of thousands of people annually.[1]

Population growth was low, with growth rates not exceeding 1.3 per cent; the mortality rate only began to decline after 1920, while the birth rate declined after 1930. However, even with low population growth, there was a growth of urban areas, with special emphasis on Lisbon and Porto, the only metropoles in the early 20th century with more than 100.000 inhabitants, accentuating a movement of population displacement to the coast and a passage of labour from the primary sector to the secondary and tertiary sectors.

Continental Portugal marked a considerable economic advance in the last decades of the 19th century, associated with a strong increase in public works, especially in the construction of roads, bridges, railways, ports, and the establishment of several industries, such as textiles, metallurgy, and chemical products. In the consolidation of liberalism, the various administrative reforms and the publication of general legislation deriving from the Constitution, such as the Administrative, Penal, and Civil Codes, which transformed society and social relations, were of great importance.[2]

The economic situation worsened after 1890 due to the English ultimatum surrounding the dispute over the African territories and the international crisis that led the bank Baring & Brothers, the main financier of the Kingdom's public works, to bankruptcy.

---

[1] Joel Serrão and A.H. Oliveira Marques, *Nova História de Portugal*, Vol XI (Lisbon: Editorial Presença, 1995),13–36; Nuno Valério (ed.), *Estatísticas Históricas Portuguesas*, Vol. I (Lisbon: Instituto Nacional de Estatística, 2001), 33–126. There were several migratory peaks in this period, with emphasis on the 1890s and the 1911–13 triennium. Only in these three years it is estimated that more than 300,000 people left the country. The numbers of legal emigration indicate that more than 1.8 million Portuguese left the country between 1860 and 1939. Emigration, on the other hand, represented the massive entry of remittances.

[2] Since the Constitution of 1822, Portugal has had several administrative codes, which advocated the division of territory. The most important, which was adapted in 1940 and lasted until 1976, is the Administrative Code of 1878. The first Portuguese Penal Code with effective applicability was that of 1852, having undergone successive changes, until it was replaced by the Code of 1886, which was in force during most of the 20th century. The first Civil Code is from 1867 and was replaced only in 1968. See Serrão and Marques, *Nova História*, 281–340.

The government was forced to remove the *real* currency from the gold standard in an attempt to curb inflation, but the country was plunged into a serious financial crisis with huge social repercussions due to a lack of food and raw materials. At the same time, the political crisis was worsened by the republicans who, in Porto in January 1891, mounted the first attempt to overthrow the monarchy.

The revolution would be successful on 5 October 1910. The Republic (1910–1926) was a liberal-democratic regime, which provided for the separation of powers. The parliament, called the Congress, was made up of a Chamber of Deputies, with direct elections every three years, and a Senate, also elected directly every six years. The President of the Republic was elected by Congress in non-successive periods of four years and appointed the president and the ministers of the government. The Republic always experienced moments of great instability and tension in the power struggle, which often continued on the street. There were scores of political killings, including several ministers, and thousands of people were killed by gunfire in riots and armed clashes.[3] It should be borne in mind that the illiteracy rate for those over seven years old in 1911 was 70.3 per cent of the population. In 1890 the rate was 75.9 per cent and in 1930 61.8 per cent.[4] One of the great programmes of the Republic was precisely to increase the education of the Portuguese.

Portugal was a rural country, with more than 85 per cent of the population living in the countryside in 1910. The capital Lisbon and the city of Porto absorbed 68 per cent of the urban population. Urbanization was slow, although the cities on the outskirts of Lisbon and Porto recorded rapid growth from the 1920s. The main cities were attractive to a large and varied population, indigent and illiterate, looking for a manual labour, often related to agriculture, a place in a factory or workshop, or learning a trade. Men, women, and children would come to the cities in search of work, often on a daily or weekly basis, and would shelter where possible, in rented rooms, in tents, in the houses of the "ilhas" or in the cubicles of the "pátios" and "vilas," close to the workplace to save on transportation, but usually paying expensive rents for the low wages earned, forcing the whole family to work.[5] Much of this labour force was encouraged to embark for migratory destinations, for the "Americas," especially Brazil.

Lisbon and Porto were administratively delimited in 1895, with their borders far beyond the central core, which allowed the development of various economic activities within their limits. But cities were still far from having modern basic infrastructures, such as the supply of piped drinking water and sanitation. Most of the streets were not paved, the sewers were open and it was normal to be infested by the waste of animals used for food and transportation.

[3] Serrão and Marques, *Nova História*, 699–745.

[4] José Mattoso (ed.). *História de Portugal, O Estado Novo (1926–1974)*, Vol. 7 (Lisbon: Editorial Estampa, 1994), 14–29.

[5] To see wage rates in cities and wage expenditures with food and housing, see Serrão and Marques, Nova história, 207–233. In the case of the city of Oporto, see Pereira, *Famílias Portuenses*, 45–78. See also Valério, *Estatísticas Históricas*, 615–655.

Water channelling arrived in Lisbon in 1868 and in Porto in 1887. The two cities already had piped gas, but the electric light did not arrive until 1895, initially used in transport, which registered a considerable advance at the end of the 19th century.

Living in the cities was dangerous, one could contract an infectious disease for which there was no cure, and not even the elite escaped the epidemic outbreaks that swept the country from one end to the other. In 1861, the Portuguese king D. Pedro V and one of the princes died of typhoid fever. The people thought it was poisoning. The food, especially in the working classes, was deficient, not allowing the organism to cement its defences, a crucial question in the fight against tuberculosis, the main social scourge.[6]

The hygienist ideas that circulated in Europe from the beginning of the 19th century reached Portugal, but did not raise the conscience of the political decision makers. At the turn of the century a generation of young doctors emerged that warned of the need to improve the sanitary conditions of cities, whose unhealthy environment was understood as the focus of infectious diseases.

"Pauperism," which generated the lack of hygiene conditions of the working classes and workers in cities, was a distant reality for decision makers and politicians, but it was a growing concern for the medical profession, some journalists and intellectuals. Although their causes and consequences were known, decision makers understood, not in concrete terms, that industrialists and households should solve them, not intervening in the rental market or in the construction industry. This view was dominant in the bills that came to parliament during the Monarchy and may have been the cause of the delay of direct intervention in the sector, even because the housing experiments under way in Europe were known and detailed in the documents presented to the Chamber of Deputies. The legislator's ineffectiveness defined protection for the renting sector and for the existing classes, a way of satisfying the real estate investments of the elite in urban centres, following the precepts of liberalism, access to private property on the one hand and free initiative on the other. The low-skilled and fragmented construction sector maintained a very rigid cost structure with high labour costs, whether the construction was of quality or more modest.[7]

The protection of the tenant sector contributed to maintaining the housing crisis with a shortage of housing that the working families could afford, and put them in a market where the available supply was characterized by a lack of conditions and insalubrity.

---

[6] For aspects related to food in this period see Serrão and Marques, *Nova História*, 617–627; José Mattoso (dir.) and Irene Vaquinhas (ed.). *História da Vida Privada em Portugal—A Época Contemporânea* (Lisbon: Temas e debates, 2011), 56–91.

[7] Álvaro Ferreira da Silva, "A construção residencial em Lisboa," in *Análise Social* 136–137, (1996): 599–629.

DURING THE CONSTITUTIONAL MONARCHY

The first attempt to legislate on housing arose in 1883, following a health report in Lisbon and the industrial survey of 1881 which dealt with the question of housing of factory workers.[8] In this proposal, only intended for the capital, the granting of tax exemptions to the companies in the construction of houses with limited income was proposed, designated "housing of the laborious classes and less wealthy." The following year a new bill came into being, directly recognizing that the only way to achieve the goals of cheap housing was through "direct government or municipal initiative," authorizing a bank loan to the Lisbon Chamber for this purpose.[9]

The deputy Augusto Fuschini (1843–1911), in 1884,[10] focused the discussion on private initiative and on the limited rent of houses or divisions, in a proposal addressed to the whole country, differentiating between Lisbon and Porto and the rest of the territory and prohibiting subletting. It opened the possibility of selling the dwelling to the tenant, with limited profits, and widened the range of tax exemptions, either for companies that gave their houses to this market or built them for rent, or for tenants who bought them.

The next bill came seventeen years later in 1901, a hiatus that hid a complex financial, economic, and political crisis. The proposal of Guilherme Santa-Rita (1859–1905)[11] followed the same precepts of the previous one—incentives to the private initiative, concretely to the corporations that were constituted to invest in the construction of "housing of the laborious classes and less wealthy." Liabilities were limited, with differentiation between Lisbon and Porto and the rest of the country, sublease was prohibited and a set of exemptions were defined for companies and tenants who became owners. The profits of corporations, in rents and in the sale of houses, were also limited. It was the first proposal to define what could be built: one-storey houses with a garden of six metres, at the edge of the street, elevated up to 50 cm from the ground. It opened the possibility of erecting buildings with more floors, but in areas that did not exceed one third of the total.

In 1905, at the suggestion of King D. Carlos, the joint proposal of the Secretaries of State for Kingdom Business, Finance, and Public Works, Commerce and Industry,[12] reversed the philosophy of previous measures. The proposal provided that working-class neighbourhoods and groups of cheap houses should be built by municipalities (or by the state, when those had no means), associations, industrial or mining companies, and individuals. The government should enter an annual budget in order to move forward with the programme. The proposal provided for benefits and tax exemptions, land transfer and infrastructure support, which

[8] Proposed law of Fontes Pereira de Melo and Hintze Ribeiro, *Diário das Sessões da Câmara dos Deputados* (15 January 1883): 54–55. There were, however, some antecedents related to social housing in contemporary times: Decree no. 10, of 31 December 1864, approving a plan of improvements of the city of Lisbon, provided that new buildings and the opening of roads should obey a set of rules of hygiene, convenience, and public enjoyment; and the Bill of Law of 17 May 1880, exempting tenants from the low-income classes for a period of five years for tenants who paid no more than 50$000 annually (abolished in 1899).

[9] Proposed law of Deputy Rosa Araújo, *Diário das Sessões da Câmara dos Deputados* (20 February 1884): 425–426.

[10] Proposed law of deputy Augusto Fuschini, *Diário das Sessões da Câmara dos Deputados*, (17 May 1884): 1633–1646.

[11] Proposed law of the deputy Guilherme Santa-Rita, *Diário das Sessões da Câmara dos Deputados* (7 March 1901): 2–6. The project can be found in *Diário das Sessões da Câmara dos Deputados* (8 March 1901): 2–4.

[12] Proposed law of the State Secretaries of Business of the Kingdom, of the Treasury and of Public Works, Commerce and Industry by Eduardo José Coelho, Manuel Afonso de Esprequeira, and D. João de Alarcão Velasques Sarmento Osório, *Câmara dos Deputados* (22 August 1905): 14–17.

should be left to municipalities. The houses, detached or semi-detached, buildings with more floors or terraced houses with a frontage up to 100 metres, built under the Health Regulations of 14 February 1903, were for sale. The rental of dwellings was only foreseen when the houses could not be sold by public auction.

In 1908, the proposal of the Secretary of State for Foreign Affairs, Ferreira do Amaral (1843–1923),[13] proposed the creation of a High Council of Housing Hygiene that would define which private economic housing would be placed in the conditional income system and thus gain access to tax benefits and exemptions. The proposal provided incentives for companies to buy depreciated housing in order to demolish, rebuild or restore it and place it on the rental market. The dwellings could be sold to the tenants, also with fixed maximum profits.

Despite the concerns shown, housing was certainly not a priority of the governments of the Constitutional Monarchy. The legislator was divided between supporting private initiative or launching itself as a promoter in the construction of housing for the working classes and the popular classes. Between 1883 and 1908, mainstream policy was that the private market should promote the construction of cheap housing, with the support of the state, through the sale or transfer of land and the construction of infrastructures, benefiting of exemptions and tax incentives, which extended to tenants who bought the dwellings.

However, the housing offer proposed by the private initiative, targeting low-income families, was a model based on the available family income, dependent on the low wages practised by industries, workshops, and the tertiary sector.[14] Even civil servants were paid low wages. On the other hand, the proposals that foresaw the creation of a small real estate market, intended to workers and families of few resources, were even more distant from the reality of the country.

The proposals launched during the monarchy helped to cement the idea of the "house," the "airy house," and hygiene; the refuge of the working family, the individual house that allows not only the diseases of the body, epidemics, contagion, immorality to be contained, but also new ideas that are emerging in the world of work, socialist and revolutionary ideas, "diseases of the spirit," which are part of the daily life of workers and employees.[15]

[13] Proposed Law of the Secretary of State for Business of the Kingdom, by Ferreira do Amaral, *Câmara dos Deputados* (23 May 1908): 12–16. The proposal came after the regicide of D. Carlos, under the reign of D. Manuel II.

[14] Manuel C. Teixeira, *Habitação Popular na Cidade Oitocentista—As Ilhas do Porto* (Lisbon: Fundação Calouste Gulbenkian, 1996), 403–426.

[15] Gaspar Martins Pereira, *Famílias Portuenses na Viragem do Século (1880–1910)* (Porto: Edições Afrontamento, 1995), 67–68; Marielle Christine Gros, *O Alojamento Social sob o Fascismo* (Porto: Afrontamento, 1982), 91–109.

THE FIRST SOCIAL HOUSING PROGRAMMES

The establishment of the Republic provided a framework of hope for the most educated citizens and for urban and working class workers, but the regime was characterized by intense political instability, which spread to the streets in violent scenarios.[16] The workers' movement, dissatisfied with the direction of the new regime, unleashed a series of strikes between 1910 and 1914, across all sectors, which were felt in urban centres, but with repercussions throughout the country. From 1914, with participation in World War I, public finances seemed uncontrolled, with the public deficit affecting the inflation, noticing the lack of fiduciary currency, due to the introduction of the *escudo*. There was a shortage of basic necessities, which reached very high values on the black market. Life in cities became very difficult, between political violence, food shortages, and permanent unhealthiness.

In this context of intense agitation, the city of Porto played a decisive role in housing, much because of its republican elite and pressure from the "socialist minorities" in the municipal Senate. Between 1914 and 1917, the physician Eduardo Santos Silva (1879–1960), first as vice-president of the executive committee of the Oporto City Council and later as president, played a key role in launching four social housing projects that became known as "colónias operárias" (working class colonies).

The three neighbourhoods built on the initiative of the newspaper *O Comércio do Porto* between 1899 and 1904, financed by public subscription after a campaign launched by the owner of the newspaper, Bento Carqueja (1860–1935), had the technical assistance of the city council, which allowed experience and knowledge on the construction of modern houses and urbanization infrastructures to be acquired.[17] Against the socioeconomic cycle, in the face of a tremendous social crisis, Eduardo Santos Silva launched the municipality into the construction of four neighbourhoods on the outskirts of the city, next to factories, which already had a number of "ilhas" at their disposal. The working colonies of Antero de Quental [MdH DB a281], Estêvão de Vasconcelos [MdH DB a282], Dr. Manuel Laranjeira [MdH DB a290], and Viterbo de Campos [MdH DB a283], names associated with republicanism and socialism, built between 1914 and 1917, are equivalent to 312 houses. The houses were arranged in groups of four with one or two floors, following the model of the *Carré Mulhousien*, which had been introduced in the neighbourhood of Monte Pedral [MdH DB a13, a271] built by *O Comércio do Porto*. They had a WC, no yard but with a little garden in some groups, they had some public equipment, and were designed for the rental market.

[16] Serrão e Marques, *Nova História*, 699–717.

[17] On the neighborhoods of *O Comércio do Porto* see Eliseu Gonçalves and Rui J. G. Ramos, "Primeiras propostas de habitação operária no Porto: A casa unifamiliar, o *Carré Mulhousien* e a *Cité-Jardin*," *Ciudades*, 19, 1 (2016): 77–98..

Insufficient in number to overcome the housing crisis in the city, the working colonies of Porto would be the first municipal initiative in the field of social housing in Portugal and emerged at a time when the ministries of Finance and Development launched the proposal of a housing programme for the "less affluent classes" in the Chamber of Deputies.[18]

The legislative initiative proposed tax exemptions and benefits for construction cooperatives, welfare institutions, and city councils in the construction of controlled-cost houses in Lisbon, Porto, and the rest of the country. The municipalities were obliged to carry out the infrastructures on the land to be built on. The project provided for the creation of construction institutes in the municipalities of Lisbon and Porto, with access to two separate loans for the construction of houses for rent. In cases where the houses were acquired, they were considered "family assets" and could not be executed on the death of the owner. As early as April 1914, congressman Francisco de Sales Ramos da Costa advanced with his bill for "cheap or low-income houses," which was the source of a new proposal in 1916, discussed in the Finance Committee.[19] This proposal provided for the construction of housing at controlled costs and rent to be built by the same organizers of the previous proposal, but also by Caixa Geral de Depósitos and the state: houses or groups of houses on one or more floors always with a yard and, if possible, with a garden at the front, benefiting from tax exemptions. The project proposed the creation of a housing market for cheap and healthy homes, recorded in a register organized by the municipality of Lisbon; the builders or owners put the houses on this exchange, for which they received a fixed-term debt for 25 years, and buyers, heads of households with a monthly income from certain amounts, acquired the houses at the same fixed interest rate.

The first law that actually promoted a social housing programme came in 1918 with the government of Sidónio Pais (1872–1918), which resulted from a coup. Decree no. 4,137, dated 24 April 1918, is addressed to the private sector, but opens the way to public initiative (art. 15), through government transfers or credit granting.

Sidónio Pais, a charismatic military man who had been in the diplomatic service in Germany, launched a populist government, centred on his figure as the dictator, who gained authoritarian outlines; he even created a "political and social" police corps in Lisbon to tighten censorship. Initially it gained renown among the popular strata, mainly because of the aid to the poor and the launching of the working-class neighbourhoods, but then it pressed the working class hard.[20]

[18] Proposed law of the Ministries of Finance and Development, *Câmara dos Deputados* (26 February 1914): 5–11.

[19] Proposed law of Francisco Sales Ramos da Costa, *Câmara dos Deputados* (28 April 1916): 1–13.

[20] Serrão and Marques, *Nova História*, 717–721.

According to the decree, which used many of the clauses of the 1914 and 1916 proposals, the focus was on private initiative, which would be encouraged to place house prices and controlled rents on the housing market, benefiting from a set of tax exemptions and support for expropriation of land, including those where there was unhealthy housing. Joint-stock companies and cooperatives pursuing these objectives benefited from a low-interest loan. These entities were also benefited by the infrastructures that the municipal councils were obliged to set up: streets, sidewalks, a sewage network, public lavatories, fountains, lighting, schools and day-care centres. The councils must contract access to cheap transport to the new quarters with transportation companies. Based on the 1914 project, the law introduced the concept of "homestead," in which houses, if acquired by a tenant who had a certain salary, could not be executed as long as one of the spouses was alive and there were children under 21 years of age. The decree proceeded to the Regulation of Construction and Sale of Affordable Houses,[21] which defined the forms of support to the private buyer, through loans. However, housing built by private initiative under this law is not known and eventually the state moved forward with construction. In Porto, in the neighbourhood of Arrábida [MdH DB a20], which began by being called "Sidónio Pais," the first thirty-five of the 100 houses were built; in Lisbon, the state purchased the land to install the future neighbourhood of Ajuda.[22]

Sidónio Pais was assassinated in December 1918 and government was assumed by the then Secretary of State of the Navy, João Canto e Castro (1862–1934). It was a period of agitation, with several military pronouncements and the establishment of the ephemeral Northern Monarchy (January–February 1919). It was marked by the return of Portuguese soldiers from theatres of war in Europe and Africa, and by the pneumonic flu, the "Spanish flu," which left a trail of more than 50,000 dead in about a year. However, in April 1919, the government presided over by Domingos Leite Pereira (1882–1956), which lasted only three months, launched a new programme of economic housing, predicting the need to "employ public works personnel and moralize and make useful its production."[23]

The amendments to the previous legislation were considerable and defined a clear objective to please certain sectors of society. Let us see: it employed workers "who are congesting the public works and are not part of any staff of the State" (Article 2); provided for the construction of 1000 independent houses by the end of 1920; fixed the rent at 8$00/month, including water supply; directed the funds obtained from the rents to a fund that would be used in the expenses of official schools and canteens, educational theatre, nursing homes, bathhouses, playground, swimming pools, and house conservation;

[21] Decree no. 4,440, of 12 June 1918.

[22] According to Decree no. 4,163, dated 25 April 1918, a loan was opened for "construction of cheap houses for workers' housing" in the Ministry of Finance: 300,000$00 for land acquisition and construction of 120 houses in Lisbon and 250,000$00 for land acquisition and construction of 100 homes in Porto. This neighbourhood, which was part of the "Labour Colony" of Viterbo de Campos, was the only realization of this housing programme, according to Decree no. 11,324, dated 7 December 1925, although part of it was built under the 1919 legislation. On the Ajuda neighborhood, see Maria da Conceição Tiago, "Bairros Sociais da I República: projectos e realizações,"*Ler História*, no. 59 (2010): 249–272.

[23] Decree no. 5,397, of 14 April 1919.

the administration of the district would be in charge of a committee of residents and representatives of the state; and legal and regulatory formalities were waived in respect of invitations to tender, contracts, supplies, and awards. The legislation originated in the Ministry of Labour, headed by Augusto Dias da Silva (1887–1928), a member of the Socialist Party. On 26 April, a new decree was to launch the construction of four more neighbourhoods, authorizing a loan of 10,000,000$00 for the purchase of land, materials, and construction.[24]

The construction regulation, Decree no. 5,481, of 30 April 1919, clarified some aspects of the programme, emphasizing the progressive nature of the legislator. The construction of the working-class neighbourhoods, which were to be called "social neighbourhoods," was carried out by an independent board of directors, assisted by a technical council and by commanders ("comanditas"), who were groups of workers hired for the construction works. It was up to the board to monitor the works, enforce the regulations and provide information to the Minister of Labour. The technical council consisted of five architects and a doctor. Each commander was in charge of twenty dwellings. The initiative was exclusively public and intended for rent, but did not specify the type of housing, single-family or multi-family dwellings. The neighbourhoods of Ajuda [MdH DB a684] and Arco do Cego [MdH DB a216] come from this legal framework. The legislation was in force until 1922, when a new government, presided over by António Maria da Silva (1872–1950), suspended all work in the social neighbourhoods of Arco do Cego, Alcântara [MdH DB a683], Ajuda, Covilhã [MdH DB a682], and Porto [MdH DB a272], dismissing and compensating all who worked on them.[25]

The continuation of the works was dependent on a new housing programme to be approved in the parliament, which never happened.[26] The government eventually resorted to a new loan of 5,000,000$00 to complete work only in the neighbourhood of Arco do Cego.[27] The goal was to save as much as possible and move forward with a work that was already partially built: sixty-five buildings finished out of seventy-two, the equivalent to 524 homes. The Ajuda neighbourhood, which would also be almost completed, was not included in this law. The following governments continued to try to erase social housing initiatives inherited from Domingos Pereira's government.

The government of Álvaro Xavier de Castro (1878–1928), was committed to alienating the housing estates that were under the authority of the state. It transferred the land expropriated in Lisbon, Oporto and Covilhã to the municipalities, as well as the buildings and construction material.[28]

---

[24] Decree no. 5,443, of 26 April 1919.

[25] Law no. 1,258, of 5 May 1922.

[26] Proposed law of Ministry of Labour, *Câmara dos Deputados* (21–22 August 1922): 10–16. The discussion scheduled in the plenary dealt with the proposal contained in Opinion no. 278, which pointed to a new housing programme, but when deputy Alves dos Santos called for urgent action to solve the issue of "social neighborhoods," the proposal was forgotten.

[27] Law no. 1,367, dated 13 September 1922. The loan ended up not being realized.

[28] Law no. 1,594 of 26 April 1924. The city councils did not accept and the districts remained in the sphere of the state, in the Ministry of Finance.

The next government, led by Alfredo Rodrigues Gaspar (1865–1938), contracted a new loan of 5,000,000$00, with the purpose of concluding the neighbourhoods in Lisbon and Oporto, in order to submit them to public auction, maintaining the Arco do Cego neighborhood in the sphere of the state.[29] Finally, Domingos Leite Pereira returned to the head of government between August and December 1925, and his ministers of Finance and Labour issued a decree that provided for compensation to landowners expropriated for the construction of social neighbourhoods in Alcântara and Ajuda, and in Porto.[30] The diploma presents its justification to end the social housing initiative initiated precisely in Domingos Pereira's 1919 government: spending, lack of control of public finances, incompetence of commanders and the technical commission, lack of projects, and widespread ineffectiveness. Shortly afterwards, the Ministry of Labour was extinct.[31] In the preamble to the decree, signed by the head of state and the head of government, it can be read that the executive of 1919 sought to meet the needs of all those who fought for Portugal in Flanders and in Africa, through social districts, compulsory insurance, and labour markets, but, according to the legislator, all these measures were nothing more than "experimentalism."

In 1926, in the last government of the Republic, the question of social neighbourhoods, especially of Arco do Cego, was still unsolved.[32] Considering that it was not appropriate for the government to continue to build affordable houses, the administrative committee of the Lisbon social districts (in Porto this committee had already been extinguished in the previous year) was dissolved and the houses still under construction were proposed through the General Administration of the Public Buildings, which would pay the costs of a loan of 3,000,000$00 contracted for the "construction of the neighbourhood in question" [Arco do Cego].

The following month the Republic fell, with the military coup of Gomes da Costa (1863–1929). Parliament was closed and the period of the Military Dictatorship (1926–1933) began, which is characterized by persecution of trade unions and associative movements, in a climate of civil war, with several blows and revolts, but with military forces emerging as an instrument of national salvation.[33] As early as 1926, the government of Óscar Carmona (1869–1951) was still seeking to resolve the issue of the "buildings" of affordable houses in Lisbon and Porto. It began by guaranteeing the remuneration of the personnel of the General Administration of Public Works and National Monuments, who should finish the construction of the houses.[34] Once completed, they would be sold by public auction, giving preference to the then residents of the affordable houses of Porto [Arrábida], which were already inhabited.[35]

[29] Decree no. 10,132, of 27 September 1924. The neighbourhoods were not sold at all.

[30] Decree no. 11,174, of 23 October 1925.

[31] Decree no. 11,267 of 25 November 1925.

[32] Decree no. 11,592, of 17 April 1926.

[33] Mattoso, *História de Portugal, Estado Novo*, 151–158.

[34] Decree no. 12,028, of 30 July 1926.

[35] Decree no. 12,029, of 30 July 1926.

Later, in 1928, the government of José Vicente de Freitas (1869–1952) promulgated a new housing programme that revisited some aspects of the Sidonist programme of 1918, but also the proposed law of 1914.[36] The law rejected the public initiative—*"what was most proven during this period was that the works to be carried out cannot be executed by the State Administration or, on a reasonable scale, by the municipalities"*; it proposed a set of tax exemptions for construction companies and cooperatives; it set the construction cost per square metre; it defined the housing model, single-family or two-storey detached, semi-detached or terraced houses; and it promoted the acquisition of houses through the payment of an annuity, for twenty years. As in the previous legislation, municipalities were obliged to carry out the infrastructure of the enterprises and to contract access to the neighbourhoods with the transport companies. Assistance and welfare institutions, banks, and insurers could use part of their reserves in the construction, acquisition or lending of affordable housing, as proposed in the 1914 project. The diploma instituted the "homestead" principle, when houses were acquired by the tenants, as happened in 1918. The programme also authorized the construction of housing by municipalities and other state agencies, but only for their employees.[37]

EPILOGUE: THE LONG WAIT FOR A "HOUSE"

There are no known results of the 1928 legislative initiative. However, there are many aspects of the Military Dictatorship legislation that seem to resurface in the housing programmes of the Estado Novo, although, starting in 1933, the initiative was entirely in the sphere of the state, from construction to regulation, from financing to distribution. From this period of many hesitations and attempts to launch consistent policies that would run counter to the environment of housing degradation of cities, a political struggle was observed around housing and the expectations of urban families who earned regular income, albeit low. The first housing programmes now appear in a framework of authoritarianism, sometimes in a framework of progressive policies, and are eventually interrupted, with scarcely or never completed achievements. One can note the discomfort of successive governments with the construction of the neighbourhood of Arco do Cego, considered an extravagance for workers, and eventually handed over to public officials (73 per cent), mostly from the armed and police forces, during the Estado Novo;[38] or the annoyance of the government of Vicente de Freitas, when he stated in the preamble of the decree of 1928 that the legal framework introduced by the Sidonist government produced "no practical results."

[36] Decree no. 16,055, of 12 October 1928. The diploma is complemented by Decree no. 16,085, of 16 October 1928, that defines the Regulation of Construction and Sale of Affordable Houses. It should be noted that at this time António Oliveira Salazar and Duarte Pacheco were part of the government.

[37] Before the promulgation of the 1928 decree, the Lisbon Chamber was already building a neighbourhood for its employees. It is the neighbourhood Presidente Carmona, which consists of three rows of townhouses in two streets, all with a backyard and two floors. It seems likely that the financing of this group was obtained in accordance with Decree no. 16,055 of 12 October 1928.

[38] Tiago, "Bairros Sociais da I República," 249–272.

Between the end of the Constitutional Monarchy and the Republic, Portugal experienced a serious housing crisis, particularly in the two major cities, as a consequence of the social, economic, and political reconfiguration that characterized the period analysed. An illiterate and rural population that grew moderately, with high physiological indexes, moved to the coast, changing the fields for the factory or commerce, and installed itself in the "house" which it managed to pay for with the low wages earned.

It was in the cities of Lisbon and Porto, where everyone contributed in search of a salary or a promise in emigration, that the housing crisis is seen, with a large number of families living in makeshift homes, without access to water and sanitation, and where widespread dissatisfaction was growing from an awareness, on the one hand, of the new political rights, and, on the other, of the origin of deadly epidemic outbreaks.

For more than three decades, political power in the monarchy recognized the housing crisis, but because of the lack of measures, it revealed its lack of interest in intervening in the reconfiguration of cities, housing markets, and wage recomposition. The Republic began by ignoring the crisis and even the pioneering experiment of the city of Porto, but a short-lived authoritarian government, which sought to use social housing as a political weapon, launched the first state housing programme, thus inaugurating a precept inherent in all political regimes later. In the short period between the fall of the Sidonist government and the fascist dictatorship of 1933, two more housing programmes were launched, the first in 1919, socialist, the other the product of affirmation of the Military Dictatorship of 1926.

The total achievements of the housing programmes launched in this period—about 830 dwellings between 1918 and 1935—reveal the options of republican political power, influenced by the debate carried out during the monarchy: minimal intervention, option for single family dwelling under lease and possibility of sale of housing. Social housing and the housing crisis were again used as a pretext during the Estado Novo to launch politically conditioned programmes. It is the same as saying that the housing crisis in Portugal that has been experienced since the end of the 19th century only began to be abolished after World War II, with negative consequences for urban evolution and reconfiguration of socioeconomic relations.

BIBLIOGRAPHY

Gonçalves, Eliseu. "O alojamento operário portuense nas primeiras décadas do século XX: Da casa familiar ao bloco comunitário." In A Habitação Social na Transformação da Cidade, Virgílio Borges Pereira (Ed.), 9–20. Porto: Edições Afrontamento, 2015.

Gonçalves, Eliseu, and Ramos, Rui J. G.. "Primeiras propostas de habitação operária no Porto: A casa unifamiliar, o Carré Mulhousien e a Cité-Jardin." Ciudades, 19, 1 (2016): 77–98.

Gros, Marielle Christine. O Alojamento Social sob o Fascismo. Porto: Afrontamento, 1982.

Matos, Fátima Loureiro de. "Da implantação da República à primeira Guerra: As primeiras tentativas de resolução do problema habitacional das classes operárias." In A Grande Guerra (1914–1918): Problemáticas e Representações. Gaspar Martins Pereira, Jorge Fernandes Alves, Luís Alberto Alves, Maria Conceição Meireles (Eds.), 369–381. Porto: Centro de Investigação Transdisciplinar "Cultura Espaço e Memória," 2015.

Mattoso, José (Ed.). História de Portugal, O Estado Novo (1926–1974), Vol. 7, Lisbon: Editorial Estampa, 1994.

Mattoso, José (Dir.) and Irene Vaquinhas (Ed.). História da Vida Privada em Portugal—A Época Contemporânea. Lisbon: Temas e debates, 2011.

Pereira, Gaspar Martins. Famílias Portuenses na Viragem do Século (1880–1910). Porto: Edições Afrontamento, 1995.

Pereira, Gaspar Martins. Eduardo Santos Silva—Cidadão do Porto (1876–1960). Porto: Campo das Letras, 2002.

Pereira, Gaspar Martins. "As ilhas no percurso das famílias trabalhadoras do Porto em finais do século XIX." In Família, Espaço e Patrimónío. Carlota Santos (Ed.), 477–793. Porto: Centro de Investigação Transdisciplinar "Cultura Espaço e Memória," 2011.

Pereira, Virgílio Borges. "A política de habitação do Estado e os seus efeitos sociais no Porto contemporâneo: Uma perspectiva sintética e panorâmica," In Família, Espaço e Patrimónío. Carlota Santos (Ed.), 547–564. Porto: Centro de Investigação Transdisciplinar "Cultura Espaço e Memória," 2011.

Serrão, Joel, and A. H. de Oliveira Marques (Eds.). Nova História de Portugal, Vol XI. Lisbon: Editorial Presença, 1995.

Silva, Álvaro Ferreira da, "A construção residencial em Lisboa: evolução e estrutura empresarial (1860–1930)." Análise Social 136–137, 2º–3º (Vol. XXXI, 1996): 599–629.

Teixeira, Manuel C.. Habitação Popular na Cidade Oitocentista—As Ilhas do Porto. Lisbon: Fundação Calouste Gulbenkian, 1996.

Tiago, Maria da Conceição. "Bairros Sociais da I República: projectos e realizações." Ler História, 59 (2010): 249–272.

Nuno Valério (Ed.). Estatísticas Históricas Portuguesas, Vol. I. Lisbon: Instituto Nacional de Estatística, 2001.

Republican Affordable Housing: Art, Hygiene, and Modern Architecture in Portugal

ELISEU GONÇALVES
University of Porto, Faculty of Architecture, Centre for Studies in Architecture and Urbanism

ABSTRACT

Right through the history of social housing in Portugal, a first cycle can be circumscribed that closes in the 1930s. Here the degree of intervention of the central administration for the resolution of the decent housing deficit had been previously discussed, parallelly to the construction of a diverse set of solutions which functioned as models to test against slums. On the one hand, the so-called "casa barata" (cheap house) began to be seen as an important political instrument in the struggle for power and social control; on the other hand, it continued to be understood as desirable real estate integrated in the complex fabric of economic interests woven into urban housing production. Although the operations conducted in this period and dominated by the First Republic were episodic and insignificant compared to the country's housing needs, some continue to have historical relevance as test balloons in the positivist laboratory that was the universe of republicanism.[1] Some neighbourhoods were authentic condensers of the complex debate inherited from the eighteenth century, which, based on scientism, sought in this way the orderly and progressive reform of society[2] in order to, among other issues, solve the so-called Social Question in which the problem of working-class housing was included.[3]

Confronted with the overwhelming rhythms of social and technical-scientific progress of the first decades, affordable housing was to be one of the most sensitive architectural programmes in the synthesis between tradition, history, and modernity. In the disciplinary field of architecture, in many cases the economic, social, and cultural valuation of the new dwelling and its particular technical and formal constraints redirected the modus operandi and the professional interest of the architect onto other themes hitherto adjacent to the central problem of style. In this transformational process of the architectural field, one of the aspects that must be mentioned concerns the regulation and normalization imposed by the hygienist rationality, putting the binomial Art and Science at stake. Thus, the main objective of this paper is to contribute to a reading of some pre-1933 economic districts centred on the international effect of hygiene considered as scientific knowledge and, also, a programme of values. In particular, in the light of a more precise explanation of a modern breath felt in the late 1920s, the document is structured in two parts, comprising, respectively, the definition of control measures imposed on house design, and use of a formal, clearly purified, and diaphanous lexicon, determined by the triangulation between Art, Economy, and Hygiene.

BIOGRAPHY

Eliseu Gonçalves is an architect and assistant professor at FAUP, where he graduated in 1994 and obtained his PhD in architecture in 2015. In 1994 he received the Eng. António de Almeida Foundation Award. Between 1994 and 2001, he worked in Manuel Fernandes de Sá's architectural office; At the same time, he opened his own office where he developed several works of architecture and urbanism. Within the scope of his interests and academic research, he has given special attention to the relationship between architecture and construction from the perspective of the modernism culture, Portuguese social housing, modern comforts in the first half of the 20th century; and energy, climate, and architectural form within the framework of the "well-tempered house." His PhD thesis was on working-class housing in Porto at the beginning of the last century (FCT Scholarship–Fundação para a Ciência e a Tecnologia). Since 2009 he has been a member of the research group Atlas da Casa at CEAU/ FAUP. He was the coordinator of the research project "Mapping Public Housing: a critical review of the State-subsidized residential architecture in Portugal (1910–1974)."

---

[1] About republicanism in Portugal, see, for example, Fernando Catroga, "O Republicanismo Português (Cultura, história e política)," *Revista da Faculdade de Letras—História*—Porto, III Série, vol. 11(2010): 95–119.

[2] Maria Rita Lino Garnel (ed.), *Corpo: Estado, Medicina e Sociedade no Tempo da I República* (Lisbon: Imprensa Nacional Casa da Moeda, 2010), 8.

[3] Note Rui Ramos' observation when he states that housing problem was an important signal of the "Social Question." Rui Ramos, *A Segunda Fundação*. História de Portugal. Vol. 6 (Lisbon: Editorial Estampa, 2001), 211.

INTRODUCTION

The campaign to discredit the Republic led by the Dictatorship after the 1926 military coup and, in particular, the propaganda of the "Affordable Houses Programme" (Decree-Law no. 23,052, 23 September 1933) fostered a historical perspective of tabula rasa on which Estado Novo registered its policy of social housing. Notwithstanding this general reading of housing policies in Portugal before 1933—which the First Republic's "Bairros Sociais" (1918) sometimes escape—some micro-historiography has highlighted, for example, the hygienist and social economy debate around the precariousness of housing for the poor classes, that had been intensifying in Portugal from the last decade of the 19th century as republicanism thought gained influence and political power. Before the introduction of the Republic in 1910, the theme of economic housing was present in various areas of civic and political intervention, including the press.

The engineer José Maria Mello de Mattos (1856–1915) fostered, in the magazine *A Construção Moderna*, a set of reflections on the technical, designing and financial questions that working housing aroused; João Lino de Carvalho (1859–1926), one of the rare architects engaged in the debate on cheap houses and their hygiene, published, among other titles, *Healthy Settlements* and *Considerations on Housing Hygiene*;[4] José Caeiro da Matta (1877–1963), deputy for the Regenerating Party, launched the book *Popular Housing* in 1909.[5] Also, in parliament, a number of studies had been drafted by specialized committees to support the legislative initiatives that invariably clashed with the liberal majority. The Republic was to take up some of the lines previously discussed, taking them as a guide for its programme of construction of social neighbourhoods which was concretized from 1918.

Unlike the legal framework of 1933, strongly linked to preconceived architectural form—ideologically manipulated and easily reproducible—production in the first third of the century was diverse, probably enjoying the freedom allowed by the lack of an integrative view of the republican central administration and also because it was associated with a determinism of local order. Sometimes, in the diversity of some sets, under humble and contradictory forms, there is an authenticity and a modern pulse that results from the fact that they were designed from a clear programme, adapting good construction to low cost "because it was built from the economy of the gesture, subordinating originality to the use of standardized elements."[6]

---

[4] Lino de Carvalho, *Construcção Moderna. Povoações Salubres* (Lisbon: Typographia do Commercio, 1905).

[5] Caeiro da Matta, *Habitações Populares* (Coimbra: Imprensa da Universidade, 1909).

[6] Carlos Sambricio, "Introducción," in *Un Siglo de Vivienda Social (1903–2003)*. Tomo I (Madrid: Editorial Nerea, 2003), 26.

The irregularity observed in the architecture of the affordable housing estates of this period may have resulted from some "modern" disturbances, because, as José-Augusto França noted, "19th century patterns have either extended or overflowed into the 20th century,"[7] making the birth of the concept of modernism widespread in the early decades. On the historiographical problem of the "modern," França would later say that *"[. . .] between us, 'modern' always hesitated between a way of being (mode) and a way of doing (fashion), both related to what is current, of today or of recently [. . .] the way it has been assumed in Portuguese "modernismo" in its various stages and by its various proponents and users must therefore be borne in mind."*[8]

An important member of the Society of Portuguese Architects, Lino de Carvalho, mentioned above, when reporting the results of the *1st International Congress of Housing Sanitation and Salubrity* in Paris (1904) confessed that the theme of economical houses *"is a very complex, but very interesting and momentous problem of this section III: regular and solid construction, simple but elegant, perfectly salubrious and, as a special condition, at a relatively cheap price."*[9] About this kind of problem, Carvalho later declared that *"in the present day, harmonizing art and hygiene with economy is in fact the most interesting problem that is imposed on the architect."*[10] This triangulation between art, hygiene, and economy allows some readings to be put forward about the nature of the modern breath that is found in some early proposals. In the next part of this paper, we will analyse specifically how *hygienism* inhibited architecture as an art form in two ways—normalization control and aesthetics—in the context of affordable housing.

ARCHITECTURE, HYGIENE, AND ART

At the turn of the 19th to the 20th century, the largest urban settlements were on the verge of environmental rupture because of the pronounced imbalances brought about by industrial expansion. Excessive demographic and infrastructural maladaptation or residential saturation of urban centres led to severe outbreaks of pestilence, which forced tight physical and moral control as a major public health safety action. In the case of the accommodation of the most numerous social strata, Roger-Henri Guerrand demonstrated in *Les Origines du Logement Social en France, 1850–1914* that important achievements for the improvement of living conditions were possible thanks to the strong associative organization of the hygienists and their use of quantitative methods to assess reality, that placed the very high mortality rates and urban insalubrity in a direct cause-and-effect correlation.[11]

[7] José-Augusto França, *A Arte em Portugal no Século XIX*. Volume II (Lisbon: Bertrand Editora, 1990 [1966]), 359.

[8] José-Augusto França, *O Modernismo na Arte Portuguesa* (Lisbon: Bertrand Editora, 1991 [1979]), 93.

[9] Lino de Carvalho, "A Habitação," *Annuario da Sociedade dos Architectos Portuguezes*, Anno I (1905): 58.

[10] Lino de Carvalho, "A Habitação," *Annuario da Sociedade dos Architectos Portuguezes*, Anno IV (1908): 25.

[11] Roger-Henri Guerrand, *Les Origines du Logement Social en France, 1850–1914* (Paris: Éditions de la Villette, 2010 [1987]), 147.

The impact of this type of observations on the society of that time triggered firm answers for the reform of the city in several sectors. The ambition to make the city hygienic implied a reorganization of those administrative services directly involved, the inclusion of new areas of knowledge in work teams, the regulation of certain habits and rituals of citizens, and a comprehensive material modernization linked to urban sanitary engineering and housekeeping and the functional arrangement of public space and the various productive and residential activities. Because of the imperative need to cultivate healthy habits and to eliminate the most dangerous unhealthy areas, the authorities were compelled to quickly transform some of the procrastinated spaces, namely those directly related to workers' houses.

The housing of the poor classes in urban areas was observed from several angles with different media impacts. From the sanitary point of view, the results of inspections of the destitute neighbourhoods of Porto and Lisbon carried out by physicians and sanitarian engineers pointed to these places as potential hubs of pestilential diseases capable of endangering the whole urban system. This was a scientific perception of unhealthy conditions that resulted from the hygienist reform initiated by the Portuguese state at the end of the 19th century, which led to the huge administrative reorganization and consolidation of a new legal framework with a direct impact on urban planning and building regulations and consequently on the design of working-class housing.

A key figure in this reform promoted by the hygienist Ricardo Jorge (1858–1939) was the engineer Augusto Pinto de Miranda Montenegro (1829–1908) who had chaired the Council for Health Improvements (CMS) of the Public Works Ministry since 1903. Between 1903 and 1905, several health surveys were prepared to support new legislation through the CMS, especially committed to building regulations. In addition to the reports of the field work developed, Augusto Montenegro signed other titles, namely *Housing Conditions* (1904) and *Working Class Estates* (1903), highlighting *Hygiene in Housing* (1901) to *"compile, in simple and practical terms, the most important measures that modern hygienists advise for those who propose to build urban buildings."*[12] This last text corresponded to the text of the law promulgated two years later: the building act named *Regulamento de Salubridade das Edificações Urbanas* (RSEU).[13]

It is quite probable that the theoretical foundations that supported the more scientific and measurable part of the regulation (laboratorial values such as cubic air content of compartments or the area of façade apertures) was sustained by internationally knowledge acquired by Portuguese technicians.

[12] Augusto Pinto de Miranda Montenegro, "A hygiene das habitações," *Revista de Obras Públicas e Minas*, Tomo XXI, no.370–372 (1900): 399–417.

[13] *Diário do Governo*, no. 5309 (march 1903): 790–792. This act was published with comments in the section "Legislação das Construções," *A Construção Moderna*, no. 9, Anno VII (October 10 1906).

This kind of precise information was supported by laboratory science and statistics, discussed in several congresses, and disseminated via a set of magazines and books of this specialty. The *Congrès International d'Hygiène et Démographie* was attended by some important national personalities such as the physician João Lopes da Silva Martins (1866–1945), congressman in Budapest in 1894.[14] Particularly useful for the understanding of the above-quoted Portuguese legislation of 1903 is the analysis of the 10th meeting held at the International Exhibition of Paris in 1900.[15] Among the diverse topics considered, the debate about housing health and sanitation took place in the section "Salubrité: Sciences de l'Ingénieur et de l'Architecte Appliquées à l'Hygiène." The studies "Assainissement intérieur des maisons reliées à l'égout public; règles essentielles et moyens d'en assurer l'observation," and "Règles génerales d'Hygiène à observer dans la distribution, l'aération permanente et la décoration intérieure des maisons d'habitation," instructed the topic of the final report, "L'Habitation à la Ville," which attributed certain specifications to low-income houses—"La Maison à Loyer"—which we can identify in later situations, namely, in Portugal:

- That all habitable compartments of the house must be "sun-visited" or be naturally illuminated in such a way that there are no obstructions at an angle greater than 45° formed with the horizon;

- The house must be raised over well-ventilated cellars with well waterproofed paving and the ground floor will always be elevated;

- The internal spaces of the dwelling must have dimensions proportional to their use, but their air volume will never be less than 30 or 40 m3;

- Air flow will be ensured, which will be stabilized between 12 and 15°C in the core of these compartments;

- The latrines, regardless of the sewer system adopted, shall be at least 2 m2 in area and shall be insulated and separated as far as possible from the habitable compartments and a ventilated foyer may be admitted.

All these considerations take account of studies carried out in the second half of the 19th century, amongst which specific mention can be made of *Nouveaux Élements d'Hygiène. Première Partie: Sun, Eau, Atmosphère, Habitation,*[16] the influential compendium by the French hygienist Jules Arnould, the success of which made the text travel as far as Portugal.

[14] João Lopes da Silva Martins (1866–1945), physician and politician linked to the Democratic Republican Party. In 1909, he was responsible for the 13th Course—Hygiene—in the Medical School of Porto. In 1894 he was rapporteur of the International Congress of Hygiene and Demography held in Hungary. For example, in "Chapter VIII" of the report the "Hygiene of the Cities" was discussed; in "Chapter II," the discussion was about the "housing of the poor," the "bases for the organization of professional statistics" or the "mutualistic regime" for improvement of working-class standards of living. The discourse about workers' houses noted: "The state should grant loans to municipalities and class associations, either entirely without interest or at an extremely low rate, so that they promote the construction of houses for the poor." The report also indicates the tutelary figures of Bertillon, the head of the statistical department of Paris, and Émille Cacheux, the famous engineer responsible for the construction of working-class estates in France. Silva Lopes' last words were about the propositions voted by the "6th section of demography": First. That the State provide clean and cheap housing for the poor classes; Second. That the relationship between housing conditions and the development of infectious diseases through rigorous analysis must be investigated. João Lopes da Silva Martins, *Relatório do Congresso Internacional de Hygiene e Demographia. 8ª Sessão . Buda-Pesth, 1894* (Lisbon: Imp. Nacional, 1897), 207–210.

[15] An anonymous Portuguese exhibitor was referenced in the report of the jury of the "Groupe de l'Économie Sociale" relating to "Class 106"—working-class housing (the various sections of this exhibition were divided by types of promoters: Public Administration; Industrial Works; Philanthropic or Commercial Societies; or "Habitations à Bon Marché" propaganda movement). In addition to the exhibitor not being awarded, it seems that no solution of what was done in Portugal in the field of housing was exhibited, but was probably exposed alongside well-known architectural projects such as the Cité Ouvriere Noisiel (Île de France) or Crespi d'Adda (Milan). Maurice Lebon, *Exposition Universelle Internationale de 1900, à Paris. Groupe de l'Économie Sociale. Rapport au Nom du Jury de la Classe 106* (Paris: Société Française des Habitations a Bon Marché, 1900), 37 and 77.

[16] Jules Arnould, *Nouveaux Élements d'Hygiène. Première Partie: Sol, Eau, Atmosphère, Habitation* (Paris: Librairie J.B. Baullière et Fils, 1900 [1881]).

The book, which explored the latest research in thermodynamics and biochemistry, transposed the problem of air renewal in spaces into a set of premises by taking carbonic acid as an indicator of atmospheric impurity. The treaty was quoted in Portugal by some dissertations presented to Medical School of Porto, as is the case of José Rodrigues Braga's *Subsidies for Housing Hygiene. Ventilation, Illumination, Water and the Removal of Filth* of 1894, sharing the same experimental reference on the maximum amount of the said acid per volume of air: 25 m3 per individual. This fact and its corollaries established, far from speculative real estate interests, an irrefutable argument about the minimum dimension of interior space that has spread to other components of house design.

As far as its impact on working-class housing in Portugal is concerned, note should be taken of the greater percentage of holes in the opaque walls which was stressed in order to respond to the rule of 10‰ of the area surface, the elevation of the ground floor to facilitate ventilation, or the higher ceilings.[17]

In addition to these constraints imposed by the RSEU, a new architectural project validation framework was settled, subjecting the solutions to dry construction processes, incorporation of more involved ventilation mechanisms, the common use of sealing materials and special finishes with materials with non-porous surfaces complemented with concave and concave accessory parts, more complex detailing of window frames, or greater care in solar orientation.

Christian Moley states that in this period the "norm" became truly operative in the design of the accommodation which was constantly reworked in the long term by interactive processes. More than regulation, it was a doxa that established relations between culture and the agents involved in the construction of housing and the city, whether they were planners, private organizations, or public administration.[18] In the scope of housing design, hygienist regulations gave a numerical rationality to certain architectural elements, attributing a scientific character to it which was similar to what the science of materials had given to the new structural solutions of concrete or steel.[19] The hygienic conditioning was determinant in the formation of another spatial, functional, and material reference, where utilitarianism boosted the development of new aesthetic relations between building technoscience and architectural composition. On the approximation of changes that were introduced in the practice of architecture, we highlight the role of the architect-engineer Émile Trélat (1821–1907), dean of the École Spéciale d'Architecture of Paris,[20] whose work was widely read in Portugal with some of his texts deserving translation in specialty journals.[21]

---

[17] It should be noted that the 1903 regulation RSEU imposed various order restrictions, namely: Minimum height between floors should not be less than 3.25 m on the ground floor and first floor; 3.00 m on the second; 2.85 on the third and 2.75 on the successive ones (Article 6); The floor of the ground floor should have a waterproof layer or form an air box 60 cm high (Article 9); The design of the staircase should ensure the introduction of natural light inside the building and simultaneously allow the air to be renewed; The windows should be large to allow air and light, with at least 10 per cent of the floor surface of the room (habitable compartment) with a minimum of 0.8 m2 in the bedrooms (Article 11); Each dwelling must have at least an independent latrine; Possibility of installing interior latrines provided that a window with an area of 30x60 cm is secured preferably at the bottom of the corridor; Possibility of interior patios provided that, in the case of buildings less than 18 m high, they have 30 m2 of area with sides measuring at least 5 m (Article 19); The volume of air in the bedrooms corresponded to 25 m3 per user, requiring a direct connection to the exterior (Article 13).

[18] Christian Moley, *L'Architecture du Logement, Culture et Logiques d'Une Norme Héritée* (Paris: Economica Anthropos 1998), 11.

[19] See the entire development of numerical calculation models that took place during the nineteenth century, ending with the complex and intensive use of reinforced concrete structures at the opening of the new century.

[20] Before École Centrale d'Architecture, this school was initially supported by eminent figures such as Eugène Viollet-le-Duc and Henri Labrouste (1801–1875), Anatole de Baudot (1834–1915), and Émile Muller (1823–1889), who was a prominent figure of the French *Cités Ouvrieres* movement.

[21] See, in this regard, the text of Émile Trélat, "Heating and ventilation of the dwellings," published in several issues of the magazine *Engenharia e Architectura* in 1893 (Vol.II, no.19, pp. 146–148; Vol.II, no.24, 190–191; Vol.II, no.35, 273–276), translated from the original published in *Revue d'Hygiéne et de Police Sanitaire*, no. 8 (1886). This French magazine, which contains so many essays on working-class housing from authors linked to the hygienist movement, had correspondents in Portugal. In that period the Portuguese representative was Silva Amado, Professor of Hygiene, at the Faculty of Medicine of Lisbon.

From his production, the book *La Salubrité* (1899), where he introduced healthy building design problems definitively into the academic and professional environmentm, should be highlighted:

"Les ressources scientifiques auxquelles elle fait appel, the multiplicité des efforts qu'elle réclame ont fait de l'Hygiène, comme l'a dit Paul Bert, le carrefour de toutes les sciences. Médecins, physiologists, physiciens, chimistes, Ingénieurs, architectes, industriels, tous se sont unis pour alimenter les recherches et accroire les découvertes. Pasteur lui-même at mis à leur service ses travaux et son génie. L'ensemble de ces riches acquisitions, on ne peut s'en étonner, est aujourd'hui trés dispersé. J'ai voulu précisément ordonner, isoler et mettre à part, dans ce grand sujet, ce qu'on doit appeler la SALUBRITÉ."[22]

With Eugène Viollet-le-Duc (1814–1879) and others, Trélat objected to the pedagogical orientation followed at the École des Beaux Arts, which led to the foundation in 1865 of the École Centrale d'Architecture, whose academic curriculum was multidisciplinary, focused on the study of utilitarian and economic buildings and which aimed to bring the practice of architectural projects closer to the requirements of industrial society. In this context, "hygiene science" was taught in the course of civil construction and composition where working-class housing design was one of the targets. For Trélat, the practice of architecture should include in its body of knowledge the understanding of the major phenomena related to health, namely air, light, heat, water and soil.

The neglect by academia of these programmes related to the productive and housing needs revealed a major problem of the discipline that had been discussed since the middle of the century and which resulted from the denial of the communion of knowledge between art and industry, which prevented architecture from being enrolled in the "réel quotidien" where the so-called working-class housing was.[23] We can list half a dozen influential architects who brought about scientific reform on "cheap houses" from this type of advanced knowledge.

As Michael Browne pointed out to Henry Roberts (1803–1886), these *"architecte[s] sanitaire[s]—un spécialiste, créé, pour ainsi dire, par les découvertes des médecins, et par leur appréciation correcte de la forte influence exercée par des agents locaux dans la cause des maladies" established the figure of the "architecte scientifique."*[24] This observation is relevant in introducing an epistemological problem that would cross the century and was important to an understanding of architectural changes for modern times.

[22] Émile Trélat, *La Salubrité* (Paris: Ernest Flammarion, Éditeur, 1899).

[23] Roger-Henri Guerrand, "Un art nouveau pour le peuple et les «Habitations a bon marché,»" in *Le Social aux Prises Avec l'Histoire*, vol.3, ed. C. Chambelland, C. (Paris: CEDIAS, 1991), 165.

[24] Quoted from the introduction of Micheal Browne's reprint. Henry Roberts, *Des Habitations des Classes Ouvrières. Leur Composition et Leur Construction Avec l'Essentiel d'Une Habitation Salubre. Edition Revue et augmentée de 1867* (Paris: Editions L'Harmattan, 1998 [1867]), X.

Art de génie or *Art mécanique?*—This dialectic led to a disciplinary reframing typical of the early times of reaction between the academy and the avant-garde centred on redefining the artistic value of architecture by opposing the uniqueness of the classical canons to a new constructive rationality, its possibility for "technical reproducibility" and their social function.

In order to finish this approach to the triangulation between architecture, hygiene and art, as a reference it is worth mentioning an episode extensively reported in 1906 in the Portuguese magazine *A Construção Moderna*. It is the case of the philanthropic Rothschild Foundation's competition for the construction of a large low-income neighbourhood in Paris won by Augustin Rey[25] (1864–1934). Rey, who would replace Émile Trélat two years later in the Conseil Supérieur des Habitations á Bon Marché, was, according to the publication, an *"architect who was particularly knowledgeable of labour issues, [who] understood the immense social importance of these works and the influence they could exert abroad."*[26] The competition evaluation focused on space ventilation, minimal organization of dwellings and the refinement of the forms employed, as we can read below:

"To further emphasize the circulation of air, which is life, the health of the dwelling itself, Mr. Rey disposed the stairs in a particular way. These simple provisions give rise to super-abundant ventilation and must be documented by the hygienists as real progress. In this project, so meticulous and thoughtful, the kitchens must also be pointed out, whose disposal, at the same time as being very simple, are studied in thorough detail. [The] very simple façades without any frame are, however, very joyful, thanks to the skilful arrangement of the groups and to the elegant proportions of each detail."[27]

In addition, it is essential to note the jury's compliments which, focusing on the inventiveness of the solution and its progress and modernism, criticized the architect's professional group for not being adapted to new social, technical and aesthetic constraints imposed by the affordable housing programme:

"[The architect] C'est un artiste, on lui accorde. Donc il n'est bon que pour les hautes sphères où l'on s'imagine que l'art évolue. Un artiste pour construire des maisons d'ouvrier? À quoi bon ! Ils vont dépenser en ornement, en toitures de chalets suisses, en tourelles, créneaux et autres fadaises les fonds, forcément restreints, dont ils disposeront, mais ils ne feront pas 'du pratique.'"[28]

The tension established between old and modern practices facing this kind of housing shows the instrumental inadequacy and, also, the disregard of the conservative sectors. It was a problem that the aforementioned Lino de Carvalho tried to solve by keeping the

[25] Augustin Rey joined the Société française des habitations à bon marché in 1906 after leading the project team for the study of low-income housing formed by the Rothschild Foundation.

[26] *A Construção Moderna*, no.195, Volume VII, (August 1906); 21.

[27] Ibid., 21.

[28] Laurent Farge, ed., *Les Concours Publics d'Architecture—Revue Mensuelle, IX Année* (Paris: Libraires—Imprimeries Reunis, 1906), 3.

Society of Portuguese Architects on schedule. As director of the Social Economy, Hygiene and Public Assistance Group in the Portuguese section at the Universal Exhibition of Paris (1900), concerning the creation of the Higher Council for Housing Hygiene (Public Works Ministry), he complained against the exclusion of architects in that very important organization for the launch of the working-class housing stands. In the letter sent to the government to denounce the situation it can be read:

"The architect, realizing his ideal of Art in the luxurious villa, does not neglect the great problem of the working-class housing but even with the dedication of an apostle takes care of it. And is it only aesthetics of interest to him? No. He is well aware of its economic and hygienic importance, and, in all its complexity, the architects of all countries have always faced this problem. [...] Such a mission would not only represent an unjustified discredit for our class, but also damage to the good solution of this problem to which the same class has so usefully contributed."[29]

Overall, there was not a clear academic and professional interest in the working-class housing problem from Portuguese architects. The eloquence of the great drawing taught in the academies had marked the profession with a capricious knowledge and they were out of step regarding the need for simple constructions based on new principles. At least that was the certainty within other socio-professional groups dominated by engineers, reformers and hygienists, meanwhile self-proclaimed specialists in cheap houses. When the Society of Portuguese Architects expressed itself about the interest of architects in this cause, it argued that the dignity of housing for the poor could only be achieved with the presence of the architect because *"utilitarianism that guides modern ideas finds in the arts one of its best supporters; and so it was that Architecture, without abandoning its traditions of ornamental and monumental art, was integrated in this movement."*[30]

[29] "Casas baratas—Representação ao Governo," *Annuario dos Architectos Portuguezes*, Ano IV (1908): 18.

[30] Ibid., 17.

1930: FIRST MODERN BREATH IN AFFORDABLE HOUSING ARCHITECTURE

Another architect linked to the above-mentioned Rothschild competition was Henry Provensal (1868–1934), who won the second prize. About this important event, Georges Teyssot reported[31] a remarkable coincidence between some of Provensal's words from his book *L'Habitation Salubre et à Bon Marché* (1908) and a famous phrase by Le Corbusier. In the chapter "L'Esthétique de la Maison" Provensal states that the shape of the low-income house should be "l'expression dans l'espace d'état statique de la matière, représentatif des besoins agglutinés."[32] Later, he said that:

"[. . .] un goût sûr, un doigté habile, car, ici, le détail disparaît, les masses seules comptent. Les volumes seuls offrent des combinaisons multiples et variées auxquelles l'architecte demandera l'expression caractéristique. C'est dans la répartition savante des cubes et leur pénétration avec d'autres volumes, qu'il cherchera à faire jouer les masses lumineuses."[33]

Taking affordable housing construction as his main subject, the French architect interrogated the role of expression of the structural skeleton itself, or the use and visibility of new materials such as concrete, as well as the usage of industrialized building processes. In addition to that, he appealed for innovations related to ventilation, water zones, accessibility, and to the configuration of the minimum cell. To widen the reading,[34] we must state that in 1904 he had already written *L'Art de Demain*, where he rehearsed a new destiny for architecture based on the abstraction of form and the use of luminous cubic volumes. This text was read by the young Charles-Edouard Jeanneret (Le Corbusier) in 1905 following the advice of his teacher Charles L'Eplattenier (1874–1946) while attending L'École d'Art at La-Chaux-de-Fonds (Switzerland).[35]

These points of view were influenced by some Parisian intellectual elites who cultivated the idea of a new art for the people from the beginning of the century.[36] For example, concerning the loss of primitive art and the renewal and democratization of decorative arts, the poet and physician Henri Cazalis (1840–1909) wrote that *"l'hygiène déjà, est une branche encore de l'esthétique—car la santé, la propreté sont nécessairement des conditions essentielles de la beauté [. . .] Mais je demande plus: je voudrais partout ce que nous voulons en nos intérieurs, un peu d'élégance, de beauté, avec la salubrité et avec le confort."*[37]

[31] Georges Teyssot, "The Disease of the Domicile," *Assemblage*, no. 6 (Jun 1988): 94.

[32] Henry Provensal, *L'Habitation Salubre et à Bon Marché* (Paris: Librairie Génerale de l'Architecture et des Arts Décoratifs, 1908), 79.

[33] Ibid.

[34] It should be noted that, as a student, Henry Provensal was a colleague of the Portuguese architect Marques da Silva in 1891 at the Parisian academy. António Cardoso, 'O Arquitecto José Marques da Silva e a arquitectura no Norte do País na primeira metade do séc. XX" (PhD Thesis, Faculdade de Letras da Universidade do Porto do Porto, 1992), 73.

[35] H. Allen Brooks, *Le Corbusier's Formative Years: Charles-Edouard Jeanneret at La Chaux-de-Fonds* (Chicago: The University of Chicago Press, 1997), 27.

[36] It is worth mentioning the esoteric personality of the physician Henri Cazalis whose sui generis literary work included studies on William Morris with lateral incursions to the work of Ruskin. Besides the book "Habitation à Bon Marché," under the pseudonym Jean Lahor, he published in 1901 "L'Art Nouveau" dedicated to Félix Mangini (1836–1902), philanthropist, creator of the first French popular sanatorium and working-class housing estates in Lyon.

[37] "L'Art Nouveau au point de vue social." Jean Lahor, *L'Art Nouveau* (Paris: Lemerre éditeur, 1901), 92.

The sanitary measures and the new building codes improved by hygiene gradually became a programme of values aiming to create a mens sans in corpore sano—*hygienism*. This kind of doctrinaire position helped the emancipation of diaphanous, white and politically engaged architectural forms. Paul Overy blames the hygienist movement for the Neues Bauen's[38] neutral and scientific features, and generally for the geometry of simple shapes, large glazing, terraces, and shiny surfaces of early modern buildings, especially in new programmes related to health. Through this, we can match sanatorium design to new housing solutions by the similar use of materials and construction elements. It was this referential hygienist character, guarded by personalities as different as Walter Grophius (1883–1969) or Robert Mallet-Stevens (1886–1945), where we can register the "Ephemeral Modernism" mentioned by Nuno Portas in "Evolution of Modern Architecture in Portugal."[39]

After the end of the 1920s, the first proposals aligned with the international movements of Esprit Nouveau and Bauhaus emerged on the national scene. Within the cultural and technological constraints of the country, some young architects developed an abstract and functionalist effort against the dominant figurative language and the monumental aesthetic of governmental power. Until then, there had been an eclectic production with a classical matrix but contaminated by a certain utilitarianism that was closely adjusted to new programmes and technical innovations.

The complex urban and housing design of the first affordable neighbourhoods built by the republican government were signed by this generation of architects formed at the École des Beaux-Arts of Paris. Among the five neighbourhoods built we can underline the difference between the most monumental architecture of Arco do Cego [MdH DB a216] in Lisbon and the most traditional in Arrábida [MdH DB a20] located on the west side of the city of Porto, as well as being apart from the international bucolic forms of the garden-city movement. Particularly in the latter case, observing the chimneys, the flowerbeds, the eaves or the braiding forms of the balconies, one can recognise the first signs of an architecture that used uniformed elements rooted in traditional constructive culture with its theoretical support based on the ethnographic rhetoric of the "Portuguese House." By this time this was the main theoretical problem in the national architecture scenario when modernist forms arrived.

[38] Paul Overy, *Light, Air and Openness. Modern Architecture Between the Wars* (London: Thames & Hudson, 2007).

[39] Nuno Portas, "A evolução da Arquitectura Moderna em Portugal," in Bruno Zevi, *História da Arquitectura Moderna*. Volume II (Lisbon: Arcádia, 1973).

It can be argued that in the last stage in the reconfiguration of the economical house before the Affordable House Programme Act of 1933, there was a convergence of both the normative component of Hygienism—conveyed by the RSEU—and its ideological component imported through the aesthetic and political values of the Modern Movement. But most of the solutions built in Portugal were far from the new architectural and urban radical praxis stimulated by the social housing process of the Weimar Republic or the French HBM (Habitations à Bon Marché). Against the cultural, political and economic reality a lag of a modernity can be observed that was nothing more than a simple update of the housing design with new refined decorative repertoire. For example, Cottinelli Telmo's suggestions for working-class family housing in the Algarve were referred to as "beautiful models of modern architecture subordinated to a regional feeling."[40] Also, the architect Carlos Ramos (1897–1969) designed two alternatives for affordable housing in Funchal:[41] one was engaged with modern volumetric abstraction; the other—a complementary B-solution—appears in a "regionalist version," drawing on decorative and constructive elements linked to the local architectural tradition.

More reliable with European vanguardism was Ramos's solution for Olhão council [MdH DB a211] which was composed by twenty-four single-storey terraced houses with an inner courtyard organized along a private street that acted as an axis of symmetry in the composition of the plan. A model of this neighbourhood appeared in the important exhibition of 1930 entitled Salão dos Independentes[42] to state a strong relationship between its abstract forms and the cubist atmosphere of the Algarvian traditional village. This was an ability and a way to make propaganda for the Modern Movement in Portugal.[43] This need for contextualization was suppressed in another municipal neighbourhood [MdH DB a686] proposed in 1931 under the Funchal Improvement Plan. Here, Carlos Ramos was unequivocal in the use of a formal lexicon in tune with the functionalist postulates out of the 1929 Frankfurt CIAM—"Die Wohnung fur das Existenzminimum"[44]—about the relation between "minimal space," "light," "air" and "free space." As opposed to the solution of row houses mentioned above, the collective housing building presents a volumetric composition that makes use of the stairs as an object to punctuate the entrance in a complex set of shadows that also associates the volumes of the balconies. The facade emphasized the multiple vertical access, a solution which was constantly censored for moving away from the single-family ideal.

[40] "Casa de 9 compartimentos, para o sul do país," *A Arquitectura Portuguesa*, Ano XXVI, no. 8 e 9 (August and September 1933): 71.

[41] For a detailed reading of the work of architect Carlos Ramos, see: Bárbara dos Santos Coutinho, "Carlos Ramos (1897–1969): Obra, pensamento e acção. A procura do compromisso entre o Modernismo e a Tradição" (Master's dissertation in History of Contemporary Art, Faculdade de Ciências Sociais e Humanas da Universidade Nova de Lisboa, 2001).

[42] First of two exhibitions held at the National Society of Fine Arts (Lisbon) aimed at the dissemination of modern works in various areas, namely, architecture. José Augusto França, *História da Arte em Portugal: o Modernismo* (Lisbon: Editorial Presença, 2004), 59. Ricardo Agarez observes that the event was noticed outside Portugal, namely, in the German magazine called Wasmuths Monatshefte, Baukunst & Städtebau, August 1931.

[43] Cottinelli Telmo would also use this comparison to justify his proposal for poor family houses as "beautiful models of modern architecture subordinated to a regional sentiment." "Casa de 9 compartimentos, para o sul do país," 71.

[44] Theme of the 2nd CIAM Congress (Frankfurt 1929)—"Housing for minimum living conditions."

This new breath is also found in the "Plan for a Garden City" by author architect Rogério de Azevedo (1898–1983), located in Viana do Castelo. From the analysis of the preliminary project dated 1932, we can observe a spatial and morphological matrix which was sufficiently flexible to form typologies for up to four rooms, which could be aggregated in line or detached. The use of simple glazing and a sloped roof pitched to the back facade, with the consequent formation of a vast area of blind wall in the front elevation, contributed to underlining the nakedness and lightness of the volume. In addition to the use of these kind of formal devices, the interior space solution reveals a distinct way of organizing domestic life. For example, if we dwell on the bath and kitchen compartments we perceive a new complexity in the layout and space dimensions which probably has to do with the introduction of modern household equipment.

A final example of the effort to align with international avant-garde experimentation was the Conde de Monte Real affordable housing estate designed in 1932 by the architect Jorge Segurado (1898–1990) for Cascais. The solution was based on a rectangular web with row houses arranged in parallel repeated bars, in an order that suggests the plan of the Siedlung Dammerstock by Walter Gropius (1883–1969) built in 1928 and which Segurado visited in 1931. If fully completed, the project would give rise to 133 type A houses and 123 type B, a school, playgrounds, a library and a cooperative headquarters. The two types corresponded to single-family houses with one or two bedrooms, with a distributive nucleus formed by the "common room" to which a small cooking zone and a bath were added. In the municipal report presented by the mayor António Rodrigues Cardoso, the following was written about the architect:

"Aware of his value, which is great, he never compromises with habits of the past that were rule in matters of aesthetics in this county. He put in order what was out of it, putting each one in his place: the foremen, the project amateurs, and the creators of styles."[45]

In a photograph from that time [see page 16–17] we can see groups of four houses with the same sun exposure, rear gardens simply divided by fragile hedges. The flat roofed volumes feature a dark chromatic tone that contrasts with the delicate design of the frames made of steel profiles. These particularities that coined the modernist character of this neighbourhood were to be quickly transformed to be compatible with the formal repertoire of the Estado Novo, namely, eaved roofs; small two-leaf windows in light tones.

[45] Quoted from José D'Encarnação, *Recantos de Cascais* (Lisbon: Edições Colibri, 2007), 24.

CONCLUDING NOTE

In its broadest sense, the definition of modern corresponds to a greater degree of moral, cultural and artistic awareness of a historical process in a "state of rupture" with that in force for the improvement of material conditions of life and modification of power relations between social groups. Now, in these first decades dominated by republicanism, this awareness never became collective or institutional and therefore the construction of modernity in architecture was never committed to a sustained programme of social transformation. When compared to the vanguard, modern national works were circumstantial, inconsequential and eminently imported visual phenomenon but that did not fail to incorporate the vast sanitary and social burden of hygiene and its influence on the spatial and expressive emancipation of the architectural forms of social housing.

Apart from the fact that these latter proposals are mostly based on the single family, they contradict what would become the model implemented by the Estado Novo dictatorship. The affordable housing architecture that António Salazar wanted for the country embodied the picturesque aspects of simple pastoral houses taken as the last vestiges of the profound roots of Portugal as a unique nation.

Science and Technique in the Service of More Modern and Salubrious Cities

ANA CARDOSO DE MATOS
University of Évora, Interdisciplinary Centre for History, Culture and Societies

ABSTRACT

In this paper we intend to analyse the problems created by industrial development and the concentration of the population in the main industrial cities. The pollution created by industrial establishments, as well as the insufficient supply of water in good conditions and the lack of sewage systems, created an unhealthy urban environment that favoured the emergence of diseases and did not correspond to the hygienist ideas of the time. Thus, the idea of progress and urban wellbeing was associated with the introduction of modern infrastructures that could solve these problems. On the other hand, the development of sciences such as chemistry or medicine allowed a better understanding of the reasons for the epidemics and to realize that there could only be good public health if the problems that affected individual health were solved.

In the process of urban modernization and the resolution of health problems affecting cities, doctors, chemists and engineers played a decisive role with their scientific knowledge and technical skills. Their action also benefited from their contacts abroad, and from the solutions to urban problems adopted in other countries. Political-administrative institutions also tried to take measures to eliminate or reduce the risk of disease or pollution, in order to create urban spaces in conformity with the standards of the more developed cities. The ideas for the modernization of cities were also linked to the introduction of gas and electricity in public lighting, as well as the ideas of better planning of urban spaces and the creation of more beautiful and pleasant cities, with more gardens and green areas. Similarly, the introduction of electrical transportation favoured the population's mobility in urban space, which gradually increased.

The introduction of basic sanitation and energy networks had an influence on living space, of course, although at first this alteration was particularly felt in the most important cities and the higher social strata. In this text we intend to analyse some of the issues mentioned, covering the late 19th century and the first decades of the 20th century.

BIOGRAPHY

Ana Cardoso de Matos is Associate Professor at the Évora University–Department of History, Vice-director of the Institute for Advanced Studies and member of the board of Research Centre CIDEHUS/UE. She is responsible for the EMM TPTI–Techniques, patrimoines, territoires de l'industrie at Évora University. She is a member of: the advisory council of the Portuguese National Railway Museum Foundation, Comité d'Histoire de l'electricite et de l'energie, Foundation EDF; International Railways History Association (IRHA); Associação Ibérica de História Ferroviária; the editorial board of the journals HoST–Journal of History of Science and Technology; TST–Transportes, servicios y telecomunicaciones; Comité scientifique of Journal of Energy History/Revue d'Histoire de l'Énergie. She was Visiting Professor at EHESS–Paris (2010 and 2012). She publishes regularly both in national and international journals and is author or co-author of 6 books, co-editor of 9 books and has collaborated in several books. Two of her last publications are "Technological Nocturne: The Lisbon Industrial Institute and Romantic Engineering (1849–1888)," Technology and Culture, 2017, vol. 58, 2 (with Tiago Saraiva) and "La Russie, l'Espagne, le Portugal et l'Empire ottoman. Deux siècles de politiques technoscientifiques à l'épreuve des approches comparatistes" (with Irina Gouzevitch and Darina Martikanova) in Mina Kleiche-Dray (dir.) Les ancrages nationaux de la science mondiale XVIIIe–XXIe siècles, Paris, 2017.

INTRODUCTION

The 19th and early 20th centuries were characterised by a rising demographic concentration in Portugal's main cities, largely because of industrial development, while at the same time there was growing attention to making cities modern and beautiful. Thus, the construction of gas or electrical plants allowed, on the one hand, for the public lighting of cities, thereby creating a safer environment, while on the other hand solutions were sought for the supply of water in decent conditions to urban centres, and for the basic sanitation of cities. The pollution caused by factories and the flaws in basic urban sanitation, however, did not allow cities to enjoy the conditions of hygiene and salubriousness required by the modern hygienist theories which had been developing since the 1800s, based on the progress of sciences such as chemistry, medicine and engineering. As a consequence, the issues of salubriousness and public hygiene were a constant concern to both political-administrative institutions and doctors, chemists, and engineers. Several laws were passed to solve the problems of environmental pollution and to build more modern and functional facilities, such as slaughterhouses and marketplaces, in order to free the streets from hotspots of dirt and pollution. These new facilities used materials such as iron, glass, and tar to ensure better hygiene. Simultaneously, measures were taken to create gardens and plant trees along the main roads—both for the sake of beauty and the enjoyment of leisure time and for creating a more salubrious environment. To improve living conditions for the under-privileged classes, public housing construction was begun[1] and some industrialists took the initiative of building boroughs to accommodate their employees.

1. DOCTORS, CHEMISTS, AND ENGINEERS: APPLYING TECHNICAL AND SCIENTIFIC KNOWLEDGE IN THE CITIES

In urban modernization, and in the initiatives undertaken to improve the quality of life in cities, doctors, chemists, and engineers were decisive, and their actions helped cement both their professional status and their appreciation in society. Doctors endeavoured to regulate collective behaviour and to take measures that would prevent, rather than solve, epidemic situations. In 1899, when there was an epidemic of bubonic plague in Porto, the action of the doctor Ricardo Jorge (1858–1939) allowed the diagnosis to be based on microbiological analyses. It was thanks to the written output and the measures taken by Ricardo Jorge that, for the first time, "improving public health at home was more important than preventing foreign and exotic epidemics from entering Portugal."[2]

---

[1] Luis Urteaga, "Miséria, Miasmas Y Micróbios. Las Topografías Médicas Y el Estudio del Medio Ambiente em el Siglo XIX," *Geocrítica. Cuadernos Críticos de Geografia Humana*, Ano V, no. 29 (1980). url: http://www.ub.edu/geocrit/geo29.htm

[2] Rita Garnel, "Disease and Public Health (Portugal)," in Ute Daniel, Peter Gartrell, Oliver Janz, Heartther Jones, Jennifer Keene, Alan Kramer, and Bill Nasson (eds), *1914–1918—online. International Encyclopedia of the First World War* (Berlin: Freie Universitat Berlin, 2014)

In that same year, in another initiative by Ricardo Jorge, the Instituto Central de Higiene (Central Institute of Hygiene) was created in Lisbon. Its aim was to give doctors and engineers specialized training in the tasks of public health, already covered by courses on sanitary medicine and engineering.[3] In April 1911, this institute was placed under the pedagogical tutelage of the Faculdade de Medicina de Lisboa (Lisbon Medical School).[4] The year 1915 saw the publication of the *Proposta de organização do Instituto de Higiene da Faculdade de Medicina do Porto do curso especial de Higiene Publica* (Proposal by the Instituto de Higiene da Faculdade de Medicina do Porto to organize a special course on Public Hygiene).[5] However, by 1923, Ricardo Jorge thought that all the efforts made since the beginning of the century had not yielded very positive results[6]: *"no Portuguese town was properly sanitized, sewers were still a novelty in most parts of the country, and the supply of contaminated water continued to be responsible for typhoid epidemics."*

Concerns over disease prevention were closely associated with analyses of water quality supplied to cities, as well as with the quality of foodstuffs that reached them.[8] The analyses run on air and water led to the publication of legislative measures which aimed to control the use of rivers and the operation of industrial establishments. At the same time, inspections were set up to oversee the practical application of the legislative measures and the appearance of epidemic focus.[9] In these inspections, chemists and engineers played a decisive role, since they had the scientific and technical knowledge allowing them to appraise the causes of the pollution provoked by industrial operations, and they could propose solutions.[10] Engineers saw hygiene and salubriousness as essential elements of the modernity and progress of cities.[11]

The position of these men on the issues of public health and the pollution of the urban environment benefited from their contacts abroad, and from the solutions to urban problems found in other countries—an area in which innovations were being introduced all the time. Urban space, in fact, witnessed the introduction of "some of the most important technological and economic transformations" in the closing decades of the 19th century.[12] The publication of technical papers on urban infrastructure, from company reports to theoretical works and recommended projects, made it easier to systematize knowledge in this field, and to disseminate the corresponding technologies. As stated by M. Leguez, a sewage engineer from Paris, in his preface to the *Traîté des Égouts* by J. Hervieu, this handbook, which sought to systematize the most important knowledge concerning the construction of an urban sewage network, was—despite being very difficult to put together—enormously useful for French and foreign engineers alike.[13]

[3] Decree of 28 December 1899. However, this Institute was only formalized in 1901 by the Decree of 24 December 1901.

[4] On this matter see Ângela Salgueiro, *Ciência e Universidade na I República* (PhD Diss., FCSH-UNL), 61 and Luís Graça, "História e memória da saúde pública," *Revista Portuguesa de Saúde Pública*, vol. 33, no. 2 (2015), 126.

[5] *Annuario de Medicina do Porto. 1913–1915* (Porto: Tip Portuguesa), 329–331.

[6] Ricardo Jorge, "A Propósito de Pasteur. Discurso proferido em comemoração do centenário pastoriano na Faculdade de Medicina de Lisboa aos 25 de Abril de 1923" ["Remembering Pasteur. Centennial lecture presented at the Lisbon Faculty of Medicine on 25 April 1923"], Lisbon 1923, 58

[7] Rita Garnel, "Disease and Public Health (Portugal)," 10.

[8] This was the reason behind the creation of a laboratory in Porto, during J. A. Correia de Bastos' term as a councilman, "to perform analyses like those made in other European cities, showing unexpected attention to the fields of Bromatology, or the chemistry of food." Jorge Fernandes Alves; Rita C. Alves, "Ferreira da Silva e o Laboratório Químico Municipal do Porto (1884–1917), in *Histórias da Saúde, Estudos do século XX*, 12 (2012): 15.

[9] Sabine Barles, La *Ville Délétère, Médecins et Ingénieurs dans L'Espace Urbain XVIII – XIX Siècle* (Paris: Éditions Champ Vallon, 1999).

[10] Ana Cardoso de Matos, "Indústria e ambiente no século XIX," *Ler História*, 42 (2002): 150–151.

[11] On the importance of engineers and men of science for the modernization of cities, see Ana Cardoso de Matos, "O papel dos 'homens de ciência' e dos engenheiros na construção das cidades contemporâneas. O caso de Lisboa." Comunicação ao XVIII Encontro da Associação de História Económica e Social. Lisbon, 1998.

[12] Álvaro Ferreira da Silva and Ana Cardoso de Matos, "Urbanismo e modernização das cidades: o "embellezamento" como ideal. Lisboa, 1858–1891," *Scripta Nova. Revista Electrónica de Geografia y Ciencias Sociales*, no. 69 (30) (2000). url: http://www.ub.edu/geocrit/sn-69-30.htm

[13] Christiane Blancot and Bernard Landau, "La direction des travaux de Paris au XIXe siècle.» In *Le Paris des Polytechniciens. Des Ingénieurs dans la Ville*, edited by Bruno Belhoste; Francine Masson; Antoine Picon (Paris : Délégation de l'action artistique de la *ville de Paris*, 1994), 173.

In effect, when Portuguese municipalities took steps to modernize the urban space under their administration, they sought information on the technological options and the regulations existing in the most important European cities. Whenever necessary, they resorted to doctors, chemists, and engineers, whose scientific training enabled them to clearly understand the importance of planning the city, improving gas and water supply and solving the problem of urban sanitation. Among doctors we should name, as an example, the already mentioned Ricardo Jorge. Among the chemists were, among others, Júlio Máximo de Oliveira Pimentel,[14] in Lisbon, and Joaquim António Ferreira da Silva, in Porto. The former, who served as councillor (1853–1855) and mayor (1858–1860) of the Lisbon City Hall, was permanently concerned with the issues of hygiene in the city. In the report he produced at the end of his term as mayor, he sketched a general overview of the city's condition at the time.[15] In it he mentioned his worries about public hygiene and sanitation in Lisbon, calling attention to *"the defective plumbing for disposal of waste matters... the great accumulation of corrupt substances choking up the pipes and letting off repugnant smells."*[16] Moreover, being a chemist, he carried out several chemical analyses on the waters which the population might come to use.

In Porto, Joaquim António Ferreira da Silva played a fundamental role, not only by running the Laboratório Químico Municipal (Chemical Laboratory of the municipality), but also by writing a report on the waters of the Sousa river, in 1881, at a time when there was a demand for policies regarding the supply of water to the city of Porto.[17] In addition, in 1905 he founded the journal *Revista de Chimica Pura e Aplicada* (Journal of Pure and Applied Chemistry) with Alberto de Aguiar and Pereira Salgado, his collaborators at the Laboratório Municipal.

As we have said, engineers were just as important in this field. In the words of Melosi, "they promoted themselves as problem solvers, especially through growing professional networks and organizations."[18] As an example, let us consider the city of Lisbon. Up until the third quarter of the 19th century, attempts to transform basic sanitation were isolated and unsuccessful: they failed to implement the model that combined the water supply and sewage systems—*water carriage sewage system*—which already prevailed in other countries.[19] Only after 1874, when the engineer Ressano Garcia (who had completed his training at the École de Ponts et Chaussés in Paris,[20] was appointed to the post of Engineer at the Lisbon City Hall, could the municipality count on a Committee for Municipal Works and Improvements.

[14] On this chemist, see Ana Cardoso de Matos, "Matemático por formação, químico por paixão: Júlio Máximo de Oliveira Pimentel, um "politécnico" no Portugal Oitocentista." In *Metamorfoses da Cultura, Estudos em Homenagem a Maria Carlos Radich*, edited by Ana Maria Pina; Carlos Maurício; Maria João Vaz, . (Lisbon: CEHC-IUL, 2013),165–189.

[15] The report also provides indicators on the state of the relationship between the municipal powers and the central government. Ana Barata, *Lisboa Caes da Europa* (Lisbon: Edições Colibri, 2010), 25. The document the author quotes is called "Exposição da gerência anterior pela comunicação dos factos consumados, das medidas adoptadas, projectos em estudo, das questões ventiladas e das ideias concebidas e propostas."

[16] Quoted in Barata, *Lisboa Caes da Europa*, 31.

[17] António Joaquim *Ferreira da Silva, As Águas do Rio Sousa e os Mananciais e Fontes da Cidade do Porto* (Porto, 1881).

[18] Martin V. Melosi, *Effluent America: Cities, Industry, Energy and the Environment* (Pittsburgh: University of Pittsburgh Press, 2001), 229.

[19] Álvaro Ferreira da Silva, "Uma máquina imperfeita: Tecnología sanitária en Lisboa en la segunda metade del siglo XIX" in *Maquinismo Ibérico*, edited by António Lafuente, Ana Cardoso de Matos and Tiago Saraiva, (Madrid: Doce Calles, 2007), 371–400.

[20] This engineer had already done some works for the Belém City Hall and for the Division of Public Works in Lisbon.

It was made up of five council members and Ressano Garcia, and its role was to evaluate every urban development project and make decisions affecting infrastructures, which became objects of public responsibility (sewage, slaughterhouses, markets).[21] The continued existence of this committee[22] from 1874 to 1909 enabled a more sustained and continuous action in municipal matters having to do with urban planning and intervention in urban facilities. Doctors, chemists, and engineers, to sum up, were the professionals who best understood the environmental consequences of industrial development and looked for solutions to solve the environmental problems of cities.

2. INTERVENTION BY POLITICAL-ADMINISTRATIVE POWERS IN THE SANITATION OF CITIES

While there were specific professional groups which, as we have just seen, made significant contributions to improving standards of living in the cities, political-administrative powers had an important intervention, too, in the technical-juridical framing of the cities' technical networks: *"despite differences in scale regarding technologies, raw materials, and entrepreneurial behaviour, the networks put in place in the 19th and 20th centuries kept their trend of constant growth."*[23]

As mentioned by João Pato, solving problems "of hygiene and public health in urban context" fell exclusively to the Ministry of Public Works, Trade, and Industry (MOPCI) "concerning technical guidance and planning of the works which local corporations should undertake."[24] Thus, in 1899 a *Junta Central de Melhoramentos Sanitários* was created within this ministry, with the competence to issue legal opinions on major sewage and drinking water supply works, and also to control the operation of those services. In 1901, this Junta was replaced by the *Conselho de Melhoramentos Sanitários*, an organ with an essentially consultative capacity, like other boards already in existence within this ministry,[25] implying the creation of two sanitation areas, one in the north and another in the south of the country.[26] The *Conselho de Melhoramentos Sanitários* was supposed to *"issue consultative opinions regarding public works which concern hygiene, and lay down the rules and requisites which, from the perspective of sanitation, must be followed by buildings especially made for living."*[27] With the same purpose of improving the living conditions of urban populations, the *Regulamento de Salubridade das Edificações Urbanas* ("Regulations on the Salubriousness of Urban Buildings") was published in 1903 and, in the following year, the *Regulamento de Fiscalização das Águas Potáveis Destinadas a Consumo Público* ("Regulations on the Inspection of Drinking Water for Public Consumption").[28]

[21] Water and energy supply, as well as urban transportation, remained private concerns.

[22] This was later renamed Service of Public Works.

[23] Mercedes Arroyo and Ana Cardoso de Mato "La modernización de dos ciudades: las redes de gas de Barcelona y Lisboa, siglos XIX y XX." *Scripta Nova. Revista Electrónica de Geografía y Ciencias Sociales.* Barcelona: Universidad de Barcelona, vol. XIII, núm. 296 (6) (2009). url: http://www.ub.edu/geocrit/sn/sn-296/sn-296-6.htm

[24] João Howell Pato, *História das Políticas Públicas de Abastecimento e Saneamento de Águas em Portugal* (Lisbon: Ed ERSAR, 2011), 31.

[25] Conselho de Obras Públicas e Minas, Monumentos Nacionais e Tarifas.

[26] Decree of 24 October 1901, Article 17.

[27] Idem

[28] For systematic knowledge regarding legislation on this subject in the 19th and 20th centuries, see João Howell Pato (org), *História das Políticas Publicas de Abastecimento e Saneamento de Águas em Portugal—Cronologia e Depoimentos* (Lisbon: ERSAR, 2016).

3. STREETS, GARDENS, AND TRANSPORTATION AS STRUCTURING ELEMENTS OF URBAN SPACE

The urban modernization from which cities were meant to benefit from the second half of the 19th century onwards also implied greater planning of urban space. This would make it possible to open wider streets, thereby facilitating air circulation and the layout of technical networks which served the population—water supply, sewage, gas or electricity. Following the influence of Haussmann's interventions in the city of Paris, or those by Ildefonso Cerdá in Barcelona, the main Portuguese cities strove to open great gardens and tree-lined avenues, to facilitate the mobility of people and vehicles, render urban space more beautiful and make air circulation easier. Implementing this new vision of the city implied, in the words of Joan-Anton Sánchez de Juan, a "creative destruction" which constituted "the language of urban reform."[29]

When it came to urban planning and development, however, there was a very diverse reality around the turn of the 19th century. While some innovative urbanistic projects provided housing for the bourgeois classes in the new avenues, the working class huddled together in dense neighbourhoods that lacked water, electricity, and basic sanitation, which constituted one of the great scourges of major cities. In Lisbon, the Avenida da Liberdade replaced the public garden before the end of the 19th century, and later on the Avenida 24 de Julho was opened and new gardens and leisure areas were created,[30] but at the same time there appeared the *pátios* and the *vilas operárias,* where overcrowding generated situations of poverty and delinquency. The city of Porto saw the spread of "ilhas" ("islands")— ground-floor houses measuring around 4 metres at the side, lined up at the back of elegant buildings and housing entire families, in an even more dramatic situation than that of the capital. Only in 1916 did the city of Porto see the opening of the Avenida dos Aliados.

The diffusion of new means of transportation contributed decisively to the growth of cities and, while throughout the 19th century they benefited from innovations which made them quicker and more efficient, only with the use of electricity did urban means of transportation—namely trams and, in the 20th century, the underground railway[31]—assume decisive importance in the organization and definition of urban spaces. They contributed to the concentration of third-sector activity in the centre of town, while at the same time the residential and industrial areas were being relocated to the margins of urban space.

---

[29] Joan-Anton Sánchez de Juan, "La «destrucción creadora»: el lenguaje de la reforma urbana en tres ciudades de la Europa mediterránea a finales del siglo XIX (Marsella, Nápoles Y Barcelona." *Scripta Nova. Revista Electrónica de Geografía y Ciencias sociale, no.63* (2000), http://www.ub.edu/geocrit/sn-63.htm»

[30] Raquel Henriques da Silva, *O Urbanismo— Caminhos e Planos. Lisboa em Movimento, 1852–1920.* (Lisbon: Livros Horizonte, 1994), 47.

[31] On the history of the Lisbon underground, see Maria Fernanda Rollo e António Alves Martins, *Um Metro e uma Cidade: História do Metropolitano de Lisboa* (Lisbon: Metropolitano, 1999–2001).

4. THE INTRODUCTION OF GAS AND ELECTRICITY NETWORKS AND THE LIGHTING OF PUBLIC SPACES

The modernization of cities was linked to the introduction of gas and electricity networks that enabled their lighting and ensured greater security in public spaces. In Portugal, public lighting by gas dates back to 1848 in Lisbon, followed by the cities of Porto and Coimbra. Only in the 1880s, however, we did see a wave of initiatives in the country's main cities to generalize this form of lighting,[32] often managed by concessions to foreign companies. The spread of gas lighting was slower elsewhere in the country, and by 1896 there were only 11 gas plants in the whole territory, a figure which remained unchanged until 1907.[33] During the First World War, the gas industry faced great problems with fuel supplies. This led to the closing down of some plants and to cuts in the hours of lighting in cities, and even in some cases to the replacement of gas by olive oil as fuel.

The period between the wars made a slow recovery of the gas industry possible, although in some cities gas lighting was gradually replaced by its electrical alternative. In the case of many smaller cities, electricity came first because gas had not yet arrived[34] and so these cities had no gas lighting contracts to bind them.[35] The pre-existence of public gas lighting resulted in different situations regarding the creation of urban electricity grids. In some cases, there appeared companies to deal with the production and distribution of electricity which, operating in parallel with the gas lighting market, supplied electricity for private consumption.[36] The introduction of electric lighting in smaller urban spaces often benefited from the use of electrical power by local industries, which sold the energy needed by public lighting the night time, thereby monetizing their investments. Such was the case of the Companhia Elvense de Moagens a Vapor (Elvense Company of Steam Grinding) which, in 1901, began supplying energy for public lighting in the city of Elvas.

During the Republican period, several laws were passed in an attempt to normalize the concession of public lighting by municipalities. With this goal, on 30 November 1912 the General Board of Post and Telegraphy published its *Caderno de Encargos-tipo para a Concessão por uma Câmara Municipal duma Distribuição de Energia Eléctrica* (Set of Specifications for the Concession of Electrical Energy Distribution by Municipalities), which held good until 1923. From the same year came the *Regulamento das Concessões de Licenças para o Estabelecimento e Exploração de Instalações Eléctricas* (Rules on the Concession of Licenses for Establishing and Exploiting Electrical Installations). In 1913 a law was published which granted municipalities the right to decide on the "municipalization of local services" (7 August 1913).

[32] Ana Cardoso de Matos, "Urban Gas and Electricity Networks in Portugal: Competition and Collaboration (1850–1926)," *Quaderns d'Història de l'Enginyeria*, vol. 12 (2011): 125–145.

[33] Portugal, Ministério da Fazenda. *Anuário Estatístico* (Lisbon; Imprensa Nacional, 1907), 362.

[34] Examples of this were the inauguration of electrical public lighting in Braga in 1893, and the same again in Vila Real the following year.

[35] In some cities and towns, the introduction of electric lighting was hindered by the pre-existence of gas-powered public lighting. This was, in most cases, exploited by companies enjoying monopolies guaranteed by the concession of pubic lighting for periods which normally ranged from 30 to 60 years.

[36] This was the case, for instance, in Porto and in Évora.

This law also contemplated the possibility of several municipalities coming together to jointly manage one or more public services, e.g. the supply of water or energy. Following the 1st Congress of Alentejo Municipalities, held in 1915, in which the advantages of the municipalization of services were discussed—and supported— by the attendants, several cities considered municipalizing their sanitation and public lighting services. In few instances, however, were these intentions put into practice straight away. In 1927, although the municipalization of certain public services was already a reality,[37] the fact was that only around 15 per cent of municipalities directly exploited the services of lighting or water supply.

Based on the data that appeared in the *Estatística das Instalações Eléctricas* from 1928, we can see that the cities of Lisbon and Porto still carried decisive weight in the global consumption of electricity. This state of affairs endured until the Second World War, although the relative weight of these two cities kept falling gradually. This trend reflected the rise of electricity consumption in other regions of the country. That rise, nevertheless, was marked by great regional disparities: the coastal areas advanced faster than the hinterland, just as the northern regions advanced faster than the south.

Electricity was very important, too, for the development of urban transportation: trams were introduced in the city of Porto in 1895. In Lisbon, they first appeared in 1901, and by 1910 the main spots in the city were already linked by them, with a network which totalled an extension of 114.7 km. The highly profitable exploitation of this system allowed fares to be lowered, which favoured wider use of this means of urban transportation. In 1910, the number of passengers transported in Lisbon rose to 49,925,176, reaching an average of 317 passengers per car/day. In 1904, this improvement was extended to Coimbra, and in 1914 to Braga. In the same year, the first elevators in Lisbon were electrified—those of Bica, Lavra, and Glória, all of them belonging to Companhia dos Ascensores (Lifts Company). Despite all this, in the opening years of the 20th century, very little energy was still used for traction; a significant increase only occurred when electrical energy was applied to trains. The first railway line to be electrified, in 1926, was the Cascais line, of growing importance both to residents along the line who worked in Lisbon and to the development of Estoril as a summer resort.

In the early 20th century, the telephone was still a luxury item— accessible only to companies, public services, and a few private citizens—and it could only be found in Lisbon. But by the 1920s, its use had spread to other Portuguese cities, although mostly in networks serving a very small number of users, e.g. Alenquer, which had fourteen phone lines in 1924, or Vila Franca de Xira, with

[37] Decree no. 13,350, 25 March 1927.

thirty-two lines in the same year. In the years that followed the networks were expanded, and on 17 May 1928 the direct telephone line linking Lisbon and Madrid was inaugurated. The interest in wireless telegraphy led, after a complex process, to the creation of the Companhia Portuguesa Rádio Marconi, S.A. (Portuguese Company Radio Marconi, S.A.).

Apart from its use in communications, electricity was also important to ensure the provision of water to several urban centres, since it enabled the capture of water at deeper levels. Thus, in 1925 electrical pumps for water lifting were installed in Coimbra, and in 1927 the Companhia das Águas de Lisboa (Lisbon Water Company) installed an electricity plant to capture water.

5. THE MODERNIZATION OF CITIES AND ITS IMPACT IN THE HOME

While, as Ricardo Jorge mentioned, the problem of public health and contagion could only be solved by improving health in the home, the fact is that the drive to eliminate the problems of water supply to cities and to solve the problem of sewage—in addition to the regulations issued in the 20th century on the conditions that must be satisfied by the construction of housing—was essential to change the living conditions in houses[38], even though at first only the wealthier part of the population could reap the benefit of those measures. In effect, as mentioned by A. Lafuente and T. Saraiva, *"making cities hygienic implied the transformation of the life of their inhabitants: it meant inventing new types of civic spirit."*[39] Regarding the salubriousness of houses, only in 1903 was the *Regulamento de Salubridade das Edificações Urbanas* published, which pushed for these to be constructed on adequate sites, i.e. in those areas of the city where salubriousness was already guaranteed. These rules also expressed concern over the quality of the waters supplied through plumbing, and with the sewage which should be separated from the former so as to avoid the risk of contamination.[40] On the other hand, after the First World War the domestic consumption of gas showed a tendency to increase, which mirrors a wider use of gas not only for private lighting but in the kitchen and for heating as well.[41]

In fact, from early on, a series of advertisements sought to illustrate the advantages of using gas in the kitchen, as opposed to coal. The rise in gas consumption continued until the end of the 1940s, when the trend was inverted due to the great increase in production and distribution of electricity. The growth in consumption of the latter benefited from measures taken during the 1940s, including the adoption of regressive tariffs.

[38] On this issue see Rui Jorge Garcia Ramos, Eliseu Gonçalves, and Sergio Dias Silva, "From the Late 19th Century House Question to Social Housing Programmes in the 30s: The Regulation of the Picturesque in Portugal," *DOCOMOMO*, 51 (2014): 61–67.

[39] António Lafuente and Tiago Saraiva, "The Urban Scale of Science and the Enlargement of Madrid," *Social Studies of Science*, 34, (2004): 532

[40] On this subject, see João Cosme, "As preocupações Higio-Sanitárias em Portugal (2ª metade do século XIX e princípio do XX)," *Revista da Faculdade de Letras. História*, Porto, III série, vol. 7 (2006): 188–189.

[41] As in other European cities, for example Barcelona. See Mercedes Arroyo, "Gas en todos los pisos. El largo proceso hacia la generalización del consumo doméstico del gas." *Scripta Nova. Revista Electrónica de Geografía y Ciencias Sociales*, Barcelona: Universidad de Barcelona, vol. VII, núm. 146 (135) (2003) http://www.ub.es/geocrit/sn/sn-146(135).htm

The introduction of gas and electricity brought with it important changes in planning the domestic space: in the kitchen, electric or gas ovens do not take up so much space as the old firewood ovens, just to give an example. On the other hand, the arrival of these new forms of energy to the elite, haute bourgeoisie, brought houses a series of comfortable features: heating and lighting, powered by gas or electricity, or the convenience of vacuuming the floor with the famous Electrolux vacuum cleaners.

CONCLUSION

The use of electricity in urban spaces was related to the concepts of technical progress and urban modernization that characterized the 19th and 20th centuries. With the aim of putting into practice the ideas of the day on urbanism and hygiene, and ensuring the safety, health, and wellbeing of urban populations, a series of measures were taken to create, or modernize, the systems of lighting, water supply and sewage. The creation of urban infrastructures, requiring an analysis of situations of insalubriousness in urban spaces, and their respective technical solutions (sometimes complex), constituted a field of technical innovation which spread throughout different urban centres, starting with those which boasted higher social-economic progress and greater modernization of equipment and infrastructure. Doctors, chemists, and engineers played a decisive role in the transfer of scientific knowledge and the later adoption of these solutions: they alone had the knowledge which permitted them to understand the causes of sanitation problems, and to tailor the solutions to the characteristics of each urban space. The use of gas and electricity in public and private lighting and in transportation, which emerged in the last decades of the 19th century, also owed much to the spread of technical-scientific knowledge. The improvements introduced into the public space were mirrored in the domestic space. Besides becoming increasingly salubrious, the latter began to be planned differently, turning into a place of growing comfort and well-being.

ACKNOWLEDGMENTS

This text was supported by the project CIDEHUS
UID/HIS/00057/2013 (POCI-01-0145-FEDER-007702)

BIBLIOGRAPHY

Alves, Jorge Fernandes, and Rita C. Alves. "Ferreira da Silva e o Laboratório Químico Municipal do Porto (1884–1917)." *Histórias da Saúde, Estudos do século XX*, no. 12 (2012): 13–30.

Annuario de Medicina do Porto. 1913–1915. Porto: Tip Portuguesa.

Arroyo, Mercedes, and Ana Cardoso de Matos. "La modernización de dos ciudades: las redes de gas de Barcelona y Lisboa, siglos XIX y XX." *Scripta Nova. Revista Electrónica de Geografía y Ciencias sociales*. Universidad de Barcelona, vol. XIII, no. 296 (6) (2009). http://www.ub.edu/geocrit/sn/sn-296/sn-296-6.htm

Arroyo, Mercedes. "Gas en todos los pisos. El largo proceso hacia la generalización del consumo doméstico del gas." *Scripta Nova. Revista electrónica de geografía y ciencias sociales*, Universidad de Barcelona, vol. VII, núm. 146 (135) (2003). http://www.ub.es/geocrit/sn/sn-146(135).htm

Barata, Ana. *Lisboa Caes da Europa*. Lisbon: Edições Colibri, 2010.

Barles, Sabine. *La Ville Délétère, Médecins et Ingénieurs dans l'Espace Urbain XVIII – XIX Siècle*. Paris : Éditions Champ Vallon, 1999.

Blancot, Christiane, and Bernard Landau. "La direction des travaux de Paris au XIXe siècle." In *Le Paris des Polytechniciens : Des Ingénieurs dans la Ville*, edited by Buno Belhoste, Francine Masson, Antoine Picon, Jacques Chirac and Christian Marbach. Paris: Délégation de l'action artistique de la ville de Paris, 1994.

Cosme, João. "As preocupações Higio-Sanitárias em Portugal (2ª metade do século XIX e princípios do XX)." *Revista da Faculdade de Letras. História*, III série, vol. 7 (2006): 181–195.

Ferreira da Silva, António Joaquim. *As Águas do Rio Sousa e os Mananciais e Fontes da Cidade do Porto*. Porto, 1881.

Garnel, Rita. "Disease and Public Health (Portugal)." In *1914–1918-online. International Encyclopedia of the First World War*, edited by Ute Daniel, Peter Gartrell, Oliver Janz, Hearther Jones, Jennifer Keene, Alan Kramer, and Bill Nasson. Berlin: Freie Universitat Berlin, 2014. DOI: 10.15463/ie1418.10494

Graça, Luís. "História e memória da saúde pública." *Revista portuguesa de saúde pública*, 33 (2) (2015): 125–127.

Jorge, Ricardo. *A Propósito de Pasteur. Discurso Proferido em Comemoração do Centenário Pastoriano na Faculdade de Medicina de Lisboa aos 25 de Abril de 1923*. Lisbon: Portugália, 1923.

Juan, Joan-Anton Sánchez de. "La «destrucción creadora»: el lenguage de la reforma urbana en tres ciudades de la Europa mediterránea a finales del siglo XIX (Marsella, Nápoles Y Barcelona)." *Scripta Nova. Revista Electrónica de Geografía y Ciencias sociales*. Universidad de Barcelona, no. 63 (2000). url: http://www.ub.edu/geocrit/sn-63.htm»

Lafuente, Antonio, and Tiago Saraiva. "The Urban Scale of Science and the Enlargement of Madrid." *Social Studies of Science*, no.34 (2004): 531–569.

Matos, Ana Cardoso de. "Indústria e ambiente no século XIX." *Ler História*, no. 42 (2002): 119–152.

Matos, Ana Cardoso de. "Urban Gas and Electricity Networks in Portugal: Competition and Collaboration (1850–1926)." *Quaderns d'Història de l'Enginyeria*, vol. 12 (2011): 125–145.

Matos, Ana Cardoso de. "Matemático por formação, químico por paixão: Júlio Máximo de Oliveira Pimentel, um "politécnico" no Portugal Oitocentista." In *Metamorfoses da Cultura, Estudos em Homenagem a Maria Carlos Radich*, edited by Ana Maria Pina, Carlos Maurício and Maria João Vaz, 165–189. Lisbon: CEHC-IUL, 2013.

Matos, Ana Cardoso de. "O papel dos 'homens de ciência' e dos engenheiros na construção das cidades contemporâneas. O caso de Lisboa." Comunicação ao XVIII Encontro da Associação de História Económica e Social. Lisbon, 1998.

Melosi, Martin V. *The Effluent America. Cities, Industry, Energy and the Environement*. Pittsburgh: University of Pittsburgh Press, 2001.

Pato, João Howell. *História das Políticas Públicas de Abastecimento e Saneamento de Águas em Portugal*. Lisbon: Ed ERSAR, 2011.

Pato, João Howell (org), *História das Políticas Publicas de Abastecimento e Saneamento de Águas em Portugal— Cronologia e Depoimentos*. Lisbon: ERSAR, 2016.

Portugal, Ministério da Fazenda. *Anuário Estatístico*. Lisbon; Imprensa Nacional, 1907.

Ramos, Rui Jorge Garcia, Eliseu Gonçalves, and Sergio Dias Silva. "From the Late 19th Century House Question to Social Housing Programmes in the 30s: The Regulation of the Picturesque in Portugal." *DO.CO.MO.MO*, no. 51 (2014).

Regulamento de Salubridade das Edificações Urbanas. Lisbon: Imprensa nacional, 1912.

Rollo, Maria Fernanda, and António Alves Martins. *Um Metro e uma Cidade: História do Metropolitano de Lisboa*. Lisbon: Metropolitano, 1999–2001.

Salgueiro, Ângela. "Ciência e Universidade na I República." PhD Diss., FCSH-UNL.

Silva, Álvaro Ferreira da, and Ana Cardoso de Matos. "Urbanismo e modernização das cidades: o "embellezamento" como ideal. Lisboa, 1858–1891." *Scripta Nova. Revista Electrónica de Geografia y Ciencias Sociales*, no. 69 (30) (2000). url: http://www.ub.es/geocrit/sn-69.htm

Silva, Álvaro Ferreira da. "Uma máquina imperfeita: Tecnología sanitária em Lisboa en la segunda metade del siglo XIX." In *Maquinismo Ibérico*, edited by António Lafuente, Ana Cardoso de Matos and Tiago Saraiva, 371–400. Madrid: Doce Calles, 2007.

Silva, Raquel Henriques da, "O urbanismo—caminhos e planos." In *Lisboa em Movimento, 1852–1920*, 41–68. Lisbon: Livros Horizonte,1994.

Urteaga, Luis. "Miséria, Miasmas Y Micróbios. Las Topografías Médicas y el Estudio del Medio Ambiente en el Siglo XIX." *Geocrítica. Cuadernos Críticos de Geografia Humana*, Ano V, no. 29 (1980). url: http://www.ub.edu/geocrit/geo29.htm»

Homes Fit For Heroes

MARK SWENARTON
University of Liverpool, School of Architecture

ABSTRACT

The "homes fit for heroes" programme of 1919–21 marked a turning point in the history of public housing in Britain in both quantity and quality. Whereas before the First World War local authorities had accounted for only about 2 per cent of new dwellings, in the years 1919–23 the figure was 60 per cent and for the interwar period as a whole nearly 30 per cent. At the same time, the standard of what was built was transformed, in line with the recommendations of the Tudor Walters Report (1918), with much higher standards of space and equipment and the adoption of the low-density model developed by the garden city movement before the war.

My treatment of the subject comprises two parts. In the first, a wide-angle view is taken, setting the post-war housing in the context of the major developments—economic, technological, political, social, and intellectual—taking place in the advanced economies in the early twentieth century. These included the growth of social democracy as a political force; the revolution in production techniques associated with Henry Ford; and the commercial, and eventually military, rivalry between Britain and Germany. Within this context we see the emergence both of housing as a political issue and of the garden city movement, with its influential designer/theorist Raymond Unwin.

The second part focuses on the "homes fit for heroes" campaign itself. It shows how the social crisis that emerged in Britain at the end of the war led the government to promise a "land fit for heroes," with the construction of 500,000 houses that were to be strikingly different from working-class housing of the past. Under the 1919 Housing Act, local authorities were required to provide for the housing needs of their areas and an open-ended grant from central government was introduced to enable them to do so. The format of these new houses and new estates was set out by the government, with Unwin—first at the Ministry of Munitions, then as principal author of the Tudor Walters report and finally as chief architect at the Ministry of Health—playing a central role.

Once the post-war crisis had passed, the housing programme was brought to a halt; but subsequent governments found that the issue could not be ignored. The result was that the 1920s as a whole saw the widespread construction by local authorities of garden suburbs based on Unwin's principles.

BIOGRAPHY

Mark Swenarton is an architectural historian, critic, and educator. He studied history at Oxford University and history & theory of art at Sussex University before taking his PhD in architecture at the Bartlett (University College London). From 1977 to 1989 he taught history of architecture at the Bartlett, where in 1981 with Adrian Forty he set up the first architectural history master's degree in architectural history in the UK. He was founding editor of the international scholarly journal *Construction History*, which he edited from 1985 to 1989, and in 1989 with Ian Latham founded the independent monthly review *Architecture Today*, which he edited for 16 years. In 2005 he was appointed head of the Oxford School of Architecture (Oxford Brookes University) and in 2010 took up the James Stirling Chair of Architecture at Liverpool University, where he is now Emeritus Professor of Architecture. He is a fellow of the Royal Historical Society and the Royal Society of Arts and an Honorary Fellow of the Royal Institute of British Architects. His books include *Homes Fit for Heroes* (1981; 2018), *Artisans and Architects* (1989), *Building the New Jerusalem* (2008), *Architecture and the Welfare State* (2015) and *Cook's Camden: The Making of Modern Housing* (2017).

Launched under the Housing Act of 1919, the programme to build half a million "homes fit for heroes" in the immediate aftermath of the First World War marked a major turning-point in both the scale and the quality of public housing in Britain.[1] Whereas in the twenty-five years before 1914 local authorities accounted for only about 2 per cent of new dwellings, between 1919 and 1923 they accounted for more than 60 per cent, and in the interwar period as a whole for nearly 30 per cent.[2] And at the same time as this increase in scale, there was a substantial uplift in quality. Local authorities were told categorically in the 1919 *Housing Manual* that *"it is the intention of the Government that the housing schemes [...] should mark an advance on the building and development which has ordinarily been regarded as sufficient in the past."*[3]

This advance involved both standards and design. The new houses were to conform to the generous space standards laid down in the Report of the Tudor Walters Committee (1918), and were to include features such as upstairs bathrooms and linen-cupboards that previously had been found only in the houses of the middle classes. In terms of design, they were to follow not the example of bylaw housing—houses built at the maximum permitted densities in long rows, surrounded by nothing but tarmacadam—but the very different, low-density model offered by the garden city movement.

The *Housing Manual* specified that estates were to be laid out at low densities (not more than twelve houses to the acre), with gardens, trees, and open spaces, in the manner established by Raymond Unwin at Hampstead Garden Suburb and elsewhere before the war. With Unwin himself installed as chief architect supervising the housing programme, the housing schemes built under the 1919 Act were strikingly different from the housing to which the majority of the working class was accustomed.[4]

The first comprehensive study of this phenomenon was given in my book *Homes Fit for Heroes: the Politics and Architecture of Early State Housing in Britain* (1981) which, reprinted in 2018, remains the standard account [Figure 1]. In subsequent years I extended the investigation, looking both backwards, at the intellectual tradition from which these architects emerged (*Artisans and Architects: the Ruskinian Tradition in Architectural Thought*, 1989), and forwards, at the shaping of housing policy later in the 1920s, especially by the Conservative politician Neville Chamberlain (*Building the New Jerusalem: Architecture, Housing and Politics 1900–1930*, 2008).[5]

My treatment of the subject here draws on both these extensions as well as the original study. It falls into two parts.

---

[1] Marian Bowley, *Housing and the State, 1919–1944* (London: Allen & Unwin, 1945), 15; Harry W Richardson and Dennis H Aldcroft, *Building in the British Economy between the Wars* (London: George Allen & Unwin, 1968), 164.

[2] Figures for pre-1914 calculated from *Parliamentary Papers* 1916, Cd 8196 xii, 44th Annual Report of the Local Government Board, 1914–15, Part II, Housing and Town Planning: 20–21; Brian R Mitchell and Phyllis Deane, *Abstract of British Historical Statistics* (Cambridge: Cambridge UP, 1962), 236–7. Figures for 1919 onwards from Bowley, *Housing and the State*: 271.

[3] Local Government Board, *Manual on the Preparation of State-Aided Housing Schemes* (London: HMSO, 1919), 4.

[4] Local Government Board, *Manual*: 4–9 and Appendices I and IV.

[5] Mark Swenarton, *Artisans and Architects: The Ruskinian Tradition in Architectural Thought* (Houndmills: Macmillan, 1989); Mark Swenarton, *Building the New Jerusalem: Architecture, housing and politics 1900–1930* (Garston: IHS-BRE Press, 2008).

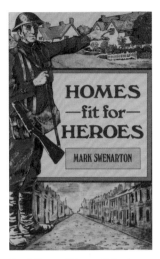

Fig. 1 Cover of Homes fit for Heroes by Mark Swenarton (1981)[6]

The first looks at the broader changes taking place in the first three decades of the twentieth century, which provided the context—economic, political, and cultural—for the post-war housing campaign. The second looks at the housing programme initiated by the 1919 Housing Act in more detail, in terms of its politics, design, and lasting significance.

The period 1900–1930 in western Europe was one in which politics, housing, and architecture all underwent enormous change. These years saw the emergence of social democracy as a major political formation; of building housing for the working class as a legitimate (albeit contested) area of state activity; and of a new concept of the social role of architecture and the architect. Of course the three were closely entwined. Housing was one of the main planks of social democratic (in Britain, Labour) politics and, in response, one of the areas in which their opponents (in Britain, primarily the Conservatives) considered it essential to make their mark. Architects saw in the advent of social democracy, with its state-funded programmes, both the opportunity and the necessity for a new kind of architecture, both as symbol and midwife of the new society emerging from the old. And it was through their claim to hegemony in the design of housing for the working class—never before seen as a major area of architectural endeavour—that architects staked their claim to their role as "experts" in the new polity. Nor, equally, did the changes to this triad take place in isolation from the other changes—economic, technological, cultural—that were transforming the developed world at this time.

[6] Mark Swenarton, *Homes Fit for Heroes: The Politics and Architecture of Early State Housing in Britain* (London: Heinemann Education, 1981; Abingdon:Routledge, 2018). The most substantial additions to the literature since 1981 are Murray Fraser, *John Bull's Other Homes: State Housing and British Policy in Ireland 1883–1922* (Liverpool: Liverpool UP, 1992) and Lou Rosenburg with John Rosser, *Scotland's Homes Fit for Heroes: Garden City Influences on the Development of Scottish Working Class Housing 1900 to 1939* (Edinburgh, Word Bank 2016).

The "factory system," first identified as a phenomenon in Britain in the early nineteenth century, had matured and spread across the globe, generating not just the organised labour movement that was to provide the basis for social democratic politics but also the intense commercial competition between industrialised countries, notably Britain and its latter-day economic rival, Germany, that was to culminate in the outbreak of hostilities in 1914—and thus lead indirectly to the "homes fit for heroes" campaign. But the kind of things that were being made in factories, and the way that they were being made, were also changing.

Thanks to its growing affluence, the working class was increasingly recognised as a consuming class; and fortunes were to be made on both sides of the Atlantic by those who, like Ford in America or Cadbury in Britain, perfected the methods of producing commodities for this new market, whether cars or chocolate. With these advances, many coming from the USA, there also arose new approaches to the organisation of production—scientific management, Taylorism, standardisation—which, at least until the USA lost its allure with the Wall Street crash in 1929, seemed to offer the answer to every problem. Nowhere was the appeal of this new approach greater than in relation to construction, with its hopelessly pre-scientific ("rule of thumb") procedures and its chronic inability to deliver a decent home that the working class could afford. For architects this suggested that the ideal might lie not in the past (which to many started to appear quaint and outdated) but in the technology and organisational sophistication of the modern age. And, while the "example of Henry Ford" attracted attention worldwide, not least in the UK, nowhere was it more potent than in a Germany reconstructing its economy in the 1920s on the back of American capital. If Henry Ford could do it for cars (as it seemed he had, with the Model-T after 1912), why couldn't the same be done for housing?

At the epicentre of all these changes stood "the war to end wars." Developments that had been taking place before 1914—the growing power of the labour movement over governments and the growing involvement of governments in the economic life of the country; the call for governments to promote or provide housing for the working class; the increasing reliance of governments on architectural experts for advice on housing provision and design—were accelerated a hundredfold. In particular the working class was no longer needed just to make and consume things; now it was needed to bear arms and therefore had to be trained in military skills. The creation of a mass army (in Britain, five million men by 1918) transformed the relationship between government and the governed: as the Home Office told the Cabinet in 1920, "in the event of rioting, for the first

Fig. 2 Photo of Hampstead Garden Suburb

time in history the rioters will be better trained than the troops."[7] In this context, working-class demands and grievances—not least, over the shortage and inadequate standard of housing—assumed a new urgency which governments across Europe (and even, albeit briefly, in the USA) sought to address.[8] In doing so the model to which these governments turned, overwhelmingly, was that developed in Britain in the decade or so before 1914 by the garden city movement, above all by Raymond Unwin.[9]

The garden city movement was not, as the name might imply, a homogeneous group with a single ideology, but was rather a heterogeneous collection of different groups and interests, linked by a common commitment to bringing about a transformation in what was termed "the housing and surroundings of the people." There were three main strands. In chronological order, these were the model villages built by industrialists, namely Lever's Port Sunlight (1887–), Cadbury's Bournville (1893–), and Rowntree's New Earwick (1902–); the garden city itself, expounded in print in 1898 by Ebenezer Howard in his book *Tomorrow: A Peaceful Path to Real Reform* and founded at Letchworth in 1903; and the garden suburbs, of which by far the most celebrated was Hampstead Garden Suburb in London, started in 1905 [Figure 2].

[7] National Archives, CAB 24/111 CP 1830 (2 September 1920), quoted in S R Ward, "Intelligence Surveillance of British ex-servicemen 1918–20," *Historical Journal* 16, no. 1 (1973): 179.

[8] For the USA see National Housing Association, *Housing Problems in America: Proceedings of the Seventh National Conference on Housing, Boston, November 25–27 1918* (New York: National Housing Association, 1919); Roy Lubove, "Homes and 'A Few Well Placed Fruit Trees': An Object Lesson in Federal Housing," *Social Research* 27 (1960): 469–486.

[9] For facsimile copies of all the major writings of Raymond Unwin, plus the Tudor Walters Report, see CD included in Swenarton, *Building the New Jerusalem*. On Unwin and the garden city movement see also Mervyn Miller, *Raymond Unwin: Garden Cities and Town Planning* (Leicester: Leicester UP, 1992); Mervyn Miller, *English Garden Cities: An Introduction* (London: Historic England, 2010); Stephen V Ward, *The Peaceful Path: Building Garden Cities and New Towns* (Hatfield: Hertfordshire Publications, 2016).

A major reason for the success of the garden city movement was its political ambiguity, which allowed it to appeal to capitalists and socialists alike. The model villages were conceived explicitly as adjuncts of capitalist industrial production and in the garden city, both as a concept and as realised, one element that was taken over unchanged from existing towns was the factory system. Garden suburbs were purely residential and therefore by definition left the basic economic relationships of capital and labour unchanged. While for socialists like Unwin the garden city movement was the way to make an immediate and unparalleled improvement in the lives of the people, for capitalists like Lever it was the way to make the workforce more contented (and thereby more productive) without altering the basic relationships of capitalist production. It was this latter that was to make it so appealing to governments faced with the crisis of demobilisation and social turmoil at the end of the First World War.

Of all the projects initiated by the garden city movement, Letchworth Garden City and Hampstead Garden Suburb were the two most famous. Both were designed by the architectural partnership of Parker & Unwin. While Barry Parker was a designer and artist-architect in the arts and crafts mould, Unwin was a planner and strategic thinker with a formidable intellect. In an age when Fordism was entrancing the world—when every problem could be subjected to the scrutiny of "the expert"—Unwin became, so far as housing was concerned, the expert's expert.

While Unwin had designed showpiece projects for each of the three strands of the garden city movement—he and Parker were also the architects of Rowntree's New Earswick—it was as the advocate of the garden suburb that he became best known. Whereas with the garden city Ebenezer Howard wanted to abandon the existing city and start from scratch in the agricultural countryside, Unwin's vision of the garden (or "satellite") suburb started with the powerful forces of suburbanisation that were already at work around towns and cities and sought to tame them so they delivered the desired environmental transformation—a far more realistic prospect [Figure 3].

In the years leading up to the First World War, Unwin set out his ideas in a series of cogently argued and lucid texts. First came *The Art of Building a Home* (1901, with Barry Parker) and *Cottage Plans and Common Sense* (1902), dealing with the design and planning of the individual house. Then, following the appointments to Letchworth and Hampstead, his attention turned to the urban scale, with *Town Planning in Practice* (1909), his magnum opus, generalising the lessons of Hampstead Garden Suburb, and *Nothing Gained by Overcrowding!* (1912), presenting the economic rationale for the low-density

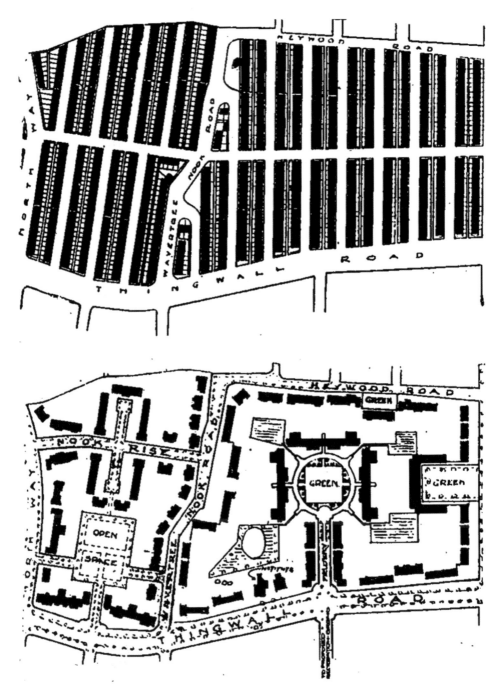

Fig. 3 Conventional versus Garden City layout (1912)

development ("twelve houses to the acre") promoted by the garden city movement. At this point, sensing that it was through government policy that real change could be affected, Unwin started to move closer to government, acting as consultant to the Admiralty on the design of the township for the new naval base at Rosyth and from 1912 serving on two government committees advising on the design of rural housing.[10] In 1914 the move was completed when Unwin left his partnership with Barry Parker to join the Local Government Board, the government department responsible for housing.

Based within central government, Unwin's ideas fed directly into the post-1918 housing programme and his appointment in 1919 as chief architect at the Ministry of Health (the successor to the Local Government Board) consolidated his position at the heart of the nationwide housebuilding programme (see below). But in other countries as well, the model developed by Unwin provided the currency of post-war thinking about housing, whether in France, where in 1921 Henri Sellier planned a series of garden suburbs for Paris based on *Town Planning in Practice*, or in Germany, where from 1925 a series of satellite developments (as garden suburbs were now called) was projected by the city architect of Frankfurt, Ernst May, who had been one of Unwin's pre-1914 assistants at Hampstead Garden Suburb.[11]

But while by 1918 Unwin's work was viewed in largely technocratic terms, its origins and formation lay in very different ground. The fundament of Unwin's thinking was shaped by his immersion in the radical socialist movement of the 1880s and above all by his encounter with the poet, philosopher, and socialist campaigner Edward Carpenter. In 1884 Carpenter gave Unwin a copy of his rambling prose-poem Towards Democracy (1883): as Unwin later recalled, this description of "a soul's slow disentanglement from [the] sheath of custom & convention" was a "revelation" that "opened [the] door to [a] new world."[12]

In Carpenter's thinking, the fundamental opposition was between "convention" derived from existing society (artificial, unnatural, repressive, unhealthy, and unnecessary) and the "real needs" of life (simple, natural, open, non-exploitative, and supportive of spiritual development). These needs could be met only by rejecting convention and adopting instead the "simple life." For Carpenter, a major aspect of this emancipation was sexual—the freedom to love, and live openly with, another man. Although Unwin did not share this sexual orientation, Carpenter was his friend, mentor, and hero (when the Unwin's son was born, he was named Edward and Carpenter was his godfather) and the main terms of Unwin's thinking were derived from Carpenter.

[10] For this little-known part of Unwin's career, see Swenarton, *Homes Fit for Heroes*, 42–44. On Rosyth see Rosenburg, *Scotland's Homes Fit for Heroes*, 144–149.

[11] Swenarton, *Building the New Jerusalem*, 77–83 and 67.

[12] Raymond Unwin, Notes for lecture on Carpenter, 3 July 1939, quoted in Swenarton, *Artisans and Architects*, 133 and 132.

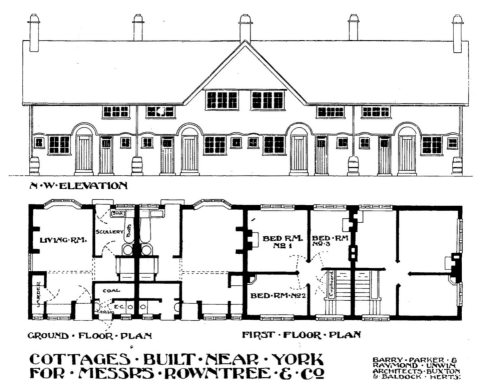

Fig. 4 Cottages built near York by Parker & Unwin (1902)

Thus for Unwin, commerce and convention were the enemies; what was needed was a rupture with convention that would both encourage and express a new way of living, in which a spirit of co-operation would replace competition and humanity would again live in harmony with nature. In terms of housing, this meant abandoning the conventional bylaw format developed by the profit-seeking builder, which, "sacrificed to convention and custom, neither satisfies the real needs of its occupants nor expresses in any way their individuality," and replacing it with a new form of housing that would meet the spiritual and collective, as well as the individual, needs of the people who lived there.[13] Such was the proposition, matured during Unwin's architectural partnership with Barry Parker from 1896, that was unveiled in print in *The Art of Building A Home* in 1901 and *Cottage Plans and Common Sense* in 1902 and on the ground, with the first houses at New Earswick in 1902–3 [Figure 4].

[13] Barry Parker and Raymond Unwin, *The Art of Building a Home: a Collection of Lectures and Illustrations* (London: Longmans Green, 1901), 1.

A similar philosophy informed the design of Hampstead Garden Suburb, both on the ground and as expounded in Unwin's magisterial *Town Planning in Practice*. *"Our towns and suburbs express by their ugliness the passion for gain which so largely dominates their creation,"* he wrote.[14] Instead of cramming the maximum possible number of houses onto the site in the manner of the speculative builder, with long rows of terrace houses, site layout should proceed from nature (i.e. both orientation and the topographical condition of the site, as established by a contour survey,) and the "real needs" of the inhabitants, as opposed to what was merely conventional. In place of the standard format of the bylaw street, good design meant—in the words of the Tudor Walters Report—*"taking advantage of all the opportunities offered by the site, position and aspect of each house in order to secure the greatest comfort and so obtain the best value for building cost."*[15] This of course meant that each layout had to be "specially planned" by a person with the necessary skills, i.e. an architect or town planner.[16]

While the years immediately following the end of the First World War saw an enormous increase in the scale of public sector housebuilding, it was by no means the beginning of state housing. Long before the First World War the state had acted to relieve certain aspects of the housing question—most notably where the health of the classes that controlled the state was threatened by the existence in the cities of large areas of festering slums. The clearance of slums was often constrained by the shortage of working-class housing and under the 1890 Housing Act, local authorities were given powers to address this shortage by building houses beyond the slums. The outcome in London was the construction by the London County Council of two major slum clearance schemes, the architecturally celebrated Boundary Street and Millbank schemes, followed by the commencement of four cottage estates in the suburbs, in Tooting, Croydon, Tottenham and Hammersmith.[17]

In the decade prior to 1914, problems of housing, not least the increase in its cost following from the rise in the rate of interest as Britain re-armed against Germany, led the government to take further measures and made housing into a subject of national debate. Nonetheless, up to 1914 housing policy at Westminster remained essentially a passive response to problems outside. The most significant development in these years was the emergence of the garden city movement. But while admiration for the garden city movement extended across the political spectrum, the response of the state was constrained by the limited nature of state intervention in housing provision. Thus the 1909 Housing and Town Planning Act attempted to promote garden city development but without increasing the state's expenditure on housing; and even with Lloyd

[14] Raymond Unwin, *Town Planning in Practice: An Introduction to the Art of Designing Cities and Suburbs* (London: T Fisher Unwin, 1909), 11.

[15] *Parliamentary Papers* 1918, Cd 9191 vii, Report of the Committee appointed by the President of the Local Government Board and the Secretary for Scotland to consider questions of building construction in connection with the provision of dwellings for the working classes in England and Wales, and Scotland, and report upon methods of securing economy and despatch in the provision of such dwellings (the Tudor Walters Report), paragraph 152.

[16] *Parliamentary Papers* 1918 Cd 9191 vii, paragraph 58.

[17] See London County Council, *Housing of the Working Classes in London* (London, London County Council: 1913); Susan Beattie, *Revolution in London Housing: LCC Architects and Their Work 1893–1914* (London: Greater London Council, 1980).

George's Land Campaign of 1913–14, which saw Unwin taking a semi-official role as a government adviser, the limited role envisaged for state housing remained an effective constraint on the promotion of garden city housing.

The position at the end of the First World War was very different. In the wake of the armistice of November 1918, the government believed that unless drastic action was taken Britain would follow Russia and Germany into a "Bolshevik" (i.e. communist) revolution. How was a mass army to be induced to return peaceably to a civilian life, the realities of which—poverty, unemployment, insecurity, bad living conditions—were so unattractive, when they held the weapons that could be used to overthrow those realities? This was the overwhelming question that preoccupied the prime minister Lloyd George and senior members of the Cabinet. The answer, they decided, was not force—which against five million trained fighting men could scarcely be effective—but ideas. In March 1919 Lloyd George told the Cabinet:

"In a short time we might have three-quarters of Europe converted to Bolshevism[...] He believed that Great Britain would hold out, but only if the people were given a sense of confidence [...] We had promised them reforms time and again, but little had been done. We must give them the conviction this time that we meant it, and we must give them that conviction quickly [...] Even if it cost a hundred million pounds, what was that compared to the stability of the State? So long as we could persuade the people that we were prepared to help them and to meet them in their aspirations, he believed that the sane and steady leaders among the workers would have an easy victory over the Bolsheviks among them."[18]

The key was to persuade the soldiers that the Britain to which they were returning was the not the Britain of the "bad old days" but something quite different, a "land fit for heroes" where a bright future awaited them, without any need for a revolution. Accordingly, the months following the armistice saw the government promising a wide-ranging programme of social reform with, at its heart, a great house-building programme. Under the government's scheme, enacted as the Housing Act of 1919, local authorities were required to build houses for the working class and were protected from any loss above a strictly limited amount by an open-ended grant from central government. The cost to the public finances would be enormous but in face of the danger facing the state, money was no object; as the Chancellor of the Exchequer (i.e. finance minister) Austen Chamberlain told the Cabinet, "we ought to push on with it immediately, at whatever cost to the State."[19]

[18] National Archives, CAB 23/9 WC 539, 3 March 1919. Lloyd George claimed a precedent in what had been done to address social unrest in Ireland by an earlier Conservative government: Fraser, *John Bull's Other Homes*, 187.

[19] National Archives, CAB23/9, WC 539, 3 March 1919.

To show the troops and the public how much better life was going to be, the new houses had to be, as one member of parliament put it, "on quite different lines" from those of the past and "a great improvement on anything we have."[20] The model was provided by the low-density format developed by the garden city movement, which with its cottages with gardens set in semi-rural surroundings was unmistakably different from the usual working-class housing of the pre-war years. The government undertook to provide 500,000 houses of this sort, built to a standard unprecedented in local authority housing, with a bathroom, parlour (i.e. additional living room), and other luxuries, providing visible evidence of the great improvement in the conditions of life [Figure 5]. The detailed specifications for these houses were set out in the *Tudor Walters Report* of 1918, as summarised in the *Housing Manual* the following year, and, so long as the goal of the housing programme remained unchanged, it was houses of this quality that were built. In mounting the housing campaign, the government drew directly on the experience in emergency housebuilding that it had gained during the war. To meet the needs for shells and other armaments, existing production facilities, such as the Royal Arsenal at Woolwich in south-east London, were expanded dramatically and entirely new ones, such as the explosives factory at Gretna in the north-west corner of England, were constructed. To provide housing for (at least some of) the workforce, new developments were constructed at breakneck speed, including most famously the Well Hall estate at Woolwich, built by the Office of Works under Frank Baines in 1915, and the Gretna and Eastriggs townships built by the Ministry of Munitions under Raymond Unwin in 1916–17 [Figure 6]. But Baines and Unwin did not see eye to eye—whereas Well Hall was a flamboyantly picturesque re-creation of an "old English village," the housing at Gretna was simple if not austere— and although both were members of the Tudor Walters Committee, Baines resigned in September 1918, shortly before the report (which was largely authored by Unwin) was published.[21]

It was thus the war-time housebuilding programme of the Ministry of Munitions that provided the basis for the national post-war programme. From the Ministry of Munitions came the Cabinet minister responsible for the 1919 Housing Act, Dr Christopher Addison; the architectural driving-force, Raymond Unwin, together with many of his colleagues who likewise moved from the Ministry of Munitions to the Ministry of Health; and its doctrines on housing design, as set out in the Tudor Walters Report. These were essentially the principles and techniques of low-density design as developed by the garden city before the war, with both passages of text and drawings from *Town Planning in Practice* now re-appearing within official government publications.

[20] 114 HC Deb, 7 April 1919, column 1762, James Gilbert (Liberal MP for Southwark).

[21] *Parliamentary Papers* 1918 Cd 9191 vii, 3. On the munitions housing programme see Simon Pepper and Mark Swenarton, "Home Front: Garden Suburbs for Munition Workers 1915 to 1918," *Architectural Review* 163, no. 976 (June 1978): 366–375.

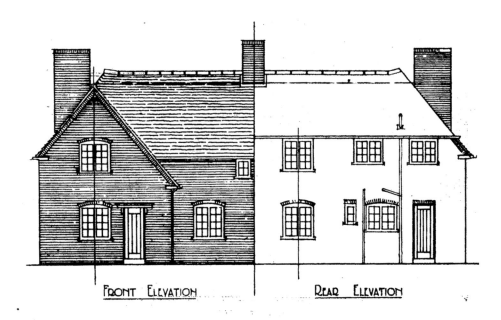

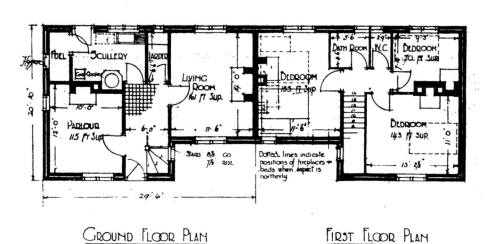

Fig. 5 Plan from Ministry of Health's Manual (1919)

Fig. 6 Photo of housing at Gretna

In only one significant respect was the garden city legacy amended. The architecture of the garden city movement had been, generally, romantic and individualistic; but a considerable body of architectural opinion (notably at the department of civic design at Liverpool University established in 1909 with funds provided by Lever) had grown up against this picturesque tradition, which was regarded as particularly inappropriate for mass housing. For the design of the new state houses, "simplification and standardisation" provided an alternative doctrine. As Unwin had argued before 1914, for low-cost housing, simplification was the most economical approach and, dressed in neo-Georgian attire, it appealed to the architectural ideologues at Liverpool and elsewhere. Above all, "simplification and standardisation" suggested a ruthlessly efficient mass-production programme that would "solve" the housing shortage (with all that that meant in political terms) as effectively as Henry Ford had "solved" the problem of mass-producing motorcars.[22]

The housing programme of 1919 was essentially an insurance against revolution: its purpose was to ensure the survival of the status quo. Behind the smokescreen of a "land fit for heroes," the old social order remained intact, largely ruled as before by the interests of finance and industry. The attitude of industry towards the housing programme was ambivalent: on the one hand industrialists wanted housing for their employees but on the other they did not want labour or materials that they needed for their own purposes transferred to housebuilding. The financial world was hostile to the housing programme and did all it could to oppose it. The result was that the resources needed to build the promised 500,000 houses were not made available and, with the demand for

[22] On the "standard cottage", see Simon Pepper and Mark Swenarton, "Neo-Georgian maison-type," *Architectural Review* 168, no. 1002 (August 1980): 87–92.

capital, labour and materials far outrunning supply, the rate of housebuilding was extremely slow and the cost extremely high. By March 1920, 16 months after the armistice, only 1,250 houses had been completed and the average cost per house doubled from the estimated figure of £600 in 1918 to an actual figure of £1,200 or more in 1920.[23] In response, all sorts of expedients were adopted to try to circumvent these shortages, including new methods of construction, the introduction of unskilled labour and the deployment of alternative agencies such as the Office of Works. All were attempts to conjure up labour and materials for housing without withdrawing them from the private sector and thereby resolve the contradiction between the post-war world presented by official propaganda and the post-war world as it was in reality.

In 1921 the government put an end to the contradiction by abandoning the image presented by its slogans. In the preceding months the entire political and economic situation had been transformed, with the economy turning from boom to slump in the winter of 1920–21, the feared General Strike (of miners, railwaymen and transport workers) falling through in April 1921 and in May 1921 the ex-servicemen forming not the Red Guard that had once been feared, but the British Legion.[24] In the changed conditions, the social reforms so readily promised in the wake of the armistice took on the appearance of unnecessary and unjustifiable extravagance, for which heads should roll. In March 1921 Addison was removed from the Ministry of Health and in July 1921 his successor, Sir Alfred Mond, announced that no further contracts would be let beyond those for the 176,000 houses completed or contracted at that date.[25] At the same time, and for the same reasons, the high standards adopted in 1918–19 were jettisoned and from early 1921 the government pressed local authorities to adopt smaller and cheaper house types, which economised both on the size and number of rooms and on the level of equipment, a process that accelerated thereafter [Figure 7].

As the *Municipal Journal* noted approvingly in July 1922, these smaller houses showed that the government was no longer "led astray by visionaries" but was simply supplying "the cheapest form of housing which will actually provide accommodation for the poor."[26] But the announcement of June 1921 did not mark the end of the government's involvement in housing. In the critical period following the armistice, the government had done everything in its power to persuade the country that the housing programme proved that there was no need for revolution. After July 1921 the government was no longer prepared to finance the housing programme but it found that, having been accorded this unique status, housing could not be simply ignored or treated as though the promises of 1918

[23] Swenarton, *Homes Fit for Heroes*, 122.
[24] Swenarton, *Homes Fit for Heroes*, 130.
[25] Swenarton, *Homes Fit for Heroes*, 134.
[26] *Municipal Journal*, 31 (7 July 1922): 487, quoted in *Homes Fit for Heroes*, 161.

and 1919 had never been made. The fundamental material problem of a severe housing shortage remained, which government was expected to address. Thanks to the time lag involved in building operations, for some time after July 1921 the government was able to point to the large number of houses being completed (67,000 in the 12 months to March 1922); but as these began to dry up the government came under increasing pressure to introduce new measures. In 1923 the newly elected Conservative government, with Neville Chamberlain as Minister of Health, passed a Housing Act which introduced a fixed subsidy for private builders for houses completed by 1925. The following year with the Housing Act of 1924 the short-lived minority Labour government, with John Wheatley as Minister of Health, introduced in addition a more generous (albeit still fixed) subsidy for local authorities.[27] Most important of all in terms of numerical output, when the Conservatives got back into power in the autumn of 1924, Chamberlain retained Wheatley's subsidy for local authorities. But to reduce competition with the private sector, at the same time he decided on a special and extremely generous grant (£200 per house) for local authorities that would adopt non-traditional methods of construction, pumping money into the Building Research Station to establish which methods were suitable.[28]

The result was that the 1920s as a whole became a decade of large-scale construction of garden suburbs by local authorities, often using the sites purchased under the 1919 Act, and in a number of cases using non-traditional construction—as at the London County Council's estates including White Hart Lane in Tottenham and the enormous Becontree estate in Essex, the largest municipal housing scheme in the world [Figure 8].[29] While it did not match up to the standards of 1919–21, the council housing built on these municipal garden suburbs in the remainder of the decade was nonetheless of a reasonable quality—forming a still conspicuous element in many towns and cities across the country as well as a monument to a particularly turbulent period in Britain's history.

[27] The legislation is summarised in Stephen Merrett, *State Housing in Britain* (London: Routledge & Kegan Paul, 1979), 42–47.

[28] Swenarton, *Building the New Jerusalem*, 171–172 and 175–184. On the Tudor Walters Committee 1917–18, and as chief architect at the Ministry of Health from 1919, Unwin played a key role in the promotion of building research.

[29] See London County Council, *Housing: With Particular rReference to Post-war Housing Schemes* (London: London County Council, 1928); Terence Young, *Becontree and Dagenham: A Report made for the Pilgrim Trust* (London: Becontree Social Survey Committee, 1934); Andrzej Olechnowicz, *Working-class Housing in England Between the Wars: the Becontree Estate* (Oxford: Clarendon Press, 1997). See also Darrin Bayliss, "Revisiting the cottage council estates: England, 1919–39," *Planning Perspectives* 16 (2001): 169–200.

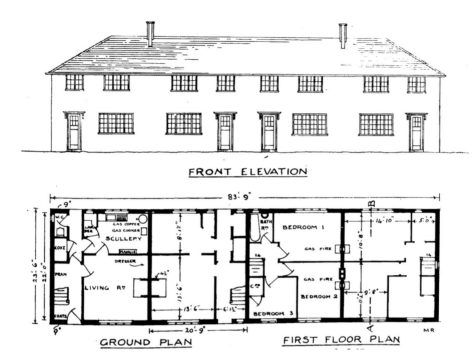

Fig. 7 Plan published by Ministry of Health (1921)

Fig. 8 Photo of White Hart Lane estate

BIBLIOGRAPHY

Bayliss, Darren. "Revisiting the cottage council estates: England, 1919–39." *Planning Perspectives* 16 (2001): 169–200.

Beattie, Susan. *Revolution in London Housing: LCC architects and Their Work 1893–1914*. London: Greater London Council, 1980.

Bowley, Marian. *Housing and the State, 1919–1944*. London: Allen & Unwin, 1945.

Fraser, Murray. *John Bull's Other Homes: State Housing and British Policy in Ireland 1883–1922*. Liverpool: Liverpool UP, 1992.

Local Government Board. *Manual on the Preparation of State-Aided Housing Schemes*. London: HMSO, 1919.

London County Council. *Housing of the Working Classes in London*. London: London County Council. 1913.

London County Council. *Housing: With Particular Reference to Post-war Housing Schemes*. London: London County Council, 1928.

Lubove, Roy. "Homes and 'A Few Well Placed Fruit Trees': An Object Lesson in Federal Housing', *Social Research*, 27 (1960).

Merrett, Stephen. *State Housing in Britain*. London: Routledge & Kegan Paul, 1979.

Miller, Mervyn. *Raymond Unwin: Garden Cities and Town Planning*. Leicester: Leicester UP, 1992.

Miller, Mervyn. *English Garden Cities: An Introduction*. London: Historic England, 2010.

Mitchell, Brian R, and Phyllis Deane. *Abstract of British Historical Statistics*. Cambridge: Cambridge UP, 1962.

National Housing Association. *Housing Problems in America: Proceedings of the Seventh National Conference on Housing, Boston, November 25–27 1918*. New York: National Housing Association, 1919.

Olechnowicz, Andrzej. *Working-class Housing in England between the Wars: the Becontree Estate*. Oxford: Clarendon Press, 1997.

Parker, Barry and Raymond Unwin. *The Art of Building a Home: a Collection of Lectures and Illustrations*. London: Longmans Green, 1901.

Parliamentary Papers 1916, Cd 8196 xii, "44th Annual Report of the Local Government Board, 1914–15, Part II, Housing and Town Planning."

Parliamentary Papers 1918, Cd 9191 vii, "Report of the Committee appointed by the President of the Local Government Board and the Secretary for Scotland to consider questions of building construction in connection with the provision of dwellings for the working classes in England and Wales, and Scotland, and report upon methods of securing economy and despatch in the provision of such dwellings" (the Tudor Walters Report).

Pepper, Simon, and Mark Swenarton. "Home Front: Garden Suburbs for Munition Workers 1915 to 1918." *Architectural Review* 163, no. 976 (June 1978).

Pepper, Simon and Mark Swenarton. "Neo-Georgian maison-type." *Architectural Review* 168, no. 1002 (August 1980).

Richardson, Harry W, and Dennis H Aldcroft. *Building in the British Economy between the Wars*. London: George Allen & Unwin, 1968.

Rosenburg, Lou, with John Rosser. *Scotland's Homes Fit for Heroes: Garden City Influences on the Development of Scottish Working Class Housing 1900 to 1939*. Edinburgh: Word Bank, 2016.

Swenarton, Mark. *Artisans and Architects: The Ruskinian Tradition in Architectural Thought*. Houndmills: Macmillan, 1989.

Swenarton, Mark. *Building the New Jerusalem: Architecture, Housing and Politics 1900–1930*. Garston: IHS-BRE Press, 2008.

Swenarton, Mark. *Homes fit for Heroes: The Politics and Architecture of Early State Housing in Britain*. London: Heinemann Education, 1981; Abingdon: Routledge, 2018.

Unwin, Raymond. *Town Planning in Practice: An Introduction to the Art of Designing Cities and Suburbs*. London: T Fisher Unwin, 1909.

Ward, S R. "Intelligence Surveillance of British ex-servicemen 1918–20." *Historical Journal* 16, no. 1 (1973).

Ward, Stephen V. *The Peaceful Path: Building Garden Cities and New Towns*. Hatfield: Hertfordshire Publications, 2016.

Young, Terence. *Becontree and Dagenham: A Report Made for the Pilgrim Trust*. London: Becontree Social Survey Committee, 1934.

The President of the Portuguese Republic, Marshal Óscar Carmona, cuts the ribbon on the newly-finished Affordable Houses Estate of Belém, in Lisboa, in 1938.

Empresa Pública Jornal O Século, Albuns Gerais no. 57, doc. 2180M
PT/TT/EPJS/SF/001-001/0057/2180M. Image from ANTT.

2. HOUSE, FAMILY, AND STATE (1933–1946)

God, Homeland and Family—the three pillars of the New State (Estado Novo), the corporatist dictatorial regime imposed by a new Constitution following the military coup of 1926.

Focusing on private property and family life, state-subsidized housing followed the British lessons and centred its action in single-family houses estates near the main urban centres.

Frankfurt am Main: A Shared Life

CARMEN ESPEGEL
Technical University of Madrid, School of Architecture

ABSTRACT

As the architecture and urban planning councilman of the city of Frankfurt and with the support of the social ideals of the Weimar Republic, Ernst May understood that the new city for the working class required not only the rationalization of the housing unit, the mechanization of the construction process or the normalization of elements, but that there was also a need to inquire into new forms of collective living. The aim was to create a life in common and a shared reality in a city for all that led to the transformation of established programmes and fostered the rise of a feeling of community that, up until then, had been inexistent. A crucial step to achieve this was to overhaul land use policies. 15,000 were units built between 1925 and 1930, which at the time represented more than 90 per cent of the finished houses in the city, a number that would not have been reached without the effort put into economic efficiency from their design to their construction.

The urban strategy implemented for this programme contemplated a decentralized layout based on the polynuclear growth of the city, producing several satellite complexes with collective services that functioned as self-sufficient colonies in direct contact with their natural surroundings. Key to this rationalization was the establishment of the size of the minimum dwelling, even though research into rationalizing the economy of the home centred on what become known as the Frankfurt kitchen designed by Margarete Schütte-Lihotzky, with its reduction in size and optimization of use. In order to economize the process, the mechanization of building systems was also needed; in this case, large-sized, prefabricated, concrete panels were developed in order to reduce construction times. At the same time, May insisted on improving the quality of building elements, such as doors, windows or handles, so he carried out a careful study to homologate and standardize these features establishing the Frankfurter Register, which had to be accepted by all the contractors. Lastly, the Frankfurt team understood the importance of spreading their objectives, especially when it came to raising awareness of these issues among housewives, therefore their research was shown in exhibitions, conferences, books, magazines or films. With this global understanding of the urban realm, Frankfurt am Main became an experiment in the matter of working class housing with a widespread impact.

BIOGRAPHY

Carmen Espegel (Palencia, 1960) is a Spanish PhD Architect and Full Professor of the Design Department at the School of Architecture (ETSAM) of the Universidad Politécnica de Madrid (UPM). Her career is based on three complementary fields: academia, research, and professional practice. She has lectured in Italy, USA, Belgium, Holland, Mexico, Colombia, Brazil, Argentina, and Portugal. In the academic sphere, she leads a Studio Design and Housing Theory Design Module in the Master's Degree in Collective Housing (MCH). She participates in the Housing doctoral programme at the School of Architecture of Porto, and lectures in the Master's Degree in Housing (MH) in the University Roma Tre. Her research is focused on housing (heading the Research Group "Collective Housing"– GIVCO) and gender architecture. In Women Architects in the Modern Movement (2018), the two volumes on Collective Housing in Spain 1992–2015 (2016) and 1929–1992 (2013), Eileen Gray: Objects and Furniture Design (2013), Aires Modernos, E.1027: Maison en bord de mer by Eileen Gray and Jean Badovici (2010), she denotes her critical thinking regarding architectural production. In 2002, she founded the office espegel-fisac arquitectos with Concha Fisac. Their works have received awards and have been published in prestigious books and magazines.

Fig. 1 Lino Salini, Sieben Frankfurter (Seven Frankfurters) 1927. Caricature of the period showing the members of the local government of Frankfurt am Main led by the mayor Ludwig Landmann.
Source: Hamburgisches Architekturarchiv, Hamburg.

For Aristotle the *polis* was, above all, a form of architectural virtue and wisdom, since it organized the framework and the matter of the citizenry. In this sense, when the economic and social "policies" of Frankfurt am Main were conceived, supported by the ideals of the Weimar Republic, an unprecedented change of mentality took place. In this understanding, the new city for the working class required not only the rationalization of the housing unit, the mechanization of its construction process or the normalization of elements, but that there was also a need to inquire into new forms of collective living. The aim was to make possible a life in common and a shared reality in a city for all that would lead to the transformation of established programmes and foster the rise of "a social conscience and feeling of community that, up until then, had been inexistent."[1]

At the beginning of the 1920s, Frankfurt am Main was growing much like its larger counterparts did. By establishing a new model, the mayor of the city at the time, Franz Adickes, set the foundations for a decentralized city.

[1] Carlos Sambricio. *L'habitation Minimum*. Facsimile edition of Julius Hoffmann's original, 1933 (Zaragoza: Delegación de Zaragoza del Colegio Oficial de Arquitectos de Aragón, 1977), 26.

The First World War and the halt of construction it caused, along with a rise in the marriage rate and the arrival of population from other regions, drastically raised the need for housing in the city.

In 1924, the socialist Ludwig Landmann, who had been the housing and finance councilman, was elected mayor. Based on his experience, Landmann decided to maintain the policy of urban expansion and turn Frankfurt am Main into a commercial, transportation and exhibitions hub. To achieve this he realized that the implementation of a "general construction plan" had to be the basis for his housing and development policies.

The coordinated work of the mayor, Ludwig Landmann, the architecture and urban planning councilman, Ernst May and the finance councillor, Bruno Asch, made this new approach to urban planning possible [Fig 1]. The architect Ernst May became the head of what was known as the Construction Office for the new developments of the city of Frankfurt am Main, which was established in June 1925 reflecting the importance of creating a team with its own identity.[2] It was formed, both on a permanent and a temporary basis, by prestigious professionals from many fields, in accordance with their understanding of the city as a complex phenomenon requiring a multidisciplinary approach.

Wilhem Schütte, Max Cetto or Adolf Meyer were among the architects that coordinated the Office; Eugen Kaufmann was given the task of researching new typologies; Margarete Schütte-Lihotzky[3] was in charge of outfitting the kitchens; Ferdinand Kramer designed the standardized furniture; Leberecht Migge addressed the landscape issues; Hans Leistikow was responsible for the graphics department and Loecher for the models. Franz Schuster, Anton Brenner, Mart Stam, Walter Gropius, Martin Weber, Hans Bernoully and Walter Dexel were some of the freelance architects that collaborated with the team and lastly, the movie director Paul Wolff was trusted with the project outreach [Fig. 2].

For Ernst May, in order to eradicate substandard housing from the city of Frankfurt land, law reform was crucial, and this, to him, was the first step to be taken in order to enable the city government to expropriate the lots needed to raise the new homes. Along with this, he proposed establishing a property tax to be collected by the city itself. Part of this revenue would be used to build new housing projects (44.5 per cent) and another part to fund administrative functions (55 per cent).[4] Lastly, he understood that the construction of new housing complexes could not be addressed individually, but under a global urban concept.

[2] Adolf Meyer, who before becoming part of this team directed Walter Gropius's office, wrote to May about his experience there: "The range of work is extensive, the constellation unusually favourable. Positive encouragement of the new building ethos all along the line." Quoted in Claudia Quiring, Wolfgang Voigt, Peter Cahola Schmal, and Eckhard Herrel, *Ernst May 1886–1970* (Munich/London/New Prestel Verlag and Frankfurt am Main: Deutsches Architekturmuseum, 2011), 63.

[3] Carmen Espegel, *Women Architects in the Modern Movement*. (New York: Routledge, 2018), 164–98.

[4] Peter Noever (ed.), *Margarete Schütte-Lihotzky. Soziale Architektur Zeitzeugin eines Jahrhunderts* (Vienna: Bóhlau Verlag, 1996), 72.

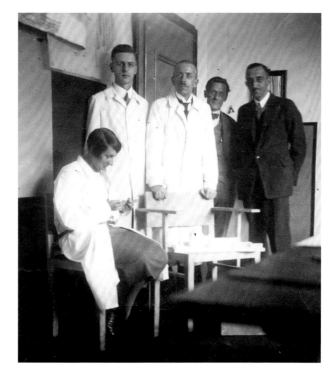

Fig. 2 Margarete Schütte-Lihotzky with her colleagues of the Construction Office, Frankfurt am Main. Source: University of Applied Arts Vienna, Collection and Archive.

[5] Carlos Martí Arís, *Las Formas de la Residencia en la Ciudad Moderna* (Barcelona: Ediciones UPC, 2000).

[6] Rosemarie Höpfner and Volker Fischer (ed.). *Ernst May und Das Neue Frankfurt 1925–1930*, Catalogue of the Exhibition at the Deutschen Architekturmuseum, Frankfurt am Main. (Berlin: Ernst & Sohn, 1986). Praunheim, which was built in three phases between 1926 and 1929, was a collaboration with Eugen Kaufmann, Margarete Schütte-Lihotzky, Martin Weber, and Max Cetto among others. It was the testing ground for the prefabricated concrete panel system and where the Frankfurt kitchen was installed for the first time. The cold, austere but gleaming Römerstadt, with its close to 1200 homes, was raised between 1927 and 1928 by Carl Hermann Rudloff, Franz Schuster, Martin Elsaesser, Wilhem Schütte, and Margarete Schütte-Lihotzky, among others. It stands out due to the way it adapts to the topography and the construction of water-retaining walls along the Nidda River. The Höhenblick *Siedlung*, erected with Carl Hermann Rudloph between 1926 and 1927, is unique because of its small size (100 units) and the way it adapts perfectly to the crossroads, made volumetrically manifest by highlighting the corners of the blocks. At Heimat 850 housing units were erected between 1927 and 1930 with the collaboration of Franz Roeckle, Herbert Boehm, and Fritz Berke. This is probably one of the most intense proposals design-wise, combining modernist orthodoxy in the repetition of the block with the diversity of angled buildings on the corners making the public spaces unique. The 654 units at Bruchfeldstrasse, built with the collaboration of Carl Hermann Rudloph in three phases between 1926 and 1927, stand out because of the definition of its large central courtyard surrounded by zigzagging blocks and delimited by the communal services building erected between 1930 and 1932 with a total of 800 units. Its morphological and typological richness is undeniable; its different kinds of window openings and its unique long balconies at the ends of the block must be highlighted.

The urban strategy proposed by May for the expansion of Frankfurt contemplated a decentralized plan based on the polynuclear growth of the city, generating several satellite complexes with their own collective facilities, thus functioning as self-sufficient, practically autarchic, colonies. To the northwest, on the shores of the Nidda river, May proposed the creation of sprawling settlements in direct connection with their natural surroundings, like the Praunheim [Fig. 3], Römerstadt or Höhenblick *siedlungen*, which were separated from the traditional urban core by a green ring. In the middle of the countryside, these developments functioned autonomously; they had their own schools, shopping centres, and restaurants. As for their general layout, it was based on the mechanical repetition of rows of houses, strictly and rationally set on an east-west orientation, even though the way they adapted to the topography, the road network or pre-existing features provided them with a variety of rich urban spaces for which specific solutions were adopted. Up to twenty-three settlements were built around the old city, among which, besides the ones mentioned above, Heitmat,[5] Bruchfeldstrasse and Hellerhof[6] stand out.

The 15,000 units built during May's tenure represented over 90 per cent of the houses finished during that period. This astounding figure would hardly have been possible without the effort put into their economic efficiency, from their design to their construction. The dissolution of the central city forced Ernst May, with his strong sense of social activism, to provide all kinds of services to the new workers' colonies, thus introducing the abstract notion of the neighbourhood as an independent entity equipped with a vast range of collective facilities [Fig. 4]: schools, swimming pools, laundromats, childcare centres, restaurants or shopping areas. Likewise, these minimum dwellings required a series of centralized services to facilitate domestic chores.

The basis for this rationalization was the definition of the size of the housing unit. This value did not depend in the surface area of the house as much as it did on the number of beds it could accommodate. The bed became the unit measurement around which all daily functions revolved, establishing the spatial proportions of the living and dining room, kitchen, bathroom, etc. Once this dimensional relationship was established, the configuration of the distribution was studied in order to guarantee optimal natural light and ventilation parameters. May reduced every feature of the house until they reached the correct size according to inhabitational functions, in an attempt to respond in the best possible way to the most pressing needs of working-class homes.

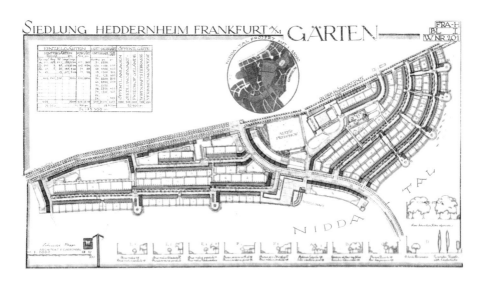

Fig. 3 Leberecht Migge, Römerstadt (Heddernheim) Siedlung in Frankfurt am Main and its garden design, 1928. Source: *Gartenschönheit* 9, 1928, 48.

Fig. 4 Covered public swimming pool in Frankfurt am Main, by the architect Martin Elsaesser, 1929. Source: *Ernst May und das Neue Frankfurt, 1925–1930*. Exhibition catalogue from the Deutsches Architekturmuseum Frankfurt am Main. Berlin: Wilhelm Ernst & Sohn Verlag, 1986, 153.

This process of extreme rationalization led to the unification, normalization, and optimization of the housing units, and with this he achieved the maximum social benefit with the minimum economic effort. This efficient distribution brought about the creation of different building typologies: one- and two-storey row houses; corridor blocks with units on different floors connected by galleries accessed by one or more staircases; low-rise buildings in which the staircases led to two houses per floor. This last type became the most commonly used in Frankfurt; even though it was not as economically efficient as the corridor block due to the existence of more staircases, it offered the houses with two completely free facades, and therefore the best orientation, ventilation, and lighting possible. By following a linear and additive process and organizing the units into a residential typologies, the rationalist "design technique" gave shape to the building; by organizing the buildings to ensure their adequate orientation, the optimal distance between them and a correct relationship with the streets and other infrastructures, the neighbourhood was created;

and by organizing the neighbourhoods and providing them with facilities, public spaces and meeting areas that improved the quality of life of the users, the city was configured.

In 1928, the first results of this construction effort proved the need to create even smaller units in order to provide the working class with affordable homes. In the autumn of the same year, the Construction Office, in agreement with local authorities, decided that half of the programmed units had to become two-room minimum dwellings. One of the types May promoted was the house for two families (Zwofa), which provided a small garden for each to compensate for the small size of the unit (between 40 and 42 sq m), foreseeing that as the economy improved it could turn into a single family house. Due to their reduced dimensions, these minimum dwellings were rented out fully furnished because the only way to make the most of the space was with custom-made furniture. Thanks to the versatility of the furniture, spaces could change functions; for example, foldaway or retractable beds enabled the living room to be turned into the bedroom and vice versa [Fig. 5].

This objective approach—this *sachlichkeit,* accentuated by the reality of construction costs—led, inevitably, to the formulation of standards for a spatial typology (for a minimal existence) that became the contentious issue of the second CIAM Congress held in Frankfurt in the autumn of 1929. May, who had participated in the first congress in Switzerland, showed the work he had been carrying out under the title *Die Wohnung für das Existenzminimum* (the house for a minimum existence). From within the Office, Margarete Schütte-Lihotzky and Eugen Kaufmann were in charge of preparing the Congress.

Fig. 5 Images of the living room with daytime and night-time furnishings at the Praunheim Siedlung, 1926–1929. Source: *Das Neue Frankfurt* 6, (June 1929): 128.

In order to highlight the idea of typology, the 105 housing units chosen were shown comparatively with the use of the systematic and objective graphic representation of plans, sections, and groupings. No references were made to the authors of the plans to avoid personal references, but other objective information was provided: the names of the cities in which the projects had been built, the income level of the social classes affected and the usable floor area as well as the volume of the units and the zones lit naturally. As Josep María Montaner states, *"this experience is one of the standard bearers of rationalism and reveals the confidence shown in objective comparative methods. It is no coincidence that this CIAM, dedicated entirely to rationalist housing, was celebrated in the city that spearheaded the promotion and construction of social housing under the guidance of May."*

Just as the Office had set out during the precedent years, the Congress pointed out the need to reduce the floor area of housing units and raise their hygienic, natural ventilation and lighting conditions with the goal of providing every adult member of the family with a bedroom, and to prioritize collective housing projects over single-family homes in big cities. Germany and the Netherlands were the only two countries in which this concept, based on an ideal separation of functions, was implemented. These progressive ideals were written into the Athens Charter of the 4th CIAM in 1933.

"In contrast with Le Corbusier's 'idealistic' appeal for an 'existence-maximum', May's minimum standards were dependent on the extensive use of ingenious storage, fold-away beds, and above all on the development of the ultra-efficient laboratory-like kitchen, the Frankfurter Küche, designed by the architect G. Schütte-Lihotzky. Escalating costs finally led May to pioneer prefabricated slab construction, the so-called 'May system' being used by the Praunheim and Höhenblick housing sectors started in 1927."[8]

Another aspect worth highlighting is the fortunate coexistence between architecture and nature that takes place in these modernist *siedlungen*, and their forceful relationship, due to either their physical contiguity with their surroundings or how these developments visually dominate them: "light, air, and sun" was the motto of these new building ideals [Fig. 6]. In May's case, his critical rationalism was mitigated by his appreciation of tradition, and the concern for the design of public space and landscape he had inherited from his masters, Theodor Fischer in Munich and Raymond Unwin in London. Thus, for him, one-storey buildings represented the ideal form of inhabitation. Behind each row of houses there was an elongated and narrow yard, conceived as a vegetable garden, and beyond it there was a back street.

[7] Montaner, *La Arquitectura de la Vivienda Colectiva. Políticas y Proyectos en la Ciudad Contemporánea*, 22–24.

[8] Kenneth Frampton, *Modern Architecture: A Critical History* (London: Thames & Hudson, 2007), 137–138.

Fig. 6 Garden in the Praunheim Siedlung, 1936. Source: Leberecht Migge, *Jedermann Selbstversorger*. Jena: Eugen Diederichs Verlag, 1918.

On the boundaries of these colonies, in the transition towards the countryside, small parks were located for the use and enjoyment of all of the city dwellers. When the units were arranged into blocks, three-storey buildings were the preferred configuration. All of the units, regardless of their size, had an open space in direct connection with their almost natural setting: the dwellings on the ground floor had small gardens attached to them, those on the intermediate level opened onto a veranda or gallery and the ones on the top floor made use of the roof [Fig. 7]. The kitchen became the key factor in the Office's endeavour to rationalize and economize the construction of housing in Frankfurt: its size was reduced, but in exchange, its functionality was improved. The kitchen proposed in 1926 by Grete Schütte-Lihotzky owes its success to all of the knowledge gathered by the American domestic engineers during the end of the nineteenth century and the beginning of the twentieth.

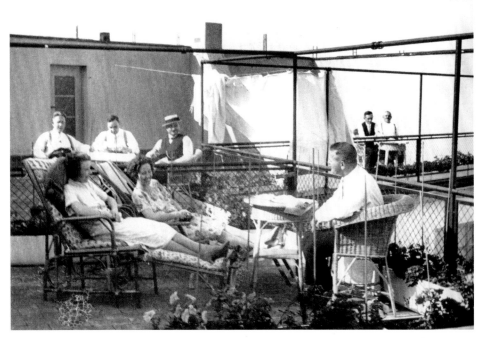

Fig. 7 Photograph taken by Paul Wolff of the roof terrace overlooking the "zigzag courtyard" in Bruchfeldstrasse Siedlung, c. 1927. Claudia Quiring; Wolfgang Voigt; Peter Cahola Schmal; Eckhard Herrel.
Source: *Ernst May 1886–1970*. Munich/London/New York: Prestel Verlag and Frankfurt am Main: Deutsches Architekturmuseum, 2011. Exhibition catalogue, 108.

The manuals written by Catharine Beecher,[9] Christine Frederick[10] and Lillian Gilbreth[11] had a huge impact on the way domesticity was conceived in the German residential programmes. The Frankfurt model follows the rationalization principles proposed by these researchers years before.[12] Margarete's radical innovation was the transformation of what had been the traditional kitchen-space into a kitchen-working machine. With its 1.90 by 3.40 metre floor plan and its standard layout, the time employed to make a meal was drastically reduced, resulting in an efficient space resembling a device, an installation, a machine for the minimum dwelling. Among some of the improvements that this kitchen introduced was the notion of separating the clothes washing area from the cooking area, thus doing away with what had been the traditional washroom-kitchen space. The diagrams showing the reduction of the number of steps needed to carry out chores and therefore the distance covered to do so, which had already been described by Frederick, were put into practice by Schütte-Lihotzky.

[9] Catherine Beecher and Harriet Beecher Stowe, *The American Woman's Home or Principles of Domestic Science Being a Guide to the Formation and Maintenance of Economical Healthful Beautiful and Christian Homes* (New York: J. B. Ford and Company, 1869).

[10] Christine Frederick, *The New Housekeeping: Efficiency Studies in Home Management* (Garden City, New York: Doubleday, Page & Company, 1913).

[11] Lillian Gilbreth, *The Psychology of Management: The Function of the Mind in Determining, Teaching and Installing Methods of Least Waste* (New York: Sturgis & Walton Company, 1914).

[12] Carmen Espegel and Gustavo Rojas, "The Trail of American Domestic Engineers in European Social Housing," *PPA Proyecto, Progreso y Arquitectura* 18 (May 2018): 58–72.

However, in Frankfurt these design innovations were taken further by including the installation of the kitchen furniture during the construction process of the house, in order to finance them by including their cost in the rent. In a certain way, the Germans were the first to reach the American dream with this first mass-produced kitchen. The furniture was arranged taking different aspects into consideration: storage; the correct height of the work surface (the turning chair that the kitchen incorporates makes it possible for the housewife to work, for the most part, sitting down); movement efficiency; the perfect artificial lighting of different areas thanks to a movable lamp, the light cone of which was calculated according to the width of the room and the height of the countertop.

Fig. 8 Photograph by Hermann Collischonn of the Frankfurt Kitchen. View from the entrance looking towards window.
Source: University of Applied Arts Vienna, Collection and Archive.

Likewise, the window was adapted to the shape of furniture and the main work area was placed under it; its generous size enabled the efficient lighting and correct ventilation of the kitchen. The furnishings were placed over a concave concrete plinth to make cleaning easier, while ceramic tiles were used for the floor [Fig. 8]. Grete also emphasized the importance of colour, since she considered that it helped to make the use of the space understandable: blue was applied for the furniture, black for the horizontal surfaces, and ochre for the wall above the work surface. In this way, architecture and furniture became an indivisible whole.[13]

"But there were some new elements in the Frankfurt Kitchen that had not existed before: the fold-out ironing board, the suspended dish rack and most notably the food stock drawers, which Schütte-Lihotzky had developed with the German aluminium company Harrer. The sink, faucets and pot cupboard were also made in cooperation with companies and could be serially manufactured."[14]

By linking the furniture to a broader strategy, costs were reduced thanks to mass production and the construction of the kitchen was ensured. Even so, Margarete had to prove that a small, fully-equipped kitchen optimized the built volume and therefore cut general construction costs at a rate equivalent to the price of the furniture itself. Behind all of these issues was the design of a new kitchen that could benefit the housewife, one that could save her time and therefore enable her to either find a paid job outside the home or have more time for herself.[15]

The exhibition *Die neue Wohnung und ihr Innenausbau, der neuzeitliche Haushalt*[16] (the new house and its interior design, the modern household) at the 1927 Frankfurt Fair was the best showcase for the Frankfurt kitchen. Margarete Schütte-Lihotzky was in charge of setting up the exhibition showing the state of the housing construction enterprise underway. The exhibition included a section created by the association of Frankfurt housewives titled "Household tasks of the new times," for which the five kitchen types designed by the architect were installed at a scale of 1 to 1, thus revealing just how important the work on these domestic issues was in these projects. The idea was to make housewives understand that their contribution was not only aesthetic but that they also had a say in technical and functional improvements. Thanks to the interest raised during the Fair, an Advice Centre was established within the Construction Office to decide the distribution of these kitchens in order to economize domestic chores.

[13] Noever (ed.), *Margarete Schütte-Lihotzky. Soziale Architektur Zeitzeugin eines Jahrhunderts*, 83–123.

[14] Sophie Hochhäusl, "From Vienna to Frankfurt Inside Core-House Type 7: A History of Scarcity through the Modern Kitchen," *Architectural Histories* 1, (2013): 1–19.

[15] Hilde Heynen, "Taylor's Housewife on the Frankfurt Kitchen," in *SQM The Quantified Home* (Zürich: Lars Müller Pub., 2014), 40–47.

[16] Werner Nosbisch, "Die neue Wohnung undihr Innenausbau, der neuzeitliche Haushalt," *Das Neue Frankfurt* 6 (July–September 1927): 129–33.

In retrospect, Margarete saw her sojourn in Frankfurt in the following terms:

"The team of specialists did everything they could in order to obtain the best, at the functional as well as the formal level, within what was technically and economically possible in the Germany of the late twenties. Once more I was part of a community, proscribed at the time, the community of modern architects, who defended certain architectural principles and ideas, and they fought for them without concessions. The whole elite of the architectural profession that Ernst May had brought together, first had to make people understand their ideas. A chain without break was then established for all the work, from the representation at public associations that Ernst May performed, through the architects who started with their first sketches, through basic plans and working drawings, building details, budgets, contracts, construction, through the finished dwelling, even beyond, advising the inhabitants in matters of furniture and use of what had been distributed. Everything was in the hands of the designing architect, and it functioned marvellously well, a rare case in a state operation."[17]

As Habraken points out, the profuse technical development that went hand in hand with the development of the modern house for the masses clearly shows the scope of May's research and *"Perhaps the best way of grasping this would be to list the hundreds of technical subsystems and new materials that were invented, developed and applied during this relatively short period, systems that nobody had never heard about before making unprecedented designs and forms of construction possible."*[18]

In Frankfurt, specifically, another important point to economize housing production was the mechanization of the building process, mainly by reducing construction times. To achieve this, large-format, prefabricated, concrete panels were developed that could be used both for walls and floor slabs [Fig. 9]. It only took twenty days to raise the first experimental block, which included 10 housing units for the Praunheim colony. May showed this system in several forums: he displayed these prefabricated elements at the *Haus der Technik* (The House of Technology) in Königsberg during its 1926 Autumn Fair, and at the 1927 Werkbund Exhibition in Stuttgart, he set up an entire home made out of this system, including the furniture designs and the kitchen.

For May, the house, like any other article for the masses, could only be built with economic rigor and criteria if it was typified, if its components were standardized and if the construction process was mechanized.

[17] Margarete Schütte-Lihotzky, *Erinnerungen, Vortrag in der Gesellschaft für Architektur, Vortragsmanuskript*, 1980. Quoted in Noever (ed.), *Margarete Schütte-Lihotzky. Soziale Architektur Zeitzeugin eines Jahrhunderts*, 82.

[18] N. John Habraken. "Antes y después de la vivienda moderna," in Josep Maria Montaner, *La Arquitectura de la Vivienda Colectiva. Políticas y Proyectos en la Ciudad Contemporánea*. Barcelona: Ed. Reverté, 2016, 10.

Fig. 9 Mounting the prefabricated reinforced concrete panels.
Source: University of Applied Arts Vienna, Collection and Archive.

Rationalizing the house involved, above all, the homologation of everything ranging from knobs, doors, and windows, to ceilings and roofs, including the combinable furniture designed by the architects Ferdinand Kramer and Franz Schuster. This normalization of domestic objects was formalized into the *Das Frankfurter Register*, and it had to be accepted by all contractors.

Lastly, the Frankfurt team understood the transcendence of spreading their research and work. In this sense, they participated in exhibitions and conferences, published books and articles and made movies, understanding the importance of efficiently raising awareness of these ideas among housewives. To do so, photographers of the standing of Hermann Collischonn, Max

Göllner, Alfred Lauer, Grete Leistikow or Hanna Reeck and such well-known cinematographers as Paul Wolff meticulously and iconically registered all of the construction activity surrounding the *siedlungen* and the new form of life that they gave rise to.[19]

In the autumn of 1926, May founded the monthly review *Das Neue Frankfurt* (The New Frankfurt),[20] in which he documented the building activity underway and created an international debate forum focusing on new construction methods, the art of the avant-garde, publicity, furniture design, and urban development policies. The magazine published critical articles such as "The New City" penned by Raymond Unwin or "The prefabrication of buildings" by Walter Gropius. It also addressed urban policy issues in "Division and urban land use in Frankfurt am Main, then and now," and participated in the typological debate in "Past and Modern Minimum Dwelling Types in Frankfurt," the latter an article by Eugen Kaufmann.

Technical matters were also approached, such as the construction of flat roofs, with articles like "Towards an aesthetic of the flat roof" by Adolf Behne, or J.J.P. Oud's "The flat roof in Holland." The final issue of the magazine in 1930 ends with an epilogue by May in which he reviewed the entire endeavour he had directed: "Five years of residential building activity in Frankfurt am Main."

Schütte-Lihotzky wrote a host of articles focusing on her research themes: the Frankfurt kitchen, kitchens for educational facilities and for cooking schools, and housing for the working woman. In these writings she extolled the benefits that rationalization[21] provided for the domestic economy, such as more time for leisure, culture, and the education of children. She also explained that the serial production of housing significantly reduced rental costs and that the minimum dwelling required a series of centralized services in order to facilitate domestic chores, such as automated laundromats with modern appliances and kindergartens. Her goal was to make women understand that they had to call for better houses since they were the most affected by their design, and that to do so they had to overcome the conventionalities of household organization.

In 1928, May commissioned Paul Wolff with the task of spreading the work that was being carried out in Frankfurt in the form of a four-part documentary [Fig. 10]. The films had a didactic approach to teach and provide housewives with the necessary tools to inhabit their new homes, even though they were also very propagandistic in the way they showed the results of the Frankfurt am Main experience. The first movie, *Die Frankfurter Kleinstwohnung*, was dedicated to the minimum dwelling as seen through the eyes of a young couple during a day in their lives.

[19] Michael Stöneberg, "Through focusing screen and viewfinder. The photographers of the New Frankfurt," in *Ernst May 1886–1970*, 79–87.

[20] Ernst May y Fritz Wichert (eds.), *Das Neue Frankfurt: Fünf Jahre Wohnungsbau in Frankfurt am Main* (Frankfurt am Main: Henrich Editionen, 2011). Facsimile of the issues of the international review *Das Neue Frankfurt*.

[21] Grete Lihotzky, "Rationalisier ungim Haushalt," *Das Neue Frankfurt* 5 (April–June 1927): 120–23. Translated into English in: Anton Kaes, Martin Jay, and Edward Dimenberg. *The Weimar Republic Sourcebook*: "Grete Lihotzky. Rationalization in the Household" (Berkeley: University of California Press, 1994), 462–65.

The second film, *Die Frankfurter Küche*, emphasized how unpractical traditional kitchens were and the advantages of the impeccable new design the Frankfurt team was proposing. With the use of a movement diagram similar to the one conceived by Christine Frederick, the efficiency of the space was proven. The distance covered to make a meal was now 8 metres, compared to the 90 metres needed to do so in the conventional kitchen. The point was made by depicting an old-fashioned looking woman toiling in a larger traditional kitchen in stark contrast with a young working woman with short hair happily preparing a meal and cleaning up in her somewhat smaller but seemingly more spacious and well-lit Frankfurt kitchen. The film not only showed the benefits of Lihotzky's design, it also made it clear that the work of housewives had to be taken seriously. As the subtitles suggest, the design of the new kitchen likens the housewife to a clerk or a factory worker.

The third documentary, *Neues Bauen in Frankfurt am Main* (A new form of construction in Frankfurt) dealt with prefabrication techniques. In it, the housing construction phenomenon in Frankfurt is portrayed in more generalist terms.

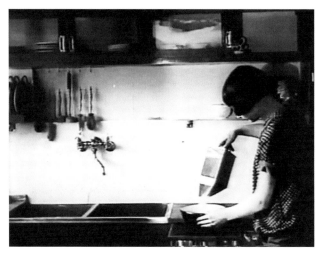

Fig. 10 Image from the film directed by Paul Wolff: Neues Bauen in Frankfurt am Main, 1928. Frankfurt: Wolff-Film, 1928.

Lastly, it is important to point out that the system by which the state subsidized this enterprise became unsustainable in the aftermath of the stock market collapse of 1929. During the Great Depression, international trade all but disappeared, loans were no longer given and once again Germany fell into political and economic chaos. This made public opinion shift to the right of the political spectrum, spelling the doom of the *Neue Sachlichkeit* and changing the destiny of German architects. Many decided to leave the country and emigrate to different places depending on their political inclinations.

May moved to the Soviet Union at the beginning of the 1930s with a team of seventeen architects and urban planners to work on the Master Plan for the steel town of Magnitogorsk in the Urals. This team included the Schütte-Lihotzky couple, as well as Werner Hebebrand, Hans Schmidt, Frend Forbat, Gustav Hassenpflug, Walter Schwagenscheidt, and Mart Stam. Hannes Meyer also left the country and took on a teaching position in Moscow.

The interminable theoretical disputes within the Russian architectural avant-garde led the Soviet authorities to quell this infighting by inviting the socialist architects of the Weimar Republic, who were more pragmatic and had more experience to tackle the First Five-Year Plan with their standardized planning and production methods. Frankfurt [Fig. 11] became a full-fledged experiment in the construction of social housing and it had a greater impact than originally expected since, to paraphrase Habraken, "with modern architecture everyday housing became a part of 'architectural design' for the first time in the history of human settlements."[22]

[22] Habraken, "Antes y después de la vivienda moderna," in Montaner, *La arquitectura de la Vivienda Colectiva. Políticas y Proyectos en la Ciudad Contemporánea*, 7.

Fig. 11 Photograph taken by Grete Leistikow of the old branch of the Nidda with the Praunheim Siedlung in the background. Source: Deutsches Kunstarchiv Im Germanischen Nationalmuseum, Nürnberg.

BIBLIOGRAPHY

Beecher, Catherine, and Harriet Beecher Stowe. *The American Woman's Home or Principles of Domestic Science Being a Guide to the Formation and Maintenance of Economical Healthful Beautiful and Christian Homes.* New York: J. B. Ford and Company, 1869.

Borngraeber, Christian. "Les prétentions sociales de la nouvelle architecture et leur échec dans le nouveau Francfort," in *Paris-Berlin 1900–1933: Rapports et contrastes France-Allemagne 1900–1933.* Exhibition catalogue. Paris: Centre Georges Pompidou, 1978.

Borngraeber, Christian. "Francfort, la vie quotidienne dans l'architecture moderne," *Les cahiers de la recherche architecturale* n17. Paris: Éd. Ministère de la Culture et de la Communication, Direction Générale du Patrimoine, September 1985.

Buekschmitt, Justus. *Ernst May: Bauten und Planungen.* Stuttgart: Koch Verlag, 1963.

Bollerey, Franziska; BÉRET, Chantal Béret, Roman Cieslewicz, Jean-Louis Cohen, Françoise and Centre de Creation Industrielle. *Architectures en Allemagne 1900–1933, catalogue d'exposition.* Paris: Centre Georges Pompidou/CCI, 1979.

Bullock, Nicholas. "Housing in Frankfurt, 1925–1931, and the new Wohnkultur." *Architectural Review* 976 (June1978): 335–42.

Bullock, Nicholas. "First the Kitchen—then the façade." *AA Files* 6 (May 1984): 58–67.

Claire, Jean. *Les Années 20, l'Âge des Métropoles.* Montreal: Musée des beaux-arts de Montreal, Gallimard, 1991.

Espegel, Carmen. *Women Architects in the Modern Movement.* New York: Routledge, 2018.

Espegel, Carmen Espegel, and Gustavo Rojas. "La estela de las ingenieras domésticas americanas en la vivienda social europea." *PPA Proyecto, Progreso y Arquitectura* 18 (May 2018): 58–72.

Frampton, Kenneth. *Modern Architecture: A Critical History.* London: Thames & Hudson, 2007.

Frederick, Christine. *The New Housekeeping: Efficiency Studies in Home Management.* Garden City, New York: Doubleday, Page &Company, 1913.

Gilbreth, Lillian. *The Psychology of Management: The Function of the Mind in Determining, Teaching and Installing Methods of Least Waste.* New York: Sturgis & Walton Company, 1914.

Grassi, Giorgio (dir.). *Das Neue Frankfurt 1926–1931.* Bari: Ed. Dedalo libri, 1975.

Heynen, Hilde. "Taylor's Housewife on the Frankfurt Kitchen." In *SQM The Quantified Home.* Zürich: Lars Müller Pub., 2014, 40–47.

Houchhäusl, Sophie. "From Vienna to Frankfurt Inside Core-House Type 7: A History of Scarcity through the Modern Kitchen." *Architectural Histories* 1 (2013): 1–19.

Höpfner, Rosemarie, and Volker Fischer (ed.). *Ernst May und Das Neue Frankfurt 1925–1930.* Exhibition catalogue at the Deutschen Architekturmuseum Frankfurt am Main. Berlin: Ernst & Sohn, 1986.

Kaes, Anton, Martin Jay, and Edward Dimenber. *The Weimar Republic Sourcebook.* Berkeley: University of California Press, 1994.

Klein, Alexander. "Les tracés de plans. Nouvelle méthode pour la comparaison et l'évaluation des plans." *L'Architecte.* France: July 1930.

Lihotzky, Grete. "Rationalisierung im Haushalt." *Das Neue Frankfurt* 5. (April–June 1927): 120–23.

Martí, Carlos. *Las Formas de la Residencia en la Ciudad Moderna.* Barcelona: Ed. Universidad Politécnica de Cataluña, 2000.

May, Ernst. "La politique de l'habitation à Francfort-sur-le-Main." *L'Architecte.* France: January 1930.

May, Ernst, and Fritz Wichert (eds.). *Das Neue Frankfurt: Fünf Jahre Wohnungsbau in Frankfurt am Main.* Facsimile of the issues of the international magazine Das Neue Frankfurt. Frankfurt am Main: Henrich Editionen, 2011.

Miller, Barbara. *Architecture and Politics in Germany 1918–1945.* Cambridge: Harvard University Press, 1968.

Montaner, Josep María. *La Arquitectura de la Vivienda Colectiva. Políticas y Proyectos en la Ciudad Contemporánea.* Barcelona: Ed. Reverté, 2016.

Murard, Lion, and Patrick Zylberman. "Esthétique du taylorisme. L'habitat rationnel en Allemagne: de la stabilisation du mark à la stabilisation d'Hitler (1924–1933)," *Paris-Berlin 1900–1933: Rapports et Contrastes France-Allemagne 1900–1933.* Paris: Centre Georges Pompidou, 1978. Exhibition catalogue.

Noever, Peter (ed.). *Margarete Schütte-Lihotzky. Soziale Architektur Zeitzeugin eines Jahrhunderts.* Vienna: Bóhlau Verlag, 1996.

Nosbisch, Werner. "Die neue Wohnung und ihr Innenausbau, der neuzeitliche Haushalt." *Das Neue Frankfurt* 6 (July–September 1927): 129–33.

Quiring, Claudia, Wolfgang Voigt, Peter Cahola Schmal and Eckhard Herrel. *Ernst May 1886–1970.* Munich/London/New York: Prestel Verlag and Frankfurt am Main: Deutsches Architekturmuseum, 2011. Exhibition catalogue.

Sambricio, Carlos. *L'Habitation Minimum.* Edición facsímil de la de Julius Hoffmann, 1933. Zaragoza: Delegación de Zaragoza del Colegio Oficial de Arquitectos de Aragón, 1977.

Corporatism and Affordable Housing in the Portuguese Urban Environment (1933–1974)

PAULA BORGES SANTOS and JOSÉ MARIA BRANDÃO DE BRITO
NOVA University of Lisbon, Institute of Contemporary History | University of Lisbon, School of Economics and Management

ABSTRACT

This article introduces a historiographical approach to the theme of affordable housing programmes developed by the authoritarian state in the Portuguese urban environment, between 1933 and 1974. It presents the housing policy as part of the authoritarian social policy and discusses the evolution of affordable housing programmes, valuing their diversity and distinguishing between the normative, political, economic, and financial tools operated for their implementation. A large number of programmes were developed following five main typologies, namely: Affordable Houses, Affordable Rent Houses, Rent-controlled Houses, Houses for Poor Families, and Houses for Fishermen. This article will scrutinize only three of these typologies, which involved greater financial investment, required the construction of a more extensive normativity, had larger national coverage and remained for a long period of time: affordable houses, affordable rent houses, and rent-controlled houses.

Using a historiographical approach, the analysis is focused on the creation of these three typologies of programmes in the sphere of the executive and legislative powers. From a legislative point of view as well as from a budgetary and financial allocation perspective, it inquires into the protagonists and circuits of political decision. Furthermore, a chronology is outlined for the investment in these typologies of housing programmes, following the changes in the government orientation and regarding the financial means applied, credit policies, and income. By way of illustration, the practical effects of some actions will be mentioned, as well as the reactions that they have aroused among various agents, namely the applicants for residents and the tenants of these houses. Finally, this article aims to verify whether the affordable housing policy of Portuguese authoritarianism, integrated in the sphere of social action of the administrative bodies, corporatist organisms, and social welfare institutions, did in fact favour the corporatist project of the state (for example, by adding heritage to it or by promoting social cohesion), or whether, on the contrary, it contributed to exposing its limitations and weaknesses.

BIOGRAPHY

Paula Borges Santos (Beja, 1976). Doctorate in Contemporary History from the Faculty of Social and Human Sciences of the New University of Lisbon (NOVA FCSH). Full-time researcher in the Institute of Contemporary History (IHC) of the NOVA FCSH, where she coordinates the Research Group Justice, Regulation and Society. In the last five years, she has published one book as author (doctoral thesis), and edited one book and eight supplements for the Dictionary of the History of Portugal (1974–1976). Author of seven chapters in books, ten articles and six specialized dossiers in international academic journals, published in the UK, Italy, Spain, and Brazil. She has given communications in Portugal, Spain, Italy, and Brazil. She was visiting professor at the Pontifical Catholic University of Rio Grande do Sul (2015). She gave master's classes at UNED and UA Madrid.

José Maria Brandão de Brito (Lisbon, 1947). Economist and Emeritus Professor at the Lisbon School of Economics & Management, University of Lisbon. He was administrator of TAP, Chairman of RTP's Board of Directors, member of the General Board of EDP, and vice-rector of the Technical University of Lisbon. He is also a member of the think tank Missão Crescimento (Order of Economists, Order of Engineers, and Forum of Business Administrators) as well as an life member of the Society of Geography. Currently he is an administrator of the EBRD (London) and member of the High Council of the European University Institute. He is an integrated researcher at the Institute of Contemporary History (NOVA FCSH). He is the author of multiple books and articles focused on the Portuguese economy and society as well as on contemporary economic history.

1. HOUSING PROGRAMMES AS A DIMENSION OF THE SOCIAL POLICY OF AUTHORITARIANISM

In a speech explaining the meaning of the economic principles that shaped the 1933 Constitution, Salazar described the condition of Portuguese workers, in the light of what had gone before, as being deeply characterized by unprotected work and as a target of exploitation (especially child and women) by the competition and low labour costs as well as by an estranged relationship with their families and workplace. It was an intervention which leaned strongly towards propaganda, ideologically grounded on an antiliberal and anti-socialist framework, in which the discourse was intentionally inflated, and as such constructed a kind of defence against the danger of what, in the ruler's understanding, could follow: the struggle of workers' associations against the state, against employers and even against the workers themselves, without solidarity or protection, and uninterested in technical improvement. The solution was found in the organization of a "new economy," able to achieve the maximum socially useful production in which the state, throughout its administrative activity, should arbitrate individual and collective interests, must guarantee the morality and the public hygiene and withdraw its presence from fields of activity where private initiative was sufficient. Work was here taken as a social duty which should be fairly remunerated (without an upper limit, but with a lower one), while excluding the participation of workers in the company profits. The professional association, added the ex-university professor, should avoid the class struggle approach, embracing intellectual and moral interests but without expecting to achieve national representation. Within this scope, the sociability of work was not left to chance; in harmony with society's organicist referential composite that animated the ruling political class and had led to the corporatist reorganization of the state, the sociability of work was in itself subject of organization both through the unions and the family. The latter gave meaning to the existence of private property and inheritance, which were safeguarded by constitutional precepts. In the same sense, the notion of family dignity would require women to withdraw from labour activity as well as home ownership.[1]

The implementation of this programmatic statement, firstly expressed in the constitutional text,[2] took some time to be claimed by the legislation that shaped the social policy of the regime, taking corporatism as a structuring element. This policy—claimed under a doctrinal point of view, over distinct conjunctures of governance, as a facet of the revolutionary experience of founding a new state as well as a novel social system—comprised different dimensions:

[1] António de Oliveira Salazar, "Conceitos económicos da nova Constituição," in *Discursos 1928–1934* (Coimbra: Coimbra Editora Lda, 1935), 190–208.

[2] Some principles of the 1933 Political Constitution claimed: the right to property and its transmission in life or death (Article 15); the duty of the states and local authorities, on behalf of defence of the family, to promote "the constitution of independent and healthy homes" and the institution of the *casal de família* (Art. 13, 1).

work organization; welfare; assistance; health; leisure and sports. It also comprised affordable housing programmes. In all these domains, the solutions proposed were critical about the way the Portuguese liberal state managed the social crisis that had devastated it and carried on the idea of overcoming the dualism between the individual, considered as sovereign in itself, and the state. Built on another perception of society—that of an organism constituted by differentiated individuals, with different activities hierarchized in their natural differentiation—such solutions sought adhesion to the state project, leaning towards the strengthening of the well-being of the "social body." This was the argument that allowed a leap to be taken towards the idea of a general interest, only accomplished by the state's intervention and freed from the evaluation of individual interests. Nevertheless, the social policy did not appear as an end of the state's action or as a legitimizing source of its power. Rather, it was a means of asserting the vocation, the impetus of achievement, and the avant-garde position that the regime believed it had.[3] Consequently, in the solutions adopted in the various domains of social policy the ability of state's interventions to guide and influence the development of the mentioned domains, on one hand, and the conceding of private sector autonomy, in its shape and extent, on the other had always been at stake had always been at stake. Grounded in this broader picture, this article reconstructs the evolution of the affordable urban housing programmes, under the Estado Novo action (1933–1974), valuing the diversity of such programmes and distinguishing between the normative, political, economic, and financial tools handled by successive executives for their implementation. It aims to confirm whether the affordable housing policy of Portuguese authoritarianism—part of the sphere of social action of administrative bodies, corporatist bodies, and social welfare institutions—really favoured the corporatist state project (for example, by adding heritage to or by promoting social cohesion) or whether, on the contrary, it contributed to exposing the state's limitations and weaknesses.

The State created five typologies of programmes, namely Affordable Houses, Affordable Rent Houses, Rent-controlled Houses, Houses for Poor Families, and Houses for Fishermen. This article focuses on the three typologies that involved greater financial investment and required the construction of a more extensive normativity, that had greater national coverage and were implemented during a long period of time: affordable houses, affordable rent houses, and rent-controlled houses. The analysis was built around the abovementioned programmes in the sphere of both executive and legislative powers. From the legislative, budgetary, and financial viewpoints, it will inquire into the protagonists and circuits of political decision expressed between distinct entities:

[3] The idea of a vanguard position of the regime, confirmed by achievements in social policy, was also present in Italian fascism. Read Irene Stolzi, "Politici sociale e regime fascista: un'ipotese di lettura," *Quaderni Florentini* 46 (2017): 257.

the Presidência do Conselho de Ministros [Presidency of the Council of Ministers], the Ministério das Obras Públicas (MOP) [Ministry of Public Works], the Ministério das Corporações e Previdência Social (MCPS) [Ministry of Corporations and Social Welfare, a sub-secretariat of state until 1950], the National Assembly, and the Corporatist Chamber. The inclusion of other powers, such as local power, or the action of social welfare agencies, is taken here for mere illustrative purposes—the complexity of these interventions should be the subject of another study, requiring an empirical survey based on another type of sources. Moreover, the architects and town planners' interventions as well as the civil construction industry involved in the programmes approved and implemented, will not be examined. It is, however, possible to identify how their expertise was integrated into the ministerial design of affordable housing programmes.

The option to include statistical elements published in technical and propaganda documentation was adopted, but it is important to mention that such elements are scarce and "deserving of little confidence," especially those related to the adjacent islands[4]. In assuming this assessment, we are incorporating a criticism made after 1972, at the end of the regime, which was found in the opinions of the Corporatist Chamber and is taken here as useful, however exceeding the purpose of this study and the possibilities of the time expended by the authors on this research. Nonetheless, the record of this statistical insufficiency is still important to historicize and exemplify the constraints that affected the planning projects, for example in the reports of the Fundo do Fomento da Habitação [Housing Development Fund] or the Planos de Fomento [Development Plans]. In fact, some of the first series published by the National Statistics Institute (INE), such as those related to the number of houses built annually, their area characteristics and cost, are considered as questionable. In the same sense, the elements available from the census had created further difficulties in 1973, when calculating the housing deficit (1960 was the last year for which official data were available) and the replacement deficit (calculated for the period 1960–1970, followed by a recommendation from the European Economic Community). Furthermore, certain realities were omitted in the elements provided by the 1960 census, such as the so-called clandestine constructions or conditions of habitability. In a kind of contamination effect—since, at the origin, the INE's elements were sometimes "imprecise and incomplete"—the statistical indicators drawn up by different technical offices of the several ministries should be read with some caution, concerning the accuracy of what they wanted to require or design.[5]

[4] "Opinion no. 56/X: Projeto do IV Plano de Fomento para 1974–1979," in *Pareceres (X Legislatura)*, vol. III. (Lisbon: Câmara Corporativa, 1973), 247.

[5] "Opinion no. 56/X": 248, 256–59, 278–9.

2. "RUPTURE" IN ECONOMIC HOUSEHOLD POLICY: AN IDEA BUILT BY PROPAGANDA

The affordable house model was taken as the key choice under Salazarist action, in order to solve the housing problem for employees, workers, and other wage earners, members of the national syndicates, civilian and military individuals, trade unions, workers of the permanent staff of the state services and municipal councils. This choice was not unprecedented in the history of the Portuguese housing crisis—understood as a critical manifestation of the so-called "social issue." Nor was it intended to stimulate construction sector activity. Furthermore, there was no significant improvement regarding the relevant problems of the hygiene and health conditions, emphasized by the urban dramatic expansion—indeed, it was in line with what had already been discussed in the nineteenth-century public sphere across Europe and with the different programmes carried out in the several countries, as well as in Portugal.[6]

However, from a financial point of view, the methods of construction were significantly distinct from the experiences carried out at the turn of the twentieth-century—first supported by Sidónio Pais and established by Decrees no. 4,137 and 4,447 of 1918, later under the direction of the Executives of the Nova República Velha [New Old Republic], by Law no. 858 and by Decrees no. 5,397 and 5,443 of 1919.[7] Another difference involved the type of entities that were allowed to construct or intervene in the building process of affordable houses, which in beginning was exclusively performed by public entities (city councils, corporatist administrations, and bodies, in collaboration with the government). The rigidity of such determination—specified by the first Decree-Law no. 23,052 of 23 September 1933, which addressed the problem of affordable housing in the scope of the Estado Novo's corporatist project—was, however, fine-tuned over the Portuguese authoritarian period. As we shall see later, other solutions that had already been distinguished in Article 15 of Decree no. 4,137 of 25 April 1918—in which it is admitted that the state as well as the administrative bodies could build affordable neighbourhoods or houses—permitted the building process to be extended to other kinds of institutions such as social welfare and assistance and charitable or similar institutions, and industrial companies when exploring any privilege, or by state grant.

These aspects were cleverly disguised by the dictatorship's engine of propaganda, ideologically committed to validating this new housing policy, on one hand, and depreciating the previous experiences of the "social neighbourhoods" conducted during the First Republic (1910–1926), on the other.

[6] For the development of this topic see: Margarida Acciaiuoli, *Casas com Escritos. Uma História da Habitação em Lisboa* (Lisbon: Editorial Bizâncio, 2015), 353–59.

[7] On the analysis of the housing problem in Portugal in the first decade of the twentieth century, see: Rute Figueiredo, *Arquitectura e Discurso Crítico em Portugal (1893–1918)* (Lisbon: Edições Colibri/ IHA–Estudos de Arte Contemporânea, Faculdade de Ciências Sociais e Humanas da Universidade Nova de Lisboa, 2007), 276–86.

This criticism oscillated between the financial matters—namely the very expensive investments made in the construction of social neighbourhoods—and the administrative gaps in organization leading to their delayed implementation. In some cases, the conceptions that inspired this solution were attacked, under the judgment that "they did not follow the sources of the problem."[8] The "problem," as it was equated in Salazarism at the beginning, had several facets: economic, since the demographic increase and migratory flows towards the main cities had generated a great demand for houses; social, because the limitations of the housing stock implied wasting results being reached in the areas of social security, health, and care, "through medical-social services, sanatoria, dispensaries and subsidies of all kinds"; moral, as the lack of housing conditions favoured the nonconformity and man's exhaustion with life, competed for promiscuity and produced the failure of the family in their legitimacy and indissolubility, as well as "the abandonment of youth to the street and dangers of vice."[9] In this line of thought, the anti-classist spirit that animated the ruling class led to the rejection of the worker's housing[10] and to the acclamation of the "independent home." Thus, it was argued that the latter was a way to protect the workers' families, *"a source for the conservation and development of the race, discipline and social harmony, and foundation of all political order."*[11] This reflection was not exactly a novelty, despite often being emphasized as such by the literature on social public policies or the Salazarist propaganda apparatus. In fact, beyond ideological rhetoric, this discourse had several contact points with the thinking of the lawmaker in 1918. In order to justify the promotion of the affordable house's construction, he had also pointed out that of several families in small cubicles destroyed "all the notions of morality," prevented feelings of *"love for his house [...] arousing not ideas of peace, quietness and happiness, but feelings of hate and revolt,"* leading towards "the tavern, brothels and addiction houses" as the only resource "to forget so many pains."[12]

The attribution of houses to lower-income workers, through a process based on the payment of contributions in which the tenant became the housing owner, had a double aim, not openly expressed: firstly, to discipline the worker in financial terms, forcing the better organization of the domestic economy, thus keeping the regular payment of the housing rent; and, secondly, to discipline the worker's behaviour, in order to be admitted during the selection process for the housing occupancy, and to preserve this "right" once attained. Moreover, this policy was also important to maintain a certain isolation of the worker from the community, guiding him into the house and away from the "phalanstery."[13] In other words, this method for the regeneration of workers was outlined in dialogue with what was considered strongly dangerous:

---

[8] *Diário das Sessões* no. 51 (1 de Março de 1944): 169.

[9] *O Pensamento de Salazar. 32 Anos ao Serviço de Portugal. Revolução Corporativa* ([Lisbon]: Ed. Lit. António Cruz, 1960), 193–94.

[10] Salazar, "Conceitos," 202.

[11] Instituto Nacional do Trabalho e Previdência, *Dez Anos de Política Social 1933–1943* (Lisbon: Oficinas Gráficas da Casa Portuguesa, 1943), 175.

[12] Decree no. 4,137 of 25 April 1918. This diploma recovered a huge part of the norms defined in two other diplomas submitted to the Chamber of Deputies, which were the subject of evaluation by parliamentary committees but that were never discussed in plenary: one was the draft law presented on 26 February 1914, by the then Minister of Finance, Tomás Cabreira; another was the bill of the deputy Francisco Sales Ramos da Costa, submitted on 20 August 1915, which renewed the initiative.

[13] Instituto Nacional do Trabalho e Previdência, *Dez Anos de Política Social*, 176.

the worker's involvement in political and syndicalist struggles. Accordingly, the organization of workers' free time and leisure constituted the other side of this disciplinary vision. However, these positions were not established without conflict. In fact, the state was theoretically founded on a corporatist republic and, therefore, it was supposed to structure a social policy capable of neutralizing the individualistic positions and promoting the encounters between the individual and his natural groups, developing associative capacities. In the mid-1930s, this perspective raised, unsurprisingly, some disagreements among the various protagonists involved in political decisions, shaping political and ideological struggles that would get stronger over time. Two distinct understandings were at the centre of such a conflict: one, arguing that the involvement of the individual in the community should always be guided by the state's invisible hand—through its multiple institutions—, acting in harmony with what was considered to be the right and the morality of the regime; and another, convinced that a true corporatism of association would naturally imply the state's action retreat in the social and economic organization. Thus, the housing policy was set up on this never completely solved polarization: should the afordable housing programmes compete for the segregation of certain classes or categories of workers? Or was it more prudent to rebuild the diversity and complementarity of the labour community in general?

3. CONSTRUCTION AND SALE OF AFFORDABLE HOUSES DURING THE MILITARY DICTATORSHIP: A NON-NEGLECTED HERITAGE

The options taken at the beginning of Salazarism were closely related to what had been the building and sales policy structured under the Military Dictatorship (1926–1933) for the affordable housing problem—which had inherited the failure of the first affordable housing programmes that started in 1918 and ended only in 1926. The action of the international trend was reflected in these first experiences, with the effects of World War I on civil construction activity, accompanied by many other national factors: high interest rates that affected the construction industry, the devaluation of the currency that had cut investment in the sector, the rise in prices of materials, and the abolition of contractual freedom of the tenancy system. Therefore, between 1926 and 1933, several ministries undertook multiple actions in order to minimize the above-mentioned difficulties. As part of this, around 26.000$00 was made available to conclude the construction programme, seeking to compensate the cooperatives and firms involved in it.

Furthermore, new normative conditions were created, with the intention of to redefining governmental intervention in the field of construtcion of affordable houses.[14] The main distinction from the previous experiences was made through a new understanding of the state's action in this domain: the problem of affordable housing should be equated with greater rationality, namely in fiscal and credit matters, the regulation and protection of the construction industry, the organization of labour and land policy.

It was precisely this orientation that made the question of affordable housing dependent on two ministries: the Ministry of Finance, both before and after António de Oliveira Salazar; and the Ministério das Obras Públicas e Comunicações (MOPC) [Ministry of Public Works and Communication] headed by Duarte Pacheco. Although it was the latter who took the responsibility for launching the first affordable houses programme in the dictatorship, the validation of this programme was dependent on directives from the Minister of Finance, in accordance with the sustainability of the ongoing actions for the replacement of the state's financial equilibrium, as well as the resources allocated for the housing policy. Part of the financial resources allocated for the implementation of the first affordable houses initiative came from tax revenue and involved the problem of unemployment, as well. For example, inheritance and gift tax rates were increased and an additional 2 per cent fee was added to the Unemployment Fund. This Fund, introduced by Decree no. 21,699 of 30 September 1932, came from the establishment of the Comissariado do Desemprego [Unemployment Commissariat], also structured by the Minister Duarte Pacheco, which was intended to create an opportunity to mitigate the problem of skilled labour in civil construction, specifically assisting its concentration. Among the four larger groups of the unemployed regulated by diploma[15]—in the preamble of which it was claimed "we do not give alms, we want to give work"—Group III, with an estimated number of 6000 individuals, including officers, assistants and apprentices from any branch of civil construction, should be allocated to urban upgrading works (where the Affordable Houses could be found), under the responsibility of the Direção-Geral dos Edifícios e Monumentos Nacionais (DGEMN) [Directorate-General for Public Buildings and Monuments], and also allocated to improving the water and sanitary system, under the action of the Administração Geral dos Serviços Hidráulicos e Elétricos [General Administration of Hydraulic and Electrical Services].[16]

On the one hand, financial income was collected from the urban landowners, whereas on the other hand, it was decided to multiply state financial aid to builders and acquirers of affordable houses, as occurred on 30 March 1928, through the decree with force of Law

---

[14] Preamble of Decree no. 16,055 of 22 October 1928. See also: José Fernando Nunes Barata, "Habitação," in *Dicionário Jurídico da Administração Pública*, ed. José Pedro Fernandes, V vol. ([s. l.]: [s. ed.], 1993), 45.

[15] Pedro Teotónio Pereira, *Memórias. Postos em que Servi e Algumas Recordações Pessoais*, I vol. (Lisbon: Verbo, 1972), 139.

[16] In 1931, a year earlier, the Minister of Trade and Communications Antunes Guimarães, through Decree no. 19,502, promoted the annual plan of works, covering all municipalities in the country, in which the construction of water supply under good hygienic conditions was already accomplished. Other diplomas, such as Decrees no. 21,696, 21,697 and 21,698, also dated 30 September 1932, had also sought to stimulate the civil construction sector by directing it towards urban improvements, in particular with regard to the "realization of urban plans."

no. 15,289, modified by several subsequent decrees. In Article 34, the diploma attributed property exemption for ten years to buildings constructed until the end of 1930. This exemption was extended by Article 24 of Decree no. 16,731 to the new parts of urban buildings; the *sisa* (property transfer tax) was reduced to 1 per cent for the acquisition of land destined for that constructions by Article 103 and the same minimum rate of 1 per cent for sisa was maintained by Article 102 for the first transmission of the buildings constructed, provided that this occurred within a period of two years from the date of their habitability. The exemptions from property tax granted by these diplomas ended only in 1939, such that the number of temporarily exempt taxpayers was 4,506 in Lisbon and 2,251 in Porto, as published in the Statistical Yearbook of Contributions and Taxes. Exemption was granted to buildings constructed until the end of 1931 by Decree-Law n.º 18,738 of 9 August 1930, reducing the term of the property tax to nine years. The renewal of fiscal favours was an instrument intensively applied until it ended in 1940.[17]

Through the decree with force of Law no. 15,289, the National Fund for Buildings and Economic Rents was also instituted under the Ministry of Finance, structured to financially support the private construction initiative and to reduce rent (house and room) expenses for the middle and working classes (Art. 48). The latitude of financial support increased significantly and transcended the horizon of affordable housing. In fact, they were trying to solve the problem of the large number of buildings whose construction had been paralyzed during the previous years (Art. 52, point 4), thus stimulating their conclusion and further occupation. It was also a way to avoid the distortions of the renting market, felt since the publication of the Lei do Inquilinato [Law of Tenancy] (1910).

Hence, a free system to fix the rent for buildings constructed since the publication of this decree was established, whether or not they had been supported with loans granted by the Fund (Art. 54, [18][19]§ 1). Attempting to balance the protection given to tenants, owners, and landlords, eviction of tenants was allowed once the term of the lease had expired and the owners put a house at the disposal of the tenants with a corresponding rent identical to the one they were previously paying (Art. 55). It was accepted that eviction could be avoided as long as the tenants agreed to pay the updated rent, as determined by the application of the coefficients set forth in § 1 of Article 30. In truth, the results of these provisions are not totally known. However, the complexity and persistence of subleasing situations, the protests of landlords and owners and the lack of investment in the conditions of habitability of buildings all raised suspicions about the real impact of these legal provisions on the problem they aimed to solve.[20]

[17] *Diário das Sessões* no. 51 (1 de Março de 1944): 169–70.

[18] The Fund had an administrative committee composed of two sub-committees: one technical and the other administrative. The first had responsibility for designing the projects, choosing materials and the methods of construction, land and interior division, which would allow affordable construction of houses. The same commission drew up the budgets and made the inspection of constructions subsidized by the Fund. (Art. 50, § 1.º).

[19] On the circumstances of the appearance of the Law of Tenancy and its effects, see Manuel C. Teixeira, "As estratégias de habitação em Portugal, 1880–1940," *Análise Social* 115, n.º 1 (1992): 76.

[20] Acciaiuoli, *Casas com Escritos*, 387–89.

A few months later, Decree no. 16,055 of 22 October 1928, published specific guidelines for the construction and sale of affordable houses. In contrast with the diploma of 30 March, the affordable housing was identified here as specific accommodation for the "low-income classes" (Art.1), as such excluding the middle class. Among the guidelines published in the legal document it is possible to identify aspects of a different nature. Firstly, the extension of benefits to builders—for example, giving a deadline of ten years for the construction. Secondly, the agreement to involve public entities in order to obtain capital applications in the construction business. Thus, the institutions of assistance, mutuality, and charities could participate with 25 per cent of their assets (Art.17) as well as insurance companies with the same percentage of their reserves (Art. 18). The Caixa Geral de Depósitos (CGD—a major public bank in Portugal) could allocate part of the funds (under the agreement of both the Finance Ministry and the Trade and Communications Ministry) to loans for construction companies, with a payment of 2 per cent interest (Art. 25). Third, the reduction of the plague of incomplete buildings was kept as an important aim. In fact, it became mandatory to sell these buildings by public auction, as long as the owner did not conclude them within one year (Art.26), which could, however, be extended by one further year in exceptional cases. Fourth, the land expropriations for works carried out by the municipalities and by the state (Arts. 11 and 13) were also enabled to make it quick and with administrative quality. The same criteria guided the compensation to be paid to expropriated persons (Art. 12), without increasing the cost, the price, and the housing rent. Finally, following the example of the English legislation, already applied in other European countries, the possibility that tenants of affordable houses could amortize their houses via monthly instalments within twenty years (Art. 19, § 2).

Three years later, the institutionalization of the authoritarian state, as previously mentioned, did not promote any significant rupture with the policy that had been adopted for affordable housing in the urban environment. More than founding new conceptions for affordable housing programmes, the abovementioned Decree no. 23,052 of 23 September 1933 fine-tuned the already existing system. Indeed, the government kept the promotion of affordable houses in coordination with municipal councils, administrative corporations, and state agencies. The possibility of attributing the property to the tenant was also rethought, establishing that, in relation to the framework of 1928, the tenant could acquire the house over twenty-five years via monthly instalments, which included—in addition to the part related to the amortization of capital—the interest rate and premiums related to death, disability, sickness, unemployment and fire risks. During the amortization period, the so-called resident-acquirer owned the house under the system of *propriedade resolúvel* (resolvable property) and, at the end of that time, would acquire it as absolute property. It was the progressive development of a policy (activated in the year 1933) that, throughout the Estado Novo, tended to establish rent systems compatible with the family rent, simplifying access to owning housing.

The set of transformations introduced by Decree no. 23,052 also pointed out, as will be described below, the reorganization of the state services and their functions, and the creation of new financial instruments, capable of supporting the affordable housing programme. This new legislation did not revert the regulation of the private initiative involved in the civil construction sector, remaining operative in the construction of affordable houses as defined until then. However, after 1935, a new aspect was introduced: the regulation of the professional exercise of the builder, given the relevant implications of the professional activity in this sector and on the municipalities' level of construction. To this end, a commission of technicians was appointed to balance the access to the labour market between individuals who had graduate from school and those who had no diploma but had practice in construction. Ten years later, the results of this work led to the publication of Decree-Law no. 35,721 of 26 June 1946, which recognized as civil builders all individuals who had sufficiently proved their competence and had expressed good moral and civil behaviour.[21]

Despite the regime's propaganda apparatus trying to connect the corporatist doctrine guidelines with the governmental aims outlined in the housing issue, the housing policy plan continued to be dominated by government action, under an ever-present propensity towards centralization. Nonetheless—as the Minister Duarte Pacheco pragmatically explained in a conference held at the Teatro de S. Carlos—the ideas framed within the cycle promoted by the recently corporatist legislation, created in 1933, *"do not illuminate such a strong light yet, nor does their renovative thinking finds itself so clearly that people than apostles or teachers can or should speak of it."*[22] For this reason, the first subvention of the new regime for the construction of affordable houses in Lisbon and Porto, in the amount of 20,000$00, had been made possible by Decree-Law no. 22,909 of 11 July 1933, without waiting for the regulatory diploma for the construction of affordable houses (Decree no. 23,052), then in the final stages of writing. A few months earlier, another way of fighting the problem of housing, in population segments of low or very low economic conditions, was created by Decree no. 21,697 of 30 September 1932.

[21] This legislative measure sought to staunch the problem of the irregularities evidenced in builders' work in several municipal councils, however avoiding their compulsory removal as this "would cause disruption in the wake of the on-going constructions." The last major change, before 1946, was operated through Law no. 1670 of 15 September 1924, which blocked the acceptance of projects not signed by graduate technicians and limited the exercise of the profession of civil builder to graduates and registered contractors in the Municipal Councils of Lisbon and Porto. The diploma had little effect, however, and the local authorities continued to contract unlicensed builders. Cf. Preamble to Decree-Law no. 35,721 of 26 June 1946.

[22] With this reference, Duarte Pacheco excluded himself from this group of ideologues of the corporatist project and showed his scepticism about it. Cf. Pereira, *Memórias*, 140.

In order to promote urban improvements, this diploma had permitted—over the following years until 1948—the construction of houses for fishermen in several fishing centres in the country,[23] by bodies and administrative corporations, as well as commissions of initiatives funded by the state budget, from the sum allocated by the MOPC.

4. THE FIRST CYCLE OF IMPLEMENTATION OF THE AFFORDABLE HOUSES PROGRAMME (1933–1945)

It is possible to distinguish two cycles of implementation of the affordable houses programme during the Estado Novo, taking into account the type of capital that stimulated its construction and also the norms for its attribution and distribution. The first cycle, defined for the period between 1933–1945, was associated with the reorganization of services and the financial instruments produced by Decree no. 23,052. The housing construction was supported by the Fundo das Casas Económicas (FCE) [Fund of Affordable Houses], made possible by: funds allocated by the government; contributions from city councils, administrative corporations, and corporatist organisms; income from securities protected by the CGD and cash deposits from the Fund; private donations; and the amounts collected from the instalments of affordable houses. In addition, the Unemployment Fund also contributed to the construction of affordable houses, without any possibility of recovering the funds invested, contrary to what happened with the FCE.[24]

To safeguard the capital invested by the Unemployment Fund, Salazar determined by Dispatch of 24 March 1936 that the monthly instalments amounts should include the regular amortization by the committed co-participating entity. The sums that exceeded that amortization constituted revenues for the FCE. These provisions, related to the financial discipline of the affordable houses programme, emphasise the rigour of the investment plan, with the requirement of the state's capital return and the purpose of avoiding financial slippage. By Decree-Law 33,278 of 24 November 1943, it was further established that the state financed, without interest, half of the cost expended on new constructions of affordable houses in Lisbon, Porto, Coimbra, and Almada. The remaining 50 per cent would be assured by the respective city councils, at 4 per cent interest rates and with the possibility of special loans. The municipalities were also responsible for providing the necessary land and urbanization. If the product of the houses' sales did not reach the cost of acquisition of the total area, the Unemployment Fund could share the expenses with the urbanization up to the amount of the difference.

[23] Until 1947, according to the information available in the Exposição de Obras Públicas (Exhibition of Public Works), held in Lisbon in 1948, 672 and 1648 houses were built for fishermaen and were already approved and under construction. Cf. Comissão Executiva da Exposição de Obras Públicas, *Quinze Anos de Obras Públicas 1932-1947*. II vol. ([Lisbon]: Imprensa Nacional de Lisboa, [1948]), 148.

[24] Dispatch [24 March 1936] in *Diário do Governo*, I série, n.º 77 (2 April 1936). The destination given to the National Building and Economic Income Fund is unknown. However, since the previous legislation had not been revoked, it may be possible that it had continued to contribute to these constructions. Another possibility is that its capital had been integrated into the Affordable Houses Fund.

The intervention of the Government in the implementation of the Affordable Housing Programme remained, in line with what had hitherto taken place, under the responsibility of the MOPC, creating the Affordable Houses Section in the DGEMN for this purpose. This public entity had the responsibility for developing the plans, projects and budgets, choosing the land, administering the funds for the buildings and inspectig the actions of building conservation and improvement. Since the housing policy represented a key aspect of the state's corporatist project, the Sub-Secretariado das Corporações e Previdência Social (SSECPS) [Sub-Secretariat of Corporations and Social Welfare] received additional attributions, throughout the Repartição das Casas Económicas [Office of Affordable Houses] which was created at the Instituto Nacional do Trabalho e Previdência Social (INTP) [National Institute for Work and Social Welfare], namely: drawing up the plans for the distribution of affordable houses; the supervision of the benefits collected; guaranteeing hygiene in the neighbourhoods; and the payment of the various insurance and insurance premiums required. This division of powers and competencies did not differ so much from what had been stipulated for the two sub-commissions that comprised the Fundo Nacional de Construções e Rendas Económicas (FNRE) [National Fund for Construction and Affordable Rents].

The affordable houses were instituted under a regime of resolvable property, with an obligation to constitute the "casal de família"—recovering what had been legislated in the Military Dictatorship by decree no. 18551 of 3 July 1930, which had consecrated that institution, making it indivisible and inalienable, either voluntarily or coercively.[25] In the wake of the protection of the family—understood as an institution—recommended in the constitutional text (Art. 13, 1) and reinforced by the corporatist ideas outlined by the regime, the "casal de família" embodied the notion of unity, endurance and durability.[26] It also represented an asset for the family patrimonial property; it should be instituted by the head of the family and could assume several modalities.[27]

The reception of this legal norm, however, raised new difficulties. The most delicate issue was the granting of absolute ownership over affordable houses (achieved when the last instalment of the contract was paid or when a death occurred before that), in the cases of non-compliance with the obligation to establish a casal de família—because it was not permitted to sell or lease the house acquired, with the obligation to ensure its transmission by death. Observed by distinct judicial entities, the problem has received contradictory analysis and decisions.

[25] Teles de Sousa, *O Regime Jurídico das Casas Económicas* (Porto: Athena Editora, 1982) V–VI. The conception "casal de família" was established by Decree no. 7,033 of 16 October 1920, in line with the studies promoted by the lawyer Adriano Xavier Cordeiro.

[26] On this topic see: Álvaro Manuel Viegas Soares, *O Casal de Família como Fórmula de Unidade* (Bachelor thesis, Universidade de Lisboa, 1942).

[27] The "head of family" could be every Portuguese citizen, of both sexes, enjoying their full civil rights, who were, or not, married and in charge of the support of one or more descendants, siblings or descendants of these. Married women or widows could institute a *casal de família* in their property, but only for the benefit of their children or other descendants. The *casal de família* could embody one of the following modalities: the housing in which the owner (the head of the family) and his family lived; or separately or cumulatively, house and a) the premises necessary for the exercise of any mechanical work performed and operated directly by any of the members of the family, in benefit of these, or (b) one or more fields, at a contiguous or neighboring location, farmed under direct family management. Cf. Mário Raposo, "Casal de família," in *Enciclopédia Luso-Brasileira de Cultura*, IV vol. (Lisbon: Editorial Verbo, [s. n.]), 1309.

In 1960, the Procuradoria-Geral da República [Attorney General's Office] considered that the absolute propriety of the affordable housing would only be inalienable once it existed and while the "casal de família" remained there, but if the acquisition had been given to the acquirer, the Administration could not proceed with the onerous alienation of the affordable house. In 1962, the Supreme Court of Justice decided that the transmission of the affordable housing in favour of the acquirer required the incorporation and registration of the "casal de família," even if the term of discharge granted him full ownership of the house. Finally, in 1968, the Supreme Administrative Court argued that the beneficiary acquired full control of the household with the payment of the last house instalment, regardless of whether or not he fulfilled the obligation to set up the "casal de família."[28]

This question played an important and critical role in the corporatist regime. Claiming to favour and respect the property right, the State acted in an opposite direction, limiting and contradicting the general principle of alienability consigned in several articles of the Civil Code of 1867 (in force until 1966).[29] Not only was the alienation of the affordable houses incorporated in the regime of absolute property permitted, but also this permission was under the dependence of the executive power (through the Under-Secretary of State and then the Minister of Corporations and Social Welfare). Accordingly, the affordable house never went to a regime of free availability, remaining in the dependency of the state. Therefore, the increase of restrictions on the nature of the property's rights was established, as a consequence of what was commonly called as its social function (that is to say, its exploitation in accordance with a collective purpose, dissolving the sovereignty of the owner in the social utility), in keeping with the programmatic assertions of both the Constitution (Art. 35) and the Estatuto do Trabalho Nacional [National Work Statute] (Art. 13).[30]

In some cases, the casal de família was not complied with, as situations not contemplated by the legislator regarding the profile of the acquirer raised doubts about what was meant by the "head of the family." This is the case of single applicants for an affordable house, although with a dependent family. The proportion of the problem is inferred from the publication of successive opinions clarifying what was understood as head of the family and it was decided that single individuals—with ascendants, siblings or nephews in charge—could not be excluded from this designation (administrative decision hierarchically undertaken in SSECPS[31]), recognising that this type of household could have more economic and social difficulties than couples without children.

[28] During the transition to democracy, by Decree-Law no. 566/75 of 3 October, it was no longer compulsory to establish the *casal de família* in the cases in which such legal requirement had not yet been fulfilled. Cf. Teles de Sousa, *O Regime Jurídico*, VI and VIII.

[29] For a legal analysis of these issues see: Cf. Feliciano Resende, "A inalienabilidade das casas económicas," *Estudos Sociais e Corporativos*, (1965): 14. The new Civil Code of 1966 embodied the idea that the owner enjoyed full and exclusive rights of use, fruition and disposition of the things that belonged to him, within the limits of the law and complying with the restrictions imposed by it.

[30] The limitations on ownership were also dispersed among the administrative legislation. The Civil Code of 1966 did not correct this aspect: it only created a pole of concentration of all the restrictions placed on the content of the property right, by the Article 1,305. Cf. Júlio de Castro Caldas, "Sobre o Novo Código Civil," *O Tempo e o Modo. Revista de Pensamento e Acção*, no. 46 (1967): 185–86.

[31] The final decision was the subject of Dispatch by the Under Secretary of State for Corporations and Social Welfare (24 May 1934). The succession of opinions within that body can be consulted in: Cachulo da Trindade, *Casas Económicas, Casas de Renda Económica, Casas de Renda Limitada, Casas para Famílias Pobres. Legislação Anotada* (Coimbra: Coimbra Editora, 1951), 14–6.

The resolvable property right and the regime of succession applicable to the ownership of affordable houses were also problems that concerned the authorities and deserved important administrative decisions (taken into the circuit of decision formed by the INTP and the MCPS). Recalling the same attitude of preserving morality and family cohesion, it was defined that in case of divorce—and as long as the INTP did not promote the rescission of the contract—the right of resolvable property of the house had to be shared.[32] Greater complexity assumed the issue of the succession regime, following in genera the precepts in civil law. In cases of marriage under the general community of goods system or in an acquired community of goods system, it was stressed that the property belonged jointly to both spouses.[33]

Regarding the practical application of Decree no. 23,052, numerous difficulties arose for both the INTP and the beneficiaries for the distribution and the acquisition of affordable houses, despite the regulatory detail present in these aspects. In the first years, doubts immediately emerged about whether national syndicates could (or not) accept effective members and contributing members for the acquisition of affordable houses. It was decided that only the former had this possibility.[34] Another doubt was linked to the applications of effective members in the residence district who exercised their professional activity in a different district. The authorization of such applications was granted, considering that there was no restrictive criterion on the subject.[35] These questions are, nonetheless, associated with a more comprehensive problem: the success rate of occupancy of this type of constructions in the housing programme. From what could be ascertained, the system presented several imperfections, which ended up generating situations of non-occupation of buildings, due to the lack of demand among eligible candidates. Several other failures were also denounced in the urban planning, concerning not only the housing but likewise its insertion in the environment. This was the case, for example, in the neighbourhood of Encarnação (Lisbon) [MdH DB a19], where the 648 houses put out to tender in 1944 did not have enough candidates. The INTP justified this case that the lack of means of transportation made access difficult and allocated the houses to applicants, in addition to the thirty-day period indicated in the advertisements. This solution raised suspicions of undue favour at a time of strong housing demand (coinciding with the creation of bus routes to the neighbourhood).[36]

[32] *Boletim do Instituto Nacional do Trabalho e da Previdência*, no. 20, (1946): 412.

[33] *Boletim do Instituto Nacional do Trabalho e da Previdência*, no.16, (1946): 370.

[34] *Boletim do Instituto Nacional do Trabalho e da Previdência*, no. 19 (1946): 402.

[35] *Boletim do Instituto Nacional do Trabalho e da Previdência*, no. 13 (1947): 238.

[36] *Boletim do Instituto Nacional do Trabalho e da Previdência*, no. 20 (1946): 520.

5. THE SECOND CYCLE OF IMPLEMENTATION OF THE AFFORDABLE HOUSES PROGRAMME (1946–1974)

Although the problems with the allocations and distributions of affordable houses had arisen in the 1930s, only in the early 1950s were new models defined for their functioning, in a period that can be considered as a second phase in the implementation of the affordable houses programme. The update of the income limits for the qualification of the affordable houses and an amendment of some norms related to the classification of the applicants were promoted by Decree-Law no. 39,288 of 21 July 1953. In a certain way, it tried to correct discrepancies that had been exacerbated by the expansion of the classes of affordable houses, stimulated by Decree-Law no. 33,278 of 24 November 1943. Classes A and B, created in 1933, were transferred to classes C, D and E (2nd class judges, 2nd class plenipotentiary ministers and full professors were included in this), and the social benefit of housing ceased to cover the poor classes exclusively. The main novelties of Decree-Law no. 39,228 were, however, represented in the authorization of loans for the residents and in the institution of social service in this type of housing neighbourhoods.[37]

Later on, Decree-Law no. 43,973 of 20 October 1961 established an age limit for the admission of applicants, regardless the class of houses to be assigned, introducing the payment of the subpraxis for the over-aged cases; it changed the income limits for the allocation of an economic house, calculated now in accordance with the values of the benefits (and not in uniform quantities connected with the economic class), fixed, in its turn, in keeping with factors dependent on the different localities; it mitigated the consequences of contract rescission, due to misbehaviour by the head of the family or of his/her spouse, offering the possibility of renting the house to other members of the household; and it provided compensation for improvements in the houses to be redistributed. To a larger extent, the pressure made for the publication of this Decree-Law stems from the fact that more and more houses were available but not put out to tender. The reasons for delaying the opening of tenders varied. The lower classes of affordable houses had always had a small number of applicants. More common were the requests for transference between acquiring residents, of a particular class, that wanted to move to the class immediately above. The services made these transferences difficult in the case of households of the same class and type, as well as within the same neighbourhood—exception was made for specific reasons accepted by the MCPS.[38] Once the housing was distributed, other kinds of problems emerged, namely regarding the compliance with the instructions for use, stipulated in the house's regulations.

---

[37] The construction of general interest equipment was foreseen by Decree-Law no. 33,278, 24 November 1943, which underlined: the "school, centre for moral and social education, church, places for sales and playgrounds for children" (Art. 1.º, § 2.º).

[38] Historical Archive of Secretaria Geral do Ministério do Trabalho, Solidariedade e Segurança Social, Collection Dr. José Carlos Ferreira, Caixa 3: Parecer n.º 671–58.

Despite the warnings given at the moment that marked the reception of the house's keys,[39] as well as an increased surveillance, unauthorized works (ex. trellises, fence walls, wooden coops, wooden crates, etc.) were carried out. The penalties involved fines, requirement of legalization or demolition of the various works undertaken. The works of conservation, which were compulsory, required the permission of the municipal councils for their implementation.[40] It must be underlined that this second phase of implementation encompassed two new characteristics. One is the increase of the MCPS's intervention in the housing policy, stimulated by Decree-Law no. 39,978 of 20 December 1954, which assigned to the Minister of Corporations the choice of the places where economic housing neighbourhoods should be built, the decision of the number of houses and, more importantly, the percentages of distribution of acquirers by class of houses. This last point was extremely relevant in a political moment in which discriminatory aspects of the distribution of affordable houses among their beneficiaries were discussed. The tendency to favour syndicate members over civil servants was subject of correction and the latter increased their presence in the system from 25 per cent or 50 to 80 per cent, depending on the type of housing class.[41]

Another characteristic was the shift towards the promotion of construction of affordable houses within a framework that included the capital of social welfare institutions. This modality had originated, albeit superficially, in Decree-Law no. 35,611 of 25 April 1946, of which article 18 allowed the application of capital from social welfare institutions in affordable houses (as well as in affordable rent houses), but only in Lisbon and Porto. This orientation has not ceased to be deepened, following the policy of diversifying the types of economic housing programmes in urban areas, as will be clarified below. The authorities' argument for justifying this strategy was based on the idea that this was the direct application of the labour remuneration in works that revert in favour of those who constituted those same values. Dignifying the worker, took the centre of the discourse and, because it was a redistributive cycle, income tax exemptions were rejected. The free or almost free house was presented as incompatible with the guarantee of the right to the house.[42] The model endorsed by Decree-Law no. 35,611, however, did not work, since it was not possible to receive the state contribution through the Fundo de Desemprego [Unemployment Fund] (as was foreseen there initially). Without such support the social welfare institutions avoided the construction of affordable houses, since the monthly rent payments to be paid by the acquirers were fixed by law and undermined the profitability required in the application of their capital. A few years later, Decree-Law No. 40,426 of 6 July 1955 sought to create more favourable conditions to social welfare institutions that invested in the construction of affordable houses.

[39] The reception of the affordable house's keys was made during a solemn session, which could be presided over by the Minister of Corporations and Social Welfare or by the President of the Republic (as in the case of the 3000th and 2000th keys of the affordable rent houses). These were moments with good press coverage and served the authorities to promote the housing policy followed.

[40] Archive of the Secretaria Geral do Ministério do Trabalho, Solidariedade e Segurança Social, Pasta Casas Económicas: Circular P.4/7 of 20 January 1954, with clear instructions to the residents who acquired affordable houses included in the neighborhood of Restelo.

[41] Archive of the Secretaria Geral do Ministério do Trabalho, Solidariedade e Segurança Social, Ministério das Corporações e Previdência Social, Direção Geral do Planeamento e Habitação Económica, Pasta "Barracas": "Nota entregue ao Dr. Mota Veiga," 2 de Dezembro de 1957.

[42] *A Cooperação das Instituições de Previdência e das Casas do Povo na Construção de Habitações Económicas* ([Lisbon]: FNAT/ Gabinete de Divulgação, 1957), 29–31.

They were allowed to deposit their sums in the Fundo das Casas Económicas (FCE) [Fund for the Affordable Houses], managed by the Direção Geral de Previdência (DGP) [Directorate-General for Social Welfare], with an interest rate of not less than 4 per cent. The repayment of the invested funds and their interest would be in keeping with the amortization schedule approved by the MCPS.[43]

The changes in the type of financing of affordable houses coincided with the denunciation, in the early 1950s, that the legal provisions related to the reimbursement of the sums invested by the city councils in the construction of those houses had not been fulfilled. It was the case of the buildings established by Decree-Law no. 35,602 of 17 April 1946. The product of the subdivisions of the city councils was no longer deposited in the FCE. This was due to the suspension or reduction of loans granted by Caixa Geral de Depósitos, Crédito e Previdência to municipalities at the same time that the Ministry of Finance continued to include in the budget of the funds of the DGEMN to meet these charges. In 1956, after this case was examined by a commission appointed by the Minister of Finance, it was decided to solve the problem of reimbursement to the city councils by granting a new request for new loans. The restoration of the sums in the Treasury's coffers would be the responsibility of the Fund, on account of its own income. Consequently, the DGEMN avoided the allocation of a budget for construction, in view of the estimated costs, without having been assured that credits had been granted for the construction plans.[44]

6. EXPANSION IN THE ECONOMIC HOUSING POLICY: THE DEVELOPMENT OF NEW PROGRAMMES

In the post-war period, affordable houses ceased to be the main focus of the affordable housing policy and new programmes emerged, creating affordable rent houses and rent-controlled houses. Another novelty was the involvement of the Casas dos Pescadores [Fishermen's Houses] in the policy of affordable housing, as determined by Decree-Law no. 35,732 of 4 July 1946. Indeed, the Junta Central das Casas dos Pescadores [Governing Board of the Fishermen's Houses] had the possibility of borrowing from the CGD in order to proceed with the construction of buildings. The revenues and funds of the Fishermen's Houses served as collateral for the loans, which could be repaid in twenty years.[45] The programme of demountable houses, which had already been explored in previous years, was also recovered and adapted, although with a very limited scope and designed to deal with housing situations of extreme poverty in different parts of the country.[46]

[43] *A Cooperação das Instituições de Previdência*, 19 and ff.

[44] Archive of the Secretaria Geral do Ministério do Trabalho, Solidariedade e Segurança Social, Ministério das Corporações e Previdência Social, Direção Geral do Planeamento e Habitação Económica, Pasta "Barracas": "Problema dos Reembolsos do Estado: Posição das Câmaras na matéria," [1956]; Pasta Casas para Funcionários Públicos: "Nota," 23 de Janeiro de 1960.

[45] At the present stage of this investigation, it is not possible to determine the extension of this housing programme or to characterize its success or failure, given that we do not know the number of housings that were built under its dependence. Even without empirical confirmation, we can admit the hypothesis that this programme was based on the experience of the construction of houses for fishermen, strongly promoted after 1932, which stems from the context of the urban improvement policy.

[46] These had been the cases of government permissions for: the construction of housing for poor families, in the Funchal district by the municipalities of Funchal and Câmara de Lobos, in 1936 (Decree-Law no. 24,488 of 1 April 1936); construction of demountable houses in Lisbon (Decree-Law no. 28,912 of 12 August 1938); construction of demountable houses in Lisbon and Porto, by the cities councils, in 1943 (Decree-Law no. 33,278 of 24 November 1943); construction of demountable houses in Celas, by the city council of Coimbra, in 1944 (Decree-Law no. 34,139 of 24 November 1944).

To be sure, the new programmes were a response to demographic growth in the areas of greater urban concentration and to the problem of aging buildings, although, in the best estimates of the late 1960s, they would only provide a cover of 20% of the replacement deficit.[47] They also had other objectives, namely the aim to impose greater regulation on the construction sector itself as well as to avoid speculation on the price of construction materials and on the land.

The construction of Affordable Rent Houses created for middle class families was foreseen by Law no. 2,007 of 7 May 1945. Its novelty resides in the liberalization of construction for cooperative or anonymous societies and firms, industrialists or concessionaires of public services, with sufficient capital to assume the cost of the land before the municipalities, although it did not prevent the participation of social welfare, corporative, and economic coordination organizations. In order to attract such investors, who could only receive a fixed maximum amount of dividends, the State guaranteed them the acquisition of land at compatible prices, tax benefits (such as exemption from sisa for the acquisition of land and for the first transmission of buildings or industrial contribution as well as the stamp and transmission taxes in the acts of constitution, dissolution and liquidation) or loans provided to the construction companies (with an interest rate of 4% for a maximum term of two years). The houses built could be for sale and rent, or only for rent, but in the latter case there were limits—it would have to be done with an income contained within the base income offered by the builder at the time of land acquisition. Total or partial subleases were prohibited. In this programme, the rents were lower for the acquirer due to the fact that life, sickness, disability, and unemployment insurance obligations ceased.[48]

The programme of rent-controlled houses would emerge two years later, created by Decree-Law No. 36,212 of 7 April 1947. It included the construction of income buildings, in which there was "a maximum rent to be charged for floors intended for housing, with decreasing bids on the rent and from a base defined in public advertisements, as well as the concession of important facilities, namely the concession of municipal land at affordable prices and not subject to competition, and the exemption from the sisa (property transfer tax) when buying the same land and in the first transmission of the buildings and in the propriety tax for a period of twelve years."[49] The increase of the two above-mentioned housing modalities implied a definition of several matters, such as expropriations, surface, and fixation rights and the need to update the housing rent. This adjustment was achieved through Law 2,030 of 22 June 1948, which consigned the principle that the rights of individuals could not be an obstacle to the realization of public utility purposes

[47] Gonçalves de Proença, *Discurso na Cerimónia de Entrega da 3000 Chave das Casas de Renda Económica do Bairro dos Olivais e da Inauguração do Centro de Recreio Popular da Encarnação em 7 de Abril de 1968* ([Lisbon]: [s.ed.], [1969]), XII.

[48] *Diário das Sessões*, no. 51 (1 March 1944): 170–1. It should be underlined that neither in the National Assembly nor in the Corporate Chamber was there any enthusiasm for the diploma's proposal, received in February 1944, which gave rise, after amendments, to Law no. 2007 of 1945. The prosecutor António Vicente Ferreira, in charge of reporting the opinion to the Corporate Chamber, considered that this was not a commercially viable investment. He insisted on the lack of qualitative and quantitative studies that would allow us to conclude that the new housing programme met the needs of urban housing. In his opinion it would be necessary to carry out a survey on economic and social aspects (house rents and household income) of urban housing, as was done in Belgium, Spain and England (Op. Cit., 425–7). In the National Assembly, critics argued that it was more important to improve housing and public spaces than to build new houses; they also required the reform of the tenancy law and suggested the creation of twenty-year urban plans for Lisbon, as well as the establishment of a central body endowed with powers and means of study in order to define the public housing policy (*Diário das Sessões*, No. 136 (8 February 1945): 295; no. 137 (9 February 1945): 304).

[49] "Opinion no. 48/X: Regime das Casas de Renda Limitada" in *Pareceres (X Legislatura)*, I vol. (Lisbon: Câmara Corporativa, 1974), 175–76. The legal regime of houses with controlled rent was later improved by Decree-Law no. 41,532 of 18 February 1958, in particular with regard to the alienation of municipal land and the sale of the houses under horizontal property, which was done by lottery between applicants for its acquirement.

pursued by the state, as long as they were compensated with just indemnity. In assuming this position, the Executive amplified the action and the ends of the state, following the evolution that also covered the expropriations for public utility.[50]

The situation in regard to expropriations was also clear: the rights of the expropriated were compressed while those of the expropriator were enlarged. The expropriated lost the full recovery of indirect capital gains; besides, the process that guaranteed the exact fulfilment of the legal criteria that determined the compensation value underwent a greater process of jurisdiction. Nonetheless, it allowed the state and local authorities to reserve the recovery of future capital gains. Additionally, the municipalities were still in possession of the so-called surface right, that is to say, the reserve of construction sites for shopping centres in the cities, hoping to encourage the construction of family houses. Another important innovation of Law 2,030 was that it allowed the Government to subscribe part of the capital of public limited companies for the construction of affordable rent houses and rent-controlled houses. As for rent, the legislator refused to give a definitive structure to the institution of tenancy; whenever possible, it followed the principle of raising old rents to a fair amount and reducing the highest of the recent ones.[51] With this option, it was reinforced the protection provided to tenants was reinforced. Landlords could not choose the tenants, nor alienate the houses or fix the rents. With the intervention of the administration and the predominance of rules of public law on the income buildings, investors and builders of the affordable houses were negatively affected in the short-term. For this reason the core of their business tended to move to the construction sites and materials, given that they could obtain reimbursements of public funds or resources for the construction of buildings of free rent.

Within the new housing programmes created in the aftermath of the post-war period, the only one that did not establish relations with the corporatist or economic coordination agencies, nor with the social welfare (not even with the private sector) was the housing programme for poor families or homeless people (related to urbanization works or others of public interest), created by Decree-Law No. 34,486 of 6 April. This endeavor was imposed by the government on administrative bodies and on the Misericordia, which could, for this purpose, benefit from subsidies of 10,000$ per house, granted in equal parts by the state and the Unemployment Fund. The MOPC, through the Direção-Geral dos Serviços de Urbanização [Directorate-General for Urbanization Services], was responsible for the approval of projects.

[50] By Decree no. 19,881 of 12 June 1931, had been enshrined the principle that from simple approval of the projects would result in the immediate recognition of public utility.

[51] *Diário das Sessões*, no. 132 (5 February 1948): 281.

These were demountable houses, which should be grouped according to the availability of the land, and whose acquisition and urbanization were determined by the administrative bodies and the Misericórdias. The rents of the houses of this programme were set by the Ministry of Finance and the license to occupy such houses was granted on a precarious basis in the form of a permit. Decree-Law No. 35,106 of 6 November 1945, which regulated the distribution of houses to poor families, forced the municipal councils to demolish the previous houses, after the installation of these families in the new housing.

7. WELFARE INSTITUTIONS TRANSFORMED INTO MAIN FINANCING ENTITIES

The transformation of social welfare institutions into the main financing entities for affordable housing, based on Law no. 2,092 of 9 April 1958, took place at a moment when the construction of affordable rent houses, the raising of capitals and the administrative burden had been given to particular entities—but it was an unsuccessful initiative. This difficulty had manifested itself just a year after the publication of Law No 2,007 of 1945[52]. Regarding the type of affordable rent houses, the Federação de Caixas de Previdência—Habitações Económicas (FCP-HE) [the Federation of Welfare Fund—Affordable Housing (FCP-HE)], created in 1946 and subject to the INTP, was responsible for their construction in collaboration with the municipal council.[53] But it must be noted that, among other competencies the Minister of Corporations and Social Welfare was responsible for formulating the agreements between the Federação and municipalities to implement the construction and the corresponding contract works.

The rent to be fixed was also subject to the approval of the Minister, taking into account the cost of the buildings, the profitability of the capitals, and the economic capacity of the applicants. The principle of compensation of charges, calculated on the basis of the social interest to be achieved, allowed the attribution of fixed lower rents to beneficiaries of lower wages or incomes. The financial compensation required by these cases was obtained from the rents of the beneficiaries with the best incomes, which exceeded their technical limits. It must be noted that it was possible to update rents under certain circumstances. Affordable rent houses could be converted into buildings under horizontal ownership, as long as all tenants requested this capacity and were in the required conditions. The distribution of affordable rent houses was made through a call for tenders, announced by the repartição das Casas Económicas da Direção Geral de Previdência [the Division of Affordable Houses of the Directorate-General for Social Welfare] (through notices in the newspapers of greater circulation),

[52] *A Cooperação das Instituições de Previdência*, 17.

[53] On the FCP-HE and its practices, see: Nuno Teotónio Pereira, "A Federação das Caixas de Previdência—1947–1972," in *Escritos (1947–1996, selecção)* (Porto: FAUP Publicações, 1996); Maria Tavares, "Habitações Económicas— Federação de Caixas de Previdência: uma perspetiva estratégica," in *Actas 1.º CIHEL, Desenho e Realização de Bairros para Populações com Baixos Rendimentos* (Lisbon: Argumentum, 2010), 47–51.

according to the Regulation approved by order of 28 June 1960 of the MCPS. Each tender was normally valid for two years[54]. Also falling within the scope of the social welfare institutions and following the publication of Decree-Law No. 43,186 of 23 September 1960, the state and the real estate market set up a new relationship grounded on two axes. The first created a real estate credit policy, allowing the welfare institutions to also allocate their capital to loans as a mean to purchase housing for their beneficiaries. Expenses resulting from such loans were expected to be mitigated by reimbursable contributions from the Fundo Nacional do Abono de Família [National Family Allowance Fund]. The value of the loan should be lower than that of the property and it would be subject to credit guarantee[55]. The second, rooted in the same law, allowed pension funds to allocate their capital not only to affordable housing (affordable rent houses, affordable houses), but also to: 1) properties in order to establish services and commerce; 2) buildings framed by a horizontally owned regime; and 3) free rent buildings. In 1962, the Social Welfare reform, established by Law no. 2,115 of 18 June, redefined the application of the amounts invested by social welfare institutions.

This new strategy opened up novel perspectives on the urban real estate property trade, but the intervention of public funds generated some anomalies. Regarding the lending to welfare beneficiaries for construction or acquisition of their own house, there were unconformities that particularly affected the economically disadvantaged classes. Also disturbed by the inaccessibility of rents promoted by the free market regime, these populational segments continued to resort to subleasing, overcrowding, and sheltering in shacks.[56] In this scenario, cluster construction increased sharply, despite being discouraged since it leads to the "segregation of certain classes or professional categories." Its expansion was, however, based on the fact that it allowed rents compatible with the economic possibilities of the recipients.[57]

By the end of 1970, the FCP-HE had built 12371 homes and 4966 were under construction, for a total investment of 2 104 000$. The modality of affordable rent housing had proved, apparently, to be better structured than that of the rent-controlled houses, whose regime was not replaced until 1967. In the same year, it was acknowledged that the latter programme had led to misuses and frauds against the law.[58] Under the rule of Marcelo Caetano, its replacement was defended and gave rise to the presentation of the law project no. 11/X, approved, with changes, in the Parliament. The military coup of 25 April 1974, while it overthrew the dictatorship ended up by precluding the diploma's publication.

[54] *Instituições de Previdência: Aplicações de Valores* ([Lisbon]: [s. ed], [196?]), 25–31.

[55] *A Cooperação das Instituições*, 36–37, 49–51.

[56] "Opinion no. 56/X," 230–31.

[57] "A Política Habitacional da Previdência," 11.

[58] "Opinion no. 48/X," 172.

Likewise, it remained to be revealed what was the impact of the successive administrative and legislative measures taken from 1970 onwards (in correspondence with what had been designed for the Third Development Plan), in the housing and urban planning domains, namely: the creation of the Secretariat of State of Urbanism and Housing (the new coordinating entity for housing policy),[59] drafting of urban plans,[60] "land law"[61] and their systematic expropriation plans therein contained,[62] as well as the regime for urban renewal plans.[63]

8. FINAL CONSIDERATIONS

The policy of affordable housing in the urban environment during the Portuguese authoritarian state was extensive. Yet it was not a successful story. It lasted for several decades, being maintained, without interruptions, by the executive throughout the life cycle of the regime. It was diversified in numerous terms, namely in the housing programmes implemented, the coverage of the national territory (mainland and islands) and the funders (not only the government, the municipal councils, corporative bodies and social security institutions, but also Portuguese banking). It reached a new level of modernization, helped by the reorganization of the state and, in particular, by its new institutions, which also operated in a new kind of functionality, identified in doctrinal terms as corporatist.

However, this policy generated just a small part of the housing production, since the financial resources were mainly "channelled into the free and speculative housing market." The increase in the number of shacks in the main cities of the country, from the 1950s on, and the inability of the authorities to contain this plague is a perfect example of the lack of resources and means used to counteract the negative effects of urbanism, which was in continuous expansion. While state intervention solved some conjunctural problems, such as the crisis of the construction industry, through the granting of stimulus packages to the sector—largely subsidized by the various public institutions—at the same time it created new constraints, as the increase in speculative construction or the constant increase in rents demonstrated. Grounded on a complex legislative production, the multiple housing programmes set the trend for the predominance of the rules of public law and the intervention of the administration in the private law domain, thus curtailing private property rights as well as the freedom to negotiate and choose.

[59] Decree-Law no. 283/72, 11 August. Followed by Direção-Geral dos Serviços de Urbanização (Decree-Law no. 605/72, 30 December) and Fundo de Fomento da Habitação (Decrees-Law no. 473/71 6 November, and no. 583/72, 30 December).

[60] Decree-Law no. 560/71, 17 December, and Decree no 561/71, same date.

[61] Decree-Law no. 576/70, 24 November.

[62] Decree no. 182/72, 30 May.

[63] Decree-Law no. 8/73, 8 January.

On the whole, the policy of affordable housing embedded in the peculiar social policy of the Estado Novo did not have the necessary strength to benefit broad segments of the population—with low and average incomes—as it was advocated by the government agents. In truth, it was very fragmented and created exclusions among the segments of beneficiaries. It eventually strengthened differentiations between classes and within them. As in the previous political regimes, the inequality between landlords and tenants was maintained, with a greater sense of protection for the latter, who were supposed to be safeguarded from the dangers of economic inequality with the help of the state.

Finally, it should be pointed out that the affordable housing programmes did not enhance the consolidation of the corporatist project aimed for by the state but contributed to the acceleration of its transformation and evolution into a "mixed economy," which was not very different from Western Europe at that time. This path was supported by employing compromise solutions between public and private capitals (present in the construction of affordable rent houses and rent-controlled houses), as early as the mid-1940s, but also in opening up the development of cooperative societies, which were promoted from the end of the 1960s. This path is also suggested by the political-legislative dimension of affordable housing policy, since it contributed to providing the public administration (central and local) with new means to constrain the development of construction (for example, by the consecration of expropriation by public utility or by the introduction of the notion of surface right). This characteristic helped to encourage the intervention of local authorities in an active policy of construction, namely in the sphere of affordable housing. Nevertheless, this modernization had a meaning: the transition from a regulatory state to an intervening state that promoted institutional distinctions, thus helping entities without corporatist representation and upon which no attempt was made to incorporate them into the corporatist organizational structure.

ACKNOWLEDGEMENTS

The authors would like to thank Anabela Cristovão and Teresa Carvalho for their valuable help and advice in consulting documents not yet inventoried at the Arquivo da Secretaria Geral do Ministério do Trabalho, Solidariedade e Segurança Social.

REFERENCES

PRIMARY SOURCES:

I—Archive sources

. Biblioteca do Gabinete de Estudos e Planeamento do Ministério do Trabalho, Solidariedade e Segurança Social: Fundo de Desenvolvimento da Mão de Obra: Pastas 02.01/07, 02.01/08, 02.01/12, 02.03/03.

. Arquivo da Secretaria Geral do Ministério do Trabalho, Solidariedade e Segurança Social: Acervo Dr. José Carlos Ferreira: Caixas 1–4; Ministério das Corporações e Previdência Social, Direção Geral do Planeamento e Habitação Económica: Pasta "Casas Económicas," "Barracas."

II—Published sources: journals and reviews

Boletim do Instituto Nacional do Trabalho e da Previdência, 1946–1947.

Elo. Serviço Social Corporativo e do Trabalho, 1970.

Estudos Sociais e Corporativos, 1962–1965.

III—Published sources: other

A Cooperação das Instituições de Previdência e das Casas do Povo na Construção de Habitações Económicas. [Lisbon]: FNAT/ Gabinete de Divulgação, 1957.

Comissão Executiva da Exposição de Obras Públicas. 15 Anos de Obras Públicas 1932–1947. Volumes I and II. [Lisbon]: Imprensa Nacional de Lisboa, [1948].

Diário das Sessões, 1944–1968.

Edificações Urbanas. Urbanização. 2ª ed.. Porto: Livraria Lopes da Silva Editora, 1946.

Instituto Nacional do Trabalho e Previdência. *Dez Anos de Política Social 1933–1943*. Lisbon: Oficianas Gráficas da Casa Portuguesa, 1943.

Pareceres (X Legislatura). III vol. Lisbon: Câmara Corporativa, 1973.

O Pensamento de Salazar. 32 Anos ao Serviço de Portugal. Revolução Corporativa. S. l.: Ed. Lit. António Cruz, 1960.

Pereira, Nuno Teotónio. Escritos (1947–1966, selecção). Porto: FAUP Publicações, 1996.

Pereira, Pedro Teotónio. *Memórias. Postos em que servi e algumas recordações pessoais*. Vol. I Lisbon: Verbo, 1972.

Proença, Gonçalves de, *Discurso na cerimónia de entrega da 3000 chave das Casas de Renda Económica do Bairro dos Olivais e da inauguração do Centro de Recreio Popular da Encarnação em 7 de Abril de 1968*. [Lisbon]: [e.ed.], [1969], II–XV.

Salazar, António de Oliveira. "Conceitos económicos da nova Constituição," Discursos 1928–1934. Coimbra: Coimbra Editora Lda, 1935, 185–209.

Trindade, Cachulo da. Casas Económicas, Casas de Renda Económica, Casas de Renda Limitada, Casas para Famílias Pobres. Legislação Anotada. Coimbra: Coimbra Editora, 1951.

BIBLIOGRAPHY

Acciaiuoli, Margarida. *Casas com Escritos. Uma história da habitação em Lisboa*. Lisbon: Editorial Bizâncio, 2015.

Barata, José Fernando Nunes. "Habitação," *Dicionário Jurídico da Administração Pública*. Ed. by José Pedro Fernandes. Vol. V [S. l.]: [s. ed.], 1993, 41–62.

Caldas, Júlio de Castro. "Sobre o Novo Código Civil," O Tempo e o Modo. Revista de Pensamento e Acção. 46 (1967): 175–190.

Figueiredo, Rute. *Arquitectura e Discurso Crítico em Portugal (1893–1918)*. Lisbon: Edições Colibri/ IHA—Estudos de Arte Contemporânea da Faculdade de Ciências Sociais e Humanas da Universidade Nova de Lisboa, 2007.

Raposo, Mário. "Casal de família," Enciclopédia Luso-Brasileira de Cultura. Vol. VI Lisbon: Editorial Verbo, [s. n.], 1309–1310.

Resende, Feliciano. "Casas económicas: propriedade resolúvel e absoluta," Estudos Sociais e Corporativos 4 (1962):

Resende, Feliciano. "A inalienabilidade das Casas Económicas," Estudos Sociais e Corporativos 14, (1965): 83–109

Soares, Álvaro Manuel Viegas. "O casal de família como fórmula de unidade." Graduate Thesis in Historical-Juridical Science. Lisbon: Faculdade de Direito da Universidade de Lisboa, 1942.

Sousa, Teles de. *O Regime Jurídico das Casas Económicas*. Porto: Athena Editora, 1982.

Stolzi, Irene, "Politici sociale e regime fascista: un'ipotese di lettura," Quaderni Florentini 46, 2017, 241–291.

Tavares, Maria, "Habitações Económicas—Federação de Caixas de Previdência: uma perspetiva estratégica." Actas 1.º CIHEL, Desenho e realização de bairros para populações com baixos rendimentos. Lisbon: Argumentum, 2010, 47–51.

Teixeira, Manuel C. "As estratégias de habitação em Portugal, 1880–1940," Análise Social 115, 1992: 65–89.

Progressively Picturesque, Reluctantly Modern: Building a Timeline of the *Casas Económicas* (1933–1974)

SÉRGIO DIAS SILVA
University of Porto, Faculty of Architecture, Centre for Studies in Architecture and Urbanism

ABSTRACT

Informally organized at first, densely bureaucratized not long after, the *Casas Económicas* (CE–Affordable Houses) Programme was a housing initiative created by the Portuguese *Estado Novo* in 1933 to develop a nationwide response to the demand for dwellings for lower-income families. It was soon transformed into a form of social control and conditioning of the inhabitants, later evolving into a reward system for layers of support for the regime, focusing on public workers and top employees of private companies.

This paper will focus on the work of three architects within the Affordable Houses Programme, each representing one generation of architectural and urban thought and one phase of the development of the programme.

Focusing on the family as the core of society, the *Casas Económicas* used the individual, isolated house as a symbol for a new social order and a new, content middle class, apolitical and in line with a stratified society in which each hierarchical line would not contaminate the next.

The archives connected to the Programme open the door to the study of a history of transformation—the evolution of the Portuguese dictatorial regime's views on housing architecture, urban design, community life, family matters, and social control—and bring to light an attempt to create real-scale models of a new social order.

BIOGRAPHY

Sérgio Dias Silva (Porto, 1982) is an architect (FAUP, 2007) currently developing a doctoral thesis on the *Casas Económicas* of the Portuguese *Estado Novo*. He is a member of CEAU and of the MdH Project Team since 2013. He has collaborated with Paulo Providência Arquitetos Associados (2007–2008), Manuel Fernandes de Sá Lda. (2008–2010), and MVCC Arquitetos (2015–2017), and was a technical assistant at Parque Escolar EPE (2010–2013). In 2013 he formed the architecture collective e.*studio* with Pedro Monteiro and Rodrigo Cruz. His research interests focus on the development of modern architecture in Portugal, its origins, influences, and cultural references.

INTRO

The *Casas Económicas* Programme (PCE–Affordable Houses Programme) was created in 1933 by the *Estado Novo* (New State) regime, in what appears at first to be an attempt to aggregate under the State's auspices a set of housing initiatives started by city councils in response to demands for cheap housing for families with low resources. Informally organized at first, densely bureaucratized not long after, the Programme is one of the few constant elements in the Portuguese dictatorial regime from its inception to its demise; it outlasted the hyperactive Duarte Pacheco[1] and the master of ceremonies Antonio Ferro[2] and it survived cosmetic operations in the State's core organization in the aftermath of the war and after the rise of Marcello Caetano.[3] Only the fall of the regime would mean the true end of the Programme, which grants us the opportunity to analyse the architectural production of a housing initiative that was central to the regime and was managed by top figures in proximity to the dictatorship.

THE REGIME AND THE PROGRAMME

1933 was a pivotal year in the development of the Portuguese dictatorship. In April, the new constitution was published, instituting an authoritarian, Catholic, conservative, corporatist, and antiparliamentarian State. Limitations to freedom of speech and reunion were decreed in the weeks after, and the next few months were of intense preparation and analysis[4] of the laws that would structure the organization of work—the institutionalization of corporatism. In August 1933, drafts of the main decrees of the organization were published in national papers, launching a (fairly limited) discussion of the corporatist organization to come. This set of decrees form the basis for the concretization of a corporatist State, basically structuring a new order for labour, with the division between Grémios (Guilds) and Sindicatos (Unions) and the institutional regency of that relation, with the Instituto Nacional do Trabalho e da Previdência (INTP–National Institute for Work and Welfare) and the Estatuto do Trabalho Nacional (ETN–National Labour Charter). Amongst that sequence of decrees, one set the basis for the PCE, the first housing initiative in Portugal set on a national scale.

The programme was based on a principle of a monthly rent/instalment for a period of twenty years of conditional private property ("propriedade resolúvel," resolvable property), depending on the social behaviour of the buyer. This principle represented a constant threat over ownership and was guaranteed not only by a fear of being observed but also, very soon into the programme, by

---

[1] Duarte Pacheco (1900–1943) was a Portuguese civil engineer who served as Minister of Education in 1928 and Minister for Public Works from 1932 to his death in 1943. In spite of having a top seat in the Salazar dictatorship, he became a rather unanimous figure as the author of a large public works programme and is remembered as such today.

[2] Antonio Ferro (1895–1956) was a Portuguese journalist, writer, and politician. After a series of very popular interviews with the dictator Salazar, he was invited in 1933 to head the Secretariado da Propaganda Nacional (SPN–Secretariat for National Propaganda) and create a modern public image for the dictatorship, blending epic views of the past with the exultation of local traditions.

[3] Marcello Caetano (1906–1980) was a Portuguese jurist and university teacher who replaced Antonio Oliveira Salazar (1889–1970) as Presidente do Concelho de Ministros (President of the Council of Ministers), and was in charge of the dictatorship from 1968 to the fall of the regime in 1974. He had been an important figure in the formation of the corporatist state from the beginning of the 1930s, collaborating in the writing of the 1933 Constitution and held several posts in the dictatorship, such as head of the paramilitary organization Mocidade Portuguesa (Portuguese Youth) from 1940 to 1944, Chairman of the Câmara Corporativa (Corporatist Chamber) from 1949 to 1955 and Minister for Colonies from 1955 to 1958.

[4] Fátima Patriarca, *A Questão Social no Salazarismo 1930–1947* (Lisboa: Imprensa Nacional Casa da Moeda, 1995).

actually being observed, as the regime instituted the figure of the "fiscal," one or more according to the dimension of the estate—a professional *neighbourhood watch* that reported to the INTP.

Initially two types of houses were created, A (smaller) and B (larger), to be distributed according to the family's income, each with three variations (one, two, and three rooms), according to the size of the family. The decree established a few generic principles for the estates but the main concept that was present was that of the isolated house, with a small flower garden in the front and a kitchen garden in the back. The goal: to create a new middle class of homeowners, supporters of the regime, eliminating class struggle and suppressing the germination of criticism of the regime or revolutionary ideas.

THE ARCHIVE

The *Casas Económicas*'s architectural production and revision was centralised in a service of the Direção-Geral dos Edifícios e Monumentos Nacionais (DGMEN, Directorate for Monuments and Public Buildings) resulting in a concentration of data in the archives of that organization, discontinued in 2007.

The collaboration between MdH and the Instituto da Habitação e Reabilitação Urbana (IHRU–Institute for Housing and Urban Refurbishment) was reflected in the participation in the H100PT Project, a celebration of 100 years of public housing laws in Portugal (1918–2018) and allowed for the consultation of the existing raw data in the DGEMN archives.[5]

That data, of which there is still not a systematic registry, is of great importance to the study of a large period of public investment in Portugal, not only in housing but in a large variety of public buildings. The analysis that was developed for this investigation was as deep as possible, but still only begins to scratch the surface of a rich compilation of information that will take years, first to fully register and later to analyse, an enterprise that is probably only possible to launch and achieve on a state level. That endeavour would certainly result in a rich contribution to the study of Portuguese architecture in the 20th century and to the questioning and completion of the views of those who were simultaneously fundamental historians and essential characters of that architectural history, such as Nuno Portas and Pedro Vieira de Almeida.

The time span of the *Casas Económicas*, more than 40 years, implies that several generations of architects were involved in its development and in its contradictions.

[5] This paper is an extension of my collaboration in the article that was a part of that participation. Virgílio Borges Pereira, João Queirós, Sérgio Dias Silva and Tiago Castro Lemos, "Casas Económicas e Casas Desmontáveis: Génese, estruturação e transformação dos primeiros programas habitacionais do Estado Novo," in Ricardo Agarez, *Habitação: 100 Anos de Políticas Públicas em Portugal 1918-2018* (Lisboa: Instituto da Habitação e Reabilitação Urbana, 2018), 83–117.

I have selected three 20th-century Portuguese architects who played important roles in the development of the PCE and in the transmission of international references and influences on the programme's architecture.

The archive suggests the possibility of several lines of analysis that could complement the understanding of the regime's approach to housing. The most interesting information, however, is often not found in designs, but in correspondence. One has to take the designs with a grain of salt, as what was kept in the official archives were not drafts, ideas, and polemical proposals; what we find in there are mostly final versions of designs that had been thoroughly reviewed and are therefore in keeping with the State's objectives and beliefs. Some surprises have survived, but a lot of reading between the lines is necessary in order to filter through this immense amount of information.

Fig. 1 Casas Económicas Estate of Alto da Serafina (Lisbon, 1934–38), Arch. Raul Lino. Source: Fotografia Alvão, Lda., "Bairro de casas económicas de Lisboa," PT/CPF/ALV/005133. Centro Português de Fotografia.

PHASE ONE (1933–1938):
RAUL LINO AND THE *PICTURESQUE*

Raul Lino (1879–1974) is a household name in Portuguese architectural history. Perhaps the only Portuguese author who is a best-seller in that field,[6] he is known as the symbol of Portuguese house authorship; he is credited with creating a catalogue of traditional Portuguese elements of construction, a claim that he himself would probably vehemently reject. He was a spearhead for the creation of the imagery of the regime, responsible for the refurbishment of national monuments from the end of the 1930s and the fuel for a great polemic within the architecture field in the 70s, when Pedro Vieira de Almeida dared to call him Modern—another statement Lino would possibly scoff at. Modernity is nowadays seen as a broader concept, and Lino's own modernity, particularly in his residential buildings of the beginning of the 20th century, is not violently disputed, so to find traces of modern concepts of housing design in his work in the *Casas Económicas* is not so shocking; whether it is possible to attribute the designs to Lino is another question.

Lino participated in the Portuguese presence in the 1929 Sevilla World Exhibition, which was followed by the publication of a book on "The Portuguese House," a subject he would return to later. At this point, Lino was already seen as an expert in the matter and that is the justification used by Fernando Jacome de Castro,[7] head of the Affordable Houses Section at Direção-Geral dos Edifícios e Monumentos Nacionais (DGEMN–Directorate-General for Public Buildings and Monuments), when he officially proposed Lino be hired to draw façades—and only that, at first—for the *Casas Económicas*; the specificity of the contract suggests the house plans were developed prior to Lino's arrival. In 1932, Duarte Pacheco had invited Porfírio Pardal Monteiro[8] to develop an Affordable House, but while the design's description is described in a letter from the architect to the Public Works Minister—mentioning, for instance, the eventual use of low-cost industrial materials—, the resulting design is unknown.[9] In 1935, Lino travelled to Brazil for a series of lectures, one of which focused on the *Casas Económicas*.[10]

The first Affordable House type is a minimal dwelling, with a small kitchen, a bathroom, and two to five rooms of similar size, of which one hoards functions: entrance hall, living room, dining room, drawing room, and family room all in one; if we add to that the standardization of construction elements, only an archetypal roof and a frugally decorated façade—a glimpse of colour in the wall base or, at most, a plaster trim on doors and windows—separates these experiments from other minimal dwellings built in the decade before in central Europe.

[6] Ricardo Agarez, *Algarve Building: Modernism, Regionalism and Architecture in the South of Portugal, 1925–1965* (Routledge, 2016).

[7] Fernando Jacome de Castro (1892–1964) was a Portuguese civil engineer and member of the military who was the head of the Secção das *Casas Económicas* (SCE–Affordable Houses Section) of the DGEMN from the beginning of the programme until the end of the 1940s and a member of the Conselho Geral das Obras Públicas (Public Works General Council).

[8] Porfírio Pardal Monteiro (1897–1957) was a Portuguese architect, very close to Duarte Pacheco, who commissioned him to design some of the most representative works of the first years of the dictatorship, such as the Instituto Superior Técnico (Lisboa, 1927) and the Instituto Nacional de Estatística (Lisboa, 1931). He was the Portuguese correspondent of the French magazine *Architecture d'Aujourd'hui* and his office housed its headquarters during the Second World War.

[9] Sérgio Dias Silva and Rui J.G.Ramos, "Housing, Nationalism And Social Control: The First Years Of The Portuguese *Estado Novo*'s Affordable Houses Programme," in *Southern Modernisms: From A to Z and Back Again*, Joana Cunha Leal et al (eds.) (Porto: Centro de Estudos Arnaldo Araújo–CESAP/ESAP, Instituto de História da Arte–FCSH/UNL, 2015), 255–274

[10] Marta Rocha Moreira, "O Valor do Tempo: O Programa Intelectual e Arquitectónico de Raul Lino." (PhD Thesis, Faculdade de Arquitetura da Universidade do Porto, 2017).

If Lino's participation in the development of the Affordable House types is unclear, some estates may be attributed to him, according to the archive. There can be found signed plans both of Alto da Serafina (1934–1936) [MdH DB a224], the first estate built in Lisbon, and Terras do Forno (also known as Belém, 1934–38) [MdH DB a225], an estate where the transition from the first to the second phase of the programme is clear. Establishing authorship in designs developed by central services, with most drawings unsigned, is a tricky path, but cross-referencing several notes we may draw a scheme of Lino's work with the programme. He was hired to draw façades for and collaborate in several estates,[11] including visits to the estate of Vila Viçosa, in Alentejo; drawings of Affordable House types are available in his personal archive;[12] the human resources file of another architect at DGEMN, Joaquim Madureira, notes their collaboration in the first estates built as part of the programme in the North of Portugal (Ilhéu [MdH DB a220] and Condominhas [MdH DB a8] in Porto, and Bragança [MdH DB a217]).

Crossing these historical connections between estates and analysing their designs, we find a set of similar cases that allow us to clearly establish an image not only of the first phase of the programme, but specifically of the regime's initial view for the Affordable House. Ilhéu, Condominhas, Serafina, and Belém have a common urban setting that is very easily transposable to Lino's views and education. These relatively small estates (fifty-four, 102, 204, and 200 houses respectively) resort to references of romantic and picturesque tradition, setting narrow winding paths in front of the houses, respecting topography and with every main façade facing the sun.

The cities of Lisbon and Porto have very clear block structures, the former a descendant of the city's transformation after the earthquake of 1755 and the latter a reminiscence of medieval property division, with narrow plots, main façades directly over the public space and rear façades facing private backyards. The principle of the isolated single-family house, or at most the semi-detached house, evokes the idea of the Garden City but the concretization is mostly just a refusal of urban life, with a self-dependency focused on the family nucleus—the father's job and the kitchen garden for small-scale production—and not on a communal view of the estate. The approach to urban design clearly follows influences of Camillo Sitte (1843–1903), an inspiration easily explained by Lino's education in Germany.[13]

The programme's first phase, then, is structured around this very peculiar paradox of a *progressive Picturesque*, crossing an exercise in *existenzminimum* with a reproduction of a mythical country family life that is, in itself, a mirror of the contradictions in the regime.

---

[11] Process «PTDGEMN:DSARH-PESSOAL-0572/01– Raul Lino» (Sistema de Informação do Património Arquitetónico, Forte de Sacavém).

[12] Raul Lino's estate is partially located at the Art Library of the Calouste Gulbenkian Foundation, Lisbon.

[13] Irene Ribeiro, *Raul Lino, Pensador Nacionalista de Arquitectura* (Porto: Faculdade de Arquitetura da Universidade do Porto, 1995).

António Ferro, head of state propaganda, devoted his mandate to a precise balance of these necessities of celebrating tradition—inventing it when reality did not suffice—and absorbing innovation—taming it when it was deemed too dangerous for weaker minds.

With two areas, one to the north following the principles described above, and one to the south with a more *urban* approach to street design, Belém is a transition estate. It is an example of the transformation that was operated in the programme after 1938, when Duarte Pacheco returned to the post of Minister for Public Works with his mind set on the 1940 celebrations of the anniversaries of the Portuguese kingdom (1140) and independence from Spain (1640).

The Centennials became a synonym for the *Estado Novo*, particularly as public buildings that symbolize this era—schools, banks, post offices—were built all across the country.[14] Housing-wise, the new *epic age* of the regime is reflected in a 1938 law that established a new programme of temporary housing—*Casas Desmontáveis*[15]—to address the housing needs of those evicted by large public works in Lisbon and determined that the one-storey type was to be avoided in the *Casas Económicas*, as it was connected with the idea of poverty.[16] Raul Lino, then almost 60 years old, had been since 1936 responsible since 1936 for the organization of national monuments refurbishment and the next generation of architects, most of whom were already working for/with the regime, was called upon to transform the Affordable House.

PHASE TWO (1938–1956): PAULINO MONTEZ AND THE *CITY BEAUTIFUL*

Paulino Montez (1897–1988) was an architect and urban planner who had a very active role in the profession, in politics, and in academia.[17] He obtained the title of architect in 1923 from the Fine Arts School in Lisboa (EBAL), was part of the administrative bodies of the Lisbon Municipality in the 1930s and participated in the management of the Costa do Sol Urban Plan, the first major initiative in urban planning launched by the *Estado Novo*. He was honoured by the state in 1937 and again in 1943, following a close cooperation with the regime in several urban plans and in the organization of several exhibitions and commemorative events. He was a member of the National Board of Education, the National Fine Arts Council, and the National Fine Arts Society, and was the director of EBAL from 1949.

[14] The public works of the Portuguese dictatorship have been subject to several in-depth studies recently. Joana Brites, *O Capital da Arquitectura: Estado Novo, Arquitectos e Caixa Geral de Depósitos 1929–1970* (Lisboa: Prosafeita, 2014); Marta Prista, "Discursos sobre o passado: investimentos patrimoniais nas pousadas de Portugal" (PhD Thesis, Faculdade de Ciências Sociais e Humanas, Universidade Nova de Lisboa, 2011); Luís Miguel Correia, "Monumentos, Território e Identidade no Estado Novo: da definição de um projecto à memorização de um legado" (PhD Thesis, Faculdade de Ciências e Tecnologia, Universidade de Coimbra, 2016); Maria Tavares, "'Habitações Económicas' da Federação de Caixas de Previdência: Arquitectura e Modos de Actuação no Exercício do Projecto" (PhD Thesis, Faculdade de Arquitectura da Universidade do Porto, 2015);

[15] Literally "demountable houses," these were effectively demountable in the three estates built in Lisboa–Boavista [MdH DB a539], Furnas [MdH DB a541], and Quinta da Calçada [MdH DB a540]—not so much in those built in Porto [MdH DB a555] and Coimbra [MdH DB a554]; while Coimbra's estate still stands, all others have been demolished after several decades of *temporariness*.

[16] Decreto 28,912, 12 August 1938.

[17] Paulino Montez published several works on the topics of the Arts, Architecture, and Urban Planning: Paulino Montez, such as *A Estética de Lisboa: da Urbanização da Cidade* (Lisboa, 1935); *Da Educação Estética: Algumas Observações Sobre a Finalidade da Cultura do Sentimento do Belo na Formação da Juventude* (Lisboa: Casa Portuguesa, 1941); *Do Ensino de Belas Artes em Portugal Através dos Séculos* (Lisboa, 1960), among others, including a series of books on his own urban designs.

Paulino Montez's participation in the *Casas Económicas* is centred in two of the most recognizable designs within the programme, both located in Lisbon: the Alvito Estate (1937–1944) [MdH DB a235] and the Encarnação Estate (1939–1944) [MdH DB a19]. As we've seen, by the end of the thirties the Affordable House model was in need of revision; the new houses should be bigger, and the estates themselves would become bigger too—Encarnação would be the largest estate, with about 1,000 houses, until the construction of Olivais Sul in the 1960s. DGEMN services were no longer sufficient for the demand for housing projects and several architects were hired to develop new designs. These contracts were made basically among a group of experienced architects that had been working on public buildings—Paulino Montez, Luiz Benavente, Carlos and Guilherme Rebello de Andrade, among others—and consequently the designs would be fairly conservative both in their approach to city planning and in the house design itself. That idea is reinforced when it is noted that the typologies used are the same for several of the estates[18]—possibly following an initial design by Luis Benavente (1902–1933)[19]—with each architect developing his own façade design for those typologies.

As other housing initiatives were launched, the *Casas Económicas* set their focus on an audience with higher income, and as a consequence two new types were created in 1943,[20] C and D, with bigger areas and more complex interior designs. If the first phase of the Affordable Houses the focus was on a minimal house, the second phase would invest in a bourgeois view of housing, with an increase in the specificity of room usage. Gone were the days when Jacome de Castro said he did not see the need to build garages as the tenants in these estates would not be able to afford cars;[21] in the forties and fifties, drawing rooms, maids' rooms, and entrance halls enter the vocabulary of the *Casas Económicas*, complexifying the house and tending to the demands of an upper class of candidates.

Paulino Montez's designs for the programme were developed in the last years of the 1930s, and therefore did not use the new C and D types, but construction works would last until the end of the following decade. The suggestion of a new target audience for the programme is, however, already clear in his designs.

Alvito, with 100 houses, is a peculiar case within the programme, both in structure and in design. It is an initiative of a pension fund for city council workers[22] and it was designed and built to the northwest of Lisbon between 1937 and 1938; by 1942, however, it remained unoccupied. It was bought by the State to be integrated in the *Casas Económicas*. It is an early example—for the Portuguese context, naturally—of a modern approach to housing design. The

---

[18] Some of the drawings at SIPA were used as basis for copies and have a list of estates to which they apply.

[19] Luís Benavente, "Projecto de Casas Económicas" (Arquivo Nacional da Torre do Tombo, Lisboa).

[20] Decree 33,278. 24 November 1943.

[21] An internal memo of the DGEMN signed by Jacome de Castro and dated 19 January 1944 reads "Within the way of life that is current in our country, I don't understand, and most would not understand, how Affordable Houses of classes A and B could have any type of garages." Process "CE–Assuntos Diversos." Forte de Sacavém: Sistema de Informação do Património Arquitetónico.

[22] Caixa de Socorros e Reformas dos Operários e Assalariados da Câmara Municipal de Lisboa

estate featured flat roofs—for which Montez referenced the traditional construction of the South of Portugal—and only two typologies (two and three rooms) used in three-storey buildings with a common staircase and in two-storey buildings with a private exterior stair for the upper floor. Placed facing south, the estate grows in width and in height towards the north, with the two-storey buildings placed around a social centre and a public garden and the three-storey buildings to the back of the estate. A central line marks the garden, the social centre, and the main street, and establishes an axis of symmetry. Although there is a similar approach to street design to that seen in Lino's proposals, turning façades to backyards, it does not seem far-fetched to find more than a few similarities between Montez's project and the design by Alexander Klein (1879–1961) for the Bad Durrenberg Siedlung (1928–1930) in Germany; Klein was certainly a familiar figure within the Portuguese architecture community by the end of the 1930s, and his investigation would be directly quoted by Jacobetty Rosa (1901–1970) when developing housing types in the following decade[23] as a new, different programme was under development by the regime.

[23] Jacobetty Rosa, "Grandes Problemas de Lisboa: A Construção de Casas de Renda Económica," *Revista Municipal*, no. 26. (1945): 33–41.

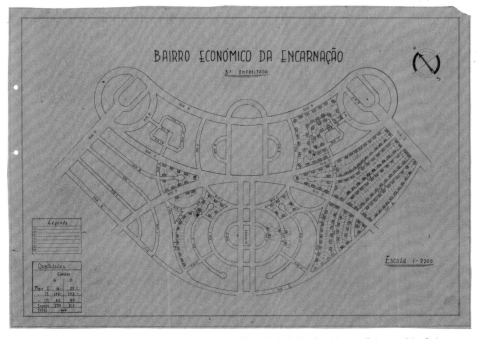

Fig. 2 *Casas Económicas* Estate of Encarnação (Lisbon, 1939–45), Arch. Paulino Montez. Scheme of the 3rd construction stage. Source: Luis Benavente Collection, Cx. 17, pt. 111, PT/TT/LB/C/001/0111. ANTT.

Symmetry is also a theme in Encarnação (about 1,000 houses). It is a large estate—the semi-detached house model with front garden and kitchen garden implies a quite extensive urban occupation[24]—organized between a central axis, the main tree-lined street with central gardens, and two narrower axes to the north and southeast that form two geometrically identical halves. The geometry of the urban plan suggests it was developed along the lines of a Beaux-Arts approach to urbanism, probably with the influence of foreign urbanists hired by the regime in the thirties and forties—particularly Alfred Agache[25]—and other classical-based plans such as those of the City Beautiful Movement in North America. Encarnação's plan works as a graphical piece, self-contained, and self-relating, to be seen from above and achieving a *picturesque monumentality*, reinforced by decorative pieces, such as the special types of houses with small "towers" without practical use to mark the entrance to the estate's central axis.

PHASE THREE (1956–1974): JOÃO ANDRESEN AND THE MODERN CITY

João Andresen (1920–1967) was an architect and urban planner who, because of his death at a young age, has a very limited presence in the historiography of Portuguese architecture. However, since obtaining the title of architect in 1948 he had a very active professional life, both in his residential designs (such as Casa de Caxias, 1953–1955) and public works (Lisbon's Palace of Justice, with Januário Godinho, 1962–1970), but is mainly remembered for his 1956 winning proposal for the Monument to the Infante de Sagres, a 15th-century Portuguese prince who was one of the main sponsors of the start of the Age of Discoveries and a central figure in the mythology of the New State. He was the author of the urban plan of the Affordable Houses Estate of Viso (1959–1965), [MdH DB a11] in Porto, and Cedro (1959–1965) [MdH DB a261] in Vila Nova de Gaia. The Viso estate process is particularly interesting at this point of the programme, as for the first time the Ministry for Public Works accepted—on a trial basis—the use of collective housing in the programme, following a decades-long quest by the regional offices of DGEMN at Porto,[26] probably with some influence from the Municipality.[27] In 1956, a new type of Affordable House was created—type "a"— that brought the programme back to its attempted origins by developing a type that was hierarchically below the existing ones and that would have lower construction costs and, consequently, lower rent. To achieve considerable reductions in cost, two methods were tested by the programme: the creation of shared areas and slabs, that is, collective housing types, and the return to minimum single-family houses with small areas and poor construction quality.

[24] Encarnação occupies an area of approximately 47 ha.

[25] Donat-Alfred Agache (1875–1959) was a French architect and urban designer. He developed urban plans for the Lisbon area between 1935 and 1936 and deeply influenced the irst generation of Portuguese urban designers. Margarida Souza Lôbo, *Planos de Urbanização: A Época de Duarte Pacheco* (Porto: Faculdade de Arquitetura da Universidade do Porto, 1995).

[26] Joaquim Madureira, while working at the Porto branch of the DGEMN, developed a collective housing design for the Pasteleira area, later the location of the Marechal Gomes da Costa Affordable Houses Estate [MdH DB a3]

[27] The Porto council developed a collective housing design for the Rua Duque de Saldanha in 1937, against the will of the government. Ramos, R.J.G., Gonçalves, E., Silva, S.D, "Segregation in Housing and Urban Forms: An issue of private and public concern," *Social Sciences* 7, no.9:145.

Fig. 3 Casas Económicas Estate of Viso (Porto, 1958–65), Arch. João Andresen. Perspective drawing of shared exterior areas. Source: Cristiano Moreira collection. Photo by the author.

João Andresen was part of a *"brand new generation"*[28] of Portuguese architects that would step into the profession in the second half of the 1940s and would be the first to fully embrace—but not apply—the full orthodoxy of the Modern Movement. Up to date on the architectural debate and conscious of the ever-varying focus of the top publications, this generation would clash several times with the intentions of the dictatorial regime, and Andresen was not only not an exception to that rule but is a symbol and a pawn of the game of give and take that the New State used to its advantage. In 1956, Andresen won a international competition to design a monument for the Infante de Sagres at the promontory of Sagres, in the southwest corner of Portugal, which, had it been built, would be the prime achievement of the New State, celebrating the mythical era of Portuguese Expansion. It was the third attempt by the New State to build that monument, after two failed competitions in the 1930s, and it was never built; it is said that Andresen's proposal was too modern for the liking of Salazar and therefore would not be funded. The intricate story of the Sagres competitions has been told and analysed[29] and what matters to this text is that it seems that as a compensation for not building the monument, João Andresen got a few public contracts for Lisbon—with Januário Godinho—and Viana do Castelo.[30] In 1959, Andresen was hired—by ministerial decree—to design both the urban plan and the architectural design for the estate of Viso, in Porto.

[28] Nuno Portas, "A responsabilidade de uma novíssima geração no Movimento Moderno em Portugal," *Arquitectura* no. 66. (1959): 13–14.

[29] Pedro Vieira de Almeida, *A Arquitectura no Estado Novo: Uma Leitura Crítica* (Lisboa: Livros Horizonte, 2002).

[30] Sérgio Dias Silva, "João Andresen: Uma Ideia de Arquitectura" (Architecture Degree Diss., Faculdade de Arquitetura da Universidade do Porto, 2007)

Building a Timeline of the Casas Económicas (1933-1974)

Andresen had been an assistant professor of Urbanology in the Fine Arts School of Porto since graduating in 1948 and had developed very profound research in the field of urban design that is mostly unknown, except for the dissertation he prepared to achieve tenure in 1961 and self-published the year after. "Para Uma Cidade Mais Humana" (Andresen, 1962) (which can be translated as "Towards a More Humane City") is a critique of two of the most mediatic urban designs of the time, Brasilia by Lucio Costa and Niemeyer and Chandigarh by Le Corbusier and Pierre Jeanneret (adapting existing plans by Albert Mayer and Matthew Nowicki), where Andresen lamented the loss of the human scale in those designs. These remarks are closely connected to the writings of Lewis Mumford and reflect Andersen's critical analysis of the development of modern urban design.

The adoption of collective housing models in the *Casas Económicas* is coeval to the introduction of more radical intentions for urban and communal spaces. These were new concepts solely in the programme's perspective, as they had been introduced in Portuguese public housing programmes through Nuno Teotonio Pereira's intervention in the Habitações Económicas (HE–Affordable Housing) and could already been seen as dated in an international context. Since the HEs were fairly independent from state scrutiny, the introduction of these models in the *Casas Económicas*, still pretty much a battle ground for a conservative view of housing within the regime, in fact represented a considerable compromise on the part of the state, a *reluctant Modern*. It is inevitable to see in this a tacit admission of failure of the single-family house model as a viable response to the lack of affordable housing. Andresen's works for the *Casas Económicas* would introduce *density* to the programme's development, concentrating the lower-rent typologies in collective housing buildings and consequently liberating vaster areas for green and communal spaces, separating walking paths from the circulation of cars and, probably for the first time in the *Casas Económicas*, developing spaces for the *community*.

The higher-rent typologies would maintain the single-family model in these estates, reinforcing the separation between the estates' low and high rent inhabitants; ironically, the conservative fear of collective buildings as growing fields for socialist thought had delayed a much more noticeable class hierarchization in public housing. Although Andresen was hired to design new types of houses for these estates, of which some drawings are found in his archive, the DGEMN services would opt for a different solution, developing a type that would be used not only in Viso and Cedro but also in other estates of the same period, such as Olivais Sul, in Lisboa [MdH DB a586], Rossio ao Sul do Tejo, in Abrantes [MdH DB a258] and in the 2nd phase of the Entroncamento estate [MdH DB a256].

RETURN TO THE ARCHIVE

The Mapping Public Housing project has been set around an effort to list and recognise a set of possibly minor architectures that are charged with untold and unknown histories and stories. To survey state-subsidized housing architecture is to find not only hidden chapters of Architectural History but also their connections to the social and political views that fed and transformed them.

I have suggested just one of the ways how the identification of a corpus of case studies that are not connected by their authors, their dates or their influences, but simply by their funding and bureaucratical organization, may contribute to set new timelines of architectural history in Portugal. The *Casas Económicas* is but an example of how the study of a mostly unknown initiative creates new narratives of the evolution of architectural though, its social, economic or political context, and its acceptance not only by younger generations but progressively by more conservative architects, by the population and, finally, by state institutions more averse to change and transformation.

I have also tried to expose various *degrees of modernity*. From the experiments on minimal housing hidden in a colourfully popular shell right at the start of programme—the "progressive Picturesque"—to the acceptance of by then already questionable principles of urban design—the "reluctant Modern"—, this study, and this research project, reflect an attempt at reviewing clean historical sequences that followed the architectural discussion of the avant-garde but mostly ignored its translation to daily life of the profession.

This review will only be possible by revisiting the archives, crossing information and making it available to academic and general publics, as the history of housing is a fundamental part of the history of private life and, consequently, the history of the community.

ACKNOWLEDGMENTS

Sergio Dias Silva has a PhD Studentship from the Fundação para a Ciência e Tecnologia (SFRH/BD/114961/2016). Access to SIPA archives was possible through the H100PT Research Project–100 Anos de Políticas Públicas de Habitação em Portugal 1918–2018 Coordinated by arch. Ricardo Agarez at the Instituto da Habitação e Reabilitação Urbana.

BIBLIOGRAPHY

Agarez, Ricardo. *Algarve Building: Modernism, Regionalism and Architecture in the South of Portugal, 1925–1965.* Routledge, 2016.

Almeida, Pedro Vieira de. *A Arquitectura no Estado Novo: Uma Leitura Crítica.* Lisboa: Livros Horizonte, 2002.

Brites, Joana Brites. *O Capital da Arquitectura: Estado Novo, Arquitectos e Caixa Geral de Depósitos 1929–1970.* Lisboa: Prosafeita, 2014.

Moreira, Marta Rocha. "O Valor do Tempo: O Programa Intelectual e Arquitectónico de Raul Lino." PhD Dissertation, Faculdade de Arquitetura da Universidade do Porto, 2017.

Patriarca, Fátima. *A Questão Social no salazarismo 1930–1947.* Lisboa: Imprensa Nacional Casa da Moeda, 1995.

Portas, Nuno. "A responsabilidade de uma novíssima geração no Movimento Moderno em Portugal." *Arquitectura* no. 66. (1959): 13–14.

Ribeiro, Irene. *Raul Lino, pensador nacionalista de arquitectura.* Porto: Faculdade de Arquitetura da Universidade do Porto, 1995.

Silva, Sérgio Dias. "João Andresen: Uma Ideia de Arquitectura." Architecture Degree Diss., Faculdade de Arquitetura da Universidade do Porto, 2007.

Silva, Sérgio Dias, and Rui J.G.Ramos. "Housing, Nationalism And Social Control: The First Years Of The Portuguese *Estado Novo*'s Affordable Houses Programme." In *Southern Modernisms: From A to Z and Back Again*, edited by Joana Cunha Leal et al, 255–274. Porto: Centro de Estudos Arnaldo Araújo–CESAP/ESAP, Instituto de História da Arte–FCSH/UNL, 2015.

Tavares, Maria. "'Habitações Económicas' da Federação de Caixas de Previdência: Arquitectura e Modos de Actuação no Exercício do Projecto." PhD Dissertation, Faculdade de Arquitetura da Universidade do Porto, 2016.

Rosa, Jacobetty. "Grandes Problemas de Lisboa: A Construção de Casas de Renda Económica." *Revista Municipal*, no. 26. (1945): 33–41.

Plain Façades and Exuberant Rooms:
A Tour of Casas Económicas

ELIANA SOUSA SANTOS
University of Coimbra, Centre for Social Studies

ABSTRACT

This essay presents a parallel between two descriptions of spaces that present a contradicting interior and exterior. One is the definition of Plain Style by the historian Julio de Castilho, and the other is the description of the writer Mary McCarthy's tour of several examples of Casas Económicas—part of the social housing programme of the Estado Novo regime. The idea of Plain Style according to the original term used by Castilho characterizes an austere façade that camouflages more exuberantly decorated interiors. This contrast was absent in George Kubler's appropriation of the concept as Plain Architecture, given that it focused mainly on the overall simplicity of religious architecture built in Portugal during the sixteenth and seventeenth centuries; this defined the architectural practice of a poor country that was resourceful in creating great spatial effects with scarce resources. In this essay we will return to Castilho's definition to look at its inherent contradiction—the simplicity of the public façades and lavish interiors of palatial homes. A similar contradiction is found in the description that McCarthy gave of her tour of some of the homes that were built under the Casas Económicas programme. McCarthy's perspective, and her debates with Hannah Arendt on the distinction between the social and the political will shed light on the nature of the social housing programmes developed in Portugal during the twentieth century.

BIOGRAPHY

Eliana Sousa Santos is an architect, researcher, and assistant professor of architecture. She was the recipient of the Fernando Távora Prize 2016/17. She curated the exhibition The Shape of Plain (Gulbenkian Museum Lisbon), an associate project of the Lisbon Architecture Triennial 2016. She was a visiting postdoctoral research fellow at Yale University in 2013/14, and is currently researcher at CES, University of Coimbra. She taught at ESAD. CR, presently she is a guest assistant professor at ISCTE-IUL. She has a degree in architecture from the Technical University of Lisbon, a master's degree from the University of Coimbra, and a PhD from the University of London.

PLAIN FACADES AND EXUBERANT ROOMS

The term Plain Architecture—deriving from the expression Plain Style, or Estilo Chão, in Portuguese—is well established in the historiography of architecture in Portugal. It has a genealogical history that can be summarized as follows: the term Plain Style was first used by the historian and founder of Lisbon Studies, Júlio de Castilho[1] and was much later adopted by the art historian George Kubler to characterize the architecture of a specific period of Portugal's history between the sixteenth and seventeenth centuries "during an age when resources were scarce."[2]

Kubler's retroactive analysis of Plain Style classified it as in the same formal family of Modernism, and consequently the book secured a place in the historiography of art in Portugal. The expression Portuguese Architecture became equivalent, during recent decades, with a kind of architectural practice that can be classified within the family of Plain Architecture and not only as a qualifier to architecture built within the country's borders or designed by a Portuguese architect.[3]

Thus, the term *Plain* in its relation to architecture became coloured by Kubler's appropriation and to some extent it revealed his experience in Portugal during the 1950s, where he spent a considerable length of time. Some of Kubler's photographs of Portugal, as in the image depicting Lisbon's aqueduct, inadvertently frame something else, other realities beyond the architectural object represented. Often, these images capture signs of poverty that eventually seeped into Kubler's main argument, that Plain Architecture was a characteristic of a poor country's resourcefulness.

In the 1961 *Arquitectura Popular em Portugal*, a survey of Portuguese vernacular architecture commonly described as a project of a progressive group of Portuguese architects,[4] a common ground is described as follows:

"Isn't there, in this plurality, something common, specifically Portuguese? We believe it is so, that there are some constants, of subtle distinction, perhaps, but real. They are not about a unity of types, forms or architectural elements, but something of our people's character that is revealed in the buildings it produces—something that is difficult to define rigorously, but that had enough power to 'domesticate' the formal eccentricities of the Baroque and transform them, within us, into a humble exuberance."[5]

Whereas in the more conservative publication *Breviário da Pátria para Portugueses Ausentes*, sponsored by the propaganda department in 1946, a similar description about the taming of the Baroque is described by the historian Reynaldo dos Santos:

---

[1] Júlio de Castilho, *Lisboa Antiga: O Bairro Alto*, Edited by Gustavo de Matos Sequeira, 3rd ed. (Lisbon: Câmara Municipal de Lisboa, 1954).

[2] George Kubler, *Portuguese Plain Architecture: Between Spices and Diamonds, 1521–1706* (Middletown, Conn.: Wesleyan University Press, 1972), xv.

[3] Paulo Varela Gomes, "Arquitectura Não Alinhada," *JA Jornal Arquitectos*, no. 200 (2001): 4–9.

[4] See Joana Cunha Leal, "Plain, Pombaline and (Post)Modernism: On Some Pre and Post-Kublerian Narratives on Portuguese Architecture," *CES Contexto, Debates*, no. 3 (2013): 7–15, 10.

[5] Translated from the Portuguese by the author: "Não existirá, contudo, nessa diversidade de feições, qualquer coisa comum, especificamente portuguesa? Cremos que sim, que há certas constantes, de subtil distinção, por vezes, mas reais. Não dizem respeito a uma unidade de tipos, de feitios ou de elementos arquitectónicos, mas a qualquer coisa do carácter da nossa gente, revelada nos edifícios que constrói—qualquer coisa difícil de definir com rigor, mas que assim mesmo teve poder bastante para "domesticar" os desvarios plásticos do Barroco e torná-los, entre nós, humildes na sua exuberância." Francisco Keil do Amaral, *Arquitectura Popular Em Portugal* (Lisbon: Sindicato Nacional dos Arquitectos, 1961), xi.

Fig. 1 Lisbon Aqueduct. Photo by George Kubler. Source: Portuguese Album 1953. Yale University Library, New Haven, Manuscripts and archives, George Alexander Kubler Papers, MS 843, 97-M-22, Box 20.

"The Baroque of the sixteenth and seventeenth centuries [. . .] presents in Portugal a very different character of these epochs, through the different influences and through the national character it expresses. The art of the seventeenth century reveals in its austerity, in its near pride in poverty, its interior strength. . ." [6]

The notion of Plain Style was thus characterized by a relationship between the "virtuous character" of the "nobility" of Portugal and their tastes in simple and austere architecture, which was thus passed through and used by different ideologies. But let us dwell on the notion as defined by Castilho; he uses the expression Plain Style as an equivalent for noble austerity and a tasteful dislike of manifesting wealth that he attributes to the character of the Portuguese aristocracy; he goes to some length to describe these characteristics formed into an "unostentatious" architecture, thus creating the moral aura of Plain Architecture:

"This way, revealed perhaps in their orderly life, in the exact commitment to their duties, in their unostentatious and sincere charity, in their observance of religious and civil laws, accorded with the plain style of architecture, that certainly wasn't that opulent Gothic of the fifteenth century, which produced many wonders of the type of private houses abroad." [7]

[6] "O barroco dos séculos XVII e XVIII [. . .] apresenta em Portugal um carácter muito diferente nas duas épocas, quer pelas influências diversas que traduz quer pelo sentido nacional que exprimiu. A Arte do séc. XVII traduz na sua austeridade, na sua pobreza quási orgulhosa, na sua fôrça interior. . ." in Reynaldo dos Santos. "A Evolução e o Sentido Cultural Da Arte Portuguesa," in *Breviário Da Pátria Para Os Portugueses Ausentes*, 269–78. (Lisboa: Secretariado Nacional de Informação, 1946), 276.

[7] "Essa feição, revelada talvez no viver pautado, no cumprimento exacto do dever, na caridade sincera e não ostentosa, na observância dos preceitos religiosos e civis, casava com o estilo chão da arquitectura, que não era certamente aquele opulento gótico do século xv, que no género de habitações particulares tantas maravilhas produziu lá fora." in Júlio de Castilho, *Lisboa Antiga*, 144.

It was this narrative of noble austerity as materially manifest in the exteriors of the aristocratic residences that served to shape the "austere nature" of the architecture read by Kubler as modern. However, on the same page, Castilho stresses that this austerity was only evident in the facades, whereas the interiors housed many luxuries, such as vast tile panels, frescoed ceilings, exotic woods, and imported textiles.[8] The character of Plain Architecture defined by Kubler as innately simple and as precursory of modernism only works if we ignore this contradiction. The narrative of austerity and sobriety in taste misses the insight that the simplicity of the exterior of the buildings camouflaged a lavish interior.

A TOUR OF CASAS ECONÓMICAS

A similar contradiction between sparse exteriors and opulent interiors is particularly explicit in the description of Casas Económicas in Lisbon by the American writer Mary McCarthy, who in 1954 was invited by SNI–Secretariado Nacional de Informação, the department of propaganda of the Estado Novo regime—to visit a series of neighbourhoods of the social housing development programme. Her host was Mr. Rodriguez, whom she presumed to be a "vice-chieftain" of the SNI. These housing projects aimed to create a solution to the housing shortage that afflicted the country then, and continued to do so in the following decades. The Casas Económicas programme aimed to promote the ownership of property by state functionaries or corporate employees by providing a home lease during a 25-year period.[9]

McCarthy—who at the time was already a fairly established author in the United States[10]—wrote two articles about her visit to Portugal published in *The New Yorker* magazine[11] and *Harper's* magazine.[12] The argument of these articles was, however, already sketched in a private letter she wrote to her friend, Hannah Arendt, on the first days of her stay in Lisbon. In this letter, she describes bits and pieces of her tour of the capital that Arendt knew. In her witty and implacable description she tries to convey the contradictions she finds in Lisbon and attempts to sketch an opinion about the most prominent activity she saw: ". . .everywhere, in the suburbs, and even in the city itself, Housing Projects are springing up. I must say, they do them better than we do."[13] Later, upon further reflection, she would question the housing projects she had seen and even compared them with the evictions that she knew about in New York, where entire populations were being removed,[14] and seriously ponder if the examples in Lisbon were really as good as she had first assumed.

[8] As in ."..the cupoladed ceilings of chambers and salons, the walls and doors, were sometimes made of Oriental wood, inlaid, with paintings and gold leaf of a certain value [. . .]. The luxury allowed to these owners to a large extent was indeed the tiles; not only did they shimmer in the turrets of churches, but they decorated the interior of rooms and stairways of the houses that people called palaces. We will concede [to these noblemen] their panels of good tiles covering the lower part of the walls, which were whitewashed and naked, covered however (probably), in the summer; by the celebrated gilded leather panels." Translated by the author from the Portuguese ". . .os tetos da cúpula de câmaras e salões, e as paredes e portas, eram por cá alguma vez de madeira do Oriente, marchetados, com pinturas e dourados de certo custo [. . .].Um luxo que os proprietários se permitiam com larga mão era o azulejo; esse sim ; não reluzia só nos coruchéus dos templos, nas enfeitava por dentro as salas e escadarias dos casarões a que se chamava palácios. Concedamos pois a estes os seus silhares de bom azulejo orlando a parte inferior das paredes, de si caiadas e desnudadas, revestidas porém (é provável), no verão; dos célebres panos de guadamecins,. . ." in Júlio de Castilho, *Lisboa Antiga*, 145–46.

[9] There were several more of such programmes in place from the 1930s to 1969, when Fundo de Fomento à Habitação was created. McCarthy saw some of these different housing programmes: "During the course of our tour, we saw not only "Economic Homes," Mr. Rodriguez' own domain, but Prefabs, Free Housing, Limited Rent Housing, and Free Rent Housing." Mary McCarthy . "Mister Rodriguez of Lisbon," in *On the Contrary*, 132–45. (New York: Farrar, Straus & Cudahy, 1961), 136.

[10] McCarthy's first novel *The Company She Keeps* (1942) had been a success. At the time she visited Portugal she wrote for the Partisan Review and was in the process of publishing the novel *The Group* (1954).

[11] The subject of McCarthy's visit and description of poverty was briefly noted in Eliana Sousa Santos, "Portuguese Plain Architecture: When History Creates a Myth," in *Papers from the International Scientific Thematic Conference EAHN 2015: Entangled Histories, Multiple Geographies Belgrade* (Belgrade: University of Belgrade, 2017), 286–90.

[12] See: Mary McCarthy. "Letter From Portugal." The New Yorker, 1955. http://archives.newyorker.com/?i=1955-02-05# and Mary McCarthy. "Mister Rodriguez of Lisbon."

[13] Letter to Hannah Arendt in Carol Brightman, ed. *Between Friends: The Correspondence of Hannah Arendt and Mary McCarthy, 1949–1975* (London: Secker & Warburg, 1995), 17.

[14] "I held my peace, mindful of the New York slum dwellers who had been dispossessed to create Stuyvesant Town and Peter Cooper Village." in McCarthy, "Mister Rodriguez of Lisbon," 143.

McCarthy wrote repeatedly how, for her, Lisbon was a city that on first impression seemed to be prosperous and pretty, populated by well-dressed and polite people, but that after pondered observation, these happy facades seemed to be camouflaging widespread poverty. In the three texts that McCarthy produced about her visit to Portugal, even in the letter she sent to Arendt, she confessed finding the country "quite puzzling on the economic level, a strange mixture of prosperity and poverty,"[15] and she repeatedly manifested her bewilderment over the gap between the cost of products and most people's earnings.

McCarthy often tried to calculate what kind of products were affordable to the working class—she had the habit of asking the people employed at the places she visited how much they earned— and realized that it would be impossible for most people to afford a basic middle-class living. The sights of poverty were very evident but her hosts seemed to politely ignore this; when McCarthy asked about the plight of the poor in Portugal she was told that the living conditions she saw in the streets of Alfama were a matter of choice rather than condition. Nevertheless, remarks about a certain pride in poverty abounded in the general discourse, specifically one shared by her host, paralleling the life of Salazar, who she describes as "the so-called dictator," who "lived very simply and austerely, stayed up late at night, working, always working"—with his policies—"saving, always saving, till the national debt was paid."[16]

As mentioned in her letter to Arendt, McCarthy's impression of Lisbon was also marked by the numerous social housing projects being built, so that the sight of them becomes a running gag throughout her texts:

"'What's that?' I kept asking, pointing to orange-roofed white buildings, gleaming new, that were spread out on the green hills of Lisbon's suburbs. 'Housing project,' the old man invariably answered, simply and proudly. This was the first thing I found out about the Estado Novo; whenever you point to anything, the answer is 'Housing project.' After a few days, I learned to frame the question the other way around. 'Housing project?' I would cautiously inquire. 'Sim, Senhora.'"[17]

McCarthy had been invited to tour several homes of the Casas Económicas described as "the backbone of the building programme" by McCarthy's host—Mr Rodriguez—who considered himself to be the "patriarch of 10,084" of these homes "occupied, according to his estimate, by 40,336 persons."[18] The houses that McCarthy visited were in the Madre de Deus [MdH DB a233] neighbourhood, in the eastern part of Lisbon and had been completed a few years before, so that its occupants were already established in their homes.

[15] in Brightman, ed. *Between Friends*, 17.

[16] Mary McCarthy, "Letter from Lisbon," 83.

[17] Ibid.

[18] Mary McCarthy, "Mr. Rodriguez," 133.

McCarthy knew that the Casas Económicas dwellings were divided "into four classes, according to [residents'] occupation: unskilled; skilled; white-collar; and professional (college graduate or equivalent)."[19] These classes were labelled from A (unskilled) to D (college graduate and professional). McCarthy was especially concerned and curious about the plight of poverty and thus she asked to see the houses of classes A and B, rented to tenants with lower income.

As McCarthy toured the neighbourhood at Madre de Deus, she was as usual calculating the value of most objects she saw and comparing their cost to a workers average wage. When entering the first house, she was astonished with the quality of the furnishings. The house was Class A, assigned to a worker of the lowest category, but the door was opened by a uniformed maid and when inside:

"The house was furnished in the height of Portuguese bourgeois taste. There was a huge crystal chandelier in the small boxlike living room; there were carved cabinets, heavy embossed draperies, a wall-to-wall armoire in the Chinese style, Oriental-type rugs, floppy velvet dolls, lace antimacassars on dark, overstuffed chairs. The dining room and the upstairs were furnished with the same abandon; the only room that could be called economic was the maid's room, which had nothing in it but a bed, a cheap chest of drawers, and the toys of the son of the house."[20]

[19] Ibid., 134.
[20] Ibid., 139.

Fig. 2 Madre de Deus neighbourhood, Lisbon, 1944. Photo by Eduardo Portugal. Source: Arquivo Municipal de Lisboa.

After visiting three houses and seeing that they were all to some extent the home of middle class families, McCarthy thought to herself: "A sort of tact prevented me from asking the indelicate question pulsing through my mind: "Are there any poor people in these houses?"[21] Out of politeness, McCarthy never asked difficult questions out loud; however, she allows the reader to access her thoughts while describing situations which sometimes create humorous contrasts, but most often reminds us of the instrumental role of politeness in autocratic contexts. This contrast between what is said and what is thought is most blatant when McCarthy describes her surprise during her visits:

"The houses were very nice, I said repeatedly, to comfort Mr. Rodriguez—very clean, very clean. And I did not bother to speculate, even inwardly, as to how these owner-tenants had qualified for their homes: had they concealed their assets or were they devoted members of Salazar's National Union or did they have a cousin or a godfather in Mr. Rodriguez' office?"[22]

It happened that the "vice-chieftain" of the Propaganda Department also lived in a Casa Económica, in another area of the city that McCarthy doesn't identify, and what she describes as "Mr. Rodriguez' own home, Class D, Type 3—college graduate, two or more children of different sexes":

"Their house was large and sunny, more restrained in its decorative appointments than any we had yet seen. It had a splendid modern kitchen, two baths, bedrooms for the children and the parents, a comfortable book-lined study for Mr. Rodriguez, and a small bare room for the maid."[23]

McCarthy's description of her visit to the "new man" of the "New State" is, as usual, a sharp and witty description of the social and cultural context. She describes the pride of the tenant showing the modern conveniences, although banal for American standards, such as the hot water shower and his family's insistence that the American guest try all the food and typical sweets from the different regions of the country. In short, McCarthy manages to convey the slightly ridiculous situation of this family that strove to achieve a middle-class status supported by an autocratic regime.

Studies about the nature of the various social housing programmes established in Portugal during the twentieth century by the different political regimes show that these were mainly concerned with the needs of the middle classes, and presented policies inconsistent with their main objectives to solve the deficit of housing for poor families.[24]

[21] Ibid., 141–2.

[22] Ibid., 142.

[23] Ibid., 144.

[24] Fernando Gonçalves. "A Mitologia Da Habitação Social—o Caso Português." *Cidade Campo*, no. 1 (1978): 21–83.

Most recently this is thoroughly argued in the doctoral thesis *Políticas Sociais de Habitação (1820–2015): Espaço e Tempo No Concelho de Lisboa* by Gonçalo Antunes. This thorough and transversal study proves McCarthy's suspicions about the unfair distribution of housing in Portugal. Moreover, Antunes argues that this unfairness happened throughout the twentieth century and is still a recurrent problem.[25]

SOCIAL HOUSING AND SOCIAL JUSTICE

The need for building affordable housing in Portugal remained one of the most pressing problems of the country throughout the twentieth century. The different political regimes created several programmes aimed at tackling the problem. However, as noted by Antunes in his study of all the policies, these programmes did not solve the housing needs of the most economically disadvantaged population, and mostly catered for the middle classes:

"According to the statements and legal diplomas analysed, social housing policies were aimed at 'economically deprived classes' and 'working classes' and other similar nomenclatures, which seemed to be directed to socially disadvantaged groups. However, the reality demonstrates the opposite; that is, most housing policies were destined for the middle classes and excluded the disadvantaged population directly or indirectly."[26]

The urgency of these issues is apparent in the writings of the architect Nuno Teotónio Pereira, who worked at Habitações Económicas/Federação de Caixas de Previdência from 1948 on, and for whom the housing problem in Portugal was essentially a matter of social inequality. In 1969, Teotónio Pereira coined the expression "housing for the masses"—"*habitação para o maior número*"—the title of an essay addressing the disparity between the vast numbers of people who needed housing, and the nature of that being built in the country. In the text, Teotónio Pereira reveals that the results of a national survey showed that 90 per cent of the country's population did not have resources to acquire or rent any kind of housing,[27] and made a clear distinction between solving the housing problem and building more housing, recognizing that this structural issue was part of a vaster and more complex network of problems.

Despite Teotónio Pereira's call to action, by the mid-twentieth century the housing problem was still being treated as a political issue rather than a social crisis. Here, it is useful to note the terms defined by Hannah Arendt as a distinction of the political and the social, in which she makes a point specifically about housing.

[25] This is the main argument of the study, see: Gonçalo Antunes. "Políticas Sociais de Habitação (1820–2015): Espaço e Tempo No Concelho de Lisboa." (PhD Diss., Nova University of Lisbon, 2017). https://run.unl.pt/handle/10362/28056.

[26] Translated by the author from the Portuguese: "Segundo os preâmbulos da maioria dos diplomas analisados no presente trabalho, as políticas de habitação social destinavam-se às "classes economicamente desfavorecidas," às "classes trabalhadoras" e outras expressões similares, o que transmitia a ideia de que eram dirigidas aos grupos socialmente desfavorecidos. Todavia, a realidade demonstra o contrário, ou seja, as políticas de habitação eram destinadas maioritariamente à classe média e excluíam de forma directa ou indirecta a população mais desfavorecida." in Gonçalo Antunes, "Políticas Sociais de Habitação," 411.

[27] Nuno Teotónio Pereira, "Habitação Para o Maior Número," in *Teoria e Crítica de Arquitectura–Século XX*, 610–13. (Vale de Cambra: Caleidoscópio, 2010), 611.

In 1972, in a conference about Arendt's body of work,[28] a question about the distinction between the political and the social is made by none other than Mary McCarthy:

"I would like to ask a question that I have had in my mind a long, long time. It is about the very sharp distinction that Hannah Arendt makes between the political and the social. It is particularly noticeable in her book On Revolution, *where she demonstrates, or seeks to demonstrate, that the failure of the Russian and the French revolutions was based on the fact that these revolutions were concerned with the social, and concerned with suffering—in which the sentiment of compassion played a large role. Whereas, the American Revolution was political and ended in the foundation of something. Now, I have always asked myself: 'What is somebody supposed to do on the public stage, in the public space, if he does not concern himself with the social?' That is, what's left?"*

McCarthy's question addresses a fundamental area of Arendt's thought that was open to much criticism, arguing essentially that the social question cannot be detached from the political question, as Arendt proposes. In synthesis, Arendt is against the politicization of poverty, the kind of abject poverty that constrains and limits freedom, which she defined previously as *"more than deprivation, it is a state of constant want and acute misery whose ignominy consists in its dehumanizing force; poverty is abject because it puts men under the absolute dictate of their bodies, that is, under the absolute dictate of necessity..."*[29] Further along in the debate, Arendt tried to clarify her position by framing the question of housing as a social question rather than a political question:

"Let's take the housing problem. The social problem is adequate housing. But the question of whether this adequate housing means integration or not is certainly a political question. With every one of these questions there is a double face. And one of these faces should not be subject to debate. There shouldn't be any debate about the question that everybody should have decent housing."[30]

Arendt's argument, originally published in the book *On Revolution*, aimed at analysing the failings of the successive revolutionary movements of the eighteenth century. It has a very wide scope, and thus it misses many of the minutiae necessary for a thorough analysis. However, the core of the argument focuses on problem of poverty and its instrumentalisation by the political field, and this is the reason for Arendt's proposed separation.

[28] "In November 1972, a conference on "The Work of Hannah Arendt" was organized by the Toronto Society for the Study of Social and Political Thought sponsored by York University and the Canada Council. Hannah Arendt was invited to attend the conference as the guest of honor, but replied that she would much prefer to be invited to participate." in Hannah Arendt, *Thinking Without a Banister: Essays in Understanding, 1953–1975*. (New York: Schoken Books, 2018), 443.

[29] Hannah Arendt, *On Revolution*. (London: Penguin Books, 1990), 60.

[30] Hannah Arendt, *Thinking Without a Banister*, 457.

Following Arendt's argument, one might try to classify the numerous programmes of affordable housing that were implemented in Portugal as political tools rather than as instruments to achieve social justice. In particular, the programme of Casas Económicas had the purpose of creating a link between the tenants and the regime, since the stability of their own life, and the possibility of owning a home, was dependent on the stability of the regime. One might be uncomfortable with Arendt's radical separation, and rightly so. Nevertheless, Arendt's view is not that the social realm should be ignored, but that the social question is indisputable, and therefore should not be used as a camouflaging tool for political purposes.

ACKNOWLEDGEMENTS

This essay was co-financed by the POPH programme of the European Social Fund and by National Funds by FCT Foundation for Science and Technology, with a postdoctoral grant with the reference SFRH/BPD/68962/2010.

BIBLIOGRAPHY

Antunes, Gonçalo. "Políticas Sociais de Habitação (1820–2015): Espaço e Tempo No Concelho de Lisboa." PhD Diss., Universidade Nova de Lisboa, 2017. https://run.unl.pt/handle/10362/28056.

Arendt, Hannah. *On Revolution*. London: Penguin Books, 1990.

Arendt, Hannah. *Thinking Without a Banister: Essays in Understanding, 1953–1975*. New York: Schoken Books, 2018.

Brightman, Carol, ed. *Between Friends: The Correspondence of Hannah Arendt and Mary McCarthy, 1949–1975*. London: Secker & Warburg, 1995

Castilho, Júlio de. *Lisboa Antiga: O Bairro Alto*. Edited by Gustavo de Matos Sequeira. 3rd ed. Lisbon: Câmara Municipal de Lisboa, 1954.

Cunha Leal, Joana. "Plain, Pombaline and (Post)Modernism: On Some Pre and Post-Kublerian Narratives on Portuguese Architecture." CES Contexto, Debates, no. 3 (2013): 16–28. http://www.ces.uc.pt/publicacoes/cescontexto/index.php?id=8350.

Gonçalves, Fernando. "A Mitologia Da Habitação Social–o Caso Português." *Cidade Campo*, no. 1 (1978): 21–83.

Keil do Amaral, Francisco (coord.). *Arquitectura Popular Em Portugal*. Lisbon: Sindicato Nacional dos Arquitectos, 1961.

Kubler, George. *Portuguese Plain Architecture: Between Spices and Diamonds, 1521–1706*. Middletown, Conn.: Wesleyan University Press, 1972.

McCarthy, Mary. "Letter From Portugal." *The New Yorker*, 1955. http://archives.newyorker.com/?i=1955-02-05#

McCarthy, Mary. "Mister Rodriguez of Lisbon." In *On the Contrary*, 132–45. New York: Farrar, Straus & Cudahy, 1961.

Santos, Reynaldo dos. "A Evolução e o Sentido Cultural Da Arte Portuguesa." In *Breviário Da Pátria Para Os Portugueses Ausentes*, 269–78. Lisboa: Secretariado Nacional de Informação, 1946.

Sousa Santos, Eliana. "Portuguese Plain Architecture: When History Creates a Myth." In *Papers form the International Scientific Thematic Conference EAHN 2015: Entangled Histories, Multiple Geographies Belgrade*. Belgrade: University of Belgrade, 2017. 286–90

Teotónio Pereira, Nuno. "Habitação Para o Maior Número." In *Teoria e Crítica de Arquitectura–Século XX*, 610–13. Vale de Cambra: Caleidoscópio, 2010.

Varela Gomes, Paulo, ed. *Points de Repère: Architectures Du Portugal*. Brussels: Fondation pour l'Architecture, 1991.

Varela Gomes, Paulo. "Arquitectura Não Alinhada." *JA Jornal Arquitectos*, no. 200 (2001): 4–9.

Between the Survey of Rural Housing and the Survey of Popular Architecture: The Housing of Settlers by the Internal Colonization Board (1936–1960)

FILIPA DE CASTRO GUERREIRO
University of Porto, Faculty of Architecture, Centre for Studies in Architecture and Urbanism

The Internal Colonization Board (JCI) was created in 1936 and throughout approximately twenty-four years, built seven agricultural colonies, where 512 farmhouses were established. The establishment and configuration of the seven colonies, and of each particular colony, was not the result of a single, specific, and closed project, but instead the consequence of a long process, mirroring the pressure, visions, programmes, and paradoxes that combined the creation and maturing of the Board itself and the economic and socio-political background of the country. In this circumstance, the diversity of the territory structuring models, the conformation of settlements and the architectural expression of the buildings and of the projects for settlers' housing are highlighted.

The delimitation between four moments allows the interpretation of that diversity, the comprehension of the specific goals of the colonizing programme and thus, the understanding of the existence of different constraints of the commission of architecture. In the first moment moment (1936–1942), that refers to the creation of the organism, the relationship between the Board and the Superior Institute of Agronomy (ISA) was decisive for the definition of goals and work methods. In this context, awareness of the extremely poor conditions of rural life and their systematized awareness (and recognition) in the *Survey of Rural Housing* had a decisive role in the debate around settlers' housing, particularly in the definition of their requisites (hygiene, health, and morals) and their minimum programme. In the second moment (1942–1946), farmhouse buildings became the object of representation of the state's ideology. The debate, now including architects, focused on the architectural expression of the whole and its regional rooting. In the third moment (1947–1953), we see a displacement of the state's means of expression to public buildings for assistance and groups of "social centres." The designs of the farmhouse buildings were revised by the architects now incorporated in the Board's technical structure, in order to cut construction costs. During the fourth moment (1954–1960), reflective of the Portuguese architectural debate of the 1950s, not only is the model of the single-family home replaced by semi-detached or terraced buildings, but the projects mirror the search for an overview between modern and popular architecture.

Regardless of the composition and architectural expression adopted in each moment, the common premise between the various Board farmhouse projects was the search to root the buildings in the region's architecture, promoting emotional ties between the settler and the building.

BIOGRAPHY

Filipa de Castro Guerreiro. Viana do Castelo, 1976.

Architect, Assistant Professor of the Faculty of Architecture of the University of Porto (FAUP), Holder of a doctorate degree in Architecture with the thesis "Portuguese Agricultural Colonies built by the Internal Colonization Board between 1936 and 1960. The house, the settlement and the territory" under the supervision of Sergio Fernandez, Marta Oliveira, and Maria Manuel Oliveira. Researcher in the Centre for Studies in Architecture and Urbanism in FAUP– "Architecture Theory Project History."

Collaborated with architect Álvaro Siza between 1999 and 2000. Founded the Laboratório da Arquitectura in 2001, with Tiago Correia and Bruno Figueiredo. Founded the Atelier da Bouça In 2008 with Tiago Correia, an architect with whom she has developed several partnership projects since 2000, of which the enlargement of the EPRAMI Paredes de Coura is highlighted (Prize Young Architect, Arquitectura em Tijolo de Face à Vista CVG 04/05), the CEIA da Paisagem Protegida do Corno do Bico (finalist of the FAD Prizes 2008 and nominated for the Mies van der Rohe Award 2009), and two houses in Bouça das Cardosas (nominated for the Mies van der Rohe Award 2015). Member of the OASRN Governing Board between 2005 and 2010.

INTERNAL COLONIZATION BOARD

The Internal Colonization Board was created in 1936 with the purpose of, among other factors, settling farmhouses on common land and state properties and in fields that were irrigated, in the meantime, by the Agricultural Hydraulics Plan. The goals were to increase the agricultural productivity of the country, balance the mainland characterized by two polar conditions—a green, densely populated north, with overly fragmented parcels and a dry, deserted, large-parcelled South, and to promote "social calm" through the conversion of agricultural workers into property owners. Through the advocacy of the need for a "healthy, strong, loyal rural population, guarantor of nationality" the internal colonization programme would fulfil a national mission, one of "racial establishment and territorial appreciation,"[1] defined by the preservation of a rural population, based on property and the family institution that a home would belong to. In this sense, other than the agricultural issues, the Board's activity also had a moral dimension, one of education and social control. These ideas, clearly expressed in the early 1940s in the "Cadernos de Ressurgimento Nacional" (National Resurgence Notebooks)[2], fit into a programme that was, at the time, afoot in several European countries. Despite the clarity and large early dimension of their goals, over 25 years, while seeking to respond to different political objectives and suffering innumerable social pressures, the Board was only able to organize 512 farmhouses in seven agricultural colonies. Over this period, the visions and contexts that governed the Board's projects were various.

Intended for the housing and agricultural outbuildings of the settlers, eighteen projects are known, of which eight were built. The debate on rural housing in this period is inextricably linked to the debate around the "Portuguese House" and, in this context, the Board farmhouse's projects materialize show signs of the "resistance to the Portuguese House Movement" that João Leal refers to:

"The starting shot for these resistances [to the Portuguese House Movement] *is provided by the Survey of Rural Housing, organized in the framework of the Superior Institute of Agronomics, whose results would be published in the 1940s. Ten years later, with the Survey of Popular Architecture in Portugal, organized by the National Syndicate of Architects, it is the time for a new generation of architects to distance themselves from the Portuguese house. Finally, while the 'new' architects were roaming the country in search of their own version of popular architecture, Veiga de Oliveira and his collaborators from the Centre for Studies of Peninsular Ethnology of Porto and later, from the Lisbon Museum of Ethnology were also starting to come up with their version of the theme, once again distinct from the one suggested by the Portuguese House."*[3]

---

[1] SNI, *Colonização Interna* (Lisboa: SNI, 1944),15–16.

[2] Ibid.

[3] Leal, João. *Etnografias Portuguesas, 1870–1970: Cultura Popular e Identidade Nacional* (Lisboa: Dom Quixote, 2000), 145.

To understand the signals expressed in the premises that govern the projects developed by the Board for the farmhouses, it is important to organize their interpretation according to four specific moments phases in the activity and ideological framework of the Board, that allow the identification of context, references, influences, and topic crossover and the subsequent architectural translation.

1936–1942 | THE MORALS, HYGIENE, AND HEALTH OF THE HOUSING

The first moment was restricted between the establishment of the organism in 1936 and the presentation, in 1942, of the colonization project of Herdade de Pegões [MdH DB a658–660], the first project developed from the ground up by the Board with the intention of creating a "doctrinally well-conceived and functionally well-founded" example.[4] Centred mostly around the issues of sizing and establishment of the agricultural farmhouse, the set of actions carried out is guided toward the setting of a development methodology of the colonization projects. Due to the shared knowledge and interests, the incorporation and guidance of previous studies in the established methodology and the viability of many of the studies developed by trainee students, collaboration with the ISA[5] constitutes an indelible mark in the success of this seminal goal.[6]

In the four developed projects—Agricultural Colony of Milagres [MdH DB a274/292/477], Martim Rei [MdH DB a483], Herdade de Pegões and Mata Nacional da Gafanha [MdH DB a538], of which only the first two were built according to the projects developed at the time—the design of settlements is a mere reflection of the agronomic issues, and it corresponds to a dispersed population of autonomous tillage settlements. In the projects for the settlers' farmhouse buildings, the references and themes of the design are restrained to the construction experience of the agronomists thatwhich, at the time, was diffused in several agricultural construction manuals.

The premises emerge naturally from the discussion generated from the papers around the "Survey of Rural Housing," a project developed by the Senate of the Technical University of Lisbon and directed by agricultural engineers Eduardo Alberto Lima Basto and Henrique de Barros.[7]

[4] *Projecto de Colonização da Herdade de Pegões* (Lisboa: JCI, 1942),16.

[5] The relationship between the two institutions was formally expressed through the presence of the "professor of general agriculture" in the technical council of the JCI (no. 2 of the Article 176º).

[6] Frederico Ágoas, "Saber e poder. Estado e investigação social agrária nos primórdios da sociologia em Portugal" (PhD Thesis in Sociology, Faculdade de Ciências Sociais e Humanas, Universidade Nova de Lisboa, 2011), 110.

[7] In this first moment, the agricultural engineers José Garcês Pereira Caldas and Henrique de Barros, professor in the ISA, constituted the ideologists of the JCI's activity.

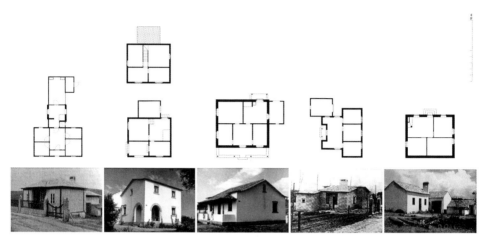

Fig. 1 Farmhouses refurbished and built during the first moment–Existing farmhouses in the Agricultural Colony of Milagres type I, II, III, and IV [architect Norberto Correia 1926–27] / Farmhouse built by the JCI in the Agricultural Colonies of Milagres and Martim Rei [technical engineering agent Dâmaso Constantino, 1937].
Source: author's composition with her own designs and images from (Fortes 1935) and (JCI [194–?]).

The issues raised by the Survey, as well as the analysis of the rural constructions in the region, when it comes to morals, hygiene, habitability, and health of the housing, are key in the minimal housing programme: three bedrooms (parents, sons, and daughters), kitchen and a space outside the house for the toilet; a physical separation between the spaces for man and animals; and the existence of lighting and ventilation devices for every space.

Apart from the issues mentioned above, in this first moment, the design of the farmhouse buildings was the subject of other debates. The matter of who should build the farmhouses (the Board or the settlers themselves) was discussed and the process of self-construction was argued. In the agricultural colonies of Milagres and Martim Rei, however, the decision was for the construction of the farmhouses by the Board, based on the urgency in the reorganization and execution of the colonies. In the early 1940s, in the colonization projects of the Mata Nacional da Gafanha and Herdade de Pegões, there was an attempt to set action principles for the JCI and give projects an educational aspect to create examples to be followed in the region.[8] A project, which constituted an interpretation of "typical rural housing" to be built by the settlers in Gafanha was developed.[9] For Herdade de Pegões, four farmhouse types that differ individually in housing design were proposed. However, no colony followed the principle of self-construction.

[8] This intention fits also in a broader activity of the Ministry of Economics, of the publishing of a set of manuals on rural housing and agricultural dependences: Basto, E. A. Lima Basto, *A Casa Rural. Campanha da Produção Agrícola. Série B–No.25* * Lisbon: Ministério da Economia, Direcção Geral dos Serviços Agrícolas, 1942) [The rural house]; Macedo, Mário Botelho de Macedo, *A Casa Rural. A habitação. Campanha da Produção Agrícola. Série B–No.26* (Lisboa: Ministério da Economia, Direcção Geral dos Serviços Agrícolas, 1942). [The rural house. Housing] and *A Casa Rural. O Silo. Campanha da Produção Agrícola. Série B–No.35* (Lisboa: Ministério da Economia, Direcção Geral dos Serviços Agrícolas, 1942) [The rural house. The silo]. With these manuals, agronomists claimed for themselves and their practice, the solution for the rural housing problem and demonstrated their loathing for the job, the recurrent time, the ornamental imagination of the Portuguese House, arguing that "good taste" and the "beauty of the rural house stems mostly from simplicity" and of the suitability of their needs. Macedo, *A Casa Rural. A Habitação.*, 9.

[9] *Plano geral de Colonização do Perímetro da Gafanha* (Lisboa: JCI, 1942).

The project of the farmhouses built in the late 1930s in the Agricultural Colony of Milagres and Martim Rei established as a principle the observance of the tillage yard as a founding and structuring element of the set of buildings. With no concession or element of the relationship that allows articulation with the remaining volumes, the building arises from the juxtaposition of several volumes, each one designed and sized exclusively according to the conditions and needs for its function. This condition of structure, and the fact that the whole perimeter of the yard is not closed, allows the adding of another volume at any time. The house is centred in a rectangular volume split into four compartments—the kitchen and three bedrooms. The toilet area is an autonomous volume located near the agricultural outbuildings. The house and its entrance, like all the other volumes, overlook the patio, establishing a direct and exclusive link with the space for agricultural activities, thereby closing the access path. Between the two colonies, the project varies only in the implementation of the agricultural annexes, maintaining the housing design. Fundamentally, the isolated volume of the house is close to the characteristics of the Affordable Houses built by the state, during the same period, in several Portuguese cities, and of the models of the rural houses disseminated in the agricultural construction manuals of the beginning of the century;[10] and of the projects built in Spain by the *Instituto Nacional de Colonización*, up to the early 1950s.

1942–1946 | THE "AGGRANDIZEMENT"[11] OF THE HOME IN THE "FARMHOUSE-TYPE" FOR THE REGION

In the second moment, which coincided with the final years of the Second World War, most of the Board's interventions were planned. Architecture was called upon to not only dignify and exalt the image of the Home, the symbol of the family, the basis of a nation, but also to give shape and clarity to the settlements. For the colonies in Trás-os-Montes and Minho, the first concentrated settlements were planned, where the spot's location was carefully defined through geographic premises, maximum distance between the house and the agricultural parcels, and the connection with the existing network of territorial population. The ideological framework was significantly altered, the panorama of minimum resources and prevalence of agricultural premises was replaced with the search for a sense of representation of state-defined values—identity, rurality, and order—and, like the state's actions regarding the contest for the "Most Portuguese Village in Portugal," a display of the conscious intention to create a landscape.

[10] For example, Maria José Soroa y Pineda, *Construcciones Agrícolas*. 4th edition (Madrid: Ruiz Hermanos, 1930).

[11] Acciaiuloli, Margarida. "Os Anos 40 em Portugal. O País, o Regime e as Artes. 'Restauração' e 'Celebração'" (PhD Thesis in History of Contemporary Art, Faculdade de Ciências Sociais e Humanas, Universidade Nova de Lisboa, 1991), 305.

The design matrix for the settlements reveals a series of references and themes recovered from the international debate of that time. The Garden City, however, is the only reference assumed.[12] With the non-assumed, but undeniable participation of architects, especially Eugénio Corrêa,[13] in the Board's projects, the theme of regionalized projects, under discussion in the General Directorate of Buildings and National Monuments from the 1930s, became part of the projects for the farmhouses. The rural house, "legitimate daughter of geography,"[14] made up the programme where the theme could be explored in all its dimensions. In this, it was possible to overcome the superficial in the mere use of region-specific materials and interpret the relationship between the spatial and volumetric shape of the house and the consequences of its climatic and geographical condition—which are key in the direction of agricultural and animal production and in everyday family life.

Other than the publication of the first volume of the *Survey of Rural Housing*[15] from the point of view of insight into rural housing, the 1940s were marked by the publication of the regional differentiation studies by Amorim Girão[16] and Orlando Ribeiro,[17] and the beginning of the ethnology studies by Jorge Dias, Benjamim Pereira, and Ernesto Veiga de Oliveira.[18] The geographer's studies are recognized in the JCI's documents, which also mention Amorim Girão.[19] The three farmhouse projects developed in this period—for Barroso [MdH DB a663], in Trás-os-Montes; for Boalhosa [MdH DB a661], in Minho; and for Pegões, in Ribatejo—clearly reflect the geographical readings of the rural house developed by these authors. For each region, the proposed "form" reinterprets the popular architecture of that region, summoning new premises of hygiene and morals and social organizing and does not refrain from manipulation for the creation of a space capable, through its values, of conditioning the everyday life of a man who the state wants to "civilize."

Overall, the focal point of the project is no longer the functionality of space for agricultural work, but the strong image of the building of the agricultural farmhouse as a pillar of the family-owned agricultural enterprise. The idea of an edified set conformed to a compound disappears with the objectification of the building, magnified by the concentration of programmes in a single volume, located in the centre of the allotment. The symbols of home—fireplace and chimney—are externally inflated, and the space for the kitchen, the centre of family life, is carefully designed. The option for a single volume constitutes a clear rupture with the premises of previous projects—distance between animal and human areas and the absence of a sense of representation. The way the organization of the house is reinterpreted around a yard or courtyard, however, can be read as the search for a sense of rooting of the settlers

---

[12] *Projecto de Colonização dos Baldios de Montalegre e Boticas: I Parte–Freguesia de Chã* (Lisboa: JCI, 1944), 59.

[13] The participation of Eugénio Corrêa constitutes a plausible hypothesis even though, currently, it was undocumented in JCI's projects.

[14] Girão, *Geografia de Portugal*, 249.

[15] E. A. Lima Basto and Henrique de Barros. *Inquérito à Habitação Rural. Vol. I: A Habitação Rural nas Províncias do Norte de Portugal (Minho, Douro Litoral, Trás-os-Montes e Alto-Douro)* (Lisboa: Universidade Técnica de Lisboa, 1943).

[16] Aristides de Amorim Girão, *Atlas de Portugal* (Coimbra: Gráfica de Coimbra, 1941), *Geografia de Portugal* (Porto: Portucalense Editora, 1941).

[17] Orlando Ribeiro, *Portugal, o Mediterrâneo e o Atlântico* (Coimbra: Coimbra Editora, 1945).

[18] Even though most of these authors' works were not published until much later in the series "Portugal de Perto" [Ernesto Veiga de Oliveira and Fernando Galhano, *Arquitectura Tradicional Portuguesa*, Colecção Portugal de Perto (Lisbon: Publicações Dom Quixote, 1992)] in the 1990s, some of the studies were initially published in the 1940s and 50s, in scattered scientific articles, as stated by Benjamim Pereira [Nuno Faria, *Os Inquéritos [à Fotografia e ao Território]. Paisagem e povoamento*. (Guimarães: Centro Internacional das Artes José de Guimarães, 2015), 311–351]. It was during this time that Jorge Dias, after finishing in 1944 his doctorate in Ethnology from the University of Munich, with the thesis "Vilarinho da Furna, Um Povo Autárquico da Serra Amarela," took over the administration of the sector of Ethnography in the Study Centre of Peninsular Ethnology in 1947. José Manuel Sobral. "DIAS, António Jorge," in *Dicionário de Historiadores Portugueses: da Fundação da Academia Real das Ciências ao Final do Estado Novo (1779–1974)*. http://dichp.bnportugal.pt/historiadores/historiadores_dias_jorge.htm. accessed 30 May, 2018.

[19] *Projecto de Colonização do Núcleo da Boalhosa* (Lisboa: JCI, 1948), 1.

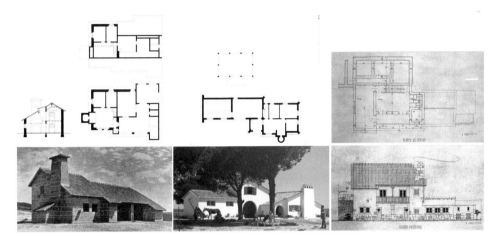

Fig. 2 Farmhouses projected during the second moment–"Farmhouse-type for the Barroso region" [architect Eugénio Corrêa (?), 1943] / "Farmhouse for the Herdade de Pegões" [architect Eugénio Corrêa (?), 194?] / "Farmhouse-type for the nucleus of Boalhosa" [architect Maurício Trindade Chagas, 1946].
Source: author's composition with her own designs and images from (Lobo and Antunes 1960) / (Novais, JCI [material gráfico] / Estúdio Mário Novais s.d.)/ (JCI 1948).

through spatial organizations that come close to their habits while still maintaining acceptable levels of hygiene and health. This sense of rooting, which, according to Orlando Ribeiro, correlates to a consciousness that "[. . .] technical solutions must be subordinate to a caring understanding of the local needs and uses,"[20] forms one of the components of the idea to establish regional types as opposed to a single model to be implemented across the territory.

Identified by Amorim Girão and Orlando Ribeiro, the first major difference between the northern and southern rural house is the structure on one or two floors, and the spatial relationship between the housing and the agricultural outbuildings, themes interpreted by the Board's projects. Therefore, in the proposal for Barroso, the house is organized around a covered courtyard that mediates the relationship between the house and the agricultural outbuildings. The space for the kitchen is designed like an interior patio, which centralizes domestic life and structures the house into two floors. Apart from the integrated construction in granite stonework, the proposed thatched roof (subsequently amended) stands out. Expressed with a reference to its usage, during the same period, in houses in Germany, France, and England, this proposal was highly employed in the Barroso region during this time.[21]

[20] Orlando Ribeiro, "A concentração urbana e os seus males. Documentos e perspectivas de estudo [1957]," in *Opúsculos Geográficos. Volume V–Temas Urbanos* (Lisboa: Fundação Calouste Gulbenkian, 1995), 134.

[21] *Projecto de Colonização dos Baldios de Montalegre e Boticas: I Parte–Freguesia de Chã*, 43.

The farmhouse projected for Herdade de Pegões, initially planned in adobe, displays the house and agricultural outbuildings on a single floor, with completely independent entrance spaces, even though each programme functions autonomously. The presence of a porch in the house stands out, a space for the relationship between the interior and the exterior whose programme surpasses a simple entrance and becomes the statement for a living space.

In the unbuilt project for the farmhouse of Boalhosa, the building adapted to the steep topography and is structured on three floors. The agricultural outbuildings were aligned on the ground floor building at the front of the yard, and on the mid floor, where the kitchen and the barn were located, the great balcony complemented and made the living spaces more flexible. While also projected in granite stonework, the wall planes of the housing part were plastered and whitewashed. In their solidity, construction quality, and architectural expression—capable of creating a vehicle of representation of the state's values, these three farmhouses are similar to the houses of the forest guards, road menders, and coastguards, designed during the same period.

1947–1953 | THE ECONOMICAL REDESIGN OF THE FARMHOUSE AND THE NEW ARCHITECTURAL EXPRESSIONS OF PUBLIC BUILDING

The third moment corresponded to the post-war period during which, even though the colonies were still being built, there was already an awareness that the colonizing programme would not be fulfilled to its whole extent. Now a part of the Board's structure, the architects were asked to redesign the projects for the farmhouse buildings to reduce construction costs. The state's redirection, to modernize and industrialize the country, led to the displacement of the favoured means of expression—the agricultural farmhouse—to the public buildings of assistance and the groups of "social centres." It was at this time that most colony-assisting buildings were designed and built.

Three new farmhouses were projected—for the Agricultural Colony of Alvão [MdH DB a669–675] and Barroso, the Agricultural Colony of Pegões and the Agricultural Colony of Gafanha. Overall, the proposals corresponded to a redesign of previous projects, but leading to a reduction of area and cost and to small changes in the agricultural programme. To simplify, buildings underwent some losses both in the previous perspectives of reinterpretation of popular housing (i.e. the farmhouse for Trás-os-Montes which became a single floor) and the quality of volumetric composition of the set (like the farmhouse in the Agricultural Colony of Pegões).

The proposal for the Agricultural Colony of Gafanha, the only one designed from scratch, followed the same premises. However, the proposed set was clearer and more balanced, not related to the redesign of a previous project. The project is particularly interesting due to the way the silos gain visibility, revealing the agricultural programme of the set, whose presence is explored with plastic expression in playing with the building's volumes.

But if architectural expression was not questioned in the farmhouses, nor was any experimentation undertaken, and rooted and tested materials, forms, and construction techniques were maintained. In the projects for the public buildings, the Board revealed a new stance that mirrored the circumstance of the national architectural debate of the early 1950s. Aside from the beginning of the industrialization process of the country, the downfall of fascist regimes in the Second World War allowed a détente of the cultural point of view.

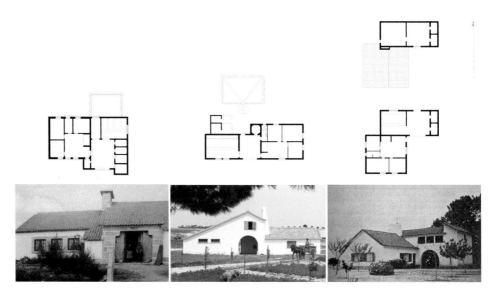

Fig. 3 Farmhouses built during the third moment–"Project of the farmhouse for settlers to be built in Alvão" [architect Trindade Chagas, 1950] / "Project of the farmhouse in Herdade de Pegões" [architect António Trigo, 1949] / "Project of the farmhouse of Gafanha" [architect Trindade Chagas, 1950].
Source: author's composition with her own designs and images from (Barriga 1964) (Novais, JCI [material gráfico] / Estúdio Mário Novais s.d.)/(Lobo and Antunes 1960).

With the "new democratic façade"[22] that the state wanted to convey, and that allowed the First National Congress of Architecture, where architects' criticism of stylistic impositions was heard and registered, there was now, within the Board, room for proposals with different architectural expressions. At the same time, and for the same space in some cases, proposals were developed with different premises concerning their architectural expression. Projects that still sought the expression and symbols of a "alleged national architecture"[23]— buttresses, eaves, classical compositions with axes of symmetry that sought monumentality—lived with projects that proposed a modern experimentation with local materials—brick domes in Ribatejo, free planes of granite stonework in Trás-os-Monte; and also with projects that sought to level a typology and a general construction system, regardless of the use. Stemming from a close reading of popular constructions (and in this sense intersecting with the architectural proposals of architect Keil do Amaral) they sought to express great unity, reduce maintenance needs and simultaneously ensure great flexibility in their internal organization, adapting to the different requests of the programme.

[22] Pereira, Nuno Teotónio. "A Arquitectura de regime, 1938–1948," in *Portugal: Arquitectura do Século XX* (Munchen, New York, Frankfurt, Lisboa: Portugal–Frankfurt 97, S.A., Deutsches Architektur-Museum, Prestel-Verlag, 1998), 37.

[23] Nuno Teotónio Pereira, "Um testemunho sobre a arquitectura nos anos 50," in *Escritos. 1947–1996, Selecção* (Porto: FAUP publicações, 1996), 259.

During this path, Eugénio Corrêa's proposal around the "Paraboloides" construction system stands out. This system, through the reading of traditional construction techniques, sought to respond to the need to construct numerous houses and public buildings quickly, economically and with acceptable comfort levels. By means of a model, photographed by the Studio Mário Novais,[24] he illustrated the adjustment of the system to some of the routine programmes in the agricultural colonies—different sized houses, stables, school, and church. As an essential programme of construction for the colonies, Eugénio Corrêa's proposal was not welcomed by the JCI, leaving the set of Santo Isidro de Pegões as nothing but an isolated experiment of construction of public buildings—church and schools—and housing for the staff—teachers and a priest. Here we see the unwillingness of the Board to risk experiments in construction for the facilities, and reserve tested and rooted solutions for the settlers' buildings, which would be the targets of long-term loans and could not be used as guinea pigs for potentially unsuccessful experiments.

1954–1960 | THE SITED PROJECT WITH MODERN EXPRESSION

The fourth and final moment corresponded roughly to the second half of the 1950s. During this period, there was already an awareness that colonization was restricted to the seven colonies. The settlement in the colony of Boalhosa was designed and built and several other unrealized projects were developed for the second stage of the colony of Gafanha. Pending projects were closed and cooperative structures were implemented. Landscape designers joined the teams of Board technicians and carried out territory-wide work, participating in colonization projects, and settlement-wide work, developing landscape management projects. There was a significant change in the design matrix for the settlements. More complex compositions were structured, organized via the disposition of plot strips, with two-way access, and which defined spaces of streets and squares, where there was a demand for a sense of community.

The knowledge accumulated from previous experiences allowed a certain autonomy for the architects, of whom pragmatism was generally required. Reflecting the architectural debate of the 1950s, the isolated single-family home model was abandoned, and other typologies were tested—semi-detached and terraced buildings.

[24] Estúdio Mário Novais. "Arquitecto Eugénio Correia [Material gráfico]/Estúdio Mário Novais." Biblioteca de Arte da Fundação Calouste Gulbenkian. s.d. http://www.biblartepac.gulbenkian.pt. Accessed 30 May 2018.

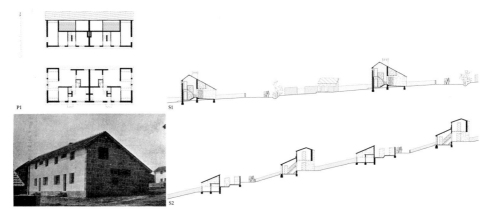

Fig. 4 Farmhouses projected during the fourth moment for the Agricultural Colony of Boalhosa –P1 and S1 Farmhouse for the Núcleo de Vascões for the Agricultural Colony of Boalhosa [architect José Luiz Pinto Machado, 1956] / S2. Farmhouse in Boalhosa [architect Henrique Brando Albino, 1954].
Source: author's composition with her own designs and images from (Lobo and Antunes 1960).

Although only farmhouses were built in the centre of Vascões in the Agricultural Colony of Boalhosa, three other farmhouse projects were developed, two for the same agricultural colony, and another for the settlement of Videira in the second part of the Agricultural Colony of Gafanha. In all projects there was an abandonment of the understanding of the building as a type generalizable to the region, favouring projects that adapted to the shape of the settlement and location-specific conditions—with great attention to topography.

The projects that were developed for the farmhouses of the Agricultural Colony of Boalhosa brought attention back to the spatial references of the popular housing of the region that were discussed with the modern premises that were already under discussion by the Board. In this regard they anticipated and accompanied the architectural debate, raised in Portugal by the Survey of Popular Architecture, around the qualities of vernacular architecture, and approached projects developed shortly after the *Habitações Económicas da Federação de Caixas de Previdência*.

The first farmhouse proposal developed for the centre of Vascões of the Agricultural Colony of Boalhosa was projected by architect Henrique Albino in 1954. It was the only project in which both farmhouses, organized continuously, and the settlement were designed by the same architect.

The project, regardless of the permanence of the continuous building, debated both the theme of monotony and the theme of identification of individuality of each farmhouse, through the differentiation of materials and plans and the juxtaposition of volumes of the silos and chimneys. The farmhouse design retrieved the "shed" from the region's housing as a paramount space for family life, using it along with the "kitchen-dining room," as an organizing central space. In order to completely implement it in the municipality of Paredes de Coura where most of the colony's agricultural lands are located, the settlement's location was reconsidered two years after the design of the project. A new project for the ensemble and the farmhouses was developed. António Trigo designed the village and José Luiz Pinto Machado was the architect that signed the farmhouse projects. The proposal, although it was now organized into semi-detached buildings, clearly stemmed from the project of Henrique Albino, revealing, however, a greater knowledge of the workings of agricultural life and a greater ability to economize and systematize the design of spaces.

When it came to the total of the house and outbuildings (agricultural annexes included) the project drastically reduced its gross area to 145 m2 (the first farmhouse built in the Agricultural Colony of Barroso was 233 m2 and the last farmhouse projected for the Agricultural Colony of Gafanha was 170 m2) coming close to the first farmhouses projected for the Agricultural Colony of Milagres and Sabugal. Just like the proposal of Henrique Albino, the project sought to minimize the need for earth moving, faced with a steep terrain, adapting the buildings to the sloping terrain. All the settlement's farmhouses had roughly the same solar orientation, ensuring that the houses were south-facing. This factor was one of the more highlighted premises of the project in the documentation, and it has direct consequences in the internal organization and volumes of the proposal. The house was organized as a vertical, two-floor volume, facing south—to ensure the heating of spaces and visibility to the courtyard area and the valley's agricultural terrains. The thermal issue is still complemented by the fact that the agricultural outhouses surround the volume of the house to the north and its sides. The rooftop is uncentred to allow a single floor to the north, constructed with a slightly higher elevation than the two southern floors. The interior of the building is also structured through the "shed." The entrance to the house and the vertical circulation space are marked by the presence of a granite stonework wall, completely free, around which there is a stairway enclosure, creating direct visual connections with the shed's gap and upper floor.

A SENSE OF ROOTING

Around most of the construction pathway of the JCI's agricultural colonies, their projects and the constructed works mirror the themes of architectural debate of the time. These were themes that the Board's architects also debated, and in some respects were pioneers of, even if it did not have the dimension, disclosure, and visibility to be a model, example or reference.

The debate on the sense and depth of the search for a regional architecture and its nuances hovers over the JCI's projects. This is a pursuit in which, if we understand it as a conservation and maintenance of tested forms and techniques, considering that the changes for continuing to ensure the adequate premises envisaged, we find a sense of conservative traditionalism that doesn't necessarily have a pejorative meaning; but it is also a stake in safe values, with a reduced margin for experimentalism, and, consequently, for evolution. However, it may mean a rooting of shapes and of the relationships between the spaces in the region's popular architecture, through the search for an interpretation of the essence between shape and circumstance, adapting them to new premises of hygiene and morals. It can thus be understood as a modern posture, even if the new man is not the free man dreamed of by the Modern Movement.

Even if in specific circumstances, the approach to popular architecture can be read according to one of these perspectives. It may reveal the posture of a specific architect, or the constraints of a particular context of commissioning, but we understand that in the whole path of the agricultural colonies' construction, the interest in popular architecture constituted a means of seizing mechanisms of approach to the settlers' culture for whom buildings were intended. Buildings in which, albeit with the intention of altering the parameters of health and morals, there is a search for identification, a rooting that contributes to the success of colonization.

ACKNOWLEDGMENTS

The present text is derived from the research carried out within the doctoral thesis "Portuguese Agricultural Colonies built by the Internal Colonization Board between 1936 and 1960. The house, the settlement and the territory" and the project "Housing: 100 years of public policies in Portugal 1918–2018" promoted by the Portuguese Institute of Housing and Urban Refurbishment.

BIBLIOGRAPHY

Acciaiuloli, Margarida. "Os Anos 40 em Portugal. O País, o Regime e as Artes. 'Restauração' e 'Celebração'." PhD Thesis in Contemporary Art History, Faculdade de Ciências Sociais e Humanas Universidade Nova de Lisboa, 1991.

Ágoas, Frederico. "Saber e poder. Estado e investigação social agrária nos primórdios da sociologia em Portugal." PhD Thesis in Sociology, Faculdade de Ciências Sociais e Humanas, Universidade Nova de Lisboa, 2011.

Barriga, António Manuel Serrano Ribeira. Relatório de Tirocínio do Curso de Regente Agrícola. Évora: Escola de Regentes Agrícolas, 1964.

Basto, E. A. Lima. A casa rural. Campanha da Produção Agrícola. Série B–No. 25. Lisboa: Ministério da Economia, Direcção Geral dos Serviços Agrícolas, 1942.

Basto, E. A. Lima and Henrique de Barros. Inquérito à habitação rural. Vol. 1: A habitação rural nas províncias do Norte de Portugal (Minho, Douro Litoral, Trás-os-Montes e Alto-Douro). Lisboa: Universidade Técnica de Lisboa, 1943.

Faria, Nuno. Os Inquéritos [à Fotografia e ao Território]. Paisagem e povoamento. Guimarães: Centro Internacional das Artes José de Guimarães, 2015.

Fortes, Mário Pais da Cunha. "Colónia Agrícola dos Milagres." Separata do Boletim de Agricultura, Ano II–n.º 4 e 5, III Série (April 1935).

Girão, Aristides de Amorim. Atlas de Portugal. Coimbra: Gráfica de Coimbra, 1941a.

Girão, Aristides de Amorim. Geografia de Portugal. Porto: Portucalense Editora, 1941.

Guerreiro, Filipa de Castro. "Colónias Agrícolas Portuguesas construídas pela Junta de Colonização Interna entre 1936 e 1960. A casa, o assentamento e o território." PhD Thesis in Architecture, Faculdade de Arquitectura da Universidade do Porto, 2016.

JCI. Colónia Agrícola dos Milagres [Photo album]. Lisboa: JCI, [194–?].

JCI. Plano geral de colonização do Perímetro da Gafanha. Lisboa: JCI, 1942.

JCI. Projecto de Colonização da Herdade de Pegões. Lisboa: JCI, 1942.

JCI. Projecto de Colonização do Núcleo da Boalhosa. Lisboa: JCI, 1948.

JCI. Projecto de Colonização dos Baldios de Montalegre e Boticas: I Parte–Freguesia de Chã. Lisboa: JCI, 1944.

Leal, João. Etnografias Portuguesas, 1870–1970: Cultura Popular e Identidade Nacional. Lisboa: Dom Quixote, 2000.

Lobo, Vasco, and Alfredo da Mata Antunes. Problemas Actuais da Pequena Habitação Rural. Coimbra: MOP–Direcção Geral dos Serviços de Urbanização, Centro de Estudos de Urbanismo, 1960.

Macedo, Mário Botelho de. A Casa Rural. A Habitação. Campanha da Produção Agrícola. Série B–No. 26. Lisboa: Ministério da Economia, Direcção Geral dos Serviços Agrícolas, 1942.

Macedo, Mário Botelho de. A Casa Rural. O Silo. Campanha da Produção Agrícola. Série B–No. 35. Lisboa: Ministério da Economia, Direcção Geral dos Serviços Agrícolas, 1942.

Estúdio Mário Novais. "Arquitecto Eugénio Correia [Material gráfico]/Estúdio Mário Novais." Biblioteca de Arte da Fundação Calouste Gulbenkian. s.d. http://www.biblartepac.gulbenkian.pt Accessed May 30 2018.

Estúdio Mário Novais. "JCI [material gráfico]/Estúdio Mário Novais." Biblioteca de Arte da Fundação Calouste Gulbenkian. s.d. http://www.biblartepac.gulbenkian.pt. Accessed 30 May 2018.

Estúdio Mário Novais. "JCI [Material gráfico]/Estúdio Mário Novais." Biblioteca de Arte da Fundação Calouste Gulbenkian. s.d. http://www.biblartepac.gulbenkian.pt. Accessed 30 May 2018.

Oliveira, Ernesto Veiga de, and Fernando Galhano. Arquitectura Tradicional Portuguesa. Colecção Portugal de Perto. Lisboa: Publicações Dom Quixote, 1992.

Pereira, Nuno Teotónio. "A Arquitectura de regime, 1938–1948." In Portugal: Arquitectura do Século XX. Munchen, New York, Frankfurt, Lisboa: Portugal–Frankfurt 97, S.A., Deutsches Architektur-Museum, Prestel-Verlag, 1998.

Pereira, Nuno Teotónio. "Um testemunho sobre a arquitectura nos anos 50." In Escritos. 1947–1996, Selecção. Porto: FAUP Publicações, 1996.

Ribeiro, Orlando. "A concentração urbana e os seus males. Documentos e perspectivas de estudo [1957]." In Opúsculos Geográficos. Volume V–Temas Urbanos. Lisboa: Fundação Calouste Gulbenkian, 1995.

Ribeiro, Orlando. Portugal, o Mediterrâneo e o Atlântico. Coimbra: Coimbra Editora, 1945.

SNI. Colonização Interna. Lisboa: SNI, 1944.

Sobral, José Manuel. "DIAS, António Jorge." In Dicionário de Historiadores Portugueses: da Fundação da Academia Real das Ciências ao final do Estado Novo (1779–1974) http://dichp.bnportugal.pt/historiadores/historiadores_dias_jorge.htm. Accessed 30 May 2018.

Soroa y Pineda, Maria José. Construcciones agrícolas. 4th edition. Madrid: Ruiz Hermanos, 1930.

The Portuguese People as Peaceful and Intuitive Artists: Propaganda, Folk Art, and the Legitimation of Salazar's New State

VERA MARQUES ALVES
University of Coimbra, Faculty of Sciences and Technology

ABSTRACT

Salazar's New State was a traditionalist and anti-democratic regime that instituted an organic vision of society inspired by a conservative vision of rural communities. Salazar, the son of poor farmers, was himself an anti-liberal who never missed an opportunity to glorify the moral superiority of the folk communities. In 1933, the same year that the New State was institutionalized, Salazar created a propaganda office—the Secretariat of National Propaganda—and appointed the writer and journalist António Ferro to be its director. Ferro's intervention would be of paramount importance in shaping an idyllic image of Portugal and its people in tune with Salazar's ruralist ideology. He did it through the organization of a series of folkloristic events and folk art exhibitions that spoke of a peaceful people composed of obedient and well-behaved peasants, entirely devoted to their traditions and absolutely alien to the conflicts of modern times.

All the parodic, transgressing manifestations of folk culture were omitted from this picture. Also obliterated were the violence, poverty, and indigence occurring in Portuguese rural life. As we shall see, the highly selective approach of Ferro and his team to the universe of folk material culture was decisive in the building of such an image. Through the exhibition and dissemination of "folk art" objects, the secretariat constructed an image of rural life as that of an existence mysteriously detached from its economic and social constraints. Those objects were in fact used to celebrate Portuguese peasants and artisans, not as workers, but as intuitive artists and poets of a special kind. António Ferro was also one of the first public figures to emphasize Salazar's strong connection to his country roots, thus claiming the sharing of a substantial essence between the chief and the people he governed. Both Salazar's rural portrayal and the idyllic image of the people reinforced and legitimated each other, offering to the working and middle classes a pattern of conduct consistent with the anti-democratic, corporatist and conservative ideology of the regime.

BIOGRAPHY

Vera Marques Alves was born in Lisbon, on 16 May, 1969. In 2008, she received her PhD in Anthropology, from ISCTE, Lisbon. Her thesis examined the nationalist uses of folk culture during the Portuguese New State. She has taught several anthropology courses at the University of Coimbra. She has, also, developed postdoctoral research at the Centre for Research in Anthropology (CRIA-UC), and at the Interuniversity Centre for the History of Science and Technology (CIUHCT-UL). Her main research interests include History of Anthropology; Museum Anthropology and Material Culture; National Identity, Folklore, and Popular Arts and Cultural History in the 20th Century. She is the author of several journal articles and book chapters on the above mentioned topics. She has also published a book on the politics of folk culture in the context of Salazar's Dictatorship.

In 1933, António Ferro, by then a famous writer and international reporter, was nominated director of the Secretariat of National Propaganda (SPN–Secretariado da Propaganda Nacional), the Portuguese New State's propaganda office. With a modernist past, Ferro had been involved in different projects in order to redesign and modernize Portugal's physiognomy. For instance, in 1921, he reorganized the weekly magazine *Ilustração Portuguesa*, with the stated intension of styling up the Portuguese nation; in 1925 he created the New Theatre company (Teatro Novo), staging plays by Jules Romains and Piradello. Meanwhile he travelled the world, from Brazil and the United States to several European countries. In 1932, he wrote an article to the daily newspaper *Diário de Notícias* where he claimed urgency in changing the habits of the elite, so that the country could occupy the pages of modern magazines—the Portuguese bourgeoisie should go out and practice sports, enjoy open air activities and make art and good taste part of their daily lives, urged António Ferro. And what about the people? Was there a place for the people in this picture? Well, there was, but according to Ferro, only through the depiction of colourful and vivid images of its folklore.[1]

António Ferro didn't see any contradiction between the modernization of the nation's image, and the promotion of selected aspects of Portuguese folklore. He had seen the most avant-garde of artists, be they the Mexico muralists or the Ballet Russes creators, blending the modern and the traditional through the manipulation of ethnographic elements.[2] Furthermore, as a reporter, Ferro had been in contact with several cases in which folk culture was used to shape modern nations' images, particularly in international exhibitions. He advocated that Portugal, a country with rudimentary industry and an incipient scientific and economic development, could greatly benefit from the refashioning of its folk culture in order to create an exclusive image of its identity. We may find this argument in a newspaper opinion piece Ferro wrote in 1929:

"If we cannot bring machines, nor automobiles, nor planes, if we cannot stage our exhibitions with [. . .] train models and liners [. . .]—why not make a parade of regional arts and crafts, rugs, furniture, ceramics— everything that gives us character, all those poor little things which, after all, are the wealth of a nation's soul."[3]

The institutionalization of the New State in 1933 created the ideal political framework to develop such a project. Ideologically, the New State was a traditionalist and anti-democratic regime that instituted an organic vision of society inspired by a conservative vision of rural communities. Salazar, the son of poor farmers, was himself a catholic and anti-liberal who never missed an opportunity to glorify the moral superiority of the folk communities.

---

[1] António Rodrigues, *António Ferro na Idade do Jazz-Band* (Lisbon: Livros Horizonte, 1995), 134.

[2] Vera Marques Alves, *Arte Popular e nação no Estado Novo. A Política Folclorista do Secretariado da Propaganda Nacional* (Lisbon: Imprensa de Ciências Sociais, 2013), 251.

[3] António Ferro, "Portugal em Barcelona," *Diário de Notícias*, June 4, 1929. My translation.

Through a sequence of initiatives that included folk art exhibitions, folkloristic pageants, folk culture-inspired programmes of aesthetic renovation, Ferro and the SPN team developed an intensive ethnographic campaign in consonance with Salazar's organic and traditionalist vision of society. This campaign would play a decisive role, not only in the reshaping of Portugal's identity—a strong obsession of Ferro's from long ago—but also in the building and dissemination of the image of the Portuguese as a people composed of peaceful peasants that, in spite of their rustic existence, lived in a poetic and lyric frame of mind, indifferent to economic inequalities or class struggles of any sort.

THE LEADER WHO CAME "FROM THE PEOPLE"

When reading about the Portuguese New State, we often find references to the peculiarities of the persona of its chief, António de Oliveira Salazar. In fact, the profile of the Portuguese dictator was built around his quiet, almost misanthropic, personality, coincident with the image of a life entirely devoted to the study and resolution of Portugal's problems. Hence, Austen Chamberlain, the former English foreign secretary and MP, spoke of the "dictatorship of the Coimbra Professor of Finance"[4] and Dean Acheson, the USA Secretary of State between 1949 and 1953, praised the dictator as "the nearest approach in our time to Plato's philosopher-king."[5]

Meanwhile, the portrait of the strict academic went hand in hand with another image: that of the dictator as a common man; someone who, despite occupying the most powerful position in the country, still preserved the austere, peasant habits of his rural childhood. As Adinolfi and Costa Pinto have recently noted, *"the image Salazar cultivated was that of a reserved, puritanical and provincial dictator."*[6] António Ferro was one of the first public figures to emphasize Salazar's strong connection to his country roots. We can observe it in the interviews he did with the Portuguese leader in 1932, first published in the *Diário de Notícias* newspaper, and afterwards gathered in a book titled *Salazar. O Homem e a Sua Obra.*[7] In its third edition, António Ferro inserts an additional interview with the dictator, carried out in 1933, during a sojourn of Salazar in his village house. The description of the scenario couldn't be more bucolic:

"The hamlet of Vimieiro, in Santa Comba, over against Salazar's modest domain. A row of country cottages standing like beggars by the wayside. Two of them, pink-washed and faded, claim our attention. One is the school house, built by Dr. Salazar's father and where young António learnt his first letters. It is a humble establishment, a farmer's endowment, but it has borne good fruit and is still in the family.

[4] Chamberlain, Austen, "Preface," in António Ferro, *Salazar. Portugal and Her Leader* (London: Faber and Faber, 1939 [1933]), 9.

[5] Alden Whitman, "Antonio Salazar: A Quiet Autocrat Who Held Power in Portugal for 40 Years," *New York Times*, July 28, 1970.

[6] Goffreddo Adinolfi and António Costa Pinto, 2014, "Salazar's 'New State': The Paradoxes of Hybridization in the Fascist Era," in *Rethinking Fascism and Dictatorship in Europe*, ed. António Costa Pinto and Aristotle Kallis (London and New York: Pallgrave Macmillan, 2014), 157.

[7] The book was published in England in 1939 under the title *Portugal and Her Leader*. In the following quotes, I shall use this edition.

The present schoolmistress is Dr. Salazar's sister who teaches reading, writing, reckoning, and the fear of God to her young charges. The other cottage is residential. It has sash windows set two feet from the ground, with a very plain door in between. In front of each small window is a bed of flowers, hardly larger than a window-box, gay with cottage roses and marguerites." [8]

In spite of its poetic tone, there was no innocence in this piece of prose. Through the literary depiction of the dictator's rural home, António Ferro was above all claiming the sharing of a substantial essence between Salazar and the people he governed, thus naturalizing his leadership and the permanence of the New State itself. In another passage from the same book the journalist underlined once more the alleged affinity: *"I'm looking with instinctive respect on this dictator who has to go to the people's way because he himself comes from the people."*[9] Here we should notice that Ferro was referring to a particular romantic meaning of the word "people," according to which, as Peter Burke stressed long ago, "the people really means the peasants."[10] Johann Gottfried Herder was one of the first intellectuals to propose that meaning, stating that *"The mob in the streets, which never sings or composes but shrieks and mutilates, is not the people."*[11] During his activity at the helm of the New State propaganda office, António Ferro would often insist on such an assumption, repeating Herder's notion in other words: in 1936, for instance, he emphasized *"the distance between the simple people, the people who come from the land and die in the land [...] and the rhetorical people, the speech-people, falsely people, masked as people."*[12] Following Ferro's words, it's easy to identify the persons or social groups who supposedly constituted the "fake people": they were the urban and factory workers who, deviating from the "good path," demanded more rights or better living conditions, thus defying the rules imposed on them. Those would be "the speech-people," or in more current designations, the mob, the crowd, the horde. Later, he corroborated this same vision, condemning *"[...]those who say they love the people, but teach them only hate, trying to deviate the people from their natural life, replacing their instinctive and poetic wisdom with poorly conceived ideas that only create doubts and never-ending uncertainties."*[13]

The above quotes belong to two speeches which António Ferro gave in related initiatives: in 1936, at the opening of a folk art exhibition organized by SPN in Lisbon, and in 1948, at the inauguration of the Museum of Folk Art (Museu de Arte Popular), also a SPN project. From the beginning of its activity, in 1933, the SPN executed a large programme of ethnographic events, comprising several folk art exhibitions, such as the one mentioned above. These events celebrated the image of a people composed of obedient and well-behaved peasants, entirely devoted to their traditions and absolutely alien to

[8] António Ferro, *Salazar: Portugal and Her Leader*, 319.

[9] António Ferro, *Salazar: Portugal and Her Leader*, 209.

[10] Peter Burke, "The 'Discovery' of Popular Culture," in *People's History and Socialist Theory*, ed. Raphael Samuel (London, Boston and Henley: Routledge and Kegan Paul, 1981), 217.

[11] Burke, "The 'Discovery' of Popular Culture," 217..

[12] Quoted in Alves, *Arte Popular e Nação no Estado Novo*, 33.

[13] Quoted in Alves, *Arte Popular e Nação no Estado Novo*, 35

the conflicts of modern times. The industrial working classes, to say nothing of the undistinguished urban plebs, were not part of this picture. They were only praised when domesticated according to the idealized patterns of rural existence. Thus, in 1938, in yet another interview given to António Ferro,[14] Salazar remarked, while watching some families cultivating their small gardens in a Lisbon public housing neighbourhood: *"This is the way: working in one's own land is the first great obstacle to the tavern."*

We may say that during the New State, both Salazar's rural portrayal and the idyllic image of the people reinforced and legitimated each other, offering to the working and middle classes a pattern of conduct consistent with the anti-democratic, corporatist, and conservative ideology of the regime. Time and again, in each folk art exhibition or folkloristic event organized by SPN, there was a renewal of the values and concepts that sustained the New State: *"the values of resignation and obedience and the concepts [...] of a society free of politics [...]."*[15]

PEOPLE AS WELL-BEHAVED PEASANTS

Besides avoiding any mention of the urban working classes and their ways of life, the image of the Portuguese people built by SPN also entailed a highly selective approach to rural life. Following a narrow romantic concept of folklore,[16] the SPN team left aside those aspects of peasant practices and world views opposed to the bourgeois and official patterns of behaviour. They obliterated, for instance, any reference to what Mikhaïl Bakhtine[17] called "popular laughter," associated with the subversive carnival folk manifestations and its atmosphere of freedom and transgression. Instead of showing the "people who laugh"—the feast people who periodically challenge the status quo—the SPN displayed an ethereal, dematerialized people, in tune with middle-class moral standards and tastes. The archive is quite instructive on this matter, showing how the secretariat officials were sometimes genuinely disgusted at the spontaneous attitudes of the rural folk who participated in SPN events. Documents show, furthermore, how the same propaganda department spared no efforts to closely watch and discipline those peasants and artisans.[18]

Let us note, for instance, the ethnographic exhibition that took place in the Portuguese World Exhibition of 1940 (Exposição do Mundo Português). This large exhibition, staged to commemorate the foundation of the nation in 1140 and its independence from Spain in 1640[19] devoted a special place to peasant life, under the designation of "Regional Centre." In this space, everything was arranged in detail to form an attractive portrait of the country for

[14] António Ferro, "Salazar. Princípio e Fim," in *Salazar: O Homem e a Sua Obra* (Lisbon, Edições Fernando Pereira, 1982 [1938]), 280. My translation.

[15] Rita Almeida de Carvalho and António Costa Pinto, "The 'Everyman' of the Portuguese New State during the fascist era," in *The 'New Man' in Radical Right ideology 1919–45*, ed. Jorge Dagnino, Matthew Feldman and Paul Stocker (London: Bloomsbury, 2018), 131–148.

[16] On the romantic concept of folklore, see the seminal critical considerations of Mikhaïl Bakhtine, *Rabelais and His World* (Bloomington: Indiana University Press, 1984 [1968]).

[17] Mikhaïl Bakhtine, *Rabelais and His World*.

[18] On this episodes see Vera Marques Alves, "O Povo do Estado Novo," in *Como se Faz um Povo*, ed. J. Neves (Lisbon, Tinta-da-China, 2010) and *Arte Popular e Nação no Estado Novo*.

[19] Jorge Ramos do Ó, "Modernidade e Tradição: Algumas Reflexões em Torno da Exposição do Mundo Português," in *O Estado Novo: Das Origens ao Fim da Autarcia: 1926–1959*, vol. II (Lisbon: Fragmentos, 1987), 177–185; David Corkill and José Carlos Pina Almeida, "Commemoration and Propaganda in Salazar's Portugal: The Mundo Português Exposition of 1940," *Journal of Contemporary History*, 44(3) (2009): 381–399.

the urban bourgeois visitors: the SPN edified a bucolic "village," with examples of Portuguese vernacular architecture, perfectly clean house interiors and a sample of well-behaved "inhabitants" producing local craft objects. The visitors could also see peasant girls passing by in their prettiest traditional outfits and young women weaving and making lace under romantic porches. Mule drivers, ox carts, and the sound of church bells made up the rest of the scenario. Thus, in a move to offer the image of a beautiful and simple domestic folk existence, all the parodic, transgressing manifestations of folk culture were forgotten.

Also omitted from this picture were the violence, poverty, and indigence occurring in Portuguese rural life: in the Regional Centre, as in other folkloristic SPN events, everything was clean, and everybody enjoyed a blissful state of satisfaction. Furthermore, there was a regionalist approach to traditions which emphasized the local and provincial particularities, obliterating economic inequalities and social conflict.[20] In SPN initiatives, regional types were in fact ubiquitous, narrowing the geographic, economic, and social differences of the Portuguese people to a pleasing variety of costumes and artisanal practices, conjugated in the most harmonious way. Póvoa do Varzim's fishermen, the shepherds from Serra da Estrela or the Minho's farm women were just an illustration of the Portuguese identity; they appeared with no connection whatsoever to the social and economic structures that framed their existence and their working conditions. We may say of the way SPN pictured the Portuguese people what Roland Barthes said about the Blue Guide's depiction of the inhabitants of Spain: they were reduced "*to a vast classical ballet, a nice neat commedia dell'arte, whose improbable typology serve[d] to mask the real spectacle of conditions, classes and professions.*"[21]

Barthes' Ballet metaphor couldn't be more suitable in describing the SPN folkloristic programme: in the same year the Regional Centre was inaugurated, the SPN created *Verde Gaio*, a dance company inspired by Diaghilev's *Ballets Russes*, through which a romantic and rural version of the Portuguese people was once more proclaimed. Several of its ballets recreated folkloristic motifs, both in costumes and music. From a certain point of view, Verde Gaio was more fitted to show an ethereal, romantic picture of Portuguese people than other initiatives: while the Regional Centre's tableaux vivant obliged SPN officials to closely supervise the rural participants that formed its idyllic scenes, Verde Gaio, on the contrary, allowed the organization of a perfectly controlled image of the nation and its people, through the aesthetic manipulation of its ethnographic materials. It worked as a device to celebrate people's folklore without having to deal with the people as such.

[20] As the historian Christian Faure as noted in his investigation about the culture politics of Vichy France, the stress on regional dress, for instance, was a way to disguise the social divisions that, on the contrary, the urban fashion highlighted in inescapable ways. Christian Faure, *Le Projet Culturel de Vichy: Folklore et Révolution Nationale 1940–1944* (Lyon, Presses Universitaires de Lyon, 1998), 81.

[21] Roland Barthes, *The Blue Guide* (New York: Noonday Press, Farrar, Strauss & Giroux, 1991[1957]), 75.

But the main instrument used by SPN in the creation and diffusion of this poetic, dematerialized portrait of the people was, curiously enough, the rural material culture itself, by then exhibited under the designation of "folk art." Anthropologists such as Hermann Bausinger[22] have shown how the category of "folk art" appeared as a result of a gradual process of selection and reclassification, through which rural artefacts were no longer seen as part of the system of production and economic life of the populations, but rather as artistic objects. Through the notion of folk art, which comprised above all aesthetically impressive rural objects, material culture was thus transformed in a "spiritual thing"; something not very different from the folk songs or the folk tales which ethnographers and folklorists had been collecting since the 18th century. Only then did the middle classes consider rural artefacts suitable to signify the nation and as such to occupy a relevant place in their homes and leisure spaces. In line with this orientation, by concentrating on the exhibition of folk art objects, the secretariat constructed an image of rural life as that of an existence mysteriously detached from its economic and social constraints. As a consequence, those exhibits didn't speak of the Portuguese peasants and artisans as rural workers, but as poets of a special kind; poets that, instead of operating with words, used clay, wood and stones.

PEOPLE AS INTUITIVE ARTISTS

For António Ferro and his team, there were not enough metaphors to describe the SPN's folk art exhibitions: the 1936 exhibit, for instance, was publicized as a "wonderful visual rhapsody," a "symphony of colour," a "gigantic polychrome screen."[23] Drawing on the work of several Portuguese ethnographers,[24] the SPN was able to assemble a set of artefacts of high decorative quality, leaving out all those material culture elements which lacked impressive visual character. Simultaneously, the SPN events gave a special emphasis to small artefacts and miniatures of all sorts. Thus, in the speeches, editions, and catalogues that accompanied the SPN folk art exhibitions, we may find a constant glorification of the immense richness of the exhibited objects' forms, of the lavishness of their ornaments, of the artisans' meticulous craftsmanship. Underlying this eulogy of Portuguese folk art was an image continually enunciated by Ferro and his collaborators: the image of the Portuguese people as a people of peasant aesthetes and intuitive folk artists, whose poetic inclinations left aside any concerns with the crude material aspects of existence, let alone with political matters. Through this image, it was the working status of the rural people that was erased. And if the true identity of the people was that of an artist, and not a worker, why should anyone feel obliged to think about their material needs?

[22] Hermann Bausinger, *Volkskunde ou l'Ethnologie Allemande* (Paris: Editions de la Maison des sciences de l'homme, 1993 [1971]).

[23] Alves, *Arte Popular e Nação no Estado Novo*, 110.

[24] See João Leal, *Etnografias Portuguesas (1870–1970): Cultura Popular e Identidade Nacional* (Lisbon: Publicações Dom Quixote, 2000) and Alves, *Arte Popular e nação no Estado Novo*.

The most vivid embodiment of such an image was given by a collection of dozens of 60 cm dolls, dressed in regional outfits, which stood out in every SPN folk art exhibition. It was as if the peasants not only lived surrounded by playthings, but were themselves lovely little toys of a fairy-tale land. For a dictatorial and traditionalist regime such as the Portuguese New State, there could be no more convenient image of the people, a fact Regina Bendix explains while considering the general features of the political uses of folklore: *"When our eyes, ears, nose and taste buds are ensnared and pleased, we waste little effort thinking about the system of production and the nature of rule under which these aesthetic practices reached their contours."*[25] Likewise, Kirshenblatt-Gimblet[26] has also argued that by aestheticizing the cultural manifestations of certain social or ethnic groups, one tends to obliterate the marginal status of some of them.

During the forties, the relevance of Portuguese folk art would be reinforced through a SPN initiative designated the "Good Taste Campaign" (Campanha do Bom Gosto). António Ferro wanted to expand the contact of the public with folk art objects far beyond the isolated events he organized. He wanted them to invade the daily life of the middle classes, as well as their leisure environments. In this context, SPN created a set of little hotels or inns, called "Pousadas de Portugal," spread throughout the national territory. Their architecture and interior decorations used local materials and were inspired by the regional folk motifs. In the launching of this programme, the SPN promoted the renovation of an old guest house in Óbidos (a little town 80km from Lisbon), where, according to Ferro, one could appreciate the "pastoral joy" of folk pottery and simple fabrics.[27] Following this model, each one of the several inns then inaugurated was arranged with folk artefacts of the corresponding region. The secretariat could now show to the middle class how to use the rural artefacts as "good taste" decorative objects in modern habitats. The *Panorama* Magazine—also an SPN creation—was another relevant vehicle in the pursuit of this pedagogical agenda. In its pages, publicists guided the readers on how to decorate restaurants, little hotels, and private houses, declaring war against "sad furniture" and heavy dark curtains which should be substituted by regional decorative elements and folk artefacts.[28] The emotional enchantment aroused by folk art objects could now be transformed into a daily feeling of tenderness towards the Portuguese nation and its people of aesthete peasants.

[25] Regina Bendix, "Final Reflections: 'The Politics of Folk Culture' in the 21st Century," *Etnográfica*, n.º IX (1), (2005): 195.

[26] Barbara Kirshenblatt-Gimblett, "Objects of Ethnography," in *Exhibiting Cultures: The Poetics and Politics of Museum Display*, ed. Ivan Karp and Steven D. Lavine (Washington and London: Smithsonian Institution Press, 1991), 428

[27] António Ferro, *Turismo: Fonte de Riqueza e de Poesia* (Lisbon: Edições SNI, 1949).

[28] Alves, *Arte Popular e nação no Estado Novo*, 276–281.

BIBLIOGRAPHY

Adnolfi, Gofreddo, and António Costa Pinto. "Salazar's 'New State': The Paradoxes of Hybridization in the Fascist Era." In *Rethinking Fascism and Dictatorship in Europe*, edited by António Costa Pinto and Aristotle Kallis, 154–175. London and New York: Pallgrave Macmillan, 2014.

Alves, Vera Marques. "'A Poesia dos Simples': Arte Popular e Nação no Estado Novo." *Etnográfica*, vol. 11 no.1 (2007): 63–89.

Alves, Vera Marques. "O Povo do Estado Novo." In *Como se Faz um Povo*, edited by J. Neves, 183–194. Lisboa: Tinta-da-China, 2010.

Alves, Vera Marques. *Arte Popular e nação no Estado Novo. A Política Folclorista do Secretariado da Propaganda Nacional.* Lisboa: Imprensa de Ciências Sociais, 2013.

Bakhtin, Mikhail. *Rabelais and His World.* Bloomington: Indiana University Press, 1984 [1968].

Barthes, Roland, 1988 [1957], "O Guia Azul," *Mitologias*, Lisboa, Edições 70, pp. 113–115.

Bausinger, Hermann. *Volkskunde ou l'Ethnologie Allemande.* Paris: Editions de la Maison des sciences de l'homme, 1993 [1971].

Bendix, Regina. "Final Reflections: 'The Politics of Folk Culture' in the 21st Century." *Etnográfica*, vol.9, no.1 (2005): 195–203.

Burke, Peter. "The 'Discovery' of Popular Culture." In *People's History and Socialist Theory*, edited by Raphael Samuel, 216–226. London, Boston and Henley: Routledge and Kegan Paul, 1981.

Carvalho, Rita Almeida de, and António Costa Pinto. "The "Everyman" of the Portuguese New State during the fascist era." In *The 'New Man' in Radical Right Ideology 1919–45*, edited by Jorge Dagnino, Matthew Feldman and Paul Stocker, 131–148. London: Bloomsbury, 2018.

Chamberlain, Austen. "Preface." In António Ferro, *Salazar: Portugal and Her Leader*, 7–10. London: Faber and Faber, 1939.

Corkill, David, and José Carlos Pina Almeida. "Commemoration and Propaganda in Salazar's Portugal: The Mundo Português Exposition of 1940." *Journal of Contemporary History*, vol. 44, no.3 (2009): 381–399.

Faure, Christian. *Le Projet Culturel de Vichy: Folklore et Révolution Nationale 1940–1944.* Lyon: Presses Universitaires de Lyon, 1989.

Ferro, António. "Portugal em Barcelona." *Diário de Notícias*, June 4, 1929.

Ferro, António. *Salazar: Portugal and Her Leader.* London: Faber and Faber, 1939 [1933].

Ferro, António. "Salazar. Princípio e Fim." In *Salazar: O Homem e a Sua Obra.* Lisboa: Edições Fernando Pereira, 1982 [1938].

Ferro, António. *Turismo: Fonte de Riqueza e de Poesia.* Lisboa: Edições SNI, 1949.

Kirshenblatt–Gimblett, Barbara. "Objects of Ethnography." In *Exhibiting Cultures: The Poetics and Politics of Museum Display*, edited by Ivan Karp and Steven D. Lavine, 386–443. Washington and London: Smithsonian Institution Press, 1991.

Leal, João. *Etnografias Portuguesas (1870–1970): Cultura Popular e Identidade Nacional.* Lisboa: Publicações Dom Quixote, 2000.

Ó, Jorge Ramos do. "Modernidade e Tradição: Algumas Reflexões em Torno da Exposição do Mundo Português."In *O Estado Novo: Das Origens ao Fim da Autarcia: 1926–1959*, vol. II, 177–185. Lisboa: Fragmentos, 1987.

Rodrigues, António. *António Ferro na Idade do Jazz-Band.* Lisboa: Livros Horizonte, 1995.

Whitman, Alden. "Antonio Salazar: A Quiet Autocrat Who Held Power in Portugal for 40 Years." *New York Times*, 28 July, 1970.

Innauguration of the church of the Alvalade Estate in 1955. The Alvalade Estate, planned at the start of the 1940s, was until the end of the following decade the largest housing initiative in Portugal, mixing public and private investment.

Empresa Pública Jornal O Século, Albuns Gerais no. 118, doc. 1471AG.
PT/TT/EPJS/SF/001-001/0118/1471AG. Image from ANTT.

3. HOUSE, NEIGHBOURHOOD, AND DENSITY (1946–1968)

By the end of World War II, single-family houses were seen by architects, planners and some municipal entities as a limited response to the housing problem. The New State reacted by creating new housing programmes that allowed multi-family buildings and rent systems, with new target audiences, such as the urban middle classes. The focus of a new generation of Portuguese architects would shift to the Italian example.

Post-War Portugal: Between Conservatism and Modernity

MARIA FERNANDA ROLLO
NOVA University of Lisbon, School of Social Sciences and Humanities

ABSTRACT

World War II—and the post-war period—had lasting impacts and involved deep changes in Portuguese society, implying an unequivocal turning point in the country's political and economic path. It is a fact that the New State (Estado Novo) had endured—by making a clever use of the formula of neutrality. The end of the world conflict was going to boost a sense of restlessness, partly roused by awareness of the regime's uncertain continuity in the new times. The importance of the Allies' support for the survival of the New State was undeniable; nevertheless, breathed new life into the opposition forces, which, feeling strengthened, moved against the regime.

The disturbing times of military conflict were followed by the no less complex times of peace. War and peace brought about an intricate procession of deregulations and effects that generated discontent and imbalances in Portuguese society and the economy, but also introduced new opportunities. The truth was that, after World War II, nothing would ever be the same. Politically, cracks opened in the established power and it was confronted with lively and solid dissent, which left scars for years to come. However, the New State survived, protecting its vulnerabilities and rising above these difficulties; and, once the crisis had passed, it asserted itself, reinforced and unruffled.

At the same time, overcoming a few hesitations and unravelling several deadlocks, post-war Portugal started a process of economic and social development, keeping up—although far behind, of course—with the climate of prosperity that characterized the economy and society of European countries as a whole during the next two decades. It was a growth cycle that incorporated structural changes, even though there were powerful factors of social and political resistance that, by enduring, negatively affected the pace and the extent of modernizing changes. Between plans and realities and at both these levels, deep contradictions and dissensions were hidden. In the meantime, there were renewed pressures and major tensions, internal and external, bringing reformist effects that the regime was not able to repress or contain. Cultural changes, new behaviours and social expectations, urbanization, emigration and internationalization, among other dynamics, converged in a whirlwind in which the colonial issue and the assertion of the colonial peoples' autonomy movements were going to stand out drastically. In the long term, and in spite of efforts made to maintain "order" and unite wills, that process would become compromised, confronting the regime with its own limits.

BIOGRAPHY

Historian. PhD and with Aggregation in Contemporary History. Professor of the Faculty of Social Sciences and Humanities of the Nova University of Lisbon, and researcher at the Institute of Contemporary History. Coordinator of Centro República (2011–). Secretary of State for Science, Technology and Higher Education (2015–2018). President of the Institute of Contemporary History (2011–2015). Inception and coordination of the ROSSIO infrastructure (2011–2015). National Commissioner for the Celebrations of the Centenary of the Republic (2008–2011).

Her areas of research are Portuguese history in the 20th century, Portugal's participation in European economic cooperation movements, economic, industrial, engineering and innovation, contemporary history, history of the organization of science in Portugal.

Ciência Vitae F91D-2B9A-5767

After five years of widespread conflict, the end of World War II in Europe was announced on 8 May 1945. Even though Portugal did not take part in the war, the country was inevitably stuck in that all-enveloping moment, sharing the satisfaction and anguish of peace. Regardless of perspective, the world had changed, and the assumptions involving its reorganization were complex. Portuguese neutrality hadn't been able to contain the effects of the changes that pervaded the international sphere, and these, crossing borders, took the country by surprise and broke through the national reality; its permeability was perhaps even more evident than what the triple purpose which was devised and announced during the war—economic defence, moral defence, political defence[3]—had tried to prevent.

It is beyond doubt that the war was a clear turning point in our country's path, at all levels, leaving an indelible mark on 20th century Portuguese history, as in fact it did in all the other countries directly or indirectly affected by the conflict, as well as on the global international order. However, this must be especially emphasized in the Portuguese case, highlighting the extent to which the wartime context determined the emergence of the New State's first political crisis. Changing the ways in which Portuguese economic activity operated, it brought about disruption and the manifestation of new dynamics in the scenario of financial and monetary stability, forcing changes in the direction and cadence that guided the economy of the country. That disruption was clearly visible in the housing plan.

In fact, in spite of its stance of neutrality, Portugal suffered from the economic effects spread by the war, and was forced to adopt a true wartime economy. This situation, proving that national economy was strongly dependent on foreign trade (especially on supplies), exposed the importance of a set of *structural vulnerabilities*[4] that shaped the Portuguese economic reality with respect to the nature and composition of its productive fabric. This led to a reflection on the substance of Portuguese economy, raising awareness of the limits imposed by its poor performance in terms of production, particularly revealing the weaknesses of its industrial network. It opened the way for the acceptance and approval of an economic modernization programme based mainly on the adoption and implementation of an electrification plan (Law no. 2,002[5]) and on the acceptance of an industrialization programme (Law no. 2,005[6]), which would be badly compromised by varied obstacles.

The bitter denunciation of external dependence, displayed within the context of widespread scarcity, heavy restrictions, and supply difficulties imposed by the war, was joined by a complex procession of internal effects, such as inflation, the black market and contraband, along with changes made to the productive system as a

---

[1] Title of a speech made by Oliveira Salazar to the country on 25 June 1942; António de Oliveira Salazar, *Discursos e Notas Políticas, vol. III 1938–1943*, Coimbra Editora, 1st ed. 1943, 2nd ed. 1959, pp. 321–352.

[2] Fernando Rosas, *Portugal entre a Paz e a Guerra. Estudo do Impacte da II Guerra Mundial na Economia e na Sociedade Portuguesas (1939–1945)*, "Imprensa Universitária, 83" (Lisbon, Editorial Estampa, 1990), Chapter I.

[3] Law no. 2,002, Country Electrification, *Diário do Governo* (DG), I Série (26 December 1944).

[4] Law no. 2,005, "Industrial Development and Reorganization," *DG*, I Série, no. 54 (14 March 1945).

reaction to markets that operated under unusual conditions and amid increasing dysfunction. It quickly became obvious, at least to some observers, that the war after all posed a stark test to Portuguese economic capacity, especially when considered within a framework of economic autarky. Most interestingly, the procured solution took on a markedly nationalistic trait and aimed precisely at reinforcing this postulate of economic independence.

In short, the war created a context and imposed an important turning point that affected some main assumptions and forced changes upon the development strategies that then guided Portugal's economic policy, or the lack thereof, sublimating particularly in the priority plan to electrify and industrialize the country. However, it should also be emphasized that the war, by compromising the equilibria created in the 1930s, also forced its assumptions to falter. Behind the more obvious aspects mentioned above, it is possible to understand how, despite the refusal of contemporaries to admit it, in the end the effects of the war exposed and boosted the contradictions engendered by the system that shaped Portuguese economy.

The truth is that the war hit the Portuguese economy by surprise on its weakest side, simultaneously dealing a powerful blow to the theoretical postulate of corporatism that presided over its guidance—something that the system tried to solve by reinforcing that corporatism. On the whole, by adopting a wartime economy and by choosing solutions meant to be implemented during the War and in the post-war years, the situation led to a clear reinforcement of the role of the state and to its increasing intervention in the economic activity, an intervention that the effects and results of the conflict, particularly considering the accumulated wealth, would tend to enhance. Nevertheless, it should also be said that the effects of World War II in Portugal had a globally positive impact on the course of Portuguese economy, temporarily creating a space of relative prosperity and a period during which many economic agents became wealthier, including the state, at the same time as the inequality of the distribution of national wealth actually worsened. However, two fundamental issues should be mentioned.

First, the good financial situation of both the state's accounts and private entities in Portugal was accompanied by persistent inflationary pressure, which was in fact one of the main concerns of the Portuguese government's economic and financial policy. Second, evaluating the behaviour of Portuguese economy during the war and comparing it with other neutral economies highlights the unsatisfactory results of national production.

Actually, as Silva Lopes pointed out, *"national production increased very little during the war. The GDP per capita was not much higher in 1946 than in 1939. This evolution contrasted with that of Sweden and Switzerland, which, like Portugal, remained neutral during the war."* In any case, in addition to the aforementioned positive influence of the war on launching an economic modernization programme, basically through laws 2,002 and 2,005, other aspects have been identified that sustain the notion of a positive impact and relative prosperity in Portugal connected to the context of the war. Among these are the *"hitherto unknown increase of the trade balance, mainly due to the exportation of products abnormally valued due to the needs of the belligerent countries [...], the development, in Portugal, of an effort to industrialize certain activities, seeking, on one hand, to meet the needs usually covered by imports and, on the other hand, to take advantage of extremely favourable conditions brought about by the war, as well as the creation of an exceptional reserve of gold and foreign exchange in the Bank of Portugal, substantial amounts in the account of the Treasury and [...] significant increases in bank deposits."*[6]

The regime was busy preparing for peace, taking into account both the external context and the national situation. On one hand, it sought to face the new challenges, situations of uncertain outlines arising in the international stage, and to find a space to (re)position itself within the new community of nations, of which the shape was, strictly speaking, still unclear and undergoing constant adjustments. On the other hand, as a result of the sense of vulnerability stemming from its very nature, the government made obstinate efforts to assert itself internally. It was intent on annihilating the momentum of any bolder resistance, decidedly trying to acquire the means and confirm the reasons for its existence, making sure it was able to overcome a context of complex crisis bearing unmistakable and undisguised signs of dissent legitimized by growing social malaise. As time passed, however, it became apparent that the positive expectations created by the war did not develop nor fully materialize, cruelly confronting the country with the true nature of its short-lived prosperity. In fact, *"the prosperity felt at the end of the war was more apparent than real, basically because the war generated wealth but not permanent and self-sustained sources of income."*[7]

It became evident that the conjunctural effort made in order to profit from recently acquired advantages and integrate new "bearings" that would let the country prevail over the vulnerabilities of the national productive fabric, counteracting the negative effects felt during and after the war, could not have immediate effects, since it was difficult to counter long-established tendencies.

---

[5] José da Silva Lopes, "Portuguese Economy in the 20th Century," in *Panorama da Cultura Portuguesa no Século XX, 1. As Ciências e as Problemáticas Sociais*, ed. Fernando Peres (Edições Afrontamento / Porto 2001 / Serralves Foundation, 2002), 311.

[6] Maria Fernanda Rollo, *Portugal e o Plano Marshall* (Estampa, 1994) 190–191.

[7] Rollo, *Portugal e o Plano Marshall*, 191.

In addition to this situation, there were restraints imposed by Portuguese authorities, particularly in order to preserve the internal political and social balances, the constraints of corporate organization and the strict compliance with the dogmatic principles of traditional financial policy, which regulated, defined and in practice overlapped with the pursuit of that strategy.

Efforts to develop and put into practice the modernization strategy formally accepted in the context of the current political, economic and social reality met with hesitations and difficulties. In addition, the accumulated wealth would soon be depleted, since it had not been used for the benefit of durable investments able to enhance the national economy, a situation which was due to internal, public and private issues, but also to external constraints. The problem of supplies, coupled with a climate of growing dissatisfaction and social instability, worsened in face of the international situation and was apt to become even more serious due to the weaknesses of the Portuguese productive fabric, clearly incapable of meeting essential needs, now added to requirements of the economic programme which the government meant to carry out. This issue had obvious political consequences and so it came to the forefront, demanding urgent solutions. On the other hand, the effort announced to tackle the problem of the productive structure, paving the way for rapid industrialization, was neither fully accepted nor able to yield immediate results. In addition, measures adopted to counteract this trend, which predictably could worsen, particularly in foreign trade, were ineffective or clearly insufficient to present timely positive results.

The process was hard and even lengthy; efforts had to be sustained during the months following the end of the war. By the beginning of 1947, the government showed signs of having succeeded in reinforcing its political control and strongly asserting itself, at least until the next clash. However, it would take more than two years, until after the hardest part of the ongoing crisis was over, to complete the complex process of transition from a war economy to a peace economy and to set the moulds that were to guide the country's economic future. On the political front, following the events surrounding the presidential elections of 1949, the New State managed to establish a climate of internal appeasement and annulment of the oppositions that would last almost until the end of the following decade. It had no difficulty in neutralizing the candidacies of the opposition—Quintão Meireles, with the support of the more moderate sectors (Cunha Leal, Azevedo Gomes, António Sérgio, Henrique Galvão), and Rui Luís Gomes, supported by the MND (National Democratic Movement)—to the presidential elections that followed the death of Óscar Carmona, in 1951, or in electing the 120 candidates of the UN (National Union party) to the 1953 elections.

However, the Portuguese political reality was changing significantly, showing signs of a clear reinforcement of the "reformist" sector surrounding Marcello Caetano, in collusion with the new President of the Republic, Craveiro Lopes (since July 1951), potentially against a conservative current, *"ultramontana"* (ultramontanist), well headed by Santos Costa. Outside the regime, liberal opposition was growing, gathered around Cunha Leal and António Sérgio, diverging from the PCP (Portuguese Communist Party) and the MND, betting on an understanding that would encompass all those who opposed the regime—including, for a while, the PCP itself. The socialist current, trying to assert itself, was also developing around Mário Soares. The most important moment came in 1957, when General Humberto Delgado's "independent candidacy" was launched for the 1958 presidential elections. Tensions were rekindled around what was to become the biggest protest movement against the regime of Oliveira Salazar. Under the "Pact of Cacilhas," Arlindo Vicente, the PCP candidate, would withdraw his candidacy and support Delgado.

From north to south, the country watched these events anxiously. Complaining against massive electoral fraud, Delgado was defeated at the polls; Américo Tomás was elected President of the Republic. But Portugal had changed. By the end of the decade there was political unrest, coming from various quarters, popular protests and general dissent, filled with events. It should be noted that the Catholic Church began edging away from the New State. This was clearly expressed by the Bishop of Porto, António Ferreira Gomes, in a letter to Salazar (13 July 1958), where he criticized his governance and questioned the role of the Church in Portuguese society (the following year, *Dom* António Ferreira Gomes was forced into exile); or by the forty-five Catholics, among whom we find Nuno Teotónio Pereira; on 1 March 1959, they sent an "open letter" to Salazar condemning the violence and crimes perpetrated by the political police. The dissent was marked by the Revolt of the See: a revolutionary conspiracy, both military and civil, that erupted on the night of 11 to 12 March 1959, but which the PIDE managed to break up. A number of lower-ranking officers were arrested, although it was known that the conspirators had accomplices among senior figures in the military hierarchy. The regime tried to guard against possible attacks. Even the presidential elections were closed to the opposition: on 29 August 1959, when the revised constitution was promulgated, it established that the President of the Republic would be chosen by an electoral college of 602 members (deputies to the National Assembly, members of the Corporate Chamber, representatives from the administrative structures of colonial territories and representatives from municipal councils).

But it was not only internal politics that were different. In the economic field, it should be noted that, once some hesitations and deadlocks were worked out, namely the matter of foreign supplies, as well as the payment crisis of the late 1940s, post-war Portugal started on a path of economic and social development, part of the climate of prosperity that marked the international context during the next two decades, enjoyed particularly by European countries. It was undoubtedly a cycle of growth and modernization that incorporated structural changes, notwithstanding the powerful social and political factors of resistance that, by subsisting, negatively conditioned the pace and scope of the modernizing transformations.[10]

In fact, starting in the post-war period, Portugal, following the international trend, started a process of fast and sustained economic development that would last until 1973. During this period, the country's growth rate was unprecedented in national history; shortening some of its usual lag, Portugal neared and converged towards the more developed European countries. Although there are different opinions concerning time frames, it has been noted that the growth of the 1950s increased during the 1960s. Among the most relevant and "innovative" aspects that outlined the Portuguese economy during the 1950s were the intervention of the state and the adoption of an economic policy inscribed in development plans, trying to shape its economic model. One of the aspects that most clearly influenced the performance of the various European market economies over the "thirty golden years" was the adopted economic cooperation platform and its effects, namely in terms of liberalization and development of commerce, in which Portugal was also involved and from which it benefited, particularly through its participation in the Marshall Plan and the OECD.

This was to be one of the most "weighty" consequences of the effects of World War II and the post-war period in Portugal, intimately connected with the period of growth and modernization that characterized the Portuguese economy in the second half of the 20th century. In fact, it was also due to the effects of the war, especially following the events surrounding our country's participation in the Marshall Plan, that Portugal became gradually more open to outside influences and its economy increasingly internationalized: by being involved in the Marshall Plan and joining the OECD and the European Payments Union (EPU), Portugal ensured its integration in the post-war trade and payments system and its active presence in the emerging cooperation movements inside the European economy.

[8] Cf. Maria Fernanda Rollo, "Crossed Paths," in *Engenho e Obra. Uma Abordagem à História da Engenharia em Portugal no Século XX*, ed. J. M. Brandão de Brito, Manuel Heitor and Maria Fernanda Rollo (Lisbon: Publicações Dom Quixote, Lisbon, 2002) 43.

It is worth noting, however, that this approach, particularly during the 1950s, was almost inevitable, mainly due to the pressure exerted by the international context. It was not an option, but rather an inexorable reaction, proof of the weight of the international "siege," and one that the government combined with greater attention to the colonies. The war brought about an important change of tack in the attitude of the Portuguese government towards the colonies. Taking advantage of the logic behind the colonial pact, the colonies emerged as an alternative space in terms of supply and commerce, a safe haven for investment opportunities and an important rearguard of complementary resources for the metropolitan economy. The colonies were also reassessed under the light of their reserves of natural resources, worthwhile discovering and exploiting, both nationally and internationally; there was even talk of the need to industrialize those resources, under certain conditions, of course. Summing up, the regime made an effort to preserve the essential aspects of the existing reality, trying, as much as possible, to reconcile two tendentially divergent courses: autarky and internationalization.

In any case, as pointed out, the involvement and integration in the dynamics and new international institutions to which the Marshall Plan gave rise was a decisive opportunity to gain access to the European economic cooperation movement from which, perhaps, it would have been kept away. It is a fact that the return to "normality"—the crisis, home and abroad—and the change of the people responsible for economic affairs restrained the enthusiasm and euphoria of wartime years, meaning a deceleration of the passionate voluntarism used and promoted by Ferreira Dias through the laws of electrification and industrialization of the country. The truth is that the concern with stabilizing the economy of the system overcame the developmental impetus associated with "development and industrial reorganization." However, the 1950s were marked by the systematic start of economic planning (I Development Plan—1953/58) and by the final triumph of the idea of industrialization, the concept and design of which would be consecrated by the end of the decade at the II Congress of Economists and Portuguese Industry (1957).

Furthermore, the new political and economic strategy of the state, set in motion in the aftermath of World War II with a view to coherently framing the major objectives of economic policy within the then so-called "development plans," was an essential factor in the considerable evolution of Portuguese economy. It advanced, in obedience to the general tendencies of European capitalism, the conditions that would lead to a marked growth of the national industrial sector.

Agriculture was left irreparably behind, even though the government stated that industrial development was to be subordinated to agricultural development. Somewhat in line with an historical evolutionary pattern, "national farming" practically gave up on its own growth and modernization process, clinging reluctantly to obsolete farming formulas and archaic technologies that generated lasting stagnation.

Remarkably, it was (only) during the first half of the 1950s that there were significant changes in the structure of the Portuguese economy, industry clearly becoming the most dynamic and important sector. In fact, from then on the rate of growth of the industrial sector started to noticeably exceed that of agriculture. The relatively slow economic growth experienced over this decade (the GNP increased at an annual rate of 4.4 per cent between 1950 and 1960) was mainly due to the output growth of the industrial sector, contributing more and more to the GDP, instead of the primary sector. However, the new industrial policy, based on the principle that this sector's growth would in itself lead to an overall economic development of the country, soon proved to be ineffective. In fact, in the 1960s, shaking the foundations on which stood the industrialization of the previous decade, and under the backlash of a strategy that favoured industry but neglected the parallel development of the primary sector, Portugal found that the growth of its industrial production was far from guaranteeing sustained and nominally balanced economic development.

On the other hand, the late 1950s and especially the early 1960s also posed new challenges for Portugal concerning its involvement in European economic cooperation movements, entailing important decisions, and coherent strategies. By joining EFTA (formally, on 4 January 1960, by signing the Stockholm Convention), Portugal avoided staying permanently out of European integration movements; it assumed commitments of a strictly economic and commercial nature, with no issues concerning its regime or political system (as in the EEC), much less problems arising from the existence of the African colonies, given the arranged customs autonomy as far as third countries were concerned. Portugal's comparative industrial underdevelopment vis-à-vis the other member powers was safeguarded through the acceptance of the "famous" Annex G, by which Portugal was allowed a much slower tariff removal (which in Portugal's case could be extended by 20 years—twice what was granted to the other members) and, above all, it expressly authorized our country to erect customs barriers whenever the protection of new industries was involved. Incidentally, 1960 was also the year when the study of the *unification of the Portuguese economic space* was pushed forward.

The new architecture given to the colonial problem would emerge the following year, formally creating the Portuguese Economic Space—the colonial war in Angola had already begun. On another front, urbanization and tertiarization, together with industrialization, gave rise to new realities and tensions in Portuguese society.

The 1960s clearly illustrate the contradictions and imbalances inherent to the chosen development model in regard to the demographic behaviour of the Portuguese population, in addition to which there were effects from the colonial wars. Notwithstanding the positive aspects of the transition to a modern demographic regime, with modernization and overall improvement of living conditions throughout this period, the demographic behaviour, containing strong regional inequalities, was characterized by the slowing down of the annual growth rate (negative during the 1960s) and was indelibly marked by high levels of migration and emigration over the period, leading to the gradual aging of the national demographic structure.

Mainly affecting the inner countryside and rural or underdeveloped urban areas, flight from the fields was directed to the cities or abroad. The Portuguese continental population preferred Brazil at first; then, starting from 1963–1964, the more developed countries of Europe. The population from Portuguese archipelagos opted mainly for Atlantic destinations. Between 1946 and 1973, almost two million people emigrated—mostly males between the ages of 15 and 29.

Partly absorbing the rural exodus, the increasing post-war urban explosion, especially visible during the 1960s, took place mainly in medium-sized urban centres (ten to twenty thousand inhabitants) and large urban centres (more than twenty thousand inhabitants). This progressive trend reduced the percentage weight of the two main urban centres, Lisbon and Porto, a fact which can be explained by the tertiarization of the traditional urban centres, expelling part of their resident population to peripheral municipalities, where the bulk of the migrant population, who could not afford urban prices, tended to settle, looking for work in the city or on its outskirts.

The spectacular growth of suburban "mushrooms" in the peripheral districts of Lisbon and Porto, giving good reason for the labels Greater Lisbon and Greater Porto, took place in a disorderly way, with no support in terms of housing, sanitary or transport infrastructures, giving rise to an abundance of illegal housing, which grew into shanty towns, inserted in a scenario with increasing social problems and worsening living conditions.

This shows how the regime/country and its assertions was being left behind. It was confronted with impossibilities, ignoring intrinsic blockages and contradictory forces, seeking, sometimes in vain, sometimes using its authoritarianism, to contain modernizing tensions, and attempting to resist, perpetuating inertias or simply bumping into conservative apathy, taken by surprise by social and cultural changes that turned up and stood their ground.[11] However, modernity has a way of materializing and changing assumptions, as illustrated by the significant case of the Alvalade neighbourhood, analysed in this book by the text under the authorship of João Pedro Costa, giving evidence of growing technical competence and modernizing inspiration.

This, however, occurred in a city recurrently taken by surprise and outdated, conditioned, and restrained by the slow arrival of modernity—as seen in the construction of the subway, decided in 1947, after decades of deadlock; modern, technically robust, and indisputable, anchored in the competence of national engineering, but so late in coming and being inaugurated and, on top of everything, reduced to such a minimum extent that in 1959 it earned the nickname "centimetre."[12] And yet, it came to be. Porto, too, and how, as read in the essay by Virgílio Pereira, mirrored the dynamics in progress, shaping spaces, "suppressing" increasing asymmetries, watching the impressive and "silent" movement that swelled its "islands." Deep social changes took place in this context of rapidly increasing city density. Proletarianization inside heavy industries of a large part of the rural population which arrived in the cities, the birth and expansion of a modern service sector, increasing literacy levels, greater access to education, culture, and media, new forms of social life, all of this would make the urban and suburban population in the main cities and metropolitan areas an increasingly important agent for social and political intervention, particularly in Lisbon and the northern and southern banks of the Tagus. This would require and give rise to new and more adequate answers from urban planners and architects, other solutions, different approaches, reconciling ambitions and expectations, combining scientific expertise and technical competence, looking to the future, politically too, as we may find in Teotónio Pereira or Nuno Portas—see the text in this book by Tiago Lopes Dias.

Naturally, migratory movements, flight from the countryside, industrial development and ongoing tertiarization would bring about a visible change in the composition of the Portuguese working population, with a visible decrease in assets linked to the primary sector and a clear growth of assets connected to the secondary and tertiary sectors.

[9] Very interesting testimonies about the changes in the city of Lisbon, social occasions and daily events that made up these post-war years may be found at Avenue Memories (www.memoriaparatodos.pt).

[10] Maria Fernanda Rollo, *Um Metro e Uma Cidade. História do Metropolitano de Lisboa. Vol. I–1885–1975* (Lisbon: Metropolitano de Lisboa, E.P., 1999).

Moreover, the numerical increase in the active population of the secondary sector during this period and its relative distribution among the sector's various areas of activity show, to a great extent, the priority given to the country's industrialization programme.

Seeing as we can acknowledge the existence of an aggressive and pro-active industrializing strategy during the 1950s and early 1960s, it is also necessary to mention that Portugal was riddled with prolonged political and economic impasses from the mid-1960s until the 1973–74 break-up. In addition to the changes that took place in political power, ending in a new government leadership (1968), the global perspective, still nationalist and autarkic, of struggling to replace imports, hampered by an undersized internal market, was substantially altered, and gradually became a strategy to promote and replace exports.

Some events, though of a different nature, alleviated internal tensions and paved the way for this new strategy: joining EFTA, the rapid growth of emigration and the trade agreement with the EEC (1972). In fact, all these events, combined with the liberalization of foreign investment, accelerated the process of opening up the Portuguese economy; nevertheless, this was insufficient to prevent the rise of inflation and a significant increase in the trade deficit. It may be said that even though there was accelerated growth in industrial output between the late 1950s and the early 1970s, it was not satisfactorily accompanied by economic and social development. Globally, the production system failed to modernize, especially the agricultural sector, and some structural internal imbalances even worsened; on the other hand, the evolution of the economic fabric, showing effects from the concentration of capital and the growing presence of a relatively small group of important economic and financial groups, was not followed by the general development of the Portuguese population and regions.

BIBLIOGRAPHY

Brito, J. M. Brandão de. A *Industrialização Portuguesa no Pós-Guerra (1948–1965). O Condicionamento Industrial*, "Universidade Moderna, 90." Lisboa: Publicações Dom Quixote, Lisbon, 1989.

Lopes, José da Silva Lopes. "A economia portuguesa no século XX." In Panorama da Cultura Portuguesa no Século XX, 1. In As Ciências e as Problemáticas Sociais, edited by Fernando Peres. Edições Afrontamento / Porto 2001 / Serralves Foundation, 2002.

Rollo, Maria Fernanda. *Portugal e o Plano Marshall. Da Rejeição à Solicitação da Ajuda Financeira Norte-Americana (1947–1952)*. Lisbon: Editorial Estampa, 1994.

Rollo, Maria Fernanda. *Um Metro e Uma Cidade. História do Metropolitano de Lisboa*. Vol. I–1885–1975. Lisbon: Metropolitano de Lisboa, E.P., 1999.

Rollo, Maria Fernanda. *Portugal e a Reconstrução Económica do Pós-Guerra. O Plano Marshall e a Economia Portuguesa dos Anos 50*, "Biblioteca Diplomática Collection, 13." Ministry of Foreign Affairs, 2007.

Rollo, Maria Fernanda. "Percursos Cruzados." In Engenho e Obra. Uma Abordagem à História da Engenharia em Portugal no Século XX, edited by J. M. Brandão de Brito, Manuel Heitor and Maria Fernanda Rollo. Lisbon: Publicações Dom Quixote, 2002.

Rosas, Fernando. *Portugal entre a Paz e a Guerra. Estudo do Impacte da II Guerra Mundial na Economia e na Sociedade Portuguesas (1939–1945)*, "Imprensa Universitária, 83." Lisbon: Editorial Estampa, 1990.

Rosas, Fernando. *O Estado Novo (1926–1974)*. História de Portugal, Volume VII, edited by José Mattoso. Lisbon: Círculo de Leitores, 1994.

Boosting Perspectives from the Neighbourhood of Alvalade

JOÃO PEDRO COSTA
University of Lisbon, Faculty of Architecture, Research Centre of Architecture, Urbanism and Design

ABSTRACT

The development of the Alvalade neighbourhood left its mark on Portugal, both as a pivotal point in Portuguese architecture and in the practice of urbanism in the 1940s. It introduced several important innovations at the time, decisively influencing both housing and urban projects, and became a benchmark reference.

Firstly, this development broke the then dictatorship regime's approach of the "village project." The ideological stigma of the "modest nest" grounded in the rural world, idealized under a single house typology located in a controlled neighbourhood and detached from the city, was finally replaced by large-scale urbanisation of collective housing, which then became understood as part of the city's expansion. Through this shift in the direction of the promotion of public housing, Alvalade became a neighbourhood of the modern lifestyle, where the new middle classes found adequate living conditions. Its first boost in the first half of the 20th century was therefore a societal one.

Secondly, the Alvalade experience represented the effective emergence of modern housing studies; both through the elaboration of project-types for the "Casas de Renda Económica," with a detailed study on minimal habitable areas, the layout of housing functions, the reduction of lost spaces, and the standardization of the constructive process; and the large practical experimentation that took place in the various "Casas de Renda Limitada." Alvalade became a living laboratory that seems to have been the support for the elaboration of the RGEU (General Regulation for Urban Construction) in 1951.

Thirdly, Alvalade marked a new moment in Portuguese urbanism, inaugurating the profession's modernity. As has been established in the literature, it was the product of maturity of the first Portuguese Urbanist, Faria da Costa, supported by a culture of internationalisation.

Alvalade boosted new perspectives for urbanism and housing in the 1940s, but its example does not end in the past. It addressed several issues that are still key contemporary questions for the discipline, and so, what better way to seek answers for these than to get inspired by experiences from the field?

BIOGRAPHY

João Pedro Costa (Lisbon, 1970) is an architect, with a master's degree in Contemporary Architectonic Culture and a PhD in Urbanism; he qualified as a full professor in Urbanism. He is Associate Professor at the Faculty of Architecture, University of Lisbon, and member of the Board of Directors of CIAUD–Research Centre of Architecture, Urbanism and Design. He is also a Visiting Professor at the Superior Institute of Agronomy. He was the director of the professional journal Arquitecturas, from 2005 to 2016. From 2002 to 2004 he was advisor and head of cabinet to the Portuguese Secretary of State for Spatial Planning. He currently develops his research activity through the coordination and participation in international teams and networks in the areas of adaptation to climate change, urban and spatial planning policies, and urban morphology, combined with project activities at the university level, the most recent of which was the coordination of the Strategic Land Management Plan of the Island of Atauro, Timor-Leste (2016), the first strategic land management plan ever to be approved in the history of Timor-Leste. In the 2017 municipal elections, he ran as candidate for the Vice-Presidency of the City of Lisbon, for the Social Democrat Party, and is currently a Councilman on the City Council, without executive functions.

THE NEW PARADIGM OF THE 1940S ESTADO NOVO NEIGHBOURHOODS: FROM THE "VILLAGE PROJECT" TO THE "IDEA PROJECT"

The development of the Alvalade neighbourhood [MdH DB a89, a90, a581] left its mark on Portugal, both as a pivotal point in Portuguese architecture and in the practice of urbanism in the 1940s. Planned during the Second World War and built over a period of thirty years immediately after it, this new urban expansion of 240 hectares to the north of Lisbon introduced several important innovations that decisively influenced national orientations, both for housing and urban projects. It became a benchmark reference, with expression across several domains. The idea of a "Village Project" was developed with the regime's fresh approach to the city and to housing problems. After an initial period of political instability in the late 1920s and early 1930s that did not allow for an investment in housing or urban planning, the 1930s saw an increase in the rhythm of development and began responding to the existing demand for housing and public facilities.[1] Specifically in terms of urban development, a strong policy began to be established based on three main priorities: the creation of a stock of public land, eliminating the existing private monopoly; a subsidy for work; and the implementation of a large enterprise of public infrastructures, accessibilities and public buildings with a view to modernizing the country. In line with other European regimes, the *Estado Novo* devised a string of guidelines for architecture and housing programmes that emanated the values of authority, discipline and order, side-by-side with the promotion of nationalism, family, and the rural world. It was in this context that ground-breaking work began in the country, focussing on the issue of the "Portuguese House."[2]

It was this rural, Portuguese house, attached to the values associated with the traditional family, that guided the first housing neighbourhood undertakings in the scope of the 1938 General Urbanisation and Expansion Plan of Lisbon (PGUEL).[3] As presented in Chapter 2.3, several new neighbourhoods were developed with a geographical detachment from the city, as small "rural villages" composed of single houses, each one with a small plot of land. Mainly promoted by the 1933 "Casas Económicas" (Affordable Houses) Programme, these neighbourhoods included Alvito (1937) [MdH DB a235], Quinta do Jacinto (1937) [MdH DB a635], Belém (1938) [MdH DB a225], Caramão da Ajuda (1938) [MdH DB a634], Quinta das Furnas (1938) [MdH DB a541], Quinta da Calçada (1939) [MdH DB a540], Alto da Boavista (1940) [MdH DB a539], Alto da Serafina (1940) [MdH DB a224], Encarnação (1940) [MdH DB a19], Madre de Deus (1942) [MdH DB a233], Calçada dos Mestres (1943) [MdH DB a584], and Caselas (1949) [MdH DB a237].

---

[1] This acceleration in the urban development of Lisbon was caused by the private housing outbreak generated by the 1928 emergency Decree no. 15,289, which aimed to stimulate the private sector to participate in the construction of housing in the city and by the reappearance of the public construction policy, complementary to the above decree, focusing especially on the construction of public facilities.

[2] José Manuel Fernandes, "Para o Estudo da Arquitectura Modernista em Portugal," *Arquitectura*; no. 132, (March 1979): 54–65; no.133 (May 1979): 38–47; no.137 (August 1980): 16–25; no.138 (October 1980): 64–73.

[3] Etiènne de Gröer. *Plano Director de Lisboa, Relatório, Análise* (Lisbon: Càmara Municipal de Lisboa, 1948).

In the words of Oliveira Salazar, *"we will start the construction of the low-cost house, the house for the poorest, [. . .] arranged as a nest—a home for the working family, a modest, secluded, Portuguese home."*[4] These neighbourhoods configure what Filipa Serpa calls "the village project" in her interpretation of one hundred years of public housing promotion in Lisbon, from 1910 to 2010:[5]

"It is the idea of a project inspired by a village, where each family has its own house and plot, where everybody knows (and controls) each other and where social activities are limited to the spaces of the Church, the Market and the School, the triad that represents the (less urban) lifestyle promoted by the Regime. [. . .] Having a clear option regarding the architectonic typology, these projects assume very specific patterns of location and relation with the city. They are evidence of the intention to isolate the housing neighbourhoods from the city and assume them as urban and social segregated units."[6]

Alvalade became a reference firstly because it broke with the Regime's approach of the "village project." Facing strong demand for housing, the new "Casas de Renda Económica" (Affordable Rent Houses) Programme[7] was devised to respond to the housing needs of the emergent urban middle classes and to address a new scale of urban development, by allowing corporate or public limited companies to take on the construction works. The regime finally allowed the construction of collective housing, settling on a maximum of four floors; the large-scale urbanisation on 240 hectares was implemented, overriding the previous largest neighbourhood constructed of 80 hectares of single houses in Restelo (1938) [MdH DB a247].

This inflection from a "village project" into an "idea project"[8] sets up quite a different reality. In line with this type of public housing promotion, which occurred in Lisbon at a rhythm of one per decade, Alvalade "stands out by the physical dimension and by the urban cultural ancestry [. . .] supported through reference models"; an undertaking that assumes "a leading role in urban growth, due to its dimension and relation with the city."[9]

As observed, Alvalade marked a shift in urban and architectural paradigms, but it also marked a relevant shift from an intentionally isolated rural neighbourhood, which promoted a limited and controlled lifestyle, into a much larger urban expansion, in continuity with its main urban axes,[10] allowing for the introduction of a modern urban lifestyle that definitively reconfigured the living conditions of the middle class and the city from the 1950s onwards.

[4] Oliveira Salazar, quoted by Nuno Teótonio Pereira, Pereira, "A Arquitetura do Estado Novo de 1926 a 1959," In *O Estado Novo, das Origens ao Fim da Autarcia, 1926–1959* (Lisbon: Edições Fragmentos, 1988), 332. My translation.

[5] Filipa Serpa, *Entre Habitação e Cidade. Lisboa, os Projetos de Promoção Pública: 1910–2010* (PhD Diss, Faculty of Architecture, University of Lisbon, 2014)

[6] Serpa, *Entre Habitação e Cidade*, 355–356. My translation.

[7] The "Casas de Renda Económica" Programme was regulated by the Decree no. 35,611, from 25 April 1946, under the Law no. 2,007, of 05 July 1945. It can be closer observed in Chapter 3.4 of this book.

[8] Serpa, *Entre Habitação e Cidade*.

[9] Serpa, *Entre Habitação e Cidade*, 383. My translation.

[10] Carlos Nunes Silva, *Política Urbana em Lisboa, 1926–1974* (Lisbon: Livros Horizonte, Colecção Cidade de Lisboa, no. 26, 1994).

Alvalade became the first expression of the 20th century's bourgeoisie city urban expansions in Lisbon, which would be followed by several major neighbourhoods, both of public promotion, such as Olivais Norte [MdH DB a186], Olivais Sul [MdH DB a193], Telheiras [MdH DB a906, a907] or Parque das Nações, and of private promotion, like Benfica or Portela.

With Alvalade, Lisbon assumed a new dynamic of urban growth, supported by large cosmopolitan housing neighbourhoods that incorporated social diversity. This idea for housing expansion established a direction for Lisbon's urban planning, designing a modern middle-class city with social integration, and a city that would grow in successive steps.

INTRODUCING THE ALVALADE NEIGHBOURHOOD: THE 1945 MASTER PLAN AND ITS IMPLEMENTATION

This chapter takes a closer look at Alvalade, synthesizing some of the existing key literature on its context,[11] spatial planning, and architecture,[12] as well as some of its sociological[13] dimensions. The first studies for Alvalade were prepared under the scope of the 1938 PGUEL. This plan was developed by the municipal services, and combined the layout with the main development guidelines for the city. At the turning point of the 1940s, this area was located on Lisbon's northern exit, facing the site of the future airport (1942).

"In its first references (1938–39), the studies comprehended the area of the future urbanisation plan in a wider area for the expansion of the city: from the current Chile Square to the Alferes Malheiro Avenue (currently Brazil Avenue). In these first trials, plans were drawn for the United States of America Avenue (the new ring road proposed by the PGUEL) and the Rome Avenue, as well as its limits by the Alferes Malheiro Avenue, 28th of May Fields and railway belt. [...]

The first rehearsals of urban design saw continuity in 1941, with the accomplishment of the 'Joint Study of the Area South of the Alferes Malheiro Avenue,' concluded in 1942, which suffered profound changes in 1944. It is important to note that from this phase onwards, the design of Alvalade already had the participation of architect-urbanist Faria da Costa, the author of the urbanisation plan approved in October of 1945."[14]

In this respect, the Government was able to approve the "Urbanisation Plan of the Area to the South of the Alferes Malheiro Avenue"[15] in October 1945, prepared by Faria da Costa, who had graduated in Paris and had begun to work in the municipality some years before.

[11] João Pedro Costa, *Bairro de Alvalade, um Paradigma no Urbanismo Português* (Lisbon: Livros Horizonte, 2010); "O Quarteirão, Elemento Experimental no Desenho da Cidade Contemporânea," in *Os Elementos Urbanos*, ed. Carlos Dias Coelho (Lisbon: Argumentum, 2015), 122–145.

[12] João Pedro Costa, "Ler Alvalade no Tempo, Arquitectura e Urbanismo no Estado Novo, 1930/1950," *Ur–Cadernos da Faculdade de Arquitectura*, no. 8 (December 2010): 26–41.

[13] Pedro Janarra, *A Política Urbanística e de Habitação Social no Estado Novo–O Caso do Bairro de Alvalade (Entre o Projeto e o Concretizado)* (Master's Thesis, ISCTE, Lisbon, 1994).

[14] João Pedro Costa, "The Alvalade Neighbourhood (1945–1970) in the 20th Century Portuguese Urbanism and Architecture," in *Proceedings of the 13th International Planning History Society Conference* (Chicago, Illinois: International Planning History Society, 2008), 177.

[15] CML / DSUO, *Plano de Urbanização da Zona a Sul da Avenida Alferres Malheiro* (Lisbon: CML, 1945).

However, Alvalade's relation with the 1938 PGUEL did not occur merely through the development process of the plan. Under the PGUEL, a general process of land expropriation was underway in the city. Supported by legislation from 1938 and 1944, and developed until 1946, these expropriations focused mainly on Lisbon's urban expansion crown, including areas such as Monsanto, Airport, Alvalade, Caselas or Restelo, allowing the Municipality of Lisbon to become the owner of most of the approximately 240 hectares of Alvalade's master plan.[16]

In its structuring, *"the Plan area was divided into eight cells, defined by the main road structure, forming distinct urbanisation units, separated between themselves by the surrounding traffic lines. Each of these cells*[17] *was organized around the school facilities, and the simple street layouts provided access to the houses. To overcome the initial inertia and to create a strong construction dynamic in the area of the plan, the municipality provided the projects for the low rent houses*[18] *and the construction of site infrastructures, also taking on the responsibility for the construction of the first housing units."*[19]

The distribution of the different typologies of the "Casas de Renda Económica" was a central concern of the plan, which deliberately predicted the coexistence of different social category houses, integrating different classes, therefore continuing the central city's previous tradition. The different building typologies were mixed, combining families of different sizes and income levels, following an idea of social complementation. The non-controlled-cost housing envisioned in the plan was mainly located on the structural avenues, reserving urbanised plots for the free market.[20]

As planned in 1945, Alvalade was designed to integrate a population of 45,000 inhabitants,[21] corresponding to an urban density of approximately 200 inhabitants per hectare—much higher than the densities in Lisbon's public housing promotion. The plan's organization was supported by the so-called "elements of general interest," namely the main open areas, facilities, public services, and commercial areas. These were strategically located for better accessibility within the neighbourhood, *"in such a way that they could be reached by the residents of the eight cells through convenient and not extensive routes, crossing main traffic intersections only when inevitable."*[22] The urbanisation of Alvalade was promoted by the Municipality and began in 1946. The new main accesses were almost concluded by 1947 and completely transformed the previous rural landscape. The residential programme accompanied it and its implementation intentionally started on the northern part, with the construction of cells 1, 2, and 3, leaving a gap between the new urban area and the limits of the consolidated city.

[16] Victor Matias Ferreira, "Lisboa, Anos 30–40. O Processo de Expropriação de Terrenos e a Recomposição Sociopolítica do Estado Novo," *Arquitectura*, no.151 (1983).

[17] The dimensioning of each cell took into account a maximum distance of 500 metres to access the school, which was located in its centre; and a population of 4,000 to 5,000 inhabitants per cell, corresponding to the dimension attributed to a school district at the time.

[18] The "Casas de Renda Económica" considered nine typologies, according to the dimension of the family; its project, by Miguel Jacobetty, was developed simultaneously with the neighbourhood master plan and integrated its technical content.

[19] Costa, "The Alvalade Neighbourhood (1945–1970)," 177.

[20] CML, *A Urbanização do Sítio de Alvalade* (Lisbon: CML, 1948).

[21] The 45,000 inhabitants were to be distributed in four types of housing: collective housing with low-cost rents (31,000 inhabitants); collective housing for the free market (9,500 inhabitants); single-family housing with low-cost rent (2,000 inhabitants); and single-family housing for the free market (2,500 inhabitants).

[22] Costa, "The Alvalade Neighbourhood (1945–1970)," 178.

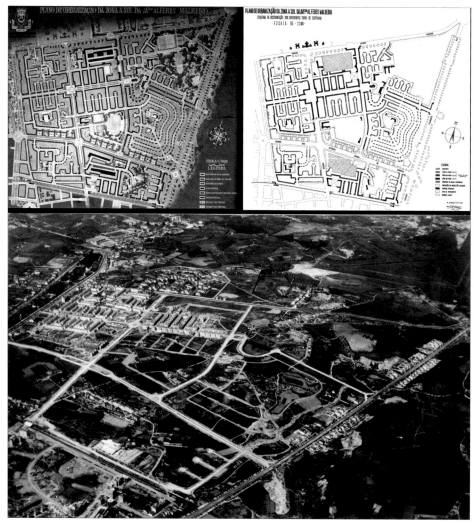

Fig. 1 Alvalade Neighbourhood: General plan and plan with the distribution of the different types of houses, 1945; aerial view of the cells 1, 2, 3 and 5 in construction, to the north of the neighbourhood, also showing the non-built areas to the south, which separated the new urban area from the consolidated city, 1950.

Sources: CML / DSUO, "Plano de Urbanização da Zona a Sul da Avenida Alferes Malheiro"; Unidentified photographer, Photographic Archives of the Lisbon Municipality, ref. PT/AMLSB/SPT/000201.

The plan was to stimulate private initiative, promote the construction sector and create a new dynamic on the site to attract investors to develop the areas between the urbanised areas. Simultaneously, the public sector responsibility for building the first cells allowed for the introduction of new technologies and to perfect the civil construction processes.[23] Assuming the role of an entrepreneur agent, the Municipality was responsible for promoting the construction of approximately 2,900 "Casas de Renda Económica" built between 1947 and 1956, located in cells 1, 2, 5, and 6. These houses accommodated a population of around 12,000 inhabitants, corresponding to an implementation rate of 38% of the programme. However, this rhythm of execution was unsatisfactory for the objectives of the Alvalade programme and the appearance in 1947 of the new legal figure of the "Casas de Renda Limitada" (Controlled Rent Houses) provided a broader range of options: it allowed the private sector to take on the construction of housing, through the alienation of the urbanised plots, the establishment of a limit to the rents and of important fiscal benefits. It also allowed commercial uses on ground floors, thus creating a new dynamic for local activities. The legal regime of the "Casas de Renda Limitada" became a key factor for the success of the implementation of the Alvalade plan and for the diversification of the urban fabric. Projected by the municipal services, each of these execution units developed its own detailed studies and architectonic language, promoting housing construction according to specific project-types. Initiated in 1949, housing construction in Alvalade was supported by the "Casas de Renda Limitada" and dominated the decade between 1950 and 1960. The construction of the neighbourhood was concluded in the 1970s.

THE LIVING LABORATORY OF ALVALADE'S HOUSING PROJECT: INTERPRETATIONS OF MODERNISM AND CULTURALISM

The new figure of the "Casas de Renda Limitada" was a decisive step for the effective implementation of the Alvalade plan. Not only did it have a strong participation from the private initiative, providing the necessary muscle for construction; but it also led to a diversification of the housing programmes in the neighbourhood. What was originally, according to the 1945 master plan, an urban fabric with two-thirds dominated by nine project-types of "Casas de Renda Económica," ended up by not occupying 20 per cent of the area, with these units mainly concentrated in cells 1, 2, and 5—and residually in cell 6. With the various "Casas de Renda Limitada" new plot division plans and housing project-types, Alvalade gained diversity in its housing typologies, in its social class orientation and in architectonic aesthetics.

[23] Luis Guimarães Lobato, "A Experiência de Alvalade," in *Separata da Revista Técnica–Revista de Engenharia dos Alunos do I.S.T* (Lisbon: IST, 1951), 209–210.

This transformation allowed the occurrence of a very rich practical confrontation between different approaches to the housing project. This transition from the original "Casas de Renda Económica" project-types to the "Casas de Renda Limitada" saw some continuities and innovations. Yet the modernist approach to low-rent housing units was a constant. In Alvalade, the urban structure resulted from a combination of the plan's top-down urban design approach with an urban fabric generated by the repetition of the building-type, which resulted from the detailed study of the housing-unit for the left-right typology. Faced with the intention of constructing a large quantity of housing, the "Casas de Renda Económica" were originally supported by intense research on the housing-unit, focusing on: (1) optimization of the minimum habitable area; (2) layout of the various housing functions; (3) reduction of lost spaces; and (4) systematization of its constructive process. The modernist idea was that the optimized housing unit would generate an efficient building, and fulfil its role in the urban fabric. *"Studies by Alexander Klein found expression in these projects, mainly through the use of the author's methods for the left-right typology housing-unit."*[24] To attest to the relevance of this research on the optimization of housing, the hypothesis below stands:

"This detailed study could have been the technical support for some housing definitions in the General Regulation for Urban Construction (RGEU), published in Portugal in 1951 and still in practice today. With reference to the peak of the modernist movement in Portugal, the profound typological and constructive study of the housing-unit in Alvalade determined: (1) the establishment of minimum areas by housing function; (2) optimum spatial layout; and (3) minimum dimensioning of constructive elements."[25]

Curiously, the very rational housing plans of the "Casas de Renda Económica" acquired an aesthetic expression that was still influenced by the theme of the "Portuguese House," mainly due to the use of traditional constructive elements, such as the ceramic roof, the standardized stonework, the window design or the use of ceramic coatings on the *façade* and chimneys.

The modernist studies on the optimized housing-unit maintained a clear influence in the development of the following "Casas de Renda Limitada" projects, the large majority of which proceeded with the left-right typology; of course, having several different projects designed by different architects now meant that several variations were introduced. Some of the "Casas de Renda Limitada" continued the design guidelines of the master plan and an aesthetic approach closer to the "Casas de Renda Económica," particularly the ones projected in the 1940s: (1) the commercial zone, in cell 3, designed by Fernando Silva in 1947/1948; (2) the Rio de Janeiro Avenue and

[24] Costa, "Bairro de Alvalade, um paradigma no urbanismo português," 162. My translation.

[25] Costa, "The Alvalade Neighbourhood (1945–1970)," 183.

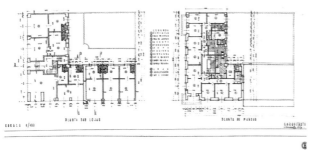

Fig. 2 Alvalade Neighbourhood, cell 3's commercial zone: view of the neighbourhood life style in 1949; Project-type 5A of the "Conditional Rental Housing Units," designed by Fernando Silva in 1947/1948: blueprints for the 1st floor and main elevations of "Street 20 and Street 10A," today the streets Marquesa de Alorna and Luis Augusto Palmeirim, 1948.

Sources: Unidentified photographer, Photographic Achieves of the Lisbon Municipality, ref. PT/AMLSB/CMLSBAH/PCSP/004/AVZ/000060; Silva, "Casas de Renda Limitada–Célula III."

Igreja Square, structural axis linking cells 3 and 6, as well the corner of cells 4 and 5, by Dário Silva and Lima Franco in 1949; and (3) the S. Miguel Neighbourhood, in the interior of cell 7, by Miguel Jacobetty, the same architect of the "Casas de Renda Económica," in 1951.

In keeping with the guidelines of the master plan, the pioneer case of the eastern housing unit in cell 8, designed by Joaquim Ferreira and Orlando Azevedo in 1949–1952, explored a linkage between the left-right typology and a modern aesthetic expression. It was the first project in Alvalade to introduce clear rationalist references in the design of the *façade* and to propose buildings at specific sites with more than four floors. Some other undertakings under the scope of the "Casas de Renda Limitada" clearly assumed the need to proceed with an evolution in the master plan design guidelines, such as: (1) the D. Rodrigo da Cunha Avenue, the structural axis that links cells 4 and 6, by Joaquim Ferreira in 1949, with its four flats distributed in two half-floors in buildings with a new perpendicular orientation to the avenue—which was developed in accordance with Faria da Costa; (2) the Bairro das Estacas [MdH DB a548], in the western interior of cell 8, by Ruy d'Athouguia and Formosinho Sanches in 1949, one of the charismatic icons of the modernist movement in Lisbon at the time; or (3) the Estados Unidos da América Avenue [MdH DB a544], developed through seven different detailed units between 1951 and 1966, with variations to the modernist block, with 7 to 12 floors, disposed perpendicularly to the avenue, although this modernist image results mostly from the combination of three left-right buildings.

It is interesting to observe that the introduction of different ideals in Alvalade marked, *"above all, an experimental evolution to which several architects of the time adhered to (as well as Faria da Costa, the architect responsible for the plan's implementation), and to which the management of the urbanisation plan was adapted, without a loss of identity. [. . .] The plan had the capacity to assimilate this evolution, without losing its structure and main concepts; on the contrary, it became clear that each urbanisation unit could have some autonomy inside the whole and that the initial urban design guidelines allowed for localized oscillations."*[26]

It was also due to this experimental and adaptive capacity that Alvalade became a reference for Portuguese housing and urban design; it attests the capacity of these large undertakings to integrate diversity and to adapt over time as a natural evolution in a long-term implementation process.

[26]Costa, "Bairro de Alvalade, um paradigma no urbanismo português," 95. My translation.

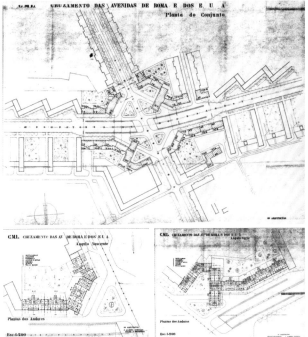

Fig. 3 Alvalade Neighbourhood: view of the crossing of the Estados Unidos da América and Roma avenues, 1969; buildings designed by Filipe Figueiredo and Jorge Segurado in 1951: assembly plan, east angle plan and north plan (both floor plans).

Sources: Armando Maia Serôdio, Photographic Archives of the Lisbon Municipality, ref. PT/AMLSB/CMLSBAH/PCSP/004/SER/S05770; Figueiredo, Segurado, "Cruzamento das Avenidas de Roma e dos EUA."

ALVALADE'S URBAN PROJECT: AN ECLECTIC SYNTHESIS OF CONTEMPORARY MODELS AND EXPERIENCES

Lastly, Alvalade became a reference due to its eclectic urban design,[27] as established in the literature: "From the experience of Alvalade we can draw a lesson on the application of models, no longer for their ideal, but from withdrawing particular techniques, forms, and concepts, defining typologies of elements of urban composition. [...] *In Alvalade, urban models and experiences constitute a syllable within the available vocabulary of urbanist speech. The discourse of the urban planners to which I refer to is their compositional capacity to find urban design solutions adapted to each reality, by means of a synthesis of their disciplinary cultural background.*"[28]

The 1945 *Plano de Urbanização da Zona a Sul da Avenida Alferres Malheiro* (Urbanisation Plan of the Area to the South of the Alferes Malheiro Avenue), by Faria da Costa, was already a rich piece of urban design during his time.[29] Here, one can identify concepts used in different urban models and in several contemporary experiences of urban design, some also constituting paradigms in the theory of urbanism. Yet the approach to the design of the plan did not elect any as a dominant reference to be followed. Neither did it simply undertake some sort of reinterpretation of one of those references. It was not inspired exclusively by a specific previous experience or model. *"On the contrary, Alvalade achieved a synthesis of variable influences, some taken initially as totally antagonistic; and the new synthesis constitutes a paradigm, at least in the context of urbanism in Portugal—hence the eclectic design."*[30] In previous research, based on the neighbourhood primary sources, it was identified that the Alvalade morphological elements emerged from:

"1) The "pre-industrial" city of regular blocks and streets, e.g.:

> The definition of urban spaces based on a rectilinear street canal, limited by marginal façade plans;
> The application of the concept of avenues and squares as structuring elements of the urban tissue [...];
> The definition of urban perspectives in its main and local structures [...].

2) The garden city, e.g.:

> The typological proposal for cell 4 [...];
> The application of the urban model of the housing impasse, proposed by Raymond Unwin in Town Planning in Practice [...];
> The application of a network of interior pedestrian paths to access the school [...];
> The multiplication of green spaces in the area encompassed by the plan [...].

[27] Costa, "Bairro de Alvalade, um paradigma no urbanismo português," 9. My translation.

[28] Costa, "O Quarteirão, Elemento Experimental no Desenho da Cidade Contemporânea," 128. My translation.

[29] Ana Tostões, "O Bairro de Alvalade," in *O Livro de Lisboa*, ed. Irisalva Moita (Lisbon: Livros Horizonte, 1994).

[30] Costa, "The Alvalade Neighbourhood (1945–1970)," 180.

3) *The Modern Movement, e.g.:*

The application of forms of functional zoning [...];
The use of the typology of the block perpendicular to the roads, in particular in the main crossing axes [...];
The systemized study of the housing unit for low-income rental housing units [...];
Localised application of the building over pilotis and of the housing block in height [...].

4) *Amsterdam Expansions, 1910s (Berlage) and 1930s (Van Eesteren), e.g.:*

[...] The intermediate stage in the opening process of the block [...];
The interior block equipment—the potential that remained to be fully developed in Alvalade[31] *[...];*

5) *From Berliner Siedlungs, e.g.:*

Morphological references of the low-cost housing buildings, with Siedlungs, as the most significant [...] Siedlung Diesdorferstrasse, J. Goderitz, Berlim 1925;
The study of the housing unit, with adoption of the methodologies used in the studies of Alexander Klein of the left-right typology;
The volume, scale, and image of the adopted architecture, in particular the first accomplishments of the "regime architecture" until 1945.

6) *The application of the "neighbourhood unit" concept, proposing housing cells of 5,000 inhabitants, centred on school facilities and developing a neighbourhood community lifestyle."*[32]

THE ALVALADE NEIGHBOURHOOD, BOOSTING PERSPECTIVES IN THE PRESENT

There are different reasons why Alvalade became a turning point in Portuguese architecture and urbanist practices. Firstly, because it broke the regime's approach of the "village project." The ideological stigma of the "modest nest," grounded in the rural world, idealized in the single-house typology located in a controlled neighbourhood and detached from the city, was finally replaced by large-scale urbanisation of collective housing. The need for large-scale housing in the city was determinant, but also the new professional competences acquired by the presence of urbanists such as Etiènne De Gröer who was responsible for the elaboration of the PGEUL, or Faria da Costa, who had just completed his specialist training at the Institut d'Urbanisme de Paris.[33] What is relevant to observe is the fact that this shift in the direction of the promotion of public housing had direct consequences. Alvalade became a neighbourhood of the modern lifestyle, where the new middle classes had found adequate living conditions.

[31] Pereira, Nuno Teotónio, *Estudo de Algumas Transformações no Bairro de Alvalade* (Lisbon: Habitações Económicas / Federação das Caixas de Previdência, 1959).

[32] Costa, "The Alvalade Neighbourhood (1945–1970)," 180–181.

[33] For a deeper understanding of João Guilherme Faria da Costa's training and practical background Patrícia Bento d'Almeida, *Bairro(s) do Restelo. Panorama Urbanístico e Arquitetónico.* (PhD Diss., Universidade Nova de Lisboa, 2013), 27–96 should be consulted.

Its first boost in the second half of the 20th century was, therefore, a societal one. An emerging bourgeoisie found its home in Alvalade, in a context of a mix of classes and a dynamic that was repeated over the next decades in the large majority of the "idea projects" in Lisbon, such as in Olivais Norte, Olivais Sul, Telheiras or in the Alta de Lisboa. More importantly, this example is very much relevant to the present day context of economic recovery in Lisbon. The city's internationalization as a housing destination, directed at the upper classes, and the boom of tourism that opened the market of local housing to owners, are the main reason for the new crises in the housing market, causing inflation of prices. It particularly affects the same middle classes that Alvalade started to boost and that are now being pushed out from the city and pulled towards the metropolitan periphery. What should the role of public housing promotion be today?

Secondly, the Alvalade experience represented the effective emergence of modern housing studies in Portugal. Both the elaboration of the project-types for the *Casas de Renda Económica*, with the detailed study on minimal habitable areas, on the layout of the housing functions, on the reduction of lost spaces and on the standardisation of the constructive process; and the large practical experimentation that took place in the several "Casas de Renda Limitada"; it constituted a living laboratory that seems to have been the support for the elaboration of the RGEU in 1951. Again, this example is very much relevant to the present day changes in the contemporary form of living and in family conditions. Society has changed radically; the evolution of technology has revolutionised lifestyles in all domains (work, mobility, socialisation, life expectancy, migration, etc.); "multiple indicators and analyses make us think that the general transformations of our society in general and of cities in particular, are just beginning."[34] There is a need to go much further than reviewing housing regulations, replacing the 1951 RGEU and harmonizing the different speciality regulations. Housing today needs a particularly deep reflection on new typologies, on different forms of ownership and on funding, adapting these to the new way of life and to new housing mobility. What types of housing do we need today?

Thirdly, Alvalade marked a new moment in Portuguese urbanism, having inaugurated the profession's modernity. Previous experiences of public housing promotions were executed in the 1930s, with the construction of the Republican Arco do Cego neighbourhood [MdH DB a216], an isolated case, and with the experience of the several "village projects," with their different sizes and locations, maintaining the rural approach inspired in the 30-year-old garden city.

[34] François Ascher, *Novos Princípios do Urbanismo. Novos Compromissos Urbanos* (Lisbon: Livros Horizonte, 2010), 19.

But in Alvalade, contemporary urban design took a step forward. It is now established in literature how Alvalade inaugurated a culture of internationalisation that would continue in the next major public housing promotions;[35] or how Faria da Costa, the first Portuguese Urbanist, achieved results of great maturity, following previous experiences upon his return to Portugal, such as in the "Plano de Urbanização da Encosta da Ajuda" (Restelo, 1938).[36]

It can be stated that urbanism, as a modern discipline that grew in Portugal in the 1940s, found a major boost in Alvalade and this statement might lead us to several questions for our present: How do our contemporary urban design and housing solutions deal with time? Are they able to become high quality and integrated parts of the city, 70 years after construction? What are we doing today to promote the same high standards of urbanism? There is no doubt that Alvalade boosted new perspectives for urbanism and housing in the 1940s. However, its example did not end in the past; it addressed several issues that are still key contemporary questions for the discipline. And to help answer them, what better way than to be inspired by past experiences from the field?

[35] Costa, "Bairro de Alvalade, um paradigma no urbanismo português."

[36] Bento d'Almeida, "Bairro(s) do Restelo. Panorâma Urbanístico e Arquitetónico," 27–96.

ACKNOWLEDGMENTS

This research work on Alvalade is supported by previous publications by the author. The major part of the fieldwork and all the archive work were developed for the author's master's thesis in Architectonic Culture, submitted to the Faculty of Architecture, Technical University of Lisbon, in 1998. It was supported by a master's scholarship provided by the JNICT–Junta Nacional de Investigação Científica e Tecnológica, Praxis Programme XXI.

BIBLIOGRAPHY

Ascher, François. *Novos Princípios do Urbanismo. Novos Compromissos urbanos*. Lisbon: Livros Horizonte, 2010.

Bento d'Almeida, Patrícia. *Bairro(s) do Restelo. Panorâma Urbanístico e Arquitetónico*. PhD Dissertation, Universidade Nova de Lisboa, 2013.

CML. *A Urbanização do Sítio de Alvalade*. Lisbon: CML, 1948.

CML/DSUO. *Plano de Urbanização da Zona a Sul da Avenida Alferes Malheiro*. Lisbon: CML/DSUO, 1945.

Costa, João Pedro. *Bairro de Alvalade, Um Paradigma no Urbanismo Português*. Lisbon: Livros Horizonte, 2010.

Costa, João Pedro. "Ler Alvalade no Tempo, Arquitectura e Urbanismo no Estado Novo, 1930/1950." *Ur–Cadernos da Faculdade de Arquitectura*, no. 8 (December 2010): 26–41.

Costa, João Pedro. "O Quarteirão, Elemento Experimental no Desenho da Cidade Contemporânea." In *Os Elementos Urbanos*, edited by Carlos Dias Coelho, 122–145. Lisbon: Argumentum, 2015.

Costa, João Pedro. "The Alvalade Neighbourhood (1945–1970) in the 20th Century Portuguese Urbanism and Architecture." *Proceedings of the 13th International Planning History Society Conference*, 171–186. Chicago, Illinois: International Planning History Society, 2008.

Fernandes, José Manuel. "Para o Estudo da Arquitectura Modernista em Portugal." *Arquitectura*, no. 132 (March 1979): 54–65; no.133 (May 1979): 38–47; no.137 (August 1980): 16–25; no.138 (October 1980): 64–73.

Ferreira, Victor Matias. "Lisboa, Anos 30–40. O Processo de Expropriação de Terrenos e a Recomposição Sociopolítica do Estado Novo."*Arquitectura*, no.151 (1983).

Figueiredo, Filipe and Jorge Segurado. *Cruzamento das Avenidas de Roma e dos EUA*. Lisbon: CML, 1951.

Gröer, Etiènne de. *Plano Director de Lisboa, Relatório, Análise*. Lisbon: CML, 1948.

Janarra, Pedro. "A Politica Urbanística e de Habitação Social no Estado Novo–O Caso do Bairro de Alvalade (Entre o Projeto e o Concretizado)." Master's Thesis, ISCTE, Lisbon, 1994.

Lobato, Luis Guimarães. "A Experiência de Alvalade." In *Separata da Revista Técnica–Revista de Engenharia dos Alunos do I.S.T.*, 209–210. Lisbon: IST, 1951.

Pereira, Nuno Teotónio. "A Arquitetura do Estado Novo de 1926 a 1959." In *O Estado Novo, das Origens ao Fim da Autarcia, 1926–1959*. Lisbon: Edições Fragmentos, 1988.

Pereira, Nuno Teotónio. *Estudo de Algumas Transformações no Bairro de Alvalade*. Lisbon: Habitações Económicas / Federação das Caixas de Previdência, 1959.

Rosas, Fernando. "Portugal e o Estado Novo, 1930–1960." In *Nova História de Portugal*, edited by Joel Serrão and António Oliveira Marques, Volume XII. Lisbon: Editorial Presença, 1990.

Serpa, Filipa. "Entre Habitação e Cidade. Lisboa, os projetos de promoção pública: 1910/2010." PhD Dissertation, Faculty of Architecture, University of Lisbon, 2014.

Silva, Carlos Nunes. *Política Urbana em Lisboa, 1926–1974*. Lisbon: Livros Horizonte, Colecção Cidade de Lisboa, 26, 1994.

Silva, Fernando. *Casas de Renda Limitada–Célula III*. Lisbon: Câmara Municipal de Lisboa, 1948.

Tostões, Ana. "O Bairro de Alvalade." In *O Livro de Lisboa*, by Irisalva Moita. Lisbon: Livros Horizonte, 1994.

"From User to Dweller": Observation, Consultation, and Involvement Processes in Housing Solutions, 1950s and 1960s

TIAGO LOPES DIAS
Technical University of Catalonia | University of Porto, Faculty of Architecture, Centre for Studies in Architecture and Urbanism

ABSTRACT

After the Second World War, careful attention to the way people use and live their cities, neighbourhoods, and dwellings fostered a new critique on the aseptic and functionalist environment promoted by the Modern Movement and pre-1947 CIAM meetings. Impelled by sociological research, architects "discovered" in ordinary and everyday life a powerful motif to reconsider their dogmas. Housing was the programme in which the process of design underwent the greatest changes. Observation and consultation processes were put in place in order to understand how users adapt to and appropriate their dwellings. From the early post-war years to the turn of the 1960s to the 1970s, these processes evolved into more ambitious ideas related to the emancipation of low-income classes from paternalistic state aid. Due to the social changes that shaped all of the Western world in the late 60s, a certain radicalism was now possible.

This text analyses how these ideas were absorbed into the Portuguese context, in a period when a dictatorial government faced a great need for housing, caused by population migration from the rural areas of the country towards the industrialized cities. The text follows the thread of French sociology applied to urban habitat, on the one hand, and the thread of the generation who would put an end to CIAM—the angry young men—on the other, and places them against research done by two Portuguese architects with relevant input in the fields of theory, criticism, and design: Nuno Portas and Pedro Vieira de Almeida.

BIOGRAPHY

Tiago Lopes Dias (Porto, 1978) holds a bachelor's degree in architecture (FAUP, 2004) and a PhD in theory and history of architecture (UPC, Spain, 2017). His research focuses on the relations between theory, criticism, history, and design in the second half of the 20th century, particularly within the European and the Iberian contexts. He is researcher at the Centre for Studies in Architecture and Urbanism CEAU-FAUP and Assistant Professor at UPC-ETSAV.

THE "AS FOUND"

In 1945, Nigel Henderson and his wife Judith moved to the working-class neighbourhood of Bethnal Green in London's East End, which had been heavily bombed during the war. Judith, the anthropologist in charge of the research project "Discover your neighbour" directed by the sociologist J.L. Peterson, was the responsible for Nigel's growing interest in the street life that had spontaneously emerged from the ruins.[1] In 1947 Henderson began to take photographs of children playing in the streets or on the thresholds of houses, of neighbours gathering on sidewalks or at snack bars, stopping by a storefront display, or immersed in some daily routine.

After five years *wandering about looking at things*, Henderson had gathered a powerful collection of images, which would eventually have a significant impact on the young couple of architects Alison and Peter Smithson. Some of these photos were included in the panel presented at the 1953 CIAM by the British delegation, to which the Smithsons belonged. The now famous "Urban Re-Identification Grid" was a manifesto that sought to question the Charter of Athens' schematic functionalism, and its voluntary omission of the complexity intrinsic to human beings and to the way they relate to their community and the balance between the individual and the collective spheres. In the panel there were also images from the Smithsons' Golden Lane competition entry, a housing complex structured around pedestrian galleries that would later be referred to as "streets-in-the-air." As Reyner Banham observed, what differentiated this solution from those studied by Le Corbusier and Ludwing Hilberseimer was not a formal issue, but the essence that presided over the gallery: it was *"intended to function socially and psychologically in the manner of the street, which—in working class areas in Britain—is the main public forum of communication, the traditional playground for children, and the only public space available for mass meetings and large-scale sociability."*[2]

Between 1953 and 1956, the year of the 10th CIAM, the Smithsons and the group of young architects in charge of the next congress (Team 10) stressed the need to abandon diagrammatic methods in favour of the study of communities as they existed and influenced each other. Very critical of *"the forms and patterns derived from the garden city movement or the rationalism of the 1930s endlessly repeated in contradiction to the climate, human habitat, location, and common sense,"*[3] the Smithsons would put forward a new way of thinking that considered each problem of urbanism as a distinct entity, a unique form of human association at a particular time and in a particular place.

[1] See: Claude Lichtenstein and Thomas Schregenberger (eds.), *As Found: The Discovery of the Ordinary* (Bern: Lars Muller, 2001).

[2] Reyner Banham, *The New Brutalism. Ethic or Aesthetic?* (Stuttgart and Bern: Karl Kramer Pub., 1966), 42.

[3] Alison and Peter Smithson, "Draft Framework #4, CIAM X," in *The Emergence of Team 10 Out of CIAM: Documents,* edited by Alison Smithson (London: Architectural Association, 1982), 41.

This new approach to urbanism was synthetized in the "section valley" diagram with the four scales of association, based on the work of Patrick Geddes. Geddes was a former biologist who later studied the transformation of human communities and pioneered survey techniques that revolutionized town planning. However, the social structure to which the urban planner had to give form after Second World War was, in the Smithsons' words, "not only different, but much more complex than ever before."[4] The inspiring theoretical propositions of the Smithsons, collected from countless activities, including close contact with a group of artists, were strong enough to shake Team 10's meetings and to precipitate the end of CIAM. One of the propositions that would later be referred to as *modus operandi* was related to Henderson's sensibility towards the ordinary:

"In architecture, the "as found" aesthetic was something we thought we named in the early 1950s when we first knew Nigel Henderson and saw in his photographs a perceptive recognition of the actuality around his house in Bethnal Green [. . .]. The "as found" was a new seeing of the ordinary, an openness as to how prosaic "things" could re-energise our inventive activity.[5]*"*

"THE SOCIAL SIDE" AND THE INFLUENCE OF CHOMBART DE LAUWE

Also in the early 1950s, a team led by the ethnographer and sociologist Paul-Henry Chombart de Lauwe ran several surveys in Paris to study the relationships between men, society, and the built environment. The analysis of everyday working class life through interviews, maps of daily movements, and ethnographic studies was one of the most innovative approaches to the study of post-war urban habitat.

The surveys were part of a sociological line of thought that had a precursor in Maurice Halbwachs. His most notable followers, Louis-Joseph Lebret, Robert Auzelle, and Chombart de Lauwe, shared the idea that "social observation" was a humanistic approach that differed from book-based education in that its methods were based on direct observation and in-depth analyses. The complex problems of contemporary human settlements could not be solved merely by a harmonious arrangement of clearly defined elements. A deeper and more comprehensive study was necessary: "Men, in themselves, elude us. Before housing them it is necessary to know them."[6]

After studying the relationships between social structures and the material framework in the great Parisian agglomeration, the team led by Chombart de Lauwe focused more directly on the study of its basic units: the family and the dwelling.

[4] Alison and Peter Smithson, "An alternative to the Garden City idea," *Architectural Design* 7 (1956): 230.

[5] Alison Smithson, "The 'as found' and the 'found'," *The Independent Group: Postwar Britain and the Aesthetics of Plenty*, edited by David Robbins (Cambridge: MIT Press, 1990), 201.

[6] Paul-Henry Chombart de Lauwe, "Sociologia da habitação. Método e perspectivas de investigação," *Arquitectura* 68 (Lisbon, 1960): 41.

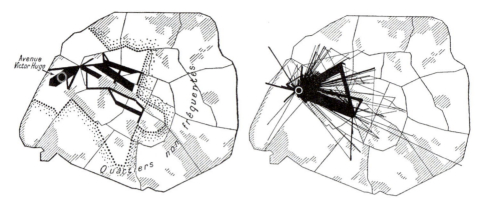

Fig. 1 Everyday life in western Paris: arteries and routes frequented by 30 residents of Av. Victor Hugo (left) and by a young woman in the span of one year (right) Source: Chombart de Lauwe, *Essais de Sociologie*, 1952–64.

This was the purpose of the seminal book *Famille et Habitation,* the first volume of which was published in 1959 by the Centre National de la Recherche Scientifique. It summarized previous research and presented the state of the art, divided into three main sections: the first on notions of family and housing, as well as those of space, necessity, and function; the second on the mid-twentieth century housing crisis; and the third on working methods and fundamental research. The last chapter included interviews with architects such as G.H. Pingusson, A. Wogenscky and Le Corbusier.

The dialogue between sociologists and architects that it intended to foster is of the utmost importance. In light of the continuous transformation of social structures, particularly within the family, Chombart de Lauwe advocated a broad and comprehensive vision of society as a whole. This effort, insurmountable for the architect who acts alone, should be entrusted to *"large teams, in which researchers from the human sciences are in close touch with architects and the many people who have responsibilities in the plans."* A significant part of Chombart's career was dedicated precisely to the study of what he called "upward communication channels": how the aspirations of a given social group could reach and be taken into account by decision-makers (politicians, urban planners, architects, and engineers). The upward movement should prevail over the movement from cusp to base, something which did not occur in most post-war housing estates.

Famille et Habitation would have a significant impact in Portugal, largely due to the interest it aroused in Nuno Portas. In the year it was published, Portas was finishing his degree thesis on social housing.

[7] Chombart de Lauwe (dir.), *Famille et Habitation. I–Sciences Humaines et Conceptions de l'Habitation* (Paris: CNRS, 1959), 211.

Presented as a methodological essay, the thesis opened with an epigraph from Chombart de Lauwe[8] and claimed the human sciences' model of methodical observation as an essential resource in the development of new housing units. An accurate analysis of reality should therefore include ideas on "the tradition of dwelling," and more specifically, the *"critical understanding of the social environment to be served, its life of relationships, family habits, connection with nature and previous historical environment."*[9] As he wrote in a coetaneous text-manifesto, such analysis should also lead to a reformulation of architectural and urban modernity:

"[The] conception of space must respond to a thorough search of human needs, finding a solution in form for all the ambiguities and contradictions of personal and social demands—not of a theoretical or future person or class, but [. . .] taken in their real existence, in their impasses and contradictions—as they have been perceived by the human sciences."

The "upward communication channels" are a pertinent matter to understanding Portas' thesis, whose genesis lies in the study commissioned by the sociologist Adérito Sedas Nunes for the Centre for Social and Corporate Studies.[10] Knowing the humanistic and deeply democratic orientation of Chombart de Lauwe's research, Sedas Nunes was aware of the impact that it could have on a highly conservative society such as the Portuguese society of the time. An example of this is the debate on the progressive incorporation of women in the service sector and its consequences for the family space: leaving home for work meant that home ceased to be the "universe of the woman," thus becoming the "universe of the family." Although this was still barely perceptible in the Portuguese context, the progressionist Catholic wing—to which Sedas Nunes and Portas belonged—shared this conception of a more egalitarian family, without the authority of the *pater familias*, in contrast with the more conservative view of other sectors of the Church. In light of this, Portas defended a redesign of the daytime living area of the dwelling, recasting it as a place where the family could gather in a *"less austere and conventional atmosphere than the one defined by the traditional family with its hierarchical structure,"*[11] while also allowing greater freedom of action and interaction among all members of the family. Examples of this are his proposals for unfolding the living room in several spaces that would allow the kitchen to link to a dining area (that could also be used as a working space), and a quieter area for reading or visitors. On the other hand, the reference to less specialized spaces such as the Italian *stanza di lavoro* or the American *big-room*, spaces of relative freedom, are in line with the reminder often repeated by Chombart de Lauwe: the architect should attend reality without giving up the responsibility of guiding a possible evolution of the family structure.

[8] «L'étude de l'habitation des hommes est un terrain excellent pour oeuvrer à l'integration des sciences humaines."

[9] Nuno Portas, *A Habitação Social. Proposta Para a Metodologia da Sua Arquitectura* (Porto: FAUP, 2004 [1960]), 90.

[10] Nuno Portas and António Freitas Leal, *Aspectos Sociais do Habitat* (Lisbon: LNEC, 1959).

[11] Portas, *A Habitação Social*, 31.

In February 1960, Robert Auzelle and Chombart de Lauwe were invited to attend a congress on the housing problem held in Lisbon. Although organized with the support of the National Syndicate of Architects, the congress was prepared according to the study commissioned by Sedas Nunes.[12] Nuno Portas and António Freitas Leal opened the afternoon sessions with lectures dedicated to the subjects covered by each in that study: dwelling cells and their forms of grouping, and neighbourhood units. In the evening, the conferences were held by the guest lecturers. Chombart de Lauwe's intervention was structured according to *Famille et Habitation:* on the first evening he presented some themes from Vol. 1, and on the second he announced the results of Vol. 2, published in April of that year with the subtitle "An essay of experimental observation." It consisted of the presentation and analysis of data obtained from inquiries to 1,500 families living in three new housing estates on the outskirts of Paris, Nantes, and Bordeaux.

Some conclusions of this observation study may appear obvious today, but were highly relevant then. Correct soundproofing of the dwellings and careful location of collective equipment were pointed out as decisive factors for the development of good relationships between neighbours. The encouragement of social relations in a building was seen as a positive factor, whenever the choice of the relations was *as free as possible.* In that respect, the connections with other neighbourhoods or parts of the city was emphasized because it allowed people "to free themselves from collective life and, for this very same reason, to take an interest in it instead of suffering its concerns."[13] Other recommendations concerned the preferences of householders for layouts with a corridor facilitating the isolation of the bedrooms, instead of layouts with bedrooms adjoining the living room; and also the aspirations of most families to a certain autonomy, that would allow them to give their houses a "personal touch." Le Corbusier's *Unité d'Habitation* in Nantes (Rezé), one of the case studies,[14] had good appreciations on the equilibrium between an idealist communal living and the possibility of having selective social relations, to which the large *rue corridor* undoubtedly contributed.

[12] "Aspectos sociais na concepção do habitat" [*Social Matters in the Conception of Habitat*] was the title of the congress, almost the same of Portas & Leal's study.

[13] P.H. Chombart de Lauwe (dir.), *Famille et Habitation II. Un Essai d'Observation Expérimentale* (Paris: CNRS, 1960), 174.

[14] The others were *La Citté de la Plaine* (Paris), a group of small scale buildings with some single houses built by a team of architects under the direction of Robert Auzelle, and *La Benauge* (Bordeaux), a housing complex with a civic and commercial centre.

THE SOCIOLOGICAL INQUIRY: ITS METHODS AND ITS CRITIQUES

The impact of Chombart de Lauwe's lectures went beyond the restricted scope of the congress.[15] In the closing session, Nuno Teotónio Pereira emphasized his contribution as scientist and humanist by making clear the architect's responsibility in the adoption of housing solutions with impact on the lives of thousands of families, a choice that shouldn't be made without knowledge of the underlying reality that it was meant to serve. In a document written as a synthesis of two intensive days of debate, the architects called for the creation of a scientific research centre, *"given that an adequate housing policy can only be founded on the analysis of the real needs of human groups, particularly the family."*[16]

An independent research centre was never built. However, the National Laboratory for Civil Engineering (LNEC) played a central role in housing research, through its Construction & Housing Department. Nuno Portas joined it in 1961 to lead an project of inquiry into state-subsidized housing complexes. Considered as a fundamental basis for a more realistic study on economic housing, this fieldwork was the beginning of a research programme that made the implementation of SAAL possible after the popular revolution of April 1974.[17] The main objective of the inquiries carried out in Lisbon and Porto between the end of 1962 and the beginning of 1963 was to implement methods of direct interviews with householders. The so-called "pilot inquiry" sought to become familiar with the way people inhabit spaces, but also to gain expertise with this kind of interviews. The information collected from similar experiences (INA-Casa and Chombart's Groupe d'Ethnologie Sociale) was very helpful for the preparation of the questionnaire and the norms of the interview. The variables to be considered were taken from Chombart's studies: the analysis of the household, the characteristics of the previous house(s), and, in the main body of the survey, the uses of the dwelling, divided into five sections: bedrooms, living, services, hygiene, and play.[18]

It is important to mention that the process unfolded differently in Lisbon and Porto.[19] In the former, architecture students were selected from the university but acted autonomously; in the latter, when LNEC proposed a collaboration with the School of Fine Arts of Porto, the fieldwork was integrated in the study programme, becoming mandatory for the students and with the support of the teachers. The fieldwork was in line with the course of Analytical Architecture supervised by Octávio Lixa Filgueiras, which was at the time conducting a very similar exercise in Matosinhos.

[15] Which was no small deal: 150 participants in a total of a few thousand architects, in a time when 8,000 dwellings were being built or designed for the new housing quarters in Olivais.

[16] "Conclusions of the congress," document not signed (LNEC: Nuno Teotónio Pereira's archive, March 1960).

[17] See: Lopes Dias, "A precedent of SAAL: the National Laboratory for Civil Engineering's housing programme in the 1960s," in *SAAL and Architecture*, edited by Bandeirinha, Sardo, Canto Moniz (Coimbra/Porto: CES/Serralves, 2016), 85–92.

[18] Ruy José Gomes and Nuno Portas, *Inquérito-Piloto Sobre Necessidades Familiares em Matéria de Habitação* (Lisbon: LNEC, 1963).

[19] The neighbourhoods studied were Alvalade [MdH DB a89], Olivais Norte [MdH DB a186], Pontinha, Quinta do Jacinto (Lisbon) [MdH DB a635/676], Pasteleira [MdH DB a196], and D. Leonor–Sobreiras (Porto) [MdH DB a195/801].

The proposal from LNEC was easily inserted in a pedagogical strategy that valorized the approach and the contact of the school with its immediate reality. Sedas Nunes, who was involved in drafting the survey, selecting the sample and conducting the pilot inquiry in both Lisbon and Porto, also wrote part of the report, in particular the section on general valuation. The most important aspects were the inquiry's operativeness concerning its structure, execution, and receptivity, in order to check its feasibility in the Portuguese context. However, some doubts about the relevance of a few of the queries pointed directly to part of Chombart de Lauwe's tour-de-force: the distinction between *obligation-needs* and *aspiration-needs*.[20] It was the case of the "preferences" about living and dining rooms: when asked to criticize the existing space, interviewees from lower socioeconomic levels were unable to express an opinion. They could not formulate their own aspirations and did not reply, a data point that should be considered null.

Despite some reluctance concerning the extent[21] and experimental character of the pilot inquiry, some of its data were used for a study on family needs and space requirements in dwellings, published one year later. Sixteen activities were listed[22] and a filing sheet was presented for each with the functional data, the standard equipment and the anthropometric requirements, and a minimal floor area was established. Nuno Portas considered the vast majority of affordable housing built in Portugal unacceptable, noting that the case studies analysed satisfied the primary need for shelter but didn't have the capacity to absorb the *aspirations*, which could soon become *obligations*. Compared to similar subsidized housing estates in England, France, Holland, Italy or Spain, Portas detected a deficiency in floor area ranging from 20% to 40%. He advised that "a much broader perspective in establishing standards for future developments" be adopted and proposed a considerable increment in floor area, distinguishing strict standards from satisfactory standards, and bringing the latter closer to the European average.[23]

On the other hand, the data collected in the fieldwork were further developed and presented in 1967 as Volume 2 of the pilot inquiry. The oral information of the interview was compared with the graphic record of the dwelling and some remarks included in the first report were framed by the demographic and sociocultural characterization of the families. The drawings consisted of a register of the locations of each activity in the plan and the annotation of the furniture layout, particularly in the living rooms. These graphic notations were considered a first step in the establishment of a suitable method for surveying the ways of inhabiting.

[20] Paul-Henry and Marie-José Chombart de Lauwe, "L'evolution des besoins et la conception dynamique de la famille," *Revue Française de Sociologie* 4 (1960), 403–425.

[21] About 100 interviews were conducted in Lisbon and Porto.

[22] 1–sleeping, 2–cooking, 3–eating (current meals), 4–eating (special meals), 5–living, 6–living (guests), 7–play (children), 8–personal activities (young), 9–personal activities (older), 10–housekeeping (clothes), 11–housekeeping (laundry), 12–housekeeping (ironing), 13–toilette, 14–outdoor activity, 15–entering/circulation, 16–storage. See: Portas, *Estudo das Funções e da Exigência de Áreas da Habitação, Vol. 2* (Lisbon: LNEC, 1964).

[23] Nuno Portas, *Estudo das Funções e da Exigência de Áreas da Habitação Vol.1* (Lisbon: LNEC, 1964), 20. In the Affordable Rent Houses Programme and the Porto City Council Programme, the dwelling areas were around 40 m2 (2 bedrooms) and 50 m2 (3 bedrooms) versus 55 m2 and 65 m2 (Habitation à Loyer Modéré, France) or 70 m2 and 90 m2 (INA-Casa, Italy) for the same number of bedrooms.

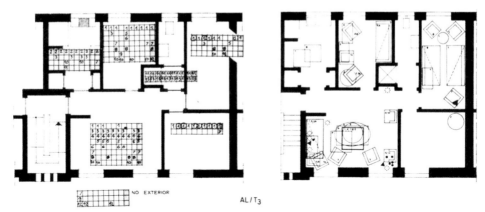

Fig. 2 LNEC's inquiry in Alvalade, Lisbon: record of the 16 activities in the dwelling (left) and the furniture display for several dwellings, overlapped (right) Source: Portas and Pereira, Inquérito-piloto... II.

Through them it was possible to recognize the "relative 'nomadism' of certain functions, as well as an almost absolute constancy of others,"[24] and to detect cultural aspects visible in the quality of the furniture and the way it was used, in the changes introduced in a partition wall or the re-adaptation of usage in a room. For instance, adapting a bedroom to a living room indicated a need for isolation from the dining area but also suggested the need for a space of greater prestige for social life.

During the 1960s, the line of research established by LNEC and coordinated by Nuno Portas pursued a double goal: to survey the needs of the families and to prepare new tools and methods to integrate this information into a more objective design process. This scientific approach—the sociological-based surveys and the processing of its data through mathematical analysis and computer calculation, based on Christopher Alexander's early studies[25]—was questioned by Pedro Vieira de Almeida.

Having written his graduate thesis on space in architecture and being a close follower of Portas' research,[26] Vieira de Almeida considered that sociological-based inquiries neglected or omitted specific architectural values, and hence they could not be a reliable basis for architecture. An alternative inquiry had to be prepared, related with the perception of space. It should analyse how residents *apprehend* and *appropriate* space through a methodology of repeated approaches to interviewees—a "system of interviews" rather than the question-and-answer routine—supported by photographic reports.[27] Studies on how the shape of an interior space influenced the way it was inhabited were already being done.

[24] Nuno Portas and Maria da Luz Pereira, *Inquérito-Piloto Sobre Necessidades Familiares em Matéria de Habitação II* (Lisbon: LNEC, 1967), 3.

[25] Namely *Community and Privacy* (1963, with Serge Chermayeff) and *Notes on the Synthesis of Form* (1964). See: Portas and Alves Costa, *Racionalização de Soluções da Habitação, 2 Vols.* (Lisbon: LNEC, 1966).

[26] Both worked in Nuno Teotónio Pereira's office in the first half of the 1960s, sharing ideas and discussing theory while collaborating on many projects. See: Lopes Dias, "Teoria e Desenho da Arquitectura em Portugal, 1956–1974: Nuno Portas e Pedro Vieira de Almeida" (PhD thesis, Polytechnic Univ. of Catalonia, 2017).

[27] This study was carried out by Pedro Vieira de Almeida between 1964 and 1967, supported by a Calouste Gulbenkian Foundation grant, but no conclusive synthesis was ever presented.

Vieira de Almeida was aware of Lennart Holm's conclusions on the relation between the size, shape, and arrangement of a living room: for areas between 18–24 m², the use of two nuclei of furniture (dining table and chairs; couch, armchair, and small table) was frequent and for areas between 20–24 m², the rectangular shape defined more precisely the order of the nuclei.[28] He thought, however, that this kind of analysis should be complemented with "quality data": the positioning and size of windows, doors, and other elements. Observing the graphic records of LNEC's fieldwork, he pointed out how the location of two windows and a wall next to the entrance door in Alvalade provided a better organization and an ambience of greater intimacy to the living area, compared with the remaining case studies.

Influenced by Gaston Bachelard's phenomenological interpretation, Pedro Vieira de Almeida would decline any technoscientific approach to the dwelling. In his opinion, economic criteria could not justify a prescriptive method by which a specific function was assigned to each space of the house, constraining the freedom of each family to appropriate space and to create its own universe. Instead, he proposed a critical revaluation of the spaces to which one specific function could not be attributed—corridors, halls, porches, loggie—those considered by the most strict functionalism as *lost spaces*.[29] The vagueness of the former (circulation devices) and the ambiguity of the latter (semi-interior or semi-exterior spaces) could balance the rigidity of uses in kitchens, bathrooms, and bedrooms. Unlike the *stanza di lavoro*, an independent room with "circumscribed malleability," *lost spaces* enhanced flexibility throughout the house. The notion of *lost space* must be understood within the debate on functionalism that framed post-war architecture. If in the Modern Movement's "heroic period," the moral commitment didn't allow any minimum portion of space to be left unused, in the sixties it was *"exactly the possibility and the necessity of setting forth spaces of indecision that became important, to architectural practice and critical reflection."*[30]

[28] Pedro Vieira de Almeida, "Da utilidade social da arquitectura," *Análise Social* 6 (April 1964): 237–248. Holm's study was "Living in flats" (1956).

[29] Pedro Vieira de Almeida, "O «espaço-perdido.» Proposta para a sua revalorização crítica," *Jornal de Letras e Artes*, 27 January 1965. See also the continuity of this article, published in the same newspaper with subheads "Evolução dos edifícios escolares" (17 February 65), "Habitação" (26 May 1965), "Edifícios de culto" (4 August 1965).

[30] Vieira de Almeida, "O «espaço-perdido»": 8.

By proposing an interpretation of the programme in terms of "space" rather than in terms of "functions," Pedro Vieira de Almeida was trading the inductive method of social and human sciences for a deductive one, in which space was no longer a receptacle for some predefined need but a source of stimuli for unexpected practices. Contrary to Nuno Portas, for whom architecture began in the programme—an interdisciplinary task with many inputs, particularly sociological data—for Vieira de Almeida architecture began in the space. "Space transcends function," Louis Kahn's epitome, might be the best definition for the *lost space*.

Although via different methodological approaches, Nuno Portas and Pedro Vieira de Almeida reached the same conclusion: a rigidly controlled programme such as economic housing should provide margins of indeterminacy, so that the house could adapt to the ever-changing situation of the family. The rational methods applied by LNEC did not eliminate the indeterminacy factor: the analysis of the information on functions and activities was aimed at visualizing the dynamics of life inside the dwelling and understanding it as a "field of tension," rather than at achieving conceptual simplicity; as Portas recognized, the sociological knowledge of inhabiting was relevant only if all the ambiguity and diversity of human behaviour was taken into account in the design process. For Vieira de Almeida, malleability wasn't possible without the reality of indeterminate spaces, with which the notion of *lost space* is directly related.

(ALL) POWER TO THE USER: A PARADIGM SHIFT?

Throughout the 1950s and 1960s, the principle of distinction between structure and complement was essential among Team 10 members. This principle was meant to deal with an increasingly complex and inscrutable society with changing needs and aspirations. The "study of communities as they exist" seemed almost impossible in a world in perpetual change (a frequent remark on the surveys concerned precisely how quick its data were outdated). In mass housing, the dichotomy between determinate and indeterminate elements made "openness" possible to both individual forms of expression and changes in time. Golden Lane's "yard-garden"—the extension of the dwelling that could eventually be occupied as another room—, Candilis-Josic-Woods' fixed core units serving multiple displays of living-rooms and bedrooms in Bagnols-sur-Cèze, and Bakema's studies for growing houses with predictable patterns of extension along the patio are just a few examples. Herman Hertzberger would later refer to *structure and infill* as the paradox of order that is conducive to freedom.[31]

A more systematic contribution came from N. J. Habraken and his research group SAR, by presenting the concept of *support* as an alternative to mass housing. It was based on the distinction between the immovable and collective elements of a building and the individual elements that each user could choose according to their needs and preferences: the *support* was the part of the structure over which the user did not have control; everything else could be altered, taken down or rebuilt, independently from the overall display. According to Habraken, a support structure *absorbs the unforeseen* and "enables the occupants to be involved via the independent dwelling."[32]

[31] Herman Hertzberger, *Lessons for Students in Architecture* (Rotterdam: 010 Publishers, 2009 [1991]). "[It is a] paradox that the restriction of a structuring principle (warp, spine, grid) apparently results not in a diminution but in an expansion of the possibilities of adaptation and therefore of the individual possibilities of expression."

[32] N.J. Habraken, *Supports: An Alternative to Mass Housing* (London: The Architectural Press, 1972 [1961]), 92.

These interpretations seem to undermine the notions of "needs" and "requirements." By the second half of the 1960s, even someone like Christopher Alexander, who believed in the possibility of writing an objectively correct building programme, preferred to speak of *tendencies*. He considered that a good environment was not so much one that satisfied people's needs as one that enabled people to satisfy their own needs by themselves.[33]

By the end of the 1960s, social turmoil allowed marginal experiences on popular initiative of self-building and self-management to be received as a refreshing input for disciplinary practice. As had happened before with the revaluation of the Casbah by Team 10, the squatter settlement in Lima, Peru, was presented by John Turner in 1968 as *architecture that works*, particularly on the social level.[34] In incipiently industrialized countries, the government did not control the material and human resources necessary for the satisfaction of basic housing needs. Turner considered that the natural resourcefulness of the *barriada*-builder[35] that he had been observing—initiative, inventiveness, perseverance, and hope—could achieve a lot more than any state aid. He advocated housing as an open system diametrically opposed to the authoritarian state-subsidized housing system, imposed from above with total disengagement from the users. For families with very low income, the *barriada* had an "existential value" translated to *"the freedom of community self-selection"* (including the place to live), *"the freedom to budget one's own resources and the freedom to shape one's own environment."*[36]

The procedure of building by stages—from a minimum provisional structure to a two- or three-storey house, according to priorities and budget—had the advantage of a *"consequent adaptability of space and structures to the changing needs and behaviour patterns of the family."*[37] Besides, the improvements were made using construction techniques which the users were familiar with. Turner would criticize the employment of advanced techniques and the use of materials and components difficult to modify or combine with other materials using hand tools in Habraken & SAR's work. By locking the users into highly industrialized forms of construction, *"they are reduced to the status of passive users or 'consumers' of subsystems that they can only assemble,"* he wrote.[38]

John Turner's radical and literal "as found" and Team 10's metaphorical "as found" would unexpectedly meet in 1969, when a UN-sponsored international competition was launched to build a low-cost neighbourhood on the outskirts of Lima, with high-density and low-rise standards and a growing courtyard house as basic cell. The impact of the Lima-PREVI[39] was due in large part to the participation of Team 10 members like Aldo van Eyck and Candilis, Josic & Woods.

---

[33] Christopher Alexander and Barry Poyner, *The Atoms of Environmental Structure* (Center for Planning and Development Research, University of California, 1966).

[34] John Turner, "The Squatter Settlement: an architecture that works," *Architectural Design* 8 (1968): 355–360.

[35] A *barriada* is the Peruvian term for squatter settlement.

[36] Turner, "The squatter settlement," 357.

[37] Turner, "The squatter settlement," 360.

[38] John Turner, "Commentary on SAR," in *The Scope of Social Architecture*, edited by Richard Hatch (NY: Van Nostrand Reinhold Co., 1984), 61–62. "Indeed, I have a great deal in common with the Supports concept as pioneered by Habraken at a time when I was only starting to articulate my own and parallel ideas."

[39] Proyecto Experimental de Vivienda (*Experimental Housing Project*). See: *Architectural Design* 4 (1970) and *Time Builds!*, edited by F.García-Huidobro, D.Torres, N.Tugas (Barcelona: GG, 2008).

For the latter, it was an opportunity to return to a vital experience: as Eric Mumford pointed out, the practice of ATBAT in Morocco twenty years earlier was fundamental for Candilis to consider housing as an evolutionary process, beginning with the provision of basic infrastructure and partially self-built units, evolving eventually to more advanced solutions.[40]

This research would be influential in a key study conducted by Nuno Portas in LNEC from 1968 onwards. *Evolutionary Housing* was meant to be an alternative to state-subsidized blocks or towers with minimum standards and rigid constructive systems with no possibility of further improvement. A fundamental distinction between public commitment and private initiative was made in the first pages of the report: the acquisition and urbanization of the land and its legislative control belonged to the state, and the improvement and extension of the basic central core and the self-management of all communitarian facilities were the responsibility of dwellers.[41]

[40] Eric Mumford, *The CIAM Discourse on Urbanism, 1928–1960* (Cambridge: MIT Press, 2000).

[41] Nuno Portas and Francisco Silva Dias, *Habitação Evolutiva. Princípios e Critérios de Projectos.* (Lisbon: LNEC, December 1971).

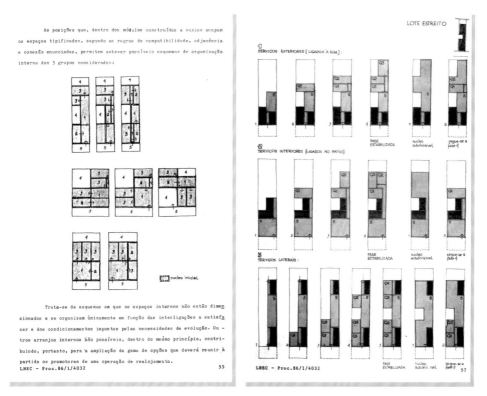

Fig. 3 Evolutionary housing: typological studies on 3 types of plots, according to 5 groups of activities (left) and growing patterns for narrowed plots (right) Source: Portas and Silva Dias, *Habitação Evolutiva*.

Three types of land plots were considered, and for each a simple set of typological rules was studied in order to allow growth along the courtyard. Although the growing patterns were supported by the 1964 study on areas and functional organization, physical and biological needs were indeed much less important than psychological and cultural values. Portas would emphasize the importance of the (semi-)detached house for the low income families, with the garden as a privileged space for appropriation.

John Turner's most influential idea was that housing could be considered as a *process or activity* instead of a "packaged product," an existentially significant activity that stimulated individual and social well-being.[42] By distinguishing housing as a process that builds community from housing as a product to be consumed, he was surprisingly in tune with French studies on social space, particularly those by Henri Lefebvre.[43] Lefebvre met Chombart de Lauwe in the Centre d'Études Sociologiques and was an admirer of his studies on everyday life, but unlike Chombart, he would defend the detached house—the *pavillon*—to the detriment of the communitarian model of the *Unité*.[44] Lefebvre observed in the *pavillon* practices of modelling and appropriation on fences, gardens, and outbuildings that he considered symptoms of a real, though limited, process of inhabiting.[45] These practices of appropriation should also invade the public space of the city in order to change the course of what Lefebvre saw as a growing *bureaucratic society of controlled consumption*. According to Nuno Portas, admittedly influenced by Lefebvre, one of the main contributions of the study on the *pavillon* was the elimination of the "left-wing ideological prejudice" towards the detached house, according to which it "would fatally lead its users to become reactionary petit-bourgeois."[46]

Although appropriation became a key concept in Lefebvre's theories on social space, it was already part of a wider reflection presented by Chombart de Lauwe in *Famille et Habitation*. Appropriation was one of the aspects that his team found absent in the work of experimental observation. Families adapted passively to their dwellings, and such acquiescence was pointed out as one of the dangers against which it was necessary to fight. The far-reaching implications of this problem were also pointed out at the social level: *"the worst that can happen is that the inhabitants of a city live in total indifference and make no personal effort to organize their existence. Here we refer to a specific problem that stands before us, but it is a general problem; it has to do with the very foundation of democracy."*[47]

---

[42] As he would later describe on *Freedom to Build* (1972), distinguishing the word "housing" as a verb (an action) from the same word as a name (a thing).

[43] See Lefebvre's work between *The Right to the City* (1968) and *The Production of Space* (1974).

[44] About Chombart and Lefebvre, see: Lukasz Stanek, "Henri Lefebvre: for and against the 'user'," In *Use matters: an alternative history of architecture*, edited by Kenny Cupers (London&NY: Routledge, 2013), 139–152; Anthony Vidler, "Troubles in theory. Part IV: the social side," In *Architectural Review* 1394 (April 2013): 83–87.

[45] See Lefebvre's introduction to: Raymond, Henri; Haumont, Nicole; Raymond, Marie-Geneviève; Haumont, Antoine. *L'Habitat Pavillonnaire* (Paris: Centre de Recherche d'Urbanisme et Institute de Sociologie Urbaine, 1966).

[46] *Cuadernos 7. Especial Nuno Portas* (Seville: Escuela de Arquitectura de Sevilla, 1971), 63. *L'Habitat Pavillonnaire* was indicated in *Habitação Evolutiva [Evolutionary Housing]* bibliography, in the subsection "Appropriation and change of the dwelling space by its users."

[47] Chombart de Lauwe (dir.), *Famille et Habitation II*, 260.

ACKNOWLEDGMENTS

This text is a revised version of a part of the author's PhD thesis, funded by European and national funds POPH/FSE; FCT–Portuguese National Funding Agency for Science, Research and Technology (grant SFRH/BD/84258/2012).

Proofreading by Sara Levy.

BIBLIOGRAPHY

Almeida, Pedro Vieira de. "Da utilidade social da arquitectura." *Análise Social* 6 (April 1964): 237–248.

Almeida, Pedro Vieira de. "O «espaço-perdido." Proposta para a sua revalorização crítica." *Jornal de Letras e Artes* (January 27, 1965): 10, 14.

Banham, Reyner. *The New Brutalism. Ethic or Aesthetic?* Stuttgart and Bern: Karl Kramer Pub., 1966.

Chombart de Lauwe, Paul-Henry (dir.). *Famille et Habitation. I– Sciences Humaines et Conceptions de l'Habitation*. Paris: CNRS, 1959.

Chombart de Lauwe, Paul-Henry (dir.). *Famille et Habitation. II– Un Essai d' Observation Expérimentale*. Paris: CNRS, 1960.

Chombart de Lauwe, Paul-Henry. "Sociologia da habitação. Método e perspectivas de investigação." *Arquitectura* 68 (Lisbon, July 1960): 41–50.

Chombart de Lauwe, Paul-Henry, and Marie-José Chombart de Lauwe. "L'evolution des besoins et la conception dynamique de la famille." *Revue Française de Sociologie* 4 (1960): 403–425.

Habraken, N.J. *Supports: An Alternative to Mass Housing*. London: The Architectural Press, 1972.

Hertzberger, Herman. *Lessons for Students in Architecture*. Rotterdam: 010 Publishers, 2009.

Lefebvre, Henri. "Introduction." In *L'Habitat Pavillonnaire*, edited by Henri Raymond, Nicole Haumont, Marie-Geneviève Raymond, Antoine Haumont. Paris: Centre de Recherche d' Urbanisme et Institute de Sociologie Urbaine, 1966.

Portas, Nuno. "A responsabilidade de uma novíssima geração no Movimento Moderno em Portugal." *Arquitectura* 66 (Lisbon, Nov./Dec. 1959): 13–14.

Portas, Nuno, and Ruy José Gomes. *Inquérito-Piloto Sobre Necessidades Familiares em Matéria de Habitação*. Lisbon: LNEC, 1963.

Portas, Nuno. *Estudo das Funções e da Exigência de Áreas da Habitação, Vol.1*. Lisbon: LNEC, 1964.

Portas, Nuno, and Maria da Luz Pereira. *Inquérito-Piloto Sobre Necessidades Familiares em Matéria de Habitação II*. Lisbon: LNEC, 1967.

Portas, Nuno, and Francisco Silva Dias. *Habitação Evolutiva. Princípios e Critérios de Projectos*. Lisbon: LNEC, 1971.

Portas, Nuno. *A Habitação Social. Proposta Para a Metodologia da Sua Arquitectura*. Porto: FAUP, 2004 [1960].

Smithson, Alison, and Peter Smithson. "An alternative to the Garden City idea." *Architectural Design* 7 (1956): 229–231.

Smithson, Alison, ed. *The Emergence of Team 10 out of CIAM: Documents*. London: Architectural Association, 1982.

Turner, John. "The Squatter Settlement: an architecture that works." *Architectural Design* 8 (1968): 355–360.

A Singular Path in Portuguese Housing: Reviewing the Work of the Habitações Económicas–Federação das Caixas de Previdência

MARIA TAVARES
Lusíada University | University of Porto, Faculty of Architecture, Centre for Studies in Architecture and Urbanism

ABSTRACT

Between 1946 and 1972, the architectural debate on programmed housing achieved new heights in Portugal. Amidst a crisis in housing for the masses, the Habitações Económicas–Federação das Caixas de Previdência (HE–Affordable Housing–Federation of Provident Funds), subordinate to the Subsecretariado de Estado das Corporações e Previdência Social (Undersecretariat of State for Corporations and Social Providence) and responsible for promoting the use of social insurance funds to design and build housing, generated, in those 26 years, new ideas and ideals on architecture for a disfavoured social class that was bereft of proper housing.

A year after the Casas de Renda Económica (CRE–Affordable Rent Houses) programme was made law, revealing a more pragmatic approach by the Estado Novo regime towards housing policies, private initiative showed little interest in applying the new legislation. The HE was therefore created as a clear response not only to the obvious housing shortage but also to the possibilities which originated from the CRE programme and which favoured the construction of housing with low rents and provided a basic tool for a dynamic generation of architects to test new housing devices for a new, modern way of life.

Faced with the reality of a country in dire need of housing and armed with a sense of social responsibility, the architects involved in the CRE decentralized their actions and spread their work field across the whole country. That social responsibility is reflected not only in the schemes implemented but particularly in the housing models they used, studying the future users' varied cultural patterns and the specificities of the context. From 1948, the remarkable role and participation of Nuno Teotónio Pereira stressed the urgency of revising housing models, complementing the housing programmes the Estado Novo had launched by affirming an experimental path for the CRE.

BIOGRAPHY

Maria Tavares (Lisbon, 1970), is an architect and an assistant professor of the Faculdade de Arquitetura e Artes da Universidade Lusíada Norte. She has a master's degree from the Faculdade de Arquitetura da Universidade Técnica de Lisboa (FAUTL 2003) and a PhD in architecture from the Faculdade de Arquitetura da Universidade do Porto (FAUP 2016) with the thesis on the work of the Habitações Económicas–Federação das Caixas de Previdência. She is an integrated member of the CITAD–Centro de Investigação em Território, Arquitetura e Design at Universidade Lusíada, a collaborating member of the investigation group Atlas da Casa, at the Centro de Estudos de Arquitetura e Urbanismo (CEAU) at FAUP, and a team member of the FCT funded investigation project "Mapping Public Housing: a critical review of the State-subsidized residential architecture in Portugal (1910–1974)." She has authored several publications and talks on the subject of state-subsidized programmed housing and coordinated the research nucleus "O arrendamento social público (1945–1969): Nova escala, novos programas e agentes" promoted by the Instituto da Habitação e Reabilitação Urbana (IHRU).

1. CONTEXT REVIEW

In 1969, during the Coloquio de Urbanismo,[1] Nuno Teotónio Pereira presented an essay—later published in the dynamic magazine Arquitectura, launching "even if with an experimental character" [2] what would become a regular section on social housing—with a critical review of the condition of Portuguese housing. In the article "Housing for the larger number"[3] Teotónio Pereira pinpointed the centre of the housing issue to the exponential character of the shortage, determined by several factors, such as demographic pressure resulting from the flux of rural populations to urban centres and the reduction of family size, among others. Whichever the response, it should be limited to the "construction of some estates,"[4] as the "larger number" was a variable reality, progressively affecting new population strata and becoming a collective issue. To recognise its dynamics in order to place it in a realistic perspective, was the only way to devise the necessary instruments to solve the issue at hand, as no visible border line clarified priority territories for intervention.[5] Going back two decades, to 1948 and the first Congresso Nacional de Arquitectura (National Congress on Architecture), Teotónio Pereira—who identified the initiative as the "turning point for the recovery of the architects' freedom of speech"[6]—then an architectural intern, presented a talk with Costa Martins on the subject of "Affordable Housing and Social Readjustment."[7] In that talk, the authors noted that building for the larger number presupposed an analysis and understanding of the social frame of the larger cities and a distinction between two target groups among those poorly housed: the working class and the middle class. To the authors, it was imperative that the upwards social movement of the working classes should grow vastly and quickly while the degradation of living conditions of the middle class should be checked, which could be achieved by building housing close together for both groups, establishing neighbourly relations among them[8].

The usual topic of building upwards, a contemporary debate analysed and presented by Gropius in the 1930 III Congrès Internationale de l'Architecture Moderne (CIAM) in Brussels, through his diagrams "Low, Mid- or High-Rise Building?," is primarily related to a demand for rationality.[9] Teotónio Pereira and Costa Martins claimed the urgency of applying that principle on a large scale, without forsaking the sociological characteristics of the target population. If the modern housing block was not designed as an isolated part of the city, it could, as stated by Ana Tostões, achieve "a new dignity" if shaped as a "repeatable piece based on urban values" and so contribute to "a more contemporary image of the civilized and internationally urban city."[10]

---

[1] Urbanism Conference in Funchal

[2] Opening remarks to the "Habitação Social" section. *Arquitectura*, no. 110 (Jul./Aug. 1969): 181–182.

[3] Nuno Teotónio Pereira, "Habitações para o maior número," *Arquitectura*, no. 110 (Jul./Aug. 1969): 181–182

[4] Ibid.

[5] Ibid.

[6] Nuno Teotónio Pereira, "A arquitectura do Estado Novo," *Arquitectura* no. 142 (Jun. 1981).

[7] Included in Topic 2, "The Portuguese Housing Problem"

[8] Nuno Teotónio Pereira and Costa Martins, "Habitação Económica e Reajustamento Social" in *Iº Congresso Nacional de Arquitectura*, ed. Ana Tostões (Lisbon: Ordem dos Arquitectos, 2008), 248, fac-simile edition.

[9] Madalena Cunha Matos, "Para o maior número: sobre a Federação de Caixas de Previdência," *JA*, no. 204 (Jan./Feb. 2002): 34.

[10] Ana Tostões, *Os Verdes Anos na Arquitectura Portuguesa dos Anos 50* (Porto: FAUP publicações, 1997), 71.

After the 1948 Congress and the resulting expectations of social transformation, the twenty years that separate the two texts frame a revision of concepts, as the architectural discourse on housing was transformed (or adapted), surpassing the rural ideology epitomized by the "self-owned, modest and properly Portuguese house"[11] which the Estado Novo had promoted. The "brand new generation"[12] of architects, as Nuno Portas described it, coordinated an operative reflexion on the coeval reality. In a context of reconstruction in Europe, it participated in a restless approach to modern solutions of simplification and standardization. A new social conscience complemented that restlessness, working towards a modernity that was slowly becoming possible in the Portuguese reality.[13] In this frame of social responsibility by the "brand new generation" and its quest for housing for the "larger number," the HE[14] was created in 1947 with the supervision of the Undersecretariat for Corporations and Social Providence.

2. AFFORDABLE HOUSING: PRAGMATISM VS EXPERIMENTALISM

World War II set a turning point in the course of housing design in Portugal, as the debate on the topic grew significantly in a new, less ideological and more pragmatic approach. The 25 April 1946 Decree no. 35,611 presented new solutions to the housing problem by opening up the execution of social works[15] such as the construction of Affordable Houses and Affordable Rent Houses to social welfare institutions, enabling the creation of the HE in the following year, with the purpose of applying capital from the Provident Funds in the promotion of housing through the Affordable Rents Houses[16] programme. That programme was seen by Nuno Teotónio Pereira, the first architect of the HE, as an "adaptation effort by the Estado Novo to the new political setting resulting from the defeat of fascist regimes in World War II."[17]

The use of Provident Funds capital over more than twenty years of work (1946–1972) by the HE generated a debate and reflexion on the subject of housing, testing a new research territory and adapting to an economically constricted reality by reducing to its essentials the proposed domestic structures. Through the transformation of the Estado Novo housing policies and the new regime of the Affordable Rents Houses, the HE became a "disciplinary research school for collective housing,"[18] focusing on a new renting system[19] and in the thoroughly debated housing block, even if limited to four stories to ensure the distance to the *"phalanstery, potential generator of social subversion."*[20]

[11] Maria Tavares, "Leituras da produção [moderna] da casa: as HE nos anos 50 e 60 em Portugal," in *Resdomus.* (Porto: FAUP publicações, 2014), 73.

[12] Nuno Portas, "A responsabilidade de uma novíssima geração no Movimento Moderno em Portugal," *Arquitectura* no.66 (Nov./Dez. 1959): 13–14.

[13] Ibid.

[14] The HE was created according to principles stated in article 11, no.3, of the Decree no. 35,611, 25 April 1946. *Diário do Governo*, no. 137, II series (15 June 1946): 3256.

[15] Decree no. 35,611, 25 April 1946, article 11.

[16] According to Law no. 2,007, 7 May 1945..

[17] Nuno Teotónio Pereira, "A Federação de Caixas de Previdência–1947–1972," in *Escritos (1947–1996, selecção)* (Porto: FAUP publicações, 1996), 205.

[18] José Manuel Fernandes, "Jorge Viana, o arquitecto de Oeiras," in *Arquitectura Portuguesa (Temas Actuais II)* (Lisbon: Livros Cotovia, 2005), 144.

[19] Renting systems were seen by the regime as pro-socialist.

[20] Pereira, "A Federação de Caixas de Previdência," 206.

The aforementioned practical approach by the state generated a strategic change in course, towards a "reinforcement of the productive apparatus, and a modernization and rationalization of the state,"[21] and the Bairro de Alvalade [MdH DB a89] in Lisbon would mark the turning point. Its first two cells, built entirely with Providence funds, pragmatically used the designs developed by Miguel Jacobetty, later presented in the 1948 Congress in the topic of Portuguese Housing. The same designs were employed in other cities, deviating from the working classes and setting their target on a middle class "whose housing needs were considered new data and whose support the regime required"[22] in a series of small interventions, far from the scale of Alvalade. The inexistence, in 1947 and in the first years of the HE, of a technical team able to respond to requests, and the disparity between the contributions and the amount of pensions paid, built up the available funds to be applied in that large new area of Lisbon[23] and transformed it into the "launching pad"[24] of the HE. Nuno Teotónio Pereira joined the HE a year after its creation and went on to become a central figure to the institution's methods and percourse. He started his professional career while still a student, in the construction works of Alvalade, monitoring them as an assistant to the lead architect, Miguel Jacobetty, and under the supervision of the engineer Magalhães Lobato. That experience generated an invitation to join the HE team as with responsibility for studies and designs at the central delegation in Lisbon. He kept a connection to the HE until its dissolution, as the only architect for the first eight years and as a consultant after the lively arrival of João Braula Reis. Due to his responsibilities in the HE, he was sent to the UIA, the International Union of Architects, where he was the Portuguese delegate for six years. He travelled across Europe looking for similar initiatives, namely the Italian INA-Casa,[25] in order to discuss and apply new models within the HE's actions. He "participated in the selection of locations and programme definition, commissioning colleagues across the country"[26] before producing evaluations of the designs "following fruitful exchanges of views,"[27] as he described them. After the first phase of Alvalade, new requests emerged from all the national territory. Working with municipalities which made terrains available following studies on local housing deficits, projects were commissioned on a freelancing principle to a select group of architects from Lisbon and Porto close to Teotónio Pereira. The new designs were developed in multiple contexts across the country, avoiding repetition of designs but using standardized details in varied combinations[28]—a curious option after the pragmatic approach to Alvalade. These external commissions[29] resulted in an experimental approach to housing production, reflecting the dynamics of the "brand new generation" in the 1950s and 1960s and the search for a renovation of modern models.

[21] Ibid.

[22] Pereira, "A Federação de Caixas de Previdência," 207.

[23] Described by Nuno Portas as an "ensanche."

[24] Pereira, "A Federação de Caixas de Previdência," 207.

[25] INA-Casa: Instituto Nazionale de Assicurazione-Casa, also known as Plano Fanfani, named after the Work Minister who created it. It started in 1949 with the main goal of reducing unemployment through building and solve housing shortage.

[26] Nuno Teotónio Pereira, "Um testemunho pessoal," in *Arquitectura e Cidadania, Atelier Nuno Teotónio Pereira* (Lisboa: Quimera Editores, 2004), 45

[27] Ibid.

[28] *Habitações Económicas–Federação de Caxias de Previdência, Colectânea de Estudos de Habitação, Publicação de Circulação Restrita*, no.9 (Out. 1963): 10.

[29] The HE was still in charge of construction management.

3. TWO STAGES, TWO LAWS, A SHARED GOAL.

AFFORDABLE RENT HOUSES

At the beginning of the 1950s, Nuno Teotónio Pereira's office was hired to design an estate in Braga [MdH DB a43], which we consider the start of a second stage of the HE, as it was the first initiative to break with the use of the Alvalade models. "In a compromise focusing on the integration in the urban fabric,"[30] the estate in the old Avenida do Marechal Gomes da Costa, today Avenida da Liberdade, open then as an expansion axis to the city, a variant of the standard block was tested, marking simultaneously a continuity of existing urban fabric and a liberation from a strict urban grid. The experience monitoring the estate of Alvalade was reflected in "the substitution of backyards for public spaces."[31]

Numerous designs followed. In a more urban context, the Bairro de Ramalde [MdH DB a22] in Porto, by Fernando Távora, stands out, presented by the O Primeiro de Janeiro newspaper as *"a truly new city, for six thousand inhabitants, that will be built [. . .] following the latest urban concepts."*[32] Not fully executed, it was the major initiative of the HE in the city.[33] In Lisbon, the great expansion of the plans for Olivais Norte, Olivais Sul, and, later, Chelas[34] were developed with a considerable presence[35] of buildings for the HE. In Gaia [MdH DB a30] and Bragança [MdH DB a51], João Andresen—who had, previously to Távora, developed a design for Ramalde with Rogério Martins—rationally reduced circulation areas, even in larger typologies than would be expected in this kind of housing initiatives. The singular set of buildings[36] designed by Chorão Ramalho in Funchal, Madeira [MdH DB a130] *"ensured a spacious setting for the buildings, surrounding them with free green areas."*[37]

Countless other designs were developed by Ruy d'Athouguia, Bartolomeu da Costa Cabral, Nuno Portas, Vasco Croft, Vítor Figueiredo, Justino Morais, Conceição Silva, Jorge Viana, and the northerners Alcino Soutinho, Lixa Filgueiras, Rui Pimentel, Luís Cunha, Arnaldo Araújo, among others. In rural settings, the same Affordable Rents House programme had a relevant presence. Contemporarily to the Survey of Popular Architecture, in which Teotónio Pereira was the responsible for the Estremadura section, designs valued local ways of living and new physical infrastructures and proposed new models of housing. In the Barcelos estate [MdH DB a42], by Teotónio Pereira, learning about future users generated new research territories.

[30] Nuno Teotónio Pereira, "Um percurso na profissão," in *Escritos*, 153.

[31] João Afonso, "Uma imensa simplicidade. A cidade que se constrói na Rua da Alegria," in *Arquitectura e Cidadania*, 88.

[32] *O Primeiro de Janeiro* (26 February 1950).

[33] The estate of Ramalde is the sole operation in the city of Porto. Later, as the FFH had already taken over, the great operation of Pasteleira was developed with a design by João Serôdio.

[34] Plan by the Gabinete Técnico da Habitação (GTH), from the 1959 Decree no. 42,454.

[35] Maria Tavares, "Habitações Económicas–Federação de Caixas de Previdência: uma perspectiva estratégica [nos anos 1950 e 1960 em Portugal]," in *Actas do 1.º CIHEL–Congresso Internacional do Espaço Lusófono* (Lisbon: Argumentum, 2010), 48.

[36] The functionally complex program included offices for the district's Caixa Sindical da Previdência (Union Provident Fund), medical services, two blocks of nine and three stories for housing and two commercial areas.

[37] Raul Chorão Ramalho, "Conjunto de Habitações no Funchal," *Arquitectura* no.87 (Mar./Apr. 1965): 47–53.

New housing models were rehearsed, simplifying the scheme by concentrating functions in a central common zone, designed as a main area for domestic life "deeply influenced by a multifunctionality of vernacular roots"[38] with a direct connection to external areas. This modern device, used by the author in several designs,[39] reduced the need for circulation areas and was adaptable to varied family structures and ideologies. As the woman performed a fundamental role within domestic work, a typically modern experimentation area was made available for her, with a complex service nucleus supported by furniture design. The set of twenty houses, in two two-storey rows,[40] *"seek a contextualized setting in place and a proximity to rural typologies while keeping with a sense of modernity."*[41]

The same concerns were present in the designs for Famalicão [MdH DB a50] and Trancoso [MdH DB a75], also by Teotónio Pereira, or in the mix of rows of houses and housing towers he developed with Nuno Portas for Vila do Conde [MdH DB a29] and Caramulo [MdH DB a128]. The distribution of commissions to architects from Lisbon and Porto connected and decentralized architectural production, in a context of participation by architects in the aforementioned Survey of Popular Architecture promoted by Keil do Amaral.

As Provident Funds capital and requests for housing grew in the 1950s, the HE felt the need to expand its technical team. The young architect João Braula Reis, who had developed a thesis on affordable housing for his graduation,[42] was hired on the suggestion of Nuno Teotónio Pereira. Teotónio Pereira became a consultant for the HE and Braula Reis became the active conductor of the institution, putting together a young team with an atelier feeling of freedom of decision and design,[43] distancing it from a bureaucratized institutional structure. The first project team, created in the second half the 1950s, was therefore headed by Braula Reis and included the architects Vasco Croft de Moura, Bartolomeu da Costa Cabral, and Justino Morais, reaching a considerable size (about twenty architects, along with engineers, inspectors, etc.). The institution's response capacity grew but some designs were still subject to external commissions. The project team had a significant role in the HE's next phase, when it created a support structure not only for design and supervision but also for building.[44]

---

[38] Rui J. G. Ramos, *A Casa, Arquitectura e Projecto Doméstico na Primeira Metade do Século XX Português* (Porto: FAUP publicações, 2010), 87.

[39] The design for Soda Póvoa, at Póvoa de Santa Iria, although located in an urban context, showed the same concerns in the organization of domestic space, as well as some later experiences at Olivais.

[40] Of six and fourteen houses respectively.

[41] Ana Tostões, "Cultura e Tecnologia na Arquitectura Moderna Portuguesa" (PhD Thesis, Instituto Superior Técnico/Universidade Técnica de Lisboa, 2002), 647

[42] His thesis included a design for a fishermen's estate in Peniche and a deep study on housing for poorer classes. Vasco Croft, *Arquitectura e Humanismo. O Papel do Arquitecto, Hoje, em Portugal* (Lisbon: Terramar, 2001), 281.

[43] Maria Tavares, "Federação de Caixas de Previdência–Habitações Económicas, Um Percurso na História da Arquitectura da Habitação em Portugal" (Masters Diss., Universidade Técnica de Lisboa, 2003).

[44] Pereira, "A Federação de Caixas de Previdência," 209.

HOUSES BUILT OR ACQUIRED THROUGH LOANS

At the end of the 1950s, new legislation was created in the field of housing provision. Decree no. 2,092 of 1958, related to accumulation of capital, permitted loans to private citizens that were contributors to Provident Funds and fulfilled certain requirements,[45] for building, acquiring or refurbishing self-owned houses.[46] Within the same framing, loans were also possible for private equity companies and Casas do Povo (People's Houses) that had plots available for construction.[47] This set dynamic new scenarios for the HE action and enabled the growth of the project team, ensuring a wider coverage of the national territory. With a team of about twenty architects and a newly-created North Delegation,[48] a network of regional architects was created through a regime of regular fees. Nine work teams directed by architects were created for nine regions: Porto (Duilio da Silveira/Rui Pimentel), Trás-os-Montes (Augusto Amaral/Arnaldo Araújo), Coimbra (Vasco Cunha), Covilhã (Pinto de Sousa), Lisboa (Justino Morais), Santarém (Vítor Figueiredo), Elvas (Manuel Bagulho), Faro (F. Modesto), and Funchal. That way, a response was available for requests from varied contexts in the country.

Public funding for the acquisition of private property increased in an open and flexible fashion. Within a period of eight years, nine thousand loans were granted for housing, surpassing every forecast.[49] However, even in a context of effective response to interested beneficiaries, an objective analysis showed that large-scale programmed housing was the only solution to the degradation of housing provision. Although the loan solution had its merits, "individual loans took their right place as complementary measures,"[50] in sporadic and spread out situations.[51] As this decentralization of architectural production took place, the central services of the HE functioned as technical support, deepening the study of affordable housing as a *métier* and developing templates for several elements and steps of the design process, such as standardized materials, details, and specifications.[52] This research, focusing on quality patterns, gave rise to a set of deeply systematized data and publications such as the *HE Bulletins* and the *Cadernos Técnicos de Circulação Restrita* (Limited Circulation Technical Notebooks).[53] The Bulletins were published irregularly from May 1962, and the limited access to the information[54] they contained did not stop Braula Reis from encouraging "the exchange of ideas that could in any way help solve the problem of social housing"[55] in Portugal. Throughout the 1960s, the enforcement of the Houses Built or Acquired Through Loans Law had some results, as the HE joined the transition and revision of modern ideas on architecture and matured its processes through enriching experiences of social transformation.

[45] Tavares, "Federação de Caixas de Previdência–Habitações Económicas," 81.

[46] After their houses were completed, beneficiaries had to place a plaque on a façade with the corresponding modality: A, Acquisition, B, refurbishment, C, new building.

[47] The HE would loan 70 per cent of the funds needed for building a house, as long as the beneficiary had the remaining 30 per cent and a plot available. In the case of contributing companies and members of the People's Houses, specific tables would apply. People's Houses and Municipalities would give the necessary support to make the plots viable and contribute with part of funding.

[48] The North Delegation was created in 1960, given the urgent need for responses to requests, as a consequence of the new law. Alcino Soutinho was in charge of the delegation, developing proposals for Trás-os-Montes, Aveiro, and the Greater Porto area.

[49] *Habitações Económicas–Federações de Caixas de Previdência, Casas de Renda Económica, Casas Construídas ou Adquiridas Através de Empréstimos* (August 1966).

[50] *Habitações Económicas–Federação de Caixas de Previdência, Moradias Construídas ao Abrigo da Lei n.º 2092* (Porto)

[51] Tavares, Federação de Caixas de Previdência–Habitações Económicas, 97.

[52] The Studies and Designs Office was divided in two sections: 1 Studies Section (norms) and 2 Design Section. The first section developed an internal work of analysis and costs control in building, house organization, and urban equipment, and produced the HE Bulletins. The second section was in charge of planning estates of Affordable Rents Houses and for People's Houses and individual loans. The two sections generated documentation to be used by regional architects.

[53] Pereira, "A Federação de Caixas de Previdência," 209.

[54] Mostly directed at close collaborators of the HE.

[55] *HE.FCP Colectânea de Estudos de Habitação, Publicação de Circulação Restrita*, no. 1 (Year 1, May 1962)

Every actor involved in this phase of the institution's activity was committed to a valorization of Portuguese domestic architecture, following João Braula Reis' challenge to approach every case individually through a directed and contextualized design, therefore refusing design templates, and to accurately study every aspect and element of affordable housing building.[56] Design repetition was to be avoided, as Nuno Teotónio Pereira noted in a statement to the HE in 1958, as even if a design was reused it should "always be adapted and perfected by the author, as it was, like every work of art, a unitary and individual creation"[57] and the contract stated that reasons for design repetition should be declared and justified.[58]

Housing for industry and rural workers generated the most representative designs of this period of the HE. Those designs focused on family life and adaptation to local conditions, but also on community living and services to support it. These initiatives, unlike the Affordable Rents Houses programme, presupposed prior discussion with the target populations or their representatives, adding new data to the design processes, as user participation was seen as key to the humanization of housing design. Geographical, anthropological, and sociological contexts, as well as knowledge of user needs and expectations, injected realism into processes, programmes, and models and forced their renovation. A wide array of examples may be indicated, but we will highlight the exemplary contributions by Vitor Figueiredo in the region of Santarém, Arnaldo Araújo in Trás-os-Montes, and Bartolomeu da Costa Cabral, with Vasco Croft, in Chamusca.[59]

Vitor Figueiredo paid singular attention to organization of internal areas, suggesting a very critical attitude towards the limitations of the architectural repertoire.[60] To him, narrow budgets were a component of the design process, not a limitation. He cited F.L. Wright and Alvar Aalto and imaginary paths to be discovered, breaking spatial constrictions by homogenizing living areas and allowing for flexible use according to the needs of the family.[61] The study of internal organization was enriched by the appreciation of what the author called "afunctional" areas in such designs as in the rural context of Benavente [MdH DB a150], Santo Estevão [MdH DB a151], Constância [MdH DB a888], and in the urban areas of Olivais Sul [MdH DB a189/549], and Peniche [MdH DB a79/80].

Arnaldo Araújo, a dynamic figure within the HE, based his approach on an understanding of popular living conditions and architecture and its rationality, an interest that was reflected in his 1957 CODA thesis (Concurso para Obtenção do Diploma de Arquiteto–Contest for Attribution of the Degree of Architect) on rural forms of housing in the North of Bragança in his participation

[56] Vasco Croft, *Arquitectura e Humanismo. O Papel do Arquitecto, Hoje, em Portugal* (Lisbon: Terramar, 2001), 281.

[57] Nuno Teotónio Pereira, *Serviços Técnicos das HE, Informação*, no. 4 (58).

[58] Article 3 of the "Condições Especiais Referentes a Casos Individuais da Lei 2.092" (Special Conditions For Individual Cases of the Law 2092).

[59] Bartolomeu da Costa Cabral and Vasco Croft developed this design as members of the HE design team and not as regional architects.

[60] Duarte Cabral Mello, "Vítor Figueiredo/Arquitecto," *Arquitectura*, no.135 (Oct. 1979).

[61] Ramos, *A Casa...*, 87.

in the Survey of Popular Architecture, in his and Fernando Távora's design for a rural community presented by the CIAM Porto team in the X CIAM in Dubrovnik and, finally, in the experimental renovation of the Espinhosela village, supported by the HE and based in his CODA thesis. As a regional architect for the HE, he and José Dias designed an estate for Torre Dona Chama [MdH DB a182], in Bragança,[62] using the fireplace as the central and symbolic element of the house and of domestic and family organization, separating family room and kitchen, eliminating circulation areas and establishing multiple relations with exterior areas, adapting modern concepts to local technical and cultural conditions.

The estate for the Casa do Povo (People's House) [MdH DB a152] in Chamusca,[63] designed by Bartolomeu da Costa Cabral and Vasco Croft, also built under the Loans Law, took an insightful approach to spatial programme and place, zeroing in on population needs but in keeping with the conceptual principles of their designs for more urban areas.[64] The common central area, with the fireplace as the centre of family life and of spatial composition, took advantage of several small devices for use and comfort, simplifying partitions and reducing circulation areas. Awareness of the role of the woman was also taken into account in the relation between working and common areas.[65] This experiment in the decentralization of architectural production added social significance to modern formal elements, scaling them according to regional values and local traditions. Housing was seen as a social service and the user as an integral actor of the design process.

4. THE LARGE INITIATIVES OF LISBON AND ESPINHOSELA

In the transition from the 1950s to the 1960s, the large urban operations in Lisbon—Olivais Norte [MdH DB a186] and Olivais Su [MdH DB a193], and, later, Chelas [MdH DB a194]—developed by the GTH (Gabinete Técnico da Habitação—Technical Office for Housing) from Decree 42,454, represented a considerable growth in size of intervention and social outreach, with a substantial presence of promotion and building by the HE.[66] In Olivais—unlike the uniformity of Alvalade—a single large-scale plan generated several independently developed designs, turning that intervention into a territory for experimentation, *"the definitive laboratory for modern architecture and architectural culture in Lisbon."*[67]

[62] This design was not built and was replaced by a design by Alcino Soutinho.

[63] Carlos Duarte and Daniel Santa Rita, "Bairro Económico da Chamusca," *Arquitectura*, no.74 (Mar. 1961).

[64] The large operation in Olivais, in which they participated, was already underway.

[65] Portas, *A Habitação Social, Proposta para a Metodologia da sua Arquitectura* (Porto: FAUP publicações, 2004), 142.

[66] The GTH coordinated the plan and distributed the plots to several entities in charge of building.

[67] Ana Tostões, *Os Verdes Anos*, 76.

We are particularly interested in the presence of the HE in this context, through a significant variety of professionals that intervened in the operations, providing a "considerable diversity of architectural experiences"[68] in typology and urban designs, an experimental laboratory on the subject of the social responsibility of architecture and of the variety of available options for social housing at a time when the values of context and ways of living were under scrutiny and revision. Works financed and built by the HEs were designed by Nuno Teotónio Pereira, António Pinto Freitas, Bartolomeu da Costa Cabral, Vasco Croft, Vitor Figueiredo, Nuno Portas, João Braula Reis, João Matoso, Pedro Cid, Fernando Torres, Vasconcelos Esteves, Palma de Melo and Pires Martins, among others.

Experimentation was the rule and "formulas for integration and coordination of financing sources and promoting entities"[69] were tested, and the HE received the majority of the building plots for Affordable Rents Houses according to Law no. 2,007. Simultaneously, in an eminently rural context, Arnaldo Araújo was commissioned with the pilot study for the village of Espinhosela. Studies for this operation started in 1960 in the Lisbon offices, with a view to restoring villages in the municipality of Bragança. A realistic renovation plan was to be implemented across the municipality, using the instruments of Law no. 2,092, and its preparation included meetings with stakeholder entities—the Municipality, Casas do Povo, parish councils, village vicars, etc.—field trips and surveys of local housing conditions, including building materials, techniques, and costs. Regular field trips were joined by others, such as Octávio Lixa Filgueiras, António Menéres, Viana de Lima (as author of the urban plan for Bragança) and the painter António Quadros. Notably, the Brazilian architect Lúcio Costa visited Espinhosela in 1961 to study aspects of rural housing after a series of conferences in Porto. Discussions on the subject of urban planning and rural and anthropological studies were therefore developed in parallel, with common elements and concerns, in a collective quest for improvement of collective housing solutions.

5. A SET OF CIRCUMSTANCES

Throughout those twenty-six years of experience, particularly in the 1950s and 1960s, a series of parallel circumstances must be considered that directly or indirectly involve the HE, through the participation of its elements in a context of political, social, and cultural agitation. Congresses, colloquiums, and meetings that were organized across that period established indispensable ground for crossing experiences, exposing concerns, and setting intervention strategies, particularly in the UIA congresses where, as we noted,

[68] Sérgio Fernandez, *Percurso, Arquitectura Portuguesa, 1930/1974* (Porto: edições FAUP, 1988).

[69] José António Bandeirinha, *O Processo SAAL e a Arquitectura no 25 de Abril de 1974* (Coimbra: Imprensa da Universidade de Coimbra, 2007), 101.

Nuno Teotónio Pereira was the national delegate on housing for six years. In an interview, he noted the importance of the topic of social housing in these congresses organized in several countries where information was exchanged in work meetings and visits were organized to local housing estates in the location of each congress.[70] In the 3rd Congress of the UIA, in Lisbon in 1953, the Sindicato Nacional dos Arquitectos (SNA–National Union of Architects) set the stage for an important moment for architects, with about six hundred participants and thirty five national delegations discussing the topic of "Architecture at the Crossroads." In February 1960, the SNA hosted a colloquium organized by Nuno Portas and others[71] to discuss "The Social Aspects of Habitat Building." The urban planner Robert Auzelle presented his work for Porto and the sociologist Chombard de Lauwe addressed the "social implications of housing use citing specific cases of massive building in France,"[72] presenting the results of renowned surveys that had taken place in large social structures in that country, concluding that unsuccessful estates were the result of inadaptation by users to new spaces as these were the result of a lack of discussion on the social and psychological traits of the target populations.[73]

Having accumulated and systematized experiences in the field of housing, the HE, namely Nuno Teotónio Pereira and João Braula Reis, was in charge of the chapter on housing and urban planning of the Intermediary Development Plan for 1965–67,[74] stressing, as stated by Teotónio Pereira, an important step finally taken to highlight housing as a significant problem in Portugal.[75] In a complex juncture of colonial war and rising emigration, new strategies were needed that included the promotion of housing.[76] Towards the end of the 1960s, a new awareness of housing problems arose, considering it not only a significantly sized social problem with urban presence but also a political problem.

The Colloquium on Housing Policies organized by the Ministério das Obras Públicas (Public Work Ministry) in 1969[77] in LNEC concluded that actions by public and semi-public sectors on the field of housing represented only 5 to 10 per cent of total building.[78] The disorder generated by a set of disperse entities was noted, and the FFH[79] was created through Decree 49,033, of 28 March, "with the goal of uniting, within a sole entity, the different forms of state intervention in the field of social housing,"[80] in an outstanding event for housing policies in Portugal which eventually led to the dissolution of the HE.

[70] Nuno Teotónio Pereira Interview. Tavares, "Federação de Caixas de Previdência–Habitações Económicas."

[71] Peres Fernandes, Rui Mendes Paula, Raul Ramalho, Bartolomeu Costa Cabral, Octávio Filgueiras and Coutinho Raposo.

[72] Bandeirinha, *O Processo SAAL*, 65.

[73] Ibid.

[74] *Plano Intercalar de Fomento para 1965–1967* (Lisbon: Imprensa Nacional Casa da Moeda, 1964).

[75] Pereira, "A política de habitação nos Planos de Fomento," in *Escritos*, 52.

[76] Bandeirinha, *O Processo SAAL*, 69.

[77] 30 June to 5 July 1969

[78] Bandeirinha, *O Processo SAAL*, 71.

[79] As announced in the Intermediary Development Plan.

[80] Pereira, "A Federação de Caixas de Previdência," 211.

6. SUMMARY OF A SINGULAR PATH

The work of the HE in Portugal was based, as stressed by Nuno Teotónio Pereira, on "an elevated sense of public duty." It was, firstly, a field for cooperation among architects and technicians from other study fields that, facing the transformation of the Portuguese reality, tested new operative approaches. As we have seen, the often circumstantial participation of members of the HE technical team in other initiatives was fundamental for the development of intervention methods and models. In the first stage, the client was seen as an entity: a majority of the population that was the architect's target when developing social housing. From the end of the 1950s, the future user became an integral part of the design process, through a revision of concepts and new legislation. More than just applying the principles of the existing legislations, HE design teams used the available means to develop a strategic approach to the problem, basing their intervention on the systematic studies by Raul da Silva Pereira on housing deficits and living conditions. In the 1950s and the 1960s, this purely social approach represented a new perspective and method for housing design and domestic architecture. The study of minimum housing and the role of the woman in domestic life, according to Nuno Porta's research[81], was the "basis for revising the concept of home organization."[82] The house went from a divided space to a continuous space, in a mix of Modern Movement formal elements and social responsibility that gave rise to pioneer studies in a field which until then had been mainly based on empirical approaches.[83] The HE action was based on the architectural culture of their time and contributed to a territory of systematic production and housing development, using the means available to them and their own research interests to surpass the limits of modernity and bring forth a new generation of professionals.

---

[81] Nuno Portas, *Funções e Exigências de Áreas de Habitação* (Lisbon: Laboratório Nacional de Engenharia Civil, 1969); *A Habitação Social*.

[82] Portas, *Funções e Exigências*, 27.

[83] Pereira, "A Federação de Caixas de Previdência," 210.

Housing Programmes and the Construction of the Portuguese City: the Realization of Modernity in the First Half of the Twentieth Century

TERESA CALIX
University of Porto, Faculty of Architecture, Centre for Studies in Architecture and Urbanism

ABSTRACT

The 1950s, in Portugal, are the years of the reunion with modernism. This late fulfilment of the Modern Movement reduced its capacity for urban achievement and assigned the mission of contributing to the expansion of the existing city to interventions. The construction of the Portuguese city that had taken place until this decade was achieved by adding "fragments" as a continuum, expanding the existing urban areas and contradicting the more comprehensive rationales of understanding and actions with greater autonomy and capacity for transformation that the Modern Movement projected.

Taking the housing programmes promoted by the state in the first half of the twentieth century as the central topic of this article, we will try to establish a relation between their evolution and accomplishment and Portuguese urban development. By placing the instruments of formal urbanism and the housing programmes in confrontation, the two practices that intersect and transform the territory, we will try to show how the principles of modern urban development have been systematically reversed: the housing areas promoted were often responsible for the implementation of new urban axes or grids and new districts of urban growth; while the plans drawn up in this period, although quite numerous and connected to the political view and promoting the image of the regime, sometimes fell short of effective realization, despite what might have been expected.

BIOGRAPHY

Teresa Calix graduated in architecture (1998), has a master's in urban planning and design (2002) and a PhD in architecture (2013), with a PhD thesis that focused on the morphologies of the contemporary city. Currently she is assistant professor at FAUP, where she is the coordinator of the study profile Dynamics and Urban Forms of the PhD Programme in Architecture and she is the head of the course Projecto 5–urban design studio–of the Integrated Master's in Architecture. She also collaborates in the course Urban Project Studio of the Master's in Spatial Planning and Urban Project (from FAUP and Faculty of Engineering of the University of Porto). Her teaching activity, particularly that related to practical exercises in the scope of the courses, workshops, and summer schools referred to, is used as an opportunity to deepen the relations with the municipalities of Porto Metropolitan Area and with experts of several areas of knowledge, bridging the gap between university/students and professionals. She is also the coordinator of the research group Morphologies and Dynamics of the Territory of the Centre for Studies in Architecture and Urbanism (MDT-CEAU-FAUP) and has participated in several research and consultancy projects.

With the aim of contributing to the debate on the production of the modern city, this article will try to establish a relationship between the evolution and the diffusion of the housing programmes promoted by the state in the twentieth century and Portuguese urban development, culminating in the processes underlying the modern city of the 1950s.

The *Centro de Estudos de Urbanismo e Habitação Engenheiro Duarte Pacheco*, a Centre for Studies in Urbanism and Housing of the Ministry of Public Works,[1] was responsible for a publication in 1963 focusing on the housing policy of the period mentioned, in which it was acknowledged that *"as the real knowledge of the country's housing needs became more acute, the government was able to face a more important intervention within an indispensable range of priorities, conditioned by the economic viability of its budgets."*[2] This document also established that the years preceding it (1955–1962) *"are characterized by a marked evolution in the housing and spatial planning sectors (which in turn will be reflected in the future) and is a positive indication of a strong government orientation."*[3]

This publication, a disclosure document from the government at the time and stating the efforts in housing, allows not only an understanding of the actions developed in the years prior to its date of release, but also the sequence of facts that it describes, which shows an overlap between different deliberations and the dependence between effects and spaces of decision in which the list of legislation produced stands out. Similarly, it is considered that the different times of production, implementation, and reformulation of the diverse measures and the evolution of the political, economic, and social circumstances directly influencing the 1950s cannot be understood without going back in time. Thus, taking the housing programmes as central to the reflection and accepting as relevant a reading bearing in mind the chain of procedures in time, the proposal that is presented assumes two cross-perspectives: one is that attending to the instruments of formal urbanism tries to show the models that influenced the elaboration of plans and the corresponding understanding about the city that these disseminate; and another that accepts that *"the identification between modern city and residential proposals of the modern architecture is valid, since these constitute the background fabric on which the idea of the city elaborated by the architectural culture of the first half of the twentieth century rests."*[4] This assumption, valid for any context, is particularly interesting for the Portuguese circumstances since, in many situations, certain elements considered structural in the scope of the urban space development have been, or are, ensured by interventions that meet the scale of architectural resolution and not by means of the direct implementation of previously produced planning instruments.

---

[1] Decree-Law 44,948, 29 March 1963, creates and defines the attributions of the *Centro de Estudos de Urbanismo e Habitação Engenheiro Duarte Pacheco* operating close to the cabinet of the Minister of Public Works. It recognizes "the advantage of promoting and disseminating the study on the problems of urban planning and housing in all aspects related to modern technical processes and systems of action in the field of national, regional, and local planning."

[2] Alves de Sousa (dir), *A Habitação em Portugal* (Lisboa: Ministério das Obras Públicas, Centro de Estudos de Urbanismo e Habitação Engenheiro Duarte Pacheco, 1963), 13.

[3] Sousa, *A Habitação em Portugal*, 13.

[4] Carlos Martí Arís, "Las formas de la residencia en la ciudad moderna," in *Las Formas de la Residencia en la Ciudad Moderna: Vivienda y Ciudad en la Europa de Entreguerras*, ed. Carlos Martí Arís (Barcelona: Edicions UPC, 2000), 3.

By placing in confrontation the two practices that overlap in the territory but do not always converge—which even allows us to show the relevance of this point of view in contemporary Portuguese territory—we will try to show how the principles of modern urban development have been systematically reversed. In fact, the new housing programmes were often responsible for the implementation of new urban axes or grids and new areas of urban growth, and also imposed the new conditions of its design, considering the influences of the international framework and the modern standards of hygiene and comfort of the dwellings.

These contributed, or not, to the accomplishment of the proposals contained in the plans that preceded them. In this context, the modern international housing proposals that are presented as alternatives *"to the speculative city generated by the nineteenth century industrial development, in which many of the features that defined the traditional city had disappeared,"*[5] will serve as references to the solutions realized in the twentieth century in Portugal. However, they will occur later in time, with specificities (and inconsistencies, associated with the political influence of the dictatorial regime of Oliveira Salazar[6]), and, above all, will reveal a scale of expansion of existing urban settlements that is much less dramatic when compared to that of the great European cities.

Indeed, while in the international context the Modern Movement evolved from the 1920s to the years after World War II, the 1950s in Portugal were the decade of reunion with modernism, following a movement of strong politicization succeeding the I *Congresso Nacional dos Arquitectos*, the first national congress of architects, in 1948. The principles of the Athens Charter were then assumed as those that must guide a response to the structural problem of housing that had dragged on and increased since the beginning of the twentieth century.

Nevertheless, the complete but late fulfilment of the Modern Movement in Portugal is reduced in its capacity of urban achievement by two orders of reasons: firstly, it was delayed in its realization due to the diffusion of the political image of fascist nationalism of the late 1930s and especially of the 1940s, which matches the apogee of its national discussion and dissemination with the beginning of its international critique; secondly, the neutrality of Portugal and its non-participation in World War I deprived it of the European reconstruction dimension, assigning the mission of contributing to the expansion of the existing city and as a continuum from it to the interventions.

[5] Martí Arís, "Las formas de la residência en la ciudad moderna," 4.

[6] Oliveira Salazar (1889–1970) was the promoter of Estado Novo (1933–1974) and its political organization; he directed the destiny of Portugal as dictatorial president of the Ministry between 1932 and 1933 and as President of the Council of Ministers between 1933 and 1968.

In this period can be recognized, on the one hand, an evolution resulting from the "affirmation of urbanism as a generalized social practice [...] as a result of the voluntarist action of Duarte Pacheco"[7] from the 1930s. However, on the other hand, while many influences of European urbanism and architecture did reach Portugal, the exaltation of the principles of the Athens Charter and the claim of a modernist city from 1948 onwards is not unrelated to the contradictions that arose alongside the undisputed weight of traditionalist ruralism, and the devices created for the exaltation and reproduction of nationalism. The latter was particularly celebrated in the 1940s, *"inflicting with a monumental and historicist flavour the 'ephemeral' modernism that at first interested to Estado Novo,"*[8] the authoritarian regime installed in Portugal.

Thus, considering that urbanism and architecture are recognized as inseparable parts of the project of modernization of cities, the specificity of the modern project of the Portuguese city requires recognition of the different moments of its evolution in the period of industrialization, despite its relatively moderate size. It also implies understanding the machine of capitalism that, in order to respond to the increase in the demanding consumption-production dichotomy, led to a significant increase in urban population and subsequent deterioration of housing conditions in the city.

For this reason, starting with a significantly synthesized historical overview, this article begins at the turn of the 20th century and focuses on the promotion of housing in the development of urban territories. It is organized in three parts, after which the final considerations follow:

- Ephemeral hygienist modernism;
- The influence of the formal model of the Garden City;
- The integration of the canons of the Modern Movement.

---

[7] Margarida Souza Lôbo, *Planos de Urbanização: A Época de Duarte Pacheco* (Porto: DGOTDU, FAUP Publicações, 1995), 13. Duarte Pacheco (1900–1943) was the Minister of Public Works, responsible for planning, transports, and all kinds of public intervention; he imposed urbanism as a generalized social practice by passing a law that created urbanization plans and gave full powers to the municipalities to take over the transformation of their territory.

[8] Ana Tostões, *A Idade Maior: Cultura e Tecnologia na Arquitectura Moderna Portuguesa* (Porto: FAUP Publicações, 2015), 377.

1. EPHEMERAL HYGIENIST MODERNISM

The Improvement Plans—*Planos Gerais de Melhoramentos*—resulting from the imposition of the Decree-Law of 19 January 1865, instated modern urbanistic concerns[9] for the first time in formal urbanism, although limited to a "regulatory pre-urbanism."[10] However, "without a great critical sense or a particular view of the shape of the city that goes beyond the effect of 'beautification' in imitation of European cities,"[11] the plans drawn up were particularly directed at controlling the relationship between private investment and public space so as "to meet the indispensable conditions of light, ventilation, water supply and drainage of sewage."[12] Thus, the shape of the city remained of secondary importance. Only in Lisbon and Porto did the plans aim a little further on the definition of the models for growth. Thus, the effort and the urgency of drawing up the plans resulting from the legislation, dragging through the first decades of the twentieth century, shows that *"Portuguese industrialization was late and mainly concentrated in Lisbon and Oporto. The effects of industrialization in these two cities were felt more intensely from the second half of the nineteenth century and constitute a catalogue of problems familiar to urban historians and common to other eighteenth-century cities: growth of the urban population and increase in housing density, development of precarious housing solutions and overcrowding of residential areas, degraded urban areas and poor sanitary conditions."*[13] The *vilas* and *pátios* of Lisbon and the *ilhas* of Porto, examples of this precariousness, increased greatly in this period.

During this period, a number of relevant urban renewal proposals were devised, although they were confined to particular urban sectors,[14] as well as some modern views of broader urban development, even though they did not materialize.[15] The political and economic difficulties of the 1920s—associated with participation in World War I and intensified by the Great Depression of 1929—and the internal migratory flows—stemming from the industrialization process of a hitherto essentially agricultural country—not only failed to provide reliable solutions as they further exacerbated *"the housing needs of a growing population, with a clear trend towards concentration among large population centres and the difficulty of most of the population in meeting the rental costs required for housing built under a free-trade regime (without direct or indirect aid of the State)."*[16] In fact, the imbalance between housing demand and supply would not diminish with the promulgation of the "Decree-Laws 4,137 of 25 April 1918, 4,163 of 29 April 1918, and 5,443 of 26 April 1919, which had the objective of encouraging the construction of good quality private housing for workers."[17]

[9] José Fernando Gonçalves, "Edifícios modernos de habitação colectiva, 1948–61: desenho e standard na arquitectura portuguesa" (Phd Diss., Department of Proyectos d'Arquitectura–UPC, 2007), 43.

[10] Lôbo, *Planos de Urbanização: A Época de Duarte Pacheco*, 16.

[11] Gonçalves, "Edifícios modernos de habitação colectiva, 1948–61," 43.

[12] Lôbo, *Planos de Urbanização: A Época de Duarte Pacheco*, 17.

[13] Manuel C. Teixeira, "A história urbana em Portugal. Desenvolvimentos recentes," *Análise Social*, vol. xxviii (121), (1993–2.º): 381.

[14] Like *avenidas novas*, the new avenues proposed by Ressano de Garcia, in Lisbon, or the future civic centre of Barry Parker, in Porto.

[15] Like the three garden cities proposed by Forestier, in Lisbon, or the prologue to the plan of the city—*Prólogo ao Plano da Cidade do Porto*—by Ezequiel de Campos, in Porto.

[16] Sousa, *A habitação em Portugal*, 9.

[17] Fátima Loureiro de Matos, "Da implantação da República à primeira Guerra: As primeiras tentativas de Resolução do problema habitacional das classes operárias," in *A Grande Guerra (1914–1918): Problemáticas e Representações*, ed. Gaspar Martins Pereira et. al (Porto: CITCEM–Centro de Investigação Transdisciplinar «Cultura, Espaço e Memória," 2015), 370.

Decree 4,137 of 25 April 1918, is actually "the first real intervention of the state in the housing sector,"[18] "establishing various measures to promote the construction of economical houses" in a particularly difficult period of the First Republic.[19] Although it gave rise to concrete interventions,[20] it can be stated that the results were limited to the construction of some working quarters entirely at the expense of the state, which limited unconditionally the volume of achievements required as a consequence of the total absorption of the financial resources available.[21] In 1918, under Decree 4,137, three neighbourhoods had been started: Ursulinas [MdH DB a685], in Viana do Castelo, Ajuda/Boa Hora [MdH DB a215], in Lisbon, and Arrábida [MdH DB a20], in Porto.

While acknowledging the low level of implementation of the aforementioned Decree, it is important to highlight at the same time its pioneering role in the interventions that would mark the decades that would follow. In the long preamble that opens the diploma, describing foreign experiences in the promotion of affordable housing, one notices that *"Of all the models, the interest in the English model stands out in the pioneering role of the construction of 'cheap houses' by cooperative societies or by the local administration and by the regime of 'rent-to-own property' that would inspire legislation and political practice in Portugal, by taking into account the symbolic value of access to property as a 'factor of regeneration' of the working classes."*[22]

After the Military Coup of 28 May 1926—which ended the First Portuguese Republic, and led to the formal establishment of the Estado Novo dictatorship through a new Constitution in 1933—Decree 23,052, of 23 September, was enacted, establishing the "Affordable Houses Programme." Pointing to a model of occupancy and housing based on the single family dwelling, it was *"the first diploma truly aimed at effectively combating the housing crisis; specially oriented for the development of economic housing for the middle and working classes, provided for the realization of houses in a rent-to-own property scheme, which would be redeemable in 20 or 25 years and included insurance for fire, disability, death, sickness and unemployment."*[23] This was followed in 1934 by the Decree 24,802, of 21 December, which *"forces the municipal councils of the continent and adjacent islands to carry out the survey of topographic plants and the drawing up of general urbanization plans"*—Planos Gerais de Urbanização—thus establishing the criteria that would determine the image of future urbanization works.

[18] Sousa, *A Habitação em Portugal*, 10.

[19] According to Maria da Conceição Tiago, "Bairros Sociais da I República: projectos e realizações," *Revista Ler História*, no. 59–*Repúblicas: Culturas e Práticas* (2010), "in that year of 1918, instability was general: there was a serious agricultural crisis, a shortage of basic necessities, a serious financial situation with high inflation, compounded by the devastating effects of the typhoid outbreak in 1917 and the pneumonic flu in 1918, which mainly affected the less salubrious neighbourhoods. At the same time, the rural exodus to the cities was increasing, particularly in Lisbon and Porto. The precarious conditions of housing for the poorer classes became more visible as a result of epidemics, enforcing the urgent need under these circumstances for intervention by the public authorities."

[20] "The construction of these neighbourhoods initiates a process of implementation of some measures of state protection, timid, small, paternalistic in their genesis and configuration" (Matos, "Da implantação da República à primeira Guerra," 370.)

[21] Sousa, *A Habitação em Portugal*, 10.

[22] Tiago, "Bairros Sociais da I República: projectos e realizações."

[23] Sousa, *A Habitação em Portugal*, 11.

2. THE INFLUENCE OF THE FORMAL MODEL OF THE GARDEN CITY

If the problem of housing and the corresponding disorder of urban settlements was recognized. *"With the rise to power of Salazar, at the end of the 1920s, the urban problem linked to the growth of the city came to definitively be included in the concerns of the state. After 1933 [. . .] a new methodology of action began, organized around the State Public Works—a policy that guided the three times of man: past (restoration of monuments); present (public facilities); future (urbanization plans)."*[24] With Duarte Pacheco at the head of the Ministry of Public Works from 1932, *"the necessary legislative measures for the acquisition and expropriation of land for the construction of economic dwellings"*[25] were promulgated, but also *"the development of large infra-structures, such as the construction of roads, bridges, dams and the spatial planning of towns and cities, with the realization of plans and an extensive programme of urban improvements."*[26] In order to promote "an urban image with which the regime identified,"[27] the housing programmes and the city promoted by the state in the 1930s and 1940s corresponded to a process of conception and urban renewal strongly marked by the influence of the morpho-typological solutions advocated by the Garden City movement.

Indeed, while these were widely diffused, the complex *Garden City model* proposed by Ebenezer Howard in *To-Morrow: A Peaceful Path to Real Reform* (1898)—an entity capable of responding to the social nature of the most pressing urban issues and meet the demands of the economy—would barely be considered. Howard's proposal, recognizing the advantages and disadvantages of the countryside and the city of the late nineteenth century, gave as a third alternative the town-country or, as it would later be called, the *garden city*. This model was based on three fundamental principles: the value of land should be shared fairly by the community, owners, and promoters, ensuring profit for all; the political leadership should be strong and present a clear vision; and the organization should take responsibility for the long-term management of community assets. The *social city*, a polycentric cluster of garden cities, clearly delimited and linked together by a network of infrastructures, would allow "all the economic and social opportunities of the giant city"[28] to be reached. While Howard's modern incremental model of the Garden City presupposed converting profits into collective gains, based on a socialist political ideology that simultaneously responded to the intents of industrial and human development, its proposal was often misinterpreted, reducing it to physical issues and scales of higher resolution and lower achievement, confusing Howard's Garden City with the morphological principles applicable to Raymond Unwin's garden suburb.

[24] Gonçalves, "Edifícios modernos de habitação colectiva, 1948–61," 44.

[25] Sousa, *A Habitação em Portugal*, 11.

[26] Lôbo, *Planos de Urbanização: A Época de Duarte Pacheco*, 36.

[27] Lôbo, *Planos de Urbanização: A Época de Duarte Pacheco*, 36.

[28] Peter Hall, *Cities of Tomorrow* (Oxford: Blackwell Publishers, 1996 [1988]), 93.

Unwin, a disciple of Camillo Sitte, was involved in the physical realization of the first experiences of the Garden City. By publishing, first, *Town Planning in Practice. An Introduction to the Art of designing Cities and Suburbs* (1909)—where he advocated an innovative understanding of the past, maintaining and elevating the traditional values of the community to future generations through a discipline based on design rather than purely technical—and then *Nothing Gained by Overcrowding* (1912)—where he claimed, above all, a less dense form of occupation—he may have contributed to the dissemination of housing areas with single-family houses, usually detached or semi-detached, as major principles and results of the Garden City. This type of occupation fostered areas with low density and where prolonged contact with nature would be compatible with a high degree of cohesion of the urban form.

Fitting into this neo-traditionalist reformist trend, where the German *Siedlungen* are also included, the usually peripheric housing units that make up the "Affordable Houses Programme" in Portugal in this period, determined relatively small and cohesive groups. However, the choice of their location defined directions for growth and promoted the consolidation of urban expansion from certain bordering territories—which later will be associated with other public programmes, as well as privately promoted housing—which influenced the development and future form of urban settlements.

Along this process of growth focused on the small scale of intervention and not on the plan—which does not mean that it occurred only in its absence but also did not guarantee its materialization—the process of elaborating the general urbanization plans was developed, obligatory for all "localities with more than 2,500 inhabitants who, between two consecutive official censuses, evidence a population increase of more than 10 per cent."[29]

In spite of some previous experiences, the influence of the Garden City movement also arrived, albeit belatedly, to Portuguese urbanism. This happened especially through the influence of the architect Etienne de Gröer,[30] who would be responsible for a significant number of general urbanization plans since the late 1930s, a period in which Portuguese urban planners with specific training were relatively scarce. Although De Gröer was visibly acquainted with Ebenezer Howard's polycentric vision, at least in what it means from the point of view of his physical conception—a network of pre-set medium-size cities[31] linked with each other—he was equally familiar with the principles of Raymond Unwin's *Town Planning in Practice*.

[29] Decree 24,802, of December 21, 1934, article 2(a).

[30] Etienne de Gröer was educated in Paris, although he was born in Warsaw, son of a Polish mother and a Russian father.

[31] Lôbo, *Planos de Urbanização: A Época de Duarte Pacheco*, 77.

De Gröer also addressed the land issue by advocating long-term lease of land in a regime similar to the surface right, which came to be enshrined in Portuguese land law.[32] He integrated some solutions of decentralization, through the proposal of satellite settlements with alternative locations to the growth of the city, although, given the distance proposed for the urban nuclei and their size, they do not present themselves as real alternatives, but rather as poles dependent on the existing urban centre.[33] He also developed design solutions with clear didactic objectives (and his work at this level is especially striking). The limit established in the cities for four-storey buildings shows especially his preference for single-family housing, based on a right-wing ideological discourse in which it is argued that "the large house is an open field to communism."[34]

Thus, the formulas of urbanism were established that the regime recognized as appropriate and which would dominate the production of instruments of territorial management, the urban renewal and the construction of new areas of expansion in the 1940s—the single-family housing and the monumental city. However, the absence of modernist proposals that gave continuity to some experiences of the Portuguese avant-garde of the 1930s showed *"the progressive hegemony in the state apparatus, of traditionalist values [. . .], a breeding ground to precipitate the crisis of the modernist architects that had already manifested itself before, [. . .], when there were apparently no univocal official guidelines to impose a national style."*[35]

"The heyday of urban planning in Portugal lies between 1944 and 1954," however, in the many studies and plans or pre-plans drawn up "we can distinguish a first period, from 1944 to 1948, in which an initial eclecticism gives rise to a specific synthesis," and a second period, since "in 1948 there was a turn marked by the first national congress of architects," when they brought into question the city and lodging instead of the traditional questions of architectural language."[36]

[32] Lôbo, *Planos de Urbanização: A Época de Duarte Pacheco*, 77.

[33] Lôbo, *Planos de Urbanização: A Época de Duarte Pacheco*, 79.

[34] Lôbo, *Planos de Urbanização: A Época de Duarte Pacheco*, 81.

[35] Nuno Portas, "Arquitectura e Urbanística na Década de 40,"in *Arquitectura(s) História e Crítica, Ensino e Profissão* (Porto: FAUP Publicações, 2005 [1982]), 291.

[36] Gonçalves, "Edifícios modernos de habitação colectiva, 1948–61," 338.

3. THE INTEGRATION OF THE CANONS OF THE MODERN MOVEMENT

With the end of World War II, Europe made a great effort to rise from its agony. Dictatorships gave way to democracies and one of the emergent phenomena in Portugal after the first national congress of architects in 1948 was the politicisation of urban issues *"to reaffirm not only the legitimacy of the creative act free of bureaucratic and censorship obstacles (being modern is not anti-Portuguese) but above all the affirmation of the need for housing policies, facilities and urban renewal that sought to push the regime against the ropes also as regards social investment."*[37] The truth is that if the detached or semi-detached house and the neighbourhood-(suburbia)-garden is that which best adapts to the preferences of the regime[38] and of the bourgeoisie that supports it, this form of space occupation and housing promotion, which involves mostly small interventions, is a political tool for normalizing society by "strengthening the institution of the family"[39] and by inserting itself *"in a wider perspective of social repression, both in the selection of beneficiaries as in the social control through the 'habitat'"*[40].

In addition, the housing shortages were not catered for by the few projects carried out and by the small size of the operations, which were generally of very low density; and if this were not the case, if the assumptions of the dominant form of intervention were maintained, the new areas to be occupied in order to meet the needs would greatly extend the existing urban agglomerations. The conclusions of the Congress thus defended the impracticability of single-family housing programmes and advocated the intensification of collective housing. As such, the adoption of architectural solutions that consider the verticalisation of buildings was proposed—the functional architecture of the massive and high forms that should be implemented considering the solar orientation on ground more available to green areas— referring to the "bases of modern urbanism,"[41] as Corbusier called it, and to the doctrinal principles defined in the Athens Charter.

It would be within the framework of the "Affordable Rent Houses"programme, enacted through Law 2007 of 7 May 1945, that the system of rent in buildings of greater heights is accepted for the first time: *"it establishes collective housing, with no more than 3 floors [or 4, as recommended by De Groer for the plans], and, pour cause, puts an end to the pretension of generalizing access to residential property by its occupants, thus legitimizing the lease."*[42] It opened *"the road to transforming the understanding of the housing problem as a matter centred on a conservative ideology, based on the assumption of the 'merit of the aligned', by the concept of the 'right to housing' and the pursuit in terms of 'objective needs', deriving from a 'technicist' and more universally legitimized ideology"*[43].

---

[37] Portas, "Arquitectura e Urbanística na Década de 40," 294.

[38] According to the Constitution, it is the responsibility of the state and the local authorities "to promote the establishment of independent residences in sanitary conditions, as well as the institution of the 'homestead', with the purpose, of course, of defending the family 'basic institution of society'. The same is to say that the type of social 'habitat' will necessarily have to be the single-family house, giving access to the property, since the discourse on the virtues of the duality of single-family house/private property has never been so flourishing." Marielle Christine Gros, *O Alojamento Social sob o Fascismo* (Porto: Edições Afrontamento, 1982), 117.

[39] Gros, *O Alojamento Social sob o Fascismo*, 122.

[40] Gros, *O Alojamento Social sob o Fascismo*, 122. Apart from the houses being distributed to heads of households according to their social categories, the elements to be considered in the order of preference are regularity of employment, moral and professional behaviour, age, family composition, and family wages.

[41] Le Corbusier, *Urbanisme* (Paris: Les Éditions Arthaud, 1980 [1925]), i.

[42] Sandra Marques Pereira, *Casa e Mudança Social: Uma Leitura das Transformações da Sociedade Portuguesa a Partir da Casa* (Casal de Cambra: Caleidoscópio, 2012), 73.

[43] Ibid.

The Bairro de Alvalade [MdH DB a89], in Lisbon, exemplifies the process of modernization through the promotion of the "Affordable Rent Houses" programme. It *"materializes in the adoption of the modern paradigm in its strictly technical and economical dimension, clearly ignoring its ideological dimension: modern housing is programmed, but the foundation of this programmatic inflection is exclusively referred to for reasons of efficiency, functionality, rationality, and economy, and never for purposes of democratization. Indeed, in this immediate post-war period, the first motivation was to expand in a planned way, economising, and if possible capitalising."*[44]

In 1955, *"the concept of 'horizontal property' or by storeys was established, whereby the extension of the regime of rental of houses of limited income was promoted to the regime of access to the property in economic conditions accessible to a wider section of the population."*[45] On this followed the possibility of granting loans for the construction and purchase of housing by households. Exemptions from property taxes, with a view to reducing burdens that would promote private initiative in fostering and accessing housing, thereby reducing State burdens, were also promulgated. Indeed, while the recognition of the right to housing was further reinforced by the "progressive" contestation, strengthened since the early 1950s, the state's inability to take on a coherent policy of housing promotion becomes even more evident: *"the decrees and declarations of intention are multiplied; and if that leads to a real complexification of the legal-administrative building, the practical reach of such a policy is far from being evident"*[46] or effective to respond to the increasing population numbers in a situation of real housing shortage increasingly forced into clandestine solutions.

The architectural and urbanistic experiences closest to the canons assumed in the European reconstruction operations succeeded. However, *"the modern city vocabulary would never be taken as a refusal of the existing city, but rather as a new possibility of dialogue that 'extends' the traditional city—the modern plans for growth in Portugal coincide in the critique of the nineteenth century city, but they are more like tests of integration than of rupture."*[47] Thus, *"the 'collectivist' city of modern architects would only appear with the Plano de Ramalde [MdH DB a22] (or the drawings for Campo Alegre), by Fernando Távora [in Porto] and, above all, with the Plano dos Olivais Norte [MdH DB a186] [in Lisbon]— the only large-scale urban intervention, where the 'Athens Charter' was tried without any ties to the traditional city."*[48] In the 1960s, Chelas [MdH DB a194] and Olivais Sul [MdH DB a193] in Lisbon promised a new panorama, stressing not only the scale of the interventions but also the explicit affirmation of the new principles of modern urbanism: although the density is increased in one perspective, it would be reduced in the other.

[44] Pereira, *Casa e Mudança Social*, 75.

[45] Sousa, *A Habitação em Portugal*, 17.

[46] Gros, *O Alojamento Social sob o Fascismo*, 139. Seeking to highlight what he designates as a "fragmented policy," Marielle Gros points out the fifteen main possible formulas of economic housing solutions in 1962.

[47] Gonçalves, "Edifícios modernos de habitação colectiva, 1948–61," 338.

[48] Gonçalves, "Edifícios modernos de habitação colectiva, 1948–61," 339.

The solution considered massive and high-built forms, which should release more green areas, ensuring a relatively low occupation density. In Porto, beginning in 1956, the implementation of the improvement plan—*Plano de Melhoramentos*—enacted by Decree-Law 42,454 of 18 August 1959, which implies a need to sanitize the many existing *ilhas*, the expansion of the municipal housing stock goes from a thousand dwellings in 1955 to more than seven thousand in 1966.[49] Corresponding to a strategy of relocation in peripheral areas, it was carried out through housing neighbourhoods that followed the principles of implementation of the Athens Charter, although considering relatively restrained areas when compared to European experiments.

However, the late entry of the Modern Movement overlapped with its internal crisis, assumed at the 1956 CIAM, International Congress of Modern Architecture, in Dubrovnik, although already announced in the 1951 CIAM when the rationalist functionalist model began to lose its strength, according to the recognition of the relationship between the social and the physical structures of the city. Therefore, although Le Corbusier remained as a reference for the formal imaginary of Portuguese architects, the *"universal recognition of the architect as a mentor of spatial forms, in which a historical-social conscience becomes objective, implies a rigorous requirement in the study of phenomena that the work will define."*[50]

The recognition of this condition implied the disclosure of critical positions, still in the late 1950s, which rejected the exclusive adoption of "certain types considered as a universal panacea."[51] This view defended, first of all, *"as outdated the essentially theoretical position of the rationalist period, which conceived an urban fabric as a standardized mesh of standard units [...] and led to the search for "ideal forms of grouping,"* which is why it challenged *"the indiscriminate claim by the Portuguese architects [in 1948] for large collective properties, taken as the only type of units suitable for social housing"*[52]; and secondly, it denounced the contradictions of the "single family house, inevitably depreciated with the economical and intensive character to which it was now subjected," a reality that could only be understood *"in the context of an ignorance of the urban problems that led to identify with injustice and simplicity, nationalism and certain forms."*[53] Thus, one can affirm that the pro-modernist radicalism of the beginning of the decade was confronted in its final years with the foundational contradictions of the Modern Movement. As regards formal urban planning and according to the Athens Charter, the plans drawn up adopted functional zonings and emphasized the circulation system, segregating the different modes where possible.

---

[49] Queirós, João, "O 'Plano de Melhoramentos para a Cidade do Porto' de 1956: enquadramento político-social e elenco de realizações," in Pereira, Virgílio Borges (coord.), *A Habitação Social na Transformação da Cidade: Sobre a Génese e Efeitos do Plano de Melhoramentos para a Cidade do Porto" de 1956*, ed. Virgílio Borges Pereira (Porto: Edições Afrontamento, 2016), 58.

[50] Nuno Portas, *A Habitação Social: Proposta para a Metodologia da sua Arquitectura* (Porto: FAUP Publicações, 2004 [1959]), 79.

[51] Portas, *A Habitação Social*, 82.

[52] Portas, *A Habitação Social*, 83.

[53] Ibid.

Moreover, the acknowledged *"inefficiency of the blueprint plan [of the 1930s and 1940s] stemming from its rigidity led to its replacement by the management plan which was more flexible and adaptable during implementation,"*[54] at the same time showing the Portuguese inability to carry out planning and even its discredit, which, despite some intervals of "enthusiasm,"[55] remains to the present day.

This process of adapting territorial management instruments, starting in the mid-1950s, in fact allowed an *"ideal of renewal 'in continuity' that did not call into question any ideological content, justified the crossing of the traditional city with the "conservative" innovation of the garden city and the growth centred on the small scale of the land division operations and not in the plan. The modern social and aesthetic assumptions could only appear in fragments, centred on the architectural object,"*[56] simplified in their ideology by reduction to a particularly formal approximation, that the housing programmes of the following decade continued to materialize. Assuming localized interventions in certain fragments of the territory, the implementation of modernist city corresponded to "units materialized through compositions of isolated blocks where collective housing predominated" that *"resulted from a unitary project, realized through operations of land division or public interventions of significant surface dimension, and, as such, presented the limits of the plot as initial reference for their configuration."*[57]

4. FINAL CONSIDERATIONS

The models that conveyed the architectural and urban production of the first half of the Portuguese 20th century, as devices for the design and production of the built space, were promoted essentially from the divulgation of a physical form, considered as paradigm of a certain set of values that it was important to advance. In fact, the underlying ideological issues in the origin of their formulation did not always determine, nor were even considered, to the appropriation of the foundations underlying the model that refers to them; it was reduced only to the principles that advocated a particular morphology or typology. Indeed, in many instances the ideology of the regime overlapped, establishing the discourse that determines the formal appropriation in the planning and implementation processes of the programmes, particularly those related to housing, which we have focused on here. However, it is important to highlight a process of resistance that would culminate in the late 1940s at the first national congress of architects, and which determined a significant turning point in the construction of the modern Portuguese city.

[54] Lôbo, *Planos de Urbanização: A Época de Duarte Pacheco*, 219.

[55] In 1994, PROSIURB (programme for consolidation of the national urban system and support for the execution of municipal master plans) was created; in the 1990s translated into the coverage of the national territory by territorial management instruments.

[56] Gonçalves, "Edifícios modernos de habitação colectiva, 1948–61," 350.

[57] Teresa Calix, "As morfologias da cidade contemporânea: uma matriz imperativa da forma urbana. O sistema urbano do Porto." (Phd Diss., Faculdade de Arquitectura da Universidade do Porto, 2013), 542.

Indeed, *"if modernity corresponds, on the one hand, to a permanent process of transformation—'a permanent revolution'—which inevitably translates into the successive metamorphosis of the physical and technological components of the urban space,"*[58] *"the end of the war, with the awakening of democracies and an opposition reinvigorated by the defeat of fascism in Europe, drew a time of cultural unrest that made the end of the 1940s particularly significant for the reflection on modern architecture in Portugal."*[59]

The perhaps debatable[60] maturity of the late 1950s coupled with the critical review of the possible (re)integration of modernist values in architecture and urban planning was not, however, strange to the intensification of the housing needs of a growing number of cities; it resulted from the process of migration associated with industrialization, determining conditions for the project of modernity (and capitalism). In this scenario, the implementation of urgent housing programmes to meet the needs was, in fact, the condition of occupation of new urban areas and promotion and dissemination of the modernist model. The Portuguese city developed in this period, hostage to possible interventions and its viability, was built by adding many fragments, contradicting the more comprehensive rationales of understanding and actions with greater capacity for transformation of the territory.

In its inaugural formulation, and under the umbrella of capitalism, the architectural interventions of modernism would have the ambition to determine and dominate the future, aiming at the action of the present and also the definition of the future. Architectural design was therefore understood as the heart of the modernization process, and through it, in the modernist period, the two disciplinary dimensions that determine urban reality—architecture and urban planning—actually tend to overlap. However, while urban planning seen as "a large-scale architecture" persisted until the 1960s in Europe, in Portugal it was the small scale of the various buildings or housing complexes that ensured the implementation, on a hybrid urban setting, of fragments of the modernist city, thus conveying some intentions of expansion previously established in plans which the Portuguese state could never fully realize.

[58] Berman (1982) apud Calix, "As morfologias da cidade contemporânea," 18.

[59] Ana Tostões. *Os Verdes Anos na Arquitectura Portuguesa dos Anos 50* (Porto: FAUP Publicações, 1997), 21.

[60] França (2013) in Tostões, *A Idade Maior: Cultura e Tecnologia na Arquitectura Moderna Portuguesa*, ii.

NOTE

The author is responsible for all the translations into English of the original texts in Portuguese.

BIBLIOGRAPHY

Calix, Teresa. "As morfologias da cidade contemporânea: uma matriz imperativa da forma urbana. O sistema urbano do Porto." Faculdade de Arquitectura da Universidade do Porto, 2013.

Gonçalves, José Fernando. "Edifícios modernos de habitação colectiva, 1948–61: desenho e standard na arquitectura portuguesa." PhD Dissertation, Department de Proyectos d'Arquitectura UPC Barcelona, 2007.

Gros, Marielle Christine. O Alojamento Social sob o Fascismo. Porto: Edições Afrontamento, 1982.

Hall, Peter. Cities of Tomorrow. Oxford: Blackwell Publishers, 1996 (1988).

Le Corbusier. Urbanisme. Paris: Les Éditions Arthaud, 1980 (1925).

Lôbo, Margarida Souza. Planos de Urbanização: A Época de Duarte Pacheco. Porto: DGOTDU, FAUP Publicações, 1995.

Martí Arís, Carlos. "Las formas de la residencia en la ciudad moderna." In Las Formas de la Residencia en la Ciudad Moderna: Vivienda y Ciudad en la Europa de Entreguerras, edited by Carlos Martí Arís. Barcelona: Edicions UPC, 2000.

Matos, Fátima Loureiro de, "Da implantação da República à primeira Guerra: As primeiras tentativas de Resolução do problema habitacional das classes operárias." In A Grande Guerra (1914–1918): Problemáticas e Representações, edited by Gaspar Martins Pereira et al, 369–381. Porto: CITCEM–Centro de Investigação Transdisciplinar «Cultura, Espaço e Memória," 2015.

Pereira, Sandra Marques. Casa e Mudança Social: Uma leitura das transformações da sociedade portuguesa a partir da casa. Casal de Cambra: Caleidoscópio, 2012.

Portas, Nuno. A Habitação Social: Proposta para a Metodologia da sua Arquitectura. Porto: FAUP Publicações, 2004 (1959).

Portas, Nuno. "Arquitectura e Urbanística na Década de 40." In Arquitectura(s) História e Crítica, Ensino e Profissão. Porto: FAUP Publicações, 2005 (1982).

Queirós, João. "O "Plano de Melhoramentos para a Cidade do Porto" de 1956: enquadramento político-social e elenco de realizações." In A Habitação Social na Transformação da Cidade: Sobre a Génese e Efeitos do Plano de Melhoramentos para a Cidade do Porto" de 1956, edited by Virgílio Borges Pereira. Porto: Edições Afrontamento, 2016.

Sousa, Alves de (dir). A Habitação em Portugal. Lisboa: Ministério das Obras Públicas, Centro de Estudos de Urbanismo e Habitação Engenheiro Duarte Pacheco, 1963.

Teixeira, Manuel C.. "A história urbana em Portugal. Desenvolvimentos recentes." Análise Social, vol. Xxviii, no. 121 (1993 [2.º]): 371–390.

Tiago, Maria da Conceição, "Bairros Sociais da I República: projectos e realizações." Revista Ler História, no. 59–"Repúblicas: culturas e práticas"(2010).

Tostões, Ana. Os Verdes Anos na Arquitectura Portuguesa dos Anos 50. Porto: FAUP Publicações, 1997.

Tostões, Ana. A Idade Maior: Cultura e Tecnologia na Arquitectura Moderna Portuguesa. Porto: FAUP Publicações, 2015.

State, Social Housing, and the Changing City: Porto's 1956 "Improvement Plan"

VIRGÍLIO BORGES PEREIRA and JOÃO QUEIRÓS
University of Porto, Faculty of Arts and Humanities, Department of Sociology; Institute of Sociology

ABSTRACT

The political regime in Portugal in the aftermath of the military coup on 28 May 1926 gradually grew into a conservative, authoritative governmental solution, of a strong nationalist bias, which came to be known as Estado Novo (New State), lasting for more than four decades. The problems of the critical housing shortage, not only in terms of number but also of the quality thereof, marked Portuguese society throughout the entire 20th century. Although the housing policies were part of the basic framework of the regime's political action, especially through the 1933 "affordable houses" programme, the priority was not on the long-standing health-hazard problems associated with contexts such as those of the working-class *ilhas* in central Porto (literally: "islands," meaning the inner-city slum-type housing). This chapter looks into the emergence and consolidation of Porto's 1956 "Improvement Plan," through the analysis of the results of a multi-method research focusing on institutional archives on public housing and on testimonials of several political agents and professionals who were involved in the making of Porto's housing policy. While this social housing plan came much later in the history of the regime's priorities, the state and the city council were eventually able to formulate a vast social housing plan for the city. Despite the peripheral location of neighbourhoods and the restrictive housing concepts underlying the development of the plan, its implementation represented a significant change in the city's physical and social landscape.

BIOGRAPHY

Virgílio Borges Pereira is an associate professor of sociology at the Department of Sociology of the Faculty of Arts of the University of Porto, where he has taught since 1994, and a researcher at the Institute of Sociology of the same university. Since 2003, he has collaborated with the Faculty of Architecture of the University of Porto, where he teaches both master's and PhD courses. His research combines sociological, historical, and ethnographic approaches, and focuses on the production of social and cultural inequalities in different spatial contexts in Northern Portugal, with a special interest in the study of the sociological legacy of P. Bourdieu's work. He has written extensively on the constitution of social spaces, class cultures, and social housing. Among his recent publications in English is: Pereira, V.B. "Urban Distinctions: Class, Culture and Sociability in the City of Porto." *International Journal of Urban and Regional Research*, 42, no. 1 (2018): 126–137.

João Queirós is an adjunct professor at the School of Education of the Polytechnic Institute of Porto, Portugal. He does research at the Institute of Sociology of the University of Porto. He also collaborates with the Centre for Research and Innovation in Education of the Polytechnic of Porto. His teaching and research interests cover: social change and urban transformations; local and regional development; community studies; and adult education. He is the author of several articles, books, and book chapters in these subjects, including *Aleixo. Génese, (des)estruturação e desaparecimento de um bairro do Porto (1969–2019)* (Porto: Afrontamento, 2019), a work on the social and political history of a council housing estate in inner city Porto, as seen throughout the last five decades.

1. INTRODUCTION

Following the military coup on 28 May 1926 and the complex process that took António de Oliveira Salazar and his political group to the highest level of state power, Portugal lived for more than four decades under a conservative and nationalist authoritarian regime, with a fascist-inspired right-wing political affiliation, self-proclaimed as "*Estado Novo.*" In a brief approach to identifying the regime's political and ideological idiosyncrasies, this chapter aims to examine how the Portuguese "*Estado Novo*" was structured and what instruments it implemented to address one of the main problems faced by Portuguese society for as long as the regime was in force: the severe hardships endured by the population, especially its most vulnerable sectors, as a result of housing scarcity and poor housing conditions. A special focus is put on the ways through which this process came into fruition in the city of Porto, by analysing the slow recognition of the need for specific housing policy measures for solving the problem of the working-class "*ilhas*" across the city, and how the city council's 1956 "Improvement Plan for the City of Porto" was implemented, contributing to a profound transformation of the city's physical and social landscape. This chapter is based on the findings of a multi-method sociological research that combined the analysis of institutional archives on public housing and of testimonials of political agents and professionals involved in the making of Porto's housing policy during the period in question.

2. THE POLITICAL CHARACTERISTICS OF "ESTADO NOVO," THE PERSPECTIVE ON THE "SOCIAL QUESTION," AND THE AIMS OF ITS HOUSING POLICY

Following the political-military uprising championed by the more socially and politically conservative sectors of the Portuguese army that led to the "March on Lisbon" on 28 May 1926, Portugal saw the end of the troubled Republican political experience in force in the country for little more than 15 years. The military dictatorship was gradually transformed into a political regime profoundly different from that which the country had known, built on a "revolutionary" project of a clear nationalist orientation.[1] Under the growing influence and subsequent political leadership of António de Oliveira Salazar and his effective group of close supporters,[2] the rise to power of the Portuguese far right was hinged on a skilful exploration of converging interests and a cunning removal of competitors and political opponents, a process that extended over many years and was a constant concern of Salazarist power.[3]

[1] A. H. Oliveira Marques, *Breve História de Portugal* (Lisbon: Presença, 2006).

[2] Manuel Lucena. *Os Lugar-Tenentes de Salazar. Biografias* (Lisbon: Alêtheia Editores, 2015).

[3] Fernando Rosas, *Salazar e o Poder: a arte de saber durar* (Lisbon: Tinta da China, 2012).

From the point of view of the regime's leading figures, with the "approval" and entry into force in March and April of the 1933 Constitution of the Republic, the self-proclaimed "*Estado Novo*" was established, along with a concrete political purpose that, despite the distancing from the original formulations and ideological plans, sought to find a "third way" between liberal democracy and communism based on a "revolutionary" compromise with the nation ("Nothing against the Nation, All for the Nation"), backed by an institutional shield with a clear "all-encompassing" focus.[4]

Prepared on earlier political and legal reflections carried out throughout the 1920s, the "necessary" institutionalisation of the "national dictatorship" established in the early years of the 1930s was accompanied from very early on by relatively systematic considerations on the role of the "*Estado Novo*" in the Portuguese society and by concrete measures that promoted the creation of an equivalent "*Homem Novo*" ("New Man"). By articulating an anti-parliamentary and anti-democratic operating framework with the activity of the *União Nacional* ("National Union")—an organisation founded in 1932 not foreseen as a party, but which in practice ended up being transformed into the sole party of the regime—Salazar explored a game of political ambiguities that led to the implementation of a form of power focused on the authority of the executive power and, in particular, of the head of government.[5]

The conservative and nationalist authoritarianism promoted by Salazar was, from the early years of the regime, based on the (re)organisation of practices and institutions especially dedicated to the use of force, with the mission of promoting the "Good of the Nation." Entities or actions such as the political police, special courts, preventive censorship, and prisons for political opponents were created to keep "order." Further to the orderly and "organic" promotion of the "Good of the Nation," several other institutions also ensured the embodiment of the regime's values. For example, the National Union, the *Legião Portuguesa* ("Portuguese Legion"), and the *Mocidade Portuguesa* ("Portuguese Youth Organisation") ensured the propaganda and assimilation of the regime.[6] This framework was extended to alternative fields which, while not neglecting the promotion of more endogenous dynamics, involved the political promotion of the regime and its values. An example of this is the work of the Secretariat for National Propaganda in matters of mass communication and culture[7] or the promotion of leisure, through the *Fundação Nacional para a Alegria no Trabalho* ("National Foundation for Joy in Work").

[4] Manuel Loff, *O Nosso Século é Fascista! O mundo visto por Salazar e Franco (1936–1945)* (Porto: Campo das Letras, 2008).

[5] Manuel Braga Cruz, *O Partido e o Estado no Salazarismo* (Lisbon: Presença, 1988).

[6] Luís Reis Torgal, *Estados Novos. Estado Novo* (Coimbra: Imprensa da Universidade de Coimbra, 2009).

[7] Rui Pedro Pinto, *Prémios do Espírito. Um estudo sobre prémios do Secretariado de Propaganda Nacional do Estado Novo* (Lisbon: ICS, 2009).

While the need to repress and integrate the population were part of the political project to be established by the "*Estado Novo*," the "organic" logic it entailed received "special" treatment when referring to the country's "Social Question." Indeed, the self-proclaimed revolutionary purpose of the "*Estado Novo*" was also based on a "national" way of handling the relations between capital and labour, and of recognising the social problems of the country. A relevant section on this matter is presented in the *Estatuto do Trabalho Nacional* (ETN, the "National Labour Charter"), like the Constitution, published in the decisive year of 1933 (in the case of the ETN, published in September). Inspired by the *Carta del lavoro* issued in fascist Italy, the ETN is, in many aspects, one of the logical consequences of the 1933 Constitution, since it establishes the basic institutional principles of Portuguese corporatism, namely, in summary form, placing the "national interest" above private interests—partial, partisan—and creating a corporative shield formed by cooperation, sensitive to the place of every person in society, between guilds and national unions.[8] As a proof of how the "national revolution" was seen by the leaders of the regime, the ETN was published together with a significant number of pieces of legislation of special relevance to the process of implementing the Portuguese "*Estado Novo*." In addition to the decrees governing the guilds, national unions and *Casas do Povo* ("Houses of the People" in a free translation), and closely related to the ETN, this legislative body was also accompanied by other significant political achievements, in this case the implementation of the *Programa de Casas Económicas* ("Affordable Houses Programme").

Having implemented laws on affordable housing, the "*Estado Novo*" recognised the need for the state to intervene in the severe housing crisis that had affected the country for several decades,[9] promoting and materialising, for the first time in the history of the Portuguese state, a policy that placed the state at the centre of the advancement of housing and with a role of urban developer. This intervention was done not only under the regime's ideological beliefs reflected in the urban morphology and in the type of houses it put forward (small individual houses in "garden-cities" located in the periphery of the country's main urban settings), but also in the recruitment of residents projected for these neighbourhoods (public servants and workers enrolled in the regime's "national unions"). As an institution, the Department of Affordable Houses depended on the management of the *Instituto Nacional do Trabalho e da Previdência* ("National Institute for Labour and Social Welfare") and of the *Subsecretariado de Estado das Corporações e da Previdência Social* ("Undersecretariat for Corporations and Social Welfare").

---

[8] Manuel Lucena, *A Evolução do Sistema Corporativo Português. O Salazarismo*. Vol. 1. (Lisbon: Perspectivas & Realidades, 1976); Fátima Patriarca, *A Questão Social no Salazarismo, 1930–1947* (Lisbon: ICS, 1995); Hermínio Martins, *Classe, Status e Poder* (Lisbon: ICS, 1998); Irene Pimentel, *A Cada Um o Seu Lugar: a política feminina do Estado Novo* (Lisbon: Temas e Debates, 2011).

[9] Manuel Teixeira. *Habitação Popular na Cidade Oitocentista* (Lisbon: FCG-JNICT, 1996).

Under this policy, it promoted access to home ownership: these were very specific, small individual houses in neighbourhoods created from scratch, intended for specific social categories, more specifically, financially sound families who were part of the more qualified segments of the working class and the petty bourgeoisie engaged in urban services, which the policy-makers sought to engage in the social and political support of the regime.[10] Although this programme was a key element of the "*Estado Novo*"'s housing policy, its response to the housing shortage in Portugal was limited and always structured around the highly hierarchised vision of social reality the regime promoted.[11] As a marker of Portuguese industrialisation, the city of Porto was one of the places that first felt the constraints from the depletion of the historical city's housing capacity.

The solution found was to build houses characterised by unhealthy conditions, such as the ones found in the "*ilhas*" (literally. "islands") in the central part of town, mostly used by industrial workers.[12] The first state measures concerning social housing were applied in this city in the second decade of the 20th century, to try to confront the nature of the city's housing shortage and lack of sanitation conditions. These were marginal and generally ineffective measures. The first initiative of the Affordable Houses Programme in Porto was the construction of the *Ilhéu* [MdH DB a220] neighbourhood, the inauguration of which in 1935 was attended by high-ranking government officials.[13] However, despite these initiatives and since the focal point of the Affordable Houses Programme was the financial capacity of the families, the problem of the working-class "*ilhas*" in central Porto persisted. The regime's ideological backbone and core ideal of access to housing through home ownership put the problem of Porto's working-class "*ilhas*" on a secondary plane.

3. THE 1956 IMPROVEMENT PLAN FOR THE CITY OF PORTO

It was only in the early years of the 1950s that Porto saw some important changes in its urban planning and housing policies. As the modernising segments of Portuguese society became more steadfast within the regime and state bureaucracy,[14] new initiatives aiming at the urban transformation of the city were put forward. The developments in 1953 and 1954 in the political leadership of the City Council of Porto and the Ministry of Public Works, when José Albino Machado Vaz in the former, and Eduardo de Arantes e Oliveira in the latter took up office, were not by chance, but rather the result of the important changes that took place at the heart of the state and of the regime. Throughout their long terms in office, these two committed engineers—who were actually very close—led the renovation of technical structures and reshaped the interventions of the institutions under their control, with visible effects on the country's urban landscape.

[10] Virgílio Borges Pereira and João Queirós, *Na Modesta Cidadezinha. Génese e Estruturação de Um Bairro de Casas Económicas do Porto (Amial, 1938–2010)* (Porto: Edições Afrontamento, 2012) and "Une maison pour le 'peuple portugais'. Genèse et trajectoire d'un quartier du programme des «maisons économiques» à Porto (1938–1974)," *Politix* 101 (2013): 49–78; Paulo Almeida. "Favor, recompensa e controlo social: os bairros de casas económicas do Porto (1935–1965)." Masters Thesis in Contemporary History, Faculdade de Letras da Universidade do Porto, 2010.

[11] Marielle Gros. *O Alojamento Social sob o Fascismo* (Porto: Afrontamento, 1982).

[12] Gaspar Martins Pereira, "Housing, household, and the family: The 'Ilhas' of Porto at the end of the nineteenth century," *Journal of Family History*, 19 (1994): 213–236.

[13] Virgílio Borges Pereira and João Queirós, *Na Modesta Cidadezinha*; Virgílio Borges Pereira, João Queirós, Sérgio Dias da Silva, and Tiago Lemos. "Casas Económicas e Casas Desmontáveis: génese, estruturação e transformação dos primeiros programas habitacionais do Estado Novo." In *Habitação: Cem Anos de Políticas Públicas em Portugal*, ed. Ricardo Agarez, 82–117 (Lisbon: IHRU, 2018).

[14] Rosas, Fernando. "Estado Novo." In *Dicionário de História do Estado Novo*–Volume I, ed. Fernando Rosas and J. M. Brandão de Brito (Lisbon: Bertrand, 1996), 318.

In the case of Porto, it was exactly after Machado Vaz took office that precepts were renewed and experiences in the construction of council houses were deepened to house families from the "unhealthy" houses demolished or to be demolished in the central areas of the city. In peripheral areas, and in the first half of the 1950s, new housing projects were built for the "poor," either as single family houses with one, two or three bedrooms for "very low income families" who lived in "slums," "makeshift shacks," and other "indecent houses," or as four-storey buildings to rehouse families from "buildings demolished for urban planning purposes" or "*ilhas* or other houses with no sanitation conditions."[15] Despite this progress, the mayor of Porto soon admitted that these efforts to solve the city's housing problem were not regular or sufficiently intense:[16]

"There have not been significant results in the way this problem has been dealt with, as what we have done is insufficient.[...] [there needs to be] a slight change in the City Council's direct actions, in order to build more, build more economically, and more modestly."

The terms of this "change of course" were made public in May 1955, when the "Sanitation Plan for the *Ilhas* of Porto" was published. Through this document, the then Mayor called on the government to support the council's ambitious building plan to be implemented within the next ten years with the purpose of "radically changing" the accessible housing situation in the city.[17] The 1955 "Sanitation Plan" was based on a survey carried out in the "*ilhas*" in 1939 by the city council, which indicated that there were more than thirteen thousand houses of this type, housing almost 45 thousand people, and echoed some of the purposes of the 1940–42 "sanitation and improvement campaign."

This plan served as the basis for the "Improvement Plan" which was approved and initiated in the following year, and proposed an integrated intervention on twelve thousand houses, involving the remodelling of each set of two adjacent houses in an "*ilha*" into one single house, and the construction of six thousand new houses in council housing neighbourhoods built from scratch to replace the eliminated "*ilhas*" houses. The 1955 "Sanitation Plan" accepted the benefits of rehousing the population involved in this large urban transformation project—an estimated 25 to 30 thousand people—in areas close to the "*ilhas*" to be demolished. It also justified the inevitability of having to build most of the new neighbourhoods on the city's periphery with the need to "reduce land use to acceptable levels" in the city centre, which were considered "blatantly excessive."[18]

[15] Câmara Municipal do Porto [CMP]. *Relatório de Gerência, 1954* (Porto: Câmara Municipal do Porto, 1954).

[16] Machado Vaz, in a statement made in December 1953, quoted in Fernando de Sousa, Coord., *Os Presidentes da Câmara Municipal do Porto (1822–2009)* (Porto: CEPESE/Câmara Municipal do Porto, 2009).

[17] Câmara Municipal do Porto, *Plano de Salubrização das «Ilhas» do Porto* (Porto: Câmara Municipal do Porto, 1955), 5.

[18] Câmara Municipal do Porto, *Plano de Salubrização das «Ilhas» do Porto* ,11.

The decentralisation of the residential and industrial capacity and the subsequent reduction in the congestion of the central area, earmarked for services and administrative and commercial activities, was one of the essential options of this Plan, thus following the principles of the "City Master Plan" approved a year before. The construction of the new council housing neighbourhoods on the outskirts of the city would also allow major savings, as the costs of expropriations and land purchase would drop significantly, which could be further increased by the economic benefits of no longer having to build single-family houses, but rather "moderately high buildings," and of reducing the common use spaces to a minimum, which would also "mitigate promiscuity" and "reduce any chance of bad or confrontational relations between neighbours."[19]

It should also be added that in order to involve private individuals in the process and to avoid excessive resistance on the part of homeowners, large plots of land for the construction of the future neighbourhoods were expropriated "for multiple purposes," to be used not only for public housing projects, but also for private real-estate purposes. In the opinion of the city officials, the fact that the new council housing projects scattered across the city would be adjacent to other types of neighbourhoods would enable the *"recommended and useful conviviality between different classes, to enable mutual help and exchange of services between the various members of society."*[20] As for the intervention in the "*ilhas*" in the city centre, the "sanitation" of which the city council also felt could trigger tensions and resistance by tenants or homeowners, they would not be done without first carrying out an inspection to determine the decision on the future use of the housing area inspected. Where the conditions of the "*ilhas*" inspected by council officials required "sanitation" works, the residents would have to vacate the properties and the "*ilha*" would have to be partly or completely demolished. If this resulted in a partial demolition, improvement works would have to be done on the remaining building. Where the inspection determined the demolition of the "*ilha*," it could either be built again, or the land could be used for "common use" purposes (green area or parking lot, for example), through expropriation and if the city council felt the conditions were not in place for new constructions.[21]

Exactly one year after the "Sanitation Plan for the *Ilhas* of Porto" was presented, and following intense political-diplomatic bustle, in which the city mayor was personally involved, the government approved Decree-Law 40,616, of 28 May 1956, which established the exact outlines of what became the broadest and most important state housing intervention in Porto.

[19] Câmara Municipal do Porto, *Plano de Salubrização das «Ilhas» do Porto* , 22.

[20] Câmara Municipal do Porto, *Plano de Salubrização das «Ilhas» do Porto*, 11–14.

[21] Câmara Municipal do Porto, *Plano de Salubrização das «Ilhas» do Porto*, 14–15.

Fig. 1 and 2 Demolished "ilhas" and an eviction process in central Porto in the mid-1950s. Source: Municipal Historic Archive of Porto [F-NP/CMP/04/02200; F-NP/CMP/04/02035 (authors and dates unknown)].

While recognising the "moral, social and political relevance" of the "problem of the *'ilhas'*," which had remained "practically unsolved" until then, despite the "efforts made across successive generations" and the "repeated public calls for tough actions for the demolition" of these housing areas, the 1956 "Improvement Plan for the City of Porto" proposed to dedicate to this problem a "new and determined effort," by building "at least six thousand houses specifically intended for the same number of families living in the *'ilhas'* and similar unhealthy neighbourhoods in the city" within ten years.

Moreover, the construction of the new houses would be followed by "the immediate demolition of vacant houses" or by mandatory "radical refurbishment works" in the cases where "a strict judgement" showed that the houses "could survive" and that the "requirements of urban refurbishment" for the land would not be compromised. As the previous improvement works on the "*ilhas*" carried out by the city council were "clearly poor and unlikely to be implemented on a wide scale," this form of intervention was proposed on an exceptional basis and would turn out to be little more than residual. In fact, what prevailed was the "massive demolition" of the "*ilhas*" houses, already foreseen in the preamble to Decree-Law 40,616, and the relocation of their occupants to the new neighbourhoods in the city periphery.[22]

The necessity of finding peripheral locations for the future council housing neighbourhoods was taken from the 1955 "Sanitation Plan." Indeed, the implementation of the 1956 "Improvement Plan" would contribute not only to solving what was considered the city's main housing and social problem, but also to solving "another problem of recognised importance for the future of Porto," that of the "creation of expansion areas requiring joint and carefully organised urban planning," within the general provisions of the "master plan" in force.

Through a "very direct intervention in all phases of the creation of the new areas," Porto City Council was taking upon itself the "inalienable responsibility of implementing a sound land development policy," with the creation of new public housing areas being only a part of a broad process of redistributing land tenure and of functionally reorganising the city. This unprecedented role of the city council in stimulating the local real estate market would enable the essential objectives of the "Plan" to be achieved and to bear the "onerous burdens of the urban transformation that Porto badly needed" and the "*deficit* from the forced undervaluation of land to be used for the construction of cheap dwellings."

[22] The quotations in this paragraph as in others refer to the preamble or provisions of Decree-Law 40,616, of 28 May 1956.

To expedite the processes and provide the "Improvement Plan" with the necessary conditions for its timely execution, all expropriations related thereto were considered of public utility and compensations were established expeditiously by an arbitration committee. The financing of the plan included a loan with the public bank, a non-refundable treasury subsidy and a contribution put forward by the local government. The preparation, organisation, and conduct of the plan were the exclusive responsibility of a technical-financial department set up for that purpose and reporting directly to the mayor. The "Directorate for Urban Improvement Services," formed by a "House Construction Office" and an "Urban Developments Office," was responsible for a wide range of duties associated to the development of the initiative initiated in 1956. This Directorate concentrated the experience and know-how of the City Council's administrative practices, which from then on continued to consolidate and eventually became autonomous.

The construction of the first "Improvement Plan" council housing neighbourhood started before the end of 1956 as soon as the legal, institutional, financial, and technical-administrative conditions were in place for the start of the operations. Taking advantage of the surplus land from the opening of a new street in the city's first periphery, Porto City Council launched the contract for the construction of the six blocks of the *Bom Sucesso* [MdH DB a691] neighbourhood, with a total of 128 houses [Figures 3 and 4]. While works were ongoing, surveys were conducted in the "*ilhas*" and in other city centre housing areas targeted for demolition with the purpose of obtaining information to support the decisions regarding the typologies of the new houses and for organising the resettlement processes.[23]

[23] On this matter, and for further information, see *A Habitação Social na Transformação da Cidade: Sobre a Génese e Efeitos do «Plano de Melhoramento para a Cidade do Porto» de 1956*, ed. Virgílio Borges Pereira (Porto: Afrontamento, 2016). See also João Queirós, *No Centro, à Margem. Sociologia das Intervenções Urbanísticas e Habitacionais do Estado no Centro Histórico do Porto* (Porto: Edições Afrontamento, 2015) on the housing policies put forward in Porto's inner city.

Fig. 3 and 4 View of the Bom Sucesso neighbourhood after its construction was completed at the end of the 1950s (left), and panoramic view over the Arrábida area, near Bom Sucesso, at the time of the inauguration of the new bridge, in the early 1960s (right) Source: Municipal Historic Archive of Porto [F-ALB/005/02/000060; F-ALB/006/00087 (authors and dates unknown)]..

Despite some difficulties in the expropriation processes, a report published in 1960 by the Directorate for the Improvement Plan Services stated that the work ran smoothly: the neighbourhoods of *Bom Sucesso* (Massarelos), *Pio XII* (Campanhã) [MdH DB a692], and *Carvalhido* (Paranhos) [MdH DB a693] were concluded within four years; the works in the neighbourhoods of *Pasteleira* (Lordelo do Ouro) [MdH DB a196, a197, a199, a200] and the first phase of the *Outeiro* neighbourhood (Paranhos) [MdH DB a694] were being finalised, and the following were ongoing: *Agra do Amial* (Paranhos) [MdH DB a695], *Carriçal* (Paranhos) [MdH DB a696], *Fernão de Magalhães* (Bonfim) [MdH DB a698], and the first phases of *S. Roque da Lameira* (Campanhã) [MdH DB a704] and *Fonte da Moura* (Aldoar) [MdH DB a706]. Overall, more than 50% of all planned houses were built or under construction by the end of the 1950s.[24] Of the neighbourhoods completed or under construction, only two were located in areas adjacent to the city centre. The remaining new council housing neighbourhoods were situated on the periphery, near recently opened, or to be opened, roads. In some cases, the new neighbourhoods were the initiators of the urbanisation processes of areas until then hardly urbanised at all or residually urbanised [Figures 5 to 8].

In the early years of the 1960s, the pace of construction of the new houses held up well. Between 1961 and 1963, the launch of the construction of the largest neighbourhoods in the "Improvement Plan"—*Cerco do Porto* (Campanhã) [MdH DB a708], with 804 houses, *Regado* (Paranhos) [MdH DB a709], with 722 houses, and *Campinas* (Ramalde) [MdH DB a710], with 900 houses—gave the momentum needed to meet the targets set in 1956: ten years on, Porto City Council owned 6,072 new houses distributed across fourteen council housing neighbourhoods.

[24] Câmara Municipal do Porto, *O Problema da Extinção das Ilhas do Porto* (Porto: Câmara Municipal do Porto/Direção dos Serviços do Plano de Melhoramentos, 1960).

Fig. 5 Vacant land in Lordelo do Ouro, where the Pasteleira neighbourhood was built, with the primary school and the "Affordable Houses" of Marechal Gomes da Costa in the background. Source: Municipal Historic Archive of Porto [F-ALB/005/03/00001; F-ALB/005/03/00063; F-NP/CMP/04/02904 (authors and dates unknown)].

Fig. 6 and 7 View of the Pasteleira neighbourhood, during the construction period (top), and the interior of a neighbourhood council house built under the 1956 "Improvement Plan" (below).
Source: Municipal Historic Archive of Porto [F-ALB/005/03/00001; F-ALB/005/03/00063; F-NP/CMP/04/02904 (authors and dates unknown)].

At the end of the ten-year period of this unprecedented state effort to build public housing, the urban and social layout of the city of Porto had changed considerably. The outskirts of the city, which had until the end of the 1950s been spared from urbanisation, were now home to medium or large neighbourhoods occupied by thousands of families that had been moved from the city centre, mostly from the "*ilhas*"; in the city centre, the demolition of these "*ilhas*" opened the way for urban development aimed at affirming the area as a business and service hub. Very possibly as the result of the proposed zoning of the city and of the need to centralise resources for the construction of the six thousand new planned houses, the effects of the 1956 "Improvement Plan" in the "*ilhas*" were almost always their demolition, with no records of there having been renovation operations capable of providing an alternative housing solution to the construction of the new neighbourhoods and the consequent relocation of families to the outskirts of the city. In fact, the prevailing intervention model introduced by the "Improvement Plan" continued beyond 1966: in that year, the City Council of Porto, headed by Nuno Pinheiro Torres, who followed José Albino Machado Vaz, began the construction of a further 1,674 new houses, distributed across the neighbourhoods of S. João de Deus (Campanhã) [MdH DB a702], Francos (Ramalde) [MdH DB a712], Aldoar [MdH DB a713], Lordelo do Ouro [MdH DB a714], and Corujeira/Monte da Bela (Campanhã) [MdH DB a556].[25]

[25] Câmara Municipal do Porto, *Plano de Melhoramentos 1956–1966* (Porto: Câmara Municipal do Porto/Direção dos Serviços do Plano de Melhoramentos, 1967), 27–29.

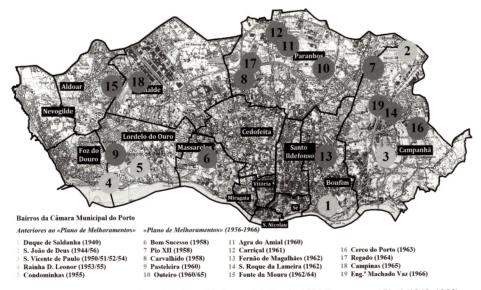

Fig. 8 Neighbourhoods built by Porto City Council before and during the 1956 "Improvement Plan" (1940–1966)
Source: The Authors and Project SFRH/BD/46978/2008.

At the political-institutional level, the exponential expansion of the city housing stock, which had gone from less than one thousand houses in 1955 to more than seven thousand in late 1966, forced the city council to focus on and provide more and more resources for these interventions. Although the investment in housing, which in the years of the "Plan" had always been close to 30 per cent, dropped to less than one fifth of the city's annual budget after 1966 (still well above the 5 to 10% given until 1955 to this sector of the city's action), the buildings that the City Council now owned implied that more technical, administrative and financial resources were provided to properly manage and maintain them. The city council had created and consolidated the "Directorate for the Improvement Plan Services," and this service would be replaced in 1966 by a strengthened "Directorate for Housing Services," which was responsible for coordinating and implementing all the intervention works in this field, as part of a reform of the city council's macrostructure. Moreover, the city council also provided considerable resources to the "Urban Developments Office," so that it could revise the city's master plan, which would culminate with the publication of the new Master Plan in 1962, and test some forms of financing and promotion of "assistance" in the housing areas under its supervision. Public bureaucracy was thus transformed to encourage urban change, and as a result of this urban change, its own structure was revamped and became more complex.

With more than six thousand new houses built, the same number of "*ilhas*" demolished, and almost thirty thousand people relocated to the fourteen neighbourhoods built over the ten years of the 1956 "Improvement Plan," the city council also faced new problems concerning the institutional framework and the "social promotion" of relocated families. Its response did not differ too much from the patronising handouts, often repressive, which had hitherto marked the action of the city's public authorities. The new tenants were repeatedly reminded of the "precarious" nature of occupancy and knew they ran the risk of being relocated or even evicted if they failed to pay the rent or breached any tenant duties, which included, besides those relating to house conservation measures and the use of common spaces, the duties of "good moral and civic behaviour."[26] It is no surprise therefore that the figure of the "inspector" took on a renewed role in these neighbourhoods, and that in the late 1960s, social intervention only served purposes of strict charity. The very running of the "social centre" facilities—which the city council wanted to build in several of its neighbourhoods—was still viewed in the light of a concept based on the distrust and moralism with which the regime invariably considered the city's working classes.

[26] Câmara Municipal do Porto, *Regulamento das Habitações Construídas em Execução do Plano de Melhoramentos para a Cidade do Porto*, Article 12 (Porto: Câmara Municipal do Porto, 1958).

The "social centres" were not only responsible for providing the needed "moral and material assistance" to residents, but also to establish within them "cultural and even recreational services" able to "distract the unprepared youth from the street or inconvenient places." The activity of these "social centres" was eventually left to the exclusive responsibility of institutions directly or indirectly linked to the Catholic Church. They were also responsible for "giving allowances for clothing and food to the more disadvantaged families" and for giving "moral assistance" to the households facing "family issues," very common among the "less educated and financially weak classes."[27]

4. CONCLUSION

This chapter set out from the identification of the fundamental social and political characteristics of the action of the "*Estado Novo*" to highlight the relevance of the "organicist" and highly hierarchised concept of society as part of the prevailing ideological guidelines of the regime. It pointed out the importance of these views in the development of the mainstream policy, including the housing policy. As the regime's housing policy was focused on initiatives such as the "Affordable Houses Programme," the path towards the recognition of the need for state intervention in structural areas of the country's housing shortage, such as those of the working class "*ilhas*" in the city of Porto, was slow. With respect to the problems raised by the social and housing situation in inner city Porto, through this analysis we identified the process that led to the emergence and organisation of the "Improvement Plan of the City of Porto" in 1956, the densest and most striking social housing public programme that the city plunged into in the second half of the 20th century, and which the regime put into practice after significant internal rearrangements. In addition to identifying the conditions for its implementation, the analysis pinpointed the main underlying social and urban effects, emphasising the profound reconfiguration of the physical and social landscape of the city after the plan was implemented, which resulted in a significant demographic shift of disadvantaged populations and in the urban development of the city's periphery. Furthermore, the analysis revealed that the implementation of the Plan triggered an increasing and more complex political, bureaucratic, and institutional situation, especially in the city council's sphere of action, but this did not translate into the effective development of a social housing policy shaped by consistent mechanisms of community development and integration of socially fragile populations.

[27] Câmara Municipal do Porto, *Plano de Melhoramentos 1956–1966* (Porto: Câmara Municipal do Porto/Direção dos Serviços do Plano de Melhoramentos, 1967), 21.

BIBLIOGRAPHY

Almeida, Paulo. "Favor, Recompensa e Controlo Social: os Bairros de Casas Económicas do Porto (1935–1965)." Masters Thesis in Contemporary History, Faculdade de Letras da Universidade do Porto, 2010.

Câmara Municipal do Porto Relatório de Gerência, 1954. Porto: Câmara Municipal do Porto, 1954.

Câmara Municipal do Porto. Plano de Salubrização das «Ilhas» do Porto. Porto: Câmara Municipal do Porto, 1955.

Câmara Municipal do Porto. Regulamento das Habitações Construídas em Execução do Plano de Melhoramentos para a Cidade do Porto. Porto: Câmara Municipal do Porto, 1958.

Câmara Municipal do Porto. O Problema da Extinção das Ilhas do Porto. Porto: Câmara Municipal do Porto/Direção dos Serviços do Plano de Melhoramentos, 1960.

Câmara Municipal do Porto. Plano de Melhoramentos 1956–1966. Porto: Câmara Municipal do Porto/Direção dos Serviços do Plano de Melhoramentos, 1967.

Carvalho, Rita Almeida de. "Eduardo de Arantes e Oliveira." In Dicionário de História do Estado Novo–Volume II, edited by Fernando Rosas and José Maria Brandão de Brito, 683–685. Lisbon: Bertrand, 1996.

Cruz, Manuel Braga. O Partido e o Estado no Salazarismo. Lisbon: Presença, 1988.

Gros, Marielle. O Alojamento Social sob o Fascismo. Porto: Afrontamento, 1982.

Loff, Manuel. O Nosso Século é Fascista! O Mundo Visto por Salazar e Franco (1936–1945). Porto: Campo das Letras, 2008.

Lucena, Manuel. A Evolução do Sistema Corporativo Português. O Salazarismo. Vol. 1. Lisbon: Perspectivas & Realidades, 1976.

Lucena, Manuel. Os Lugar-Tenentes de Salazar. Biografias. Lisbon: Alêtheia Editores, 2015.

Marques, A. H. Oliveira. Breve História de Portugal. Lisbon: Presença, 2006.

Martins, Hermínio. Classe, Status e Poder. Lisbon: ICS, 1998.

Patriarca, Fátima. A Questão Social no Salazarismo, 1930–1947. Lisbon: ICS, 1995.

Pereira, Gaspar Martins. "Housing, Household, and the Family: The 'Ilhas' of Porto at the End of the Nineteenth Century," Journal of Family History, 19 (1994): 213–236.

Pereira, Virgílio Borges, ed., A Habitação Social na Transformação da Cidade: Sobre a Génese e Efeitos do «Plano de melhoramento para a cidade do Porto» de 1956. Porto: Afrontamento, 2016.

Pereira, Virgílio Borges, and João Queirós. Na Modesta Cidadezinha. Génese e Estruturação de um Bairro de Casas Económicas do Porto (Amial, 1938–2010). Porto: Edições Afrontamento, 2012.

Pereira, Virgílio Borges, and João Queirós. "Une maison pour le 'peuple portugais'. Genèse et trajectoire d'un quartier du programme des «maisons économiques» à Porto (1938–1974)," Politix 101 (2013): 49–78.

Pereira, Virgílio Borges, João Queirós, Sérgio Dias da Silva, and Tiago Lemos. "Casas Económicas e Casas Desmontáveis: génese, estruturação e transformação dos primeiros programas habitacionais do Estado Novo." In Habitação: Cem Anos de Políticas Públicas em Portugal, edited by Ricardo Agarez, 82–117. Lisbon: IHRU, 2018.

Pimentel, Irene. A Cada Um o Seu Lugar: a Política Feminina do Estado Novo. Lisbon: Temas e Debates, 2011.

Pinto, Rui Pedro. Prémios do Espírito. Um Estudo sobre Prémios do Secretariado de Propaganda Nacional do Estado Novo. Lisbon: ICS, 2009.

Queirós, João. No Centro, à Margem. Sociologia das Intervenções Urbanísticas e Habitacionais do Estado no Centro Histórico do Porto. Porto: Edições Afrontamento, 2015.

Rosas, Fernando. "Estado Novo." In Dicionário de História do Estado Novo–Volume I, edited by Fernando Rosas, and J. M. Brandão de Brito, 315–319. Lisbon: Bertrand, 1996.

Rosas, Fernando. Salazar e o Poder: a Arte de Saber Durar. Lisbon: Tinta da China, 2012.

Sousa, Fernando de, Coord., Os Presidentes da Câmara Municipal do Porto (1822–2009). Porto: CEPESE/Câmara Municipal do Porto, 2009.

Teixeira, Manuel. Habitação Popular na Cidade Oitocentista. Lisbon: FCG-JNICT, 1996.

Torgal, Luís Reis. Estados Novos. Estado Novo. Coimbra: Imprensa da Universidade de Coimbra, 2009.

Not Houses but Cities—Not Designs, but Designers. 1950s Italy: the INA-Casa Neighbourhoods

ORSINA SIMONA PIERINI
Politecnico di Milano, Department of Architecture and Urban Studies

ABSTRACT

In February 1949 the Italian government approved the INA-Casa Plan, legislation to provide incentives for employment through the construction of low-cost housing. The Plan, in effect until 1963, led to the production of 350,000 housing units in autonomous, recognizable districts across the national territory. Many great masters of architecture and urban planning played a fundamental part in the effort, and the experimentation on the theme of the neighbourhood generated discussion and debate. In Rome the Tiburtino district by Ridolfi, or the Tuscolano project by Quaroni and Libera, corresponded to positions of dissent with respect to the schematic approach of a certain type of Modernism by returning to the scale of the village, while in Milan, at the Harar development, with Figini Pollini and Gio Ponti, or in the Feltre district, the large group of Milanese architects proposed solutions in which the compact morphology of the traditional city was abandoned in favour of attribution of value to public space and nature as a central focus. From a typological standpoint, certain *Suggestions* published by the director of the technical division Adalberto Libera indicated a preference for juxtaposed tract houses, terraced houses, and tower buildings, providing a variety of types whose interpretation and montage became the main compositional thrust of an initiative that succeeded in inhabiting and interpreting the local contexts of Italy during the reconstruction.

BIOGRAPHY

Associate Professor in Architectural and Urban Composition at DAStU, Milan Polytechnic. After taking a degree in Milan in 1989, she completed her PhD in Architectural Composition with Giorgio Grassi in Venice (IUAV) in 1995.
In 1998 she received a study grant for research with Carlos Martí Arís at the ETSAB, where she focused on Spanish architecture of the 1950s, curating with José Quetglas the exhibition on Josep Maria Sostres arquitecto and the publication of Passaggio in Iberia, 2008. Her research activity is based on an idea of architectural design that interprets the architecture of the city in its historical experience as material for contemporary design: she has published the books *Sulla Facciata, tra Architettura e Città*, 2008 and *Case Milanesi 1923–1973*, 2017. She addressed the importance of the role of housing in the urban design of the contemporary city in *Housing Primer, Le Forme della Residenza nella Città Contemporanea*, 2012. During a recent sabbatical year, she investigated the notion of architectural critique with Bruno Reichlin at the EPFL. She has lectured at many universities in Europe and elsewhere, including ETSAM Madrid, KIT Karlsruhe, Beijing University of Technology, ETSA Barcelona, Henry Van de Velde Institut Antwerpen, Bauhaus Universität Weimar, CEPT Ahmedabad, Hochschule Luzern, and Düsseldorf Kunstakademie.

HISTORY AND CONTEXT

Measures to Increase Employment, Facilitating the Construction of Housing for Workers. The title of the legislation no. 43, dated 28 February 1949, narrates the genesis of one of the most important public housing operations ever carried out in Italy. The title indicates the two problems which Italy was forced to face after World War II: working-class employment and housing. The economy had yet to restabilize, and the wartime destruction existed beside situations of residential decay that seemed to come from ancient times, in which entire families lived in unthinkably unhealthy conditions, packed into caves, basements or stairwells. The law was enacted at a particular moment of the Italian reconstruction: cities were attempting to resume normal real estate operations, but they had not yet furnished themselves with the required tools of regulation and implementation; the new master plans were still in the development phase, such as that of Milan, whose Master Plan was not put into effect until 1953.

The Plan took the name of the agency in charge of the entire operation, the "Istituto Nazionale delle Assicurazioni," INA-Casa, subsequently also known as the "Piano Fanfani" to bear the name of the Christian Democrat congressman who had guided the political initiative. A president hailing from a long Catholic and communitarian tradition, Filiberto Guala was at the helm of the operation from the outset, prior to taking vows as a Trappist monk. The plan called for the involvement of the thousands of architects existing in the territory, through competitions for the constitution of professional associations or indirect commissions. The working team was put together by Arnaldo Foschini, dean of the School of Architecture in Rome, an outstanding figure from the profession. As the head of the technical division, the choice went to an architect from Trentino with extensive experience in the field of low-cost housing: Adalberto Libera. Foschini also selected an outstanding historian as the head of the Research Centre, known for his theoretical and critical acumen: Renato Bonelli.

This was the solid structure, sustained by the Ministry of Labour, for the launch of the Plan in Italy that, after two seven-year periods of work, left behind it one of the most highly evolved forms of public development, still clearly recognizable today in the crowded panorama of the urban outskirts. From February 1949 to 1963 in Italy, 350,000 housing units were built, located in 5,000 municipalities across the peninsula, with the larger clusters in the main Italian cities. In Milan and in Naples about 29,000 housing units were built, while in Rome about 23,000 were completed, and in Turin about 15,000.[1]

---

[1] The data come from the book by Luigi Beretta Anguissola, *I 14 Anni del Piano INA Casa*, Staderini, Roma 1963. The voluminous text offers detailed documentation, with plans, aerial photographs and typological charts, of the achievements of the two seven-year periods of the Plan, organized in terms of scale: districts, housing units, development units.

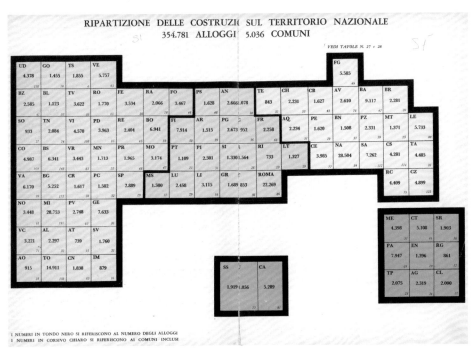

Fig. 1 Distribution of INA-CASA construction in Italy

The spread across the whole country was capillary, and the legislation stipulated that at least one third of the constructions be made in the South. During the first seven-year period, half the housing units created were put up for sale, while the other half were rented; in the second seven-year cycle, the lodgings purchased by their inhabitants reached a level of 75 per cent. Over the span of just a few years, apartments, houses, and services were created and inserted in organic urban systems,[2] in keeping with the "not buildings but cities" concept. It is worth recalling that the theme of the *Casa popolare* (low-cost housing) had already gone through a major launch at the start of the 1900s, through private initiatives connected with industry and through the establishment of independent low-cost housing authorities run by the various municipal governments. The question was later addressed in the theoretical reflections taken forward by Diotallevi and Marescotti, who had already begun to publish the volume *Il Problema, Sociale, Costruttivo ed Economico dell'Abitazione*.[3] (The Social, Economic and Construction Problem of Housing) in instalments in 1948, an impressive anthology of examples of residential complexes covered by weekly profiles with drawings and illustrations, making the entire European experience in this area accessible for comparative analysis.

[2] Paola Di Biagi, "La 'città pubblica' e l'INA-Casa," in *La Grande Ricostruzione. Il Piano INA-Casa e l'Italia degli Anni '50*, ed. Paola Di Biagi (Rome: Donzelli, 2001).

[3] Irenio Diotallevi and Franco Marescotti, *Il Problema Sociale ed Economico della Casa*, (Milan: Poligono, 1948–1949). Irenio Diotallevi was appointed to the Executive Board of the Plan.

In the immediate post-war period, the Consiglio Nazionale delle Ricerche (National Research Council) had also published the *Manuale dell'Architetto*, a work that would have a place on the drawing boards of architects for decades. The painstaking preparation of the volume, dense with drawings and particulars, analyses of materials and investigations on construction, was done for the most part by Mario Ridolfi,[4] whose work on architectural details was a distinctive part of his poetics, becoming a sort of widespread, shared language thanks to the INA-Casa Plan. Nevertheless, the Plan was soon flanked by specific publications: small design manuals, the first of which was already issued towards the end of 1949.[5] The first booklet, *Suggerimenti, Norme e Schemi per la Elaborazione e Presentazione dei Progetti* (Suggestions, Standards and Schemes for the Development and Presentation of Projects) formulated certain general principles, such as the focus on the context and local construction systems, or the use of a variety of building types: duplex terraced houses, linear buildings of three or four storeys to combine with taller structures with a central layout, of seven to eight levels. Suitable conditions of hygiene and ventilation were specified, such as air turnover rates, for example, and the use of loggias and balconies was strongly urged,[6] an element that was to become one of the earmarks of all the projects of the Plan. These guidelines were accompanied by drawings of housing prototypes: in the first booklet, we can also see the solution proposed by Mario Ridolfi with a rotated balcony, typical of his buildings in Terni and in Rome at the Tiburtino area.

These were handy publications that illustrated both good and bad examples: the second manual, *Suggerimenti, Esempi e Norme per la Progettazione Urbanistica. Progetti tipo* (Suggestions, Examples and Standards for Urban Design. Project Types) approaches the scale of urban morphological composition, with indications on the placement of buildings, on the relationship with the context and the geographical site, including suggestions explicitly drawn from Scandinavian culture, such as the projects of Backström & Reinius. All methods capable of countering a sense of repetition and monotony were strongly recommended: staggering and rotation, volumetric counterpoint, and separation into parts are the characteristic features of these buildings, for which every site would be interpreted according to the local culture, as Bruno Zevi aptly described in his presentation[7] of the Plan to the National Congress on Urbanism in 1952. A useful trove of theory and method, then, to form a precise awareness about the idea of the city or, more precisely, the fragment of the city that was going to be built: the neighbourhood. In fact, beyond the morphological experimentation connected with housing types and their groupings, each area had to create *Comunità*[8] and had to be

---

[4] *I Manuale dell'Architetto* was published by the Centro Nazionale delle Ricerche in 1946; the organizing committee, which also included Bruno Zevi and Pierluigi Nervi, was chaired by Gustavo Colonnetti, a structural engineer at Politecnico di Milano and an outstanding figure of the Italian culture in which engineering and architecture operated in synergy in the modern era.

[5] On this theme, see the essay by Patrizia Gabellini, "I Manuali: una Strategia Normativa," in *La Grande Ricostruzione*.

[6] Adalberto Libera, "Logge e Balconi," *Strutture*, no. 2 (1947): 9–11.

[7] "The unit of Via Dessiè in Milan is well-suited to a large industrial city, by now completely humanized; the Tiburtino district in Rome reprises the volumetric scale and episodic tone of the towns of Lazio and the Abruzzi that are such a characteristic feature of central Italy. The oblong form of Borgo Panigale in Bologna reflects the physiognomy of various centres in Emilia." Bruno Zevi, "L'Architettura dell'INA-Casa," in *L'INA-CASA al IV Congresso Nazionale di Urbanistica* (Venezia, October 1952), 21.

[8] As underlined by the INU President Adriano Olivetti, the enlightened industrialist and philanthropist who had constructed the model of a new society in Ivrea founded the *Comunità* editions which published the magazine of the same name, alongside many other important initiatives.

provided with public structures, to create forms of autonomy and wholeness: in this way, collective space seen as a recognizable urban factor could be structured with adequate services, such as schools or churches, as well as shops and systems of public parks. According to the stipulations of the Plan, the neighbourhoods were provided with community centres.

THE ARCHITECTURAL CONTEXT AND THE THEORETICAL DEBATE

Architectural culture was therefore ready to meet this major challenge: the solid background of the great architects who had worked between the two World Wars was now reinforced by younger disciples ready to come to terms, in operative practice, with the critique of the dogmas of Rationalism already launched on a theoretical level. The spread across the entire national territory permitted an interesting comparison of the various positions out forward by the Roman and Lombard schools, with the former more oriented towards the organicism of Wright, and the latter more closely tied to the European experience of Rationalism. A well-known example is the debate that arose regarding the creation of the Tiburtino district on the part of Quaroni and Ridolfi himself: the Rationalist culture of northern Italy opposed the picturesque character of the urban and planimetric arrangements of the Roman development, which linked back to the image of a village reinterpreted through the idea of historical montage, and in the choices of architectural language conveyed by the construction details, in which there was even talk of Neo-Realism.[9]

In several situations, as in Milan for example, the plan was an opportunity to consolidate research that had begun inside Lombard Rationalism, but would find its local interpretation in the theoretical reflections on *Pre-esistenze ambientali*[10] (Existing environmental features) put forward by *Casabella-Continuità*, in the field of both private and public residential construction. In other situations, the reference point of the international architectural culture of the period held sway, as in the interesting project of Daneri in Genoa, with its debt to Le Corbusier's idea of the *Unité d'Habitation*. In this context in which the major Italian cities would soon have to welcome thousands of workers arriving from the countryside or the south, with the resulting modification of the consolidated city limits, the opportunity to design and build large urban settlements stimulated wider-ranging thinking about the role of the neighbourhood, the relationship with the historical centre, and the constitution of new public spaces in the process of urbanization of outlying areas.

[9] See the text by Bruno Reichlin, "Figures of Neorealism in Italian Architecture," *Grey Room* 05 (Fall 2001): 78–101.

[10] This is obviously a reference to the well-known text by Ernesto Nathan Rogers published in the magazine founded in Milan in 1928, to which he added the suffix *Continuità* when he became its editor in 1953.

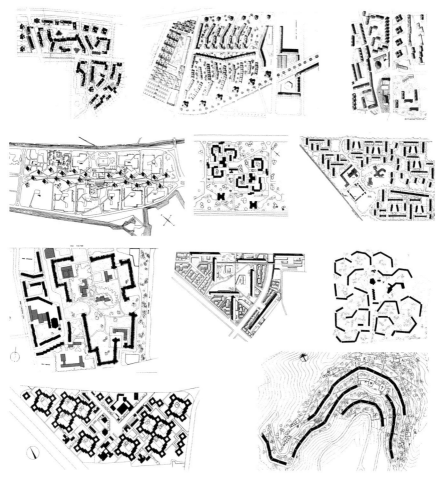

Fig. 2 Montage of plans of several INA-CASA developments: Rome Tiburtino, Rome Tuscolano, Bologna Borgo Panigale, Mestre San Giuliano, Cesate, Milan Feltre, Milan Harar, Turin Falchera, Prato San Giusto, Genoa Forte Quezzi.

In a widespread and variegated way, the exploratory research of the architects working on the INA-Casa Plan generated a testing lab on pressing themes of the modern and contemporary city, which were also soon addressed also on a European level in a critical rethinking of the Modern Movement. In the montage of the plans we can often recognize a composition based on the principle of typological variation, refined by research on the architectural language, a return to the classic themes of urban quality, such as the idea of the street or the piazza, inserted in an overall vision that would consolidate their recognition.

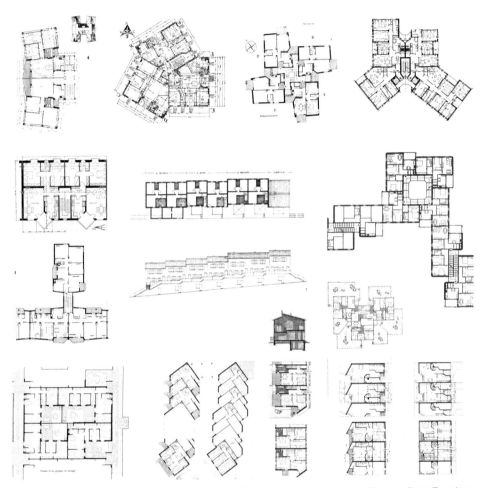

Fig. 3 Montage of plans of several INA-CASA typologies: Bologna Borgo Panigale, Rome Tiburtino, Rome Tuscolano, Milan Feltre, Naples Pontirossi, Rome Tiburtino, Prato San Giusto, Rome Tuscolano, Cesate

The relationship with modernity, on the other hand, passes through less evident features of the language, but ones that set the foundations of the relationships between constructed volumes and the layout of the housing units. The participation of architects, about 17,000 in all, was forcefully encouraged and guided, to reinforce and provide employment for not only the workers, but also for a category that was in a phase of formation: the professional associations had taken form between the two World Wars, and the social role of the professional architect had yet to find sufficient footholds of recognition.

On this theme, the Plan proceeded along two lines: on the one hand, especially in the initial phase, by organizing competitions for the formation of associations of architects, and later by assigning commissions to very large work groups. In the early phase the architects were asked to submit typological projects, while in the second phase for each large-scale project, a numerous group of professionals was formed, with a hierarchical system of group leaders who would help to "assemble" the various design proposals into an organic whole; often the entire plan was designed by one architect, almost always an outstanding figure in the culture of urbanism, such as Gianni Astengo, Saverio Muratori, Luigi Piccinato, Ludovico Quaroni, Giuseppe Samonà[11] or Giuseppe Vaccaro, for example, all figures that controlled the urban scale as well as the design of the building, in a fertile context of know-how that still called for the correlation of two figures that were to be separated in the years to follow, leading to the design of objects on one side, and the specialization of sociological studies on the other. A forceful orientation of form made it possible to control and guide the juxtapositions and the composition of the various units.

It is worth recalling another significant factor brought to light by recent research on the Plan, regarding the construction systems. It is well known that the studies on prefabrication, which in Italy were launched by the school of Colonnetti, had led to real application mainly in industrial buildings: we can state that this was first of all a political choice that imposed continuation of the construction of many developments in keeping with traditional building methods, boosting employment numbers and nurturing local small and medium businesses.[12] A choice determined for the most part by an economic system in need of reinforcement actually gave rise to unexpected architectural results, not only in terms of language and the use of specific materials, but also from the standpoint of the compositional richness of the entire building. Just consider, by comparison, the image of the large French *ensembles* made with prefabrication systems, and their rapid decay.

URBAN RESEARCH AND MORPHOLOGY

As we have already seen, the projects built during the 14 years of the Plan are still well conserved and recognizable, thanks to certain characteristics that represented their basic value: low density, typological-morphological variety, and constructive quality. If we observe the INA-Casa districts inserted in the city which has grown up around them today, we recognize differences of scale, form and proximity: they appear as large areas with extensive green zones, where the citizens have formed "communities" and take good care of their housing units.

[11] See Giuseppe Samonà, *L'Unità Architettura-Urbanistica. Scritti e Progetti 1929–1973*, ed. Pasquale Lovero (Milan: Franco Angeli, 1975).

[12] On this theme, see the essays of Paolo Nicoloso, "Gli architetti: il rilancio di una professione," and Sergio Poretti, "Le tecniche edilizie: modelli per la ricostruzione," in *La Grande Ricostruzione*.

They offer an image that is the opposite of the results of speculation, which is clearly visible in the aerial views of Rome, where the comparison with the clustering and obsessive repetition of the apartments buildings brings out, through contract, the grace of their urban textures. Again, we should remember that the low density had been indicated by the Plan at a maximum of 500 inhabitants per hectare, and that Adalberto Libera had published an article that contained substantial indications for the orientation of the projects, while offering maximum creative freedom to their authors. "To choose designers and not designs," avoiding standard types and their undifferentiated repetition, encouraging the architect's role as an interpreter in relation to the site and the function.

In the article by Libera we find precisely this concept of expressive freedom: *"The housing unit can be expressed in all the development hypotheses, from the single block of Marseille that contains all the community services of the residence, to the most extensive solutions."* The same article returns to the American tradition of "neighbourhood units" as a principle, and their relationship with the entire district, with related services suitable for the two scales: the concept of the unit reflects that of the hierarchy, on a smaller scale than that of the entire settlement, into which to subdivide spaces and inhabitants. Libera's words intertwine the expressive intent of the architect and the sensibility of the social human being.[13]

The result of the individual project is determined by the montage of the variations of the typologies developed down to the smallest details. The choice of the "suggested" building types evokes the recognizability of certain urban themes: the use of linear arrays along the main streets and bordering the space of services, the patterns of juxtaposed tract houses forming residential islands with the counterpoint of tower buildings, compact or with footprints in the form of a star or a cross. This volumetric articulation, balanced in terms of distances between buildings thanks to regulations on exposure to sunlight, soon led to the design of open spaces, of empty areas as well as full zones.

The question of individuality was addressed through the various poetics of the individual designers, who approached their fragments as whole units. In this urban context, design devices were also applied on the scale of the building: the theme of the balcony—the noble balcony of the living area, the service balcony of the kitchen—often became an opportunity for volumetric variation, especially in the compact volumes of the towers, allowing residents to have the relationship with the outdoors that would otherwise seem to be precluded by height. The theme of the entrance, in its many interpretations, was enhanced by recesses, overhangs or steps, breaking up the linear volumes.

[13] "This possibility of social contact, this tendency towards "good neighbourliness" correspond to a spontaneous aspiration of man; urban scholars have recently put an accent on this definition: *voisinage,* community, etc. [...] *Expressive interest.* To plastically express, in unity, the constructed organism, differentiating the fabric from the nucleus, means creating elements of interest: interest in their contrast and their connection; furthermore, it means sustaining the play of plastic composition with the content of real, comprehensible values." Adalberto Libera, "La Scala del Quartiere Residenziale," in Beretta Anguissola, *I 14 Anni...*

In these details that are more volumetric than linguistic in nature, we can clearly see the interpretation of the finest results of the Modern Movement: the gaps between the buildings and the focus on entrances typical of Bruno Taut, or the sculptural approach to balconies of Hans Scharoun. There is also a series of examples that works on the variation and elaboration of a single element, often the courtyard typology rediscovered from its rural origins, and urban research obtained by means of the *dispositio*, as opposed to the interventions generated by specific topographical opportunities.

In all the projects, however, there was a clear, recognizable pursuit of neighbourhood, the identity of which is reinforced through form. Today the entire INA-Casa experience offers an intensive model for reflections on "city parts" as an ongoing and very timely issue. While the traditional compact city had developed in the 1800s according to a system of large expansions of the street network, and the Rationalist city had countered this with residential segments produced as series, with the INA-Casa experience urban design entered a phase that is still very fertile today.

AN ITINERARY THROUGH THE INA-CASA DEVELOPMENTS

To outline a hypothetical voyage through the projects built in Italy from 1949 to 1963, it is useful to start with the ones that interpreted this canon in the most immediate way: these are the two largest districts built in Rome, the Tiburtino and the Tuscolano. The Tiburtino is almost a manifesto: an explicit rebuttal of the Rationalist experience is obtained by closely listening to the geographical situation, accentuated by the desire to rethink the scale of the village, where the street accompanies juxtaposed houses held together by a system of patios, balconies, and public staircases, true monuments to the collective role of circulation spaces; these are supplemented by open spaces and the careful placement of taller buildings. In this district designed by Ludovico Quaroni and Mario Ridolfi, the latter created many building types, from the tract houses described above to the linear arrays marked by the rotation of the balcony of his Siamese buildings at Terni, all the way to the tower typologies, with a star-shaped footprint, featuring the distributed composition of three residential units. From the beautiful perspective drawings, which remind us of the Townscape sketches of Gordon Cullen, we can fully grasp the objective of defining what Ridolfi himself called "ambient space," where the focus on community spaces and their mediation with respect to the domestic dimension are controlled down to the detail of the balustrades in perforated brick.

Fig. 4 Study sketches for the Rome Tiburtino district, Mario Ridolfi

The experience of the Tuscolano district is organized in three recognizable phases: while the first places linear volumes to form large urban courtyards, the second, designed by Saverio Muratori and Mario De Renzi, acknowledged masters of studies on building typology and urban morphology,[14] is based on two long orthogonal linear volumes, of which the first functions as the spine of the layout, while the second bends to form a central piazza; the footprint is then completed by buildings with wings that form a contrast with the handsome towers by De Renzi. The third phase, in which Adalberto Libera was to make one of his most famous works, seems to have been lifted from another time.

[14] Saverio Muratori, *Studi per un'Operante Storia Urbana di Venezia* (1959)

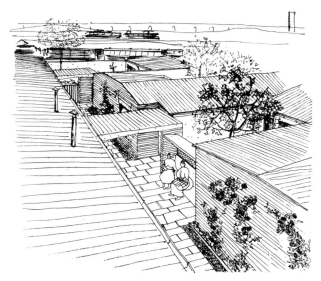

Fig. 5 Study sketches for the Rome Tuscolano district, Adalberto Libera

Fig. 6 Study sketches for the Prato San Giusto district, Ludovico Quaroni

The horizontal unit, the low and compact fabric of the patio houses concluding the herringbone of Muratori, is a skilful mixture of domestic space and relational zones. The traditional courtyard building, reduced to minimum areas here thanks to the spatial layout and the central role of the private patio, ramifies in streets inside the district, places of community life *par excellence*, designed with canopies and benches as places in which to spend time with neighbours.

At the core of this urban fabric that crosses Pompeii with Mies van der Rohe, Libera places a simple balcony building that stands on *pilotis*, rising from this apparently undifferentiated scheme. Layouts similar to those of the Roman districts, in terms of variety and counterpoint, were also applied in different geographical contexts, demonstrating the capacity to listen to the site that was one of the earmarks of the Plan.

In Bologna, in the Borgo Panigale district, Giuseppe Vaccaro extends linear volumes over the plain of the city, long porticos of shops like those of the historical centre, linear arrays of houses varied by volumetric solutions that accentuate the theme of the entrance. The idea of the street is broken down into the various housing units: the linear array that acts as the back of the layout forms an urban sequence, from the porticoes of the first segment to the image of the clustered houses of the countryside in the last segment. The entire district, with a wide range of services, offers a variety of duplex tract houses and linear rows marked by vivid volumetric shifts based on setbacks and rotations, generating different relational spaces. The rarefaction of the layout is achieved to the south with a shift of scale and proportions: from the series of the L-shaped houses to the rhythm of the tall buildings whose H-shaped footprint alludes to the small courtyards that mark the entrances of the residences. Perhaps one of the finest architectural results, this building offers a delicate solution for the graft between loggia, window, and facade, and with its two rising wings resembles the refined architectural figures of Luigi Moretti.

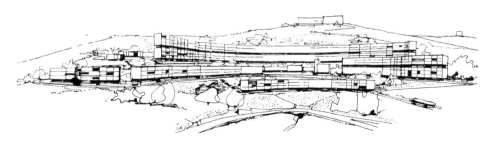

Fig. 7 Study sketches for the Genoa Forte Quezzi, Luigi Daneri

Fig. 8 Detail of the balcony and the facade in Tiburtino in Rome

The project where we can best observe the relationship between neighbourhood unit and the entire settlement is the one developed by Giuseppe Samonà and Luigi Piccinato for San Giuliano in Mestre. The plan embodies a metropolitan scale with a modern character, and it is no coincidence that we can compare it to the studies of Piero Bottoni for the Gallaratese district in Milan, organized with a similar layout relying on a central green spine; nevertheless, the contrast between the low density and traditional form of the courtyards of the neighbourhood units and the towers that pace the central axis demonstrates a very sensitive control of scales and spaces, also corresponding to careful design of primary and secondary circulation. The photographs clearly show the fragmented continuity of the low houses deployed to form a "*campiello*"[15] in the foreground, and the skilful use of the rhythmical tower to create a landmark against the background.

[15] According to a definition supplied by Giuseppe Samonà.

A similar system of organization by units, but very different in terms of scale, was applied at Cesate, on the western outskirts of Milan, in a locality served by the railway. In this context characterized by the idea of the garden city,[16] the most outstanding figures of the reconstruction of Milan made contributions: the firm BBPR,[17] Ignazio Gardella, and Franco Albini developed tract housing typologies that fully reflect the knowledge of living spaces the architects were developing in their urban works. The elegance of the houses of Gardella and the experimentation on open space seen in his work on Milanese bourgeois homes are taken to the minimum dimension of low-cost housing for workers, arranged in a variegated sequence of green areas faced by the typical vertical floor-to-ceiling windows borrowed from the Lombard tradition. Such themes were also addressed in the houses by the firm BBPR, enhanced by sloping roofs and cornices that generate a new spatial complexity in their cross-section.

The interlocks of the unique L-shaped houses by Albini, with their slight slope with respect to the new *centuratio*, form a sort of plaza that sets the single units apart, connected by a portico that marks the entrance. In this rarified construction, the definition of collective or private green spaces takes on a decisive role in determining the image of low density punctuated by sculptural finesses that gives the front entrances, terraces, and recesses, or controlled flexing of the ordering masonry elements.

[16] Warner Sirtori, Maria Prandi, *Il Villaggio INA-Casa di Cesate, Architettura e Comunità* (Milan: Mimesis, 2016).

[17] Belgiojoso, Peressutti, and Rogers, the designers—among other works in Milan—of the Torre Velasca.

Fig. 9 The Franco Albini terraced houses in Cesate

Fig. 10 Aerial photograph of the Harar district in Milan

The case of the Harar Dessiè project in Milan by Figini & Pollini and Gio Ponti, and that of the Feltre district, stand out as unique proposals on the Italian scene[18] due to the modernity of their urban approach, with the idea of the park as the central element of the system. Here the variation of the urban scale is obtained by the counter-placement of long constructed volumes, "horizontal skyscrapers" perpendicular to each other, set on the ground to enclose a large green space in which to freely organize the services. In this reversal of the idea of traditional city walls, which kept green nature outside, here low-density tract houses are placed outside, small *insulae* different from one another, to mediate the relationship with the context. The three orthogonal pairs of long buildings are designed in a very different way by Ponti and by Figini & Pollini: while the first works on the typology of linear rows, where the layout of two apartments per floor is underlined by the overhanging facade elements, in the case of the balcony building by the duo of Rationalist architects, the reference is the two-storey duplex cell, clearly inserted in a grid that forms the front.

The Feltre district in the historical industrial fabric of north-eastern Milan stands out for the proportions and radical character of the project: a single typology—a linear building ten storeys high—is organized in a sawtooth pattern to enclose a large urban park. This is a provocative proposal of a new idea of the city, positing the monumental approach to a way of living in contrast with the urban features that determined the modest character of the historical city, with its 19th-century blocks of narrow courtyards and repeated street frontage.

[18] To get an idea of the scope of the public residential projects in Milan, see the article that indicates, covering IACP, INCIS, and INA-CASA, that "over one fifth of the Milanese population found housing in subsidized constructions." Virgilio Vercelloni, "Alcuni Quartieri di Edilizia Sovvenzionata a Milano," *Casabella-Continuità*, no. 253 (July 1961): 42–49.

The group of designers was very large, and the design system was coordinated by Pollini with a system of project leaders; among the names of the many architects involved, we can mention Giancarlo De Carlo, Ignazio Gardella, Angelo Mangiarotti, Bruno Morassutti, Vittoriano Viganò. The system called for coordination of the single projects in the montage of a single linear volume that bent to form the corners of the park, in which the joint and the ends became opportunities to achieve volumetric variety. The urban composition of the parts is entirely made by means of lines that advance and retreat, which overlap to enclose a small plaza or separate to open to the landscape, even bending at the ends to become towers. The uniform language of the brick infill and fair-face concrete structures offers a clear view of the various facade solutions.

While the main part of the district takes a distance from references to the classical city, focusing on a strong idea of the modern city based on the relationship with nature, to the west the layout opens towards the existing city: low four-storey volumes act as a form of mediation, like a wing with respect to the height behind them.

Just as Feltre is organized starting with a single typological idea that is repeated, varied, and reassembled in the unity of the large central space, so in the Falchera development in Turin, designed by Gianni Astengo, a single-building typology—the linear three-storey volume broken up to border a green space—is multiplied on the terrain in an organic manner, with very low density.

Fig. 11 Aerial photograph of the Feltre district in the context.
Photo by Stefano Topuntoli.

The case of Quaroni's project for San Giusto in Prato, on the other hand, has a more stepped arrangement: the constructed unit of the courtyard building, combined with linear rows, determines neighbourhood units enclosed in larger courtyards that freely interact, forming circulation axes of constructed backdrops. This district displays a certain schematic leaning that Manfredo Tafuri interpreted as a conscious perception of the impossibility of really making a city.[19]

The case of Forte Quezzi in Genoa, designed by Luigi Daneri, of which five of the volumes were built, concludes a path that begins with the figure of the village and then fully enters the ranks of modernity by going back to the idea of Le Corbusier, that of making the residence into a large territorial infrastructure. The figure of the *Plan Obus* for Algiers is arranged here amidst the folds of the *creuze de mä*, experimenting with alignment with contour curves of the condensing building, which, as in the case of the *Unité*, would gather the complexity of the city with its services into its cross-section, all the way to the idea of the elevated street. A duplex cell and a facade grid, in their various architectural solutions, formulate this powerful figure in the landscape.

[19] "The complexity of the city cannot be tamed by dividing it into finite parts; yet this is the "condition" imposed by the policy of INA-Casa. All that remains is to embrace this contradiction and to allow for its expression," Manfredo Tafuri, *Storia dell'Architettura Italiana 1944–1985*, Einaudi, Torino 1986, p. 59.

Fig. 12 Genoa Forte Quezzi view from the street

TIMELINESS OF THE ACHIEVEMENTS OF THE INA-CASA PLAN

In spite of the many differences we have observed in this voyage across the complexity of Italy, where the North approaches design as an opportunity for morphological experimentation, the Centre recovers the characteristics of the tradition and the South often leans towards a rationalism criticized and surpassed elsewhere, certain parts of the INA-Casa experience can still be seen today as an important lesson in the field of the design of social housing.

In the awareness of a certain lack of urban character of many of these examples, where housing is often nostalgically seen in terms of a minute, fragmented image like that of villages, the Plan led to a number of important achievements. Not only the organization of the financial machinery, but also and above all the effective oxymoron of light regulation that was able to transmit precise guidelines, which had a forceful influence on the structure and form of the projects. These guidelines addressed a number of themes that are still very timely, as is demonstrated by the recent revival of figures from the 1950s like A. & P. Smithson or other members of Team X who worked on the concept of the *Community*; on spaces of mediation and typological *mixité*, all questions are also addressed in the most recent contemporary projects in this field.

BIBLIOGRAPHY

L'INA-CASA al IV Congresso Nazionale di Urbanistica, Venezia, October 1952.

Ponti, Gio. "Il Quartiere INA-Casa in Via Dessié a Milano." Domus no. 270 (May 1952).

Italia 1961. Occupazione Operaia-Case ai Lavoratori. Tivoli: Gestione INACASA, 1961.

Anguissola, Luigi Beretta. *I 14 anni del Piano INA Casa*. Rome: Staderini, 1963.

Vercelloni, Virgilio. "Alcuni Quartieri di Edilizia Sovvenzionata a Milano." Casabella no. 253 (July 1961).

Reichlin, Bruno. "Figures of Neorealism in Italian Architecture." Grey Room no. 5 (Fall 2001).

La Grande Ricostruzione. Il Piano INA-Casa e l'Italia degli anni '50, edited by Paola Di Biagi. Rome: Donzelli, 2001.

Stephanie Zeier Pilat. *Reconstructing Italy. The INA-Casa Neighborhoods of the Postwar Era*. New York: Routledge, 2016.

The Portuguese Minister for the Interior visits a new estate in Lisbon, where staircases and common hallways were enlarged to create convivial areas.

Revista Municipal de Lisboa, no. 120–121, year XXX, 1969.

4. HOUSE, URBAN SPRAWL, AND REVOLUTION (1968–1974)

A new dictator, a colonial war and growing social unrest shifted the attention of politicians to internal and external affairs, clearing the road for technicians and experts to experiment in and discuss housing and city planning in a more evolved and socially conscious manner. As in Spain, the focal point was not just the provision of housing, but the importance of *the right to the city*.

Urban Planning and Development Agency Housing Estates in Spain: Bigador's Operational Urbanism (1939–1969)

LUIS MOYA
Technical University of Madrid, School of Architecture

ABSTRACT

This paper reviews the Urban Planning and Development Agency (1959–1969) as an example of Operational Urban Planning, a process in which the Spanish Administration implemented a complete urbanization process, essentially in order to develop land quickly, hand it over to other official bodies and private promoters at a low price to generate affordable social housing and, at a later date, industrial estates as well. This process must be appreciated in its economic and political context: an autarchic military dictatorship and then an authoritarian regime driven by a liberal developmentalist philosophy. The Office head was architect Pedro Bidagor, the driving force for the establishment of modern planning in Spain, who initially enjoyed the confidence of the Regime but gradually became an impediment to its liberal laissez–faire agenda.

The paper also looks at two issues that help to explain the outcome of these actions. One was the general context of the building sector as part of the property business, a Spanish peculiarity since the start of the 20th century, in which land and property prices have been subject to speculation. One repercussion of this has been that only approx. 1 per cent of the volume of social housing is publicly owned with social rental prices. The other issue is the interesting theoretical framework encountered by the technicians in charge of urban planning and architecture, especially architects.

Finally, several conclusions are drawn from the experience of the Urban Planning and Development Agency, including the validity of Operational Urban Planning, updated to keep a pace with Spain's changed economic, political, and social context. The country has a serious shortfall in social housing, an aspect in which the growth of the global economy is not benefiting the modest layers of society. However, it is also an area in which technical expertise and tools are highly appropriate for a socially aware society which is not seeing its demands being answered by the political class.

BIOGRAPHY

PhD in Architecture. Professor in the Technical School of Architecture of Madrid (UPM) since 1985, and by the School ofArchitecture of Valladolid since 1983, and Graduate in European High Studies by the European College in Bruges (Belgium). Expertise: Town Centre Rehabilitation and Monument Restoration, Landscape and Urban Planning, and Social Housing. Five six year periods of acknowledged research experience, recognized by the Ministry of Education. Research and teaching activity in European and American Universities. Professional activity in a private office for Architecture and Urbanism; also project regarding landscape and public spaces He has published many articles and books of his research and work. Several of his professional works have been awarded. He has also taken on responsibilities in academic and cultural management. Actually direct a Group Research about Social Housing working for the municipality of Madrid and the revision of its Structure Plan.

Fig. 1 Standard blocks designed by the Urban Planning and Development Agency.

Fig. 2 Location of the Decongestion Estate, Toledo.

Fig. 3 Sector of the Decongestion Estate, Toledo.

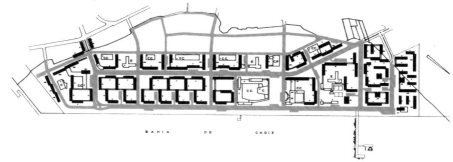
Fig. 4 Location of the Los Corrales Estate, Cadiz. 44 ha.

URBAN PLANNING AND DEVELOPMENT AGENCY HOUSING ESTATES IN SPAIN: BIGADOR'S OPERATIONAL URBANISM (1939–1969)

BACKGROUND

The "Gerencia de Urbanización" (Urban Planning and Development Agency) was set up in 1959 with the core mission of rapidly urbanising land that would be handed over at a low cost to other official agencies and private developers for the construction of affordable social housing and, later on, industrial land as well. In this paper we analyse this process and its main driving force, the architect Pedro Bidagor (1906–1996).

The Spanish economy is largely focused on the building sector as a private initiative, and in this context, Social Housing (hereinafter SH) has had a difficult history. Like other European countries, this history began at the start of the 20th century, with the Low-Cost Housing Act of 1911 drafted by the Social Reforms Commission and Institute, both bodies linked to the progressive Free Educational Institution, which was keenly aware of the exploitation of proletariat housing in the previous century.

Under the Primo de Rivera dictatorship, this Act was modified in the second Low-Cost Housing Act (1924), which outlined the destiny of SH for the rest of the 20th century—to be entrusted to private initiative, which logically approached it as a business opportunity.[1] Home rental still prevailed over ownership at the time. In 1940, after the Spanish Civil War, almost 90 per cent of dwellings were rented (in 1950, 88 per cent were rented, 6 per cent were owned and 6 per cent had other arrangements, according to Foessa). The lucrative property market has led to exactly the opposite situation today, with almost 90 per cent in ownership[2] and only 1 per cent held by the administration for social rental.

---

[1] For more details on this issue, see Luis Moya "Los Antecedentes Franquistas de la Política de VS," *Cuadernos de Investigación Urbanística*, No. 100 (2015).

[2] This situation is now changing with the likely commencement of a second property boom in 2017.

CHRONOLOGY OF URBAN PLANNING AND SOCIAL HOUSING 1939–1975

The following timeline may help to explain the trends in urban development that influenced SH and its management organisations from the end of the Spanish Civil War in 1939 until the death of Franco in 1975:

- *1939—Establishment of the following bodies: INV (National Housing Institute), technical head, José Fonseca, architect; Junta de Reconstrucción de Madrid (Madrid Reconstruction Committee), technical head, Pedro Bidagor, architect; Dirección General de Regiones Devastadas (Directorate-General for Devastated Regions); and the Instituto Nacional de Colonización (National Colonisation Institute).*
- *1941—Approval of the INV Architectural-Planning ordinances, the only regulation for public initiatives also used by the private sector. Establishment of the INI (National Industry Institute)*
- *1942—Establishment of the "Obra Sindical del Hogar" or Home Construction Union (OSH), for SH construction, and the Provincial Planning Commissions.*
- *1946—Approval of the Madrid Master Plan, Spain's first such plan and a model for other cities.*
- *1949—Establishment of the Directorate-General of Architecture and the National Planning Office under the Ministry of Government Services (now Interior) with Bidagor as head technician.*
- *1956—Passage of the Land Act, largely directed and drafted by Bidagor.*
- *1957—Establishment of the Ministry of Housing, with the architect Arrese as minister, the Directorate-General of Urban Planning, with Bidagor as head, merged with the Directorate-General of Architecture, also under the Ministry of Government Services. Approval of the Madrid Decongestion Operation (Estates).*
- *1959—Establishment of the Gerencia de Urbanización (Urban Planning and Development Agency) and approval of the General Planning Standards for Partial Plans on new Estates. Francisco Cabrero and Cesar Sanz Pastor as directors, Miguel Duran as technical author of "rationalist" regulations.*
- *1961—National Housing Plan, with "organicist" planning regulations.*
- *1964—First Economic and Social Development Plan. Commissioner Laureano Lopez Rodó.*
- *1965—2nd period of the Urban Planning and Development Agency, structural concept, fluidity. Julio Cano (architect) as head technician.*
- *1969—National Urban Planning Institute to replace the Urban Planning and Development Agency, under Minister Vicente Mortes and Director of Planning Antonio Linares, a civil engineer.*
- *1970—ACTUR Programme (Urgent Urban Development Actions).*

Fig. 5 Las Lastras Estate, Segovia. 22 ha.

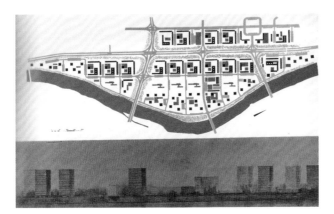

Fig. 6 Sector of Huerta del Rey Estate. 60 ha.

Fig. 7 Landaben Industrial Estate, Pamplona. 68 ha.

ESTABLISHMENT OF THE URBAN PLANNING AND DEVELOPMENT AGENCY AND ITS THEORETICAL FRAMEWORK

Large-scale urban drift from the Spanish countryside took place in the 1950s. Politicians began to worry about the shanty towns that were springing up in the cities because of their potential threat as a hotbed of subversion. Progressive church movements moved into these districts and their places of worship hosted neighbourhood and social movements. In some districts, these movements were even actually led by worker priests, some of whom became acknowledged as leaders, such as the famous Padre Llanos in the Pozo del Tío Raimundo district and Padre Jimenez de Parga in Palomeras. At the same time, a section of the Falange movement also built bridges with the social aspects of the fascist ideology, and some architects working in the political sphere were members of the Falange, including José Luis de Arrese, Minister of Housing (1957–1960), along with political technicians such as Pedro Muguruza, Director-General of Devastated Regions and Architecture, Pedro Bidagor, Director-General of Urban Planning and José Fonseca, Head Technician of the INV.

During the post-war period, Arrese stood out as a leading architect, Bidagor as an urban planner and Fonseca as a housing expert. A common aspect shared with other European dictatorships was the supreme leader's interest in urban planning and architecture, and hence the use of architects as essential allies, first of all to create a scenario and a representation of his power and, in the case of Francisco Franco, to fulfil his promise to give every Spaniard a home. He commissioned Pedro Muguruza to reorganize the profession under the Falange and to expel any architects suspected of having collaborated with the Republic, which forced many of them into exile.[3] The administration took several important steps to improve the housing situation, in view of the inoperative initiative private sector, which was not yet prepared to risk its capital on SH, investing instead in luxury and bourgeois homes and, in the 1960s, in tourism. The Land Act was passed in 1956, and in 1957 the Ministry of Housing was set up to implement a Social Emergency Plan under Minister Arrese. The main purpose of this Plan was to boost private initiatives and encourage the sector to become involved in the construction of SH with government support. At the end of the 1950s, Spain moved out of its autarchic isolation when the US, clearly interested in setting up several military bases in the country, accepted the Franco regime.

[3] On this subject see, AAVVV, *Arquitectura Española del Exilio* (Lampreave, 2015).

The Urban Planning and Development Agency was set up in 1959 as an independent body with a specific budget under the Housing Ministry's Directorate General of Urban Planning, and Bidagor was appointed as its Director. The early 1960s saw a new a phase for the National Planning Office with the construction of large estates containing anything from 500 to 10,000 homes throughout Spain, with densities of up to 500 inhabitants per hectare. The sizes of the dwellings ranged between 38 and 150 m^2, although the average was less than 60 m^2. This was all the result of the regulations set out in the 1961 National Housing Plan which was applied universally, even by private projects.

At the end of the war, the theoretical framework was heavily influenced by orthodox rationalism, in some cases with a pseudo-vernacular, ruralist veneer proposed by the fascist ideologues of post-war Spain. This is especially evident in the urban and architectural regulations drafted personally by José Fonseca for the INV in 1941. This architect had received a solid training in European functionalism in Germany during the 1930s, which explains his inclusion in these regulations of measures such as the elimination of all adornment, a tight distribution of interiors, dual-aspect apartment blocks combined with single-family terraced houses, separation of road traffic and pedestrian islands with facilities in the centre, and the spread of constructions into open and theoretically green spaces.

In the 1950s, Spain witnessed an unabashed inclusion of the principles of the organicist version of rationalism in its new SH complexes under the influence of trends in northern European countries, but without losing the ruralist touch, as indicated by their description as "poblados" or townships. This was a type of organicism that had evolved from orthodox rationalism, promoted at the fourth CIAM in 1933. It was reflected in the 1941 Athens Charter and espoused by architects like the Smithsons and Bakema, amongst others.

This approach brought in a sociological perspective, with greater priority given in the project to the encouragement of the community through appropriate spaces, although in doing so, they broke away from the hitherto undisputed priorities of solar orientation, zoning, and hygienic values in general, which were pushed into the background without being entirely abandoned.

Abercrombie and Forshaw's 1943 County of London Plan had a major influence on the Spanish planners, along with new concepts that triggered a crisis in the positivist scientism applied to urban planning, rightly criticized by people such as philosopher Henri Bergson (1859–1941) for defending the specificity of each place as opposed to a search for universal solutions, and the value of intuition in the analysis of real situations. This new organic rationalist vision was also more appropriate for the Franco Regime, which it considered to be coherent with its ideology: life in rural settings as opposed to dehumanizing parallel blocks, and an absence of places for congregation, which they went so far as to dismiss as "Republican." In 1951, Emilio Larrodera (Bidagor's successor as head designer of the 1963 Madrid Master Plan) and Manuel Ribas Piera (designer of the Barcelona plan), both Professors of Urban Planning, learned from Gaston Bardet and his theory of community steps, recommended by the 1943 Barlow Commission in England as a pattern for structuring cities. These steps and their respective facilities were defined as: neighbourhood units: 5,000 inhabitants and 10 hectares; suburb units: 20,000 residents and 40 ha.; and district units: 100,000 residents and 250 ha.[4]

In the mid-1950s, the architect Julián Laguna, Commissioner for Urban Planning in Madrid, contracted several of his young companions to design the SH townships. Many later became renowned masters of architecture: Alejandro de la Sota, Francisco Sáenz de Oiza, Romaní, Vázquez de Castro, Íñiguez de Onzoño, Carvajal and Cano, amongst others. These architects strove to incorporate the contemporary architecture they had learned about from publications or trips to northern Europe, overcoming the difficulties of a country that was slowly emerging from isolation. They implemented a creative, functional interpretation of these principles, although the circumstances forced them to design excessively economic versions.[5] The low budgets were employed to build as many houses as possible. In some cases, the planned facilities were not built, and the public spaces were left incomplete.

Later, in the 1960s, new conceptions of space emerged amongst planning theorists, especially with regard to the boundaries and isolation of communities, under the influence of the work of Catherine Bauer in the USA and Chombart de Lauwe in France. Fernando de Terán explains that they sought ."... *a continuous, fluid structure defined by relations and movements that originate in the features of the urban grid, on the basis of which experimental sociological studies provide us with an understanding and control of the so-called 'lifeblood' of the city-places that are enhanced by more frequent use, the attractiveness of different spaces, which depends on their characteristics, the impact produced by the construction of buildings and centres for certain uses.*"

[4] Gabriel Alomar's book *Comunidad Planada* (Instituto de Estudios de Administración Local, 1955) was a major reference point for technicians.

[5] Luis Moya, *Barrios de Promoción Oficial: Madrid 1939–1976* (COAM, 1983). This book was the first study of these districts, with a record of each of the 116 zones and an analysis of the socio-political context.

He also defined quite modern criteria, explaining that *".. the conceptual evolution of planning and design is now characterized by the inclusion of formal and functional complexity, the variety and combination of uses, going beyond simplistic outlines, flexibility, adaptability and the desire to include a degree of indetermination that leaves the door open to evolution and maturing by means of additions and retouches, in an attempt to incorporate something like the process of historical maturing in the planned city."*[6]

In Spain, Mario Gaviria, sociologist and disciple of Henri Lefebvre, exercised a major influence through numerous essays on the issue and lectures on urban sociology at several schools, particularly with respect to the sociology of housing at the Madrid School of Architecture in 1968, as an associate of José Fonseca.[7]

Pedro Bidagor deserves a separate section in this paper and an entire book on his work as an urban planner. He played a leading role in Spanish urban planning during the 1940s, 1950s, and 1960s, and was largely responsible for the modernization of urban planning under the Franco dictatorship, although the practical results were few.

The only doubt that may remain is how Spanish urban planning would have evolved without him. Looking at his life, his training, his starting point in 1930s Germany, his capacity for hard work and his efforts to set up a town and country planning system in Spain, one cannot help but regard him as a Quixote tilting at windmills.

At the end of the Civil War, he was convinced, along with another prominent architect and mentor, Pedro Muguruza, that the new Spain needed a new type of land planning, and he set about to create it. He organized a near-military hierarchical administrative system that worked on the entire process, from the general down to the specific. In other words, during one particular stage of his professional life, he organised the nation as a territory, he drafted the 1956 Land Act almost single-handedly, and he designed the excellent Extension of Madrid's Castellana artery.

Unfortunately, the Development Plans and the new tourist resorts ultimately distorted this territorial planning strategy, the provisions of Land Act were not respected and the morphology of the Castellana extension was changed from closed blocks to open blocks very soon after construction began, distorting the original project in order to adapt to the new private modes of housing promotion in the 1960s.

[6] Fernando de Terán, "*Evolución del Planeamiento de Núcleos Urbanos Nuevos*" Ciudad y Territorio, no.1 (1969):13-23.

[7] I was fortunate to be a member of the generation of students who received classes from him and later worked on his projects. Much later, we shared the project for the new University of Burgos campus. I was always impressed by his knowledge and innovative capacity. He died in 2018.

His professional career began with the reconstruction of a destroyed Madrid, besieged throughout the Civil War (1936–39). He was firstly appointed as Head of the Madrid Reconstruction Board (1939–46), then Technical Director of the Madrid Urban Planning Commission (1946–56), and afterwards Director-General of Urban Planning, which included the Urban Development Office (1957–69). In the Urban Planning Commission, he was appointed as Director of the Madrid Master Plan, ratified in 1946.

In all his government administrative assignments, he championed the struggle against land speculation, varying his methods with the circumstances at each moment. Proof of this can be found in the text he wrote for a Housing Ministry publication on the body's activity,[8] a section of which is included below. It deals with his attempt to control land prices from the Urban Development Office at the height of the 1960s property boom:

"These policy lines are all the more necessary due to the urgent nature of problems related to housing and industrialisation, which are of general interest to the Community, but are hampered by the resistance of landowners, accustomed as they are to easy income from speculation, waiting for the urban development to happen as a result of the efforts of others, and then reaping disproportionate financial benefits, a veritable lottery that is financially onerous and often suffocates all collective effort. Exorbitant land prices have a capricious impact on home rental and factory products. They are a direct cause of inflation, they are an impediment to building improvements and hence the health and happiness of the people, they prevent green spaces from being set aside and they make it difficult to establish social services because the exaggerated land prices are unaffordable. This state of affairs results in the serious anachronism that while the city administration authorities suffer from shortages and as a result, cannot attend to the most elementary issues such as setting up and maintaining community services, so fundamental in the life of today's society, the owners of the lands win—joyfully and avariciously—exorbitant financial benefits from the increased value of their properties that is generated by the efforts of the community, to which they have not contributed themselves."

Bidagor was responsible for a radical change to the concept of planning. Even after the Civil War, Spanish urban planning still relied on the 19th century technique of expansion districts, which were built by the city councils. Previously, under the brief Republican period, more contemporary types of territorial planning were seen in Madrid and Barcelona, but there was no time for their consolidation. Bigador drew up a centralised hierarchical national planning organisation that was based administratively and geographically in Madrid.

---

[8] *Gerencia de Urbanización, 1959-1964*, MV, 1964.

It relied largely on technical authoritarianism and expropriation for its implementation. He advocated a type of planning that focused more on function than form, with specific short-term initiatives, the avoidance of parallel private developments for speculative purposes, and municipal planning that was linked to territorial, development and tourism plans. He incorporated the time factor, so important for effective action and the prevention of speculation, with economic and financial studies and plans with different stages as part of the urban planning documents.

His rationality found itself increasingly in confrontation with totally different criteria defended by other government bodies that had more resources and were unwilling to submit to the dictates of the urban planning guidelines, and private promoters who were able to impose their interest in short-term profit by putting pressure on the undemocratic town councils of the time.

Anticipating events in the new developmentalist phase envisaged for the 1960s, he made efforts to adapt by setting up the Urban Planning and Development Agency in 1959 to implement what in Britain was known as Operational Planning. The administration was the agent that looked for the appropriate land, expropriated it (in Spain, facilitated by an authoritarian political regime), zoned it, developed it and built on it in partnership with other official bodies, or sold it, with certain conditions, at a low cost to private developers. This ensured congruence with planning guidelines, optimised locations, connections to infrastructure, facilities, and services, and also the potential for more contemporary designs and the concentration of the construction process into a given period, without holding back for speculative purposes. It also ensured full funding for the operation and helped to produce a degree of market regulation. The Urban Planning and Development Agency was an autonomous body under the Housing Ministry with a separate budget which included, when necessary, that of the National Housing Institute (INV) for residential estates, the National Industry Institute (INI) for industrial estates, and later the Development Plan Commission for both types of use. The above-mentioned 1964 publication, reviewing the first five years of the Office's operation, reports that work had been done on 226 estates that covered 14,723 hectares of land, two thirds of which were residential and one third industrial, with a capacity for 900,000 homes and 400,000 jobs respectively. The operational planning initiatives by the Urban Planning and Development Agency included an interesting land planning programme aimed at reducing Madrid's congestion with promotions in the surrounding regions, commissioned in 1960 by the Interministerial Commission.

Decongestion nodes were built in the outskirts of Toledo, Guadalajara, Manzanares, Alcázar de San Juan, and Aranda de Duero with a view to stemming the heavy urban drift towards Madrid. The Toledo initiative had 120,000 inhabitants while the others were for 60,000 residents in each case. At the time, Madrid was receiving 30,000 inhabitants per year. Morphologically and typologically, they followed the above-mentioned principles, and acted as a model for private initiative.

The First Development Plan (1964–68) and the start of the tourist boom mowed down the rational planning model drawn up by the Directorate-General of Urban Planning under Bidagor, since both of them involved the design of their own plans or *modus operandi*. The Development Plans were answerable to the Development Commission, set up under the 1959 Stabilization Plan, which became the Ministry of Planning and Development from 1967 to 1973. Commissioner and later Minister Laureano Lopez Rodó was a liberal thinker on economic matters, and therefore clashed in many respects with the Falangist *dirigisme*. Planning for the tourist industry was placed in the hands of the Ministry of Information and Tourism, set up in 1962. Its operations were mainly focused on the exhaustive exploitation of the eastern Mediterranean and Andalusian coastline. The town councils, controlled by the Interior Ministry, were influenced by local economic stakeholders and issued licenses that disregarded the approved planning guidelines or simply looked the other way.[9]

[9] In addition, each Ministry belonged to a different political clan. Urban planning and housing remained in the hands of the Falange, the economy came under the control of a new force, Opus Dei, and the administration of the dictatorship's municipal councils gradually broke away from the Falangist policies drawn up by the movement's founder, Primo de Rivera (son of the 1920s dictator) and moved towards a more accommodating regime.

FINAL STAGES OF THE URBAN PLANNING AND DEVELOPMENT AGENCY

The Urban Planning and Development Agency continued to work on these issues until 1969 when the new Minister, Vicente Mortes, with a liberal economic approach, changed its name to the National Urban Planning and Development Institute and replaced Bidagor with engineer Antonio Linares as head of the Directorate-General for Urban Planning. This new Director focused on three issues: re-establishing planning discipline—a difficult task given that the city councils responsible for its direct control were answerable to the Interior Ministry, the large-scale release of land to private initiative using rights to land—hitherto impossible because it affected the property speculation business, and ACTUR (Urgent Urban Development Actions)—the only initiative that went ahead.

The ACTUR consisted of creating new urban hubs at a certain distance from the big cities in order to decongest them. Their goals, set out in the Ministry project, were *"to facilitate the formation of integrated urban development units where housing will be built for families with different income levels, especially for workers, to provide the newly built neighbourhoods with all the collective facilities and complementary services required by modern life, and to set aside enough space for the installation of businesses which will provided jobs for the working population."*[10] The Madrid Decongestion Estates were part of a territorial strategy for the region, while the ACTUR were devised as decentralisation hubs for several large cities, interconnected with them by motorways and public transport while maintaining a degree of independence. Some of them—Tres Cantos, outside Madrid, for example—were designed to be new cities following the British and French models, but most were large-scale urban developments on the outskirts of cities. Linares represented modernity, and his Directorate was joined by a Study Cabinet commissioned to draft a new Land Act that would be more flexible than its predecessors,[11] and also to manage the ACTUR.

The ACTUR, like other Spanish government operations with the "urgent" tag attached, were declared to be "Of social interest," paving the way for land acquisition by expropriation and new developments unforeseen in the planning guidelines, in order to purchase land zoned as rural at a low cost. This trend in the final years of the decade led Bidagor to distance himself voluntarily from the urban planning sphere, which for the new department heads meant the disappearance of an obstacle to the developmentalist mindset of the new Spanish economic climate.

[10] Decree-Law of 27 June 1970.

[11] The 1975 Land Act modernised the 1956 Act and made it more flexible in several respects, one of them being the inclusion of a new classification, Non-Programmed Buildable Land.

The eight ACTUR initiatives began in the 1970s and ended in the 1980s. The sites, totalling 11,000 hectares, were planned to absorb one million residents in Tres Cantos (Madrid), Riera de Caldas, Sabadell-Tarrasa, and Martorell (Barcelona), Vilanova (Valencia), La Cartuja (Seville), Puente de Santiago (Zaragoza), and Río S. Pedro (Cádiz). The government acknowledged that despite the magnitude of this programme, it was still insufficient to halt the excessive growth of the cities, but it wanted to be an exemplary spearhead for private initiative, which at the time was generally involved in smaller-scale initiatives.

The results varied greatly, depending on the intrinsic conditions of each ACTUR site (location, infrastructure, particular objectives) and the quality of the project, and also the vicissitudes of the period that followed its approval: the death of the dictator, the birth of a democratic political system and the Autonomous Regions, the legalisation of parties including the Communist Party, which always monitored urban planning issues closely, and the power of the newly elected municipal councils by universal suffrage.

Tres Cantos, 25 km from Madrid and part of the Colmenar Viejo municipality at the time, is now an independent municipality with a motorway and a suburban rail link to Madrid. Its first residents arrived in 1982. It has a high environmental quality, with views of the nearby Guadarrama Mountains from its circumscribed built-up island. Its project has been widely praised, with balanced uses as suggested in the ministerial brief for the operation, although there is no correspondence between workplaces and residence. It has a Y-shape layout with a classic organization of concentrated facilities and services at the junction of the axes, a descending building density towards the periphery, the industrial zone is concentrated at one end of the urban area, and the planning model is a system of sectors or districts. It currently has almost 50,000 inhabitants although the Plan envisages an almost three-fold increase of this number.

All the other ACTURs can be described as districts of their respective cities. La Cartuja, Seville, is unique in sense that it is on the grounds of the EXPO'92 trade fair, where several businesses and industries are installed in the Science and Technology Park along with entertainment, administration and university facilities.

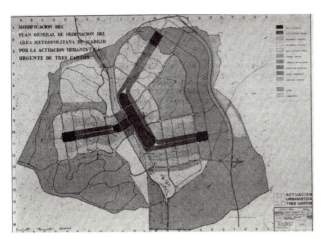

Fig. 8 ACTUR, Tres Cantos, Madrid.

CONCLUSIONS

The work of the Urban Planning and Development Agency and its Director, Pedro Bidagor, spans the history of Spanish urban planning under the Franco regime. His management was characterised by the imposition of an urban planning authority whose power diminished at the end of the country's period of post-war isolation in the 1950s and the beginning of a development-oriented government in the 1960s. Nevertheless, it maintained a firm line throughout, with support for the building industry and private housing initiatives. Social housing was part of the political-economic strategic cloud, which still continues with several positive episodes. Spain needs to double the percentage of its GDP devoted to housing in order to reach the European average, and also to ensure that this is direct investment, not a tax deduction for home buying. The large number of evictions that have occurred since the 2007 economic crisis is the result of a mortgage-based property system at a time of unstable job conditions and an unemployment rate of around 20 per cent. The contradiction that existed in the Spanish economy in the 19th century remains today. It is not possible to maintain the unstable job conditions facilitated by the latest Labour Act (2013) and at the same time encourage the property sector. The Urban Planning and Development Agency tried to get around this dilemma by prioritising developers over landowners, not with great success at the time. However, today this would be impossible without drastic measures, implemented gradually over time.

The Urban Planning and Development Agency was a well-thought-out and managed mechanism for the provision of quality, affordable social housing thanks to its capable technicians and good architects. Nevertheless, in practice it had little influence in the 1950s, even less in the 1960s, and became almost neutralised in the 1970s under the powerful emerging force of economic liberalism.

Urban planning needs stability in time and space. In a democratic system, this is achieved by agreements on the essentials—the structure and the basic rules—and ongoing negotiation over local and time-related decisions.[12] Control mechanisms also need to be in place outside the field of operations, otherwise it is difficult to overcome the pressure on the local authorities, as proven in practice. Although there is a very close relationship between politics, economics, and urban development, it is necessary to sway the balance towards technical objectivity over political opportunism, although this does not mean to say that technical expertise lacks ideology and is based on pure objective science.[13] Much can be learned from the Urban Planning and Development Agency. For this reason, I find the purpose of this book very interesting. For those of us who do not claim to be historians, history is a working tool for the design of the future, or as Fernando de Terán has put it, "the active past."[14]

[12] Bernardo Secchi and John Forester have described the current trends of urban planning in great detail.

[13] The much-criticised French centralism and the pool of national government technicians were able to achieve greater rationality in urban planning than their successors in Spain's regional governments, who are hampered by a range of laws and controls that are more influenced by economic powers than by their citizens.

[14] Fernando de Terán, *El Pasado Activo: del Uso Interesado de la Historia para el Entendimiento y la Construcción de la Ciudad* (Madrid: Akal, 2009).

BIBLIOGRAPHY

Benevolo, Leonardo. *Historia de la Arquitectura Moderna.* Barcelona: Gustavo Gili, 1979.

Bidagor, Pedro. *Gerencia de Urbanización, 1959–1964.* Ministerio de la Vivienda, 1965.

Bidagor, Pedro. "Situación General del Urbanismo en España, 1939–1964." *Arquitectura* 62 (1964).

Capel, Horacio. *Capitalismo y Morfología Urbana en España.* Libros de Cordel, 1977.

Moya, Luis. *Barrios de Promoción Oficial: Madrid 1939–1975.* COAM, 1983.

Moya, Luis. *Los Antecedentes Franquistas de la Política de VS.* Cuadernos de Investigación Urbanística 100 (2015).

Terán, Fernando. *Planeamiento Urbano en la España Contemporánea.* Barcelona: G. Gili, 1978.

Terán, Fernando. "Evolución del Planeamiento de Núcleos Urbanos Nuevos." *Ciudad y Territorio*, no.1 (1969):13-23.

Olivais and Chelas: a Large-Scale Housing Programme in Lisbon

TERESA VALSASSINA HEITOR
University of Lisbon, Instituto Superior Técnico, Centre for Innovation in Territory, Urbanism, and Architecture

ABSTRACT

Olivais and Chelas are two neighbourhoods that formed part of a large-scale social housing programme undertaken in Lisbon, beginning in the late 1950s and corresponding to one of the great Portuguese experiments in terms of town planning and architecture from the second half of the twentieth century. Far outweighing any of the government's previous attempts to provide affordable housing, this programme was conducted by the Lisbon City Council, with the political and financial backing of the central government. Its comprehensive planning process was part of the strategy to expand the city's urban fabric, deliver affordable housing and ultimately reduce its chronic housing shortage. The programme benefited from a favourable conjuncture of circumstances, which also determined its format. The combination of the government's political determination, the availability of funding and a climate that encouraged public investment in housing allowed for a significant investment to be made.

This chapter seeks to analyse how this housing programme was planned and delivered within two decades, from the end of the 1950s to the 1970s. On a wider level, it also attempts to provide an overall interpretation of the social context that influenced its conception and design, as well as the factors that determined its subsequent development processes.

The conceptual framework is founded on the premise that this housing programme was not a typical large-scale housing project, such as the ones defined by Rowe.[1] Although it involved compliance with a set of minimum standards and was conducted with the active intervention of the state, it did not apply the techniques of architectural mass production based on a series of endlessly repeated standardised housing solutions. Instead a socio-spatial differentiation was proposed that would be based on a more open and irregular, landscape-inspired design. Its clear differentiation of building types was designed to mix people from varying income groups together as a fundamental part of its rationale and its financial and operational planning.

BIOGRAPHY

Teresa Heitor was born in Lisbon, Portugal in 1959. She is Full Professor of Architecture at University of Lisbon, Instituto Superior Técnico (IST). She obtained a first degree in Architecture (1982, Escola Superior de Belas Artes de Lisboa, PT), a Master degree in Urban Design (1984, Joint Centre for Urban Design, Oxford Brooks University, UK); a PhD in Territorial Engineering (1997, Technical University of Lisbon, Instituto Superior Tecnico, Lisbon, PT), and habilitation in Architecture (2007, University of Lisbon, Instituto Superior Tecnico, Lisbon, PT). Currently she is the chair of Architecture at IST. She has been teaching post- and undergraduate students in Architecture at IST for the past 20 years. Her research interests are focused on the relationship between space, form, and function, and the development of models capable to simulate the implications of new social demands as well as on self-assessment tools to be applied along the occupancy stage. Her current research activity aims at the understanding of contemporary socio-spatial aspects of learning in urban settings, i.e., the places where structured and unstructured modes of learning, social interactions, and re-presentation of knowledge can take place. In addition to her teaching and research activity she is regularly invited to disseminate knowledge to policy-makers and the general public. She regularly undertakes higher education strategic evaluations and peer review assessments for European and national research/scientific councils.

---

[1] Peter G. Rowe, *Modernity and Housing* (Cambridge Mass. & London: MIT Press, 1993), 59–65.

1. THE BACKGROUND: A CHRONIC UNDERSUPPLY OF HOUSES FOR A GROWING CITY

The increased demand for housing generated by the migration of the population to urban areas was one of the key dimensions underlying the modernisation of Portugal in the second half of the twentieth century. Until the early 1940s, Portugal had been a largely rural country, with an urban population of only 20 per cent. The following decades were marked by an intense influx of rural populations to the country's urban centres and by a period of intense urbanisation, in which the city of Lisbon was "demographically predominant."[2]

The 1950 census revealed the demographic changes that had occurred during the previous decade: while the country's population had increased by around 10 per cent, the population of the city of Lisbon had itself risen by 20 per cent, equivalent to a further 88,000 inhabitants and corresponding to 8.4 per cent of the national population. This served to create a significant housing shortage and to increase the difficulties that the population faced in gaining access to affordable homes, since, although rents were controlled by law, they nonetheless rose faster than earnings. The "Survey of Living Conditions," which, for the first time, was incorporated into the 1950 census, revealed a considerable number of dwelling spaces that were classified as unfit for habitation, with many more households living in sub-standard conditions and facing rapidly escalating levels of urban poverty.[3] This situation deteriorated even further in the following decade as a result of the significant and persistent migration to the city of people coming from the low-employment regions inland.[4]

The strategy that the central government adopted in terms of economic modernisation initially gave priority to infrastructure and heavy industries. But, when the housing shortage became ever more acute in the main urban centres, pushing housing to the forefront of the political and economic agenda, the government was forced to assume new responsibilities. Increasingly concerned about these problems, the public authorities inevitably began to regard the provision of affordable housing for people living on low incomes as a major issue. The success of the programme for affordable rented accommodation launched in Alvalade in the late 1940s (resulting in the construction by the public and private sector of roughly 12,000 homes in just under ten years) led the government to invest even more money in delivering another large-scale initiative.

---

[2] Luís V. Baptista, "Dominação Demográfica no Contexto do Séc.XX Português: Lisboa, a Capital," *Sociologia, Problemas e Práticas*, no.15 (1994): 53–77.

[3] Raúl da Silva Pereira, "Problemática da Habitação em Portugal," *Análise Social*, vol.1, no.1 (1963): 36–40.

[4] Around 25 per cent of households lived under a system of subletting or in over-crowded dwellings, sharing their homes with one or more families, or else in shanty towns, without access to such basic amenities as electricity, sewage disposal or running water [Maria da Conceição Tavares Silva, "A sublocação em Lisboa," *Boletim do Gabinete Técnico da Habitação*, vol.1 no.1 (1964): 44–51.] In the 1960 census, when the city of Lisbon reached the threshold of 800,000 inhabitants, it was estimated that 4 per cent of the capital's population, approximately 40,000 inhabitants, lived in slums. João Reis Machado, "Plano de Chelas: V–Elementos relativos à População que habita em barracas," *Boletim do Gabinete Técnico da Habitação*, vol.1, no.9 (1965): 441–453.

2. THE HOUSING PROGRAMME

In 1959, the central government decided to launch a new large-scale housing programme, centrally managed by the Lisbon City Council and focusing heavily on public sector involvement, rather than relying on the private sector.[5]

About 737 hectares, consisting largely of farmland on the eastern fringes of the city, were allocated to the programme. This area, equivalent to approximately one tenth of the total area of the city was divided into three zones—Olivais Norte (40 ha) [MdH DB a186], Olivais Sul (186.6 ha) [MdH DB a193], and Chelas (520 ha) [MdH DB a194]. For operational reasons, the programme was divided into three distinct phases that would be implemented with significant variations. Olivais Norte (phase 1)[6] would house a population of 10,000 inhabitants in 2,500 dwellings, while Olivais Sul (phase 2)[7] would house about 38,250 inhabitants in 7,996 dwellings, and Chelas (phase 3)[8] would house about 55,300 inhabitants in 11,500 dwellings.

Fig. 1 The new expansion areas of Olivais and Chelas as part of the Master Plan of Lisbon (1938–1948) coordinated by Etienne de Groer.
Source: GEO–Gabinete de Estudos Olissiponenses, DP 1272 CMLEO

[5] The programme was officially created on 18 August 1959. Decree-Law No. 42,454 established the legislative framework for the designation, delivery, and management of the areas allocated to the housing programme. This area's peripheral location was in keeping with the strategy previously set out in the Lisbon Municipal Master Plan, implemented between 1938 and 1948 by E. de Gröer (PDUL) and subsequently maintained throughout the 1950s.

[6] The Olivais Norte Master Plan was first drawn up in 1955 in the council's town-planning department (GEU) by a team led by the engineer Guimarães Lobato. The initial version was later revised and approved in 1959 by a team led by the architect and town planner José Rafael Botelho. This team also included the architects P. Falcão e Cunha, Bartolomeu da Costa Cabral, J. Reis Machado, and A. Alves Mendes.

[7] The intervention in Olivais Sul was also coordinated by José Rafael Botelho and included Carlos Duarte, Mario Bruxelas, Celestino de Castro, and António Freitas. The building works began in 1962 and were almost complete by the beginning of the following decade, with the exception of the main civic-commercial centre, whose construction was postponed until the 1990s.

[8] The Chelas plan was also coordinated by José Rafael Botelho and included the architects Francisco da Silva Dias, João Reis Machado, Alfredo Silva Gomes, Luis Vassalo Rosa, and Carlos Worm, as well as the Engineers José Simões Coelho and Gonçalo Malheiro de Araújo. The plan was approved in 1964, indicating the year 2000 as the probable date for its conclusion.

THE GOVERNMENT TARGETS: A MIXED DEVELOPMENT

According to the programme's rationale, the Lisbon Council would enter into annual agreements for the construction of dwellings with public housing development agencies and, to a limited extent, also with private developers. The replacement housing was to be provided in the form of 70 per cent social housing and 30 per cent deregulated rent dwellings to be promoted by private entities. Within the first group, 30 per cent of the dwellings were to be delivered for the purposes of rehousing and slum clearance. The remaining homes were provided for workers and other people in employment, as well as for recipients of social security or other similar benefits, and were to be promoted by non-profit organisations acting as social partners.

Mixed-income housing was a stated objective of the government's social housing policy, with different income groups paying different rents. This mechanism was designed to prevent the creation of neighbourhoods with areas of concentrated poverty and residential segregation, while, at the same time, avoiding the building of public housing areas in which 100 per cent of dwellings would be allocated to people living in poverty. The physical composition of these areas was thus considered to be a crucial priority.[9]

Four housing categories were established, with different fixed monthly rents being calculated according to each household's level of income, and with fixed investment ceilings linked to the costs associated with housing production.[10] Category III represented the ceiling for access to social housing. Category IV represented middle-class families from wealthier socio-economic and professional backgrounds and its existence was justified only as a compensatory measure to encourage private developers to build a certain percentage of social housing units. In practice, these categories were converted simply into fixed limits of construction costs, operating with predetermined budgets, and their basic housing quality standards were never actually defined.[11]

In 1970, these housing categories were further complemented with the creation of specific "types."[12] In addition to establishing the appropriate household income level, the new classification established the minimum built area, the occupancy rates, and the quality of each home's finishes, fixtures, and fittings.[13] The debates that accompanied these changes reflected the government's desire to improve the standards of social housing. A number of studies conducted from the mid-1960s onwards[14] advocated the need to adopt the standards defined by the International Federation of Housing and Urbanism (FIHU), the so-called "Cologne Rules."

---

[9] "The new urban units to be built shall include all economic categories in order to avoid inconvenient social segregation," which was considered "alien to the traditions of Lisbon neighbourhoods" (Decree-Law No. 42,454, preamble).

[10] In accordance with this classification, changes in the household's level of income would correspond to a similar change in their housing category, in order to avoid misalignments. This concept of mixed-accommodation developments, in which people would progressively upsize or downsize throughout their lives, never in fact functioned in this way, due to the chronic housing shortage.

[11] GTH, *Classificação e Nomenclatura das Habitações de Caracter Social–Proposta de Norma–Grupo de Coordenação da Habitação* (Lisboa: GTH, 1966); H. Morgado, "Variação do Custo de Construção com o Modo de Concepção do Edifício," *Boletim do Gabinete Técnico da Habitação*, vol.3, no.21 (1971): 315–318; H. Morgado, "Olivais Sul–Estudo analítico de Projectos," *Boletim do Gabinete Técnico da Habitação*, vol. 3, no.21 (1971): 319–362; Hernâni Gandra, "Contribuição para o Estudo do problema das Áreas da Habitação Social–Análise Comparativa," *Boletim do Gabinete Técnico da Habitação*, vol.4, no.26 (1974): 219–236.

[12] Decree-Law No. 576 of 24 November, 1970

[13] Maria da Conceição Redol, "As Normas e Regulamentos na Evolução da Dimensão dos Espaços do Fogo," Congresso da Ordem dos Engenheiros, Tema 2, Comunicação 15, Lisbon 20–26 November 1977.

[14] Nuno Portas, *Funções e Exigências das Áreas da Habitação, Informação Técnica–Edifícios 4* (Lisboa: MOP–Laboratório Nacional de Engenharia Civil, 1969); FFH, *As Áreas na Habitação, Gabinete de Estudos, Proc. 101/1.6/GE de 20/7/70* (Lisboa: Fundo de Fomento da Habitação, 1970); FFH, *Estudos de Soluções Tipo de Fogos e das Características a que os Edifícios Deverão Obedecer para Estabelecimento de Princípios de Industrialização da Construção, Gabinete de Estudos, Rel. no.7/GE/71* (Lisboa: Fundo de Fomento da Habitação, 1971); FFH, *Principais Características da Habitação Económica 1970/71, Gabinete de Estudos, Rel. no.3/GE/72, Proc. 101/GE* (Lisboa: Fundo de Fomento da Habitação, 1972).

The political changes that took place in 1974 led to the extinction of these categories. Thereafter, there would be just one single category,[15] corresponding to the previous Category II.[16] Due to a greatly increased influx of vulnerable families, the new democratic government turned to social housing as the solution for their rehousing. Under this new targeted approach, social housing was allocated on the basis of need to a relatively restricted category of people, above all low-income families and those who were excluded from the labour market.

THE MANAGEMENT OF THE PROGRAMME

In order to monitor the planning, development and delivery of this housing programme, the Lisbon Council created a special department, which was given the name of Gabinete Técnico da Habitação (Technical Office for Housing–GTH) and endowed it with a high degree of administrative, financial, and technical autonomy. This department was thus able to perform a combination of different roles—acting simultaneously as client, regulator, consultant, town planner, and architect. The structure of the GTH technical staff was organised under the direction of Jorge Carvalho Mesquita in such a way as to allow for its subsequent expected expansion, which would be necessary for fully implementing the housing programme. The department also incorporated the team of town planners-architects already working in the council's Town Planning Department (Gabinete de Estudos de Urbanização–GEU[17]).

The GTH worked in close conjunction with the public and semi-public housing development agencies that were responsible for ensuring an affordable housing supply. The teams of architects and other built environment professionals, either working at or commissioned by these agencies—in particular Habitações Económicas–Federação das Caixas de Previdência (Affordable Housing–Federation of Provident Funds–HE-FCP)[18]—were able to offer a body of accumulated empirical practical knowledge, which they had gained from previous affordable rental housing developments, such as the one in Alvalade, which many people saw as the prototype for later projects.

In view of their acquired technical competence, both the GTH and the HE-FCP staff offered an informed reformist approach to social housing development policies, seeking greater fairness and social justice, something that was quite unprecedented within the framework of housing production in Portugal. They also gained a reputation for their experimental, studio-based working environment, which was particularly attractive to young practitioners and graduates.

[15] The question of the extinction of the categories had already been under discussion for some time. In "Functions and Requirements of Housing Areas" (1969), Portas questioned the lack of the standardisation that was considered indispensable for a concrete social housing policy. He presented a table of values corresponding to two categories of dwellings: one with minimum values, close to the admissible critical limits, and another equivalent to the values used in social housing programmes in other European countries.

[16] António Baptista Coelho, "Qualidade Arquitetónica Residencial" (PhD Diss., Faculdade de Arquitectura da Universidade do Porto, 1994), 95–111.

[17] GEU was coordinated by Eng. Guimarães Lobato. The team included P. Falcão e Cunha and José Sommer Ribeiro (architects).

[18] This public housing development agency was set up in 1946 under the supervision of the Subsecretaria de Estado das Corporações e Previdência Social (Under Secretary of State for Corporations and Social Security). It was responsible for designing and promoting the implementation of housing construction plans, as well as for allocating dwellings according to criteria that reflected the government's basic principles and social objectives. In 1958 a new Design Office was created within HE-FCP–Gabinete de Estudos e Projectos–under the coordination of the chief-architect João Braula Reis and the technical consultancy of Nuno Teotónio Pereira. The staff included Bartolomeu Costa Cabral and Vasco Croft Moura (architects) and Vitor Gonçalves (technical draughtsman). Later the technical staff was extended with a group of young architects [Maria Tavares, "Habitações Económicas. Federação das Caixas de Previdência. Arquitectura e Modos de Actuação no Exercício do Projecto" (PhD Diss., Faculdade de Arquitectura da Universidade do Porto, 2015), 394]. From 1959 to 1972, it was responsible for creating 26 per cent of the dwellings built in Olivais Norte and Olivais Sul. In 1972, it was disbanded and integrated into the Fundo de Fomento da Habitação (FFH–Housing Development Fund), which had been created at the Ministry of Public Works in 1969. The FFH sought to centralise the definition and implementation of social housing policy, which at that time was scattered around various government departments, by analysing and monitoring existing measures and coordinating and financing public and private initiatives in the field of social housing.

From the very beginning of the programme, the GTH introduced some measures of control, in order to ensure that the maximum authorised costs of the projects were not exceeded. This involved establishing minimum standards of quality, determining the level of infrastructure to be included in the project and using standardised building modules and other fixtures.[19] The low level of industrialisation of the national construction sector at that time limited the application of the rational building technology, prefabrication, and assembly techniques that were widely used in several other European countries. Nevertheless, some attempts were made to introduce a modular coordination of building elements in order to[20] enhance productivity and reduce building costs.[21]

In the 1960s and early 1970s, teams of architects from the private sector were increasingly commissioned to design the housing schemes, being hired mostly through direct contracts.[22] In the 1980s, as the housing programme began to be reduced, the use of outside architects was drastically curtailed. After that, the GTH relied heavily on standard and "preferred" dwelling plans, mostly designed in-house, which were seen as a way of speeding up the production of new housing. It was hoped that the provision of standardised solutions and specifications would make the design process easier, thus rendering the construction work more cost-effective by taking into account the necessary compliance codes and time criteria.

The speed of the building work undertaken in the initial phases was such that there was limited scope either for learning or for applying newly learned techniques along the way, whether in regard to design questions or in matters relating to the management of the project's finances and budget.[23] It was, however, possible to test the process for delivering the project, exploring innovative solutions and identifying the problems occurring with particular building types, which might otherwise not have been revealed before the occupation stage. This information provided valuable insights, and these experiences were passed on to the subsequent phases of the different projects.[24]

---

[19] H. Morgado, "Olivais Sul–Estudo analítico de Projectos."

[20] Ana Tostões, "Conjuntos Urbanos Planeados na Cidade," in *Arquitectura Moderna Portuguesa 1920–1970*, ed. Ana Tostões e Sandra Vaz Costa (Lisboa: Instituto Português do Património Arquitectónico, 2004), 289–296.

[21] J. Sant'Ana, E. Figueiredo and J. Antunes, "Aspectos da Intervenção do Gabinete Técnico da Habitação da Câmara Municipal de Lisboa na Construção da Habitação Social," *Boletim do Gabinete Técnico da Habitação*, vol.6, no.41/42 (2nd Semester 1982): 3–30.

[22] António H. Cardoso et al., "Projectos do Gabinete Técnico da Habitação–Alguns dados da Experiência colhida na sua elaboração e realização em obra de 1969 a 1979," *Boletim do Gabinete Técnico da Habitação*, vol.6, no.41/42 (1982): 377–384.

[23] LNEC, *Informação sobre a Situação Actual dos Empreendimentos e Necessidades da Habitação Social*, Proc. 34/0/3483, Fevereiro 1969 (Lisboa: Laboratório Nacional de Engenharia Civil, 1969).

[24] Cardoso et al., "Projectos do Gabinete Técnico da Habitação."

3. THE IMPLEMENTATION OF THE PROGRAMME: TRENDS, CONTINUITY, AND CHALLENGES

The team of town planners-architects from the GEU had been preparing the development plan and the housing programme for Olivais since 1955.[25] When the programme was finally launched, the building works were already in progress. The main road network and the basic urban services were already partly built and the housing projects had already begun to be implemented. Some short-term adjustments were needed in order to comply with the new regulations and cost control procedures.

Although this process took place at the same time as the International Congresses of Modern Architecture (CIAM) was dissolved after its 1959 Otterlo Congress,[26] there was still clearly a prevailing general consensus about the hierarchical cellular structure pertaining to the concept of a neighbourhood (establishing units of five to ten thousand people with their own dedicated facilities and amenities), which had crystallised in Europe in the post-war period[27] and in which the naturalistic tendency of the "garden city" had given way to the concept of the "city in the park."[28]

PHASE I: OLIVAIS NORTE AND THE NEIGHBOURHOOD UNIT CONCEPT

The plan for Olivais Norte typically followed the late CIAM models for new housing developments: irregular groups of buildings constructed on a large open site, based on a variety of building types, complete with schools, community services, shopping facilities, and services. Accordingly, a low/medium-density scheme was proposed, based on the integration of detached low/medium-rise single/multiple-slab blocks and towers with a variety of arrangements, different floor plan configurations, and dwelling types, which was an effective way of breaking down the "zeilenbau" effect of repetitive unarticulated buildings. A row of semi-detached single-family houses was located on the eastern periphery of the site. Mixed-use buildings were located in the more accessible spaces, together with the primary school, close to the public transport hubs, with the ground floor being used for commercial purposes and the upper floors for housing. The site's landscape was used to separate traffic and parking from the residential areas and to provide open public spaces at the heart of the neighbourhood, where households could congregate.

[25] "Olivais Norte–Extractos da Memória Descritiva do estudo Base de Olivais elaborada em 1955," Arquitectura no.81 (1964); "Olivais Sul em Discussão," Arquitectura no.127–128 (1973).

[26] At the time, the predominant discourse among the international community of town planners-architects was already marked by its criticism of the doctrines and standardising approaches of modern planning, namely "the separation of land uses, the accommodation of the automobile in the form of high-speed highways, the rejection of the street and street life, [and] the treatment of buildings as isolated objects in space rather than as part of the larger interconnected urban fabric"—Emily Talen, *New Urbanism and American Planning: the Conflict of Cultures* (New York: Routledge, 2005), 51. At stake was the search for an urban language that could promote the juxtaposition of a variety of different uses and help to restore the sense of urbanness.

[27] Frederick Gibberd, "The Master Design; Landscape; Housing; the Town Centres," in H. Evans, *New Towns, The British Experience* (London: Charles Knight & Co. Ltd., 1972), 92.

[28] Leonardo Benevolo, *História da Arquitectura Moderna* (São Paulo: Editorial Perspectiva, 1989 [1960]), 100.

As far as the different built forms are concerned, some broad typologies can be identified, divided into three very general groups relating to the different housing categories: the single/multiple-point access slab block, with four storeys (without a lift), predominated in Category I; the multiple-point access slab block with four storeys and the freestanding tower building with eight storeys predominated in Category II; and the multiple block with between nine and eleven storeys predominated in the higher categories. The higher categories were placed in the centre of the area and the lower ones spread out towards the periphery.

A group of six architects were selected to lead separate teams, one for each of the sectors identified in the plans for the housing development. Efforts were made to provide new and better solutions and, above all, to produce optimum housing typologies and floor plans, which were already familiar from modern architecture and from the welfare state experiments that were being conducted at that time in most European countries.[29]

Categories I and II were by far the ones with the most variable geometries and the most innovative and versatile solutions. Category I, Y-shaped slab buildings, designed by João Barros and Vasconcelos Esteves, allowed for the association of modules in such a way as to form different freestanding arrangements,[30] while the point-access slab blocks designed by Braula Reis and João Matoso were placed in a traditional row, defining the margins of the street. Category II developments combined four-storey gallery-access blocks with maisonettes, such as the one designed by Pedro Cid and Fernando Torres, with four-storey point-access blocks and nine-storey point-access tower buildings with several dwellings per floor, designed by Nuno Teotónio Pereira, António Freitas, and Nuno Portas. In clear contrast with the higher categories, these solutions were more in keeping with the Italian and Nordic experiments, quite clearly moving away from the more orthodox modern language used in the eight to twelve-storey point-access slab blocks with three to four flats per floor, designed by Abel Manta and belonging to Category III and the group of eleven-storey slab blocks included under Category IV and designed by Pires Martins and Palma de Melo following an arrangement of the unité plan/section type raised above open pilotis at the ground floor level, with the flats organised around a central staircase and lift shaft, and short interconnecting galleries.

A total of 1,600 dwellings were built, of which 289 were designed for rehousing purposes. In all of the categories, the dwelling's spatial and functional relationships displayed the features of contemporary living and the new modes of domesticity, separating

[29] The specialist international literature was already promoting new approaches and contributing to the dissemination of innovative experiments that had been undertaken in this area, based on the application of the late CIAM doctrines. Portuguese periodicals, such as *Arquitectura* and *Binário*, encouraged transnational exchanges of architectural practices by showing experiments that had been put to the test in different countries, justifying their pertinence and exhibiting signs of their actual completion.

[30] The base-module was organised around an open access core, keeping dedicated circulation space to a minimum and providing access to three different-sized dwellings.

the social sector from the private sector, and from the other auxiliary or utilitarian spaces. In particular, in the lower categories, some expedients were introduced in order to allow for the existence of supplementary areas and to increase the usable space, such as creating a physical permeability between the kitchen and the common room and between the interior and the exterior space by means of balconies and loggias. Some of these schemes notably offered as much amenity space, since the right type of building configuration provided a focus for residents to meet and socialise outside the dwelling areas.

Fig. 2 Aerial view of Olivais Norte
Source: Filipe Jorge–Argumentum 2015

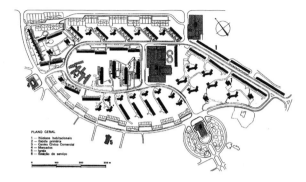

Fig. 2.1 Plan of Olivais Norte. Source: GTH.

PHASE II: OLIVAIS SUL AND THE POLYNUCLEAR SCHEME

The second phase—Olivais Sul—was marked by a shift in the conceptual strategies that had been applied in Olivais Norte. These now took account of the criticisms that had begun to be made of the earlier project at both an international and a local level, in particular its lack of a distinctive urban character, its lack of continuity and its inadequate urban services. This debate provided a different way of approaching the relationship between the housing and the neighbourhood, making this less "nodal" and more "polynuclear" in nature. It was not a question of breaking away from the functional principles of housing, work, recreation and circulation, as outlined in the Athens Charter, but rather of amplifying them and adapting them to new situations with more elaborate proposals. Such an approach reflected a changing attitude towards the relationship between physical form and socio-psychological needs. The model used in the expansion of the main Swedish cities, known as the "ABC City"[31] had become a central reference for the reflections being made on this subject by the GTH team. Vällingby, in the suburbs of Stockholm, had successfully managed to reverse its dormitory status, and attempts were being made to adapt this exemplary experiment to Olivais Sul.[32] The revision of the strategy adopted in the Mark I New Towns in the United Kingdom, which had been introduced for the first time in Cumbernauld (1956–61), in the north-east of Glasgow, was similarly arousing great interest on the part of the GTH team. The strategies adopted for the densification of the residential areas, arising from the rejection of the concept of the neighbourhood unit in favour of a "compact and nucleated" model and the inclusion of a large central multifunctional area embodying the concept of a megastructure, placed Cumbernauld at the "forefront of architectural innovation."[33]

[31] ABC is an acronym for Arbete–Bostad–Centrum, "Work–Dwelling–Centre." "The ABC concept gave way to the decentralization of the historical Stockholm city centre with the creation of a number of decentralized satellite towns connected to the core city with a newly planned metro network." R. W. Archer, "From New Towns to Metrotowns and Regional Cities," *The American Journal of Economics and Sociology*, Vol. 28, No. 3 (Jul. 1969): 257–269.

[32] Vällingby was the first prototype "ABC City." It was inaugurated in 1954 and was visited by the GTH team. Carlos S. Duarte, "Habitação e Equipamento Colectivo na Suécia," *Boletim do Gabinete Técnico da Habitação*, vol.1 no.4 (1965): 207–214; Goulart de Medeiros, "Os centros cívico-comerciais de Vallingby e Farsta," *Boletim do Gabinete Técnico da Habitação*, vol.1 no.4 (1965): 215–220.

[33] Peter Reyner Banham, *Megastructure: Urban Futures of the Recent Past* (London: Thames and Hudson, 1976).

The plan that was developed for Olivais Sul sought to increase the population density of the residential areas through the use of new and more compact forms of building aggregation and by increasing the average height of the buildings. The whole area was subdivided into six units, of which four (B, C, D and E) were to be used exclusively for housing, with a much higher density than in Olivais Norte and organised along and around a curving ring road. The proposal to build a civic-commercial centre in the heart of the area, detached from the housing units and designed to serve as a meeting point for residents, was already a reflection of the debate taking place internationally at that time, in contrast to the solution that had been applied previously.

The plan was centred around the previously adopted cellular concept for the design of its units,[34] while the polynuclear concept was expressed through the introduction of housing clusters, typically connected to pedestrian-oriented open public spaces, such as courtyards, and thereby creating a network of integrated mixed-use neighbourhood nodes. Once again, the strategy that was adopted proved to be an effective way of breaking down the effect of monotonous repetition. It was based on the use of different building typologies, ranging from clusters of freestanding towers, usually of the point-access type, and linear or serpentine-shaped slab blocks combining gallery and point-access systems (some of them using maisonettes organised in a skip-stop arrangement with dwellings on both sides of the building), to rows of semi-detached houses, marking out distinct identifiable spaces and sharing a common architectural language.

The strategy of starting the programme in Olivais Norte with fewer projects involving different housing types offered some valuable insights for the Olivais Sul development. According to the procurement model used by the GTH, a large number of different teams of architects and other built environment professionals were involved in the design of buildings.[35] In general terms, each team was in charge of various projects within the same cell and cluster. Although they had to follow the briefs established by the GTH and to comply with precise instructions in order to stay within the authorised budgets for the respective housing categories, they were surprisingly independent in terms of searching for different typological solutions in the design of the floor plans, in response to the households' lifestyles and needs, as well as in making use of the formal and tectonic aspects of the building design. All of this serves to explain the architectural variety and quality of the building programme.

[34] Tiago Oliveira, "As vicissitudes do Espaço Urbano Moderno ou o Menino e a Água do banho" (PhD Thesis in Architecture, Faculdade de arquitectura da Universidade de Lisboa, 2015.), 328.

[35] The GTH (1977) refers to the involvement of 27 teams.

In view of the budgetary constraints and the pressure to comply with minimum space standards, the floor plans, particularly in the lower housing categories, tended to introduce some versatility into the spatial organisation of functional sectors in an attempt to improve the residents' standard of living and to bring greater modernisation to the domestic sphere.[36] Typically, a clear separation was made between the social sector and the private sector, while the circulation spaces were kept to a minimum. The common room, however, was designed to be a multi-purpose space, often also becoming part of the circulation space, as it served as a passage to the private sector. The kitchen was no longer designed as an autonomous space, but became a type of open space with a dining area and an additional semi-enclosed space to be used for other domestic tasks. Also, it was common for the hall to be conceived as a versatile and usable space connected to the common room or to the kitchen.[37] In the upper categories, a greater demarcation could be observed between functional sectors, together with larger built and usable areas, including the collective spaces.

In the organisation of the four pre-defined housing categories, there was a strong tendency for the formation of a nucleus of houses from the same category. In the lower categories—I and II—the predominant solution was the multi-family slab building, combining gallery-access and point-access types with several flats per floor, with different sizes and different floor plan typologies.[38] Categories III and IV were mostly based on point-access tower and slab building types, with varying heights and configurations. The final result was a compromise between a concentration of dwellings by categories and a blending together of different categories in order to mitigate the dangers of segregation and social exclusion. This option cannot be disassociated from the prerequisite to comply with fixed budgets, which inevitably meant that the lower housing categories were obliged to occupy less accessible locations.

At the time, the supply of social housing was being subjected to greater budgetary constraints, so that new lettings necessarily focused on those in greatest need. As a result, a new low-cost housing type was integrated into this development, the so-called "zero" or "rehousing" category. The decision was to create a modular type of building to be constructed under a strictly controlled budget and scattered around the development site, forming small-sized clusters: a four-storey detached slab block, which was highly adaptable to different locations and configurations. Such buildings, designed by a team coordinated by José Daniel Santa Rita, combined open access staircases linked to galleries, with the entrances being located at the intersections between the slab segments.

[36] GTH, "Ficheiro de Projectos-Tipo para Habitação Social em Olivais Sul," *Boletim do Gabinete Técnico da Habitação*, vol.5 no.30–33 (1976/77): 209–483; Tânia Ramos, "Os Espaços do Habitar Moderno: Evolução e Significados. Os Casos Português e Brasileiro" (PhD Diss., Instituto Superior Técnico, Universidade Técnica de Lisboa, 2003).

[37] This strategy was clearly observable in Category I—four- and eight-storey slab blocks designed by Vitor Figueiredo and Vasco Lobo.

[38] Some of these were later replicated in Chelas, such as the ones designed by Vitor Figueiredo and Vasco Lobo.

Fig. 3 Aerial view of Olivais Sul. Source: Filipe Jorge–Argumentum 2015.

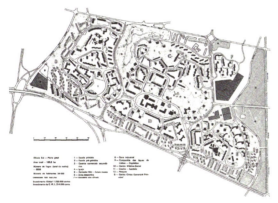

Fig. 3.1 Plan of Olivais Sul. Source: GTH.

PHASE III: CHELAS AND THE LINEAR OPTION

Encouraged by the debate that was in progress at that time, the GTH team were led to question the effectiveness of the models adopted in the previous phases. The adopted strategies had made it possible to ensure an effective link between the housing units and their immediate services and facilities. But the fact that no solution had been found for the relationship between the neighbourhood's residential function and its other productive facilities, as well as its links with the city itself, meant that both Olivais Norte and Olivais Sul were condemned to the status of "dormitory" areas. News were arriving of experiments in progress elsewhere in Europe, where the emphasis was placed on infrastructure, growth, linear organisation, and street and pedestrian networks.

In particular, the Urban Master Plan prepared by the London County Council for the construction of yet another new satellite town close to London—at Hook in Hampshire (1959–61)—raised great expectations among the GTH team of town planners-architects, so that their attentions were directed towards the linear strategies adopted.[39]

In clear contrast with the previous phases, the strategic framework adopted for Chelas favoured the linear option. This time, not as an explicit traffic-oriented scheme,[40] but rather as a denser, pedestrian-oriented neighbourhood with well-defined spaces.[41] The urban layout took the form of two parallel axes, described as "linear strips of urban activity," which spread from a central core and then branched into secondary axes that formed the structure for six residential sectors.[42] These sectors were built at higher levels and would each be afforded a different treatment, so that they would be easily recognisable. Replicated in these residential sectors was the linear concept: a tree-type solution in which the main axis ran across the whole area, bringing together housing, commercial facilities, and other social amenities. As the focus of a diversified activity, the "central core" stood out from the rest in both formal and symbolic terms.[43]

An attempt was made to interpret and recreate traditional elements of the urban form, by replacing the detached, freestanding groups of slab and tower blocks with more compact and more closely articulated built structures. The elevated pedestrian streets of Allison and Peter Smithson's projects Golden Lane (1952) and Robin Hood Gardens (1962–72), the continuous network of connected galleries at the Park Hill project in Sheffield, designed by Jack Lynn and Ivor Smith (1959–61), and the continuous linear network of "mat-buildings" with a large concentration of activities, proposed by the collective Team X of Candilis, Josic, and Woods for the new town of Toulouse Le Mirail, (1961–71), as well as the idea of a repetitive, hierarchical cluster of elements, as used in several housing projects in Holland designed by Bakema and van den Broek in the 1950s and 1960s, were some of the experiments that served as a source of inspiration. The social housing experiments carried out in Italy from the late 1960s onwards, namely the projects developed by the collectives led by De Carlo at the Villaggio Matteotti (1969–74) and by Aymonino and Rossi at the Monte Amiata Housing Development in the Gallaratese district of Milan (1967–74), were also viewed with great interest and fuelled the debate taking place among Portuguese architects, encouraging them to move up to another level in contrast to the previous housing solutions adopted in Olivais Sul.

---

[39] As Gold says, "Hook would have embraced a commitment to greater clustering to provide what would have been effectively a walking-scale city arranged on linear principles." John R. Gold, "Hook: Revisiting the New Town That Might Have Been," Introduction to London County Council, The Planning of a New Town, Studies in International Planning History Series (London: Routledge, 2015 [1961]). Although this new city was never built, the publication The planning of a New Town design based on a study for a New Town of 100,000 at Hook, Hampshire, published in 1961, was soon converted into a manual.

[40] In terms of mobility, the plan assumed that the best way of overcoming barriers to pedestrian circulation was to establish a functionally organised road network based on a hierarchy of flows and pedestrian-vehicle segregation.

[41] Implicit in this new model was the vision of a more compact, multifunctional, and socially diversified city with urban environments that were more attractive and vibrant, capable of promoting a closer-knit community with a more developed sense of neighbourliness.

[42] These five residential areas were destined for the construction of 11,500 homes, divided into five different housing categories and providing accommodation for a total of roughly 55,300 inhabitants (amounting to an average density of 160 inhabitants/hectare). For operational reasons, Area N was subdivided into two sectors: N1 and N2.

[43] As in the case of Hook, the plan was accompanied by maps that showed "the design and layout of a clustered area with a strongly demarcated centre located in a valley." Gold, "Hook: Revisiting the New Town That Might Have Been."

Fig. 4 The Master Plan of Chelas showing the main road network diagram and the connections with Olivais. Source: CML-GTH, 1964.

The economic problems that the country was passing through, further exacerbated by the fact that earlier phases of the programme were still in progress, forced the government to severely reduce its funding of the project and drastically altered the development strategy for Chelas. The integrated global operation that had been planned was interrupted and fragmented in its development, giving rise to a phased intervention. The works for the building of the road network and the infrastructures began in 1967, together with the presentation of the development plans for the first housing clusters—I, J, and N2.[44]

The built structure began to be developed in the early 1970s, with work continuing into the 1980s. As was typically the case in the schemes completed in the late 1970s and early 1980s, there was a much greater proportion of dwellings than in the earlier developments. The new rules introduced in the meantime concerning minimum space standards and dwelling areas, which were intended to reduce costs, affected the internal organisation of the dwellings and led to a more rational use of the available space.

In Sectors I and J, particular attention was given to the definition of a compact and formally coherent urban whole, so that there was a clear rejection of freestanding slab blocks and towers. Sector I[45] adopted a curvilinear configuration, based on interconnected point and gallery-access slab blocks that varied in height from five to nine storeys, in the groups adjacent to the main public areas, but increased in height from seven to twelve storeys in peripheral areas. Typically, the slab blocks looked out over open courtyards, from which there was access to ground floor lobbies in the form of open pilotis under the buildings.

While the larger courtyards were well-defined and partly landscaped, car access and parking limited their use as public spaces. The architectural vocabulary of concrete frames, narrow structural bays, and infills was developed here with the added rhythm of different bay sizes, a complex, but repetitive composition of windows, precast balustrades and balcony grilles. A solution based on a mixture of building types by categories[46] was proposed. In order to create a richer and more legible urban landscape,[47] the higher housing categories were placed along the main pedestrian spaces, together with the commercial areas, and the lower categories (I and Rehousing) were placed on the periphery of the zone, positioned in the initial segments of these axes. Category II buildings were intertwined with the others and placed along the secondary axes.

[44] Sector N was subdivided into two sectors for operational purposes.

[45] The Development Plan was drawn up at the GTH by Francisco Silva Dias, Luis Vassalo Rosa, Alfredo da Silva Gomes, João Reis Machado and José Simões Coelho. Francisco Manuel Figueira and António Alfredo also collaborated in the subsequent development of the proposals. 121 buildings with 2,590 dwellings were contemplated for the housing programme, corresponding to a population of 10,360 inhabitants. Sector J occupied an area of about 36.7 hectares and was planned for a population of 9,126 inhabitants. The GTH commissioned the architect Silva Dias to prepare a detailed plan for the area in 1967. The final version of the plan was approved in 1969. The team also included Lobo de Carvalho and Faria da Costa. A competition for the design/construction of the built area was launched in 1976, seven years after the completion of the Detailed Plan.

[46] A total of 2,272 dwellings were contemplated for this solution, of which 2,022 were subject to the imposed budgetary limits. 56 per cent of these dwellings belonged to categories 0, I, and II, and the remainder to categories III and IV. The category zero ("rehousing") and category I buildings already tested in Olivais were replicated here.

[47] F. Silva Dias and J. Lobo de Carvalho, "Plano de Urbanização de Chelas, Zona J," *Boletim do Gabinete Técnico da Habitação*, vol.5 no.27 (1st Semester 1974): 19

The Plan also contemplated the construction of towers with higher building standards, which were not compatible with the official budgetary limits. The allocation of dwellings did not adhere to the criteria initially established by the GTH,[48] thereby giving rise to a social fabric consisting entirely of socially vulnerable families. In contrast to the previous phases, a smaller number of architects were involved in the design of the building schemes, which were mostly developed in-house by the GTH teams. Furthermore, in order to control costs, a new development strategy was adopted, based on one particular building type, which was replicated at least four times.[49] This explains the greater uniformity of the housing clusters. For rehousing and category I buildings, projects were used that had been previously tested in Olivais. In Sector J,[50] a more compact built structure was proposed by the GTH team in charge of the development plan: a strip (the main nucleus) with peripheral branches (secondary nuclei), connected by a complex system of small-sized public spaces, which was inspired by the new town of Toulouse le-Mirail. The development strategy implemented by the GTH was based on a design/construction competition. With the abolition of the housing categories, the housing programme was limited to one single category and mostly destined for rehousing.

The winning solution, developed by a team coordinated by Tomás Taveira, closely followed the approach set out by the GTH in its development plan. The main nucleus, which is clearly highlighted in formal and functional terms, consists of a complex of fourteen-storey towers arranged around a central service core. These are then combined with six- to eight-storey slab blocks of different lengths, linked by external galleries and vertical connections and joined together by means of a covered gallery with commercial activities. Different floor-plan typologies were tested in the slabs, some of them making use of the "scissor section" design in order to achieve a maximum number of flats.[51] The range of different floor plans results in a more chaotic window pattern. This volumetric and typological complexity is replicated in the secondary nuclei.

As in the case of the Olivais projects, albeit on a lesser scale, several teams of architects were commissioned from outside to work on the design of the buildings for sector N2.[52] However, in contrast to the strategy adopted previously, the GTH gave the teams of architects freedom to make their own proposals for the building typologies and for the design of the public space surrounding the buildings.[53] Once again, the housing programme was converted into the use of just one single housing category, mainly destined for rehousing purposes.

[48] A significant number of dwellings still under construction were occupied illegally in the period immediately after the 1974 revolution, due to the supply and affordability gaps severely affecting the housing sector. With the abolition of the housing categories, the housing programme was mostly destined for rehousing.

[49] Cardoso et al., "Projectos do Gabinete Técnico da Habitação."

[50] The housing programme envisaged the construction of 2,028 dwellings also spread over the four housing categories, without considering the rehousing category. Due to the subsequent abolition of the housing categories, the housing programme was limited to one single category and mostly destined for rehousing.

[51] The scissor section is a complex split-level interlocking structure, developed by the London County Council and used by Kenneth Frampton of Douglas Stephen & Partners at the Corringham Housing Estate in London (1960–62). This system combines the efficiency of the access gallery with the dual orientation of the flats in question, thus improving their conditions in terms of both ventilation and sunlight. When compared to a maisonette, the split-level flat allows for greater physical cohesion between the levels. A similar system, known as the "Bakema section," was introduced into the Hansaviertel housing project in Berlin (1964) and the Elvira Flat in Delft (1964), both of which were designed by van den Broek & Bakema.

[52] The development plan was drawn up by Francisco Silva Dias, José António Lobo de Carvalho and José João Faria da Costa. The housing programme provided for a total of 1,763 dwellings and 7,925 inhabitants. As a result of this process, some changes were suggested to the GTH development plan, leading to adjustments being made to the proposed road network and the integration of some new equipment into the housing units.

[53] Reis Cabrita, "Conjunto Habitacional em Chelas," *Revista Arquitectura*, Series 4, no.140 (1979): 21–22.

Fig. 5 Aerial view of Cluster I. Source: Jose Luis de Brito, 1995.

This sector, which runs along the crest of a hill, is an overarching manifestation of linear building ideas, the latest in a modernist legacy of mega-buildings: large clusters of very long, medium-high slab buildings (of between four and twelve storeys) placed along two parallel curvilinear axes, adapted to the topography of the location and intertwined with two high-rise towers (of between fifteen and eighteen storeys) linked to the slab buildings, constituting a rather suggestive collection of gallery and point-access building types. The complexity of the area is enriched by a number of passages connecting the buildings and allowing for a great variety of raised pedestrian walks. Most of the support functions are located on steeper land backing onto the larger slab buildings and opening onto the surrounding open spaces.

The lower axis begins with a parallel row of four-storey slabs and is then intersected by a group of buildings, designed by Gonçalo Byrne and Reis Cabrita, the so-called "Pink Panther," organised around, and radiating from, a common public square defined by a cluster of five long-gallery slabs, reminiscent of the "archaeological sections" of Carlo Aymonino's Galatarese project.

The slabs around the square are joined together as two unequal blocks, connected by open rear-access galleries to create an L-shaped slab with public arcades and commercial spaces on the ground floor. The eastern slab runs parallel to a similar eight-storey slab, both containing a mixture of maisonettes and flats on each floor above and below the access level, connected to a system of galleries and staircases. Opposite the square is a long linear eight-storey gallery slab which replicates the maisonettes above and below the access level and the arcades with commercial spaces on the ground floor. Avoiding the stereotyped organisation of parallel rows of residential slab blocks, a fan-shaped building cluster designed by Vítor Figueiredo marks out a second square at the eastern intersection of the two axes. This cluster is centred around a system of five eleven-storey slab blocks of the gallery-access type. The main façades consist of horizontal bands of gallery windows and the rear façades of fully glazed linear windows. Sectors J and N2 have now been occupied for almost forty years. From the beginning, they were particularly problematical, due to a combination of social and physical problems, which are well documented. Tenants began moving in before the main road network was completed, and before the connections with the outside that would facilitate their mobility both within and outside the neighbourhood were built.

Fig. 6 Aerial view of cluster N2. Source: Jose Luis de Brito, 1995.

Unfinished public facilities were very soon vandalised. The capital flow needed for repairs, maintenance, and for installing other social services was not forthcoming. The vast spaces left beneath and around the buildings were never used as the places of social activity that the designers had intended and became empty, isolated and dangerous places. The situation improved in the late 1990s. The road infrastructure was expanded and the area's conditions of mobility were upgraded, including the building of metro stations, so that these communities were no longer so isolated. A programme was also implemented for the repair and renovation of buildings with new windows, exterior wall insulation, and repairs to the infrastructure. The failures of these projects seem to be due more to their construction processes, the performance of the authorities responsible for managing the rehousing of families, and the huge scale of the built structure, than to the actual building design.

In the remaining clusters, L, N1 and M, which began to be built in the late 1980s and 1990s, the concept of linear principles was abandoned and the residential monofunctionality became more evident. Instead, a grid system was adopted, with perimeter blocks that were open at both ends using, single point-access buildings.

Fig. 7 Aerial view of Chelas showing the central area. Source: Filipe Jorge–Argumentum 2015.

SUMMARY

A huge stock of housing was built in Olivais and Chelas during the period under analysis. Such homes were the result of the political, economic, and social climate of that time, together with a predominance of new design ideas, looking for a new format for affordable housing. When the programme was launched, the government of the time rejected the prevailing model that was to be found both in socialist societies and in the many versions of the welfare state, which regarded mass housing developments as the pre-eminent way to express equality. Instead, it looked for alternative visions for the provision of affordable housing to a mixture of different social classes, seeking, in this way, to avoid state-funded, egalitarian housing. The option was to embrace a model that was compatible with its values and its plans for economic and social modernisation, and which, at same time, would be capable of boosting the capital's global image.

In the built environment that was thus created, there was clear evidence of the desired modernisation in the adoption of the building typologies of the late CIAM models, which, at that time, were regarded as representing entirely new approaches. The rational, efficient, healthy, and functional architecture of freestanding slab and tower blocks was used as a landmark to reflect modernity. Besides making it possible to deliver higher population densities, thereby saving on land and consequently on the costs of land acquisition, it proved to be an efficient strategy for solving the problem of a phased development, without creating unnecessary flaws in the entire area. Furthermore, the generous provision of open spaces was regarded not only as a way of offering the community a series of public amenities, but it was also considered to be a means of physically dividing social groups and breaking down the zeilenbau effect of a continuous urban development. The building procurement model that was implemented, based on the development of the projects by different public and semi-public housing agencies under the sole coordination of the GTH, made it possible for a vast number of architects and other built environment professionals to become involved, thus contributing to the planned morphological diversity and architectural quality.

The drastic reduction in public investment and the alterations made in the development of the third and final phase of the programme compromised the success of the entire operation. After 1974, the key goal was to accelerate the delivery of housing designed specifically for rehousing socially vulnerable families.

This inevitably led to deviations from the programme's initial rationale, as the intended intermixing of different social groups was now limited. This, in turn, resulted in a "residualisation" of social housing, eventually contributing to the stigmatisation of Chelas.

Nevertheless, town planning and architecture were granted a prominent role in all aspects of the programme, showing an attempt to articulate urban planning and the delivery of housing, as well as approaching the relationship between the supply of housing and the size of the neighbourhood, seen also on the scale of the city itself, from the point of view of land use and the need to design and construct dwellings and other public amenities. These were two activities that until then had always been autonomous and (at least partly) uncoordinated. While accepting the limitations of a large-scale housing programme that was planned for, and built on, the periphery of the city of Lisbon in more-or-less isolated enclaves, involving various phases of construction taking place over a long period of time and under strictly controlled financing conditions, it is nonetheless undeniable that this operation stands as a remarkable example of a continuous experiment in the field of affordable housing undertaken in Portugal in the second half of the twentieth century, and, at the same time, as a sign of optimism and of a sense of common purpose.

The wide range of housing developments that were built, together with the programmatic and technical advances occurring throughout the period of the programme's implementation helped to develop a significant body of knowledge about how these different solutions performed socially, economically, and environmentally. This provides us with valuable evidence about (successful and unsuccessful) outcomes, which will certainly contribute towards the design of innovative and high-quality housing developments in the future.

BIBLIOGRAPHY

"Olivais Norte–Extractos da Memoria Descritiva do estudo Base de Olivais elaborada em 1955." *Arquitectura* no.81 (1964).

"Olivais Sul em Discussão." *Arquitectura* no.127–128 (1973).

Archer, R.W.. "From New Towns to Metrotowns and Regional Cities." *The American Journal of Economics and Sociology* Vol. 28, No. 3 (Jul. 1969): 257–269.

Baptista, Luís V. "Dominação Demográfica no Contexto do Sec.XX Português: Lisboa, a Capital." *Sociologia, Problemas e Práticas*, no.15 (1994): 53–77.

Benevolo, Leonardo. *História da Arquitectura Moderna*. São Paulo: Editorial Perspectiva, (2 edição, 1989 [1960].

Cardoso, António H., Armando F. Almeida, Carlos Reis, F. Rodrigues, and F. Sousa, F. (1982) "Projectos do Gabinete Tecnico da Habitação–Alguns Dados da Experiência Colhida na sua Elaboração e Realização em Obra de 1969 a 1979." *Boletim do Gabinete Técnico da Habitação* vol.6, no.41/42 (1982): 377–384.

Coelho, António Baptista. "Qualidade Arquitectónica Residencial." PhD Thesis in Architecture, Faculdade de Arquitectura da Universidade do Porto, 1994.

Duarte, Carlos S. "Habitação e Equipamento Colectivo na Suécia." *Boletim do Gabinete Tecnico da Habitação*, vol.1, no.4 (1965): 207–214.

FFH. *As Áreas na Habitação*. Gabinete de Estudos. Proc.101/1.6/GE de 20/7//0. Lisboa: Fundo de Fomento da Habitação, 1970.

FFH. *Estudos de Soluções Tipo de Fogos e das Caracteristicas a que os Edificios Deverão Obedecer para o Estabelecimento de Principios de Industrialização da Construção*. Gabinete de Estudos. Rel. no. 7/GE/71. Lisboa: Fundo de Fomento da Habitação, 1971.

FFH. *Principais Caracteristicas da Habitação Económica 1970/71*. Gabinete de Estudos, Rel. no. 3/GE/72, Proc.101/GE. Lisboa: Fundo de Fomento da Habitação, Março 1972

FFH. *Definição de Categorias de Habitação Social de Harmonia com o estabelecido no Decreto Lei no. 576/70 de 24 de Novembro*. Gabinete de Estudos, Sector de Tecnologia, Inf. no. 155/GE/73, Proc.47/GE. Lisboa: Fundo de Fomento da Habitação, 1973.

GTH. *Classificação e Nomenclatura das Habitações de Caracter Social–Proposta de norma–Grupo de Coordenação da Habitação*. Lisboa: GTH, 1966.

GTH. "Ficheiro de Projetos-Tipo para Habitação Social em Olivais Sul." *Boletim do Gabinete Técnico da Habitação*, vol.5, no. 30–33 (1976/77): 209–483.

Gandra, Hernâni. "Contribuição para o Estudo do Problema das Áreas da Habitação Social–Análise Comparativa." *Boletim do Gabinete Técnico da Habitação*, vol. 4, no. 26 (1974): 219–236.

Gibberd, Frederick. "The Master Design; Landscape; Housing; the Town Centres." In Evans, H. (1972) *New Towns, The British Experience*, 88–101. London: Charles Knight & Co. Ltd, 1972.

Gold, John R. "Hook: Revisiting the New Town That Might Have Been." Introduction to London County Council, *The Planning of a New Town*, vii–xxviii. Studies in International Planning History Series. London: Routledge, 2015 [1961].

Goulart de Medeiros. "Os Centro Cívico-Comerciais de Vallingby e Farsta." *Boletim do Gabinete Técnico da Habitação*, vol.1, no. 4 (1965): 215–220.

LNEC. *Informação Sobre a Situação Actual dos Empreendimentos e Necessidades da Habitação Social LNEC*, Proc.34/0/3483, Fevereiro, 1969. Lisboa: Laboratório Nacional de Engenharia Civil, 1969.

Machado, João Reis. "Plano de Chelas: V–Elementos Relativos à População que Habita em Barracas." *Boletim do Gabinete Técnico da Habitação*, vol.1, no.9, (1965): 441–453.

Morgado, H. "Variação do Custo de Construção com o Modo de Concepção do Edificio." *Boletim do Gabinete Técnico da Habitação*, vol. 3, no.21 (1971): 315–318.

Morgado, H. "Olivais Sul–Estudo analítico de Projectos." *Boletim do Gabinete Técnico da Habitação*, vol.3, no.21 (1971): 319–362.

Oliveira, Tiago. "As vicissitudes do espaço urbano moderno ou o menino e a água do banho : os Bairros dos Olivais." PhD Thesis in Architecture, Faculdade de arquitectura da Universidade de Lisboa, 2015.

Portas, Nuno. *Funções e Exigências das Áreas da Habitação. Informação Técnica–Edifícios 4*. Lisboa: MOP–Laboratório Nacional de Engenharia Civil, 1969.

Ramos, Tânia. "Os Espaços do Habitar Moderno: Evolução e Significados. Os Casos Português e Brasileiro." PhD Thesis in Territorial Engineering, Instituto Superior Técnico, Universidade Técnica de Lisboa, 2003.

Redol, Maria da Conceição. "As Normas e Regulamentos na Evolução da Dimensão dos Espaços do Fogo." Congresso da Ordem dos Engenheiros, Tema 2, Comunicação 15, 20–26 November 1977, Lisboa.

Reis Cabrita. "Conjunto Habitacional em Chelas." *Revista Arquitectura*, Serie 4, no. 140 (1979): 19–29.

Rowe, Peter G. *Modernity and Housing*. Cambridge Mass. & London: MIT Press, 1993.

Sant'Ana, J., Figueiredo, E., Antunes, J. "Aspectos da Intervenção do Gabinete Técnico da Habitação da Câmara Municipal de Lisboa na Construção da Habitação Social." *Boletim do Gabinete Técnico da Habitação*, vol.6, no.41/42 (2nd semester 1982): 3–30.

Silva Dias, Francisco, and José Lobo de Carvalho. "Plano de Urbanização de Chelas, Zona J." *Boletim do Gabinete Técnico da Habitação*, vol. 5, no.27, vol. 2 (1st semester 1974).

Silva, Maria da Conceição Tavares. "A Sublocação em Lisboa." *Boletim do Gabinete Técnico da Habitação*, vol.1, no.1, (1964): 44–51.

Silva Pereira, Raúl da. "Problemática da Habitação em Portugal." *Análise Social*, vol. 1, no.1 (1963).

Talen, Emily. *New Urbanism and American Planning: the conflict of Cultures*. New York: Routledge, 2005.

Tavares, Maria F. "Habitações Económicas. Federação de Caixas de Previdência. Arquitectura e Modos de Actuação no Exercício do Projecto." PhD Thesis in Architecture, Faculdade de Arquitectura da Universidade do Porto, 2015.

Tostões, Ana. "Conjuntos Urbanos Planeados na Cidade." In *Arquitectura Moderna Portuguesa, 1920–1970*, edited by Ana Tostões and Sandra Vaz Costa, 289–296. Lisboa: Instituto Português do Património Arquitectónico, 2004.

The Impossible Transition: Marcelo Caetano's Final Shutdown (1968–74)

MANUEL LOFF
University of Porto, Faculty of Arts and Humanities, Department of History and Political and International Studies. NOVA–New University of Lisbon, Institute of Contemporary History

In September 1968, at the age of 79, after 40 consecutive years in office, a cerebral bleed incapacitated Salazar and forced what had been built and consolidated as a personal dictatorship to find a substitute *Chefe* in Marcelo Caetano (1906–80). A professor of law as the founding leader of the authoritarian regime, Caetano had been Salazar's minister of Colonies (1944–47) and was appointed deputy head of the government (minister of the Presidency of the Council of Ministers) in 1955, mistakenly taken for an appointed successor but soon driven out of office by Salazar in 1958. Ten years later, Caetano returned to power, almost surprisingly, to replace Salazar.

Times had changed, though. The colonial war had started in Angola in March 1961 and the Portuguese government had been condemned in June that year by the UN Security Council because of its repressive action in Africa, in a vote which was to be repeated several times until 1974. Later that same year, in December, India invaded the three Portuguese enclaves of Goa, Daman, and Diu after eleven years of diplomatic stalemate imposed by Salazar's refusal to negotiate a transfer of sovereignty. Less than two years later, in 1963, war spread to Guinea-Bissau as the African Party for the Independence of Guinea and Cape Verde (PAIGC) launched its first operations against the Portuguese Army, in what would soon become the worst war scenario for the Portuguese. In 1964, it was turn of the Mozambique Liberation Front (FRELIMO) to attack the Portuguese colonial army from Tanzanian territory. Caetano led the country for the six final years of the dictatorship (1968–74) through a contradictory process of violent and repressive agony, strong economic growth (until the 1973 oil crisis) boosted by the distant war in the colonies, massive emigration (1.4 million from 1960 to 1973, of a population of 8.6 million in 1970), and social and political unrest. Out of this triumphantly emerged the military conspiracy organised by the young captains' *Movimento das Forças Armadas* (*Armed Forces Movement*, MFA) that put an end to the *Estado Novo* (25 April 1974) and opened the path for political and social revolution.

BIOGRAPHY

Manuel Loff, PhD in History and Civilisation (European University Institute, Florence), is a tenured Associate Professor at the Department of History and Political and International Studies, University of Porto, and a senior researcher at the Institute of Contemporary History/NOVA (New University of Lisbon), heading a thematic line on "Connected Histories: State-Buiding, Social Movements and Political Economy," and at the Research Centre on Dictatorship and Democracy (Centre d'Estudis sobre Dictadures i Democràcies, CEDID) of the Autonomous University of Barcelona (UAB).

He has been researching on 20th century political and social History (Fascism and Neofascism, Colonialism, International Relations and Education), Memory Studies, and 21st century authoritarian transitions through securitisation. Currently he is focused on comparative democratic transitions in the 1970s and 1980s; 21st century new authoritarian liberalism, extreme-right and neofascism; and social forms of (re)construction of collective memory on authoritarianism, coloniality, and political transitions.

Marcellism[1] was an attempt by an authoritarian regime born and consolidated in the 1930s and '40s *Age of Fascism* to rehearse political and institutional adaptations to the specific context of the late 1960s amidst deep social and economic changes. This process of calculated metamorphosis became, in fact, its final crisis and did not avoid nor probably did it really postpone the end.

In spite of Luís Reis Torgal's assumption that "there is, in fact, no political originality in Marcello Caetano's period in government,"[2] a part of Portuguese and international historiography tried to find in Marcello Caetano an equivalent, *avant la lettre*, to Adolfo Suárez, assuming that the Portuguese colonial war (1961–74) and its fatal corollary (the military's decision to finish it by overthrowing the regime) should be taken as the only truly distinctive factor that would have prevented a Spanish kind of political transition in Portugal. To a large extent, such an interpretation, widely subscribed by pretty much the whole right-wing section of the public, is based upon an overestimation of an interpretative model as equivocal as Samuel Huntington's, who, with excessive simplicity, sought to gather in a *third wave of democratisation*[3] cases as different as radical democratic transitions (such as the Portuguese Revolution of 1974–76) and *pact* transitions[4] (such as the Spanish, in the 1970s, and most of Latin America and Central Eastern Europe in the 1980s and '90s). Such historical and political accounts of the processes of democratisation, repeatedly described as historically inevitable, tend to find changes among the intentions of social and political ruling elites at the final stage of the authoritarian regimes they imposed (especially in Spain and Latin America)—changes that, once effectively put into practice, have made democracy possible. In other words, in these cases we would be talking about retroactive accounts of history, which, deliberately or inadvertently, tend to eventually *democratise* those elites and/or their political behaviour.[5]

---

[1] *Marcelismo* is used in Portuguese literature and collective memory on the 1968–74 period. Caetano's first name may be spelled both "Marcello" (an ancient form that he personally preferred) or "Marcelo," and I will use "Marcello" only when sources spell it that way. I will proceed the same way with President Américo Tomás surname (spelled "Thomaz" in most sources).

[2] Luís R. Torgal, *Marcello Caetano, Marcelismo e "Estado Social." Uma Interpretação* (Coimbra: Imprensa da Universidade de Coimbra, 2013), 15.

[3] Samuel Huntington, *Third Wave: the Democratization in the Late 20th Century* (Norman: University of Oklahoma Press, 1991).

[4] See Guillermo O'Donnell, Philippe Schmitter *Transitions from Authoritarian Rule: Tentative Conclusions about Uncertain Democracies* (Baltimore: The Johns Hopkins University Press, 1986).

[5] For a wider discussion, see Manuel Loff, "*Marcelismo* (and Late Francoism): Unsuccessful Authoritarian Modernisations," in Miguel Ángel Ruiz Carnicer (ed.), *From Franco to Freedom: The Roots of the Transition to Democracy in Spain, 1962–1982* (Brighton/Chicago/Toronto: Sussex Academic Press, 2018), 137–74.

2. THE "EVOLUÇÃO NA CONTINUIDADE" (1968–74): CAETANO'S IMPOSSIBLE REFORM

All in all, that decade during which he was drawn apart from government (1958–68) would not be long enough for the hierarchs of the regime to find an alternative to Caetano to succeed to Salazar. For a significantly longer period than Arias Navarro in Spain in 1975–76, soon after Franco's death, *Marcellism* would be the final agonising corollary of the *Estado Novo*, and Caetano had the opportunity to demonstrate the terrible limitations of his reformist agenda. Those who would be popularly known as the *ultras* (the Salazarist extreme-right equivalent to the Francoist *bunker*) during Caetano's administration, though convinced of his disloyalty, or at least disaffection, towards Salazar's heritage, were not, in the end, able to prevent him from getting a hold on power. President Tomás himself, after consulting "over forty" relevant personalities of the regime's elite when Salazar fell ill in September 1968, would not conceal to Caetano his disgust at appointing him to lead the government, a post that Caetano aspired to and would have asked the president to grant him "more than once" during the three-week interreign of Salazar's illness. Eventually, according to Tomás, "the country," or what he thought the country was, *"was increasingly [leaning] towards Marcello Caetano's solution; [. . .] his friends and supporters were feeding such an ambiance [. . .] that any other solution would be, not only misunderstood, but even unwelcome."*[6]

Caetano, as he had acted often before with Salazar, wanted to appear uninterested in assuming office. When the president finally invited him to lead the Government, nevertheless, he specifically told Tomás he would "look for the general elections to be held in 1969 [. . .] as an opportunity to allow the nation to express its point of view" about the regime's colonial policy and the war. The 1969 election outcome would remain, in fact, until the end of his days as his crucial argument not to question the choice for war in Africa. In Caetano's account, the president would have reminded him that, if the result was not "favourable to the defence of the overseas [territories] policy [. . .] the military would intervene."[7] In Tomás' account, the army, who had been "responsible for the National Revolution of 28 May 1926, assuming it was, and in fact still was, the faithful guardian of its perpetuation," had made "a formal representation," acknowledging his free choice of who would replace Salazar, expecting him to preserve and "uncompromisingly and unconditionally defend national integrity," to which Caetano "did not oppose any objection, nor even the slightest repair."[8]

[6] Américo Thomaz, *Últimas Décadas de Portugal*, vol. III (Lisbon: Edições Fernando Pereira, [1983]), 296–298.

[7] Marcello Caetano, *Depoimento* (Rio de Janeiro, São Paulo: Distribuidora Record, 1974),14.

[8] Thomaz, *Últimas Décadas*, III, 1983, 298.

2.1 ALL THE PRESIDENT'S MEN: MARCELLISTS AND TECHNOCRATS

Two cycles are usually detected in the short Marcellist rule. Fernando Rosas calls them "the two times of *Marcellism*": in the first, from autumn 1968 to 1970 (when liberalising measures for the labour unions were reversed), or 1972 (when most Marcellist liberals definitively broke with Caetano), the plan was "to try to liberalise without abandoning the war effort in the colonies"; in the second, from 1971/72 to April 1974, the move was "to keep the military effort, sacrificing liberalisation and, with it, the whole regime."[9]

Though permanently committed to assuring the *ultras* with whom he had clashed all along the 1950s that he would stay loyal to Salazar's heritage (authoritarian corporatism, refusal of any sort of concession in the colonial status quo, war in Africa to preserve them), Marcelo Caetano had, at the beginning of his time in power (1968–69), room to put forward several changes. In spite of his impersonated modesty ("for a long period [Portugal] was used to being led by a man of genius," i.e. Salazar; "from today it will have to adapt to the rule of common men"—the very same words he had used years 17 earlier, when he discussed Salazar's succession for the first time before the single Party congress in 1951), Caetano, in his inaugural address, that was to be remembered for the motto "renovação na continuidade" ("renovation within continuity"), said he was "animated" to "proceed, whenever adequate, to the necessary reforms."[10]

In 1974, soon after leaving for Brazil in exile, while describing his performance in government, he improvised the idea that "the solution adopted in September 68," taking hold of an unchanged Salazar ministerial cabinet, *"was an expedient to abbreviate the crisis"* opened by Salazar's illness, *"and everyone expected [that after the 1969 elections I would] form a government 'genuinely' of mine. It was only natural that the reforms to be undertaken were to be prepared already with this new government."*[11] But the truth is that at the end of 1969 he had already reshuffled the cabinet twice. Caetano dismissed four of the ministers of the last of Salazar's cabinets, including the last of his deputies in government (Mota Veiga, replaced by Alfredo Vaz Pinto) and the man who had led the war in Africa since 1962, General Gomes de Araújo, replaced as Minister of Defence by General Sá Viana Rebelo, who remained in office for most of Caetano's rule. He kept in office the remaining eleven ministers of the last of Salazar's cabinets, including several Marcellists with whom he had never ceased to be in contact while he was out of power. Contrary to his post-1974 narrative, he did not wait until after the November 1969 renovation of the dictatorship parliament to get rid of several other of Salazar's ministers.

---

[9] Fernando Rosas, "O Marcelismo ou a falência da política de transição no Estado Novo"J. M. Brandão de Brito (ed.), *Do Marcelismo ao Fim do Império. Revolução e Democracia* (Lisbon: Editorial Notícias, 1999), 47.

[10] Marcello Caetano, "Saibamos ser dignos desta hora," address at the Palácio de São Bento, Lisbon, 27 September 1968 (Lisbon, SNI, 1968), 4, 6.

[11] Caetano, *Depoimento*, 1974, 63.

In March 1969, six months before the election, he made his second reshuffle, replacing two other ministers; one of them, Correia de Oliveira, had been an obvious competitor for Salazar's succession as he had been chosen in 1961 by the dictator as his minister of the presidency, and then (1965) as his main economic policy supervisor. One of Salazar's technocrats, he was a hard-liner in colonial matters but, involved in a paedophile sex scandal in 1967 (known as the *Ballets Roses* affair[12]), he became hopelessly unfit to lead any sort of organised extreme-right opposition to Caetano within the regime. Getting rid of him allowed Caetano to appoint a whole new economic team made of Marcellist technocrats.[13]

During the 1969 electoral campaign, the true heavyweight of the ultra-Salazarist resistance to Caetano's new course, the Minister for Foreign Affairs Franco Nogueira, stepped down from government. He had been Salazar's minister since the beginning of the war in 1961, and in 1968 he had more chance than Correia de Oliveira of competing with Marcelo Caetano to replace Salazar. In his *Diaries*, Nogueira stated that he wanted to leave office as soon as Caetano was appointed, warning President Tomás that, on "the most serious problems and national top priorities: Defence, Overseas, and foreign policy," Caetano "had been and remained opposed to everything that has been done," implying that his appointment "could well be the prelude to the loss of the Overseas [territories]." When asked by Caetano to remain in office, he finally would have accepted to remain only "for a short period of time until beginning [1969]"[14] because President Tomás assured him that the commanding officers of the "Armed Forces Overseas" had asked for it. Nogueira eventually left government in October 1969, but remained in the National Assembly until 1973, when it became a new platform for the extreme-right watchdogs to guard the *purity* of Salazarism, and not only for the "democratic semi-opposition" Caetano wanted to co-opt into the regime's elite, as Tiago Fernandes chose to emphasise.[15]

What Marcelo Caetano described as *his* first cabinet was formed in January 1970 after his third reshuffle in sixteen months, replacing seven (out of fourteen) cabinet ministers. Only three of them had been appointed by Salazar: Army, Education, and Corporations; the latter was already a Marcellist appointed by Salazar, and none of the remaining was part of the inorganic extreme right that was clinging to President Tomás. He appointed an ambitious reformist in Education (Veiga Simão) and a loyal Marcellist, Baltasar Rebelo de Sousa, to lead two different departments (Corporations and Health). To work with him as Secretary of State for Labour, Caetano called another of his technocrats, Joaquim Silva Pinto.

[12] The *Ballets Roses* affair (1966–71) was about a network of sexual abuse of young girls involving several top officials of the Portuguese Government (including the minister Correia de Oliveira), justice, and police. In spite of the hard-line censorship, it became known by the foreign press at the end of 1967 soon after Antunes Varela (Minister of Justice) was pushed out of Salazar's government for not having prevented the investigation from getting as far as it did. Mário Soares was accused of leaking information on the case and was deported (March–November 1968) to the island of São Tomé, in Africa.

[13] The Minister Dias Rosas, Secretary of Industry Rogério Martins, Secretary of Trade Xavier Pintado, and Under-Secretary for Planning, João Salgueiro. After 1964, Martins (1928–2017) had a long career in big corporate companies; in 1983 he was elected to Parliament with the right-wing PSD, and in 1991 with the Socialist Party. Salgueiro (b. 1934) started an impressive corporate career after leaving government in 1971, interchanged with several top official positions until this day. A prominent right-wing politician, he was Minister of Finance 1981–83.

[14] Franco Nogueira, *Um Político Confessa-se. (Diário: 1960–1968)*, 3rd ed. (Porto: Civilização, [1987]), 314–316.

[15] See Tiago Fernandes, *Nem Ditadura, Nem Revolução. A Ala Liberal e o Marcelismo (1968–1974)* (Lisbon: Dom Quixote, Assembleia da República, 2005), 151–154.

The cabinet was then reduced to ten ministers; a single one (Gonçalves Rapazote, Interior) had been appointed by Salazar, significantly still in full control of the whole repressive network of the *Estado Novo*. Pushing Rapazote out of government in November 1973, immediately after the new general election and a few months before the revolution, is the only significant change in Caetano's government after 1970. With the military, political, and especially the economic situation getting extremely critical, Caetano, increasingly suspicious of everyone around him, ran short of people to work with.

Already confronted with the young army captains rebellion—the *Armed Forces Movement* was being organised since September 1973— he decided to appoint one of his *loyals* as the first civil minister of Defence (Silva Cunha), in a move resented by top- and middle-rank military officers. It became apparently so hard to find reliable military officers to work with that Silva Cunha appointed a former *Abrilada* man, Lt. Col. Viana de Lemos, to become his under-secretary for the army.[16] Already in August 1972, when the inflationary crisis and the working-class unrest were very evident, he had to let go his economic team, led by Dias Rosas. The reformist technocrats lost a considerable amount of power, "as if they anticipated the dead end"[17] which the regime was finally getting to: the war effort, inflation, and a lack of resources to implement the social policies Caetano and his technocrats thought essential to contain social unrest.

All in all, Marcelo Caetano did not have to face any hard extreme-right opposition inside the government, because, in fact, he already had room in 1968 to dismiss the most significant Salazarist hardliners and replace them with loyal Marcellists. It was he who decided to defer sacking Correia de Oliveira and Nogueira, and years later Rapazote; the choice of timing was not due to any pressure from President Tomás or the military; and when he eventually did it, nothing happened. Moreover, any serious political extreme-right opposition became even less viable with the death of two of his major enemies inside the regime (former ministers Mário de Figueiredo and Soares da Fonseca, both deceased in September 1969) and Teotónio Pereira's physical incapacity, the only alternative President Tomás had believed in 1968 would have done a better job than Caetano. Former Salazar men like Santos Costa or Costa Leite were now in the shadows, none of them with any political or institutional position since at least 1969. As could be said for the Francoist *bunker* in Spain, if Caetano had really wanted to open a reformist gradual transitional process in 1968, he would have faced on his right "a reactionary, fundamentalist and fascistising [. . .] 'paper tiger'."

---

[16] *Abrilada* is the name usually given to the April 1961 military conspiracy against Salazar, led by his own minister of Defence, General Botelho Moniz, with the support of the Kennedy administration committed to avoiding another unpredictable military conflict in Africa in which African Nationalists would be driven to seek Soviet and Chinese support. The *coup* failed even before troops were mobilised and Salazar replaced every major army commander and ordered them to push forward a military campaign in Angola. See José Freire Antunes, *Kennedy e Salazar. O Leão e a Raposa* (Lisbon: Difusão Cultural, 1991).

[17] Rosas, "O Marcelismo...," 1999, 55.

For Fernando Rosas, *"Caetano has never figured out this essential weakness on the extreme right of the regime at the crucial moment of [Salazar's] succession. On the contrary, fear of it would be a constant element obsessively paralysing his rule."*[18]

2.2 A TECHNOCRATIC SOCIAL STATE?

The *Estado Novo* understood it had to meet the challenges of post-WWII, and the need for renewal of political staff and the relative depletion of the first Salazarist generation was met by Caetano's ability to tune in with those sectors who wanted to modernise the Portuguese regime. Since the end of WWII he had cultivated his ties with several technocrats who worked in the new public and private corporations and played the role of the reformer from within.

The world war had paved the way to a very late industrialisation in Portugal: only in the post-1945 years and throughout the 1950s and '60s did the country undergo a real and intense modernising boost, while the rest of Europe was engaged in post-war reconstruction. Urbanisation, state economic planning policies, intensive private and public investment in new productive infrastructures, together with a state-controlled internationalisation of Portuguese trade produced a substantially different society. The Development Plans (*Planos de Fomento*) implemented by the dictatorship after WWII,[19] together with *"industrial growth [. . .], expansion of the education system, particularly post-secondary technical and scientific [. . .],all these trends converged towards a higher level of social and political participation, though merely illusive in some cases, of a social segment whose main characteristics were higher education, being an active part of the Public Administration's Technical Departments, of big corporations and liberal professions."*[20]

Economic planning, with all its complex bureaucratic organisation, and the expansion of the financial sector, offered a wide range of opportunities to a new generation of trained professionals. On the other hand, a more complex and resourceful Portuguese Colonial Administration was trying to adapt and to respond to the global impact of decolonisation, offering a variety of professional, political and business opportunities for Portuguese settlers. As far as the traditional Salazarist elites were concerned, both the military and the traditional (trading and landowning) bourgeoisie lost a significant amount of power to these bureaucrats who represented the more modern sections of the urban bourgeoisie, especially those connected to industrial and financial capital. Catholic reactionary scholars, close to the dictator's profile, remained, nevertheless, in control of most political higher decision-making positions.

[18] Rosas, "O Marcelismo...," 1999, 43–46.

[19] Four *Planos de Fomento* were adopted by the *Estado Novo* regime: 1953–58; 1959–64; 1965–67 (*Plano Intercalar*–Intermediate Plan) and 1968–73; a fifth (in fact, called Fourth Plan) was ready to be implemented for the 1974–79 period when the 25 April 1974 revolution suspended its application.

[20] José Manuel Leite Viegas, *Elites e Cultura Política na História Recente de Portugal* (Oeiras: Celta, 1996), 85.

All state policies had been re-designed to endorse the war effort, inevitably jeopardising the impact of the embryonic social policies the regime had been forced to put forward when it realised how potentially explosive was the swift social and economic change of the 1950s and '60s. A very significant part of national resources were now consumed by defence: 48 per cent of all ordinary tax revenue in 1973 (against 36 per cent in 1958); during this same period, social expenditure on policies such as education and health rose from 18 to 28 per cent, but remained evidently insufficient and ineffective; on the whole, defence absorbed 133 billion escudos from 1961 to 1973, while all public investment over the same period did not exceed 62 billion.[21]

Caetano's rise to power in 1968 did not change this trend: war and the *Social State* [*Estado Social*] which he kept insisting he was trying to build forced his government to raise public expenditure more than ever before: for the first time under the dictatorship public expenditure reached 26.1 per cent of GDP in 1972–73.[22] Alongside the military, that technocratic component of the civilian elite that had been ascending since 1945 kept expectations intact, hoping the regime would have to grant them more visibility to produce the necessary measures to contain social and political unrest, both in Portugal and in Africa.[23]

Caetano would soon prove impotent to change the political course of the war—if in fact he had ever wanted to—but he did try to go beyond the modernisation project of the 1945-68 period, an autarkic *industrialism*, searching instead for a "specialisation line of national production in areas in which Portugal had comparative advantage, coordinating with foreign markets, especially European," granting, on the other hand, "greater importance to social factors"—education, social welfare, health—but "disregarding the effective conditions which would have allowed or prevented these aims from being accomplished." In this sense, "Caetano and the politicians who were close to him," recruited amidst that technocratic elite of those "social segments of higher scientific and technical qualification," were apparently *"pointing towards a social state—a subtle way of changing the primary meaning of the corporative state—but evaded the problem of the regime's democratisation and liberalisation."*[24]

"I advocate a Social State—but not a socialist one," Caetano argued. *"Social because it enforces the social interest through an authority based on collective reason [. . .] while it aims to push the poorest layers of the population to accede to modern life and to protect those in labour relations who may be considered as the weak party. But not socialist because it aims to preserve, dignify and even stimulate the private sector."*[25]

---

[21] See Américo Ramos dos Santos, "Abertura e bloqueamento da economia portuguesa," A. Reis (ed.), *Portugal Contemporâneo*, vol. 5 (Lisbon: Publicações Alfa, 1989), 109–150; Eugénio Rosa, *A Economia Portuguesa em Números* (Lisbon: Moraes, 1975).

[22] See Alfredo Marques, *Política Económica e Desenvolvimento em Portugal (1926–1959). As Duas Estratégias do Estado Novo no Período de Isolamento Nacional* (Lisbon: Livros Horizonte, 1988), 184 (table 6).

[23] See Manuel Loff, "Elites and economic modernization in Portugal (1945–1995): authoritarianism, revolution and liberalism," in F. Sattler, and C. Boyer (Eds.), *European Economic Elites–Between a New Spirit of Capitalism and the Erosion of State Socialism* (Berlin: Duncker & Humblot, 2009), 153–195.

[24] Viegas, *Elites*, 1996, pp. 101ff.

[25] Caetano, speech at Porto Town Hall, 21 May 1969, *apud* Torgal, *Marcello Caetano*, 2013, 58.

Inside the regime, or at least in its co-opted semi-opposition, Francisco Sá Carneiro had easily understood that *"the Social State is no alternative to liberalisation. Saying it is social does not define ethically a state. There is no social state. Every modern state is necessarily social.[...] A Social State can be either despotic or based on the rule of law."*[26]

Caetano's "technocrats' momentum for reform lacked strong and enduring support" from a "two-headed structure of the Portuguese political system"[27] and from an "ambiguous" Caetano. *"Their inability to resolve the Europe-Africa dilemma and their resolve to continue the war in the colonies, hardly consistent with the need to modernise the economy, led to the frustration of the technocrats and their withdrawal from government,"* in fact only partial, "in the early 1972 reshuffle."[28]

2.3 CHANGING LABELS

Manuel de Lucena's 1971 pioneering interpretation of *Marcellism* was fundamentally correct. At that time, he aggregated the various aspects of what was being called Caetano's *liberalisation* under those two concepts he had used in his inaugural speech. On "continuity," Lucena was very assertive: "continuity is manifested in all key areas. Marcellism never questions the strong state and never abjured corporatism." "Chapter after chapter" of every major changes Caetano advertised, *"on constitutional reform or on redesigning corporative bodies, on the reform of labour law and Social Security [...] fidelity [to the Estado Novo principles] is by no means temporary or tactical; it is deep and visceral."*

Under "renovation," Lucena pointed out "three aspects" of the Marcellist project: "modernisation, liberalisation and integration." By *modernisation* he meant *"both the improvement of old techniques and institutions and the creation of new mechanisms and bodies that [were conceived as] an unprecedented response to emerging situations."* As for "liberalisation," Lucena believed that it was "a means and not the end of Marcellism." In 1971, he predicted that "political freedom and rights will not be taken into account and restored as such. At this level," again, "there is no distance from Salazar."[29] It was true that changes included in Caetano's bill to reform the Constitution, submitted to the National Assembly in December 1970, were consistent with a self-limited intention to alleviate some of the most evident traits of the repressive system, but, at the end of the process and in a context of "serious subversion," as the government repeatedly called the war in Africa and the opposition actions in Portugal, the whole approach seemed purely cosmetic from the beginning.

[26] Sá Carneiro, *Diário de Lisboa*, Lisbon, 25 June 1971, *apud* Manuel de Lucena, *A Evolução do Sistema Corporativo Português*, vol. 2 (*O Marcelismo*) (Lisbon: Perspectivas&Realidades, 1976), 28.

[27] González-Fernández is referring to competing roles of the head of state and the head of government.

[28] González-Fernández, "La otra modernización:...," 2016, 319.

[29] Lucena, *A Evolução do Sistema...*, II, 1976, 187.

It was, in fact, revealing his that he chose to change the names of several repressive and coercive instruments of the dictatorship without changing anything substantial about them:

(i) The political police was rebranded *Direção-Geral de Segurança* in 1969,[30] but Portuguese collective co-memory would simply remember it in the future by its former denomination (*Polícia Internacional de Defesa do Estado*, PIDE, 1945–69). Small alterations in a very few aspects of its organisational structure "were not enough to say that major changes have occurred, because in practice it all remained unchanged":[31] the capacity for the political police to conduct investigation, to prevent lawyers from being present during questionings because of the nature of the crimes political prisoners were accused of (treason and crime against state security) and the abuse of "security measures" (though slightly corrected) under which prison sentences were arbitrarily extended. Under Caetano, who posed as a defender of the "humanisation of repression,"[32] the special courts of law to which political prisoners were subject (the *Tribunais Plenários*) remained blatantly political and arbitrary. If conditions were still appalling in Portugal, they were beyond measure in the colonies, especially in those where war was being held against the African liberation movements. Again, the few parliamentary interventions of the liberal member of the National Assembly, Sá Carneiro, infuriated Caetano.[33] On the other hand, Caetano, showing full respect for the *ultras*' own role within the regime, left unmoved the militia (*Legião Portuguesa*) Salazar created in 1936, on the eve of the Spanish War.

(ii) The information and propaganda agency had already changed its name in 1968 from *Secretariado Nacional de Informação, Cultura Popular e Turismo* (SNI) to *Secretaria de Estado da Informação e Turismo* (SEIT).[34] The best sign that nothing was going to change was given by the fact that César Moreira Baptista, an old-guard Marcellist already appointed by Salazar in 1958 as secretary of the SNI, was called by Caetano in 1968 as under-secretary of the head of government for merely three weeks and was soon after appointed secretary of the *new* SEIT.[35]

(iii) The General Directorate of Censorship, created in 1933, was replaced in 1971 by several regional commissions of what became known as the *Previous Examination* (*Exame Prévio*), the new name given to the censorship system, operating at a regional scale but depending on the same national secretariat as before.[36] Censorship under Caetano had to face a much stronger, creative and pugnacious cultural dissidence in the late 1960s to early 1970s

[30] See Decree-Law no. 49,401, 19 November 1969, and no. 368/72, 30 September 1972. Irene F. Pimentel, *A História da PIDE* (n.p., Círculo de Leitores and Temas&Debates, 2007), 46–51.

[31] Fernando Rosas *et al.* (eds.), *Tribunais Políticos. Tribunais Militares Especiais e Tribunais Plenários durante a Ditadura e o Estado Novo* (Lisbon: Temas&Debates, Círculo de Leitores, 2009), 155.

[32] Marcello Caetano, *Minhas Memórias de Salazar*, 3rd ed. (Lisbon: Verbo, 1985), 565.

[33] See Caetano, *Depoimento*, 1974, 70–80.

[34] Decree-Law no. 48,686, 15 November 1968.

[35] Moreira Baptista would become Minister of Interior in the 1973 final government reshuffle.

[36] Law no. 5/71, 5 November 1971, and Decree-Law no. 150/72, 5 May 1972. See Ana Cabrera, *Marcelo Caetano: Poder e Imprensa* (Lisbon: Livros Horizonte, 2006), and Cândido de Azevedo, *Censura de Salazar e Marcelo Caetano* (Lisbon: Caminho, 1999).

and, in fact, it did not hesitate, according to the instructions conveyed by Moreira Baptista to the censors, to keep the same set of bans that had been enforced under Salazar against anything that could "attempt against principles of the constitutional order," "offend" the authorities, the armed forces, "President Salazar" or "the Christian morals traditional in the country," colonial and foreign policies, "so intimately connected," or "to establish a political antinomy between President Salazar and the President [Caetano]." Censors were asked to be "especially attentive" to "subversion," "Marxist doctrines" and "Communist activity," "wage and academic demands," "pacifist ideas," "new trends of a certain sector of the Catholic Church" or *"anything that, in literary pages and those dedicated to young people, [. . .] may endanger the upbringing of the younger generations."*[37]

(iv) Finally, Marcelo Caetano decided to rebrand the single Party, the *União Nacional* (UN), into *Ação Nacional Popular* (ANP) at the 5th Congress of the UN, in February 1970. There were grandiloquent calls for "political mobilisation," less heard within the old UN, especially aimed in the 1970s at women and young people, the two sections of society undergoing fundamental changes in a context of industrialisation and war. Yet in spite of these, the ANP remained in fact until the end the "defensive organisation" its leader, Elmano Alves, wished the single Party would cease to be in 1973.[38]

2.4 ELECTIONS AND POLITICAL PLURALISM

After a year in government, Caetano wanted to enact a democratic sanction to his rule by organising the 1969 election to the National Assembly differently. Every election had, from the beginning of the dictatorship, been systematically rigged.[39] Caetano himself had been in charge of the electoral machinery of the single Party from 1947 to 1955. Now he wanted to "the opposition to go all the way to the polls" and promised "that the election would be honest and loyal,"[40] as he wrote five years later. Caetano knew that this time he had to prevent the opposition from withdrawing their candidates. It is a fact that in 1969 there were 400,000 more voters registered than in 1965, but it was still less than a fifth of the Portuguese metropolitan population.[41] More significantly, candidates were now allowed to appoint delegates next to each polling station,[42] a possibility which, in such circumstances, could be seized by opposition election committees only in the main urban areas, and facing numerous obstacles to doing their job. But that was new, and the opposition understood it.

[37] César Moreira Baptista, Under-Secretary of the Presidency of the Council of Ministers, "Normas a observar pela Direção dos Serviços de Censura," 14 October 1968, Comissão do Livro Negro sobre o Regime Fascista, *A Política de Informação no Regime Fascista*, vol. 1 (Lisbon: Presidência do Conselho de Ministros, [1980]), 214–215.

[38] See Manuel B. da Cruz, "Acção Nacional Popular," A. Barreto, M.F. Mónica (eds.), *Dicionário de História de Portugal*, vol. 7 (Porto: Figueirinhas, 2000), 32–35.

[39] For a global appraisal of Salazarist elections, see Manuel Loff, "Electoral Proceedings in Salazarist Portugal (1926–1974): Formalism and Fraud," in ROMANELLI, Raffaele (ed.), *How Did They Become Voters? The History of Franchise in Modern European Representation* (The Hague/London/Boston: Kluwer Law International, 1998), 227–50.

[40] Caetano, *Depoimento*, 1974, 57.

[41] Manuel B. da Cruz, *O Partido e o Estado no Salazarismo* (Lisboa: Presença, 1988), 204. The electoral roll in the colonies was ludicrous: 184,000 voters in Angola (3.3 per cent of the population); in Mozambique, in 1973, after the electoral roll had been enhanced, only 111,000 voters were registered (1.2 per cent of the population). Fernando Tavares Pimenta, *Angola, os Brancos e a Independência* (Porto: Edições Afrontamento, 2008), 319, 322.

[42] Decree-Law no. 49,229, 10 September 1969.

After eight years of war in the African colonies, the student protests that emerged in 1962 became continuous at the end of the decade, and together with massive emigration, helped push up wages and provide comparatively better living standards. The regime was now facing new urban young activists who strengthened the Communist underground organisation but also a new far left that broke up with the PCP after 1963 over the Sino-Soviet split and Guevara's impulse for armed struggle against war in Africa and the dictatorship. The impact of the Colonial War in the radicalisation of the opposition movements was such that, alongside two small armed organisations completely independent from the PCP (the *Liga de Unidade e Ação Revolucionária*, LUAR, operating since 1967, and the *Brigadas Revolucionárias*, since 1971, created by former young Communist militants), even the Communists secretly decided, in 1965, to create the *Ação Revolucionária Armada* (ARA), engaged from 1970 to 1972 in sabotage operations against the Portuguese military effort in Africa.[43]

At the same time, the PCP found their favourite allies in Catholic activists in the labour movement and campaigning against the war. Together with them and some young independent Socialists, in 1969 the Communists put together the *Comissões Democráticas Eleitorais* (CDE), presenting candidates in 19 out of the 22 metropolitan constituencies. But that was not new: in the National Assembly elections of 1961 and 1965, the opposition agreed to present candidates in most constituencies; they all had been eventually withdrawn from the race, as would happen again in 1973, once all expectations on the *Marcellist Spring* were definitely over. But not in 1969: 18 of the 19 CDE lists went to the polls, having to compete in three major constituencies with the *Comissões Eleitorais de Unidade Democrática* (CEUD). Behind these was Mário Soares' *Ação Socialista Portuguesa* (ASP), created in 1964, which became the *Partido Socialista* in 1973, bringing together old-guard Republicans and young social-democrats who wanted to operate independently from the PCP.

At any rate, Caetano had no intention whatsoever of allowing any opposition candidate to be elected: according to the official results of the 1969 election, no opposition list won in any of the 18 out of 30 constituencies in which their candidates were allowed.[44] He decided, on the other hand, to co-opt a group of nineteen candidates (out of 130) into the single Party's ticket, most of them moderate Catholics no longer condoning the support of the top Church hierarchy to the dictatorship, but all the same opposing the radical democratic and anti-colonial stance of progressive Catholics. Once elected, they became known as the Liberal Wing *(Ala Liberal)*, which "virtually [became] the political nucleus publicly recognised as best representing the reformist movement."[45] Most of these liberals would create the main Portuguese right-wing party (the *Partido Popular Democrático*, PPD)[46] soon after the fall of the regime.

---

[43] See Ana Sofia Ferreira, "Luta armada en Portugal (1970–1974)" (PhD Thesis, Faculdade de Ciências Sociais e Humanas da Universidade Nova de Lisboa, 2015); João Madeira, *História do PCP. Das Origens ao 25 de Abril (1921–1974)* (Lisbon: Tinta-da-China, 2013), 567–79.

[44] Official results: UN: 980,800 votes (88 per cent); CDE: 111,095 votes (10 per cent); CEUD: 20,654 votes (1.8 per cent); *Comissão Eleitoral Monárquica* (independent Monarchists, only in Lisbon): 0.1 per cent. Abstentions: 38.4 per cent. Electoral system was majoritarian.

[45] Viegas, *Elites*, 1996, p. 86.

[46] Francisco Sá Carneiro and Francisco Pinto Balsemão were the two first right-wing Prime-Ministers (1980–83) in the democratic period and had been members of the *Ala Liberal* under Caetano. The party changed its name to *Social-Democrata* (PSD) in 1976. Since the first democratic elections (1975) it has been the largest right-wing party of the Portuguese political system.

The relationship between these liberals and Caetano was tense from the beginning. They described their political "intervention" as "free and independent," and assumed Caetano's intentions as a genuine programme of transition towards the "introduction of a Western-European kind of [political] regime," which they believed to be Caetano's "ultimate goal."[47] When he moved away from any real transitional programme, liberals found themselves standing alone by a reformist agenda which they had thought to be the new government's prime purpose. Caetano, for his part, had very different expectations of the liberals' role within the regime: they had been elected inside "a list supporting my Government, and that implied the acceptance of a certain discipline and commitment to loyal collaboration."[48] While, in fact, it was clearly his aim that *"the system remained authoritarian, although in a different setting from the past, [Caetano] used the democratic semi-opposition"*—a concept which Tiago Fernandes applies to the Liberal Wing—*"as a support in his clashes with the more conservative factions of the regime, to assure foreign respectability and to stabilise his authority within the state and institutions."* Nevertheless, as he perceived "every project of transformation of the system put forward by the semi-opposition as a way to remove [him from] power," he pushed them "to radicalisation," eventually, according to Fernandes, "withdrawing any support to the regime and getting closer to the maximalist opposition" movements[49]—which, in fact, never really happened.

2.5 CAETANO AND THE WORKERS' MOVEMENT:
FROM LIBERALISATION TO OPEN CONFLICT

In June 1969, Caetano put forward a reform of the *national unions* aiming to comply to ILO suggestions.[50] Unions were now allowed to organise themselves on a larger territorial scale, but still not on a national level, and were also allowed for the first time to appoint delegates inside companies. The most relevant change was to remove power from the Ministry of Corporations to approve every trade union's elected board. To suspend any union leader or to invalidate any election was now a matter for the courts. For the numerous occasions in which the government appointed administrative commissions to replace suspended union boards, leaving them indefinitely in office, there was now a six-month delay to call for a new election. A more rhetorical measure, however, was to formally remove from the Minister of Corporations the legal capacity to dissolve a trade union: the new law transferred this capacity to the *Conselho Corporativo* at the top of the corporative system, which, in fact, was "no more than a [smaller] council of ministers" (Presidency, Economy, Corporations, . . .). In the same sense, it was now up to the *Instituto Nacional do Trabalho e da Previdência* (INTP) and no longer the minister to allow the affiliation of trade unions in international organisations.

[47] Electoral Manifesto ("Comunicado") by Francisco L. Sá Carneiro, Joaquim Macedo, Joaquim Pinto Machado C.S., and José da Silva, 28 September 1969, Francisco Sá Carneiro, *Textos*, vol. 1 (1969–1973) (Lisbon: Alethêia, 2010), 4–5.

[48] Caetano to F. Pinto Balsemão, letter, 15 July 1971, *Cartas Particulares a Marcello Caetano*, ed. by José Freire Antunes, vol. I (Lisbon: Dom Quixote, 1985), 304.

[49] Fernandes, *Nem ditadura...*, 2005, 72.

[50] Decree-Law no. 49,058, 14 June 1969.

General policy to deny any request in that sense remained, however, unchanged, but a formal ban was abrogated.[51] In fact, the whole reform had been prepared a few months before Salazar was replaced by Caetano with Gonçalves Proença, Minister of Corporations from 1961 to 1970. According to Fátima Patriarca, only the new government's instructions to restrain the police from "any sort of intervention in [labour] conflicts," unless they were called in by the employers, though clearly limited as they were[52] and lagging "very far from any legalisation of strikes," can be inscribed in Caetano's *new course* and should be read as a response to the "unusual outbreak of social unrest beginning in the first week of January 1969." After this, "strikes spread in some of the most important manufacturing units of Lisbon and Setúbal's industrial belt." In the course of 1969, soon after Caetano came into power, ninety strikes were called, all illegal, especially in the first two months (i.e. before the labour reform), leading the government to consider that there should be "a central command controlling all these movements."[53] In search of international respectability, and in a context of very rapid social and economic change, in which Caetano wanted to look committed to building up his *Estado Social*, the regime's elite thought it more viable to open the way to actual political pluralism at the trade union level.

Nevertheless, Communists and progressive Catholics were winning control over several significative trade unions in this area at the end of the 1960s, instead of trying, or daring, any real change in the political system. The 1969 reforms, far from being, as the Salazarist ultra-right suspected, irresponsible concessions by the new government, were an obviously unsuccessful response to the workers' movement. Before Salazar stepped down from power, out of 325 *national unions* seventeen were already in the hands of left-wing democratic activists. After the 1969 reform, these numbers rose to twenty-seven in 1970, and, after the reform was reverted, they kept growing to thirty-one in 1971, forty in 1972, forty-four in 1973 and forty-eight in 1974 soon before the April revolution. As was happening in Spain and Italy, the Communists proved they were able to work together with the progressive Catholic activists, determined to oppose political and social coercion of the dictatorship, together with some Socialists and far-left activists. *Intersindical*, the Portuguese equivalent of the Spanish *Comisiones Obreras*, emerged out of this political collaboration. A first *Reunião Intersindical* ("Inter-Union Meeting"), held on 11 October 1970, called by five Lisbon and Porto trade unions, was soon followed by several other meetings bringing together representatives of thirteen different unions that decided to create the *Intersindical*, the embryo of what, after the 1974 revolution, would become the first national union confederation after 1933, when Salazar banned all free trade unions.[54]

---

[51] See Lucena, *A evolução do sistema...*, II, 1976, 57–73.

[52] According to a ministerial order of February 1969, the political police was still asked by the Ministry of the Interior to "disarticulate the criminal action of workers and their leaders [...] engaged in subversive action" (*apud* Patriarca, "Estado Social:...," 2004, 194.

[53] Patriarca, "Estado Social...," 2004, 175, 200–201.

[54] See Américo Nunes *et al.*, *Contributos para a História do Movimento Operário e Sindical: das Raízes até 1977* (Lisbon: CGTP-IN, 2011).

Caetano reacted as in any dictatorship: several union activists were arrested in the following months, liberal measures of the 1969 reform were revoked, government sanction over the trade union boards was reinstated and, at the request from the Ministry of the Interior, political police systematically checked each candidate running for trade union elections.[55] The government found itself facing street protests called on by legal trade unions against arrests and police closing down union offices. The fact that the decision to reverse liberalising measures and to return to the classical dictatorship ambiance on labour relations was taken both by hard-liners, like Rapazote (Minister of the Interior) and soft-liners, like Joaquim Silva Pinto (Secretary of State for Labour, 1970–73, and minister of Corporations, 1973–74),[56] is clearly illustrative of the very strict limits of the Marcellist new course, as well of the classist nature of its social project.

The trade union reform of 1969 appears to have been one of Caetano's wishful thinking attitudes typical of the *Marcellist Spring*. He seemed to believe that industrialisation and the general improvement in Portuguese living standards together with his rhetoric about the *Estado Social* would divert the new urban working classes from what he obsessively called *subversion*. As soon as he understood he was wrong, he revoked every change and put an end to what he, a law professor, thought was "judicialism [that] tied the hands of the Government" every time it wanted to prevent the "the corporative spirit of the Portuguese trade unionism [from] giving way to Marxism."[57]

2.6 THE 1971 CONSTITUTIONAL REFORM

In December 1970, Marcelo Caetano started the process of reforming the *Estado Novo* Constitution. It was the ninth, and last, amendment of the 1933 text in whose preparation Caetano himself had had an a significant role. On the whole, Caetano's 1971 compromise between his 1962 *defective federalism*[58] and the 1951 *integration* constitutional reform produced no more than an outdated adaptation of the *Union Française* of 1945, a neo-colonial project the French had abandoned long before the 1970s. At the end the day, the *ultras* were outraged with Caetano's *reform* of the colonial policy, the white settlers felt deceived and moved closer to separatist pipe dreams, and the African national liberation movements understood that the Portuguese regime would not come closer to a negotiation. The 1971–73 changes came too late and were completely useless to tackle the degradation of the military situation, lack of popular support for the war, and international harassment.

[55] Decree-Law no. 502/70, 26 October 1970. See Patriarca, 178–180. "Estado Social...," 2004, 175. José Barreto, "Os Primórdios da Intersindical sob Marcelo Caetano," *Análise Social*, vol. XXV (105-106), 1º–2º (Lisbon, 1990): 58 and 63–65.

[56] Silva Pinto would become one of the few members of Caetano's government overthrown by the democratic revolution of 1974 to have a long and successful political (and corporate) career afterwards, surprisingly (or not) in the Socialist Party. See his memoirs on the period in *Do Pântano Não Se Sai a Nado* and *De Marcelo a Marcelo. Caminho de Pedras Soltas* (both Lisbon: Gradiva, 2014 and 2017 respectively).

[57] Caetano, *Depoimento*, 1974, 130–132.

[58] Caetano's 1962 *federalist* memorandum on the colonial problem in João Paulo Guerra, *Memórias das Guerras Coloniais* (Porto: Edições Afrontamento, 1994), 333.

One specific amendment is particularly representative of the *Marcellist* paradox. Caetano wanted the Constitution to grant his government the power to declare, without the approval of the Assembly, the "state of emergency" in a wide range of situations, or to adopt the "necessary measures to supress subversion,"[59] which basically was the same thing as imposing a state of emergency. After 45 years of an authoritarian regime in which authorities could do without any sort of judicial independent control to enforce all sorts of repressive measures, this was a mere formality. Six months after the reform, "the Assembly passed a unanimous resolution verifying the persistence of serious subversion in some parts of the national territory."[60] Caetano had warned the Portuguese that *"in this war ... the front is everywhere terrorism [attacks] ... The front is everywhere and at every moment the enemy seeks to disseminate defeatist ideas, [...] preaching [...] an emasculated peace, made of cowardice and concessions [...] The world still belongs to those who fight. [...] There are hot areas of subversion in certain parts [...] of some overseas provinces. But there is [also] a fifth column working for them in Metropolitan [Portugal]!"*[61] A year later, in May 1972, while the government was expected to remove censorship in place since Caetano came to power in 1968, new legislation on press and information left everything unchanged, normalising the so-called *Previous Examination* due to the "subversive situation."[62]

In fact, it was the 1970–71 constitutional debate which provided the definite breakup between Caetano and the liberals. In 1970, when the liberals submitted their own constitutional amendment proposal after the government had done the same, Caetano was outraged. In May 1971, Marcelo wrote to Sá Carneiro that if he had known in 1969 that the liberals wanted to "be exempt from any political discipline" at the National Assembly, he would have "never accepted" to call them into the *União Nacional* ticket. He severely admonished the liberals against their campaign for the *"extension of freedoms [which] is mostly demanded by those who are trying to remove obstacles to the march of social revolution that soon would suppress them all."*[63]

Challenged by the constitutional reform bill submitted by the *Liberal Wing* to the National Assembly, Caetano decided to put an end to the liberals' illusions: a parliamentary expedient was used to block the debate on their bill, as the conservative majority of the Assembly decided to accept the government's project for final discussion. As they realised that it was impossible to reverse this decision, most liberals abandoned the Assembly while voting on each article of the bill took place.[64]

---

[59] Art. 109, according to the 1971 reform (Law 3/71, 16 August 1971).

[60] Caetano, *Depoimento*, 1974, 70. The National Assembly's resolution was passed on 20 December 1971 (see Portugal, *Diário do Governo*, I Série, 27 December 1971), with no reference to any specific measures to be taken by the government.

[61] Marcelo Caetano, speech in Porto, 2 April 1971, *Razões da Presença de Portugal no Ultramar* (Lisbon: Secretaria de Estado da Informação e Turismo, 1973), 50.

[62] Art. 98, Decree-Law no. 150/72, 5 May 1972.

[63] Caetano to Sá Carneiro, letter, 5 May 1971, *Cartas Particulares*, 1985, I, 318.

[64] Fernandes, *Nem Ditadura...*, 2005, 97.

3. THE IMPOSSIBLE TRANSITION

As Fernando Rosas emphasises, Caetano's political project was, while still under Salazar, to prepare "a transition within the framework of the regime." It had never been, in the least, a democratisation programme but rather *"an orderly transition, made, if possible, under the auspices of a tutelary Salazar put gracefully away from the leadership of the Government to the Presidency, or if not possible, through the constitutional mechanisms to replace the head of government,"*[65] with the president using his constitutional power to replace Salazar. In this sense, the *Marcellist* project, often associated with the so-called *technocratic* stance inside of Franco's regime, was in fact, on a Portuguese scale, not much different from the 1973 move through which Franco made room for Carrero Blanco, appointing him as the head of government while he remained as head of the state. In 1971, Manuel de Lucena thought that "Marcelo Caetano's 'liberalisation' aims for a domesticated pluralism—and no more."[66] In that same year, exasperated with the liberals he had called to the National Assembly in 1969, Caetano revealed the true ideological nature of its antidemocratic and antiliberal bias by describing liberal proposals on the freedom of the press (or rather on the lack of it) as a return to the "demoliberal bourgeois concept of 1789 taken as an ideal solution." As he would have upheld in the 1930s, *"our bourgeoisie [. . .] thinks that amidst the tremendous dispute of conceptions of life we are facing, everything is solved with. . . freedom. [Freedom] for villains, apparently,"* i.e.,*"for those who cry for freedom so they can more easily take power and use it in a totalitarian way."*[67]

In 1972, he complained against the *"bourgeoisie [who] tends to be accommodating. [. . .] There are many bourgeois who, stepping up on the protest wagon, [. . .], applaud, assist and [. . .] subsidise [. . .] [everything] from protest groups to the revolutionary press. How deluded they are! May God forbid the social revolution. [If it happened one day,] they would be the first victims."*[68] In this sense, it is surely useful to follow Torgal's advice on *"not letting ourselves to be dragged towards images that are produced about [Marcelo Caetano], especially his self-representations, in his memoirs or in those texts written in exile."*[69] It was Caetano himself who, in the late 1970s and already in exile, assumed he had to ultimately *"stop the liberalisation I had started so subversion could be fought, and to repress an increasingly permissive environment,"* claiming he had found himself *"almost alone trying to oppose the rising ideologies [sic] with a doctrine, appealing to a realistic feeling."*[70] For Rosas, *"Marcellism was, in fact, the expression of a belated triumph of the reformist undercurrent inside the Estado Novo, emerging in the aftermath of World War II, which, after several contingencies and some lost opportunities, finally came to power in 1968. [Marcellists] would once again miss [. . .] their last chance to steer the regime through a transitional process."*

[65] Rosas, "O Marcelismo…," 1999, 31–32.

[66] Lucena, *A Evolução do Sistema…*, II, 1976, 185.

[67] Caetano to F. Pinto Balsemão, letter, 15 July 1971, *Cartas Particulares*, I, 1985, 306.

[68] Caetano, address to Ribatejo's regional committee of the ANP, 21 May 1972, apud, Américo Thomaz, *Últimas Décadas de Portugal*, vol. IV (Lisbon: Edições Fernando Pereira, [1983]), 229.

[69] Torgal, *Marcello Caetano…*, 2013, 61.

[70] Caetano, *apud* Joaquim Veríssimo Serrão, *Marcello Caetano. Confidências no Exílio* (Lisbon, São Paulo, Verbo, [1985]), 170.

In fact, both from a political and a historical perspective, what seems *"essential in the history of Marcellism as a new phase of the regime is to focus on the explanation of how reformism ultimately failed as a possible output [to provide for] an evolution of the Estado Novo."*[1]

The two Iberian dictatorships fell in the 1970s. In spite of some essential differences in the way they emerged in history and were politically designed in the 1930s and early '40s, these two regimes went through fairly similar phases after 1943–45, when the predictable Allied victory and Fascist defeat forced them to find a political identity that would allow them to survive in the post-war and to plead for a place amidst the Western bloc. Although following very different paths—one through a social revolution, the other through a negotiated transitional process—the two post-authoritarian orders were a lot clearer representations of the consequences of the wide social and economic changes of the 1960s and '70s than they were the result of deliberate political choices of those who, within the two regimes, stood behind authoritarian *modernising* programmes such as Caetano's *evolução na continuidade* or the late-Francoism *desarrollo político*. Caetano's plans to blow new breath into Salazar's political heritage and enlarge the duration of the *Estado Novo* was eventually a complete failure. History abundantly shows that Caetano had never until the very end conceived any true political innovation out of the regime's institutional and ideological limits. The *liberalising* pretensions and the step-by-step strategies of the *evolução na continuidade* assumed that social and political opposition would obediently welcome the strict conditions under which these self-appointed *reformists* wanted them to act. They openly imposed the actual repressive policies which blocked any substantial evolution.

At the end of the 1960s, the regime was definitely unable to tackle social unrest, especially the unbreakable workers' and students' movements, and became ultimately exasperated with the problems of national consistency it was facing: the war in Africa and the dramatic end of the Portuguese colonial empire. In the context of the authoritarian modernisation of the 1960s and the increasing social resistance it produced, no attempt to reinvigorate the corporative social rhetoric of the 1930s would prove able to reverse the evident degenerative process of the authoritarian paradigm. These authoritarian *modernisers* were unable to predict the final outcome of these political processes. Caetano was humiliatingly overthrown by the young military officers he had earlier deceived and kept pushing again and again to return to war in Africa. From his Brazilian exile he watched, horrified, how democracy was built upon a radically liberating experience like the Portuguese revolution.

[1] Rosas, "O Marcelismo…," 1999, 16.

Before April: The Housing Issue

JOSÉ ANTÓNIO BANDEIRINHA
University of Coimbra, Centre for Social Studies

Fig. 1 Shanty town, 1970s. Photo by Alexandre Alves Costa.

BIOGRAPHY

José António Bandeirinha graduated in 1983 as an architect from the Escola Superior de Belas-Artes of Porto. Currently he is full professor in the Department of Architecture at the University of Coimbra, where he completed his PhD in 2002 entitled "The SAAL process and architecture of April 25th 1974." With the main reference of architecture and organisation of space, he has dedicated his work to several subjects—city and urban condition, housing, theatre and cultural studies. From 2007 until 2011 he held the position of Pro-rector for cultural affairs at the University of Coimbra, and from 20011 until 2013 he was the Director of the College of the Arts at the University of Coimbra. In 2012 he curated the exhibition "Fernando Távora Permanent Modernity," coordinated by Álvaro Siza. He was the scientific consultant for the exhibition "The SAAL Process Architecture and Participation 1974–1976," curated by Delfim Sardo and organized by the Serralves Museum of Contemporary Art, Oporto, Portugal, in collaboration with the Canadian Centre for Architecture, Montréal, Canada (2014–2015). He is a senior researcher at the Centre for Social Studies of the University of Coimbra. Currently he holds the position of director of the Department of Architecture at the University of Coimbra, which he held before from 2002 until 2004, and from 2006 until 2007. José António Bandeirinha has worked continuously on the urban and architectural consequences of political procedures, mainly focusing on the realities of 20th century Portugal.

At the time of the military coup on April 25th 1974, the dwelling situation in Portugal was disturbing, even when analysed from a merely quantitative point of view. 600,000 dwellings were in precarious conditions, and this number had a strong tendency to increase. Approximately 25 per cent of the mainland's population lived in dwellings lacking basic safety, comfort, health, and privacy. These ranged from degraded buildings, overcrowded spaces, "ilhas,"[1] and barracks, to houses deprived of any habitable conditions. On the one hand the absence of basic infrastructure was particularly evident in rural areas. On the other hand, in urban areas, there was an incessant increase in both the degradation of the existing housing and the development of precarious and illegal settlements: neighbourhoods of tin sheds, tents, and provisional constructions.[2] From an estimated total of two and a half million dwellings, 52 per cent lacked water supply, 53 per cent lacked electricity, 60 per cent lacked a sewage system, and 67 per cent lacked sanitary facilities.[3]

Official data shows that, in the early seventies in mainland Portugal, there was a total of 31,110 substandard dwellings—"shacks and others." Out of 2,164,965 dwellings, 64.3 per cent had electricity, 47.1 per cent had water supply, and 30 per cent had a sewage system. Out of the 2,224,020 families registered in the same area, 62.6 per cent lived in a space supplied with electricity, 45.8 per cent had domestic water supply, and only 29.2 per cent occupied dwellings equipped with sanitary facilities.[4] This situation was mainly due to the political conjuncture, which never engaged in a true and effective coordination of efforts for its resolution, despite some sporadic evolutionary experiences, mostly since the end of World War II.

Throughout the sixties, the reality characterized by these data was becoming progressively more blatant, which led the institutions of power to gradually recognize the impossibility of suppressing it. Gone were the days when the state's sole concern was ennobled around the political meaning of typological options, or the choice of an architectural language. Previously, the regime had been determined to consider the housing problem a matter of recommended styles—the so-called "national style"—or a matter of ideologically imposed typologies—the detached single family house. However, at this point in history, the regime felt the need to avoid being confronted with those urban and peri-urban "stains."[5] Besides generating dangerous internal and external divergence, the extensive deployments of shacks and barracks, clandestine neighbourhoods and the urban centres' degraded overcrowded buildings also compromised the possibility of promoting the territory as "evolution in continuity," which was the official discourse of the government, led at the time by Marcelo Caetano.[6]

[1] Speculative worker's housing built across late nineteenth century and early twentieth century in inner block spaces, specially in Oporto.

[2] Tiago Castela, "A liberal space: a history of the illegalized working-class extensions of Lisbon" (PhD diss., University of California, 2011).

[3] António Fonseca Ferreira, *Por uma Nova Política de Habitação* (Porto: Edições Afrontamento, 1987), 66.

[4] INE, *Estatísticas da Habitação (X Recenseamento Geral da População)* 1970.

[5] Nuno Teotónio Pereira, "A nódoa de Lisboa," *Seara Nova* (June 1970), in *Escritos (1947–1996, selecção)* (Porto: FAUP Publicações, 1995), 119.

[6] António Reis, "Marcelismo," in Dicionário de História do Estado Novo, V.II, ed. Fernando Rosas and J.M. Brandão de Brito (Círculo de Leitores, 1996), 546; Fernando Rosas, *O Estado Novo (1926–1974). História de Portugal*, vol. VII, ed. José Mattoso (Círculo de Leitores, 1994), 548.

Fig. 2 Clandestine developments, Brandoa, 1970s.
Photo by Alexandre Alves Costa.

Fig. 3 Clandestine developments, São Pedro da Cova, 1975.
Photo by Alexandre Alves Costa.

Before April. The Housing Issue

The first ever time there was an attempt to integrate an inclusive view of economy and society in the history of economic planning processes of the dictatorship was with "Plano Intercalar de Fomento," which covered the period between 1965 and 1967.[7] This plan was established as a desperate solution seeking to provide a conjectural response to the government's confusing set of internal contradictions and hesitations. At this time, the regime was dealing with the colonial war, the increasing wave of emigration, and the inevitable opening of the market, hence its lack of an instrument to convey strategies, to aggregate deliberations and to reunite the various tendencies within it. At the same time, this plan also began to reflect the need for economic growth to keep pace with some social concerns, among which was the housing issue. The role of private enterprise in this field was fiercely criticized and some of the reasons pointed out for its inefficiency were land value speculation, the preferential production of high-cost housing, and the uncoordinated correlation between production and urban development, which extends delays in the construction industry and exacerbates the lack of infrastructure. This critical analysis led to the need for a concrete state intervention: besides the direct construction of 21,000 dwellings, the plan proposed several initiatives to facilitate land expropriation in order to implement housing programmes, as well as initiatives which attempted to regulate the action of private investments.[8] Moreover, the plan also recommended the creation of an entity responsible for the encouragement and consequent reinforcement of these measures.

However, the "III Plano de Fomento," which contemplated the period between 1968 and 1973, later stated that the goals proposed by its antecedent plan regarding the housing problem were not fulfilled. The new plan tried to justify the failure with land-based impediments, and presented a more operative way of overcoming them: easier land reservations, increased procedural efficiency, and the promotion of the land value's stabilization. Additionally, this plan safeguarded the possibility to take special measures, such as reviewing legal procedures for land assessment and controlling speculation. Even though this idea was never really meant to be accomplished, it did instigate disapproving comments from the regime's most retrograde factions. The Reporting Committee on the subsidiary opinion of the Corporate Chamber expressed serious reservations about that possibility, alerting against radicalism and preventing hypothetical attacks on the "basic principles of social and political organization."[9] The "III Plano de Fomento" predicted the construction of 49,430 dwellings by public and semi-public entities. This was an obviously interventionist ambition, which expressed that, in order to obtain results, a more frontal and voluntary action was required, less involved in the meanderings of the usual political rhetoric.

[7] Carlos Farinha Rodrigues, "Planos de Fomento," in *Dicionário de História do Estado Novo*, V.II, ed. Fernando Rosas and J.M. Brandão de Brito (Círculo de Leitores, 1996), 740.

[8] Ferreira, *Por uma Nova Política de Habitação*, 63.

[9] Fernando Gonçalves, *Urbanizar e Construir Para Quem?* (Porto: Afrontamento, 1972), 120.

There were barely any consequences: as early as 1968, there was a decrease in almost 50 per cent of the envisaged programmes.[10] Yet, that direct allusion to the housing problem did at least have the advantage of making it clear that this sector[11] was also consolidating some modernizing positions of the state.

On September 23rd 1968, Marcelo Caetano finally rose to power. The political system's many contradictions did not prevent the recruitment of a new generation of technocrats for the government. The head of the country was counting on them to control the retrograde factions, which he could not dismiss because they were the necessary consensus for his own nomination. Also, Caetano wanted to use this new generation as the face of an ambitious economic and social development strategy, which made broad sectors of the population very hopeful. Nevertheless, in reality, this ambition was impossible to reconcile with the colonial war effort as well as the consequent isolation from the international context. Concurrently, in many state organizations which had some kind of jurisdiction over housing issues—the National Civil Engineering Laboratory, the Ministry of Public Works, the Directorate-General for Urbanization, the Federation of Pension Funds, and the municipalities, especially Lisbon—were building teams of young technicians, who were more aware of the urgency for a systematic solution to the problem. At the beginning of the 1960s, these teams—engineers, architects, social workers, economists—started to develop analytical work, methodological systems and projects, which inspired some informal training centres, less academic and more effective than universities.

This is the context that understandably led to the Ministry of Public Works' initiative to promote the Colloquium on Housing Policy, "Colóquio sobre Política da Habitação" between 30 June and 5 July 1969.[12] The Colloquium took place in Lisbon at the National Laboratory of Civil Engineering. It sought to directly state the imperative need to establish a set of measures for an integrated strategy to solve the issues related to housing, construction, and real estate development. This was already evident in the preceding development plans, especially in "Plano Intercalar de Fomento" and in "III Plano de Fomento." The Reporting Committee was presided over by the architect Ignacio Peres Fernandes and included the engineers Ferreira da Cunha, Celestino da Costa, and Ruy J. Gomes, and the architects Alves de Sousa and Nuno Portas, who was the reporter. The document Texto de Base was written before the colloquium and it began by evoking the need to stimulate dialogue between specialists with sectorial work areas.

[10] Marielle Christine Gros, *O Alojamento Social sob o Fascismo* (Porto: Afrontamento, 1982), 147.

[11] There was a very evident dichotomy between the opinions of those more politically conservative and those aligned with the Western European countries' development ideology. Since the postwar period, this dichotomy was especially pronounced in the industry sector, due to its modernization, and in the economy sector, due to the opening up of markets. The conflicts generated by this separation, often mediated by Salazar himself, encouraged the one-party assemblies, determined the government's composition, and defined the seats in the Corporate Chamber. Fernando Rosas, *O Estado Novo (1926–1974)*, 416–563.

[12] José António Bandeirinha, "Construir uma política de habitação num contexto adverso. O Colóquio de 1969," in *Habitação Para o Maior Número. Portugal os Anos de 1950–1980* (Lisbon: Instituto da Habitação e Reabilitação Urbana e Câmara Municipal de Lisboa, 2013), 62–77.

It then defined the various functions and attributions that must converge in order to establish a housing policy, such as general economic development, fair distribution of the benefits obtained from that same development and the state's intervention in market regulation, instead of merely being an exceptional housing promoter. Additionally, it characterized the housing situation, reporting shortages ranging from 350,000 to 500,000 dwellings, and it detailed the incomes of the deprived households' different social strata.[13]

The Colloquium's presentation text also included proposals, such as protection measures for a higher percentage of built dwellings, removing them from the free market and adjusting them to demand. It also mentioned the conditions for the development of a housing policy. One of them was loan and amortization regulations, which considered the possibility of "lost funds," and showed as an example the gradual increase in rents practiced by Brazil's National Bank of Housing. Other conditions stated were control of land speculation, and the possibility of phasing investments in order to obtain progressive rather than definitive results, which can be considered a bold and premonitory introduction to the possibilities of evolutionary housing.[14] Thus, the document specifically proposed the reduction of higher-standard housing construction through mechanisms to inhibit investment. They believed that this way it would be possible to reverse *"the rising prices of production derived from commercial profits of land sales, construction entrepreneurs, and intermediaries."*[15] The aim was to correct or extinguish those charges and redirect the funds to the housing sector conditioned by social needs.

Reducing the cost per dwelling was also considered in this document, providing that there were alternatives to finished construction, which the text referred to as "conventional type programmes." These alternatives were *"evolutionary type solutions— solutions that start with an elementary base and that, due to their technical design, can receive successive enlargements and enhancements as the families' conditions improve."*[16] That was when the official idea of the so-called assisted self-construction began to arise in a serious and committed way. Even though this solution was considered more appropriate to the expansion areas, they did not exclude the possibility of parallel solutions for the renovation of old degraded areas, in order to provide them with competitive levels of comfort and hygiene. The text proceeded to explain that the aim of the housing sector policies was to improve living conditions in a given area, and that improvement should not be evaluated exclusively by housing quality but also by a whole set of supplementary goods.

[13] Ignácio Peres Fernandes, A. Celestino da Costa, J.M. Ferreira da Cunha, Ruy José Gomes, Nuno Portas (reporter), J.M. Alves de Sousa, *Colóquio sobre Política de Habitação. Texto de Base* (Lisbon: Ministério das Obras Públicas, 1969 [September]), 1–3.

[14] Ignácio Peres Fernandes, A. Celestino da Costa, J.M. Ferreira da Cunha, Ruy José Gomes, Nuno Portas (reporter), J.M. Alves de Sousa, *Colóquio sobre Política de Habitação. Texto de Base* (Lisbon: Ministério das Obras Públicas, 1969 [June]), 8–9.

[15] Fernandes, *Colóquio sobre Política de Habitação. Texto de Base* [June], 10.

[16] Fernandes, *Colóquio sobre Política de Habitação. Texto de Base* [June], 17.

John F. C. Turner and Charles Abrams were quoted referring to a "set of conditions that constitute a complex value which has been designated as security in urban life."[17] The Colloquium's conclusions clearly advised the creation of a financial and administrative structure which *"must ensure the planning and legislation management of all kinds of resources and credit modalities, not just of public sector funds"*[18] The creation of a "National Fund" was recommended in order to coordinate the funding and implementation of programmes. Two hypotheses were presented: one was to make it part of a government department to be created, which carried the risk of reducing its efficiency; the other was to start an autonomous entity, which could unrestrictedly raise and direct savings and funds, for technically adjusted purposes.

It is clear that the Colloquium on Housing Policy was a striking event, due to its repercussions on the social housing sector. It undoubtedly defined an institutional shift in the way of addressing housing problems in Portugal. As previously recommended by the aforementioned "Plano Intercalar de Fomento," the creation of a housing development fund, "Fundo de Fomento da Habitação" (FFH), was finally established in the Decree-Law no. 49,033, published on 28 May 1969. This diploma's promulgation represented an attempt for change. Many of the Colloquium's discussions and interventions defended that the new fund had an organic character, which could shape its technical-administrative structure. Inevitably, this organization's legal form had to be restructured and readapted to conform to the reality.

However, the Colloquium had other consequences besides the organic structure of "Fundo de Fomento da Habitação." Both in juridical-administrative and conceptual terms, it also reinforced the possibility of building a social policy oriented to the idea of workforce reproduction. Considering the juridical consequences, it is worth highlighting "Lei dos Solos," a law approved by the Decree-Law no. 576/70 of November 24th, which set out a policy to reduce the cost of land for construction, assuring the possibility of systematic expropriation to make the property accessible and encourage private investment. However, the following should also be mentioned: Decree-Law no. 166/70 on urban intervention licensing; Decree-Law no. 278/71, on unlicensed construction control, imposing its expropriation when demolition proves impracticable; Decree-Law no. 561/71 on urbanization plan implementation; Order of 15 January 1972, which establishes rules on the use of social security funds for social housing; or Ordinance no. 398/72, 21 July, which defined a buildings' minimum conditions for habitability.

[17] "Conjunto de condições que constituem um valor complexo que tem sido designado como 'segurança na vida urbana'." Fernandes, *Colóquio sobre Política de Habitação. Texto de Base* [September], 23.

[18] Fernandes, *Colóquio sobre Política de Habitação. Texto de Base* [September], 54.

Regarding the conceptual consequences, a whole set of ideas should be mentioned. Either directly expressed or veiled in other words, these ideas clearly proclaimed the intention to call for a new institutional approach to the housing problem. On the one hand, some of these ideas almost literally translated the most advanced international perspectives on the theoretical debate. On the other hand, in their integrative coherence of common logic, they implied the conviction that the moment for great institutional and administrative reforms had finally arrived.

One of the major ideas which the Colloquium helped disseminate was the awareness that the status of citizenship directly implied the right to decent housing. Housing as an individual right of citizenship, which the state had a duty to provide, counterpointed the corporative view of the house as family's moral consecration. Furthermore, the Colloquium fought the idea of housing as mere satisfaction of the need for shelter, as it emphasized the importance of access to equipment and goods, complementing the right to decent housing with the right to a whole range of public supplies. This meant that the right to housing directly implied the right to the city. The state's recognition of these principles, its assumption that it was possible to diligently and responsibly recognize the public housing issue's social implications, was much more than a contribution to an administrative and institutional reform, it was the reform itself happening and, more than ever, it created the illusion of change. The social tendency inherent to the recognition of the right to the city indicated the overcoming of a statistical, massive, and technocratic approach to the housing issue as an isolated problem.

This social tendency, however, became unrecognizable after reading the explanations for these rights' consecration. The designated guarantees for the new housing policy's success went beyond the general political-economic framework and aimed for Keynesian-based solutions.[19] They ranged from more effective economic activities through the reproduction of the labour force, directly or indirectly induced by housing improvement, to the consequent increase in consumption levels. Another very obvious change at the time was the realization that, no matter which housing solution was adopted, the land issue was always crucial. The need to control the land and its value was referred to very assertively, for it was considered the essential and basic condition for a housing policy practice. This idea is considered the structural point of the Colloquium. It required courage to insist on this topic during such politically complicated circumstances, as well as intelligence to handle the current administrative centralization as a way to create favourable conditions for the application of measures to solve the problem.

[19] Nuno Serra, *Estado, Território e Estratégias de Habitação* (Coimbra: Quarteto Editora, 2002), 91–93.

It is also important to mention that, throughout the Colloquium, numerous planning modalities were considered. The first one was phasing the specificity of subjects and actions on the land, gradually working from the most generic to the most particular. The second one was to balance and integrate the overall coordination of phases and the different specializations. It seems obvious that, in addition to projecting a desired future, these considerations contained an implicit reproach to the existing practices. They clearly suggested that, given the gravity of the housing situation, it was necessary to move to immediate action, and also to prevent that immediacy from compromising the ambitious operations of socio-economic, territorial, urban, and architectural planning. Another important idea that the Colloquium brought up was the confirmation of the need to limit higher housing standards. In fact, it was repeatedly asserted that housing investment is excessive in qualification and deficient in quantification. The Colloquium concluded that it was possible to reverse this market strategy, intentionally regulated to keep demand levels high, by building more low-standard housing. However, due the project's optimization and enduring technical support, quality levels would not decline.

The Colloquium also sustained the idea of guaranteeing that the dwellers involved in rehousing operations had the possibility of remaining in the same place. Besides supporting the predictable direct social consequences, this idea also promoted the slow consolidation of urban fabrics, as well as the consequent dwellers' integration and sense of social belonging. In other words, the Colloquium believed in the possibility of solving the housing problem in a quantitative way, and simultaneously promoting and consolidating the sociological identification between the dwellers and the inhabited space. This was a result of the acknowledgment of some serious recent situations experienced both in Portugal and abroad generated by resettlement operations. Access to information about these situations and to interdisciplinary studies on their consequences was, of course, fundamental in considering the problem. However, there is another idea directly related to the latter, which is the idea of participation, which was certainly strongly influenced by the international debate. The intention of these participation processes was to operate not only at a formal level, but also at all decision levels; hence the necessity for users' collaboration in the definition and execution of the immediate plans and forward plans, as well as the process of executing the work; hence also the suggestion to promote dialogue and communication in order to enable participation; and also the explicit recommendation that all actions, even the most urgent ones, have organized and representative interlocutors.

Last but not least, it is interesting to highlight the diversification of housing promotion programmes. This intention to diversify the programmes was particularly important for the so-called third stratum of poor housing dwellers, which is the stratum that includes *"those who do not have a regular income, live in subsistence mode, and therefore cannot afford a minimum rent payment (yet have the capacity to work)."*[20] The conventional housing programmes were considered very likely to fail since they presupposed direct production by the state, through the use of "lost fund" solutions, without any guarantee of the value of invested capital. This is how they developed the idea of starting with an "elementary core" which could aggregate other spaces as the dwellers needs increased and as their economic capacity expanded, using both the dwellers workforce and their savings.

The project's technical quality was considered essential to accomplish satisfactory outcomes, since it would guarantee coherent and organized urban solutions. Interestingly, besides developing the notion of evolutionary housing, this solution also endorsed the notion of "evolutionary urbanization." In other words, the dwellings were intended to improve in space and in quality over time, but so were the neighbourhoods, which were intended to become more and more consolidated and develop higher quality urban infrastructures and public facilities. The concept of evolutionary self-constructed, professionally assisted housing production turned into the concept of evolutionary city development, which, as was previously mentioned, increased the technicians' responsibility to plan both urban spaces and dwellings. Therefore, the hope for an evolution of built environments became the hope for a methodological evolution of architecture and planning. Nowadays it is clear that, even though the Colloquium's consequences were not immediate, they were very significant. They did not become patent until a few years later, from 1974 on, when the country's new democracy demanded effective political measures to intervene in the housing problem. By then, the deliberation was already complete, almost all the procedures had already been suggested, namely the creation of "Serviço de Apoio Ambulatório Local" Local Ambulatory Support Service, or SAAL.[21]

All things considered, the Colloquium's consequences, albeit partially and apprehensively applied, only came later, along with the right political conditions and the eradication of dictatorship. Despite the Colloquium members' intense commitment, despite the clear social, economic, technical, cultural and legal arguments, despite the rigorous analysis based both on historic research and on realistic proposals, and despite the intention to adjust the target and organize the production process instead of increasing the investment

[20] "Aqueles que não dispõem de rendimentos regulares ou que os possuem apenas a um nível de subsistência, que não permite desviar para o alojamento o pagamento de um aluguer mínimo. (Possuem, contudo, capacidade inaproveitada de trabalho)." Ignácio Peres Fernandes, A. Celestino da Costa, J.M. Ferreira da Cunha, Ruy José Gomes, Nuno Portas (reporter), and J.M. Alves de Sousa, *Colóquio sobre Política de Habitação. Relato Final* (Lisbon: Ministério das Obras Públicas, 1969), 28.

[21] José António Bandeirinha, *O Processo SAAL e a Arquitectura no 25 de Abril de 1974* (Coimbra: Imprensa da Universidade, 2007).

values, it proved to be very difficult to establish a coordinated, integrated and committed action for the resolution of the housing problem among the many state's organizations. The lack of a concerted set of measures is consensually acknowledged by several authors, who also agree on the inexistence of a "housing policy" from an institutional point of view.[22] The housing production sector problems, which had already been described in the Colloquium's preliminary text, were deeply related to the current Portuguese political and economic system at the time. So much so that, without changing the system, those problems could not disappear nor be withdrawn.

Approximately 90 per cent of the national production was private,[23] which reflected on the Portuguese economic situation: the production forces had poor performance, purchasing power was very low and there was an excessively high monopoly of capital, but the production's accumulation of capital was too low. Regarding civil construction industry, despite the large number of micro-firms, large and medium-sized firms heavily dominated the production. The latter were, in most cases, spearheads for monopoly capital investments, most often devoted to public works, tourism, and real estate.[24] However, in the private sector, most construction companies worked both on building and real estate development, so their profits could be obtained either by production or by collecting rents. This meant that, with a few generally unimportant exceptions for public works, construction companies invested almost exclusively in tourism and luxury housing, mostly focusing on demographic groups that could offer constant demand. Large economic groups and foreign capital, which took advantage of cheap labour, invested almost exclusively in the metropolitan areas of Lisbon and Porto, as well as in a few large-scale tourist developments in the south, while the remaining urban centres "declined due to their monolithic administrative functions."[25] The dwellings' final cost, however, was twice as high due to the profit of property. That profit benefited two main active parts: the landlord who sold the land, and the promoter who sold the houses.[26]

Speculation played a prominent role in the housing sector's activity. The most defining theoretical outcomes of the Colloquium, in particular the land property issue, did not have a real significant impact, except in the industrial complexes built from scratch, like Sines. On the contrary, land speculation-based investments were having their "golden period,"[27] due to the ascending middle class's increasing purchasing power, and to emigrants investment of capital. And speculation fever also reached municipal administrations, for at this point Lisbon's city council resold important, expensive areas to the private sector, which had been claimed during Duarte Pacheco's time.[28]

[22] Ferreira, *Por uma Nova Política de Habitação*, 31; Gonçalves, *Urbanizar e construir para quem?*, 109; Gros, *O Alojamento Social sob o Fascismo*, 147–148.

[23] Ferreira, *Por uma Nova Política de Habitação*, 239.

[24] In 1973, among the main financial groups, C.U.F. had a network of 10 real estate, construction, and tourism agencies, and the Champalimaud group owned a large construction firm in addition to a bank, a cement company, and an insurance company. All other financial groups also had a strong presence in the sector: 4 real estate and tourism companies belonged to "Banco Nacional Ultramarino"; 2 real estate companies belonged to "Banco Espírito Santo"; and 2 real estate and tourism branches belonged to "Banco Português do Atlântico." Other groups such as "Banco Fonsecas and Burnay" and "Banco Intercontinental Português" had their real estate interests as well. Some multinational firms also had significant stakes in the sector, even though they were on a smaller scale and almost always in association with national groups.

[25] Maria Clara Mendes, "A habitação em Portugal: Caracterização e Politicas," in *Seminário 25 de Abril 10 Anos Depois* (Lisbon: Associação 25 de Abril, 1984), 189.

[26] Christian Topalov, "La politique du logement dans le processus révolutionnaire portugais (25 avril 1974–11 mars 1975)," *Espaces et Societés*, no.17–18 (Mars/Juin 1976), 114–115.

[27] Ferreira, *Por uma Nova Política de Habitação*, 65.

[28] Topalov, "La politique du logement," 115.

The activity of the housing sector was determined by the increase in price caused by speculation and bargaining, nearly exclusive to large companies and developers. The consequences of these circumstances are very diffuse and complex, and this is not the appropriate text to include their exhaustive enumeration and analysis. However, it seems important to emphasize the consequences which were more directly associated with the ambivalence that would later shape the historical evolution of the housing issue. The housing market's power of demand was concentrated in 2 to 3 per cent of the population, according to promoters' estimates.[29] This extreme limitation was one of the most obvious consequences and instigated two main phenomena.

On the one hand, it created the inevitable temptation to maximize the workforce's reproduction, by simultaneously raising both levels of consumption and demand. This temptation was greatly supported by the above-mentioned eminently technocratic facets of the regime, which held initiatives such as the Colloquium on Housing Policy as a part of their broader commitments. On the other hand, it created the inevitable thriving of parallel markets, which served the rest of the population, those who could not afford the practices of conventional supply. The legal land market marginalized small and medium-sized construction companies, as well as other speculators, some of them economically larger. Therefore, in suburban areas, particularly in Lisbon and its surroundings, it became common for those construction companies to purchase large non-urban parcels, provide them with basic infrastructure, and then either resell the parcels or build houses to rent. These non-legal promoters' activities were key for the growth of the cities' outskirts, especially in areas where construction was forbidden. After dividing the parcels into small lots of land, these were sold without any kind of urban facilities and without any guarantee of the possibility of construction. Shortly after buying these lots, the new owners would start building either on their own or with the help of small groups of organized construction workers, rapidly transforming these areas into degraded living spaces, or slums. This parallel market developed its own scale of value, which ranged from low-rate shacks and sheds to the considerable worth of more qualified and more densely built settlements. Simultaneously, in the urban centres, particularly in Oporto, degraded and overcrowded buildings destined for demolition propelled suspicious sublease businesses. This market's main operators were known as "subalugas." The total absence of regulation and the incessant demand, as well as a completely inhuman and submissive relationship between tenants and "subalugas," led to miserable housing conditions.

[29] Topalov, "La politique du logement," 115–117.

Fig 4 Seara Nova magazine cover, no. 1486, 1969, with a dossier on the Colloquium on Housing Policy.

Fig 5 Presentation of the Integrated Plan of Aveiro–Santiago, PIAS, and its planning history, 1979, FFH

Fig 6 Integrated Plan of Zambujal. In the foreground, the Alto do Moínho Estate, by Francisco da Silva Dias. Although designed before, it would be completed after the revolution, within the scope of the SAAL.
Source: Google Earth, 2018.

Decree-Law 49,033 was published one month before the Colloquium, and it established the creation of the housing development fund, FFH. Throughout its existence, the FFH developed intense and diversified housing promotion activity. It developed direct promotion programmes, often using so-called "Integrated Plans" (PI); and indirect promotion programmes, which provided technical and financial support to private promoters, to projects by local authorities, to SAAL, which was established in this institution after its creation in August 1974, to Economic Housing Cooperatives (CHEs)[30] to Urban Renewal comprehensive programmes, to a rehabilitation programme called "PRID" ("Programa de Recuperação de Imóveis Degradados"), and to diverse self-construction initiatives. Furthermore, the FFH also developed programmatic and spatial composition systems at a technical level, which could be applied to any context depending on a household sociological typology, and on a generic characterization of demand.

The Colloquium strongly recommended the above-mentioned integrated plans, which were directly intended strategies for combining programmes. The aim of PI was to guarantee that housing planning programmes were complemented by other services that offered appropriate and inclusive living conditions. Most of the integrated plans started in the early 1970s: Setúbal, Almada, Zambujal [MdH DB a743], Aveiro-Santiago, Porto-Viso, Guimarães, and Coimbra-Ingote. Each of these plans had different implementations and unique outcomes. Some plans followed the original expectations, from the point of view of the project and programme, and from the point of view of urban integration. Other plans remain practically unfollowed to this day.

In 1974, the architects Joaquim Cadima and Santa-Rita planned the licensing phase of Aveiro's PI. This plan envisioned a new city typology, somewhere in between Smithson's Robin Hood Gardens, in London, and George Addor's Le Lignon, in Geneva: a set of interconnected Y-shaped blocks, four to twelve floors high, with galleries accessible by common stairs, emerging from trails spread along a large green area. However, the project that was actually built was designed by three of the FFH architects, Alberto Oliveira, João Maia Macedo, and José Semide. They completely changed the previous project's intentions, opting for a classical Italian model, more aligned with Gregotti's proposal for Palermo's ZEN neighbourhood. The different results of each PI were also a reflection of the differences between the architects involved. The plans could be developed either by FFH teams, local authorities, or private companies. Arménio Losa (2nd stage), Marques de Aguiar (3rd stage), and Maria João Palla with Luís Vassalo Rosa (FFH/DUE) were the architects who worked on the Guimarães plan.

---

[30] António Baptista Coelho, "Sobre os 'anos dourados' dos conjuntos cooperativos de habitação económica, 1974–1984," in *Habitação Para o Maior Número. Portugal os Anos de 1950–1980*, ed. Nuno Portas (Lisbon: Instituto da Habitação e Reabilitação Urbana, 2013), 135–153.

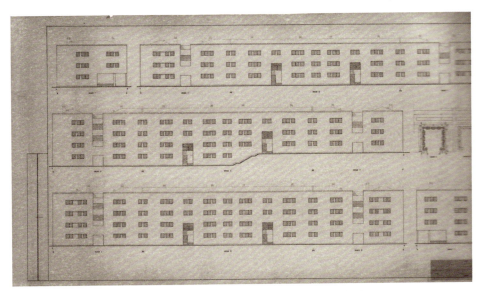

Fig 7 Vítor Figueiredo, Integrated Plan of Zambujal, 1962–75. Views 6-6' e 10-10' Set 1.
Source: IHRU/SIPA, PT VF-DES 002632.

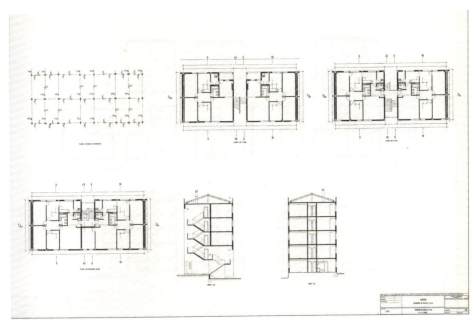

Fig 8 Vítor Figueiredo, Integrated Plan of Zambujal, 1962–75. Terraced buildings T3 and T4.
Source: IHRU/SIPA, PT VF-DES 002391.

Alberto de Oliveira and João Maia Macedo (FFH/DSP), as well as Ventura da Cruz (DHC) and José Semide (FFH/GEP) were responsible for Aveiro-Santiago. José Semide also worked on Coimbra-Ingote, but his plan was later modified and its consequences were distorted. In Zambujal the team included Duarte Cabral de Melo, José Gil, and Vítor Figueiredo, as well as Francisco Silva Dias and António Gomes; in Almada, Rui Mendes Paula, Bartolomeu Costa Cabral with Maurício Vasconcellos, Eduardo Nery, and Vassalo Rosa. In Setúbal, there were two teams, one including José Charters Monteiro, Paula Carvalho, and Galvão Lucas, and the other including Manuel Salgado and Melo Guerra. The existence of these two teams created an interesting dialectic confrontation between two urban theories, that of Aldo Rossi and that of Vittorio Gregotti.

Despite this diversity of experiences, people and institutional affiliations, these plans' common denominator was the European model initiated in the post-war welfare state, especially its strands of urban extension projects. It is fair to say that the FFH's theoretical framework resulted from a national internal debate, mainly developed in 1969 during the Colloquium. However, it was also deeply influenced by Portugal's recent participation in various international organizations, like the United Nations (UN) and the Organization for Economic Cooperation and Development (OECD), among others.[31] In addition, the implementation of FFH's broad range of action greatly depended on external funding and, subsequently, it depended on the coordination between national policies and the UN and the OECD's international guidelines. The history of the FFH is, therefore, inevitably parallel to the history of Portugal's adaptation process to Western canons during the post-revolution era. This was especially evident twice throughout FFH's existence: in 1977 and in 1983, when the IMF imposed austerity measures on the country.

In 1974, a mere three months after the revolution, SAAL was created and institutionally lodged under the FFH, which had recently been created during the dictatorship and was run by the regime's more technocratic factions. These were the last episodes of the state's intervention through direct financing in housing production. Later on, the supply became funded through outsourcing and financing of private construction industry—housing development contracts—and, finally, the demand became exclusively financed through credit acquisition.

[31] These considerations about the integrated plans and the FFH are part of an ongoing research: José António Bandeirinha, Tiago Castela, Joana Gouveia Alves, and Rui Aristides, "O Fundo de Fomento da Habitação de 1969 a 1982: ordenamento, alternativas e mercado," in *Habitação: Cem Anos de Políticas Públicas em Portugal, 1918–2018*, ed. Ricardo Agarez (Lisbon: Instituto da Habitação e Reabilitação Urbana, 2018).

ACKNOWLEDGMENTS

In the first place, I want to thank Rosa Bandeirinha, who translated this text into English. I also want to thank Tiago Castela, Joana Gouveia Alves, and Rui Aristides Lebre, with whom I carried out research co-work on this precise subject, in order to write a common text for the IHRU (Instituto da Habitação e da Reabilitação Urbana).

BIBLIOGRAPHY

Bandeirinha, José António. *O Processo SAAL e a Arquitectura no 25 de Abril de 1974*. Coimbra: Imprensa da Universidade, 2007.

Bandeirinha, José António. "Construir uma política da habitação num contexto adverso. O Colóquio de 1969." In *Habitação Para o Maior Número. Portugal os Anos de 1950–1980*, edited by Nuno Portas, 62–77. Lisbon: Instituto da Habitação e da Reabilitação Urbana and Câmara Municipal de Lisboa, 2013. [Although it was printed in 2013, it was actually presented and published in May 2014.]

Bandeirinha, José António, Tiago Castela, Joana Gouveia Alves, and Rui Aristides. "O Fundo de Fomento da Habitação de 1969 a 1982: ordenamento, alternativas e mercado." In *Habitação: Cem Anos de Políticas Públicas em Portugal, 1918–2018*, edited by Ricardo Agarez. Lisboa: Instituto da Habitação e Reabilitação Urbana, 2018.

Castela, Tiago Luís Lavandeira. "A Liberal Space: a History of the Illegalized Working-Class Extensions of Lisbon." PhD Dissertation, University of California, 2011.

Coelho, António Baptista. "Sobre os 'anos dourados' dos conjuntos cooperativos de habitação económica, 1974–1984." In *Habitação Para o Maior Número. Portugal os anos de 1950–1980*, edited by Nuno Portas, 135–153. Lisbon: Instituto da Habitação e da Reabilitação Urbana e Câmara Municipal de Lisboa, 2013. [Although it was printed in 2013, it was actually presented and published in May 2014.]

Fernandes, Ignácio Peres, A. Celestino da Costa, J. M. Ferreira da Cunha, Ruy José Gomes, Nuno Portas (reporter), and J. M. Alves de Sousa. *Colóquio Sobre Política de Habitação. Texto de Base*. Lisbon: Ministério das Obras Públicas, 1969 [June].

Fernandes, Ignácio Peres, A. Celestino da Costa, J. M. Ferreira da Cunha, Ruy José Gomes, Nuno Portas (reporter), and J. M. Alves de Sousa. *Colóquio Sobre Política de Habitação. Texto de Base*. Lisbon: Ministério das Obras Públicas, 1969 [September].

[Some of the considerations presented here were, however, developed in a previous report: Manuel Rocha, J. Ferry Borges, Francisco Silva Dias, Nuno Portas, and Ruy José Gomes. Informação sobre a Situação Actual dos Empreendimentos e Necessidades da Habitação Social. Lisbon: Ministério das Obras Públicas, Laboratório Nacional de Engenharia Civil, Serviço de Edifícios e Pontes, Divisão de Construção e Habitação, Proc. 34/0/3483, 1969 [February]. Later, this report became part of the Colloquium's works: Manuel Rocha, J. Ferry Borges, Francisco Silva Dias, Nuno Portas and Ruy José Gomes. *Colóquio Sobre Política da Habitação. Texto Complementar II*. Lisbon: Ministério das Obras Públicas.]

Fernandes, Ignácio Peres, A. Celestino da Costa, J. M. Ferreira da Cunha, Ruy José Gomes, Nuno Portas (reporter), and J. M. Alves de Sousa. *Colóquio Sobre Política de Habitação. Relato Final*. Lisbon: Ministério das Obras Públicas, 1969.

Ferreira, António Fonseca. *Por uma Nova Política de Habitação*. Porto: Edições Afrontamento, 1987.

Gonçalves, Fernando. *Urbanizar e Construir Para Quem?*. Porto: Afrontamento, 1972.

Gros, Marielle Christine. *O Alojamento Social Sob o Fascismo*. Porto: Afrontamento, 1982.

INE. *Estatísticas da Habitação (X Recenseamento Geral da População)* 1970.

Mendes, Maria Clara. "A habitação em Portugal: Caracterização e Políticas." In *Seminário 25 de Abril 10 Anos Depois*. Lisbon: Associação 25 de Abril, 1984.

Pereira, Nuno Teotónio. "A nódoa de Lisboa," *Seara Nova* (June 1970). Edited in *Escritos (1947–1996, selecção)*. Porto: FAUP Publicações, 1996.

Habitação Para o Maior Número. Portugal os anos de 1950–1980, edited by Nuno Portas. Lisbon: Instituto da Habitação e da Reabilitação Urbana e Câmara Municipal de Lisboa, 2013. [Although it was printed in 2013, it was actually presented and published in May 2014.]

Reis, António. "Marcelismo." In Fernando Rosas, J. M. Brandão de Brito, (direction), *Dicionário de História do Estado Novo*, V. II, s.l., Círculo de Leitores, 1996.

Rodrigues, Carlos Farinha. "Planos de Fomento."In *Dicionário de História do Estado Novo*, V. II, edited by Fernando Rosas and J. M. Brandão de Brito. Círculo de Leitores, 1996.

Rosas, Fernando. *O Estado Novo (1926–1974)*. *História de Portugal*, vol. VII. Edited by José Mattoso. Círculo de Leitores, 1994.

Serra, Nuno. *Estado Território e Estratégias de Habitação*. Coimbra: Quarteto Editora, 2002.

Topalov, Christian. "La politique du logement dans le processus révolutionaire portugais (25 avril 1974–11 mars 1975)." *Espaces et Sociétés*, no. 17–18 (Mars/Juin 1976).

A demonstration demanding affordable housing in 1975.

Photo by Alexandre Alves Costa.
Image from Centro de Documentação 25 de Abril, Alves Costa Collection.

5. NEW HYPOTHESIS FOR OLD PROBLEMS

Living conditions for a large part of Portuguese population were at its worse by the time the dictatorship crumbled in 1974. Urgent responses were prepared and swiftly launched, generating techical and communal discussions as never seen before. What did we learn? What did we inherit? And what can we do to make it better?

European Collective Housing in the Post-War Period: Thermal Retrofitting and Architectural Impact

FRANZ GRAF and GIULIA MARINO
École Polytechnique Fédérale de Lausanne, School of Architecture, Civil and Environmental Engineering, Institute of Architecture, Laboratory of Techniques and Preservation of Modern Architecture

ABSTRACT

"Should the *Grands ensembles* be demolished?" This question was a major preoccupation for architects in the 1990s. Incidental as it may seem today, the question is not completely old hat. The initial, progressive shift towards the practice of maintenance is to be welcomed. But we still need to be conscious, looking forward, that the qualities or values of constructions built between 1945 and 1975 are only rarely recognised and safeguarded. A tremendous variety of strategies have been adopted, and this thematic issue on collective housing's present-day relevance proposes to revisit, on the European scale, this very multiplicity of approaches.

BIOGRAPHY

Franz Graf, a graduate in architecture of the École Polytechnique Fédérale de Lausanne (EPFL), he is professor at the Accademia di Architettura di Mendrisio in 2005 and at the EPFL. Since 2010 he has been President of Docomomo Switzerland, and since 2012 member of the Comité des experts pour la restauration de l'œuvre of the Le Corbusier Fondation.

Giulia Marino has a master's degree in architecture from the University of Florence and a PhD in architecture from the École Polytechnique Fédérale de Lausanne (EPFL). Since 2007 she has been a teacher and scientist at the Laboratory of Techniques and Preservation of Modern Architecture at the EPFL. She is Vice President of Docomomo Switzerland and a member of the Swiss Heritage Society

http://tsam.epfl.ch.

From 2008 to 2012, the Laboratory of Techniques and Preservation of Modern Architecture (TSAM) at the École Polytechnique Fédérale de Lausanne was tasked with carrying out an applied research for an architectural and energy use study of the Cité du Lignon façades, in partnership with the Energy Group at the Environmental Sciences Institute, University of Geneva.[1] The heritage value of the Cité du Lignon in all its guises—architectural, technical, social, etc.—was recognized both qualitatively and quantitatively. The satellite city designed by the office of Addor and Julliard represented an exceptional case study on numerous levels and afforded an opportunity to look more widely at large-scale contemporary heritage places and their future. An intervention at a site where heritage aspects, economic limitations and energy efficiency factors intersected demanded a total strategy, with purpose-designed tools for preventive conservation whose forward-looking character can encourage the formation of a coherent regulatory framework.

[1] Franz Graf and Giulia Marino, *La cité du Lignon 1963–1971–Étude Architecturale et Stratégies d'Intervention* (Infolio, 2012).

Fig. 1 Georges Addor, Jacques Bolliger, Dominique Julliard, Louis Payot, Cité du Lignon, Geneva, 1963–1971. Photo by Claudio Merlini, Geneva, 2011.

It demanded a synthetic approach that enables the reconciliation of issues which today are not generally viewed as reconcilable. The results, founded on an exhaustive knowledge of the built object, its material identity and intrinsic characteristics, might give us insights from which we can develop new approaches that are more attentive to contemporary heritage—a sorely neglected resource—everywhere. The results are convincing, and today the 125,000 square metres of façade are under conservation/repair. From the beginning of this pioneering research, the TSAM was very attentive to European collective housing in the post-war period and in particular the architectural impact of thermal retrofitting.

This topic has come to be of wider interest, and we can say that this recent interest indicates a key cultural shift. In the last ten years, with the benefit of historical hindsight, we have begun to look again at housing schemes of the 1945–1975 period. There are so many, and they are often of considerable heritage interest; indeed they are increasingly being recognised as heritage in a way that would have hardly been thinkable not so long ago. The protection afforded to Ernö Goldifinger's Balfron Tower in London (1966–72) or the Cité de l'Etoile, Bobigny by the engineering trio of Candilis, Josic & Woods, are cases in point. We would be fooling ourselves, of course, if we thought this represented a consensus: the go-ahead has been given for the destruction of Robin Hood Gardens, by Alison and Peter Smithson (1969–72), and as we speak Britain's Prime Minister is announcing the demolition of 100 "brutal high-rise towers [. . .] that are a gift to criminals and drug dealers."[2] Nonetheless, all over Europe, and well beyond the confines of academia and the heritage lobby,[3] we are witnessing a renewed interest in the large-format housing complexes of the late 20th century, an emblematic *corpus* that has helped, in the real sense of the term, shape the contemporary landscape. Only now are these schemes beginning to be appreciated on their own terms, by users and public opinion alike.

DEMOLITION OR RENOVATION—IS THAT STILL THE QUESTION?

Conspicuous as they are, these buildings are seen as plain and ordinary. So despite a plethora of consultations, public initiatives and research intended to shed new light on the theme of the *grand ensemble*—not least in its social implications—interventions can vary immensely. Ideas about how to protect contemporary architecture and the scientific tools for cataloguing it are becoming clearer. Traditional art-historical criteria are being refined by new kinds of assessment: "technological innovation, production techniques, the aesthetic of manufacture in series."[4]

[2] David Cameron, "I've put the bulldozing of sink estates at the heart of turnaround Britain," *The Sunday Times*, 10 January 2016.

[3] For example, the good recent article in the French newspaper Libération : Tonino Serafini, Sibylle Vincendon, "Grands ensembles: démolir les clichés, pas les cités,» *Libération*, 7 October 2015.

[4] Adopted in 2011, during the conference *Zwischen Baukunst und Massenproduktion. Denkmalschutz für die Architektur des 1960er und 1970er Jahre*, the Bensberg Charter aims to "refine classical history of art assessment criteria of the period to take account of the full breadth of programmatic aspects, such as technological innovation, production techniques, the demands of flexibility and variability, the aesthetics of production in series, etc." *Charta von Bensberg zur Architektur des 1960er und 1970er Jahre* (Rheinischer Verein, 2011).

Yet current architectural practice within existing buildings is still feeling its way forward. A tremendous variety of strategies have been adopted, and this thematic issue on collective housing's present-day relevance proposes to revisit, on the European scale, this very multiplicity of approaches. But the situation is on notice. Things are not as reassuring as they could be. Only rarely are the methods defined with the aid of suitably thorough supporting studies. It is a mixed picture on the ground where interventions pay only the scantest attention, most often by accident or misapprehension, to the material integrity and the cultural values of post-war architecture, whilst landscape character is overlooked altogether. In this context, large post-war housing schemes, originally conceived as a demonstration of architectural, technological and social aspirations, are now a major target for action when it comes to issues like energy consumption.

"Should the *grands ensembles* be demolished?" This question was a major preoccupation for architects in the 1990s.[5] Incidental as it may seem today, the question is not completely old hat. The initial, progressive shift towards the practice of maintenance is to be welcomed. But we still need to be conscious, looking forward, that the qualities or values of constructions built between 1945 and 1975 are only rarely recognised and safeguarded. A real transfiguration of the contemporary city is silently underway all around us.

A SILENT TRANSFIGURATION: FROM ORDINARY HOUSING…

In his reinterpretation of the Wohnüberbauung Heuried, by Paillard and Leemann, at Wiedikon (1969), Adrian Streich hides a minutely conceived thermal upgrade in the fluid profile of his new envelopes. For the Göhnerswil-Volketswil (1969) by Marcel Meili and Markus Peter, metamorphosis provided an occasion to reflect on the methods of industrialised production by means of superimposed prefabricated timber-structured panels over the original *Plattenbau*. Lacaton and Vassal, along with Drouin and Hutin, at Cité du Grand Parc, Bordeaux, are building on the Tour du Bois-le-Prêtre experience, with an intervention that is primarily designed for economy and includes winter gardens and prefabricated concrete balconies, applied onto the façades, the original expression of which is to be utterly reconfigured. Set against landmark operations such as these, on ordinary housing to which each designer has in his own way contributed a "+Plus"[6] to the existing fabric (effectively a new building), it is a pity that more common practice generally misses the mark. Major physical interventions, clumsy on the aesthetic level never mind the heritage impact, are the norm.

[5] Françoise Moiroux, "Faut-il détruire les grands ensembles ? De l'univoque à la polyphonie…," Special Report, *D'Architectures*, 141 (2004).

[6] We refer to the research heading « + ," a rehabilitation strategy for large-scale housing schemes in France, devised by Druot, Lacaton & Vassal. Cf. Frédéric Druot, Anne Lacaton, Jean-Philippe Vassal, et al., *Les Grands Ensembles de Logement. Territoire d'Exception* (Gustavo Gili, 2007).

They are made independently of the intrinsic qualities of buildings. Tougher energy legislation is compounding the issue. New, over-insulated and ventilated façades are popping up all over, flattening modelled detail and erasing lines of force that were once described with utmost carefulness. We have metal siding and fibre-cement wrapped around volumes and cloaking balconies, losing nuanced reliefs, simplifying and impoverishing the volumetrics. Window joinery is growing thicker, replaced by heavier frames (most often in PVC) capable of supporting triple glazing. And as for colour—cliché of clichés—look no further than the "makeover" treatment of the remarkable BBPR Gratosoglio quarter in Milan (1963–71), or the Tour Super Montparnasse, Paris, by Bernard Zehrfuss (1966–69): intelligent juxtaposition of materials and textures, meticulously rendered by designers of the 1960s, ditched for a chequerboard of garish tones, "brightened by a touch of colour," usually an astonishing shade of red straight from the standard cladding industry colour chart. Even attempts to "preserve" original characteristics by adding a new external layer evoking the existing colours and materials look like caricatures. These clumsy, irreversible "thermal renovations" follow a trend for "upgrading" or, more prosaically, achieving "code compliance" that too often rides roughshod over the need for a prior determination of the value of the built object and ignores its intrinsic qualities. Undertaken at huge cost, they should give us pause for reflection.

... TO HOUSING HERITAGE

The imperatives of energy conservation—rightly recognised as inescapable—are becoming the pretext for giving buildings a new identity. In a more subtle way, it seems that even objects acknowledged as of exceptional historical importance might not be free from harm in spite of the tight constraints of the heritage planning context. While some interventions have fortunately established constraints for energy retrofitting as a priority from the outset, others cases like the Siedlung Halen, Berne-Kirchlindach (1955–61), an iconic housing estate by Atelier 5 known and admired well beyond the Swiss border, face an uncertain future.[7] In much the same vein is the recent "energy upgrade" of the Miremont-le-Crêt complex, Geneva (1956–57) by Marc J. Saugey. Listed as a *Monument Historique* in 2002, it illustrates the limitations of the exercise where there is no clear strategy setting out what is to be achieved.[8] On one level, a fruitful cooperation involving the cantonal heritage and energy efficiency authorities has spared Saugey's building from the worst effects of "code compliance"—meaning radical alteration—allowing performance below the legal consumption limits thanks to a series of well-conceived offsets.

[7] Despite "guidelines" published in 2013 by the Canton of Berne heritage conservation department, it is proving difficult to make headway with an energy retrofit project for the envelopes of the Siedlung Halen that respects the place's exceptional heritage values; Franz Graf and Giulia Marino, "Mirabilia ou ressource durable ? Le patrimoine récent à l'épreuve des enjeux énergétiques," *Kunst + Architektur in der Schweiz*, 2 (2015) : 58–65.

[8] Giulia Marino, "Kampf um Millimeter. Renovation der Wohnhäuser Miremont-le-Crêt in Genf von Marc-Joseph Saugey durch meier+associés und Oleg Calame," *werk, bauen+wohnen*, 1–2 (2016): 36–41.

But on another level, the need to demonstrate "exemplary" energy efficiency outcomes has by default sanctioned an overall "upgrade" strategy that uses a repertoire of hi-tech, thermal-performance products aiming to meet insulation values similar to those of new constructions, even though they have somewhat uncomfortable consequences in terms of the visual and architectural qualities of the original ensemble...

RESPONSIBLE WAYS FORWARD

Emblematic of these modern works, where notions of lightness and transparency play a crucial role, marrying technical and architectural innovation, the case of the "energy upgrade" at Miremont-le-Crêt encapsulates the difficulties of reconciling the cultural challenge of heritage conservation with environmental paradigms. As we have said, on another scale, built assets are repeatedly faced with hasty and all too radical transformations with no overarching strategy capable of placing limits on what is effectively a transfiguration of the contemporary city. Aside from cultural considerations—or even just the architectural ones, the general "dumbing down" of our environment—with recession on the horizon we should be looking at this practice with a new sense of urgency. The statement that *"the different strategic options for restoration stem from, among other things, a precise analysis of the existing building,"* technical guideline 2047 *Rénovation Énergétique des Bâtiments*, recently published by the *Société des Ingénieurs et des Architectes Suisses* (SIA), gives crucial indications.

This salutary stance has grown out of a number of highly significant experiences. A case in point is the guidelines developed for the impressive Barbican complex in London (1953–57)[9] which identifies the original elements as the sole traces of authentic fabric, the only evidence capable of expressing the complex's architectural qualities, including the often neglected issue of exterior spaces. In Switzerland we can point to the important work by architects Miller and Maranta in advance of the energy upgrade works to Hermann Baur's Siedlung im Lee scheme, in Basel (1963). From them we have learned that detailed knowledge of the fabric is a vital necessity for targeting thermal improvements to the built object at close quarters, to conserve its intrinsic characteristics but without rejecting substantial energy savings. By the same token, the intelligent pilot project for the upgrade of the Tscharnegut in Bern (Hans and Gret Reinhard, 1958–61), devised by Rolf Muhlethaler, which is now in progress, is a compelling demonstration of the indispensability of adaptation to current circumstances in terms of energy but also the typological needs of the sector.

[9] Barbican Estate, London, Chamberlin, Powell & Bon architects, 1953–57; listed *Grade II*, this exceptionally significant building was the subject of a series of studies by a working group composed of different institutional actors and Avanti Architects, to establish guidelines for conserving the tower blocks. Initial conclusions set out clear indications on respecting the materials and colour palette used for the original façades. Timber frames of the large window panels could easily accommodate insulated glazing units to replace the single glass of the original. Avanti Architects, *Barbican Listed Building Management Guidelines*, vol. II (October 2012).

It manages to respect the striking urban forms within this representative post-war housing scheme, an ensemble well worth preserving. Equally, the highly conclusive experience of the TSAM Laboratory and its applied academic research at the Cité du Lignon was recently extended to other late 20th-century "grands ensembles" in the Geneva area for a research project supported by the *Stiftung zur Förderung der Denkmalpflege*. An appraisal of buildings according to a wide range of constructional types—from a masonry façade with openings in the Quai du Seujet (1964–76), to the externally insulated prefabricated concrete panel of the Cité Avanchet Parc (1973–77), not to mention the "Honegger" buildings in the Carl-Vogt (1960–64) and the curtain wall of the Meyrin residential suburb (1960–64)—has shown how the balance between preserving the built object and making sizeable thermal improvements generally comes in at around 80–90 per cent of the legal requirement, depending on techniques used.

Fig. 2 Georges Addor, Jacques Bolliger, Louis Payot, Meyrin Parc Satellite Precinct, Geneva, 1960–1964. Photo by Claudio Merlini, Geneva, 2011.

Fig. 3 Honegger Frères, Cité Carl-Vogt, Geneva (1960–1964).
Photo by Claudio Merlini, Geneva, 2011.

The 10–20 per cent that still needs to be achieved to attain current standards implies heavy and highly destructive interventions which are technically challenging and therefore entail an exponential increase in build costs for an equivalent life cycle. For existing housing assets, the price in conservation terms—and more prosaically, in terms of economic investment—appears out of proportion.

In place of this "intensive therapy," which exacts such a heavy price, we should be looking at responsible steps to highlight the notion of "built heritage as resource"—essentially, something very akin to the *use value* imagined by Alois Riegl—accepting building performance ratings that, while not perhaps the best, at least favour sizeable or substantial reductions in consumption to be coupled perhaps with gains from renewable energy. As for highly significant items— "young monuments" to use the phrase suggested in a thematic issue of *werk, bauen+wohnen,* recently—an explicit stance is required: can one reasonably aim for energy excellence by demanding that an existing building with acknowledged heritage value meet the performance needs of a new building, rigidly established by rules that have evolved into extremely strict limit-values?

Fig. 4 Franz Amrhein, Walter Maria Förderer, Steiger Partner, Avanchet Precinct, Geneva, 1973–1975).
Photo by Claudio Merlini, Geneva, 2011.

The response is nuanced. In balancing preservation of the built fabric with the environment, perhaps we need to be broadening the issue and reversing the trend. In other words, the building itself should define the limit of interventions, depending on intrinsic material characteristics opportunely mapped during preliminary studies. This gets around the issue of a strict application of standards, which so often have repercussions, and potentially irreversible ones, on the integrity of objects and, more broadly, the appearance of our cities. It is not a matter of neglecting the paradigm that requires us to respect the very legitimate need to reduce energy consumption and CO_2 emissions. Rather it is a matter of calibrating performance improvements more closely to the built object, prioritising smaller, targeted interventions, *ad hoc* responses developed from closer contact with the built fabric and geared towards accommodating it in a way that improves user comfort. This pragmatic and sympathetic approach should be adopted more widely as part of the project of conservation of recent heritage. This is a "demanding brief"[10] illustrating, above all, the intelligent and culturally aware position the designer must be ready to occupy.

[10] "Editorial," *werk, bauen+wohnen*, issue Junge Denkmäler, 10 (2013): 4.

Fig. 5 Franz Amrhein, Walter Maria Förderer, Steiger Partner, Avanchet Precinct, Geneva, 1973–1975).
Photo by Claudio Merlini, Geneva, 2011.

BIBLIOGRAPHY

Graf, Franz, and Giulia Marino. Patrimoine Moderne, Énergie, Économie: Stratégies de Sauvegarde. EPFL-TSAM, Stiftung zur Förderung der Denkmalpflege, 2015

Graf, Franz, and Giulia Marino. "Mirabilia ou ressource durable? Le patrimoine récent à l'épreuve des enjeux énergétiques." Kunst + Architektur in der Schweiz, 2 (June 2015): 58–65.

Graf, Franz, and Giulia Marino. La cité du Lignon 1963–1971– Étude Architecturale et Stratégies d'Intervention, cahier hors série de la revue Patrimoine et architecture. Infolio, 2012.

Graf, Franz, and Giulia Marino. Modern and Green: Heritage, Energy and Economy, in Ana Tostoes, Liu Kecheng (dir.), Docomomo International 1988-2012: Key Papers in Modern Architectural Heritage Conservation, 183–193, 152–161. Pekin: China Architecture & Building Press, Pekin, 2012.

Graf, Franz, and Giulia Marino. "Strategien zum Erhalt moderner Architektur." werk, bauen+wohnen, no.10 (October 2013): 20–25.

Typo-Morphological Laboratories During the 20th Century: a General Overview on the State-Subsidized Multifamily Housing Projects in Portugal (1910–1974)

GISELA LAMEIRA
University of Porto, Faculty of Architecture, Centre for Studies in Architecture and Urbanism

ABSTRACT

In Portugal, although the single-family remained the preferred model for a large set of public housing initiatives until the early 1950s, multifamily buildings in the urban context played a significant part in shaping the city centres of the most important Portuguese cities, Lisbon and Porto. Particularly in the post-war period (mainly the 1950s–1970s), these residential architectures had a key role in the urban transformation of these cities, namely in their morphological consolidation and expansion.

During these decades, different sorts of promoters generated types and models carrying their own identity, either in terms of typology design, construction practices or influences from international contexts. The private promoters, real estate developers, and state housing promoters followed agendas involving divergent factors, such as political and legal frameworks, financial resources and urban settings.

In terms of public initiatives, during the first three quarters of the 20th century, several housing programmes were implemented in Portugal with the aim of providing proper dwellings for a large part of the Portuguese population. Focusing on Porto and Lisbon, for example, the public sector had been deeply involved in its urban dynamics since the 1940s, implementing housing solutions aiming not only at inhabitants with lower resources but also an emerging middle-class that took advantage of the possibility of renting or buying their houses with beneficial terms. Also, these initiatives resulted in large urban operations that were strategically connected with the planned expansion of the urban fabric through residential areas, imposing urban models which were radically different from the traditional composition systems. The constructed buildings were also a vehicle of effective typological experimentation, exploring the "minimum dwelling" principles and the rationale of renovated distribution.

Through a panoramic overview of the housing programmes which were carried out or supported by Portuguese public initiatives between 1910s–1974s, the aim is:
- to identify some of the most relevant residential estates built during this period;
- to clarify the associated regulation in terms of housing policies;
- to highlight their relevance not only in terms of their impact on the cities, morphological transformation but also regarding the proposal of new housing typologies.

BIOGRAPHY

Gisela Lameira (Portugal, Viseu, 1978) is an architect and researcher with the "Atlas da Casa" (Housing architectural design and forms of dwelling) working group of the Center for Studies in Architecture and Urbanism (FAUP, CEAU). She has a PhD in Architecture (FAUP, 2017). Her research interests include the study of architecture and urban theory and history, specifically the genesis and transformation of multifamily housing in Portugal. She worked as a research fellow on the project "Mapping Public Housing: a critical review of the State-subsidized residential architecture in Portugal (1910–1974)," hosted by FAUP/ CEAU [P2020-PTDC/CPC-HAT/1688/2014] and is currently undertaking research for the exploratory projects "Ageing in Place/Architecture4Ageing" and "ICAVI. Independent Living model," at FAUP, where she also teaches History of Contemporary Architecture for the second cycle course at FAUP.

SHIFTING PARADIGMS. THE EMERGENCE OF MULTIFAMILY HOUSING MODELS DURING THE 1ST HALF OF THE 20TH CENTURY

For almost seven decades, between 1910, the date of the implementation of the 1st Portuguese Republic (1910–1926), and 1974, the date of the fall of the *Estado Novo* dictatorship regime (1933–1974), several housing programmes were implemented. Each one showed different approaches regarding dwelling typologies in general, and multifamily housing particularly, and most of the estates built had a different impact on the cities' morphological and functional structure.

The 20th century public housing production was extensively mapped by the research project "Mapping Public Housing" [https://mappingpublichousing.up.pt/en/]. Its purpose was to identify the housing programmes subsidized by the state and their spatial concretizations during the period 1910–1974: neighbourhoods, collective buildings or single-family houses. The current status of the ongoing inventory carried out throughout this research project has allowed a comprehensive vision of the typological experimentation carried out until 1974.

The research project database currently holds about six hundred records (referring mostly to neighbourhoods built with varying dimensions), from which about two hundred include multifamily housing buildings. Within this universe, it is possible to find various types of buildings, with different number or storeys and access systems. Intermediate or hybrid solutions, i.e., buildings that have direct/individual access to the apartments from the street, were a frequent option, especially in the housing programmes implemented during the middle 1940s. A distribution gallery or vertical access cores were developed in a larger set of buildings, mainly in those constructed after 1945.

Although the multifamily type, with vertical access and several apartments on each floor, was a well-known type of building among private housing sector construction, particularly in Lisbon, clearly it was not the first option when it came to the public initiatives. During the 1930s and 1940s, the housing programmes implemented were focused on spreading low-density neighbourhoods, a sort of garden cities with single-family houses with individual small gardens. These housing policies allowed the construction of large parts of the city of Lisbon and Porto, contributing to their planned expansion and morphological restructuring, but failed to offer a global solution for the housing needs felt during that period.

HOUSING PROGRAMMES, MULTIFAMILY HOUSING BUILDINGS AND CITY MODELS. A GENERAL OVERVIEW

This panoramic overview focuses on a residential stock that frequently does not stand out for its architectural quality, defining a particular object of study—the state-subsidized multifamily housing buildings built in Portugal, a temporal frame—the period between 1910–1974, and a particular perspective of approach—the typological and morphological analysis. It aims to identify some of the most relevant residential estates built during this period, in terms of scale, morphological impact on the cities' expansion and the innovative approach regarding the design of the dwellings, framing their current regulation in terms of housing policies.

1. THE FIRST EXPERIENCES

The "Affordable Houses Neighbourhoods" (*Bairros de Casas Económicas*–BCE, Decree-Law 4,137, 25 April 1918) constitutes the first housing programme in which several provisions were promulgated on the construction and sale of affordable houses for the underprivileged classes of the urban population. Although this public initiative (and its regulatory framework) was directed towards the construction of single-family dwellings and housing in terraced houses (article 4), in the three neighbourhoods built under this programme, it is relevant to refer to the *Ajuda* neighbourhood, in Lisbon (1918–1935) [MdH DB a215], which proposed multifamily housing buildings with three storeys along with single-family buildings.

Fig. 1 and 2 President Carmona Municipal Neighbourhood (Lisbon, 1927–1935)–102 dwellings (single-family and multifamily buildings), on the left. GPS: 38.739993N 9.131524W (left); Neighbourhood of the insurance company "O Trabalho" (Porto, 1928)–18 dwellings. GPS: 38.739993N 9.131524W (right).
Photos by Gisela Lameira (2018).

Later in 1928, the "Affordable Houses System" programme (*Regime das Casas Económicas*–RCE, Decree-Law 16,055, 22 October 1928) followed this direction, also advancing some neighbourhoods with multifamily models. Two examples stand out, one in Lisbon and other in Porto, both proposing a two-storey housing block with shared vertical access to the apartments (two on each floor).

By the late 1920s, this type of buildings, close to some low-end solutions built by the private sector, sought to solve the housing needs in a more effective way, especially in Lisbon with the construction of 102 dwellings.

The implementation of the dictatorship in Portugal (*Estado Novo*, 1933) made it difficult to develop further this line of experimentation, as the regime clearly privileged the construction of single-family houses as an "instrument of social control."[1] Until the late 1950s, the first housing programme created during the *Estado Novo*, the "Affordable Houses" programme (*Casas Económicas*–CE, Decree-Law 23,052, 23 September 1933), did not produce other types of buildings for housing, nor even intermediate solutions.

According to the "Mapping Public Housing" inventory, the "Affordable Houses" programme built around 70 neighbourhoods over nearly five decades (1933–1971). Only from the late 1950s was the inclusion of multifamily housing types considered (in about 12 examples), such as the *Viso* neighbourhood (Porto, 1958–1965) [MdH DB a11], the *Cedro* neighbourhood (Vila Nova de Gaia, 1962–1966) [MdH DB a261], and the *Mira-Sintra/ICESA* neighbourhood (Agualva-Cacém, 1965–1975) [MdH DB a267].

2. THE POST-WAR PERIOD AS A TURNING POINT.

The shift to the construction of multifamily housing models, observed around the 1940s, indicates that the single-family model wasn't able to fulfil the housing needs felt at the time. In this sense, several housing programmes were then implemented, which defined a turning point in terms of public housing policies and led to intense experimentation in terms of typological solutions. The first examples built during this period pointed to intermediate solutions, housing building types with few floors, direct access to the apartments or vertical access systems serving just a few dwellings. In specific situations, architectural solutions were restricted by the legislation itself, which limited the height of the buildings to four floors. That was the case with the formulation of the 1945 Decree-Law for the "*Affordable Rent Houses*" programme.

[1] Sérgio Dias Silva and Rui J.G. Ramos. "Housing, Nationalism and Social Control: The First Years of The Portuguese Estado Novo's Affordable Houses Programme," in *Southern modernisms from A to Z and back again*, ed. Joana Cunha Leal et al (Porto: Centro de Estudos Arnaldo Araújo–CESAP/ESAP, Instituto de História da Arte–FCSH/UNL, 2015), 261.

The "Houses for Poor Families" programme (*Casas para Famílias Pobres*–CP, Decree-Law 34,486, 6 April 1945), also implemented at the same time, was meant for the most disadvantaged fringe of the population, which was ineligible for housing via other public housing offers. Although this programme started with individual houses, during the early 1950s it turned to multifamily housing types, hybrid models with two floors, and housing blocks with several floors and access galleries (about a dozen examples, from eighty-seven currently listed).

The *São Vicente de Paulo* neighbourhood (1950) [MdH DB a552] and the *Rainha Dona Leonor* neighbourhood, stage 2 (1955) [MdH DB a801], both located in Porto, are interesting cases regarding the use of galleries as optimised distribution systems in the set of examples identified in this programme. The housing buildings in the *Quinta do Jacinto* neighbourhood [MdH DB a676], with a T-shape, vertical accesses, and three apartments on each floor, added an extra layer of experimentation, through a rational plan that organized the location of the buildings according to their solar exposure.

Fig. 3, 4 and 5 São Vicente de Paulo neighbourhood (Porto, 1950)–18 dwellings, on the left. GPS: 41.154289N 8.578656W (left); Quinta do Jacinto neighbourhood (Lisbon, 1950–1957), Raúl Tojal, José de Lima Franco–180 dwellings. GPS: 38.707352N 9.176778W (middle); Rainha Dona Leonor neighbourhood, stage 2 (Porto, 1955)–100 dwellings, on the right. GPS: 41.149087N 8.662276W (right). Photos by Gisela Lameira (2018).

The "*Affordable Rent Houses*" programme (*Casas de Renda Económica*–CRE, Law 2007, 7 May 1945), implemented via Affordable Housing–Federation of Provident Funds (*Habitações Económicas/ Federação de Caixas de Previdência*–HE/FCP) was developed in a different direction. This housing initiative was intended to provide access to lower-rent houses, targeting residents who could not apply for the single-family houses constructed under the "Affordable Houses" programme in force since 1933.

During its lifespan, this housing programme constructed a relevant number of multifamily residential complexes. According to the ongoing inventory of the research project "Mapping Public Housing," about 115 neighbourhoods and 14,420 dwellings were built, from which around one hundred included multifamily housing types. This allowed effective experimentation, engaged with the proposal of new city models in line with the Charter of Athens urban paradigms, the introduction of new languages, either related to Modern Movement principles or to regionalist reinterpretations, and the design of typologies closely linked to the rationalist theories underlying the "minimum dwelling" ideal.

The project of Miguel Jacobetty Rosa for the *Alvalade complex, Cells 1 and 2* (1945–1948) [MdH DB a89], located in Lisbon, was first adopted as a typological model to reproduce across the country. During the 1950s and the 1960s, new strategies emerged, namely with the intervention of Nuno Teotónio Pereira and a large set of well known "modern" architects, such as Nuno Portas, Bartolomeu Costa Cabral, João Andresen, Ruy Athouguia, among others, who tried to approach each intervention according to local specificities, or to incorporate modern features at distinct levels. The *Alvalade* neighbourhood, Cells 1 and 2, the *Ramalde* residential unit (Porto, 1950–1954) [MdH DB a22] the *Soda Póvoa* neighbourhood (Vila Franca de Xira, 1953) [MdH DB a96], the *Cabo-Mor* neighbourhood (Vila Nova de Gaia, 1957) [MdH DB a30], and the *Caixas da Previdência* neighbourhood (Parede, 1957) [MdH DB a88] are some built examples where the authors developed rational apartment designs with regular configurations, seeking minimum dwelling areas, the optimization of circulation spaces and the compression of living spaces. Projects such as the *Santa Marta* neighbourhood (Barcelos, 1955–1962) [MdH DB a42] and *Torres Vermelhas da Pasteleira* (Porto, 1966–1972) [MdH DB a16], explored other lines of intervention, closer to vernacular references and "organic" approaches that were being explored, for example in Italy, in the INA-Casa residential complexes.

As some of these estates occupy large plots, new urban models were tested, namely the design of rational layouts with structuring axes and buildings placed parallel to each other according to the best solar exposure. The exterior areas located between the buildings were frequently planned to be green areas with pathways. On the one hand, this rationalist Charter of Athens approach can be seen in the *Ramalde* residential unit, the *Caixas da Previdência* neighbourhood (Coimbra, 1965) [MdH DB a57] or the *Cabo-Mor* neighbourhood, while the site plan distribution of *Torres Vermelhas da Pasteleira* suggests, on the other hand, the organicist influence from 1960s Italian residential settlements.

Some examples:

Fig. 6 and 7 Cabo-Mor neighbourhood (V. Nova de Gaia, 1957), João Andresen–72 dwellings. GPS: 41.119662N 8.613127W (left); Caixas da Previdência neighbourhood (Coimbra, 1965), Jorge Albuquerque–180 dwellings, GPS: 0.197993N; 8.411143W (right). Photos by Gisela Lameira (2018).

Fig. 8 and 9 Ramalde residential unit, Stage 1 & 2, (Porto, 1950–1954), Fernando Távora–426 dwellings, GPS: 41.167382N 8.655740W (left); Caixas da Previdência neighbourhood (Parede, 1957), Ruy Athouguia–160 dwellings. GPS: 38.692053N 9.349484W (right). Photos by Gisela Lameira (2018).

Fig. 10 and 11 Santa Marta neighbourhood (Barcelos, 1955–1962), Nuno Teotónio Pereira–20 dwellings. GPS: 41.534584N 8.608408W (left); Torres vermelhas da Pasteleira (Porto, 1966–1972), João Serôdio, Luís Almeida d'Eça, Rui Paixão–500 dwellings, on the right. GPS: 41.1513384N 8.6630958W (right) Photos by Gisela Lameira (2018).

Fig. 12 and 13 Alvalade neighbourhood, Cells 1 and 2 (Lisbon, 1945–1948), Miguel Jacobetty Rosa–2066 dwellings, on the left. GPS: 38.752311N 9.146895W (left); Soda Póvoa neighbourhood (Vila Franca de Xira, 1953), Nuno Teotónio Pereira–12 dwellings. GPS: 38.859693N 9.067165W (right). Photos by Gisela Lameira (2018).

The "Houses for Fishermen" programme (*Casas para Pescadores*–CP, Decree-Law 35,732, 4 July 1946) was at first supported by Law 1953, dated March 11, 1937, which establishes the bases for the creation in all fishing centres of social cooperation organizations with legal personality, known as "Fishermen's Houses," and later by Decree-Law 35,732 of July 4, 1946, that allowed the Central Board of Fishermen's Houses to borrow loans to finance the construction of the buildings. According to the current inventory, it constructed fifty-six neighbourhoods, of which fourteen included shared access to the apartments. In this particular programme, implemented in Portuguese coastal areas, the most produced building is the two-storey type with direct access to two apartments, repeated in several locations (Matosinhos, Póvoa de Varzim, Sines, etc.), although some neighbourhoods have housing blocks with several stories and vertical access.

Fig. 14 and 15 Fishermen's Houses neighbourhood, Matosinhos (stage 3, 1958), Alexandre Bastos–104 dwellings, on the left. GPS: 41.187778N 8.679868W (left); Fishermen's Houses neighbourhood, Matosinhos (stage 2, 1958), Alexandre Bastos–56 dwellings. GPS: 41.187778N 8.679868W (right); Photos by Gisela Lameira (2018).

That is the case of Fishermen's Houses neighbourhood in Matosinhos (3rd stage) and Fishermen's Houses neighbourhood of Torre in Cascais (1st & 2nd stage, 1963–1965).

From another perspective, the "Houses with Controlled Rent" programme (*Casas de Renda Limitada*–CRP, Decree-Law 36,212, 7 April 1947), tried to increase cooperation between private investment and the public sector, through the previous fixing of the maximum total rent to be charged for the apartments. Although only three neighbourhoods located in Lisbon were built, they represent remarkable examples of the interpretation of the modern movement in Portugal, both in terms of urban concept and the design of the typologies. As the dwellings built under this housing programme were intended for a sector of the population that had some resources, the apartments areas and interior distributions exposed clear differences regarding other housing programmes' solutions. The "Plan of Improvements for the city of Porto" (*Plano de Melhoramentos da Cidade do Porto*–PMP, Decree-Law 40,616, 28 May 1956), a municipal document implemented in 1956 with the aim of solving the housing needs in Porto through the construction of about 6,000 homes in ten years, gave rise to a large set of residential settlements of varying sizes that were built on the first periphery of the city, contributing to its planned expansion and urbanization. The houses built under the "Improvement Plan for the City of Porto" had a direct connection with the "Houses for Poor Families' programme of 1945, and therefore followed its main principles.

Fig. 16, 17 and 18 Estacas neighbourhood (Lisbon, 1949–1955) [MdH DB a548], Ruy Athouguia, Sebastião Formosinho Sanchez–264 dwellings. GPS: 38.746497N 9.137728W (left); Residential complex in Avenida dos Estados Unidos da América (Lisbon, 1954) [MdH DB a544], Manuel Laginha, Pedro Cid, João B. Vasconcelos–540 dwellings. GPS: 38.749121N 9.136709W (middle) Residential complex in Avenida Infante Santo (Lisbon, 1949–1955) [MdH DB a546], Alberto J. Pessoa, Hernani Gandra, João Abel Manta–184 dwellings. GPS: 38.709920N 9.165252W (right). Photos by Gisela Lameira (2018).

The 30 neighbourhoods built under this housing programme comprise buildings with a varying number of storeys (at least four) and vertical accesses or distribution galleries, following type-projects in most cases. During the construction of the Improvement Plan neighbourhoods which took place between 1957 and 1977, it is possible to underline that the design of the typologies was gradually fine-tuned, in a process of experimentation that started to connect the shape of the housing buildings and its site more closely. This can be confirmed through the comparison of the neighbourhoods of *Pasteleira* [MdH DB a196], *Bom Sucesso* [MdH DB a691], and *Carvalhido* [MdH DB a693], from the beginning of the programme (1956–1958), namely the rationality of the layouts materialized from the site plan to the apartment design, with later projects implemented in the city, such as the *Falcão* neighbourhood (1967–1972) [MdH DB a715]. Some examples:

Fig. 19 and 20 Bom Sucesso low-income housing unit neighbourhood (Porto, 1956–1958)–126 dwellings [Gallery buildings], GPS: 41.153723N 8.632201W (left); Pasteleira low-income housing unit neighbourhood (Porto, 1957)–608 dwellings [Gallery buildings/Vertical access buildings]. GPS: 41.153944N 8.659717W (right).
Photos by Gisela Lameira (2018).

Fig. 21 and 22 Carvalhido low-income housing unit neighbourhood, (Porto, 1957–1958)–264 dwellings, GPS: 41.169443N 8.622784W (left); Falcão low-income housing unit neighbourhood, (Porto, 1967–1972, stage 1)–224 dwellings. GPS: 41.158975N 8.576916W (right). Photos by Gisela Lameira (2018).

Despite the specificities that can be found in each particular project, these residential complexes share the same rationale in terms of urban concept: large plots with a layout that organized parallel housing buildings, green areas, paths and streets that would connect with the urban structure defined by the Master Plan of Porto of 1962. Nevertheless, following some principles defined in the Charter of Athens, in most cases the urban model which was achieved seems to falter regarding its coordination with the pre-existing surroundings, creating fragmented pieces of urban fabric. This remark is particularly noticeable is most settlements of the Improvement Plan, as they neither incorporate others type of structures (facilities buildings, schools, commercial areas, etc.), fundamental for the inner dynamics of the ensemble, nor do they define hierarchies in the design of the street system and its connection to existing roads.

3. BETWEEN THE LATE 1950S AND THE EARLY 1970S. LARGE SCALE INTERVENTIONS.

The analysis of the state-subsidized housing programmes implemented from the late 1950s to 1974 points towards three of the larger settlements built in Lisbon in the early 1960s, namely the neighbourhoods of *Olivais Norte*, *Olivais Sul*, and *Chelas*. The Urbanization Plan of *Olivais Norte* neighbourhood (1955–1960) [MdH DB a186], for example, incorporated 5,000 dwellings in multifamily buildings spread over a 40 ha area, while about 6,986 dwellings were built for that of *Olivais Sul* neighbourhood (1959–1962) [MdH DB a193] in a 186 ha area.[2] These residential zones were developed under the "Plan for Constructing New Housing" programme (*Plano de Construção de Novas Habitações–PCNH*, Decree-Law 42,454, 18 August 1959), which established the global strategy for the construction of low-income dwellings linked to the planned expansion of the urban structure of Lisbon. Several affordable housing promoters were engaged with this strategy. Through this Plan, the *Olivais Sul*, *Olivais Norte*, and *Chelas* ensembles turned into large-scale multifamily housing laboratories. The investment made in the design of the urbanization plans[3] and the definition of coordination and monitoring instruments (such as the creation of a Technical Office for Housing–*Gabinete Técnico da Habitação–GTH*), allowed exploration and diversity of typological projects instead of the implementation of type projects and standardized solutions. Also, the overall urban concept of the plan was characterized by several aspects that contributed to an integrated process, such as the financial autonomy enabled by the selling of the plots, the definition of street hierarchies, the incorporation of equipment buildings, or the study of built large-scale neighbourhoods from international contexts.

[2] Teresa Heitor, "Olivais e Chelas: operações urbanísticas de grande escala," Centro de Estudos em Inovação, Tecnologia e Políticas de Desenvolvimento, IST Mestrado em Engenharia de Concepção, História Económica, Tecnologia e Sociedade, 2004.

[3] *Olivais Sul*–Urbanization Plan (Lisbon, 1959–1968)–6986 dwellings. GPS: 38.763863N 9.109696W
Olivais Norte–Urbanization Plan (Lisbon, 1955–1960)–2500 dwellings. GPS: 38.775152N 9.113723W
Chelas–Urbanization Plan (Lisbon, 1962–1967–1990)–2590 dwellings GPS: 38.749126N 9.117121W

Some examples (*Olivais Norte* neighbourhood):

Fig. 23, 24 and 25 Cell A–Cat. II (Lisbon, 1957–1968), Nuno Teotónio Pereira, Nuno Portas, António Pinto de Freitas–384 dwellings. GPS: 38.776181N 9.116921W (left); Cell A–Cat. III (Lisbon, 1959–1964), Cândido Palma de Melo, Artur Pires Martins–128 dwellings. GPS: 38.775414N 9.114904W (middle); Building type IID (Lisbon, 1958–1960), Pedro Cid, Fernando Torres et al.–80 dwellings. GPS: 38.776376N 9.114732W (right).
Photos by Gisela Lameira (2018).

Fig. 26 and 27 Cell A–Y type (Lisbon, 1960), João Barros Vasconcelos Esteves–900 dwellings. GPS: 38.775749N; 9.113916W (left); Building type IC (Lisbon, 1959), João Braula Reis, João Matoso–90 dwellings. GPS: 38.775749N 9.113916W (right). Photos by Gisela Lameira (2018).

Some examples (*Olivais Sul* neighbourhood):

Fig. 28, 29 and 30 Cell C–Cat.I, (Lisbon, 1960–1964), Vasco Croft, Justino Morais, Joaquim Cadima–972 dwellings, on the left. GPS: 38.764514N 9.122760W; Cell B–Cat. II–Plot 29, 46, (Lisbon, 1960), Vítor Figueiredo, Vasco Lobo–140 dwellings. GPS: 38.766580N 9.121002W; Cell C/freestanding slabs, (Lisbon, 1958–1968), Nuno Teotónio Pereira, Nuno Portas, Bartolomeu da Costa Cabral, José Maria Torre do Valle, Pedro Vieira de Almeida, Rui Gamito (eng.)–272 dwellings, on the right. GPS: 38.765831N 9.115313W.
Photos by Gisela Lameira (2018).

Between the late 1960s and 1974, three other public housing initiatives were implemented addressing specific questions: the "Plan for Rehousing Ddisaster Victims" (*Plano de Realojamento dos Sinistrados*–PRS, Decree-Law 48,240, 17 February 1968); some neighbourhoods advanced by the "Housing Development Fund" (*Fundo de Fomento da Habitação*–FFH, Decree-Law 49,033, 28 May 1969), an organization with legal personality and administrative and financial autonomy, created with the purpose of contributing to the resolution of the housing problem; and the development of the "Department of the Sines Area" (*Gabinete da área de Sines*–GAS, Decree-Law 270, 19 June 1971), designed to promote the urban-industrial development of a specific zone in Sines. Among the neighbourhoods built via the "Housing Development Fund" (FFH), the well-known housing estate of *Alto do Zambujal* in Amadora (Buraca, 1974–1977) [MdH DB a743], designed by Vitor Figueiredo and Duarte Cabral Mello, and the *Bela Vista* neighbourhood (Setúbal, 1974) [MdH DB a744] by José Charters Monteiro and José Sousa Martins, stand out regarding the scale of the settlements and the urban models implemented. Both estates can be seen as relevant experiments regarding the morphological redefinition of the relationship between the design of collective exterior spaces and the disposition of the buildings. Their plans propose an interpretation of the housing quarter as the composition unit of the urban structure, clearly going beyond the Charter of Athens paradigm, where buildings were spread out in landscaped areas.

Fig. 31 e 32 Housing estate of Alto do Zambujal (Amadora, 1974–1977), Vitor Figueiredo, Duarte Cabral Melo–601 dwellings (multifamily housing buildings and terraced houses). GPS: 38.737508N 9.208744W (left); Bela Vista neighbourhood (Setúbal, 1974), José Charters Monteiro, José Sousa Martins–840 dwellings (distribution gallery buildings). GPS: 38.522116N 8.869128W (right). Photos by Gisela Lameira (2018).

CONCLUSIONS

This general overview of the state-subsidized housing programmes implemented during the first three-quarters of the 20th century brought together a heterogeneous set of housing solutions, with varying degrees of architectural quality and impact in the planned expansion of Portuguese cities such as Porto and Lisbon.

1. THE "ORDINARY" CONSTRUCTION OF MODERNITY. MODERN SIGNS THROUGH ARCHITECTURAL AND URBAN DESIGN.

It is possible to suggest that this overview sheds light on the history of the genealogy of the modernity brought by the less known or valued production of multifamily housing. On the one hand, influences of the Modern Movement can be clearly pointed out through specific signs regarding urban concepts (rational layouts, freestanding slabs spread, solar exposure, etc.) and buildings' architectural options (volume, materiality, building language, typology design, etc.). On the other hand, international references were also adapted and reinterpreted considering the local character of the sites, especially in some interventions carried out via the "Affordable Rent Houses" programme.

2. TYPIFICATION, DIVERSITY AND AUTHORIAL APPROACHES.

In this broad set of examples, authorship is revealed as an important fact regarding the overall architectural quality and the integration of the ensembles in the urban structure.

When municipalities were the direct developers, type projects were frequently adopted as in the case of the "Improvement Plan for the City of Porto," resulting in homogeneous settlements. Nevertheless, these neighbourhoods also incorporated Modern Movement principles from a simplified point of view, more effective in the rational design of the apartment, rather than in the proposed parcelled plan, which in most solutions revealed a fragile connection with the pre-existent urban fabric. In this case, the building innovation can be found more clearly in the apartment design, throughout the experimentation regarding the "minimum dwelling," i.e., the challenge of reducing the areas and the programme of the household. Type projects can also be found in the Fishermen's Houses, where lower resources for the building were well-defined. The first methodology led by the "Affordable Rent Houses" programme was also focused on the reproduction around the country of the building types developed by Miguel Jacobetty Rosa for the *Alvalade* complex, in Lisbon (1945). However, the involvement of Nuno Teotónio in the process enacted a significant diversification of the proposals, less abstract and much closer to the inhabitants' needs and the character of the sites. The intervention of well-known architects contributed to the overall quality of the neighbourhoods built via this housing programme, between 1945 and 1977.

3. TYPES AND MODELS. INNOVATION IN ACCESS SYSTEMS AND RATIONALIZATION IN APARTMENT DESIGN.

Regarding the implementation of multifamily type of buildings, several solutions were put forward, from low-density models with only two floors and direct access to each apartment or a vertical access serving a few dwellings, to large buildings with distribution galleries and/or vertical access cores. Among the cases studied, the most current solution regarding access to the apartments is the design of stairways that reach a small number of dwellings on each level. The exploration of the potential and effectiveness of the distribution galleries in the building's design can be found across several housing programmes, from low-end solutions built via the "Houses for Poor Families" programme (1945), to more sophisticated and qualified solutions developed in the "Houses with Controlled Rent" programme (1947) or the "Plan for Constructing New Housing" programme (1959), both developed in the area of Lisbon. Among lesser-known housing buildings from the 1950s, the design of the gallerics and stair core of the *Soda Póvoa* neighbourhood (Vila Franca de Xira, 1953), designed by Nuno Teotónio Pereira, stands out as a remarkable example of the experimentation around the access systems.

During the period under analysis, the design of efficient dwellings is a cross-cutting priority across all the housing programmes. The typological experimentation clearly focuses on the design for the minimum dwelling, producing solutions with regular configuration and compact areas, which continuously explore the possibility of reducing the living areas.

4. THE EXPANSION OF THE CITY THROUGH RESIDENTIAL AREAS. THE DEVELOPMENT OF NEW URBAN MODELS.

Among the neighbourhoods analysed it should be underlined that after a first phase where the Charter of Athens principles were tested, namely in the rational layouts developed in *Ramalde* residential unit (Porto, 1950–1954), the *Cabo-Mor* neighbourhood (Vila Nova de Gaia, 1957), or the *Caixas da Previdência* neighbourhood (Parede, 1957), other approaches were tested, experimenting with more organicist tendencies in the disposition of the buildings. This line of approach can be seen in the *Torres Vermelhas da Pasteleira* neighbourhood (Porto, 1966–1972), a medium-scale settlement, or later in large urban operations such as the urbanization plans of *Olivais Sul* (Lisbon, 1959–1968) and *Olivais Norte* (Lisbon, 1955–1960). A shift in the proposals for urban models can be seen in the mid-1970s, in the housing estate of *Alto do Zambujal* (Amadora, 1974–1977), where the design of the plan seems to point to the return of the quarter as the "traditional composition unit," redefining the morphological relationship between the outdoor spaces and the built areas.

The multifamily residential complexes built under the state-subsidized housing programmes acted as important morphological and typological laboratories during the period 1945–1974, supporting the renovation of the residential architectural codes and building standards current in Portugal over that period. This panoramic overview was only possible through the extensive inventory and information gathered by the database developed by the research project "Mapping Public Housing."

ACKNOWLEDGMENTS

This paper was written as part of the CEAU/Mapping Public Housing project, which is co-financed by the European Regional Development Fund (ERDF) through COMPETE 2020–Operational Programme Competitiveness and Internationalization (POCI) and national funds from FCT under the PTDC/CPC-HAT/1688/2014 project and the POCI-01-0145-FEDER-007744 project.

BIBLIOGRAPHY

Correia, Célia Maria Senra. "Habitações Económicas–Federação das Caixas de Previdência: Bairro de Santa Marta–Barcelos." Master's Thesis, Universidade Lusíada de Vila Nova de Famalicão, 2012.

Costa, João Pedro. *Bairro de Alvalade*. Lisbon: Livros Horizonte, 2010 [2002].

Heitor, Teresa. "Olivais e Chelas: operações urbanísticas de grande escala." Centro de Estudos em Inovação, Tecnologia e Políticas de Desenvolvimento, IST Mestrado em Engenharia de Concepção, História Económica, Tecnologia e Sociedade. 2004.

Jacobetty, Miguel. "Comunicação–Estudo de casas de renda económica." In *Relatório da Comissão Executiva. Teses, Conclusões e Votos do Congresso. 1º Congresso Nacional de Arquitectura*. Maio/Junho de 1948 [fac-simile edition 2008]. ISBN: 978-972-8897-27-7

Lameira, Gisela, and Luciana Rocha. "Adaptação e transformação na habitação apoiada pelo Estado no século XX. As Torres Vermelhas da Pasteleira enquanto laboratório." In *Congresso da Reabilitação do Património*, 131–139. Aveiro: CREPAT 2017, 2017. ISBN: 978-989-20-7623-2

Lameira, Gisela, and Luciana Rocha. "Portuguese state-subsidized housing projects. A general overview of a recent heritage." In *Heritage 2018. Proceedings of the 6th International Conference on Heritage and Sustainable Development, Volume 2*, edited by Amoêda, R; Lira, S; Pinheiro, C.; Zaragoza, J. M. S.; Serrano, J. C.; Carrillo, F. G, 1373–1383. Greenlines Institute, Barcelos, Portugal, Editorial Universidade de Granada, Spain, 2018. e-ISBN: 978-84-338-6261-7

Lameira, Gisela, and Luciana Rocha. "Portuguese state-subsidized multifamily housing projects. Emergent modernity during the mid 20th century." In *Proceedings of the 15th International Docomomo Conference–Metamorphosis. The Continuity of Change*, edited by Ana Tostões and Natasa Koselj, 164–163 . Lisbon: Docomomo International; Ljubljana: Docomomo Slovenia, 2018. ISBN: 978-989-99645-3-2.https://www.scopus.com/inward/record.uri?eid=2-s2.0-85055724228&partnerID=40&md5=ca6bb25f9f3df25ef41771e064a8b15b

Portas, Nuno. *Funções e Exigências de Áreas de Habitação. Necessidades Familiares e Áreas de Habitação. Análise de Exigências por Funções de Habitação*. Lisboa: Laboratório Nacional de Engenharia Civil–Ministério das Obras Públicas, 1964.

Silva, Sérgio Dias and Rui J.G. Ramos. "Housing, Nationalism and Social Control: The First Years of The Portuguese Estado Novo's Affordable Houses Programme." In *Southern modernisms from A to Z and back again*, edited by Joana Cunha Leal et al., 255–274. Porto: Centro de Estudos Arnaldo Araújo–CESAP/ESAP, Instituto de História da Arte–FCSH/UNL, 2015. ISBN: 978-972-8784-66-9.

Silva, Sérgio Dias. "João Andresen: Uma Ideia de Arquitectura." Master's Thesis, Faculdade de Arquitectura da Universidade do Porto, 2007.

Tavares, Maria. "Habitações Económicas–Federação de Caixas de Previdência: uma perspectiva estratégica [nos anos 50 e 60 em Portugal." In *Actas 1º CIHEL, Desenho e realização de bairros para populações com baixos rendimentos*, 47–51. Lisbon: Argumentum, 2010. ISBN: 978-972-8479-72-5.

Tavares, Maria. "Leituras de um percurso na habitação em Portugal, as Habitações Económicas–Federação de Caixas de Previdência." In *Habitação Para o Maior Número, Portugal, os Anos de 1950–1980*, edited by Nuno Portas, 21–45. Lisbon: CML, IHRU, 2013. ISBN: 978-972-98508-8-2.

Tavares, Maria. "Habitações Económicas. Federação de Caixas de Previdência: Arquitectura e Modos de Actuação no Exercício do Projecto." PhD Dissertation, Faculdade de Arquitectura da Universidade do Porto, 2015.

Tavares, Maria. "Casas a Norte: as HE num Processo de Continuidade." In *O Estado, a Habitação e a Questão Social na Cidade do Porto, vol. 2*, edited by Virgílio Borges Pereira. Porto: Edições Afrontamento, 2015.

Tiago, Maria da Conceição. "Bairros Sociais da I República: Projectos e Realizações." *Ler História* no. 59. Repúblicas: Culturas e Práticas (2010): 249–272.

Vasconcelos, Diana. "Um Bairro Moderno no Porto. O Bairro de Ramalde de Fernando Távora." Master's Thesis, Faculdade de Arquitectura da Universidade do Porto, 2009.

Further bibliographical references about each housing programme and the mentioned neighbourhoods can be found at the MdH online database/Project List:

[https://mappingpublichousing.up.pt/en/].

Between Preservation and Transformation of State-Subsidized Multifamily Housing Buildings: Current Paradigms in the Scope of the "Improvement Plan" for the City of Porto

LUCIANA ROCHA
University of Porto, Faculty of Architecture, Centre for Studies in Architecture and Urbanism

ABSTRACT

In Portugal, as in other countries, the state-subsidized and municipal housing initiatives allowed to build different types of housing buildings, from the single-family house model to multi-family housing blocks. These housing solutions express the nature of the state's commitment and the relation between ideology, welfare policies and housing architecture. When a new programme was created in the 1940s proposing smaller rental apartments, aggregated into housing blocks, public housing changed in many respects: in the urban concept (in accordance with the Charter of Athens), in architectural language (introducing modern elements in the conception of the façades), and in the development of new access systems and housing typologies in the housing buildings.

In Porto, the "Improvement Plan" from 1956 was intended to simultaneously provide housing solutions for inhabitants of old neighbourhoods and to expand the city through planned urbanization actions. The neighbourhoods built under this programme consist of housing buildings with a minimum of four storeys, access systems composed by vertical cores or distribution galleries and a rational layout; they are characterized by a common urban concept based on large ensembles with communal green areas and regular connections to the surrounding urban structure. These buildings, despite their characteristics and qualities, nowadays face constructive and architectural challenges related to the need to adjust to current requirements for comfort and domestic needs.

Through the in-depth study of specific cases built in the scope of the "Improvement Plan" for the city of Porto (1956–1966), including its extension (1966–1978), the subject of recent interventions commissioned by the Municipality, the aim is to identify and characterize the actions carried out and their effects on the preservation of the originality/identity of the buildings, and to reflect on the adaptability of these ensembles considering their main urban principles and formal aspects. Given the contemporary challenges related to urban and social changes, to what extent is state-subsidized housing architecture reacting or adjusting to the current requirements?

BIOGRAPHY

Luciana Rocha (Santa Maria da Feira, 1983) is an architect and researcher at Centro de Estudos de Arquitectura e Urbanismo (CEAU/FAUP). She has a degree in architecture from the Faculdade de Arquitectura da Universidade do Porto (FAUP, 2007) and a PhD in architecture (FAUP, 2016) with the thesis "Intervention in the Modern: Recognition, Characterization and Safeguard of Multi-Family Housing Buildings" under the guidance of Professor Ana Tostões (IST/UL) and Professor Luís Soares Carneiro (FAUP). Her research focuses on preservation of built heritage, namely the analysis of intervention strategies in multifamily housing buildings from the middle of the 20th century, questioning the adaptability and flexibility of these constructions in adjusting to the current requirements of domestic comfort.

She was a research fellow of the project "Mapping Public Housing: a critical review of the State-subsidized residential architecture in Portugal (1910–1974)" [P2020-PTDC/CPC-HAT/1688/2014] and, currently, she develops research in architectural design and intervention on built heritage with particular reference to preservation measures and sustainability strategies.

A GENERAL APPROACH TO THE "IMPROVEMENT PLAN" FOR THE CITY OF PORTO

The "Improvement Plan" (Plano de Melhoramentos)[1] for the city of Porto consisted of a housing programme approved by Decree-Law 40,616 of 28th May 1956, implemented by the municipality and supported by the state. This plan was mainly intended to provide housing solutions for the inhabitants of old neighbourhoods in the city centre but it was also an opportunity to expand the city through urbanization plans and to decongest the central areas. Thus, between 1956 and 1966 (only ten years), fourteen ensembles were built with approximately 6,000 dwellings, in the broadest public housing initiative held in Porto and one of the most intense processes of socio-territorial rebuilding noted in Portugal.[2] The new buildings were then arranged in large ensembles located in the expansion areas created in the first periphery of the city. These areas were connected with the remaining urban structure defined by regulatory plans as the Master Plan (Plano Director do Porto) from 1962. Furthermore, the extension of this plan (Decree-Law 47,443 of 30th December 1966) allowed for the construction of another 11 neighbourhoods and over 3,000 other dwellings.[3] The "Improvement Plan" is also related to the "Houses for Poor Families" programme (Casas para Famílias Pobres, Decree-Law 34,486, 8 April 1945), mainly as a supporting system, following its main principles. The main objective of this programme implemented by the Portuguese state was to promote the construction of housing for very low-income families within a simplified system, regarding the conditions required for the occupation of the previous "Affordable Houses" programme (Casas Económicas, Decree-Law 23,052, 23rd September 1933).

SIGNS OF MODERNITY AND HERITAGE VALUE

The residential complexes built under the "Improvement Plan" for the city of Porto reveal similar underlying rationales in terms of urban concept, although they are located on different sized lots and in distinct areas of the city. While the housing blocks do not stand out in terms of architectural quality, they do in fact propose a new residential model, questioning the traditional street and the urban closed block as the structuring principles in the urban system (e.g. Pio XII [MdH DB a692] and Lagarteiro [MdH DB a729] neighbourhoods). The apartments typologies face the challenge of reducing and simplifying the functional programme due to the compactness of the floor plan, mainly through the introduction of multifunctional spaces and the elimination of unnecessary circulation spaces.

[1] Cf. Câmara Municipal do Porto, Plano de Melhoramentos: 1956–1966 (CMP, Porto, 1966).

[2] Queirós, João, "O 'Plano de Melhoramentos para a cidade do Porto' de 1956: Enquadramento político-social e elenco de realizações," in O Estado, a Habitação e a Questão Social na Cidade do Porto, ed. V.B. Pereira (Porto, Edições Afrontamento, 2016), 37–64.

[3] This analysis follows the study presented by João Queirós (2016) regarding to the number of neighbourhoods and dwellings built during these plans (a total of twenty-five neighbourhoods). The thirty examples presented on the MdH database refer specifically to the period between 1910 and 1974 and separate the different phases individually.

The modern concept of the common living room, combining several functions, appears in association with different solutions: by joining living room/kitchen in a central area (e.g. Carvalhido [MdH DB a693] or Engenheiro Machado Vaz [MdH DB a705] neighbourhoods) or by incorporating the circulation areas (e.g. Contumil neighbourhood).

The experimentation of the access systems stands out for its use of distribution galleries. This system reveals its potentiality both for the economy of distribution, allowing entrance to several apartments through a single vertical communication core, and for the development of more intense human relations (e.g. Carvalhido neighbourhood). Furthermore, for example in Pereiró [MdH DB a847] neighbourhood, the exterior staircases located on the lateral façades of the buildings can be highlighted as an exceptional architectural element.

Although less obvious, some buildings also excel in terms of architectural language. The use of traditional materials in the Falcão [MdH DB a715–728] neighbourhood, such as stone in the sidewalls or the brick in the main façades, combined with new application techniques, reveals an accurate and expressive design of the ensemble. Despite the economic and political constraints from the investment point of view that naturally had an impact on the architectural standard of the buildings and affected the construction of these neighbourhoods, these characteristics are certainly signs of modernity and of architectural quality, even with different grades depending on the specific case. Thus, these neighbourhoods should be considered as identity or cultural heritage, in this case, more related to the importance of the ensemble than to the value of the individual building or dwelling.

PROPERTY REGIME

Although these buildings were originally built to be rented under a state-subsidized and municipal housing initiative, the presence of apartments on the real estate market suggests that these buildings were divided into autonomous units meant to be sold. This process found legitimization in a later legislative framework, namely Decree-Law no. 419, dated 4 October 1977, which allowed the alienation of the "Houses for Poor Families," the programme which co-financed the constructions of the "Improvement Plan." This regulation also defined the bases for that acquisition, namely regarding the terrain which remained as municipal property or the obligation to keep a limited rent when for rental purposes. The dwellings still benefit from tax exemptions.[4]

[4] Ministérios da Justiça, das Finanças e dos Assuntos Sociais, "Decreto-Lei n.º419/77 de 4 de Outubro," *Diário da República, I Série, no. 230* (1977): 2431–2433

In addition, Decree-Law no. 310, dated 5 September 1988, defined a formula for the evaluation of the autonomous units based on comfort level, conservation status, floor area, ageing, among others. This calculation also considers a possible intervention action by the municipality, which conditions the final value of the dwelling.[5]

CASE STUDIES: INTERVENTION ACTIONS

Recently and mainly during the last decade, Porto Municipal Council, through Domus Social E.M.,[6] commissioned many intervention actions to promote the rehabilitation and renovation of the social housing stock in the Porto municipality. From the twenty-five neighbourhoods built in the scope of the Improvement Plan for the city of Porto and its extension, between 1956 and 1978, only 3 ensembles (Pasteleira [MdH DB a196–197], Bom Sucesso [MdH DB a691], and Aleixo[7] [MdH DB a732]) seem to have not yet had any municipal intervention. However, most of the registered interventions are restricted to the treatment of façades, roofs, and common spaces (twenty registered cases), while very few cases have significant interventions inside the dwellings (two registered cases). Some neighbourhoods also underwent important alterations in the surrounding public spaces (six registered cases), mainly to improve the accesses and the common exterior areas.

The assembled case studies were selected to exemplify some of the different types of interventions that have been carried out, namely in public spaces, in general building maintenances or in more profound interventions with typological transformations. These examples represent intervention actions with diverse levels of transformation and distinct characterizations, potentialities, and limitations.

1. REQUALIFICATION OF THE PUBLIC SPACES

The Pio XII neighbourhood (1958, Campanhã) consists of an ensemble of six buildings of four storeys with 122 dwellings, located in Campanhã, in the eastern part of the city of Porto. This ensemble reflects the previously mentioned urban concept with a communal green area between the buildings and a single connection to the adjacent urban structure. In 2007, this neighbourhood was the subject of a public space requalification by the architects Cristina Guedes and Francisco Vieira de Campos from the *Menos é Mais Arquitectos* studio. The intervention was intended to solve the main existing problems related to the lack of parking lots and green leisure areas, as well as to improve access to the neighbourhood.

---

[5] Ministério do Planeamento e da Administração do Território, "Decreto-Lei n.º310/88 de 5 de Setembro," *Diário da República, I Série, no. 205 (1988)*: 3666–3668

[6] Domus Social E.M. is a housing and maintenance company of Porto municipality formed in 2000 under the terms of the article 19 of Law no. 50 from 31 August 2012. Cf. www.domussocial.pt.

[7] The Aleixo neighbourhood is an exception because it is awaiting the conclusion of a demolition process which was not considered, in this scope, as an intervention action.

The project consists of a global intervention to reorder the urban structure that aims to define road and pedestrian routes, including access for disabled people, to delimit parking and recreation areas and, above all, to establish a hierarchy between public, semi-public, and private spaces. The materialization of this proposal stands out for its use of prefabricated elements in reinforced concrete for the definition of guides, platforms, walls, benches, stairs or ramps, among others.[8] These elements contribute to establishing a consistent language in the ensemble, but above all they allow a solution for the accentuated slopes of the terrain or for different areas and their respective uses to be delimited. This intervention action was commissioned by Porto Municipal Council through Domus Social with the contribution of the Urban II programme. The project won an honourable mention in the IHRU 2008 Prize from the "Institute of Housing and Urban Rehabilitation" (Instituto da Habitação e da Reabilitação Urbana). In awarding this mention, the jury highlighted the space layout and the effective improvement of this area of collective use, as well as the use of durable and low-maintenance materials.[9]

The Contumil [MdH DB a736–737] neighbourhood (1977–1981, Campanhã) also underwent an intervention in the public space with a project by the same architects from the Menos é Mais Arquitectos Studio. This ensemble was originally built in three different phases: the first designed by Manuel Teles, Rui Paixão, and Alexandre Alves Costa (three buildings and 128 dwellings); the second designed by Rui Paixão (one building and sixty-four dwellings); and the third by Alberto Rosmaninho (eleven buildings and 296 dwellings). Despite the differences in lot size, urban scale (fifteen buildings with four or five storeys), and number of dwellings (488 total), the requalification project, also from 2007, reveals similarities in the concept and materiality with the one analysed in the Pio XII neighbourhood. The project is based on the same objectives and structuring principles as regards the arrangement of the urban layout, the definition of access and leisure zones and the use of elements in concrete to unify the ensemble. However, in this case the reformulation of the road structure with the intention of allowing car access to all housing buildings can be highlighted and, above all, the opening of a new road to simplify access to the neighbourhood.[10] This project was also a finalist for the Secil Architecture Prize in 2008.

The Lagarteiro neighbourhood (1973–1977, Campanhã) was built in two phases over almost a decade: the first designed by Domingos Faria with nine buildings and 248 dwellings; the second between by Florêncio de Carvalho with four buildings and 192 dwellings.

---

[8] Cf. Cristina Guedes, "Intervenção no Bairro Pio XII e Contumil, Porto," *Estudo prévio: Revista do Centro de Estudos de Arquitectura, Cidade e Território da Universidade Autónoma de Lisboa* (2014). https://bit.ly/2RqnAcd.

[9] Further information at: https://bit.ly/2EShvzm

[10] Cf. Cristina Guedes. "Intervenção no Bairro Pio XII e Contumil, Porto."

Fig 1 and 2 Pio XII neighbourhood (1957, Campanhã), [s.n.].
Photos by Luciana Rocha (2018).

Fig 3 and 4 Contumil neighbourhood (Third phase, 1977, Campanhã), Alberto Rosmaninho.
Photos by Luciana Rocha (2018).

Fig 5 and 6 Lagarteiro neighbourhood (first phase, 1968–1973, Campanhã), Domingos Faria, on the left; Lagarteiro neighbourhood (second phase, 1974–1977, Campanhã), Florêncio de Carvalho, on the right.
Photos by Luciana Rocha (2018).

This neighbourhood, characterized by a set of blocks with a predominance of four storeys and located on hilly terrain, had as its main problems the location immediately outside the city limits, the lack of accesses, and the consequent isolation in relation to the urban structure of the city of Porto. The intervention in this public space was completed in 2012 and promoted by the Porto Municipality under the Critical Neighbourhood Initiative (IBC) funded by the IHRU. The project by the architect Paulo Tormenta Pinto and the landscape architect João Ferreira Nunes had as its main objectives to redefine the connections between the neighbourhood and the urban structure, in accordance with the Municipal Master Plan (Plano Director Municipal) and to establish a greater relationship between the two sectors of the ensemble (first and second phases), solving the unevenness of the terrain. In addition, the project provides parking spaces combined with green areas and pedestrian accesses. The solution is then to establish a road network crossing the whole neighbourhood and to use concrete support walls to solve the unevenness. Also, the use of granite cubes in different shades and textures allows the distinctive areas to be accentuated, maintaining a uniform language. The first phase of this intervention was awarded with the IHRU Prize in 2012.[11]

2. BUILDING MAINTENANCE

The Carvalhido neighbourhood (1958, Paranhos) is located near Carvalhido street and the Porto beltway. This ensemble has fourteen housing blocks with four storeys and a total of 264 dwellings designed by Luís de Almeida d'Eça. The buildings follow three different axes: one main, oblique to the Sousa Pinto street, existing (eight blocks); and two secondary ones, parallel to two new streets, of less importance, Acácio Lino (one block) and Marques de Abreu (five blocks), in which the latter defines the limits of the complex. The buildings are placed parallel to each other, separated by exterior spaces constituted by green areas, open parking lots and service streets. The dwelling accesses are by gallery which serves as an intermediate space for circulation and interaction among residents.

During the last decade, two requalification actions took place, in 2007 and 2018, with reference to the façades, roofs, and collective areas such as stairs and circulation spaces. The main actions related to the treatment of façades and roofs included the application of thermal insulation and new coating materials, the replacement of existing window frames and the application of new ones in galleries and staircases, and the rehabilitation of infrastructures such as drainage of rainwater.

[11] Further information at: https://bit.ly/2Amgewi

The action of closing the galleries with aluminium window frames was one of the most significant changes of this general intervention, both in the impact on the architectural language of the building and, above all, in the reinforcement of using these spaces as an extension of the dwellings.

The Engenheiro Machado Vaz neighbourhood (1966, Campanhã) is located near the Contumil train station in the eastern part of the city, occupying a lot of considerable size. This ensemble designed by Vasco Mendes has 272 dwellings distributed in thirteen multifamily housing buildings with four storeys and vertical access. The building interventions carried out between 2016 an 2017 also focused specifically on the maintenance and renovation of façades, roofs, and common areas. The project, designed by the architect Nuno Abrantes and distinguished with the Nuno Teotónio Pereira 2017 Prize, was based on correcting evident pathologies, solving important infrastructural issues and improving the energy efficiency of the buildings. The main actions on the façades included the application of a new exterior coating with insulation and the replacement of existing window frames and the application of new ones on the balconies and stairwells to close these areas. The laundry, originally marked on the façade with horizontal elements in cement, now appear with glass brick and window frames. In the roof, it is important to underline the replacement of the structure and the installation of solar panels. The interventions in the common areas mainly concern the reinforcement of infrastructures for water supply, drainage of rainwater, electricity, gas and telecommunication systems. A recent visit to this building complex in late 2018 revealed the general maintenance works described. However, the residents seem to intervene individually, mainly in the public areas, expanding the living spaces.

The Falcão neighbourhood (1973-1981, Campanhã) is also located in the eastern part of the city, near the Corujeira garden and was originally built in two phases: the first one designed by Rui Paixão; and the second one by Florêncio de Carvalho. This article focuses on the actions resulting from the general intervention project carried out in 2017 on the dwellings built in the first phase as an example of an overall requalification. Thus, the first phase of this neighbourhood has 224 dwellings in nine multifamily housing buildings with a vertical access system. This ensemble stands out in terms of architectural language due to the expressiveness of its exterior materials, such as the stone sidewalls, the brick or the concrete in the guards of the stairs levels, and due to the design details, such as the floor slabs in the façade, the grille in the laundries or the guillotine windows.

As in the previous cases, the intervention action carried out in this neighbourhood focused on the treatment of façades, roofs, and common spaces. Accordingly, the project, designed by the architect Paulo Calapez, included the installation of thermal and acoustic insulation, the replacement of window frames and blinds, the application of new window frames in stairwells, the installation of a new grid system in the laundry areas, the application of a ventilation system in bathrooms and kitchens, the installation of solar collectors, and the reinforcement of common infrastructures, among others. However, in this case, the project excels due to preservation of the original language of the ensemble, mainly through the conservation of predominant external materials and the application of technical solutions such as the placement of insulation inside the exterior walls to solve the existing problems.

3. GENERAL INTERVENTIONS WITH TYPOLOGICAL TRANSFORMATION

The São João de Deus [MdH DB a702] neighbourhood (1941–1977, Campanhã), near the Circunvalação road and the municipality of Gondomar, was built over three decades and in three different phases. The first phase began in 1941 with the construction of the Tarrafal neighbourhood or Municipal Neighbourhood Low-income Housing of Rebordões, which in 1950 was renamed the São João de Deus neighbourhood. This municipal initiative was composed of individual or terraced houses of two storeys with a total of 144 dwellings. The development of this neighbourhood continued in the following decade with the construction of the second phase in 1956, with 152 more dwellings, now distributed in eight multifamily housing buildings. This phase was already constructed within the "Houses for Poor Families" programme. The third and final phase, with 144 dwellings in eight multifamily housing buildings, was built between 1966 and 1977 in the scope of the extension of the Improvement Plan for the city of Porto. The last two phases were later demolished by the Porto Municipal Council.

The intervention recently proposed for the São João de Deus neighbourhood, designed by the architect Nuno Brandão Costa,[12] focuses on the transformation and extension of the ensemble corresponding to the first phase. The project was based on the preservation of the existing volumes and the transformation of the 144 original dwellings into 97, by resizing the spaces (reducing the number of dwellings and increasing the area of the spaces) and complying with current regulations.

[12] Cf. André Cepeda, *Porosis: The Architecture of Nuno Brandão Costa*, ed. Daniela Sá and João Carmo Simões (Lisbon: Monade, 2017).

Fig 7 and 8 Carvalhido neighbourhood (1957–1958, Paranhos), Luís de Almeida d'Eça.
Photos by Gisela Lameira (2018).

Fig 9 and 10 Engenheiro Machado Vaz neighbourhood (1963–1965, Campanhã), Vasco Mendes.
Photos by Luciana Rocha (2018).

Fig 11 and 12 Falcão neighbourhood (first phase, 1967–1972, Campanhã), Rui Paixão.
Photos by Luciana Rocha (2018).

The new buildings thus result from the need to complete the number of dwellings lacking after the expected intervention on the original volumes, and serve as an element of conclusion for the overall project. Although the project was designed all at once, the actions were developed in different phases, from the construction of the new volumes to the intervention on the existing ones. The extension process, completed in 2017, consisted of the construction of six buildings located at the southern end of the neighbourhood, on the original site of the third phase. The buildings respect the scale and the language of the ensemble both in the predominance of the two storeys and in the configuration and size of the exterior windows. However, these volumes, designed as an intervention border, differ from the existing ones with their the flat roofs and the dark brick as predominant coating material. The dwellings superimposed in height have individual and direct access resulting from the use of the significant slope of the site. The intervention on the existing buildings, an ongoing process, thus proposes 84 updated units. The solution was then the preservation of the exterior walls in stone and the roof structure in wood and the application of insulation/waterproofing and new coating materials. The transformations in the interior spaces result from the adjustment to the new functional programme.

The updated language of the ensemble stands out due to the contrast between the white on the main façades and the black asphalt fabric on the sidewalls and roofs, and also because of the diversity of the façades caused by the arrangement of the windows. This project follows important economic constraints that affected the main general decisions: formal and functional. However, the result consists of an interpretation of the original language, despite the significant and profound intervention actions. The CTT neighbourhood in Pereiró (1956, Porto), designed by Luís de Almeida d'Eça,[13] consists of a small ensemble composed of two symmetrical four-storey buildings with a total of sixty-four dwellings (thirty-two with two bedrooms and thirty-two with three bedrooms). These buildings present numerous details such as the exterior stairwell and galleries in concrete or the window frames that reveal a strong architectural language. These elements also recall the buildings of the second phase in the Rainha D. Leonor housing complex, by the same author, although those were higher and more complex in the typological solution. During recent years, specific studies presented proposals for the refurbishment or renovation of this neighbourhood[14] not only due to the severe state of degradation and urgent need of intervention on the ensemble but also with the aim at preserving its original characteristics. However, the intervention project currently ongoing seems to present an alternative solution with profound changes both inside and outside the building.

[13] Joana Restivo et al., "Public housing in Porto: (in)extensive refurbishment," in Workshop *Physical Aspects of Design and Regeneration* (ENHR, 2015), 1.

[14] P. Conceição, F. Brandão Alves, H. Corvacho, J. Restivo, M. Quintela and J. Gonçalves, *Caracterização e Diagnóstico do Bairro dos CTT* (Porto: Domus Social. E.M./CTT–Correios de Portugal/IC–Instituto da Construção, 2010); Restivo, "Public housing in Porto: (in)extensive refurbishment," among others.

The project by the architect Carlos Coelho provides a resizing of the dwellings for a total of sixty units: thirty-two in the east block (sixteen T1 and sixteen T2) and twenty-eight in the west block (twelve T1, twelve T2, and four T3). These transformations of typologies suggest a possible adaptation to the needs of the current inhabitants, an ageing and predominantly inactive population (retired or unemployed).[15] However, the project also includes profound interventions on façades, roofs, and common areas. These actions involve significant changes in the configuration of the stairwells and in the sidewall details through the placement of lifts, the construction of new galleries and variations in the coating materials, among others. The conclusion of this intervention was planned for September 2019.

The same author of the CTT neighbourhood in Pereiró—Luís Almeida d'Eça—also designed the Rainha D. Leonor [MdH DB a195/801] housing complex[16] (1953–1955). This project, a municipal initiative, was a result of the urban restructuring that preceded the Plano Regulador da Cidade do Porto [1952] and a response to the necessary rehousing of the resident population in precarious conditions in the scope of the "Houses for Poor Families" programme.[17] The project was divided into two construction phases: the first, completed in 1953, comprised 150 houses, placed in a set of buildings with two levels and direct access. The second phase included 100 dwellings in five blocks of four storeys with a distributed system in a gallery, which was concluded in 1955. The first phase of the Rainha D. Leonor housing complex was the subject of a requalification project approved in 2005. The project by the Inês Lobo architectural studio proposed a set of intervention actions for both the inside of the dwellings, via the implementation of new typologies, and the private and common exterior spaces, for the requalification and maintenance of the public spaces.[18] This proposal presented the alternative solution of joining two dwellings horizontally, which doubled both the interior area and private exterior area. The new internal organization succeeded in significantly reducing the circulation spaces, providing a more autonomous kitchen space and adding a laundry space and storage spaces. The living room represented the central living space. On the outside, the main action was the removal of the outbuildings in the gardens to recover the initial use of these spaces. In September 2015, the Porto City Council announced a new tender for the rehabilitation of the second phase of the housing complex. The work, awarded to Aythya–Investimentos Imobiliários, Lda. in February 2016, aimed to demolish the existing blocks and build new buildings with at least fifty-eight social housing units to accommodate resident households. In return, in order to reduce costs for the municipality, this model provided for the transfer of part of the land to the developer.

---

[15] Restivo et al., "Public housing in Porto: (in)extensive refurbishment.," 6.

[16] Or Sobreiras housing complex, name used due to the location in the *Sobreiras* area, between *Lordelo do Ouro* and *Foz*, in Porto.

[17] Although this housing complex isn't included in the "Improvement plan," but in the programme which co-finances the plan, it serves as an exceptional example of a significant intervention for a comparative analysis on this topic due to the few registered cases.

[18] Cf. Ana Lima, "Habitação mínima e apropriação do espaço: O Bairro Rainha D. Leonor," (Integrated Master's Thesis, FAUP, Porto, 2012).

Fig 13 and 14 São João de Deus neighbourhood (expansion, 2017), Nuno Brandão Costa, on the left; São João de Deus neighbourhood (intervention, ongoing), Nuno Brandão Costa, on the right.
Photos by Luciana Rocha (2018).

Fig 15 and 16 CTT neighbourhood in Pereiró (Porto, 1956), Luís de Almeida d'Eça, on the left; CTT neighbourhood in Pereiró (intervention, ongoing), Carlos Coelho, on the right.
Photos by Luciana Rocha (2018).

Fig 17 and 18 Rainha D. Leonor neighbourhood (first phase–intervention, 2005), Inês Lobo architectural studio.
Photos by Luciana Rocha (2018).

Fig 19 and 20 Rainha D. Leonor neighbourhood (second phase, 1955), Luís de Almeida d'Eça, on the leftRainha D. Leonor neighbourhood (second phase–intervention, ongoing), Aythya–Investimentos Imobiliários, on the right. Photos by Luciana Rocha (2018).

CONCLUSIONS AND FUTURE CHALLENGES

The study of recent interventions in specific case studies built under the "Improvement Plan" for the city of Porto allowed analysis of different actions regarding changes in the urban space, outside the buildings and common areas or inside the dwellings. The main goal was to reflect on the adaptability and tolerance to change of these neighbourhoods and to identify the main potentialities and limitations of each type of intervention. The analysis reveals that these housing buildings, as a general rule, have great potential for transformation and consequent adaptation. Most of the identified actions consist of general interventions on facades, roofs, and common areas that occasionally involve small interventions in unoccupied dwellings. This type of intervention mainly solves thermal problems with the application of insulation and new window frames, and technical issues with the alteration of the infrastructures. However, it does not contribute to the significant adaptation of the dwellings' interior to the current requirements of domestic comfort. The changes introduced by this type of intervention may cause a greater (e.g. Carvalhido) or smaller (e.g. Falcão) impact in the exterior language of the buildings; however, they tend to preserve an overall rationale (e.g. Engenheiro Machado Vaz). The fact that the inhabitants stayed in the buildings during these works contributes to lower logistics and associated costs.

Interventions with typological transformation, identified in a smaller number of cases, are more demanding in terms of costs and logistics, given that they imply the temporary move of the inhabitants, which usually results in an increase of income after the intervention actions. However, it responds in a more efficient and definitive way to the necessary adaptation to the comfort requirements of both buildings (e.g. insulation, window frames, solar panels) and dwellings (e.g. areas, functional distribution, equipment), which results in a significant improvement in the living conditions of the inhabitants. This type of intervention, however, results in very variable solutions: on the one hand, it allows the language of the ensemble to be restored (e.g. first phase of Rainha D. Leonor Housing Complex); on the other hand, it can lead to profound transformations with changes in original architectural characteristics (e.g. Pereiró). In addition, there are also reinterpretations of the original language in order to improve the living conditions (e.g. São João de Deus neighbourhood) or total demolitions for the construction of new projects, which results in significant losses of housing complexes (e.g. the second phase of Rainha D. Leonor Housing Complex). The interventions in the surrounding public space stand out for the integration of the housing complexes (e.g. Pio XII and Contumil) and the improvement of the connections between the ensembles and the adjacent urban structures (e.g. Lagarteiro). The identified actions are related to the general reorganization of routes (pedestrian and car), access to persons with reduced mobility, and the definition and hierarchy of different areas and their uses. The adaptability results from the tolerance to changes introduced throughout time which appear due to the original flexibility. Tolerance to changes and the ability to adapt are essential characteristics, which influence the permanence and durability of spaces. The housing buildings are in constant transformation and permanent adequacy to comfort needs. What can be transformed or easily adapted tends to stay throughout time, while the rigid imposition of a structure, form or function decreases in durability.

The flexibility of housing buildings and domestic spaces involves a resistance to time and to social alterations. In this specific context, the main characteristics that give evidence of flexibility of these ensembles are the general use of a typified project and the rational structure and layouts of the buildings. The façades present a plain language with clearly defined modern elements. From a preservation point of view, the intervention actions must be adjusted to each case, considering the specificities and qualities inherent to the project and the potentialities and limitations of each intervention type. As a conclusion, two future challenges are highlighted in order to improve the valorisation and preservation of these ensembles:

DISSEMINATION AND RECOGNITION OF THIS ARCHITECTURAL HERITAGE

One main challenge is raising both the residents' and the experts' awareness of the importance of this recent architectural heritage. In this context, the database developed by the research project "Mapping Public Housing" is an essential instrument for identifying and geo-referencing the housing programmes and respective initiatives. This platform, available online, gathers the process documents (memoirs, reports, and assessment procedures, etc.), bibliography and photographic references, as well as the legal framework for each operation/estate/building. Furthermore, a specific section focused on the intervention actions comprises the main information about the projects carried out since the original construction of the buildings (author, client, year) with the level (slight, moderate, profound, and total), type (alteration, demolition, extension) and location (public space; façade, roof and common spaces; domestic spaces) of each intervention. This analysis contributes to identify the main actions and corresponding results. For future interventions, this will serve as a basis for a proper evaluation of each specific building.

THE ANALYSIS OF THE INHABITANTS' EXPERIENCES AS AN INDICATOR

Another challenge is acknowledging the inhabitants' experience as an indicator of the architectural quality through the analysis of the confrontation of the spatial design and the practice of its everyday use. Moreover, the importance of the user's experience should be recognized in developing future intervention strategies to improve living conditions and, in this way, to promote an effective engagement of the population on the housing maintenance. Very often in the cases analysed, the residents find themselves outside the decision-making process with their individual action being diminished. Even when the interventions actions are both outside and inside the dwellings, the residents continue to carry out individualized interventions to improve and increase the housing space (e.g. Rainha D. Leonor housing complex, first phase). Therefore, decisions about interventions actions in housing buildings should always be made in consultation.

ACKNOWLEDGMENTS

This paper was written as part of the CEAU/ Mapping Public Housing project, which is co-financed by the European Regional Development Fund (ERDF) through COMPETE 2020–Operational Programme Competitiveness and Internationalization (POCI) and national funds from FCT under the PTDC/CPC-HAT/1688/2014 project and the POCI-01-0145-FEDER-007744 project.

BIBLIOGRAPHY

AA/VV, "Conjunto de habitação municipal Rainha D. Leonor, Porto." JA 236 Ser Pobre, quarterly journal of Association of Architects–Portugal (2009). ISSN-0870-1504

[s/n], Plano Director da Cidade do Porto, Gabinete de Urbanização da Câmara Municipal do Porto, Câmara Municipal do Porto, Vol. 3, 1962

Câmara Municipal do Porto, Plano de Melhoramentos: 1956–1966, CMP, Porto, 1966

Cepeda, André, Porosis: The Architecture of Nuno Brandão Costa, Daniela Sá and João Carmo Simões (ed.), Monade, Lisbon, 2017. ISBN 9789899948525

Cepeda, André; Costa, Nuno Brandão, São João de Deus, Dafne Editora, Porto, 2019. ISBN: 978-989-8217-47-9

Conceição, P.; Brandão Alves F.; Corvacho H.; Restivo J.; Quintela M. and Gonçalves J., Caracterização e Diagnóstico do Bairro dos CTT, Porto, Domus Social. E.M./CTT–Correios de Portugal/IC–Instituto da Construção, Porto, 2010

Costa, Nuno Brandão, São João de Deus Neighborhood, Conversation with the author about the intervention project, FAUP, Porto, February 2019

Cruz, Marta, "The inhabitants' experiences as an architectural quality indicator," 24th ENHR Conference, Lillehammer, Norway, 2012, Online publication

Guedes, Cristina. "Intervenção no Bairro Pio XII e Contumil, Porto." Estudo prévio: Revista do Centro de Estudos de Arquitectura, Cidade e Território da Universidade Autónoma de Lisboa, Lisbon, 2014, UAL

Lameira, Gisela and Luciana Rocha. "Adaptação e transformação na habitação apoiada pelo Estado no século XX. As Torres Vermelhas da Pasteleira enquanto laboratório." in Congresso da Reabilitação do Património. Aveiro. CREPAT 2017: 131–139, 2017. ISBN: 978-989-20-7623-2

Lameira, Gisela, and Luciana Rocha. "Portuguese state-subsidized housing projects. A general overview of a recent heritage." in Heritage 2018. Proceedings of the 6th International Conference on Heritage and Sustainable Development Volume 2. Amoêda, R; Lira, S; Pinheiro, C.; Zaragoza, J. M. S.; Serrano, J. C.; Carrillo, F. G. (eds.), 1373–1383. Greenlines Institute, Barcelos, Portugal, Editorial Universidade de Granada, Spain, 2018. ISBN: 978-84-338-6261-7

Lameira, Gisela, and Luciana Rocha. "Portuguese state-subsidized multifamily housing projects. Emergent modernity during the mid 20th century." in Tostões, Ana, and Koselj, Natasa (eds.), (2018) Proceedings of the 15th International Docomomo Conference–Metamorphosis. The Continuity of Change. Lisbon: Docomomo International; Ljubljana: Docomomo Slovenia, 2018, 164-163. ISBN: 978-989-99645-3-2

Lima, Ana. "Habitação mínima e apropriação do espaço: O Bairro Rainha D. Leonor." Integrated Master's Thesis, FAUP, Porto, 2012.

Ministérios da Justiça, das Finanças e dos Assuntos Sociais, "Decreto-Lei n.º 419/77 de 4 de Outubro," Diário da República, I Série, N.º 230, 1977: 2431–2433

Ministério das Obras Públicas e Comunicações (Gabinete do Ministro), "Decreto-Lei n.º 34486," Diário da República, I Série, n.º 73, 1945: 232–234

Ministério do Planeamento e da Administração do Território, "Decreto-Lei n.º 310/88 de 5 de Setembro," Diário da República, I Série, N.º 205, 1988: 3666–3668

Pereira, Virgílio Borges. A Habitação Social na Transformação da Cidade. Sobre a Génese e Efeitos do "Plano de Melhoramentos para a Cidade do Porto" de 1956, Porto, Edições Afrontamento, 2016. ISBN: 978-972-36-1478-7

Queirós, João. "O 'Plano de Melhoramentos para a cidade do Porto' de 1956: Enquadramento político-social e elenco de realizações." In V.B. Pereira (org.), O Estado, a Habitação e a Questão Social na Cidade do Porto, Porto, Edições Afrontamento, 2016: 37–64

Restivo, Joana, F.B. Alves, P. Mendonça, and J.A. Ferreira. "Public Housing Renovation in Porto: Typology versus Occupancy Density," in International Journal for Housing Science, Vol. 36, N. 1, 2012: 9–16

Restivo, Joana. "Habitação Pública no Porto: Intervir para Qualificar," PhD Thesis, FEUP, Porto, 2014

Restivo, Joan, J.A. Ferreira, F.B. Alves, and P. Mendonça. "Public housing in Porto: (in)extensive refurbishment," in Workshop Physical Aspects of Design and Regeneration, ENHR, 2015

Further bibliographical references about the neighbourhoods referred to can be found at the MdH online database/ Project List: [https://mappingpublichousing.up.pt/en/].

The New State, Architecture and Modernism

JOANA BRITES
University of Coimbra, Faculty of Arts and Humanities, Centre for 20th Century Interdisciplinary Studies

ABSTRACT

This paper aims to address the architecture of the Portuguese New State (1933–1974) and discuss its modernist nature. Firstly, the historiographic interpretation which opposes the two phenomena is characterised and questioned. Secondly, an alternative proposal for interpretation is presented and grounded. The fully modernist nature of the architecture of New State is argued by the agency of two major contributions: the international historiography on the relationship between modernism and fascism, which has been increasingly questioning and overcoming the previously identified contradiction between the terms; and the historiography of the development of other areas during the New State that show no contradiction in the mobilization of science and technology for the pursuit of a societal project contrary to the liberal political matrix of the Enlightenment. The maximalist definition of modernism advanced by Roger Griffin is adopted, thus explaining it as a heterogeneous set of palingenetic reactions, developed between the second half of the nineteenth century and the end of the Second World War, which aimed to counterbalance the consequences of the process of western modernisation perceived as adverse.

In the light of this analytical framework, which also allows rethinking the classification of the political-ideological nature of the Portuguese New State, a demonstration is sought of how the architecture of the regime integrated the project of social regeneration conceived and applied with relative success. Furthermore, the ways in which this architecture reflects the rationalisation of the governmental practice, characteristic of modernity, are highlighted. It is argued that the New State radicalised and further implemented on an unprecedented scale the transformation which the 19th century operated within the framework of urbanism and building design: its conversion into two distinct technologies of power, albeit articulated: the disciplinary and the regulatory. Moreover, a similar radicalisation and institutionalisation are detected regarding the 19th-century demand for a national art. The search for a national modern (an architecture that was both contemporary and adequate to the specific character of the country or the region), recognisable in countries with different political matrices, is thus differentiated regarding its fascist implementation. The palingenetic nature underlying this artistic agenda, not at all diminished by the use of historicist or traditionalist references, is emphasised, and a parallel is established between the selective and negotiated methodology that operationalised it and the syncretism that can be recognised in other areas of intervention of the New State.

BIOGRAPHY

Joana Brites (Coimbra, 6/12/1982) is an assistant professor of Romanticism, Modern Art, Theory and Methodologies of Art History and Heritage Studies at the Faculty of Arts and Humanities of the University of Coimbra (UC), where she is the director of the Undergraduate Programme Studies in Art History. She completed her master's and the doctorate in art history (field: Portuguese architecture of the 20th century) at UC and during the development of the research for both academic degrees, received a scholarship from the Foundation for Science and Technology. She worked as an art historian in the office responsible for the application of the University of Coimbra for World Heritage Status. She is an associate researcher in the Centre for 20th Century Interdisciplinary Studies (CEIS20) where she coordinates a line of research. Her research focuses on the following areas: the relationship between fascism and modernism; the art of authoritarian/totalitarian regimes; spheres and mechanisms of artistic control; "dissonant heritage" and collective memory. She supervises postgraduate theses in the field of 19th- and 20th-century art and heritage, participates in various national and international research projects, provides scientific consulting services to different institutions, and has two books and several articles published in national and international journals.

The historiography on the relationship between modernism and architecture during the New State continues to show remnants of an antipodal interpretation. Indeed, despite its already significant problematization, targeted by several monographic studies which have contributed to a more complex and conciliatory vision of the apparent paradoxes of the New State's cultural policy, the historiographical reading which was first established on the phenomenon continues to affect its overall analysis. It is important, therefore, even at the risk of extreme simplification, to commence from its characterisation to further our enquiry and suggest alternative perspectives.[1]

According to this reading, in the initial phase of its institutionalisation, the New State would have adopted or somewhat tolerated an architectural language that posited itself between *art deco* and modernist rationalism. The reason for such could be twofold: either because the image of effectiveness and novelty mattered to a regime that was also presented as a national revolution, or due to the fact that the New State's desired type of architecture had not yet been envisioned. This would happen, according to the previously mentioned historiographical interpretation, in 1938 with the design of the Areeiro Square in Lisbon [Fig. 1] by the architect Luís Cristino da Silva or, more markedly, with the holding of the Portuguese World Exhibition in 1940, in the capital. This exhibition would thus signalize the "death" or the "reversal" of a modernism of compromise labelled as superficial (of false front, not based on a solid theory) and ideologically uncommitted (therefore detached from the democratic or socialist booklet, which are considered to be part of the foundations of the Modern Movement).

Accordingly, the architecture of the New State would be conceived, despite the occasional traces of modernity, as mostly anti-modern, conservative, and traditionalist, given that it resorted to historicist forms, from classic to baroque, or regionalist motes, both inculcated and fantasized, without critical basis previous to the Survey of Portuguese Regional Architecture, whose results were broadcast at the beginning of the 1960s. The fifties, which corresponded to a new generation of modern architects who were increasingly politicized with the end of the Second World War, and that strengthened—around the First National Congress of Architecture (1948)—their class consciousness, would hence be characterized by the implantation of the ideological component of the Modern Movement, the same that had been amputated in the 1930s. During the 1960s, this would lead to a revision of that same Modern Movement characterized, both in Portugal as well as internationally, by the exploration of a supposedly critical regionalism, which

[1] For additional or different interpretive readings of the one exposed in this chapter, see, among others: N. Portas, "A evolução da arquitectura moderna em Portugal: uma interpretação," in *História da Arquitectura Moderna*, ed. Bruno Zevi (Lisbon: Editora Arcádia, 1973), vol. 2, 687–744; J. A. França, *A Arte em Portugal no Século XX: 1911–1961* (Lisbon: Livraria Bertrand, 1974); N. T. Pereira, and J. M. Fernandes, "A arquitectura do fascismo em Portugal," *Arquitectura* 142, (July 1981): 38–48; P. V. Almeida, and J. M. Fernandes, *História da Arte em Portugal. A Arquitectura Moderna* (Lisbon: Alfa, 1986); S. Fernandez, *Percurso. Arquitectura Portuguesa. 1930/1974* (Porto: FAUP, 1988); M. Acciaiuoli, "Os Anos 40 em Portugal: o País, o Regime e as Artes. «Restauração» e «Celebração»" (PhD diss., Universidade Nova de Lisboa, 1991); A. Tostões, "Arquitectura portuguesa do século XX," in *História da Arte Portuguesa*, ed. P. Pereira, (Lisboa: Círculo de Leitores, 1997), vol. III, 507–591; A. Tostões, *Os Verdes Anos na Arquitectura Portuguesa dos Anos 50*. 2nd ed (Porto: FAUP, 1997); A. Tostões, A. Becker, and W. Wang, eds., *Portugal: Arquitectura do Século XX* (Munich, New York, Frankfurt, Lisbon: Prestel/DAM/PF97, 1997); J. P. Martins, "Portuguesismo: nacionalismos e regionalismos na acção da DGEMN. Complexidade e algumas contradições na arquitectura portuguesa," in *Caminhos do Património*, ed. M. Alçada and M. I. T. Grilo (Lisbon: DGEMN, 1999), 115–32; P. V. Almeida, *A Arquitectura no Estado Novo: Uma Leitura Crítica. Os Concursos de Sagres* (Lisbon: Livros Horizonte, 2002); J. M. Fernandes, *Português Suave. Arquitecturas do Estado Novo* (Lisbon: IPPAR, 2003); N. Rosmaninho, *O Poder da Arte: o Estado Novo e a Cidade Universitária de Coimbra* (Coimbra: Imprensa da Universidade, 2006); A. Tostões, *Idade Maior: Cultura e Tecnologia na Arquitectura Moderna Portuguesa* (Porto: FAUP, 2015).

Fig. 1 Areeiro Square (now Francisco Sá Carneiro Square), Lisbon. Architect Luís Cristino da Silva, 1938–1949. Source: Studio Horácio Novais, undated. Col. Mário Novais Studio [CFT164.45118], Calouste Gulbenkian Foundation–Art Library and Archives.

would be capable of reconciling architecture with a certain specific geographical character without promoting a reactionary agenda of folklorization of the landscape and of mentalities.

The argumentative structure just laid out has several limitations, among which the most significant will be further highlighted. Firstly, the operability of such a reading, in particular the part concerning the decades of the 1930s and 1940s, was established according to a highly selective presentation of traces. Indeed, among the buildings constructed during the New State, only those which corroborated and illustrated the various steps that—in cohesive and linear form—could be identified in the development of the architecture of the regime were chosen. Amongst the constructions available in the 1930s, the historiographic gaze focused on those closest to the international functionalism archetype. For its part, for the next decade, mainly nationalist prototypes of historicist and regionalist nature were selected. The perpetuations and concomitances of the above-mentioned aesthetical strands, along with their hybridity, were disregarded. They were only natural in a country where the teaching of architecture remained—until the reform of 1957[2]—faithful to the broadly internationally diffused eclecticism of the French matrix, which was marked by the propensity for the treatment of the exterior as an autonomous casing and for the manipulation and combination of different styles.

[2] G. C. Moniz, "O Ensino Moderno da Arquitectura. A Reforma de 57 e as Escolas de Belas Artes em Portugal (1931–69)" (PhD diss., Universidade de Coimbra, 2011).

The compartmentalisation of the architectural reality implies a depreciation of the fact that modernity and tradition have established a dialogue, albeit tense, since the 19th century, introducing this dilemma in the 20th century as well. This is not to deny that the appeals in favour of building adaptation to a national or regional context become more systematic and incisive from the end of the 1930s onwards. Be that as it may, I intend to emphasize the absence of definitive cuts and to reiterate that the attempts to agglutinate the contemporary formal and constructive novelties with the history and/or national landscape, not only mobilized a much broader set of agents (and, therefore, hardly constitute a mere *top-down process*), as well as being something prior to the institutionalisation of the New State in 1933.

Furthermore, the attempts of compromise between tradition and modernity are far from characterising an exclusively Portuguese phenomenon. The regime headed by António de Oliveira Salazar radicalised and operationalised the demand for a national art in the contemporary era on a scale and with efficiency without precedent. This demand, in Portugal as in the globality of European countries, was born from the impact of the French Revolution, the moment from which architecture was requested to express and strengthen the national character.[3]

The second vulnerability of the historiographical interpretation presented as still dominant concerns the association between modernism and democratic or socialist values. In order to question it—without rebutting what was, in fact, a authoritarian mode to produce and experience architecture—it is worth remembering the parallels between the depurated monumental classicism of the public architecture built between the years of 1920 and 1940 in democratic or liberal democratic countries as well as in authoritarian or totalitarian regimes.[4] Additionally, it is crucial to keep in mind that the negative reaction to international functionalism, far from being exclusive to the extreme right or the extreme left, stretched across the entirety of the political spectrum, even reaching the epicentres of the Modern Movement. It is of equal importance to note that, with the furthering of the knowledge of the architectural practices of the 20th century, the perception of the relationships between these professionals and the political regimes under which they lived likewise became more complex. Architects who were politically conservative projected paradigmatic works of international modernism, while progressivist architects—or even those who joined the totalitarian and authoritarian opposition—conceived architectural and urbanistic interventions that historiography has considered reactionary.

[3] Barry Bergdoll, *European Architecture: 1750–1890* (Oxford: Oxford University Press, 2000), 139.

[4] Franco Borsi, *The Monumental Era: European Architecture and Design. 1929–1939* (London: Lund Humphries, 1987).

To these frailties, already mentioned and recognized in various monographies, one may add the potential of problematization galvanized by two themes that continue to require fresh historiographic investment:[5] the First National Congress of Architecture (1948) and the Survey of Portuguese Regional Architecture (carried out between 1955 and 1960; printed under the title *Inquérito à Arquitectura Popular em Portugal*) published in 1961, both of which were carried out under the Government's sponsorship and validated by the state seal. Characterized as tokens of cultural opposition to the New State (and as a result, acquiring an ideological-political antagonism character as well), and as events that stimulated an architectural counter-narrative, the weight assigned to both events has been excessively inflated. Indeed, what remains to be extensively examined is the actual impact of the Survey and the Congress on the regime's architecture erected from the decade of 1950 onwards. We should, therefore, evaluate the extent to which the changes for which they are accountable were indeed executed: the first, a withdrawal from the stylistic impositions of the regime and a shift in the design of public initiative housing; the second, the ultimate deposition of the belief in the existence of *the* Portuguese house and the setting of the bases for a "critical" regionalism.

Partial analytical contributions, which either focused on a particular typology or on a specific geographical area, have allowed the questioning of such assumptions. Concerning the Congress of 1948, its influence seems to be more productive in enhancing the architects' class consciousness than at the level of the design practices themselves. Regarding the context of the housing promoted by public initiative or support, it is useful to thoroughly analyse the development of collective vertical housing projects (an alternative model to the single-family dwelling, supposedly the most suitable to the regime's ideology). Thus it can be seen if its origins lie in the Congress or if the latter was primarily a vehicle for the expansion and awareness of a transformation that had been underway since the end of the Second World War. Regarding the retraction from the guidelines of the regime, the analysis of the construction campaign of certain typologies of public buildings since the decade of the 1930s up to 1970 does not disclose any rupture in 1948 or the years immediately following the meeting of this assembly. It is, however, an observation made from a single case study.[6] It would hence be beneficial to test their general applicability through the examination of a more comprehensive set of buildings promoted by the government. In turn, the results of the Survey of Portuguese Regional Architecture, despite discrediting the existence of *the* Portuguese house (a thesis erroneously attributed to Raul Lino[7]), in light of the country's geographical diversity of

[5] However, the contributions should be underlined of contemporary rereadings of the First National Congress of Architecture at the time of the facsimiled edition of its Minutes, in July 2008, on the occasion of the 10th anniversary of the Ordem dos Arquitectos—A. Tostões, ed., *1.º Congresso Nacional de Arquitectura* (Lisbon: Ordem dos Arquitectos, Conselho Directivo Nacional, 2008)—as well as the more recent work of historiographical review of the Survey of the Portuguese Regional Architecture, among which are: M. H. Maia, A. Cardoso and J. C. Leal, *Dois Parâmetros de Arquitectura Postos em Surdina. Leitura Crítica do Inquérito à Arquitectura Regional* (Porto: CESAP/CEAA, 2013); M. H. Maia, A. Cardoso and J. C. Leal, *To and Fro: Modernism and Vernacular Architecture* (Porto: Centro de Estudos Arnaldo Araújo, 2013); Ricardo Agarez, *Algarve Building: Modernism, Regionalism and Architecture in the South of Portugal (1925–1965)* (London: Routledge, 2016); M. L. Prista, "A memória de um Inquérito na cultura arquitetónica portuguesa," in *1.º Colóquio Internacional Arquitetura Popular* (Arcos de Valdevez: Município de Arcos de Valdevez, 2016), 273–88.

[6] J. Brites, *O Capital da Arquitectura. Estado Novo, Arquitectos e Caixa Geral de Depósitos (1929–1970)* (Lisbon: Prosafeita, 2014).

[7] See: R. Lino, *A Casa Portuguesa* (Lisbon: Imprensa Nacional, 1929); P. V. Almeida, "Raul Lino. Arquitecto moderno," in *Raul Lino, Exposição Retrospectiva da sua obra* (Lisbon: Fundação Calouste Gulbenkian, 1970), 115–88; P. V. Almeida, *Dois Parâmetros de Arquitectura Postos em Surdina. O Propósito de Uma Investigação* (Porto: Centro de Estudos Arnaldo Araújo, 2010); N. Rosmaninho, "A «casa portuguesa» e outras «casas nacionais,"" *Revista da Universidade de Aveiro–Letras* 19/20, (2002–2003): 225–50.

vernacular architecture, reinforced the conviction that there indeed existed "in this diversity of features, a common thing, specifically Portuguese," i.e., *"certain constants, perhaps of subtle distinction, nonetheless real,"* that did not concern *"a unity of types, shapes or architectural elements, but some recognizable aspect of the character of our people."*[8] The Manichaean contrast established by historiography between the regionalism practised before and after the Survey (inconsistent and conservative vs critical and progressive) has, for its part, already been challenged.[9]

Furthermore, it should be clarified that the Survey's real influence on the design of public works did not undermine the agenda of architecture's "reportuguesifying" advocated by the regime, nor did it displease those responsible for project evaluation. Instead of being the Trojan horse of its contemporary architects (a government-sponsored initiative that would invalidate its own perception of a contemporary national architecture), the Survey decisively contributed to the recognition—by a generation that asserts itself after the Second World War, demonstrates a larger political commitment and that more strongly subscribes a Modern Movement of international nature—of the creative potential of architecture's adaptation to the local context.

After recognising the need for further expanding on the reading of the New State's architectural production, as well as the necessity to overcome a purely formal definition of modernism, it is vital to contemplate a reassessment of the regime's architecture. I consider it a fully modernist phenomenon. To substantiate this fact, it may be appropriate to draw upon two contributions. Firstly, the international historiography that has been produced in the last three decades on the relationship between modernism and fascism, in which is outlined a growing tendency to consider as modernist the artistic production of regimes included within this political typology[10]. Secondly, the most recent Portuguese historiography that, while aiming its attention at the reality of other sectors during the New State (from agriculture to external and internal colonization, taking into account the development of social sciences as well[11]), showed no contradiction in the engagement of science and technology for the pursuit of a societal project adverse to the liberal political matrix of the Enlightenment and, therefore, to liberal and democratic values. Regarding the interpretation of the New State's architecture, the maximalist definition of modernism proposed by Roger Griffin[12] is adopted.

---

[8] *Arquitectura Popular em Portugal*. (Lisbon: Sindicato Nacional dos Arquitectos, 1961), XI.

[9] Agarez, *Algarve Building*.

[10] See., namely: D. P. Doordan, *Building Modern Italy: Italian Architecture 1914–1936* (New York: Princeton Architectural Press, 1988); W. L. Adamson, *Avant-Garde Florence: From Modernism to Fascism* (Cambridge, Mass.: Harvard University Press, 1993); A. Hewitt, *Fascist Modernism: Aesthetics, Politics, and the Avant-garde* (Stanford, CA: Stanford Univ. Press, 1993); R. Griffin, "Nazi Art: Romantic Twilight or Post-Modernism Dawn?," *Oxford Art Journal* 18, no. 2 (1995): 103–07; M. Antliff, M. and M. Affron, eds., *Fascist Visions: Art and Ideology in France and Italy* (Princeton: Princeton University Press, 1997); E. Braun, *Mario Sironi and Italian Modernism: Art and Politics Under Fascism* (New York: Cambridge University Press, 2000); M. Antliff, "Fascism, Modernism, and Modernity," *The Art Bulletin* 84, no. 1 (March 2002): 148–169; E. Gentile, *The Struggle for Modernity: Nationalism, Futurism, and Fascism* (Westport, CT: Praeger, 2003); C. Lazzaro and R. J. Crum, *Donatello Among the Blackshirts: History and Modernity in the Visual Culture of Fascist Italy* (Ithaca: Cornell University Press, 2005); M. Antliff, *Avant-garde Fascism: The Mobilization of Myth, Art, and Culture in France, 1909–1939* (Durham, NC: Duke University Press, 2007); M. Fuller, *Moderns Abroad. Architecture, Cities and Italian Imperialism* (London/New York: Routledge, 2007); R. Griffin, *Modernism and Fascism: The Sense of a Beginning under Mussolini and Hitler* (Basingstoke: Palgrave Macmillan, 2007); R. Griffin, "Modernity, Modernism, and Fascism: A 'Mazeway Resynthesis'," *Modernism/Modernity* 15, no. 1 (January 2008): 9–24.

[11] See, among others: F. Ágoas, "Saber e Poder. Estado e Investigação Social Agrária nos Primórdios da Sociologia em Portugal" (PhD diss., Universidade Nova de Lisboa, 2010); F. Ágoas, "Economia rural e investigação social agrária nos primórdios da sociologia em Portugal," in *O Estado Novo em Questão*, ed. N. Domingos and V. Pereira (Lisbon: Edições 70, 2010), 197–231; F. Ágoas, "Estado, universidade e ciências sociais: a introdução da sociologia na Escola Superior Colonial (1952–1972)," in *O Império Colonial em Questão (Sécs. XIX–XX). Poderes, Saberes e Instituições*, ed. M. B. Jerónimo (Lisbon: Edições 70, 2012), 317–347; C. Castelo, "Ciência, Estado e desenvolvimento no colonialismo português tardio," in *O Império Colonial em Questão (Sécs. XIX–XX). Poderes, Saberes e Instituições*, ed. M. B. Jerónimo (Lisbon: Edições 70, 2012), 349–387; M. B. Jerónimo, "The States of Empire," in *The Making of Modern Portugal*, ed. L. Trindade (Newcastle upon Tyne: Cambridge Scholars Publishing, 2013), 65–101.

[12] Griffin, *Modernism and Fascism*.

Without the restriction of the phenomenon to the sphere of aesthetics, Griffin conceives it as a heterogeneous set of palingenetic reactions, developed between the second half of the 19th century and the end of the Second World War, which aimed to counterbalance what was then perceived as the adverse consequences of the process of western modernisation. Along these lines, the aspects identified as "pathological" as well as, and above all, their forms of correction and overcoming were varied. Between them stood out, alternately or cumulatively: the diffusion of rationalism, liberalism and secularism, along with the cult of progress and the widespread faith in scientific-technological developments, urbanisation and industrialisation, the development of a society of masses and the globalisation of capitalism. The plurality of experiences encompassed by the concept of modernism (among which fascism itself) shared the search for transcendence and regeneration as a common denominator against the alleged anarchy and decadence that resulted from the transformation of institutions, social structures, and the system of traditional beliefs. Such manifestations wanted, thus, to inaugurate an "alternative modernity."[13]

In light of this analytical grid, if applied to the artistic field, it is possible not only to exceed a formally limited understanding of modernism but also, within the same interpretive category, to reconcile experiences that at first sight would appear so distinct as the conception of a row of standardized dwellings and the recovery and reinvention of the folk traditions and the traditional customs of a particular people. If the first intended to respond to the pressing needs of the contemporary city, acting upon the imbalances that could promote social revolution, the second aimed to counter the amnesic and denationalising globalisation, seen as an "invasion" of foreignism and/or cosmopolitanism.

Although the typological definition of the Portuguese New State does not meet with unanimous accord in the historiographic community, I opt to include it in the maximalist category of fascism,[14] notwithstanding its specific traits (on a par with any historical phenomenon) and the systematic self-defence of its originality within the framework of modern dictatorships. Arising out of the military dictatorship (1926–1933) which put an end to the First Republic (1910–1926), it organised and consolidated itself as a right-wing dictatorship, tendentially totalitarian. Nationalist and centralist, imperialist as well as protectionist, interventionist and corporatist, the Portuguese New State was radically opposed to liberal, liberal democratic, democratic, and socialist alternatives.

[13] Griffin, *Modernism and Fascism*, 55.

[14] On the debate concerning the classification of the New State, cf., among others: M. B. Cruz, *O Partido e o Estado no Salazarismo* (Lisbon: Editorial Presença, 1988); A. C. Pinto, *O Salazarismo e o Fascismo Europeu: Problemas de Interpretação nas Ciências Sociais* (Lisbon: Editorial Estampa, 1992); L. R. Torgal, "«Estado Novo» em Portugal: ensaio de reflexão sobre o seu significado," *Estudos Ibero-Americanos* XXIII, no. 1 (June 1997): 5–32; F. Rosas, "O salazarismo e o homem novo: ensaio sobre o Estado Novo e a questão do totalitarismo," *Análise Social* XXXV, no. 157 (2001): 1031–54; J. P. A. Nunes, "Tipologias de regimes políticos. Para uma leitura neo-moderna do Estado Novo e do Nuevo Estado," *População e Sociedade* 8, (2002): 73–101; A. C. Pinto, ed. *The Nature of Fascism Revisited* (New York: Columbia University Press, 2012); A. C. Pinto and A. Kallis, eds. *Rethinking Fascism and Dictatorship in Europe* (Basingstoke: Palgrave Macmillan, 2014).

In comparison with other fascist regimes, the Portuguese case presents lower levels of "ideological radicalism," either during Salazarism, or, and especially, during Marcelism.[15] This relative moderation, verifiable both at the level of the exercise of power as in the degree of clarity of its ideological enunciation, is understandable in view of conjunctural and structural, endogenous and exogenous constraints, the need to balance conflicting interests within the internal level, and the top leadership profile of the regime and its intermediate leaders.[16] However, it is believed that such factors did not jeopardise the totalizing project that the New State applied to Portuguese society, nor did it limit its future-oriented dimension. Architecture, as a social technology capable of influencing the behaviour of bodies (in terms of spatial management) and minds (as an ideological discourse expressed visually and a reference for the continuous reshaping of identity), incorporated both aims.

The nationalist, historicist, and ruralist strands patent in architecture—in likeness with other areas of intervention of the regime—despite exhibiting resistance to the process of modernisation, were far from hindering the modernist vocation of the dictatorship led by António de Oliveira Salazar. It is in the context of public initiative housing that one may find some of the clearest evidence of this thesis. It should be sought not in the projects that, in the second half of the 20th century, are closer to the architectural and urban planning ideals of several international modernist currents, nor in the participation of project designers that were part of the cultural and political opposition to the New State. In order to further substantiate the endorsed interpretative approach, it would be more productive to focus our attention on the analysis of the decades of the 1930s and 1940s.

The construction of clusters of single-family housing units [Fig. 2], the model that first characterised the politics of the regime regarding this sector for an extended period, translated the new social order—manufactured, designed, implemented, and supported by devices of censorship and repression—that was to be enforced. The spatial conception of these clusters, small villages idealised for urban space or its periphery, not only reflected a political-ideological programme but also created the conditions for its own implementation and social internalisation, based on what was perceived by the regime as the "irreducible cell" of the nation: the family. It is an exemplary exercise of palingenesis. Its revolutionary nature and its drive for regeneration relied precisely on the enforcement of aesthetic formulations and models of familial existence that would be considered, if not utterly outdated, at least widely challenged by the contemporary demands.

---

15 J. P. A. Nunes, "A memória histórica enquanto instrumento de controlo durante o Estado Novo. O exemplo do anti-semitismo," *Revista de História das Ideias* 34, (2016): 141.

16 J. P. A. Nunes, "A memória histórica," 142–143.

Fig. 2 Single-family houses in the Affordable Houses neighbourhood of Belém, Lisbon. Architect Raul Lino, 1933–1938. Source: Mário Novais Studio. Col. Mário Novais Studio [CFT003.023724.ic], Calouste Gulbenkian Foundation–Art Library and Archives.

The recovery of the nation's origins, of its genuine and wholesome core, on which the national rebirth would be based, contained a programme of radical social transformation under the cover of the alleged rescue of authenticity. In this way, the demand for authenticity was entirely artificial. It translated the action of the "Gardening State"[17] which, in favour of the reorganisation of the national garden, enforced the elimination of weeds in the interest of the growth and proliferation of regular plants. The summoning of a "healthy" past acted, therefore, as curative and as prophylaxis simultaneously: not only did it eliminate the degenerative symptoms already present but it also prevented future deviations. In any case, this excursion into the past always assumed a scheduled return to the present, where a "battle" of "salvation" was fought, and a "mission" of "regeneration" of an allegedly sick nation, weakened by a century of monarchical and republican liberalism, was put into motion.

[17] Z. Bauman, *Modernity and Ambivalence* (Ithaca: Cornell University Press, 1991), 20.

It is within this context that the architecture of Portuguese fascism must be understood. It is one of the social engineering mechanisms exploited by the regime. It reflects, therefore, a modern political practice that, although applied on behalf of an agenda far from the political and social illuminist ideals, corresponds to the Enlightenment's assumption that it was possible to shape and improve human nature.

Furthermore, the development of architectural programmes so methodically organised and on such scale, operating within a structured legal framework and implying such technical know-how, rationalisation, and bureaucratisation as the one fostered by Salazarism, could only have materialised within a modern state. Indeed, the New State radicalised and further implemented on an unprecedented scale the transformation which the 19th century operated within the framework of urbanism and building design: its conversion into two distinct technologies of power, albeit connected: the disciplinary and the regulatory.[18] The former aims to control the body, by the agency of mechanisms for the spatial management of individuals, in order to normalise their behaviour. The latter, targeting the population as a whole, establishes the rules and patterns of leasing, house credit, health insurance and pensions, hygiene and sanitation as well as the organisation of the urban fabric, etc.

Both of these mechanisms (disciplinary and regulatory) can be found in the architecture of the New State. Each public building obeyed, according to its nature, certain spatial distribution criteria designed to ensure the correct and orderly performance of its allocated functions (courthouses, agencies of the state bank, stations of post offices, telegraphs and telephones, etc.). This control, practised over the body, protruded further in the infrastructures dedicated to education (schools, colleges, universities), to the organization of free time (holiday camps, among others), to health and social care (hospitals, sanatoriums, houses of the people, etc.), to the housing of public initiative (affordable houses programme, among others) and to correction/punishment (jails, prisons, etc.), the design and construction of which in most cases entailed specialized administrative entities—primarily consisting of engineers and architects—which studied their configuration.

This research could require trips to other countries for the observation of the most advanced typological proposals. Although many of the architectural typologies that have just been mentioned can be traced back to the 19th century, and therefore not an invention of fascism, it is with this regime that such functional programmes tend to undergo a standardisation, to be centrally planned and systematically deployed.

[18] M. Foucault, *"Society Must be Defended."
Lectures at the Collège de France, 1975–76* (New York: Picador, 2003), 250–251.

Its sole purpose was not the satisfaction of functional requirements. It also aimed to architecturally materialise the multiform state apparatus of domain, domestication, inculcation, and ideological repression. Regarding the mechanisms of a regulatory nature, there was an effort to establish a legal framework for project assessment, supervision and execution of public works, as well as policies concerning urban planning, social welfare and housing of public initiative, leasing and expropriation, construction, hygiene, health and sanitation.

These concerns, which emerged in the final stages of the constitutional monarchy and during the First Republic, experienced a decisive legislative reinforcement at the hands of the military dictatorship and especially with the formalisation of the New State in 1933. On the one hand, this shows an increasing governmental aptness regarding this specific course of action and understanding it as a priority. On the other hand, it reveals a process of complexification and bureaucratisation, enshrined in an increasing legislative detailing and densification which, in turn, helped to reduce the margin of error and enhanced the standardisation of aesthetical options and outcomes.[19]

On a par, knowledge and scientific procedures were mobilised (with a particularly relevant role played by social sciences) to map and meet the reality that was to be transformed with the greatest possible accuracy. One could refer, for instance, to the implementation of the Survey of Rural Housing in the 1940s, which was part of the set of studies and surveys that sought to justify the reform of the economy and rural societies, put in motion by the regime from the second half of the 1930s onwards.[20]

Secondly, the New State's architecture reflects the rationalization of the governmental practice, characteristic of modernity. The development of the regime's architecture occurs within the framework of a campaign of infrastructural works, urban planning and equipment construction. This was carried out by Salazarism, following the improvement of the country's financial and economic situation, in response to specific conjunctural (the Crisis of 1929 and the Great Depression) and structural traits (the transformation of the modes of socio-economic regulation and the growth of state's intervention in the economy). Its planning, implementation and monitoring was the responsibility of the socio-professional group of the engineers, a technocratic elite which played a major role in the theorization and conduction of a modernisation that, alongside conservative traditionalism, found expression both in its actions as well as in the composition of the middle and upper state boards of the regime.[21]

[19] Brites, *O Capital da Arquitectura.*

[20] F. Ágoas, "Saber e Poder."

[21] See, among others: F. Rosas, *Salazarismo e Fomento Económico (1928–1948)* (Lisbon: Editorial Notícias, 2000).

The campaign of public works obeyed to a hierarchical, specialized and centralized organization, achieved through the confluence of two operating principles. With the first, commenced during the military dictatorship, the aim was for all responsibility referring to the preparation, execution, and supervision of construction or renovation of public buildings to be aggregated in the Ministry of Public Works and Communications (MOPC)[22]—created interim. The second resulted from the awareness of the considerable volume of works, many of which were urgent in nature, and of the specific technical knowledge which they would imply. Such conditions led to the establishment of a panoply of organisms—councils, delegations and administrative committees, consisting of an independent body of technicians (autonomous or under the remit of the Directorate General of National Buildings and Monuments albeit, in any case, still dependent on MOPC)—to which was assigned the task of coordinating the planning and construction of the body of public buildings belonging to distinct typologies throughout the national territory.

Accordingly, a division of labour guided by criteria of rationality, efficacy, and efficiency, such as the determination of action plans and the listing of intervention priorities, was likewise enacted. To this can be added the growing tendency for the typification of the programme(s) to be adopted in each architectural typology (stations of post offices, telegraphs and telephones; courts; agencies and branches of the Caixa Geral de Depósitos; barracks; schools; health care units; prisons, among others) and the establishment of a standard bureaucratic method for the evaluation and approval of architectural projects, financed either partially or entirely by the government. This course of action, marked by the intervention of different spheres of decision-making, proved to be able not only to influence but also shape any architectural proposal, regardless of its potential initial radicalism.

Alongside the legal system established to oversee the architectural practice, Salazarism created mechanisms for the ideological surveillance and indoctrination of architects. In addition to being the primary contractee of architectural projects and chief promoter of the most significant percentage of exhibitions at the national and international levels, the government also assured, among other aspects, a compulsive class corporatization, the monopoly of the teaching of architecture, as well as the censure of the essays and scientific discourse concerned with it. Moreover, it established institutions and programmes for the framing and/or disciplining of the artistic phenomenon (among others, the Superior Council of Fine Arts, the National Academy of Fine Arts, the Secretariat of National Propaganda, the Board of National Education, the artistic

[22] Created in July 1932, from the processing of the previous Ministry of Commerce and Communications, the Ministry of Public Works and Communications became designated only as Ministry of Public Works (MOP) from December 1946.

awards and the so called "Missões Estéticas de Férias," programmes that supposedly immersed the artists, during their vacation, in the national landscape subsequently promoting the realization of creative work within this framework[23]).

Adequately inserted into a specific framework, the discipline of architecture and its professionals was subsequently summoned to participate not only in the construction of the (non-static) image of the regime, but also in the recasting of the nation, contributing to the transformation of sociabilities and the worldview that was underway. Its modernist nature expressed itself at the level of its aesthetic language, which was another means, only artificially separated, of the pursuit of an alternative modernity. This was, as the expression itself suggests, a selective process, syncretic and negotiated, which can be further recognised in other areas of intervention of the New State. The search for a national modern—an architectural language that was, at the same time, contemporary and appropriate to the specific nature of the country and/or region—it is the common denominator, despite adopting different formulations, of the entirety of the architectural production of the regime. In essence, it coincides with the agenda pursued by other fascisms, such as the German, Italian or Brazilian, whose artistic realities were met with the admiration of some Portuguese architects and critics.[24] Moreover, it is also possible to find corresponding parallels with the cultural worldviews of radically different political systems. As an example, we could mention the North American and Finnish cases, whose architecture was praised both in generalist and specialist periodicals of the time.[25]

The compulsion to associate contemporary buildings with its geographical and/or historical-cultural specificity was not a concern exclusive to fascist regimes. Thus, one might wonder what ascribes them a particular political and ideological nature in architecture. In my view, it is their mode of production (a short interval between the maximum and minimum limits of creative freedom, the negotiation of aesthetic options and the containment of differences), how their use and occupation was stipulated and encouraged, as well as the high degree of ideological and political propaganda that charged them. The specificity of fascist architecture should not, therefore, be correlated to a putative degree of aesthetic cohesion and uniformity regarding its built heritage, nor to the alleged level of the discipline's knowledge present in the discourse of the dictators. Both interpretations have been already widely challenged by artistic historiography, including the one which looked on National Socialism,[26] the case that would express the presence of these two assumptions with higher probability.

[23] On the intervention of the State in the cultural field, see, among others: J. R. Ó, *Os Anos de Ferro: O Dispositivo Cultural Durante a Política do Espírito, 1933–1949: Ideologia, Instituições, Agentes e Práticas* (Lisbon: Editorial Estampa, 1999).

[24] R. Lino, Carta a António de Oliveira Salazar (7 Março 1933) (*Arquivo Nacional Torre do Tombo: Arquivo Oliveira Salazar.* AOS/CP-156, pasta 4.3.7/21); T. R. Colaço, "Nota," *A Arquitectura Portuguesa* 24, (Março 1937): 25; T. R. Colaço, "O exemplo do Brasil," *A Arquitectura Portuguesa* 23, (Fevereiro 1937): 1,8; G. C. Branco, "Manifestação cultural. A moderna arquitectura alemã através da interessante exposição que vai abrir nas Belas-Artes," *Diário de Lisboa* 6807, (3 November 1941): 5,7.

[25] "Arquitectura de hoje pelo estrangeiro," *A Arquitectura Portuguesa* 37, (Abril 1938): 37, 22; "Arquitectura das cidades finlandesas," *Diário da Manhã* 4552, (5 January 1944): 3.

[26] B. M. Lane, *Architecture and Politics in Germany: 1918–1945* (Cambridge Mass.: Harvard Univ. Press, 1985).

The ambiguity of the motto of fascist architecture and its consequent hegemonic "pluralism,"[27] instead of hinting at the absence of a singular cultural policy, attest to the inclusive logic that these regimes employed in the artistic field, similar to the way in which they managed conflicting forces and agents in the political, social and economic spheres.

The demand for a national modern was nebulously enunciated and, therefore, expressed more clearly what it disapproved of rather than what proposed. In Portugal, it encompassed aesthetic narratives as diverse as the simplified update of historicisms, regionalisms, *art deco* and the International Style. Its hybridisation—by which the eclectic modus operandi of the 1900s is prolonged in the next century—was achieved to a greater extent via the juxtaposition of stylistic references than by its synthesis.

[27] M. Stone, "The State as patron: making official culture in Fascist Italy," in *Fascist Visions: Art and Ideology in France and Italy*, ed. M. Antliff and M. Affron (Princeton: Princeton University Press, 1997), 208.

Fig. 3 Branch of Caixa Geral de Depósitos (State Bank), in Leiria. Designed by architect Luís Cristino da Silva between 1940 and 1942 (demolished decades later). Source: Mário Novais Studio. Col. Mário Novais Studio [CFT003.23702], Calouste Gulbenkian Foundation–Art Library and Archives.

As a consequence, the buildings often exhibited facades that conciliated different aesthetical references [Fig. 3]. The questionable critical character of this intersection was no impairment, however, to the modernist intention that presided over its creation. The exercise itself did not represent a rejection of modernity, but its correction; not the rebuke of artistic modernism, but the amendment of what was perceived as a stateless and disaggregating internationalism, and that did not agree with the climate, landscape or the nature of the country.

In conclusion, an attempt to explain the modernist nature of the New State's architecture does not require the disclosure, within itself, of formal vestiges of the Modern Movement. This procedure would maintain of a evaluative scale regarding the interpretation of modernism and the subsequent detection of levels of completeness and impurity. Modernism in architecture includes the Modern Movement, although it is not limited to this phenomenon, nor should it be taken as a model of analysis for disparate proposals. Despite its traditionalist camouflage, and to a greater extent because of it, the architecture of the New State was an instrument used to reshape Portuguese society and to modify its way of conceiving and being in the world. In this way, the more archaic or historicist characteristics of this architecture do not disturb in the slightest its palingenetic nature, namely, its purpose of social regeneration. The selective use of the past bolstered a project for the future. Far from being an unwavering path, it should be more accurately described as reactive and corrective. In parallel, what justifies the interpretation of the New State as a modernist phenomenon must not be confined to the identification of the developmental traits that Portuguese fascism comprised. Likewise, it should predominantly depart from the recognition of the existence of a societal project and the intended making of a "new man," and focus on the analysis of how these goals, rejecting some of the premises of the process of modernisation, were sought after with the use of instruments and procedures which are characteristic of modernity.

NOTE
The author submitted this chapter in April 2018. Although further literature has been published on the subject in question, the text remained unaltered until its final publication.

BIBLIOGRAPHY

Acciaiuoli, M. "Os Anos 40 em Portugal: o País, o Regime e as Artes. «Restauração» e «Celebração.»" PhD dissertation, Universidade Nova de Lisboa, 1991.

Adamson, W. L. Avant-garde Florence: From Modernism to Fascism. Cambridge (Massachusetts): Harvard University Press, 2010.

Agarez, Ricardo. Algarve Building: Modernism, Regionalism and Architecture in the South of Portugal (1925–1965). London: Routledge, 2016.

Ágoas, F. "Economia rural e investigação social agrária nos primórdios da sociologia em Portugal." In O Estado Novo em Questão, edited by N. Domingos, and V. Pereira, 197–231. Lisbon: Edições 70, 2010.

Ágoas, F. "Estado, universidade e ciências sociais: a introdução da sociologia na Escola Superior Colonial (1952–1972)." In O Império Colonial em Questão (Sécs. XIX–XX). Poderes, Saberes e Instituições, edited by M. B. Jerónimo, 317–347. Lisbon: Edições 70, 2012.

Ágoas, F. "Saber e Poder. Estado e Investigação Social Agrária nos Primórdios da Sociologia em Portugal." PhD dissertation, Universidade Nova de Lisboa, 2010.

Almeida, P. V. "Raul Lino. Arquitecto moderno." In Raul Lino, Exposição Retrospectiva da Sua Obra, 115–188. Lisbon: Fundação Calouste Gulbenkian, 1970.

Almeida, P. V. A Arquitectura no Estado Novo: Uma Leitura Crítica. Os Concursos de Sagres. Lisbon: Livros Horizonte, 2002.

Almeida, P. V. Dois Parâmetros de Arquitectura Postos em Surdina. O Propósito de Uma Investigação. Porto: Centro de Estudos Arnaldo Araújo, 2010.

Almeida, P. V., and J. M. Fernandes. História da Arte em Portugal. A Arquitectura Moderna. Lisbon: Alfa, 1986.

Antliff, M. "Fascism, Modernism, and Modernity." The Art Bulletin 84, no. 1 (March 2002): 148–169.

Antliff, M. Avant-Garde Fascism: The Mobilization of Myth, Art, and Culture in France, 1909–1939. Durham, NC: Duke University Press, 2007.

Antliff, M., and M. Affron, eds. Fascist Visions: Art and Ideology in France and Italy. Princeton: Princeton University Press, 1997.

"Arquitectura das cidades finlandesas." Diário da Manhã 4552, (5 Janeiro 1944): 3

"Arquitectura de hoje pelo estrangeiro." A Arquitectura Portuguesa 37, (Abril 1938): 37, 22.

Arquitectura Popular em Portugal. Lisbon: Sindicato Nacional dos Arquitectos, 1961.

Bauman, Z. Modernity and Ambivalence. Ithaca: Cornell University Press, 1991.

Bergdoll, Barry. European Architecture: 1750–1890. Oxford: Oxford University Press, 2000.

Borsi, Franco. The Monumental Era: European Architecture and Design. 1929–1939. London: Lund Humphries, 1987.

Branco, G. C. "Manifestação cultural. A moderna arquitectura alemã através da interessante exposição que vai abrir nas Belas-Artes." Diário de Lisboa 6807, (3 Novembro 1941): 5,7.

Braun, E. and Mario Sironi. Italian Modernism: Art and Politics Under Fascism. New York: Cambridge University Press, 2000.

Brites, J. O Capital da Arquitectura. Estado Novo, Arquitectos e Caixa Geral de Depósitos (1929–1970). Lisbon: Prosafeita, 2014.

Castelo, C. "Ciência, Estado e desenvolvimento no colonialismo português tardio." In O Império Colonial em Questão (Sécs. XIX–XX). Poderes, Saberes e Instituições, edited by M. B. Jerónimo, 349–387. Lisbon: Edições 70, 2012.

Colaço, T. R. "Nota." A Arquitectura Portuguesa 24, (Março 1937): 25.

Colaço, T. R. "O exemplo do Brasil." A Arquitectura Portuguesa 23, (Fevereiro 1937): 1,8.

Cruz, M. B. O Partido e o Estado no Salazarismo. Lisbon: Editorial Presença, 1988.

Doordan, D. P. Building Modern Italy: Italian Architecture 1914–1936. New York: Princeton Architectural Press, 1988.

Fernandes, J. M. Português Suave. Arquitecturas do Estado Novo. Lisbon: IPPAR, 2003.

Fernandez, S. Percurso. Arquitectura Portuguesa. 1930/1974. Porto: FAUP, 1988.

Foucault, M. "Society Must be Defended." Lectures at the Collège de France, 1975–76. New York: Picador, 2003.

França, J. A. A Arte em Portugal no Século XX: 1911–1961. Lisbon: Livraria Bertrand, 1974.

Fuller, M. Moderns Abroad. Architecture, Cities and Italian Imperialism. London/ New York: Routledge, 2007.

Gentile, E. The Struggle for Modernity: Nationalism, Futurism, and Fascism. Westport, CT: Praeger, 2003.

Griffin, R. "Modernity, Modernism, and Fascism: A 'Mazeway Resynthesis'." Modernism/Modernity 15, no. 1 (January 2008): 9–24.

Griffin, R. "Nazi Art: Romantic Twilight or Post-Modernism Dawn?" Oxford Art Journal 18, no. 2 (1995): 103–07.

Griffin, R. Modernism and Fascism: the Sense of a Beginning under Mussolini and Hitler. Basingstoke: Palgrave Macmillan, 2007.

Hewitt, A. Fascist Modernism: Aesthetics, Politics, and the Avant-Garde. Stanford, CA: Stanford Univ. Press, 1993.

Jerónimo, M. B. "The States of Empire." In The Making of Modern Portugal, edited by L. Trindade, 65–101. Newcastle upon Tyne: Cambridge Scholars Publishing, 2013.

Lane, B. M. *Architecture and Politics in Germany: 1918–1945.* Cambridge Mass.: Harvard Univ. Press, 1985.

Lazzaro, C., and R. J. Crum. *Donatello Among the Blackshirts: History and Modernity in the Visual Culture of Fascist Italy.* Ithaca: Cornell University Press, 2005.

Lino, R. *A Casa Portuguesa.* Lisbon: Imprensa Nacional, 1929.

Lino, R. Carta a António de Oliveira Salazar (7 de Março de 1933). Arquivo Nacional Torre do Tombo: Arquivo Oliveira Salazar. AOS/CP-156, pasta 4.3.7/21.

Maia, M. H., A. Cardoso, A., and J. C. Leal. *Dois Parâmetros de Arquitectura Postos em Surdina. Leitura Crítica do Inquérito à Arquitectura Regional.* Porto: CESAP/CEAA, 2013.

Maia, M. H., A. Cardoso, A., and J. C. Leal. *To and Fro: Modernism and Vernacular Architecture.* Porto: Centro de Estudos Arnaldo Araújo, 2013.

Martins, J. P. "Portuguesismo: nacionalismos e regionalismos na acção da DGEMN. Complexidade e algumas contradições na arquitectura portuguesa." In *Caminhos do Património*, edited by M. Alçada and M. I. T. Grilo, 115–32. Lisbon: DGEMN, 1999.

Moniz, G. C. "O Ensino Moderno da Arquitectura. A Reforma de 57 e as Escolas de Belas Artes em Portugal (1931–69)." PhD dissertation, Universidade de Coimbra, 2011.

Nunes, J. P. A. "A memória histórica enquanto instrumento de controlo durante o Estado Novo. O exemplo do anti-semitismo." *Revista de História das Ideias* 34, (2016): 137–168.

Nunes, J. P. A. "Tipologias de regimes políticos. Para uma leitura neo-moderna do Estado Novo e do Nuevo Estado." *População e Sociedade* 8, (2002): 73–101.

Ó, J. R. *Os Anos de Ferro: O Dispositivo Cultural Durante a Política do Espírito, 1933–1949: Ideologia, Instituições, Agentes e Práticas.* Lisbon: Editorial Estampa, 1999.

Pereira, N. T., and J. M. Fernandes. "A arquitectura do fascismo em Portugal." *Arquitectura* 142, (Julho 1981): 38–48.

Pinto, A. C. and A. Kallis, eds. *Rethinking Fascism and Dictatorship in Europe.* Basingstoke: Palgrave Macmillan, 2014.

Pinto, A. C. *O Salazarismo e o Fascismo Europeu: Problemas de Interpretação nas Ciências Sociais.* Lisbon: Editorial Estampa, 1992.

Pinto, A. C., ed. *The Nature of Fascism Revisited.* New York: Columbia University Press, 2012.

Portas, N. "A evolução da arquitectura moderna em Portugal: uma interpretação." In *História da Arquitectura Moderna*, edited by Bruno Zevi, vol. 2, 687–744. Lisbon: Editora Arcádia, 1973.

Prista, M. L. "A memória de um Inquérito na cultura arquitetónica portuguesa." In *1.º Colóquio Internacional Arquitectura Popular*, 273–88. Arcos de Valdevez: Município de Arcos de Valdevez, 2016.

Rosas, F. "O salazarismo e o homem novo: ensaio sobre o Estado Novo e a questão do totalitarismo." *Análise Social* XXXV, no. 157 (2001): 1031–54.

Rosas, F. *Salazarismo e Fomento Económico (1928–1948).* Lisbon: Editorial Notícias, 2000.

Rosmaninho, N. "A «casa portuguesa» e outras «casas nacionais.»" *Revista da Universidade de Aveiro–Letras* 19/20, (2002–2003): 225–50.

Rosmaninho, N. *O Poder da Arte: o Estado Novo e a Cidade Universitária de Coimbra.* Coimbra: Imprensa da Universidade, 2006.

Stone, M. "The State as patron: making official culture in Fascist Italy." In *Fascist Visions: Art and Ideology in France and Italy*, edited by M. Antliff, and M. Affron, 205–238. Princeton: Princeton University Press, 1997.

Torgal, L. R. "«Estado Novo» em Portugal: ensaio de reflexão sobre o seu significado." *Estudos Ibero-Americanos* XXIII, no. 1 (Junho 1997): 5–32.

Tostões, A. "Arquitectura portuguesa do século XX." In *História da Arte Portuguesa*, edited by P. Pereira, vol. III, 507–591. Lisbon: Círculo de Leitores, 1997.

Tostões, A. *Idade Maior: Cultura e Tecnologia na Arquitectura Moderna Portuguesa.* Porto: FAUP, 2015.

Tostões, A. *Os Verdes Anos na Arquitectura Portuguesa dos Anos 50.* 2nd ed. Porto: FAUP, 1997.

Tostões, A., A. Becker, and W. Wang, eds. *Portugal: Arquitectura do Século XX.* München, New York, Frankfurt, Lisbon: Prestel/DAM/PF97, 1997.

Tostões, A., ed. *1.º Congresso Nacional de Arquitectura.* Lisbon: Ordem dos Arquitectos, Conselho Directivo Nacional, 2008.

Readings and Re-Readings of the Estado Novo

VICTOR PEREIRA
University of Pau and Pays de l'Adour. Identities, Territories, Expressions, Mobility.

ABSTRACT

This chapter aims to provide a synthetic overview of the Estado Novo's historiography. Its goal is to describe the main developments of this field of study and to highlight some shortcomings, in particular the insufficient openness to the various social sciences.

The historiography of the dictatorship began even before the Carnation Revolution and was consolidated under the democratic regime. The question of the nature of the regime—fascist or not—has been a significant one for many years, at the risk of closing this field of research to a relatively small universe of problems. This question remains a sensitive one, as demonstrated by the debate in the press between several Portuguese historians in 2012. However, we can now question the heuristic scope of this debate, which has largely neglected a social history of the dictatorship and a concrete study of the governmentalities deployed by the State.

BIOGRAPHY

Victor Pereira, historian, PhD (Institute of Political Studies–Paris), is associate professor (maître de conférences) at the Université de Pau et des Pays de l'Adour (France). His research focuses on Portuguese emigration and twentieth-century Portuguese history.

He published La Dictature de Salazar face à l'émigration. L'État portugais et ses migrants en France (1957–1974) in 2012 (Paris: Presses de Sciences-Po). This book was translated in Portuguese in 2014 (Temas & Debates). With Nuno Domingos, he co-edited, O Estado Novo em Questão in 2010 (Lisbon: Edições 70). He is one of the Editors of the journal Lusotopie (Brill) and Histoire@Politique (Centre d'Histoire de Sciences-Po). He is also the director of the Presses Universitaires de Pau et des Pays de l'Adour (Pau University Press).

The historiography of the *Estado Novo* was born while the dictatorship had not yet fallen. It is mainly outside Portuguese borders that these first works were developed, either by Portuguese in exile or by foreigners interested in a country on the fringes of the West, stuck in colonial wars that appeared archaic. Among the first to emerge was Hermínio Martins, living in Great Britain, and Manuel de Lucena, who presented an academic dissertation on Portuguese corporatism in Paris in 1971.[1] These pioneering works fit into the more global framework of research carried out by exiles on contemporary Portugal—some preparing doctoral theses—in order to understand the dictatorship that forced them to leave their country. This research is articulated with a political commitment: knowledge appears as a political weapon to unveil the dictatorship, to grasp the foundations of its sustainability and, in consequence, to fight it better. Among the foreigners going to Portugal to study a dictatorship often presented as archaic, we can mention Philippe Schmitter[2] and Howard Wiarda[3] who, like Lucena, looked at Portuguese corporatism. By studying Portuguese corporatism, Schmitter assumed the role of a '"political palaeontologist" who finds a fossil in an obscure museum and is convinced that, if he succeeds in deciphering its meaning, it will reveal to him the deep and sinister secrets of the hideous interwar period'.[4] In the context of the colonial wars (1961–1974) and the Lisbon government's refusal to concede the independence of its colonies, the Portuguese Empire in Africa also attracted attention. Douglas Wheeler, René Pélissier, Allen Isaacman, and Clarence Gervase-Smith thus travelled to Portugal and its colonies and their works made incursions into the *Estado Novo* period. It should not be forgotten, however, that the Salazarist dictatorship was able to count on foreign panegyrists, presenting the dictatorship as a necessity in order to end the chaos provoked by the First Republic (1910–1926) and as making Portugal a great nation again. The Portuguese corporatist experience had been analysed with admiration by journalists, essayists, and economists since the 1930s.[5] From that time, some historians described the early years of the regime, which they believed ended several decades of chaos.[6]

In Portugal itself, a rigorous study of the dictatorial regime was hardly conceivable because contemporary history, considered potentially subversive, was banned from school and university curricula. Access to sources was very much reduced if not totally impossible. For example, Howard Wiarda and Philippe Schmitter were able to conduct interviews with senior officials. Schmitter even managed to obtain documents enabling him to know the background of Portuguese parliamentarians.[7] Historians close to the regime, depicting the 19th and the beginning of the 20th century as a period of long decadence, painted a glowing portrait of

---

[1] Hermínio Martins wrote the chapter dedicated to Portugal in a collective book on European fascisms published in 1968 and directed by Stuart Woolf: Hermínio Martins, "Portugal," in *European Fascism*, edited by Stuart Woolf (London: Weidenfeld and Nicolson, 1968). This chapter, along with other works, was published in the 1990s: Hermínio Martins, *Classe, Status e Poder e Outros Ensaios Sobre o Portugal Contemporâneo* (Lisbon: Imprensa de Ciências Sociais, 1998). The thesis that Manuel de Lucena defended in 1971 at the Institute of Social Sciences of Labour at the University of Paris I was published in Portuguese after the Carnation revolution: Manuel de Lucena, *A Evolução do Sistema Corporativo Português*, 2 vols (Lisbon: Perspectivas e Realidades, 1976).

[2] The works published by Schmitter have been compiled in a book: Philippe Schmitter, *Portugal. Do Autoritarismo à Democracia* (Lisbon: Imprensa de Ciências Sociais, 1999).

[3] Howard Wiarda, *Corporatism and Development. The Portuguese Experience* (Amherst: The University of Massachusetts Press, 1977).

[4] Schmitter, *Portugal*, 12.

[5] To mention only the case of French admirers of the Estado Novo: Emmanuel Hurault, "Le modèle portugais," in *Serviteurs de l'Etat*, edited by Marc-Olivier Baruch, Vincent Duclert, (Paris: La Découverte, 2000), 439–447; Frédéric Rozeira de Mariz, "Le Portugal de Salazar et la droite extrême française, 1928–1945," *French Politics, Culture & Society*, 23, no. 2, (2005), 28–42; Alain Chatriot, "Les nouvelles relèves et le corporatisme. Visions françaises des expériences européennes," in *Les Relèves en Europe d'un Après-Guerre à l'Autre. Racines, Réseaux, Projets et Postérités*, edited by Olivier Dard, Etienne Deschamps, (Brussels: Peter Lang, 2005), 173–196; Olivier Dard, Ana Isabel Sardinha-Desvignes, *Célébrer Salazar en France (1930–1974). Du Philosalazarisme au Salazarisme Français* (Brussels: Peter Lang, 2018).

[6] Jesus Pabón, *La Revolución portuguesa*, 2 vols. (Madrid: Espasa-Calpe S.A., 1945); Paul Descamps, *Histoire sociale du Portugal* (Paris: Firmin-Didot, 1959).

[7] Schmitter, *Portugal*, 29.

dictatorship and its restorative action. Historians linked to the various opposition movements, when they were not forced into exile and had the financial means to continue their research, preferred other historical periods. However, some of their works make references to the *Estado Novo*, such as those of Vitorino Magalhães Godinho[8] or António de Oliveira Marques. The latter, a medievalist by training, even published a history of Portugal, going as far as the government of Marcelo Caetano,[9] and collections of texts, annotated and presented, on the first years of the dictatorship.[10]

The fall of the dictatorship in April 1974, the development of contemporary history in universities and the foundation of master's degrees linked to the study of this period, the creation of journals and books collections, access to archives (Salazar papers and the political police archives are open to all since 1994) and the massification of the school system allowed the multiplication of studies on the *Estado Novo*, by both Portuguese and foreign researchers. The field of history of the *Estado Novo* is now consolidated, supported by a curiosity of the general public not only in scientific works but also works of journalists, documentary or fictional films or television programs.[11] As well as access to the archives, many working tools are now available: historical dictionaries,[12] biographical dictionaries,[13] and publications of the private and public correspondence of Salazar.[14] However, the *Estado Novo* is not a historical object like any other: the political and memorial stakes remain intense, as illustrated by the numerous articles published by historians during the summer of 2012 around the chapters devoted to the dictatorship by Rui Ramos in a History of Portugal.[15]

In this short historiographical review—which is an exercise to which many other historians have devoted themselves[16]—we want to quickly take stock of the works that have been carried out and the different evolutions in this field, but also to point out some gaps or approaches that need to be further developed. One of the limits of the works on the *Estado Novo* lies in the compartmentalization of this field which is insufficiently open to the contributions of other social sciences. Works which, although essential to write a social history of this period, are often totally neglected. If total history is a difficult goal, it is harmful that the debates on the *Estado Novo* are locked into a universe of relatively closed books, sources, and methods. A final caveat: the historiographical review exercise can sometimes lead to some injustices: this or that forgotten article, this or that neglected thesis. In addition, the brevity with which the various works are evoked sometimes leads to simplify their richness and their contributions, which can not be summarized in a few lapidary words.

[8] Vitorino Magalhães Godinho, *Estrutura da Antiga Sociedade Portuguesa* (Lisbon: Arcádia, 1971).

[9] António de Oliveira Marques, *História de Portugal. Desde os Tempos Mais Antigos até ao Governo do Sr. Marcelo Caetano*, 3 vols (Lisbon: Ágora, 1972).

[10] António de Oliveira Marques, *História do Portugal Contemporâneo. A Unidade da Oposição à Ditadura, 1928–1931* (Lisbon: Europa-América, 1973); António de Oliveira Marques, *História do Portugal Contemporâneo. A Primeira Legislatura do Estado Novo, 1935–1938* (Lisbon: Europa-América, 1974).

[11] Luís Reis Torgal, *História, que História?* (Lisbon: Temas e debates/Círculo de Leitores, 2015).

[12] Fernando Rosas, José Maria Brandão de Brito, ed., *Dicionário de História do Estado Novo* (Venda Nova: Bertrand, 1996); António Barreto, Maria Filomena Mónica, ed., *Dicionário de História de Portugal*, 3 vols (Porto: Figueirinhas, 1999).

[13] Manuel Braga da Cruz, António Costa Pinto, ed., *Dicionário Biográfico Parlamentar (1935–1974)*, 2 vols (Lisbon: Imprensa de Ciências Sociais, 2004); Mário Matos e Lemos, Luís Reis Torgal, ed., *Candidatos da Oposição à Assembleia Nacional do Estado Novo (1945–1973). Um Dicionário* (Lisbon: Texto editores, 2009).

[14] See, for instance, João Miguel Almeida, *António Oliveira Salazar, Pedro Teotónio Pereira, Correspondência Política (1945–1968)*, (Lisbon: Temas e debates, 2008).

[15] Rui Ramos et alii, *História de Portugal* (Lisbon: Esfera dos livros, 2009); Filipe Ribeiro Meneses, "Slander, Ideological Differences, or Academic Debate? The 'Verão Quente' of 2012 and the State of Portuguese Historiography," *E-Journal of Portuguese History*, 10, no. 1 (2012); Bruno Monteiro, "Penser l'État. Une relecture de l'historiographie récente sur l'Estado Novo (2010–2015)," *Histoire@politique*, 29 (2016) https://www.histoire-politique.fr/index.php?numero=29&rub=dossier&item=276#_ftnref97

[16] Fernando Rosas, "Bilan historiographique des recherches sur l'État nouveau," *Vingtième siècle. Revue d'Histoire*, 62 (1999): 51–60; Luís Reis Torgal, *Estado Novo, Estados Novos. Ensaios de História Política e Cultural*, vol. 2 (Coimbra: Imprensa da Universidade de Coimbra, 2009): 323–413; Francisco Carlos Palomanes Martinho, "O Estado Novo na historiografia portuguesa: sobre a questão do fascismo," in edited by João Paulo Avelãs Nunes, Américo Freire, *Historiografias Portuguesa e Brasileira no Século XX. Olhares Cruzados* (Coimbra: Imprensa da Universidade de Coimbra, 2013): 111–146.

REASON AND UNREASON OF "CLASSIFICATORY LOGIC"[17]

Fascist or not? This question has structured part of the historiography of the *Estado Novo* since the 1970s. It continues to provoke debates, sometimes vehement, because it touches closely on the memory of the struggle against the regime. Historians who consider that Salazarism is not fascism but rather authoritarianism are sometimes accused by others of whitewashing the dictatorship, obscuring the violence it exerted, challenging the cardinal values of Portuguese democracy born after a revolution that radically broke with the regime that preceded it. This questioning—which affects other regimes of the interwar period—is based on friable foundations because the very definition of fascism is the object of deep struggles and disagreements in the field of history or political science, both in Portugal and at the international level. As there is no agreement on a definition of fascism, the debate seems insoluble.[18] Guided by this debate on the nature of the regime that acts as a compass, until now, research has focused on repression (the political police,[19] policing,[20] exceptional justice,[21] and censorship[22]) and on the characteristics that could place Salazarism in the family of fascist dictatorships during the interwar period: the single party[23] and mass mobilization.[24] From this perspective, one of the most studied areas is propaganda. António Ferro, leader of propaganda in the 1930s, has, since the 1980s, been the subject of many studies seeking to understand the "politics of the mind" which he built. A globetrotting journalist, an adept of modern cultural products—such as jazz—surrounded by avant-garde artists, Ferro is a fascinating paradox for many historians because he was the main architect of the propaganda of a conservative, even reactionary, regime emphasizing traditional and rural values.[25]

During the 1970s and 1980s, Salazarism was massively assimilated to fascism. The first academic symposium on this period, held in 1980, was published under the title "Fascism in Portugal." However, since the 1980s, some foreign researchers—such as Jacques Georgel—have placed this regime in the family of authoritarian regimes. The lack of mobilization of the majority of the population, the absence of a project to build a "new man," the maintenance of traditional structures (Church, army, provincial notables), Salazar's reluctance to modernize a backward country, the inexistence of a cult of the leader (Salazar was not very charismatic), the desire to stay away from international conflicts and the apparent lesser use of violence lead certain historians to define Salazarism as authoritarianism. Based on a comparative approach, on works carried out in history, historical sociology, and political science on the dictatorships of the interwar period and conducting a study of the "blue shirts," a movement claiming to be fascist that the Salazar

---

[17] This expression is taken from Michel Dobry, "La thèse immunitaire face aux fascismes. Pour une critique de la logique classificatoire," in *Le Mythe de l'Allergie Française au Fascisme*, edited by Michel Dobry, (Paris: Albin Michel, 2003): 17–67.

[18] Many books review the abundant historiography of fascism. Among them, see Olivier Forlin, *Le Fascisme. Historiographie et Enjeux Mémoriels* (Paris: La Découverte, 2013).

[19] Tom Gallagher, "Controlled repression in Salazar's Portugal," *Journal of Contemporary History*, no. 14 (1979), 385–402; Douglas Wheeler, "In the service of order: the Portuguese political police and the British, German and Spanish intelligence, 1932–1945," *Journal of Contemporary History*, no. 18 (1983): 1–25; Maria da Conceição Ribeiro, *A Polícia Política no Estado Novo, 1926–1945* (Lisbon: Estampa, 1995); Irène Flunser Pimentel, *A História da PIDE* (Lisbon: Temas e Debates/Círculo de Leitores, 2007); Duncan Simpson, "The 'sad grandmother', the 'simple but honest Portuguese' and the 'good son of the Fatherland': letters of denunciation in the final decade of the Salazar regime," *Análise Social*, no. 226 (2018): 6–27.

[20] João Madeira et alii, *Vítimas de Salazar. Estado Novo e Violência Política* (Lisbon: Esfera dos livros, 2007); Diego Palacios Cerezales, *Portugal à Coronhada. Protesto Popular e Ordem Pública nos séculos XIX e XX* (Lisbon: Tinta da China, 2011).

[21] Fernando Rosas et alii, *Tribunais Políticos. Tribunais Militares Especiais e Tribunais Plenários durante a Ditadura e o Estado Novo* (Lisbon: Temas e Debates, 2009).

[22] Graça dos Santos, *Le Spectacle Dénaturé: le Théâtre Portugais sous le Règne de Salazar, 1933–1968* (Paris, CNRS éditions, 2002); Ana Cabrera, *Marcello Caetano: Poder e Imprensa* (Lisbon: livros horizonte, 2006); Joaquim Cardoso Gomes, *Os Militares e a Censura. A Censura à Imprensa na Ditadura Militar e Estado Novo (1926–1945)* (Lisbon: Livros Horizonte, 2006); Ana Cabrera, *Censura Nunca Mais! A Censura ao Teatro e ao Cinema no Estado Novo* (Lisbon: Alètheia, 2013).

[23] Manuel Braga da Cruz, *O Partido e o Estado no Salazarismo* (Lisbon: Presença, 1988).

[24] Simon Kuin, "A Mocidade Portuguesa nos anos trinta: a instauração de uma organização para-militar de juventude," *Análise social*, no. 122 (1993): 555–588; Luís Nuno Rodrigues, *A Legião Portuguesa. A Milícia do Estado Novo, 1936–1944* (Lisbon: Estampa, 1996).

[25] Heloísa Paulo, *Estado Novo e Propaganda em Portugal e no Brasil. O SPN e o DIP* (Coimbra: Minerva, 1994); Ernesto Castro Leal, *António Ferro. Espaço Político e Imaginário Social (1918–1932)* (Lisbon: Cosmos, 1994); Jorge Ramos do Ó, *Os anos de Ferro: o Dispositivo Cultural durante a "Política do Espírito" (1933–1949)* (Lisbon: Estampa, 1999); Daniel Melo, *Salazarismo e Cultura Popular* (Lisbon: Imprensa de Ciências Sociais, 2001); Vera Marques Alves, *Arte Popular e Nação no Estado Novo* (Lisbon: Imprensa de Ciências Sociais, 2013); Orlando Raimundo, *António Ferro. O Inventor do Salazarismo* (Alfragide: Dom Quixote: 2015).

regime banned[26], António Costa Pinto[27] claimed in 1992 that Salazarism was an authoritarian regime.[28] Although Salazar can be considered a "strong dictator" because he followed government management very closely on a daily basis for more than 30 years,[29] Costa Pinto claims that the *Estado Novo* never attempted to change the country's social structure as fascist regimes did. The traditional control of the population continued and ministers were massively recruited within universities and the army.[30] Through publications in English, Costa Pinto's theses have been widely disseminated in the international field of study of interwar dictatorships.[31] In France, for example, Yves Léonard comes to close conclusions, in line with the works led by René Rémond, Pierre Milza and Serge Berstein on the dictatorships between the wars and fascism.[32] In a work published in 1996, Léonard also considers that Salazarism is not fascism but an authoritarian regime.[33]

However, the debate is not over and many historians—such as Fernando Rosas, Manuel Loff, or Luís Reis Torgal—continue to consider Salazarism as fascism or as a variant of a "generic fascism." We can question the heuristic scope of this debate. Indeed, controversies have often limited the field of questioning and neglected certain themes considered secondary. This focus has been confined to an elitist and institutional vision of politics, leaving aside approaches from social history. In these debates, the regime has often been apprehended as a monolith which lasted four decades. Thus, the main contributors to this debate focus on the 1930s, with little or no consideration in their reflections for the period after the Second World War. This focus on the first Salazarist period leaves some questions open. For instance, if multiple quotations from Salazar's discourses or writings are mobilized to prove his rejection of modernity, how can we explain that in the last years of his long reign, the country experienced significant economic growth and a significant rural exodus? However, the main perverse effect of the debate has been to restrict itself to very limited sources and archives. For these controversies, the public discourses of Salazar and some prominent figures of the regime such as António Ferro or Marcelo Caetano have often been sufficient. Historiography has been very much concerned with what leaders said, but more rarely with what they did concretely. For example, based on Manuel de Lucena's seminal book, published in 1976, one of the most studied elements of the *Estado Novo* is the corporatist system, the set of organizations regulating Portuguese capitalism.[34] Hating liberalism and the principle of competition, the leaders of the *Estado Novo* gradually established multiple organizations to regulate markets, often in a persnickety manner. Raw materials were subject to quota, prices were fixed and industry's production capacities were controlled.

[26] *O Fascismo em Portugal* (Lisbon: A Regra do Jogo, 1982).

[27] Jacques Georgel, *Le Salazarisme. Histoire et Bilan* (Paris: Éditions Cujas, 1981).

[28] António Costa Pinto, *O Salazarismo e o Fascismo Europeu: Problemas de Interpretação nas Ciências Sociais* (Lisbon: Estampa, 1992); António Costa Pinto, *Os Camisas Azuis. Ideologia, Elites e Movimentos Fascistas em Portugal, (1914–1945)* (Lisbon: Estampa, 1994).

[29] António Costa Pinto, "Elites, single party and political decision-making in Fascist-era Dictatorships," *Contemporary European History*, no. 3 (2002): 429–454.

[30] António Costa Pinto, "O império do professor, Salazar e a elite ministerial do Estado Novo (1933–1945)," *Análise social*, no. 157 (2001): 1055–1076.

[31] António Costa Pinto, *Salazar's Dictatorship and European Fascism. Problems of Interpretation* (New York: SSM–Columbia University, 1994); António Costa Pinto, *The Blue Shirts. Portuguese Fascists and the New State* (New York: SSM–Columbia University, 2000); António Costa Pinto ed., *Ruling Elites and Decision-Making in Fascist-Era Dictatorships* (New York: Columbia University, 2009); António Costa Pinto, Aristid Kallis ed. *Rethinking Fascism and Dictatorship in Europe* (Basingtoke: Palgrave Macmillan, 2014).

[32] Pierre Milza, *Les Fascismes* (Paris: Seuil, 1991); Serge Berstein, Pierre Milza, *Dictionnaire Historique des Fascismes et du Nazisme* (Bruxelles: Complexe, 1992); Marie-Anne Matard-Bonucci, Pierre Milza (eds), *L'Homme Nouveau dans l'Europe Fasciste (1922–1945). Entre Dictature et Totalitarisme* (Paris: Fayard, 2004).

[33] Yves Léonard, *Salazarisme et Fascisme* (Paris: Chandeigne, 1996).

[34] In addition to the works of Schmitter, Wiarda and de Lucena already mentioned, see also Fernando Rosas, *O Estado Novo nos Anos Trinta. Elementos para o Estudo da Natureza Económica e Social do Salazarismo (1928–1938)* (Lisbon: Estampa, 1986); Fátima Patriarca, *A Questão Social no Salazarismo, 1930–1947*, 2 vols. (Lisbon, Imprensa Nacional–Casa da Moeda, 1995); Fernando Rosas, *Salazarismo e Fomento Económico (1928–1948)* (Lisbon: Editorial Notícias, 2000); Nuno Luís Madureira, *A Economia dos Interesses. Portugal entre as Guerras* (Lisbon: Livros Horizonte, 2002); José Luís Cardoso, Maria Manuela Rocha, "Corporativismo e estado-providência (1933–1962)," *Ler História*, no. 45, (2003):111–135; António Costa Pinto, Francisco Carlos Palomanes, ed. *O Corporativismo em Português. Estado, Política e Sociedade no Salazarismo e no Varguismo* (Lisbon: Imprensa de Ciências Sociais, 2007); Fernando Rosas, Álvaro Garrido, ed. *Corporativismo, Fascismo, Estado Novo* (Coimbra: Almedina, 2012).

Inspired by the ideas of corporatism, developed particularly by the Catholic Church at the end of the 19th century, the *Estado Novo* claimed to ensure the collaboration of classes and suppress the struggle between capitalists and proletarians. Nevertheless, as Manuel de Lucena proved in the early 1970s, despite the discourses about improving workers' living conditions, the corporatist system was mainly used to fight and muzzle the labour movement. Strikes, demonstrations, and free trade unions were prohibited. Studies on the corporatist system have relied mainly on the discourse of leaders and on the abundant legislative and regulatory corpus devoted to corporations. They notably described a hiatus that Portuguese and foreign observers had already pointed out in the 1930s.[35]

While the regime's ideologues boasted a corporatism of association, in which professional groups managed their field of activity, it is a state corporatism that imposes itself. More than corporations, which only appeared in the 1950s, state-controlled organizations of economic coordination regulated the various markets. This gap suggests that it is impossible to accurately grasp practices from discourse and laws. It is necessary to go as close as possible to the functioning of these organizations, to study their concrete practices, to seize the balance of power within the state, a space of struggle and competition between institutions and individuals, but also to analyse the different relations between state and employers. If such studies have been carried out, based on consultations of the archives, on the fisheries[36] or wine[37] sectors for instance, they are still too rare. One of the difficulties lies in locating and accessing the archives of these organizations. Dulce Freire, Nunes Estêvão Ferreira, and Ana Margarida Rodrigues highlighted the following paradox: if corporatism has been the subject of several researches and is considered a central element of the *Estado Novo*, *"there is no systematic record of the organizations that have constituted the system, just as we do not know the documentary resources that can be consulted."*[38] Worse, several archives of the organizations that formed the corporatist system were simply destroyed, either to free up space or because these funds were considered useless. This paradox highlights one of the shortcomings of the historiography of the *Estado Novo*: a focus on discourse, on legislation, on a few archive collections (most notably the António de Oliveira Salazar papers deposited in the National Archives) while many archive collections remain unlocated, not inventoried or even destroyed.

It is true that, after the Carnation Revolution in 1974, there was a desire to preserve and make certain archives accessible in order to unveil the dictatorship and, mainly, the repression that it carried out.

---

[35] Odette Samson, *Le Corporatisme au Portugal* (Paris: Librairie technique et économique, 1938).

[36] Álvaro Garrido, *O Estado Novo e a Campanha do Bacalhau* (Lisbon: Círculo de Leitores/ Temas e Debates, 2010).

[37] Dulce Freire, *Produzir e Beber. A Questão do Vinho no Estado Novo* (Lisbon: Âncora Editora, 2010).

[38] Dulce Freire, Nuno Estêvão Ferreira, Ana Margarida Rodrigues, *Corporativismo e Estado Novo. Contributo para um Roteiro de Arquivos das Instituições Corporativas (1933–1974)*, Working Paper ICS, 2014.

Thus, in 1977, the government created the commission of the black book on the fascist regime which published several books between 1979 and 1991 reproducing archive documents, notably from Salazar's papers.[39] Nevertheless, to understand the state on a daily basis, the administrative apparatus in action, to grasp, in Foucauldian terms, the "governmentalities" deployed under the *Estado Novo* by a set of actors and institutions located at different hierarchical levels, it is necessary to consult archives from various organizations (general directorates of ministries, municipalities, corporations, etc.). Limiting oneself to laws, decrees or other texts condemns us to not apprehending "the discretionary power"[40] that many civil servants could exercise, mobilizing in the plethora of texts those which fit with their interests. It also obscures one of the salient features of the Portuguese state that Boaventura de Sousa Santos calls the "dual state":[41] in parallel with the formal State, which promulgates laws, there is an informal State that does not enforce its own laws and leaves a wide field of manoeuvre to civil servants who develop clientelist practices. Thus, without the consultation of archives—sometimes austere—it is impossible to grasp the various interactions between state agents and the population and the way in which the latter obeyed, adapted and sometimes resisted or bypassed the desiderata of those who wished to govern.

The non-use of archive collections from ministries and different administrations has often been compensated by the using Salazar' papers, available at the National Archives since the 1990s. Undoubtedly, this fund is extremely rich and the practice of the power deployed by Salazar—a "strong dictator" as António Costa Pinto characterizes him—often makes it unavoidable. However, it is far from sufficient because it represents only the tip of the iceberg of political and administrative work.[42] On the one hand, not all aspects of state management went back to Salazar. On the other hand, many documents, once passed through the Prime Minister's Office, returned to departments and other jurisdictions. Finally, focusing on Salazar's interventions postulates that his decisions were then faithfully executed by the ministries, by the agents on the ground, all of whom were considered to be deprived of agency. This view explains why many works on the *Estado Novo* contain Salazar in their title, reducing certain processes and phenomena to their relationship with the dictator, even in the areas in which he was hardly involved. Salazar thus appears to be the "owner" of the power that would circulate perfectly in a top-down way and impose itself on a population considered apathetic. This conception of power obscures the role and actions of many other actors and institutions. Recent sectoral studies have demonstrated the need to study different fields—with their specific rules, their actors with different capitals—beyond only their relationship with Salazar.[43]

[39] Filipa Raimundo, *Ditadura e Democracia. Legados da Memória* (Lisbon: Fundação Francisco Manuel dos Santos, 2018): 62.

[40] Alexis Spire, *Étrangers à la Carte. L'Administration de l'Immigration en France (1945–1975)* (Paris: Grasset, 2005).

[41] Boaventura de Sousa Santos, *Portugal. Ensaio Contra a Autoflagelação* (Coimbra: Almedina, 2011): 121. Also see Boaventura de Sousa Santos, *O Estado e a Sociedade em Portugal (1974–1988)* (Porto, Afrontamento, 1990).

[42] Victor Pereira, "'Ainda não sabe qual é o pensamento de Sua Excelência Presidente do Conselho'. O Estado Português perante a emigração para França (1957–1968)," in edited by Nuno Domingos, Victor Pereira, *O Estado Novo em Questão* (Lisbon: Edições 70, 2010): 41–79.

[43] Rahul Kumar, *A Pureza Perdida do Desporto. Futebol no Estado Novo* (Lisbon: Paquiderme, 2017).

FOR A SOCIAL HISTORY

The approaches favoured by the historiography of the *Estado Novo* have neglected a social history of the dictatorship. There are certainly many definitions of social history: a history in which the social is the main determinant of historical processes, a history that attaches itself to the dominated actors (slaves, workers, peasants), a history that is concerned with social classes, a history that privileges social relations. Whatever the chosen definition, this social history is seldom summoned in the historiography of the *Estado Novo*. For example, in propaganda studies, the focus is placed on institutions, discourses, intellectuals, and artists.

The works (writings, films, paintings, buildings, etc.) of the propaganda are inscribed, from an internalist perspective, in literary, artistic or intellectual currents. But, on the one hand, this research tends to diminish the weight of cultural productions belonging to a popular and transnational mass culture (such as the Hollywood film industry). On the other hand, the question of the reception of this propaganda—taking into account the high rate of illiteracy throughout the dictatorship—is often the great absence of the works which are only interested in the offer. Fernando Rosas, in particular, defends the idea that there was a "totalitarian project" that has unfolded through *"a vast bureaucratic complex of organisms of general ideological enunciation and complementary instruments of authoritarian and unambiguous inculcation of these values at all levels of everyday sociability, from family to workplace, through school and leisure."*[44]

But did propaganda, built in literate urban circles, really reach the countryside? In what form? Was the propaganda appropriated by a poorly literate population? Ignored? Received with "oblique attention," to use Richard Hoggart's words? The few works based on oral interviews tend to nuance the idea that the *Estado Novo* had the "infrastructural power"[45] to transmit its propaganda throughout the territory, to all social classes. For example, Maria Alice Samara and Raquel Pereira Henriques showed the distance of the inhabitants of the countryside from literate culture (the newspaper) and from most media. They quote the testimony of a peasant born in 1920 in the central region of the country: "There was neither radio nor television. Information circulated mouth-to-mouth, with delays".[46] It is also significant that a whole literature on the popular classes —first and foremost the peasantry—is only very rarely mentioned in the works on the *Estado Novo*.[47] The research led by José Cutileiro[48], Manuel Carlos Silva[49] or José Manuel Sobral[50] attempts to explain the rural populations' ways of seeing.

[44] Fernando Rosas, *Salazar e o Poder. A Arte de Saber Durar* (Lisbon: Tinta da China, 2012): 189.

[45] Michael Mann, "The autonomous power of the State: its origins, mechanisms and results," *Archives Européennes de Sociologie*, no. 25 (1984): 185–213.

[46] Marie Alice Samara, Raquel Pereira Henriques, *Viver e Resistir no Tempo de Salazar* (Lisbon, Verso da Kapa, 2013).

[47] Virgílio Borges Pereira, Yasmine Siblot, "Comparer les classes populaires en France et au Portugal. Différences structurelles et histoire intellectuelles," *Actes de la Recherche en Sciences Sociales*, no. 219 (2017): 56–79.

[48] José Cutileiro, *A Portuguese Rural Society* (London: Oxford University Press, 1971).

[49] Manuel Carlos Silva, *Resistir e Adaptar-se. Constrangimentos e Estratégias Camponesas no Noroeste de Portugal* (Porto: Afrontamento, 1998).

[50] José Manuel Sobral, *Trajectos: o Presente e o Passado na Vida de uma Freguesia da Beira* (Lisbon: Imprensa de Ciências Sociais, 1999).

Rural populations had a strong distrust of the state, mainly perceived as an external and constraining entity that could jeopardize survival strategies by raising taxes, requiring licenses of all kinds or enlisting young men in military service. As in the historiography of Nazism[51] or Vichy regime in France,[52] where the opinions of different fractions of the population were analysed from different materials (letters, reports from the authorities, etc.), it would be necessary to study the daily life of the popular classes, their experiences, their conceptions of politics. These questions would make it possible to scrutinize the "hidden discourses"[53] of these populations, not to be confined to the image of an apathetic population. Alice Ingerson's work, realized in the early 1980s, shows that workers were able to use the "weapons of the weak"[54].

For instance, they use and manipulate the language of the authorities in order to obtain some advantages[55]. The workers studied by Ingerson know how to divert to their advantage the discourses constructed by the dictatorship without complying with them. Similarly, their tactics are not based on the positions of the Portuguese Communist Party, which also tried to inculcate its views. This point should also encourage us to conduct a history of the opposition to Salazarism less focused on its elites and organizations. Indeed, it is the main leaders of opposition movements that have been studied[56]—particularly in the context of the biography that has developed considerably in recent years, sometimes cutting individuals from the social context in which they were formed and evolved—as well as the evolution of organizations,[57] doctrines and political ideas.[58] We still know very little about the working class sociability, urban but also rural,[59] which has been the basis for militant commitments, or on "militant careers."[60]

[51] Ian Kershaw, *L'Opinion Allemande sous le Nazisme. Bavière 1933–1945* (Paris: CNRS éditions, 1995); Alf Lüdtke, "'A Grande massa é indiferente, tolera tudo...' Experiências de dominação, sentido de si e individualidade dos trabalhadores alemães antes e depois de 1933," in *A Política em Estado Vivo. Uma Visão Crítica das Práticas Políticas*, edited by Bruno Monteiro, Virgílio Borges Pereira, (Lisbon: Edições 70/ Le Monde Diplomatique, Edição portuguesa, 2013): 71–106.

[52] Pierre Laborie, *Les Français des Années Troubles. De la Guerre d'Espagne à la Libération* (Paris: Seuil, 1990).

[53] James C. Scott, *Domination and the Arts of Resistance. Hidden Transcripts* (New Haven: Yale University Press, 1990).

[54] James C. Scott, *Weapons of the Weak. Everyday Forms of Peasant Resistance* (New Haven: Yale University Press, 1985).

[55] Alice Ingerson, *Contos, Cartas e Conversas: Três Histórias de Família e de Classe no Vale do Ave* (Porto: Instituto de Sociologia–Universidade do Porto, 2012).

[56] For instance, a monumental biography of Álvaro Cunhal, in several volumes, is being published. Already published: José Pacheco Pereira, *Álvaro Cunhal. Uma Biografia Política*, vol. 1, *"Daniel", o Jovem Revolucionário* (Lisbon: Temas e debates, 1999); *Álvaro Cunhal. Uma Biografia Política, vol .2, "Duarte", o Dirigente Clandestino (1941–1949)* (Lisbon: Temas e Debates, 2001); *Álvaro Cunhal. Uma Biografia Política, vol. 3, O Prisioneiro* (Lisbon: Temas e debates, 2005); *Álvaro Cunhal. Uma Biografia Política, vol. 4, O Secretário-Geral* (Lisbon: Temas e debates, 2015). About Cunhal see also José Neves, ed., *Alvaro Cunhal. Política, História e Estética* (Lisbon: Tinta da China, 2013).

[57] Susana Martins, *Socialistas na Oposição ao Estado Novo* (Lisbon: Casa das Letras, 2005); Irene Flunser Pimentel, *História da Oposição à Ditadura, 1926–1974* (Porto: Figueirinhas, 2013); Susana Martins, *Exilados Portugueses em Argel. A FPLN das Origens à Rutura com Humberto Delgado (1960–1965)* (Porto: Afrontamento, 2018).

[58] José Neves, *Comunismo e Nacionalismo em Portugal. Política, Cultura e História no século XX* (Lisbon: Tinta da China, 2008); Miguel Cardina, *Margem de Certa Maneira. O Maoismo em Portugal. 1964–1974* (Lisbon, Tinta da China, 2011); João Madeira, *História do Partido Comunista Português. Das Origens ao 25 de abril (1921–1974)* (Lisbon: Tinta da China, 2013).

[59] Paula Godinho, *Memórias da Resistência Rural no Sul. Couço (1958–1962)* (Oeiras: Celta Editora, 2001); Dulce Freire, Inês Fonseca, Paula Godinho, *Mundo Rural. Transformação e Resistência na Península Ibérica (Século XX)* (Lisbon: Colibri, 2004).

[60] Guya Accornero, *The Revolution Before the Revolution. Late Authoritarianism and Student Protest in Portugal* (New York: Berghahn, 2016).

"PORTUGAL IS NOT A SMALL COUNTRY"

In recent years, two fields of research have experienced a strong process of dynamism: the history of international relations and colonial history, both of which are strongly connected because diplomacy was one of the main weapons of the dictatorship to safeguard its empire.

The first research on the foreign policy of the *Estado Novo* were partly related to the question of the nature of the regime. Indeed, in analysing Salazar's foreign policy in the 1930s and during the Second World War, the aim was to understand to what extent the *Estado Novo* had collaborated with other—mainly fascist—European dictatorships and how diplomacy Portuguese had wavered between the Allies and the Axis during the Second World War in order to ensure its sustainability once peace came.[61] One of the episodes studied early on is the Spanish Civil War, a conflict in which the Portuguese government helped the nationalists who defeated the Republic in various ways. Portugal was a place of refuge for nationalist conspirators and a transit point for the weapons intended for the troops led by Francisco Franco.[62] The dictatorship organized the sending of "volunteers" (*Viriatos*) to fight "communism" and gave diplomatic support to the Burgos government. Moreover, in the context of the Spanish War, the Portuguese dictatorship experienced a radicalization process with the creation of different structures aimed to control the population—mainly urban—the increase of imprisonments and the creation of a concentration camp on an island in Cape Verde where the opponents of the regime (mainly communists and anarchists) were sent.

The other element that has attracted the attention of historians is the evolution of the relationship between Portugal and Britain, Portugal's oldest ally and the world's leading maritime power until the Second World War.[63] The first researches were embedded, often in an underlying way, in the questions raised by the Latin American "theory of dependency" and in the vigorous denunciation of US imperialism (in a context where the Vietnam War had only recently ended). What were the diplomatic, economic, and political forms of British rule over Portugal, a rule that was reinforced at the beginning of the 19th century during the Napoleonic wars? How was the British democracy satisfied with a dictatorship in Portugal, or did it even promote its consolidation? These questions then arose to analyse the links between Portugal and the new main world power after the Second World War: the United States.[64] How did the United States finally, despite some tensions, support a dictatorship that was trying to keep its colonies against the "wind of change"?

---

[61] António José Telo, *Portugal na Segunda Guerra (1941–1945)*, 2 vols. (Lisbon: Vega, 1991); Fernando Rosas, *Portugal entre a Paz e a Guerra (1939–1945)* (Lisbon: Estampa, 1995).

[62] César de Oliveira, *Salazar e a Guerra civil de Espanha* (Lisbon: O Jornal, 1987); Fernando Rosas, ed., *Portugal e a Guerra civil de Espanha* (Lisbon: Colibri, 1998); Valentim Alexandre, *O Roubo das Almas. Salazar, a Igreja e os Totalitarismos (1930–1939)*, (Alfragide: Dom Quixote, 2006); Dulce Simões, *A Guerra de Espanha na Raia Luso-Espanhola. Resistências, Solidariedades e Usos da Memória* (Lisbon: Colibri, 2016).

[63] Fernando Rosas, *O Salazarismo e a Aliança Luso–Britânica. Estudo sobre a Política Externa do Estado Novo nos anos 30 e 40* (Lisbon: Fragmentos, 1988); David Castaño, *Paternalismo e Cumplicidade. As Relações Luso–Britânicas de 1943–1949* (Lisbon: Associação dos Amigos do Arquivo diplomático/MNE, 2006); Pedro Aires Oliveira, *Os Despojos da Aliança. A Grã-Bretanha e a Questão Colonial Portuguesa* (Lisbon, Tinta da China, 2007).

[64] José Freire Antunes, *Kennedy e Salazar. O Leão e a Raposa* (Lisbon: Difusão Cultural, 1991); Luís Nuno Rodrigues, *Salazar–Kennedy. A Crise de uma Aliança* (Lisbon: Editorial Notícias, 2002).

The research does not all draw an impervious line between foreign and domestic politics because, to perpetuate itself as a regime and as an empire, the Portuguese dictatorship had to ensure the support—or tolerance—of the main Western powers.[65] To show how these different dimensions are connected, Fernando Rosas stressed that Portugal is *"structurally dependent on Great Britain, but simultaneously a colonizing power and creator of dependencies. In the context of the international division of labour in a world already marked by the rise of the economic and political phenomenon of imperialism, Portugal is in an intermediate position between the centre and the periphery."*[66]

Studying the diplomatic policy pursued by the dictatorship after the Second World War, historians are less concerned with the nature of the regime. Rather, they attempt to understand two contradictory processes. On the one hand, how did Portugal, despite its dictatorial nature, its corporatist organization and its imperial integration policy, not completely remain outside the European construction? Many studies follow, sometimes step by step, the negotiations that led Portugal to benefit from the Marshall Plan, join the Organization for European Economic Cooperation (OEEC), join the GATT (General Agreement on Tariffs and Trade), be a founding member of the European Free Trade Association and sign a trade agreement with the European Economic Community in 1972.[67] It is not only diplomatic negotiations that have been analysed, but also the effects of these accessions on trade, on the circulation and the diffusion of new ideas and economic practices (often in contradiction with corporatist doctrine).[68]

Portugal's participation in these international organizations sharpened the struggles among Portuguese political, economic, and administrative elites with different perspectives on economic and social policies and Portugal's economic integration into the world-system.[69] This research thus makes it possible to place the evolution of state practices—and of governmentalities more generally—not only within the restricted framework of a Portuguese corporatist system cut off from the rest of the world, but in the context of internationalization and the transnationalization of trade, administrative practices and methods of human resource management.[70] The analysis of the dissemination, the appropriation, and the transformation of the practices and the ideas diffused by international organizations such as the OEEC or the International Labour Organization makes it possible to nuance the discourse of the dictatorship which considered itself a model apart, a coherent and "national" model.

[65] António José Telo, Hipólito de la Torre Gómez, *Portugal e Espanha nos Sistemas Internacionais Contemporâneos* (Lisbon: Cosmos, 2000).

[66] Rosas, *O Estado Novo nos Anos Trinta*: 55.

[67] Maria Fernanda Rollo, *Portugal e o Plano Marshall* (Lisbon: Estampa, 1994); António José Telo, *Portugal e a NATO: o Reencontro da Tradição Atlântica* (Lisbon: Cosmos, 1996); José Manuel Tavares Castilho, *A Ideia de Europa no Marcelismo (1968–1974)* (Porto: Afrontamento, 2000); António Costa Pinto, Nuno Severiano Teixeira, eds, *A Europa do Sul e a Construção da União Europeia–1945–2000* (Lisbon: Imprensa de Ciências Sociais, 2005); Elsa Santos Alípio, *Salazar e a Europa: História da Adesão à EFTA* (Lisbon: Livros Horizonte, 2006);Nicolau Andresen Leitão, *Estado Novo, Democracia e Europa. 1947–1986* (Lisbon: Imprensa de Ciências Sociais, 2007); José Maria Brandão de Brito, Maria Fernanda Rollo, João Ferreira do Amaral, eds., *Portugal e a Europa. Testemunhos de Protagonistas* (Lisbon: Tinta da China, 2011).

[68] Cristina Rodrigues, *Portugal e a Organização Internacional do Trabalho (1933–1974)* (Porto: Afrontamento, 2012).

[69] Carlos Manuel Gonçalves, *Emergência e Consolidação dos Economistas em Portugal* (Porto: Afrontamento, 2006).

[70] Nuno Domingos, "Desproletarizar. A FNAT como instrumento de mediação ideológica no Estado Novo" in edited by Nuno Domingos, Victor Pereira, *O Estado Novo em Questão* (Lisbon: Edições 70, 2010): 165–196.

Although Portugal joined several international organizations, the central objective of its foreign policy was to preserve its empire. Portugal's ability to obtain the necessary assistance (purchase of weapons, support in the United Nations, while the newly independent countries of Africa and Asia criticized Portuguese colonialism) has been the subject of several publications.[71] In this context, studies on Portugal's relations with several Western powers (the United States, Great Britain, France,[72] and West Germany[73]) were carried out, relying on Portuguese and foreign diplomatic collections as well as on diplomats' memoirs (which must, however, always be used with the critical spirit that suits historians).

The study of colonial policy was not limited to these diplomatic aspects. The various evolutions—far from linear—of Portuguese colonialism in Africa were examined: the sending of settlers,[74] the public work projects (dams, roads, ports),[75] the improvement of population and labour force control[76] the growth of the repressive apparatus[77] or, also, the diffusion of the ideology of lusotropicalism[78] that took over part of Gilberto Freire's work, in order to legitimize the refusal of decolonization. Nevertheless, the end of Portuguese colonialism was marked by long military conflicts, conflicts, that caused profound changes in Portuguese and colonial society. Several hundred[76] thousand men—[77]both metropolitan and African—were mobilized and a substantial part of the budget was devoted to the war. Both the war and its memories—often traumatic—are now dynamic fields of research.[78]

---

[71] José Freire Antunes, *A Guerra de África (1961–1974)*, 2 vols (Lisbon: Temas e debates, 1996); António José Telo, "A prioridade à África (1959–1974)" in *Nova História Militar de Portugal*, edited by Manuel Themudo Barata, Nuno Severiano Teixeira, vol. 4 (Lisbon: Círculo de leitores, 2004): 463–495; António Costa Pinto, Miguel Bandeira Jerónimo, eds., *Portugal e o Fim do Colonialismo. Dimensões Internacionais* (Lisbon: Edições 70, 2014); Valentim Alexandre, *Contra o Vento. Portugal, o Império e a Maré Anticolonial (1945–1960)* (Lisbon: Temas e debates, 2017).

[72] Daniel da Silva Marcos, *Salazar e de Gaulle. A França e a Questão Colonial Portuguesa (1958–1968)* (Lisbon: Instituto Diplomático/MNE, 2007); Amaral da Silva Lala, "L'Enjeu Colonial dans les Relations Franco-Portugaises, 1944–1974," PhD Diss., Paris, Institut d'études politiques de Paris, 2007.

[73] António Muñoz Sánchez, "La socialdemocracia alemana y el Estado Novo (1961–1974)," *Portuguese Studies Review*, no. 13 (2005): 477–503; Ana Mónica Fonseca, *A Força das Armas. O Apoio da República Federal da Alemanha ao Estado Novo (1958–1968)* (Lisbon: Instituto Diplomático/MNE, 2007); Rui Lopes, *West Germany and the Portuguese Dictatorship 1968–1974. Between Cold War and Colonialism* (Baskingtoke: Palgrave Macmilan, 2014).

[74] Cláudio Castelo, *Passagens para África. O Povoamento de Angola e Moçambique com Naturais da Métropole (1920–1974)* (Porto: Afrontamento, 2007).

[75] Victor Pereira, "A economia do império e os plano de fomento," in *O Império Colonial em Questão. Poderes, Saberes e Instituições*, edited by Miguel Bandeira Jerónimo, (Lisbon: Edições 70, 2012): 261–295; Nuno Domingos, Elsa Peralta, eds., *Cidade e Império. Dinâmicas Coloniais e Reconfigurações Pós-Coloniais* (Lisbon: Edições 70).

[76] Todd Cleveland, *Diamonds in the Rough: Corporate Paternalism and African Professionalism on the Mines of Colonial Angola (1917–1975)* (Athens: Ohio University Press, 2015); Diogo Ramada Curto, Bernardo Pinto da Cruz, Teresa Furtado, *Políticas Coloniais em Tempo de Revoltas–Angola circa 1961* (Porto: Afrontamento, 2016).

[77] Yves Léonard, "Salazarisme et lusotropicalisme, histoire d'une appropriation," *Lusotopie*, no. (1997): 211–226; Cláudia Castelo, *'O Modo Português de Estar no Mundo'. O Luso-Tropicalismo e a Ideologia Colonial Portuguesa (1933–1961)* (Porto: Afrontamento, 1998); Marcos Cardão, *Fado Tropical. O Luso-Tropicalismo na Cultura de Massas* (Lisbon: Edições Unipop, 2015).

[78] Elsa Peralta, Bruno Góis, Joana Oliveira, eds, *Retornar. Traços de Memória do Fim do Império* (Lisbon: Edições 70, 2016); Ângela Campos, *An Oral History of the Portuguese Colonial War. Conscripted Generation* (Cham: Springer, 2017); Miguel Cardina, Bruno Sena Martins, eds., *As Voltas do passado. A Guerra Colonial e as Lutas de Libertação* (Lisbon: Tinta da China, 2018).

CONCLUSION

It is impossible in such a short text to reproduce all the approaches and questions that have been raised about the *Estado Novo* dictatorship over a period of 40 years. In tune with the international historiography in which global history is on the rise, there has been a diversification of issues in recent years, including greater attention to transnational processes and changes in the colonial domination. This insertion of the Portuguese dictatorship into a broader framework allows analysis to go beyond the discourse that the regime itself promoted, discourse highlighting its singularity and its isolation—the famous "proudly alone." Nevertheless, it is necessary to see these global dimensions in relation to the local scale, analysing finely the social configurations from diversified sources. As we have seen, one of the main shortcomings of the historiography of the *Estado Novo* is the insufficient attention given to social history and more particularly to the practices, the ways of seeing and the agency of the population, in its social, territorial and gender diversity. A vision that the dictatorship defended remains: that of a power, dominated by a man, who governs a country made up of obedient and apathetic individuals. This exaltation of the leaders converges in recent years, with the return in force of the biography, a process allowed by the decline of the *Annales* school and holistic approaches.[79] It is not insignificant that the biographies of leaders—both of dictatorship[80] and the opposition—have multiplied over the past decade. Nevertheless, this focus on leaders does not allow us to grasp more closely the "governmentalities" that took place during the dictatorship.

To overcome an elitist view of the dictatorship, it would be necessary to better use the archive collections that have not disappeared or been destroyed and not be limited to those concerning Salazar or Marcelo Caetano. It would also be necessary, as anthropologists and sociologists have done for many years, to continue to collect histories of life and to use oral sources rigorously. It would then be possible to write a history in which a large part of the historical actors would not be absent.

---

[79] François Dosse, *Le Pari Biographique. Ecrire une Vie* (Paris: La Découverte, 2005).

[80] Filipe Ribeiro de Meneses, *Salazar. Uma Biografia Política* (Alfragide: Dom Quixote, 2010); José Manuel Tavares Castilho, *Marcelo Caetano. Biografia Política* (Coimbra: Almedina, 2012); Francisco Carlos Palomanes Martinho, *Marcello Caetano. Uma Biografia 1906–1980* (Lisbon: Objectiva, 2016).

Agualva-Cacém

PHOTO ESSAY BY TIAGO CASANOVA (2018)

The Affordable Houses Estate of Agualva-Cacém, that is now the parish of Mira Sintra, near Lisbon, represented a late effort by the regime to salvage the most politically charged of its housing programmes, and the first of its housing initiatives, the *Casas Económicas*, that focused on the creation of a class of homeowners, through a resoluble rent system that effectively excluded low-income families. It became simultaneously an instrument of social control and a reward system for loyal subjects.

Agualva-Cacém is a symbol of the hesitations, contradictions and of the evolution of the Portuguese dictatorship's view of housing. The design started in 1965 and was one of the first instances of a new town in Portugal, a prototype for the Planos Integrados, the large scale housing initiatives that marked the state's intervention in housing in the 1970s. Crossing low-rise and high-rise, density and green areas - designed by Gonçalo Ribeiro Telles (1922-2020), the Portuguese master landscape architect -, it was still under construction in 1974, when the regime fell.

BIOGRAPHY

Tiago Casanova studied Architecture at Faculdade de Arquitetura da Universidade do Porto, where he was one of the founders of Scopio - International Photography Magazine in 2010. He was also one of the founders of the XYZ Books Publishing house and Bookshop in 2013, A ILHA (Gallery and Art Space) in 2014, and Estúdio Bulhufas in 2017. Has been exhibiting his work regularly in solo and group shows since 2006. Besides the work he produces in the context of his artistic investigation and practice, he also develops a professional career as an editor, book-maker, curator and exhibition designer. In 2012, he was the recipient of the BES Revelação Photography Award and of an Honorable Mention at Novos Talentos Fnac Fotografia. In 2014, his work was mentioned for the best work selection at Plat(t)form - Fotomuseum Winterthur, and in 2015 he won the Jury Award at Festival A3 Bandas in Madrid. He is represented by Galeria Carlos Carvalho (Lisbon). He is currently based in Lisbon and Porto.